Cultural Anthropology

Cultural Anthropology

CONTEMPORARY, PUBLIC, AND CRITICAL READINGS

Keri Vacanti Brondo

University of Memphis

OXFORD UNIVERSITY PRESS

NEW YORK   OXFORD

Oxford University Press is a department of the University of Oxford.
It furthers the University's objective of excellence in research,
scholarship, and education by publishing worldwide.

Oxford New York
Auckland Cape Town Dar es Salaam Hong Kong Karachi
Kuala Lumpur Madrid Melbourne Mexico City Nairobi
New Delhi Shanghai Taipei Toronto

With offices in
Argentina Austria Brazil Chile Czech Republic France Greece
Guatemala Hungary Italy Japan Poland Portugal Singapore
South Korea Switzerland Thailand Turkey Ukraine Vietnam

For titles covered by Section 112 of the US Higher Education
Opportunity Act, please visit www.oup.com/us/he for the
latest information about pricing and alternate formats.

Published by Oxford University Press
198 Madison Avenue, New York, New York 10016
http://www.oup.com

Library of Congress Cataloging-in-Publication Data

Names: Brondo, Keri Vacanti, author.
Title: Cultural anthropology : contemporary, public and critical readings/Keri Vacanti Brondo.
Description: Oxford ; New York : Oxford University Press, [2017] |
Includes bibliographical references.
Identifiers: LCCN 2016011466| ISBN 9780190253547 (pbk. : alk. paper) |
ISBN 9780190253554 (instructor edition : alk. paper)
Subjects: LCSH: Ethnology.
Classification: LCC GN316 .B78 2016 | DDC 306—dc23 LC record available
at http://lccn.loc.gov/2016011466

Printing number: 9 8 7 6 5 4 3 2

Printed in the United States of America on acid-free paper

To Amalie and Keegan, and to my past, current, and future students, who inspire me to be a better teacher.

Contents

Part 1: Thinking Anthropologically   9

Part 2: Communicating Culture: Language and Expressive Culture   53

Part 3: Belief Systems   99

Part 10: Violence, Conflict, and Mobility in the 21st Century

Part 11: Visual and Media Anthropology

Part 12: Careers in Engaged and Applied Anthropology   477

Acknowledgments

This book exists due to the incredible support and guidance from Oxford University Press. Their editorial team is simply extraordinary. Sherith Pankratz, Meredith Keffer, Elizabeth Kelly, Lisa Grzan, and Simon Benjamin provided exceptional support and guidance throughout the process, from development to production.

I am indebted to my colleagues and friends who collectively brainstormed a long list of "dream" selections that they would want in a contemporary reader for their classes. It was a difficult task to cull the initial list of outstanding new work in engaged, public, and applied anthropology while also retaining some of the "old gems." I thank James Bielo, Holly Dygert, Ruthbeth Finerman, Tara Hefferan, Kari Henquinet, Beth Rose Middleton, Suzanne Kent, Micah Trapp, Luis Vivanco, and Michael Walker for their ideas on readings and anthropologists to profile. I am also grateful to Shannon Blanton, Sara Bridges, and Randy Floyd for their insights and sage advice during this development stage. Finally, twelve reviewers provided critical feedback on the earliest prospectus and initial table of contents, providing me with critical feedback to strengthen the depth and range of geographic and topical areas, as well as author diversity and perspective regarding anthropological application.

This book is special for many reasons, but one is because several individuals agreed to submit original case studies or be interviewed for an "Anthropology in Practice" profile. I greatly appreciate the following people who worked with me so responsibly and eloquently on their submissions: Natalie Bourdon, Jillian Cavanaguh, Melissa Cefkin, Ray Codrington, Shirley Fiske, Andrea Freidus, Robert Hahn, Tara Hefferan, Hsain Ilahiane, Barbara Rose Johnston, Ippy Kalofonos, Fabiana Li, Tanya Luhrmann, Laura McNamara, Karen Nakamura, Michael Perez, Bernie Perley, Neera Signh, Megan Springate, Don Stull, Micah Trapp, Luis Vivanco, and Michael Walker. I am also very grateful for Daniel Vacanti's review of several overview essays and for Katherine Lambert-Pennington's thoughtful feedback on the introductory chapter.

Once the contents were finalized, the editorial labor was supported by outstanding undergraduate and graduate students at the University of Memphis. Several Department of Anthropology student workers assisted with scanning and compiling materials. Kyle Simpson and Jessica Stanley-Asselmeier aided with the tedious formatting and reformatting as files went through a pdf-to-Word conversion. Jessica also provided outstanding support with final formatting for the entire manuscript, all within just one month of beginning her graduate study. I am full of gratitude for both, each of whom is extremely conscientious, detail-oriented, and generous in their support.

Lastly, I wish to thank my family for their love and support. Amalie, Keegan, and Daniel, you make life easy.

Manuscript reviewers

Alexa S. Dietrich, Wagner College

Meghan E. Ference, Brooklyn College, CUNY

Jay Gabriel, Rowan University

Landon Karr, Augustana College

Rocky L. Sexton, Ball State University

Natalie H. Thompson, California State University, Bakersfield

Dean H. Wheeler, Glendale Community College

Sara Withers, University of New Hampshire

Aníbal Yáñez-Chávez, California State University, San Marcos and three anonymous reviewers

To the Student

Instructors have a wealth of textbooks and readers to choose from when they are making decisions about what they will assign you, making their decision quite challenging. Each selection they make is intentional, items chosen to serve the learning objectives of the course. In choosing this reader, I would like to think that your instructor made the decision they did because they are hoping to introduce you not just to the old "gems" (which are also featured in this reader) but also to contemporary examples from public, critical, and applied anthropology.

While there has been a shift in introductory readers to be more inclusive of the aforementioned forms of practicing anthropology, this inclusiveness is most commonly represented in textbooks through the addition of a separate section on applied anthropology, often featured at the end of a book. In contrast, your book embeds practicing anthropology throughout; after all, we anthropologists are applying our knowledge and skills all the time, not as an afterthought. Other special features to illustrate anthropological application include "Anthropology in Practice" and "In the News" summaries and web links. The profiles capture anthropological praxis, meaning translating anthropological theories and ideas into action. Interviews with public, engaged, and practicing anthropologists, as well the "In the News" coverage offers contemporary examples of application that have been featured in the mainstream news media, bringing anthropology squarely into the public realm. The final part of the book includes selections dedicated to unpacking the variety of ways in which anthropologists might "engage" and provides career advice for practicing anthropology.

Finally, if you were assigned this book, chances are you are enrolled in a college or university in the United States. While the selections in this reader represent a broad spectrum of geographic and cultural areas, the reader also includes a high number of U.S.-based case studies to inspire you to think anthropologically "in your own backyard."

To the Instructor

The goal of this reader is to help students "think anthropologically" by introducing core concepts from the discipline through engaging case studies. The book is designed primarily for undergraduate introductory courses in cultural anthropology. However, there are a handful of selections that attend to critical debates in biocultural anthropology or applied archaeology and therefore may also be appropriate for general anthropology courses.

While there are several "classic" selections, the majority (39 of 55) are contemporary pieces, published from 2005 onward, 24 of which were published after 2012. These pieces treat timely topics that should resonate with U.S. college students and generate discussion regarding the value of an anthropological perspective in the modern world. While the overall selections represent a range of geographic and cultural areas, the reader includes a high number of selections that discuss U.S.-based fieldwork so students are inspired to think anthropologically "in their own backyards."

Selections emphasize critically engaged, public, and applied anthropology; several case studies are examples of anthropology in practice, and each part of the reader includes special features that profile anthropological application through "In the News" and "Anthropology in Practice" features. The news pieces present a contemporary story or debate published in the U.S. national media. The "Anthropology in Practice" features are short interviews with anthropologists working in the subject area under focus in each part (e.g., anthropology of religion, environmental anthropology, visual anthropology), demonstrating how anthropologists put their knowledge to use as applied, public, or critically engaged scholars.

This book was intentionally designed to align with Oxford's two existing introductory textbooks: (1) Robert L. Welsch and Luis A. Vivanco's *Cultural Anthropology: Asking Questions About Humanity* (November 2014), and (2) Emily A. Schultz and Robert H. Lavenda's *Cultural Anthropology: A Perspective on the Human Condition*, 9th ed. (November 2013). Figure x.1 details the alignment between this book's 12 parts and the chapters in the two textbooks.

This Reader	Welsch and Vivanco	Schultz and Lavenda
	CHAPTER	CHAPTER
Part 1 – Thinking Anthropologically	1–3, 5	1–3
Part 2 – Communicating Culture	4	5
Part 3 – Belief Systems	14	6,7
Part 4 – Marriage, Family, Gender and Sexuality	12–13	10–12
Part 5 – Race, Ethnicity, Class and Inequality	11	12
Part 6 – Medical Anthropology	15	1, 13
Part 7 – Taste and Foodways	7	9
Part 8 – Environmental Anthropology	8	9
Part 9 – Globalization, Development and Culture	6	4
Part 10 – Violence, Conflict and Mobility in the 21st Century	1, 6, 10	8
Part 11 – Media and Visual Anthropology	16	6
Part 12 – Careers in Engaged Anthropology	1	1, 14

Figure x.1

Chapter alignment with Oxford University Press' cultural anthropology texts.

While it was designed to ease bundled textbook adoptions for instructors working with Oxford University Press, the reader can also serve as a standalone volume for those who prefer to teach key terms and core ideas through lecture, case studies, and other educational resources. Each part of the book includes an overview essay to orient students to central areas of study within the general research domain (e.g., language and communication, belief systems, taste and foodways); the overview essays also highlight the central themes that cut across each part's selections. While these introductory essays cover some key terms, instructors should bear in mind that they are far from exhaustive, limited to the topics featured within the case study selections. For example, while Part 5's Race, Ethnicity, Class, and Inequality overview essay introduces definitions of race, racism, and whiteness, it does not cover castes, the "one-drop rule," or primordialism and instrumentalism in social theories of ethnicity. Therefore, instructors using this as their core text will need to supplement with lecture or other materials.

Instructors might also choose to disregard the reader's parts altogether, as the decisions to put one piece in a certain part over another may appear arbitrary. Just as postmodernism has unraveled the treatment of culture as a bounded and static entity—it's more of a "garage sale" than "a museum" (Rosaldo 1989)—several selections easily fit into more than one category. Why put Andrea Freidus' "Policing Childhood Through The Learning Channels' *Toddlers in Tiaras*" (Reading 11.3) in Part 11: Visual and Media Anthropology and not in Part 4: Marriage, Family, Gender, and Sexuality, where one might discuss the social construction of childhood and mothering? Should Annette Wickström's "Virginity Testing as a Local Public Health Initiative" (Reading 4.4) be featured in Part 6: Medical Anthropology instead of Part 4: Marriage, Family, Gender, and Sexuality? Given the nebulous nature of the overall organization, each case study is introduced with a short paragraph which allows instructors to customize the volume and assign some pieces earlier or later. For example, Lila Abu-Lughod's "Do Muslim Women Really Need Saving?" (Reading 10.1) might be used as a framing piece at the start of a class to introduce and discuss cultural relativism and human rights, rather than to discuss war and peace, a topic featured toward the end of this book. Or, Shalini Shankar's "Speaking Like a Model Minority" (Reading 2.4) could be used in Part 5: Race, Ethnicity, Class, and Inequality to discuss the racialized implications of speech practices. The list here goes on.

Practicing Anthropology Today: Being Critically Applied and Publicly Engaged

The Neoliberal Moment

The contemporary moment is marked by neoliberalism, a term that you will encounter in several readings, but one that often remains undefined. Therefore, it will be important for you to have a basic understanding of its meaning from the start. Neoliberalism refers to a set of political and economic policies and programs that presume human well-being can be best enhanced through encouraging efficient economic markets, free trade, and strong property rights, while also limiting the role of the state by privatizing public services (e.g., schools, hospitals, railways, road maintenance, banks, electricity, fresh water) and engaging in massive governmental deregulation (e.g., remove restrictions on manufacturing, barriers to commerce, impose zero tariffs) (Edelman and Haugerud 2005; Harvey 2005). This is likely the only political-economic system you have ever known, but it was not always this way. At the turn of the twenty-first century, such free-market universalism came to dominate global development policy, replacing past approaches that had encouraged modernization, redistribution with growth, and meeting the basic needs of the poor (Edelman and Haugerud 2005, 8).

All of the contemporary pieces in this reader take place with the context of neoliberalism. Collectively they illustrate the effects of neoliberal policies, which radically reduced—or altogether eliminated—the safety net for the poor and the concept of "the public good," replacing it with a "pull yourself up by your bootstraps" mentality where individuals are expected to be responsible for finding solutions to their own well-being. What decades of anthropological research on the impacts of global neoliberalism have shown is that such policies have significantly widened the gap between rich and poor, with the poorest and most socially marginalized communities having been hit the hardest.

Neoliberalism has also impacted higher education. Major cuts in governmental funding for universities across the United States have meant that there are now fewer tenure-track academic jobs available. What this means for new graduates in anthropology is that most will end up working outside of university settings. For the few who remain within universities, resources to support teaching and research have also been significantly reduced or eliminated in the neoliberal context, and academics are placed under increased pressure to secure their own funding and to "do more with less." This context produces higher levels of collaboration between universities and other sectors also struggling to achieve their goals with fewer resources. Various forms of anthropological engagement emerge in such a context, along a continuum that includes partnerships with government, nongovernment, and private sectors on research to problem-solve within the confines of neoliberalism at one end, and activist work to critique and advocate for a structural overhaul to the current global political-economic system at the other end. You will find examples from both ends of the continuum in this book.

What's in a Label?

That the selections represent a great range in approaches to anthropological research and engagement is quite intentional. As students of anthropology, you will have a choice in how you wish to represent yourself vis-à-vis your community of research. Do you envision yourself to be a somewhat detached observer of cultural phenomena, one who will eventually transform your ethnographic work into a cultural snapshot, a somewhat static report of another way of being in the world? Or, will you co-create the reality which you represent? Do you believe anthropology's tools should be "put to use" (van Willigen 2002, 8) to solve the problems of humanity? Do you see yourself as "action-oriented" or as an activist?

A great deal of attention has been given to the various forms of engagement an anthropologist can take, and to teasing out the meanings behind such labels as "engaged," "applied," "activist," "action," and "public" anthropology. This section provides a brief accounting of these labels, to help you familiarize yourself with some of the core differences and debates over meaning and provide some guidance as to what the identity you assume as an anthropologist might signal to those around you.

Applied Anthropology and Practicing Anthropology

Applied anthropology is defined as the practical application of anthropological knowledge, theory, and methods to solve specific societal problems. Simply stated, it is "anthropology put to use" van Willigen 2002, 8). It is goal-oriented and aimed at changing a human behavior to ameliorate a contemporary problem. Applied anthropology has a long history, and up through World War II it comprised the majority of work that anthropologists pursued, shaping and defining the discipline into what it is today (Ervin 2005; Kedia and van Willigen 2005; Nolan 2013; Rylko-Bauer et al. 2006).

Some people distinguish applied anthropology from *practicing anthropology* by identifying the place of employment of the anthropologist. When one speaks of "practicing anthropologists" they are usually referring to non-academic anthropologists, those who are employed outside of university settings, for practical purposes (Erwin 2005, 4; Nolan 2013, 1). Applied anthropologists often are employed by universities, but doing applied work outside of the university setting, on a project that has been commissioned by an outside organization. In this fashion, applied anthropologists put their knowledge and skills to use to problem-solve either as a consultant for a government or nongovernmental agency, a business enterprise, or as the principal investigator on their own research. Conversely, practicing anthropologists put their knowledge and skills to work *within* their places of employment.

Nolan reminds us that this distinction in terms of place of employment is what sets practitioners apart from applied, action, or engaged anthropologists. The work that practicing anthropologists do is not "optional" or part-time; they are full-time employees of the organization sponsoring their work, and the context in which they work is significantly different from university settings. A university professor may do "applied" research, but this is a choice in positioning the kind of research they do; at the end of the day, they are still employed by a university and receive their support and security from that institution. In contrast, for "practitioners," the scope and nature of their work is defined by or in conversation with their employers (Nolan 2013, 1).

In recent decades, new labels for the use of anthropological theories and methods have emerged. When just a few decades ago there was "applied" anthropology and "pure" anthropology, today several different names are available to distinguish one's work. Some feel strongly that a distinct label is crucial to underscore the intentionality behind a specific goal and audience for one's anthropological practice (e.g., Borofsky on public anthropology); others find the newer labels distract from the shared goals of our discipline and create distance between anthropologists themselves (e.g., Rylko-Bauer et al. 2006; Singer 2000, 7).

Given the extensive literature on these debates, in this chapter I focus solely on providing simple definitions for terms used by those who advance specific labels, and I refer the reader to the now exhaustive literature if they wish to explore further (e.g., Baba and Hill 2006; Bennett 1996; Besteman 2013; Borofsky 2011; Hale 2008; Field and Fox 2007; Lamphere 2004; Lassiter 2005; Low and Merry 2010; Mullins 2011; Sanford and Angel-Ajani 2006).

Cultural Critique and the Theory-Practice Divide

Part of the rationale for new terms like "engaged" or "public" anthropology (discussed later) is a longer-standing—false—division between applied and academic anthropology. Academic anthropologists see the work they do bringing a "critical perspective" to contemporary societal problems (Nolan 2013, 2), drawing on theoretical approaches within the discipline to analyze and make sense of cultural phenomena. Critical approaches replaced early anthropological theories such as functionalism and structural-functionalism, which treated peoples and cultures as static and bounded entities, and did not attend to the flow of power or the influence of outside forces like colonialism, development, or globalization on culture change.

Cultural critique continues to be a common approach to research and writing in which the researcher pays attention to power, deconstructing how knowledge is produced and championing the subaltern. Academic anthropologists involved in cultural critique are typically not focused on finding a "solution" to a human problem, but rather work to unpack why that problem exists in the first place and to document who is the most deeply impacted as a result. Conversely, applied and practicing anthropologists are working toward change and are expected to find solutions. This focus on problem-solving has meant that applied and practicing anthropologists are often criticized for being "atheoretical."

The only evidence to support the claim that applied and practicing anthropology lack theory is that practicing anthropologists often do not publish their findings in peer-reviewed journals, as do academic anthropologists. The expectation for practitioners to publish their findings is unrealistic in a number of ways. Two key assumptions are behind this impractical expectation: (1) it assumes that part of a practitioner's job description includes publication; otherwise practicing anthropologists would need to be writing for journals in their spare time; and (2) it assumes that the anthropologist is permitted to publish the results of their work; much more commonly, information is proprietary, or privately owned by the organization that commissioned the work (Nolan 2013, 6).

Understanding of the nature of applied and practicing anthropology and the realization that all anthropology is indeed theoretical is improving in recent years (Rylko-Bauer et al. 2006, 184–185). There have been recent shifts in publicizing applied and practicing work. For example, our professional organizations are increasingly recognizing non-traditional publication methods and venues, like agency reports, museum exhibits, white papers, or even blogs, as legitimate forms of scholarship of equal status. The American Anthropological Association has even created guidelines to aid peers in evaluating the merit of such non-traditional works (see http://www.americananthro.org/AdvanceYourCareer/Content.aspx?ItemNumber=1667). The Society for Applied Anthropology has a journal dedicated to anthropological practice (*Practicing Anthropology*), and mainstream academic journals have moved to include an emphasis on practicing anthropology (e.g., *American Anthropologist's* public anthropology section).

Times are indeed changing. In 1994 Baba (182) reported that there existed a "prestige gap" among practicing and academic anthropologists, citing studies of anthropologists working in the private sector who got the sense that their graduate professors felt they "sold out the discipline" and that the work they did was not "real" anthropology. Today, anthropology students are just as often entering the field with plans to work beyond the university as they are within. As further evidence of this change, you will notice that several of the anthropologists profiled in this volume refuse to choose a label (e.g., applied, public, or engaged), shutting down the divisiveness that such labels create through their comments about the future of the discipline (see, e.g., Shirley Fiske in Part 8).

Being Engaged

In 2010, anthropologists Setha Low and Sally Engle Merry organized a special seminar and publication on *engaged anthropology*, producing a well-circulated article that outlines dilemmas and opportunities for doing engaged work. Low and Merry (2010) cast a wide net in thinking about what engaged anthropology is, or can be. For them, being an *engaged* anthropologist takes many forms, including (1) sharing and support (e.g., building friendships, possessing a commitment to social justice or social change); (2) teaching and public education (e.g., training and mentoring, public workshops, outreach); (3) social critique (i.e., using methods and theories to uncover power relations and structures of inequality); (4) collaboration (e.g., sharing leadership over research process with community members); (5) advocacy (e.g., expert witnessing, providing testimony, assisting communities in their organizing efforts); and (6) activism (which differs from advocacy in its commitment to confronting violations or suffering) (Low and Merry 2010, S207–S211). Importantly, for Low and Merry (and I might add for most anthropologists who identify as engaged scholars), these are not discrete categories, but they may—and often do—overlap.

Because Low and Merry's framing of engaged anthropology is so broad, many of the contemporary pieces in this reader fall within its definition. From the friendships and relationships John Jackson built in his study of race and class in contemporary black America (featured in Reading 5.4) to Vicanne Adams' uncovering of the structural causes of widespread suffering among the poorest and most marginalized in post-Katrina New Orleans (Reading 9.3), to Jacqueline Copeland-Carson's advocacy work within community development agencies to improve financing options for immigrant communities in Minnesota's Twin Cities, each is an example of engagement. Some have questioned if Low and Merry's definition of engagement might be a bit too wide (Low and Merry 2010, S222–S223). To respond to this questioning and add some nuance, I turn now to other definitions of engaged anthropology.

For Catherine Besteman (2013) and Kay Warren (2010), engaged anthropology is an anthropology that is values-driven and self-consciously works toward addressing power differentials rather than reinforcing them. It is an anthropology concerned with social justice, one that is reflexive and critical, attending to power differentials between researchers and the communities under study, and sharing findings with the broader community (Besteman 2013, 3; Warren 2010). For some engaged scholars, such as Dana-Ain Davis (2010), whose work appears in Reading 6.4, to be an engaged anthropologist means you are *politically* engaged.

Davis (2010) has described her approach as grounded in the work of Paolo Freire, the famous Brazilian educator who advocated for critical pedagogy and an education of liberation, whereby education must be relevant to, and emerge in conversation with, participants. Freire's (1993) work in popular education, or the self-reflective approach to collective and participatory production of knowledge, formed the basis for participatory action research

(PAR), an approach to research in which all parties are equal partners and gain something out of the research experience. PAR has influenced a number of action-oriented anthropologists, including Keisha Khan-Perry (Reading 8.3) and Barbara Rose Johnston (Profile, Part 9).

Some anthropologists frame their engagement under a growing university trend toward *engaged scholarship*. Stan Hyland (2010) defines engaged scholarship as research that (a) is collaborative, involving reciprocity among partners, and (b) leads to the production of new (and shared) knowledge. Further, Hyland advocates for engaged work to be *policy-relevant* and interdisciplinary. Shirley Fiske (Profile, Part 8) shares this perspective, encouraging budding practicing anthropologists to familiarize themselves with law, policy, and key issues and major players in the area in which they wish to specialize within their careers. Katherine Lambert-Pennington's (2012, 111–125) work with the Memphis Urban Transformation Initiative offers an example of an engaged scholarship agenda that employs the characteristics of effective engagement as identified by Hyland and Fiske.

The Memphis Urban Transformation Initiative was a collaboration informed by a participatory action research orientation that resulted in the creation of comprehensive planning documents for two Memphis urban neighborhoods (Lambert-Pennington 2012). The research team was interdisciplinary in nature, including anthropologists, urban planners, architects, civil engineers, social workers, and public health faculty and students. These university-based academics worked alongside and collaboratively with neighborhood residents, social service providers, local businesses, nonprofit organizations, and educators to produce planning documents and action strategies for implementing programs that addressed locally identified priorities. Lambert-Pennington (2012, 116–117) identifies five characteristics that set this work apart as an example of democratic and social-justice–centered engaged scholarship. These include: (1) its holistic and comprehensive understanding of social issues, which were identified collaboratively; (2) the linkage of a variety of academic units; (3) the diversity within the research team members and their skill sets and experiences; (4) shared ownership of data and collaboration on the production of tangible results; and (5) an explicit connection from the research activities to products, advocacy, and action.

More and more universities are moving to embrace civic engagement and engaged scholarship as part of their core missions. Yet there is room for some healthy skepticism about the potential risks of institutionalizing engaged scholarship within higher education, especially if it is un- or under-compensated, and valued under market. Academics that engage in this work may be impelled to do so out of their social and political commitments. Nevertheless, if the pursuit of such work without adequate resources (human, economic, and social) to back it supports an exploitative model whereby students and faculty are pursuing work that would otherwise be paid, and universities are able to capitalize on faculty and students "doing more for less," academics might think twice about pursuing these activities. Checker (2014) points out that with the trend toward civically engaged universities, engaged scholars are often pressured to build relationships that lend credibility to their institution. Checker (2014, 418) warns that these relationships can tend to be superficial and distract from the time and resources necessary to build a truly transformative anthropology.

Activist Anthropology

Activist anthropology is an anthropological practice that (a) helps unveil and understand the root causes of inequality and human suffering, (b) is carried out in collaboration with a collective of people subject to those conditions of suffering or oppression, and (c) is put to use with the people in question to develop strategies to transform the conditions of inequality and gain the power to ensure these strategies are effective (Hale 2001, 13). This definition of activist research by Charles Hale provides a challenge to the long-standing dichotomy and division between "pure" and "applied" research. As discussed previously, culture critique unveils the way in which power operates. It sets up the need for activist research, but ironically, Hale (2001) points out, it then does very little in terms of suggesting methodologies for action. In essence, while critical anthropologists are able to uncover the core issues in need of addressing, they usually stop short of application. Cultural critique is therefore largely an academic exercise, striving for intellectual production that is uncompromised by broader political struggles (Hale 2006). Whereas with activist research, one is compromised (and also enriched) by being positioned "squarely amid the tension between utopian ideals and practical politics" (Hale 2006, 100).

To be an activist anthropologist is not as straightforward as it sounds. There are questions about loyalties and practicalities, all of which impact one's ability to "act." Hale (2006) argues that activist anthropologists are loyal to both the space of critical scholarly production and the principles and practices of people who struggle outside academic settings. The work that academically based anthropologists pursue is constrained in specific ways by the expectations associated with tenure and promotion, including demands on one's time to publish and secure funding in addition to teaching and professional service (Checker 2014; Checker et al. 2014; Hale 2001). Being an activist anthropologist is not necessarily "easier" (or less constrained) if one works as a practicing anthropologist, employed by a nonprofit, NGO, government agency, or community-based organization. A collection of essays written by feminist activist anthropologists employed within development organizations (Eyben and Turquet 2013) reveals that bureaucratic structure and hierarchical managerialism can impede upon the success of their activist work. The underlying message that several activist anthropologists have made (Checker et al. 2014; Eyben and Turquet 2013; Hale 2006; Heyman 2011) is that even those with some degree of power (e.g., university professors or feminist human rights activists in development organizations) are subjected to the same structural forces of those who their research seeks to empower (in a nutshell: the forces of neoliberalism).

Public Anthropology

In her reflection on pubic anthropology, its strengths and constraints, the tensions it creates and compromises it makes, Catherine Besteman (2013) notes that the key difference between engaged anthropology and public anthropology is messaging. Unlike engaged anthropology, which can be either "inward" or "outward" facing, public anthropology is necessarily "outward facing," oriented toward promoting anthropological knowledge to a primarily non-academic public, and focused on expanding anthropology's public image (Besteman 2013, 4; Besteman and Gusterson 2004). According to Robert Borofsky (2011), who runs the Center for Public Anthropology, a 501(c)(3) nonprofit organization dedicated to "fostering accountability in higher education," public anthropologists are those who "address public problems in public ways." Examples of public anthropology, as so defined, are numerous and can be found throughout this volume, especially within the "In the News" and "Anthropology in Practice" features. The American Anthropological Association's Race: Are We So Different? project and Ray Codrington's discussion of his coordination of the b-boying/girling (dance) performances during the "Hip Hop for Social Change" event that he organized at the Field Museum in Chicago are two clear examples featured in Part 5 of the book.

Borofsky (2011) finds that the current structure of higher education impedes upon the ability of academics to pursue public anthropology, a point developed earlier in this introduction. While more and more cultural anthropologists find themselves engaging the non-academic public, or attempting to contribute to human problem-solving through sharing anthropological knowledge in public spaces, anthropologists who work within academic settings face a range of constraints in their ability to pursue these activities in full. The institutional pressure to publish and secure external funding in order to advance through tenure and promotion means that scholars are forced to spend more of their time writing for peer-reviewed publication in journals that are read by specialists in their field, written in obscure theoretical language rather than in styles or venues that are accessible to popular audiences (see also Low and Merry 2010, S213). Given this situation, Borofsky advocates for a revision to current academic accountability standards where anthropologists are evaluated less by the number of their publications and more by an evaluation of the degree to which their work actually addresses social problems. The American Anthropological Association (AAA) "Guidelines for Evaluating Scholarship in the Realm of Practicing, Applied, and Public Interest Anthropology for Academic Promotion and Tenure" is a positive step in this direction, as it sends a strong signal that our discipline's largest professional association of anthropologists recognizes the value in this work.

Borofsky's (2011) form of public anthropology also advocates for a revision to our ethical code, moving from "do not harm" toward "do some demonstrable good." In 2015, anthropologists Elizabeth Briody and Tracy Meerwarth Pester, professional anthropologists with extensive careers working outside of the academy in ethnographic consulting and employed for decades by General Motors, raised this same question in an AAA Ethics Blog. In reviewing the AAA Code to consider whether or not it reflected the kind of work they perform as practicing anthropologists, they were surprised by its "preoccupation with the concept of 'harm' with no corresponding emphasis on the concept of 'help'" (Briody and Pester 2015). The two argue that professional or practicing anthropologists are typically working toward a goal, and that is to produce a more effective system, toward "doing some good." The idea of "doing good" brings us back to issues of power, and the question that remains for most who are putting anthropology to use is, for whose good am I serving?

Practicing Anthropology Today: Being Critically Applied and Publically Engaged

After reading the preceding text, one can see that all approaches share a common theme as sociocultural anthropologists, and that is a concern with how "local knowledge is put to work in grappling with practical problems of everyday life and with basic philosophical problems of knowledge, truth, power, and justice" (AAA definition of sociocultural anthropology, AAA 2015). As you read the case studies, news pieces, and interviews, you might attempt to place each within a specific tradition: applied, cultural critique, public, engaged, and so forth. Or, you may notice that the content does not lend itself to a label, and maybe a particular anthropologist explicitly refuses to be labeled. This author wishes to remind readers of Barbara Rylko-Bauer and colleagues' (2006) concern that labeling and othering within our own discipline can be counterproductive and serve to overlook or erase significant areas of accomplishment. Writing to "reclaim and position" applied anthropology, Rylko-Bauer et al. (2006) forcefully argue against the misconceptions that applied work is uncritical, atheoretical, or disengaged, calling for a convergence of approaches.

A meaningful convergence of methodologically sound, critical, reflexive, and engaged anthropology—a convergence that builds on and learns from the extensive past experiences of putting anthropology to use—will free us up to focus on differences that actually do matter in the real world: the compelling divides that separate those who have from those who have not, those who are honored from those who are stigmatized, those wielding disproportionate power from those with limited agency and voice, and those who are central from those who are marginalized (Rylko-Bauer et al. 2008, 187).

Regardless of the label under which the authors of the selections in this book put their skill sets to use as anthropologists, they all share in common an interest in "putting anthropology to use" for the good of humanity (Rylko-Bauer et al. 2008).

Finally, all of the more contemporary pieces in this reader are clearly contextualized within the neoliberal moment. This political-economic context has had jarring sociocultural effects including rising inequality in access to critical resources, from economic resources to healthcare services to water. To practice anthropology today, regardless of from where (from a university center, from a nonprofit, government agency or corporation), or under what "hat" (as a public, applied, action, or activist anthropologist), one cannot escape anthropological "engagement" informed by critical theory. Thus, for this author, to be practicing critically engaged anthropology today is to be working to communicate anthropological knowledge about human and cultural diversity effectively, either in conservation or partnership with those we study, in addressing public audiences, or in effecting policy or programmatic change.

PART 1
Thinking Anthropologically

Anthropology professors often say that one of their goals in introductory courses is to teach students how to "think anthropologically." But what does it mean to think anthropologically? Anthropology, as the study of humankind across time and space, seeks to understand and explain human behavior in all of its diversity. To think anthropologically, anthropologists approach the study of culture through three interrelated core tenets: holism, cross-cultural comparison, and cultural relativism. The holistic approach means we examine culture as a whole, rather than as distinct parts. Through cross-cultural comparison, we consider practices and beliefs in one culture as they appear in other cultures. This comparison is not done to create a ranking system or hierarchy of cultural behavior but rather to lead us to generalizations about human behavior, shedding light on what it means to be human. Critical to cultural understanding and paramount to avoiding ethnocentrism (or the assumption that your own cultural worldview is the best or correct way of seeing the world) is the principle of cultural relativism. Cultural relativism refers to understanding another culture in its own terms, according to their worldview, ethics, and values. In pursuit of cultural understanding, anthropologists employ a variety of qualitative and quantitative research methods, but the hallmark of cultural anthropology is the ethnographic method, which involves long-term intensive immersion and participant observation within a community.

Readings in this initial section are intended to provide the building blocks of anthropological thought and engagement. John Monaghan and Peter Just's "A Dispute in Donggo" (Reading 1.1) and Claire Sterk's

"Tricking and Tripping" (Reading 1.2) introduce readers to the subfield of cultural anthropology, describing and defining ethnography and the ethnographic method. These pieces illuminate some of the challenges of "doing" fieldwork, including how anthropologists go about gaining trust within a new community, and negotiating complicated ethical dilemmas in the field, including protecting the identities of informants and maintaining trust among those engaged in illegal activity.

As noted previously, one of anthropology's core tenets is cultural relativism, which provides us with an intellectual and moral commitment to withhold judgment about cultural beliefs and practices that may seem different or strange (Welsch and Vivanco 2014). Carolyn Fluehr-Lobban's piece, "Cultural Relativism and Universal Human Rights" (Reading 1.3), takes up the following conundrum: Can there ever be such a thing as universal human rights, or are human rights also culturally relative? Drawing on her own research in the Sudan on female genital mutilation, Fluehr-Lobban explores the role of anthropologists in international human rights dialogues. Here readers will again be confronted with the role of the anthropologist vis-à-vis their community of study. Reflexivity, or considering and describing one's own social position in relation to those they study, became an important addition to anthropological writing in the 1980s and continues even now. The "positionality" of the researcher—that is, who she or he is in terms of race, ethnicity, class, gender, sexuality, education, experience, and so forth—shapes both what information an anthropologist has access to and how they come to understand what they hear and experience. Reflecting on one's positionality is a tool anthropologists use to situate themselves within the social context and power structure, allowing for a clearer understanding of how the researcher came to their conclusions. Positionality is considered in the last two selections.

In "Maxwell's Demons" (Reading 1.4), Janet McIntosh considers the impact that anthropologists have in changing the perspectives of their research informants, and vice versa. She shares her journey as an agnostic anthropologist studying Giriama beliefs in spirits and witchcraft alongside Maxwell, an aspiring faith revival leader, and how each began to change the other's belief systems over the course of the research. As anthropologists, we are constantly seeking to understand to the world from "the native's point of view." McIntosh's reflection on her journey illustrates both her and her research assistant's oscillation between emic (insider) and etic (outsider) perspective, and raises questions about which is preferable. The pursuit of an emic understanding has long been considered by many in the field to be the goal of ethnographic work. This has led some to argue that ethnographic work is best performed by "native anthropologists," where there is a close cultural and linguistic familiarity between the anthropologist and the people being studied. The assumption here is that such a close match will provide for easier access to the community, resulting in a higher degree of rapport, empathy, and understanding (see Tsuda, this volume). In "Is Native Anthropology Really Possible?" (Reading 1.5), Takeyuki Tsuda, a Japanese American studying Japanese Americans, provides an interesting counterpoint to this perspective, arguing that "difference" between the researcher and research participants is productive and essential for fieldwork; difference is "good to think with."

Part 1 closes with the profiles of two high-level anthropologists, Afghanistan's President, Dr. Ashraf Ghani Ahmadzai, and Dr. Jim Yong Kim, the twelfth President of the World Bank. While some may argue about whether each of these high-profile persons fits the goals of "public anthropology," without question they are very "public" figures, representing our discipline in positions of significant power.

KEY TERMS:

- Ethnography
- Ethnographic method
- Fieldwork
- Participant observation
- Emic and etic
- Subjectivity

- Positionality
- Ethics
- Cultural relativism
- Universal human rights
- Female genital mutilation
- Native ethnography

1.1 A Dispute in Donggo: Fieldwork and Ethnography

JOHN MONAGHAN AND PETER JUST

How do anthropologists "do" anthropology? From this selection, out of a short book introducing students to the field of sociocultural anthropology, the reader will learn what ethnography is, how anthropologists go about "doing fieldwork" (and how this has changed over the years), as well as some of the practical and ethical challenges ethnographers face in doing their work. The selection begins with a story from one of the author's fieldwork experiences as a means to illustrate the distinct interpretive lens anthropology offers as compared to other social science approaches.

Questions

1. Compare how a historian or a sociologist may have analyzed the case of la Ninde's assault on ina Mone to how the anthropologist did? What are the advantages of the ethnographic method?
2. What is the "ethnographic present," and why has it been largely abandoned in ethnography writing?
3. How does subjectivity impact the ethnographic process, including the study of and writing about culture? Is ethnographic subjectivity a "problem" that must be overcome?

As has often been said, if you want to understand what anthropology *is*, look at what anthropologists *do*. Above all else, what anthropologists do is *ethnography*. Ethnography is to the cultural or social anthropologist what lab research is to the biologist, what archival research is to the historian, or what survey research is to the sociologist. Often called—not altogether accurately—"participant observation," ethnography is based on the apparently simple idea that in order to understand what people are up to, it is best to observe them by interacting with them intimately and over an extended period. That is why anthropologists have tended traditionally to spend long periods—sometimes years at a stretch—living in the communities they study, sharing the lives of the people to as great an extent as they can. It is this approach that has defined our discipline and distinguished it from other social sciences. Now, we certainly do not dismiss the methods more characteristic of other disciplines, such as the use of questionnaires or the collection of quantitative behavioural data. But anthropologists have long felt that approaching the study of human beings in those ways is likely to produce an incomplete—even misleading—understanding of the people studied, especially when those people are members of foreign or unfamiliar societies. . . .

Let us begin with a story, a story that shows you not only how anthropologists work, but what is distinctive about anthropology as a discipline. This is a story about Peter's fieldwork with the Dou Donggo and how he came to be interested in the anthropology of law.

One night I was sitting in the house of a friend in Doro Ntika, the village where I was conducting fieldwork. One of my friend's relatives burst into the room, shouting that his sister-in-law, a

John Monaghan and Peter Just. "A Dispute in Donggo: Fieldwork and Ethnography." 2000. *Social and Cultural Anthropology: A Very Short Introduction.* New York: Oxford University Press, 13–33. By permission of Oxford University Press.

woman named ina Mone, had been assaulted by a young man, la Ninde. We rushed over to ina Mone's house to see what had happened. Ina Mone sat on the floor of the room, one side of her face painted with a medicinal paste, where she said la Ninde had struck her. She also showed us the shirt she had been wearing and that had been torn in the assault. Her male relatives were angry, and talked of "taking down the spears and sharpening the bushknives," anxious to exact an immediate revenge on la Ninde. But everyone became calmer when ama Tife, one of the principal elders of the village, came by to assure us that he and the other elders of Doro Ntika would convene a court and exact justice according to tradition. The next morning they did just that. La Ninde was brought before a group of elders with most of the village looking on. Ina Mone showed her medicated face and torn shirt as evidence. La Ninde admitted to having shouted at her, but denied having laid hands upon her. A spirited and tumultuous drama ensued, as members of the court, led by ama Panci, berated la Ninde and finally extracted a confession. He was assessed a minor fine and was made to kneel before ina Mone begging forgiveness. She gave him a symbolic slap on the head, and he was let go.

Later that afternoon, I chatted with a friend. I said. "Wasn't that terrible, what la Ninde did, assaulting ina Mone like that?" He answered, "Yes, it was. But you know he never really hit her." I was surprised. "What about the torn shirt and her face?" I asked. "Well," he said, "anyone can tear a shirt, and who knows what's under the medicine." I was deeply shocked. "But that means la Ninde is innocent. Isn't this terribly unfair?" "Not at all," he replied. "What la Ninde was convicted of was more true than what really happened." He then proceeded to fill me in on what everyone else in the village knew, indeed, what they had known all along. Ina Mone had seen la Ninde hanging around la Fia, a young woman who was betrothed to another young man, absent from Doro Ntika. Ina Mone had complained to la Ninde's mother, who in turn had admonished la Ninde. Furious at having been ratted out, la Ninde had gone to ina Mone's house and threatened her—a serious breach of etiquette—but had not in fact assaulted her.

This story is an account of a real event in the real world, as witnessed by an ethnographer. How would this event have been recorded and analysed by a historian or a sociologist? To begin with, to a historian who works primarily with archives or court records, the case of la Ninde's assault on ina Mone would be completely invisible. The Dou Donggo do not keep written records of disputes settled by village elders, so this case and the great majority of cases would not appear in a form accessible to the historian working in an archive. Even a historian who adopts the ethnographic methods of an anthropologist and takes down oral histories might have difficulty in accessing this case, for among the Dou Donggo it is an accepted practice that one never discusses a dispute after it has been settled. Only because he was on the scene at the time the dispute erupted was Peter able to record it and explore its meaning.

How would this case have appeared to a sociologist or a criminologist? Although some sociologists and criminologists are adept at using ethnographic methods, it is far more common for them to rely on surveys, questionnaires, and the analysis of official statistics. Again, to those relying on official statistics, this case would have been completely invisible. La Ninde's "assault" might have appeared as a "data point" in a survey of disputes in the community undertaken by a sociologist. But it seems unlikely that a survey would be so artfully constructed as to see beyond the superficial evidence of the case, or, more importantly, to uncover the notion that la Ninde's conviction of a crime he did not commit was "more true than what really happened." If the case *had* been recorded officially, researchers (including anthropologists) who rely on such data would probably assume the case of la Ninde was one of simple assault, leading to conclusions about Dou Donggo society that would be seriously incomplete, if not misleading.

Very well, then, what might the case described mean to an ethnographer? How might an anthropologist analyse this event to learn more about what the Dou Donggo believe and how they behave? First, after considerable questioning, it became clear to Peter that the case had little to do with assault and a very great deal to do with respect for the institution of marriage. Why had ina Mone complained to la Ninde's mother about his flirtations with la Fia? Because ina Mone had a real and vested interest in protecting the integrity of betrothals, particularly betrothals contracted by the family of ama Panci.

Why? Because ina Mone's daughter was betrothed to ama Panci's son, and another of ama Panci's sons was betrothed to la Fia!

One lesson, then, that Peter learned was that in disputes (at least among the Dou Donggo) things are often other than what they appear to be. A case of "assault" may really be a case about "alienation of affection'". What made this sort of realization possible? First of all, Peter was there to witness the event to begin with, something that would not have been possible had he not spent almost two years in this village. The ability to observe unusual, unique events is one of the principal advantages of the ethnographic method. It is important to recognize, as well, that Peter was able to observe the case in question from the outset not only because he lived in Doro Ntika for a long time, but because he lived there around the clock and as a member of the community. The case came to his attention not because he was seeking out information on disputes or even on betrothals, but because he just happened to be chatting with friends in a nearby house, long after a conventional "working day" was over. It is this openness to the serendipitous discovery that gives the ethnographic method strength and flexibility not generally available to highly deductive social science methods, such as survey or statistical research. Indeed, anthropologists often find themselves doing significant research on unanticipated subjects. While there are those research topics we take with us to the field, there are also topics imposed upon us by the actual circumstances and events of people's everyday lives. Peter had not intended to study dispute settlement when he set off for Indonesia, but neither could he ignore the research opportunity he encountered that evening. The randomness of ethnographic serendipity is compensated for by the length of time a good ethnographer spends in the field; eventually, one hopes, one will accidentally encounter most social phenomena of significance.

Prolonged exposure to daily life in Doro Ntika also made Peter aware that it was necessary to look beyond the superficial events of the case, made him aware that issues like the fidelity of fiancés was a sensitive, even explosive, topic in this community. In other words, after more than a year living in this community, Peter had a rich and nuanced context into which the events of this case could be placed. The discrepancy between what a social event is apparently about and what it might "really" be about is almost impossible to discern without the experiential context ethnographic fieldwork makes available. That is one of the advantages

that anthropologists have traditionally relied upon for the insights they derive from their research and it is why traditional ethnographic fieldwork has placed a premium on long duration—often as much as two years for an initial study. Moreover, Peter was able to discover what the case was "really about" because his long residence in the village had allowed him to build up relations of trust with people who were willing to confide in him and to explain events and motivations beyond superficial appearances. Having long-term cordial relations with people in the village—having friends, if you like—also enabled Peter to persist in his questions beyond the superficial and to evaluate the content of the answers he received.

What implications might an anthropologist see in the lessons of this case? Every ethnographic description at least implicitly participates in the cross-cultural comparisons that also engage anthropologists. Anthropology has long been engaged in relating the description of local beliefs and practices to categories of universal, pan-human significance. The case of la Ninde compelled Peter to bring into question his understanding of legal categories like "evidence" and "liability," to question the universality of the idea of "justice" itself. What does it mean that virtually everyone in the village knew the physical evidence presented by ina Mone was false, yet was nonetheless accepted? What might it mean for our understanding of liability and responsibility if la Ninde could be convicted for what he *might have done*, rather than for what he actually did, without producing a sense among the villagers that he was a victim of trumpery or injustice? If evidence and liability could be handled in this way, what does that mean if we are to try to construct a sense of what justice means to human beings at large? It is interplay between the specific and the general, between the local and the universal that gives anthropology much of its value as a social science. For not only are we engaged in recording the "customs and manners" of people around the world, we are constantly bringing our appreciation of local knowledge to bear on a more general understanding of what it means to be a human being. . . .

Fieldwork: Strategies and Practices

. . . An ethnographer goes to the field with the intention of studying some particular aspect of social life, which might range from ecological adaptation to indigenous theology, to relations between the genders, to grassroots political mobilization, and so on. . . . The ethnographer does not enter into the enterprise unprepared. . . . Most anthropologists begin their preparation with several years of study in the history and previous ethnographic literature of the region in which they propose to do fieldwork. Because anthropologists have felt it imperative that they conduct their fieldwork in the language of the people they study without using translators, an ethnographer may need to acquire at least passable fluency in several languages. In addition to such general preparation, ethnographers are usually trained in more specialized fields concerning the kind of problem they intend to investigate. A researcher who intends to study the medicinal use of plants among an Amazonian people, for example, needs to learn not only a good deal of conventional botany, but also needs to be familiar with how various of the world's peoples have categorized and used plants. Anthropologists are always anthropologists *of* something and somewhere: John is an anthropologist of religion and a Mesoamericanist; Peter is an anthropologist of law and a Southeast Asianist.

An ethnographer's first task is to become established in the community. This is often a protracted and difficult process, during which more than a few projects have foundered. Once the ethnographer has found a source of funding for the project, it is often necessary to secure a variety of permits from various levels of government, local research institutions, and the host community. This can consume more than a year of the ethnographer's time, before he or she even sets foot in the field site. One colleague carrying out a research project at the headquarters of a major industrial concern needed to have his proposal reviewed by the company's lawyers before he could even enter the building to talk with anyone. Once they have arrived, ethnographers face many of the same problems anyone would encounter when moving into a new community, problems complicated by unfamiliarity with the language and the challenges of daily life in places lacking many of the amenities they may have been used to at home: electricity, indoor plumbing, or easy access to healthcare, news, or entertainment. Many anthropologists work in cities and suburbs in Europe and North America, where the challenges are of a different nature. . . .

The ethnographer faces more subtle difficulties, too. Locally powerful individuals may try to use the ethnographer as a prize or a pawn in their rivalries. Members of the community may have an exaggerated idea of what the ethnographer can do for them, and make persistent demands that cannot be met. At the same time, the ethnographer often experiences the great joy of making new friends and the thrill of seeing and doing things he or she would never otherwise have been able to see or do. As a day-to-day experience, fieldwork can be filled with abruptly alternating emotional highs and lows. At its heart the process of doing ethnography really is participant observation. By living among the people of the community as they themselves live, the ethnographer stands the best chance of becoming established.

Dialogue is the backbone of ethnography. While anthropologists make use of a variety of techniques to elicit and record data, the interview is by far the most important. Interviews can range in formality from highly structured question-and-answer sessions with indigenous specialists, to the recording of life histories, to informal conversations, or to a chance exchange during an unanticipated encounter. Ultimately, the key to ethnographic success is *being there*, available to observe, available to follow up, available to take advantage of the chance event. Beyond the apparently simple techniques of interview and dialogue, ethnographers also employ a variety of more specialized techniques. Audio recording of speech and music, photography, film, drawing, genealogy, mapping, census-taking, archival research, collecting material culture, collecting botanical or other natural samples, all have their ethnographic uses, depending on the ethnographer's specific research project.

Leaving the field can be almost as difficult as entering it: considering the effort required to establish oneself in a community, parting company with friends and now-familiar ways of life can be a wrenching experience. On an intellectual level, there are often nagging worries about whether one has really completed the research topic—a concern that is often justified. In a sense, no ethnographic research project is ever truly complete; it is always possible to learn more, to expand the temporal or spatial scope of one's understanding, or deepen the subtlety of that understanding. . . .

Critiques of Ethnographic Fieldwork

. . . The very strengths of classical ethnographic research have sometimes also proved to be weaknesses. One problem with participant observation has been a temptation for the ethnographer to present the community in a kind of temporal and spatial isolation. Many ethnographers, particularly in the "classic" accounts of the 1930s and 1940s, employed what came to be called the *ethnographic present* in which communities were presented as frozen in time, outside any historical context, and without reference to neighbouring societies or encapsulating states. For example, one of the most admired classics, Raymond Firth's *We the Tikopia*, described the social organization and traditional religion of the Tikopia without reference to the fact that half the population had recently converted to Christianity. Indeed, anthropologists may sometimes be carried away by the romance of their own enterprise and value the "unspoiled" traditions of a society far more than the people themselves do. A friend of ours visited Tikopia some twenty years after Firth had lived there, and was taken to a grotto by the sea where offerings to the gods of the old religion had been made. Seeing a single old offering, he asked his guide who had left it there, and was told "Fossi left it there." "Fossi," of course, is the Tikopia pronunciation of Firth's name. Ethnographers are not always successful in guarding against a temptation to romanticize the "otherness" of the people they study. Another criticism of the "ethnographic present" has concerned the tendency of ethnographers to write in an omniscient third-person voice, as if they had not been actively involved in eliciting the information they present. For better or worse, the past ten years has seen the emergence of a genre of ethnography that seems as intent on conveying the ethnographer's personal experiences in collecting the data as in presenting the data themselves.

Participant observation—characterized by long-term intense interaction with relatively small groups of people—may allow the ethnographer to dig deeply into the complexities and subtleties of a community's social life. But how representative of larger social and cultural wholes can this be? Based on participant observation alone, it would be impossible for Peter to say to what extent the beliefs and values uncovered in the case of la Ninde are typical of the Dou Donggo in general, or of the regency of Bima, or of Indonesia, or of Southeast Asia. In approaching these problems we recall once again that ethnography is incomplete without the cross-cultural comparisons which allow the uniqueness of ethnographic description to find a comparative spatial and temporal context. . . .

There are also persistent questions about the "objectivity" of the data collected by means of participant observation. When a chemist sets out to analyse a sample, she might use a spectroscope. Like any scientific instrument, a spectroscope can be *calibrated* so that the scientist can be reasonably sure that data collected with

one spectroscope will be comparable to data collected with a spectroscope calibrated in another time or place. But what—or, more appropriately, who—is the instrument of data collection in anthropology? Obviously, it is the ethnographer, and calibrating a human being is a far more daunting prospect than calibrating a spectroscope. Each ethnographer is a unique individual, the product of a unique upbringing and education, replete with all the psychological predispositions—hidden as well as obvious—that constitute any human being. There have been notorious instances in which two anthropologists have studied the same community but come to very different conclusions about them. How, then, can we reconcile the inevitable subjectivity of participant observation with our desire for a calibrated uniformity of data collection? The short answer is that we can't, and it is this, more than anything else, that distinguishes social sciences such as anthropology from natural sciences such as chemistry, whatever their own problems of observer bias.

Can the problem of ethnographic subjectivity be overcome? The origins of participant observation as the hallmark method of anthropology began at the end of the last century as an attempt to compensate for the variable reliability of descriptions of non-Western peoples. Not content to rely on travellers' tales, missionary accounts, and official colonial reports of "customs and manners," W. H. R. Rivers, Bronislaw Malinowski, Franz Boas, and others among the founders of modern professional anthropology insisted on the first-hand collection of ethnographic data by trained observers. It was their hope that training would suffice to compensate for the prejudices of the observer. . . .

Other notable attempts to overcome these epistemological problems have included re-studies and studies undertaken by teams of ethnographers. One would think that a scientific approach to gathering ethnographic data would encourage anthropologists to re-study communities that had been studied before by other ethnographers as a check against subjectivity or bias. But this is far from common. To some extent this has been due to a sense of urgency among anthropologists to conduct "*salvage ethnography.*" Many have been concerned that most of the world's smaller societies and traditional ways of life are fast disappearing and that it is more important to record those that have never been studied than to confirm results already collected. It must also be admitted that many anthropologists were first attracted to the field by the romantic image of the lone, intrepid explorer, and that an unspoken ethnographic "machismo" has attached itself to those who have studied the previously unstudied. There has been, altogether, an understandable if misguided sense of proprietorship on the part of an ethnographer for "his" or "her people" which has made it very difficult for one ethnographer to "poach" on the "territory" of another. Finally, it has been rare for ethnographers working in communities that have been studied before to approach those communities interested in precisely the same theoretical or ethnographic issues as their predecessor. And because societies can change rapidly, separation in time of even a few years between an initial study and the next study also makes it difficult for re-studies to provide a check on ethnographic objectivity.

On occasion, anthropologists have engaged in the study of a particular community by a team of researchers, partly to provide greater comprehensiveness and partly to compensate for individual observer bias. . . . [I]t is not clear that the data collected by teams of ethnographers are significantly less subjective than those collected by groups.

More recently, some anthropologists have argued that "objectivity" is a false issue. Our bias—that is, our social and historical situation—is what gives us a point of view, and hence constitutes a resource we should openly draw upon in our interpretations. Others contend that any form of representation is an exercise in power and control. To these critics, the whole enterprise of ethnographic description is suspect so long as asymmetries of power persist between the observer and the observed. These critiques have occasioned new styles of ethnographic writing. In contrast to the language of omniscient objectivity that characterized earlier ethnography, some now favour the presentation of relatively unedited texts representing a variety of "voices" other than the ethnographer's. Other ethnographers have adopted the inclusion of a more autobiographical style of presentation, in which the ethnographer's background and relations with his or her subjects become a central topic of the ethnography. . . .

All the same, isn't it an act of extraordinary hubris for someone to propose to present a definitive account of another people, even when it is based on long-term "participant observation"? And isn't it problematic that the vast majority of ethnographers are Westerners when the vast majority of their subjects have been non-Western? To some extent this is a self-correcting problem: more and more non-Western students are trained as anthropologists and more and more nations are developing their own traditions and styles of anthropological research. For example, most of the ethnography of Mexican communities is today written by Mexicans, in Spanish, which was not the case twenty years ago. The same can be said to be true of gender: women, who now constitute a majority of recent doctorates in American anthropology, are frequently engaged in the study of women, both at home and elsewhere. By the same token, a number of non-Western ethnographers have begun to turn their attention to the study of Western societies. The discipline as a whole can only benefit from additional perspectives. After all, Alexis de Toqueville's description of American society remains unsurpassed by any observation made by an American. In the same way, anthropologists have long regarded the "outsider's perspective" they bring to their subjects as one of the principal advantages of ethnographic method. A person studying his or her own culture can be likened to a fish trying to describe water. While the insider is capable of noticing subtle local variations, the outsider is far more likely to notice the tacit understandings that local people take for granted as "common sense" or "natural" categories of thought. The outsider status of the ethnographer, then, can be regarded as strength as well as a weakness, even as a strength crucial to the success of the enterprise.

The Ethics of Ethnography

The nature of ethnographic work is such that the researcher develops a unique set of relationships with the people he or she studies, with host institutions and governments, and with colleagues. As anthropology has matured, the moral issues raised by these relationships have become matters of concern. Various professional associations have debated the issues and framed codes of ethical conduct. For fieldworkers the first imperative is to ensure that one's research does not harm the people one studies. For example, John and a colleague wrote a history of a Maya town in Guatemala. In a book review, a geographer questioned their expertise and political commitment by noting that the book failed to mention and criticize the establishment of an army garrison in the town in the 1980s. John and his colleague had certainly been aware of the army's presence (in 1979 a drunken soldier fired a machine gun into the house where John was sleeping). But John and his colleague declined to discuss the army in their book because, given the political situation in Guatemala at the time, and their close work with certain individuals and families in the town, critical mention of the army could have led to retaliation against their friends. Similarly, Peter's account of the case of la Ninde makes use of pseudonyms to protect the anonymity of the parties concerned—a fairly standard practice among anthropologists. Like other anthropologists, he also uses pseudonyms to refer to the places where he has worked.

A persistent source of ethical dilemma for ethnographers is to be found in the extent to which it is appropriate for ethnographers actively to influence the social, religious, or political life of the communities in which they work. In one celebrated case, for example, an ethnographer was presented with a situation in which members of her host community held the traditional belief that twins are inhuman and should be allowed to die of neglect. When twins were born to a village woman during her stay, she faced the dilemma of whether to intervene and if so, in what way. Should she try to persuade the mother not to abandon her newborn babies? Should she offer to adopt them herself? Should she inform village or government officials who disapproved of the traditional practice? Or, out of respect for the beliefs of her hosts, should she do nothing? For all our efforts to frame codes of professional behaviour, there is no consensus among anthropologists as to how such dilemmas are to be resolved. Admittedly, most of the dilemmas anthropologists face are not matters of life and death, but the degree to which the participant observer should really participate in the affairs of the community remains a persistent and vexing problem. In a similar vein, John has frequently been asked by Mixtecs to aid them in entering the United States without a visa. How should he respond? On the one hand he feels a deep sense of obligation to people who have been his friends and hosts in Mexico. On the other hand, helping them in this way violates the laws of his own country.

At the same time, ethnographers have often felt compelled to become advocates for the people they study. The peoples anthropologists study have often been among those most vulnerable to colonial and neocolonial oppression, genocide, displacement, poverty, and general powerlessness in the face of governments and other institutions. Anthropologists sometimes (although hardly always) have access to media and other means of publicizing the plight of the people they study and many have made use of this access.

Advocacy has not been without risk to these anthropologists, who have suffered deportation, imprisonment, and even assassination in retaliation for their actions.

One ethical issue that has received increasing attention concerns intellectual property rights. Anthropologists have been criticized for "profiting" from the "expropriation" of indigenous cultural knowledge. Are indigenous peoples entitled to copyright knowledge that has traditionally been in the public domain? Should communities be able to exercise control over the publication of cultural knowledge? Should they be entitled to pass binding editorial judgement on the interpretations ethnographers make? Are ethnographers obliged to share what profits, if any, they make from the sale of ethnographic accounts with the subjects of their accounts?

Ultimately, we have to confront more general ethical issues. To whom does an ethnographer owe his or her greatest allegiance? Is it to the people studied, to the sovereign government of the country where research takes place, to the agency or foundation that funds the ethnographer's research, to the academic or research institution that employs the ethnographer, or to the community of scholars to which the ethnographer belongs? Should ethnographers be expected only to add to humanity's knowledge of itself or should they be expected to provide more tangible benefits to the people they study or to the world at large? Should ethnographers be held to a higher standard than the one applied to journalists, filmmakers, or photographers who also report on their fellow human beings? These, too, are unresolved questions, subject to lively debate.

What can we expect of ethnography and the ethnographer? For all of the claims made for and against the products of participant observation, anthropology has always relied on what amounts to a good-faith effort on the part of ethnographers to tell their stories as fully and honestly as possible. Similarly, we have relied on the common decency of ethnographers to act with due regard for the integrity of their profession. We all recognize that complete descriptive objectivity is impossible, that a comprehensive understanding of any society or culture is unattainable, and that ethical problems are more easily posed than resolved. That we continue to pose these questions is perhaps the best indication of the fundamental health of anthropology as both an academic discipline and a humanistic enterprise.

1.2 Tricking and Tripping: Fieldwork on Prostitution in the Era of AIDS

CLAIRE E. STERK

How do cultural anthropologists go about learning about other cultures? What methods do they use during their fieldwork? This excerpt from Claire Sterk's book provides a nice overview of her use of qualitative methods and prolonged participant observation to gain an in-depth understanding of the lives of female prostitutes in New York and Atlanta. Sterk describes the process by which she gained entrée into this community, how she built trust, and the ethical dilemmas she faced as a researcher seeking to understand the complexities of illegal activities and drug dependence.

Questions

1. How does ethnographic research differ from other research approaches?
2. How do in-depth interviews and participant observation compare with structured questionnaires?
3. How does an ethnographer go about building trust and rapport?
4. How does a researcher's relative privilege shape the research process for ethnographers working in marginalized communities?
5. What did being given a street name symbolize to Sterk?
6. What ethical dilemmas arose for Sterk?

> *Prostitution is a way of life. IT IS THE LIFE*
> *We make money for pimps who promise us love and more,*
> *but if we don't produce, they shove us out the door.*
> *We turn tricks who have sex-for-pay.*
> *They don't care how many times we serve every day.*
> *The Life is rough. The Life is tough.*
> *We are put down, beaten up, and left for dead.*
> *It hurts body and soul and messes with a person's head.*
> *Many of us get high. Don't you understand is a way of getting by?*
> *The Life is rough. The Life is tough.*
> *We are easy to blame because we are lame.*
>
> —PIPER, 1987[1]

Claire E. Sterk. 1999. *Tricking and Tripping: Fieldwork on Prostitution in the Era of AIDS.* Putnam Valley, New York: Social Change Press, 1–19, 166–167.

One night in March of 1987 business was slow. I was hanging out on a stroll with a group of street prostitutes. After a few hours in a nearby diner/coffee shop, we were kicked out. The waitress felt bad, but she needed our table for some new customers. Four of us decided to sit in my car until the rain stopped. While three of us chatted about life, Piper wrote this poem. As soon as she read it to us, the conversation shifted to more serious topics—pimps, customers, cops, the many hassles of being a prostitute, to name a few. We decided that if I ever finished a book about prostitution, the book would start with her poem.

This book [excerpt] is about the women who work in the lower echelons of the prostitution world. They worked in the streets and other public settings as well as crack houses. Some of these women viewed themselves primarily as prostitutes, and a number of them used drugs to cope with the pressures of the life. Others identified themselves more as drug users, and their main reason for having sex for money or other goods was to support their own drug use and often the habit of their male partner. A small group of women interviewed for this book had left prostitution, and most of them were still struggling to integrate their past experiences as prostitutes in their current lives.

The stories told by the women who participated in this project revealed how pimps, customers, and others such as police officers and social and health service providers treated them as "fallen" women. However, their accounts also showed their strengths and the many strategies they developed to challenge these others. Circumstances, including their drug use, often forced them to sell sex, but they all resisted the notion that they might be selling themselves. Because they engaged in an illegal profession, these women had little status; their working conditions were poor; and their work was physically and mentally exhausting. Nevertheless, many women described the ways in which they gained a sense of control over their lives. For instance, they learned how to manipulate pimps, how to control the types of services and length of time bought by their customers, and how to select customers. While none of these schemes explicitly enhanced their working conditions, they did make the women feel stronger and better about themselves.

In this [excerpt], I present prostitution from the point of view of the women themselves. To understand their current lives, it was necessary to learn how they got started in the life, the various processes involved in their continued prostitution careers, the link between prostitution and drug use, the women's interactions with their pimps and customers, and the impact of the AIDS epidemic and increasing violence on their experiences. I also examined the implications for women. Although my goal was to present the women's thoughts, feelings, and actions in their own words, the final text is a sociological monograph compiled by me as the researcher. Some women are quoted more than others because I developed a closer relationship with them, because they were more able to verbalize and capture their circumstances, or simply because they were more outspoken.

The Sample

The data for this [work] are qualitative. The research was conducted during the last ten years, in the New York City and Atlanta metropolitan areas. One main data source was participant observation on streets, in hotels and other settings known for prostitution activity, and in drug use settings, especially those that allowed sex-for-drug exchanges. Another data source was in-depth, life-history interviews with 180 women ranging in age from 18 to 59 years, with an average age of 34. One in two women was African-American and one in three white; the remaining women were Latina. Three in four had completed high school, and among them almost two-thirds had one or more years of additional educational training. Thirty women had graduated from college.

Forty women worked as street prostitutes and did not use drugs. On average, they had been prostitutes for 11 years. Forty women began using drugs an average of three years after they began working as prostitutes, and the average time they had worked as prostitutes was nine years. Forty women used drugs an average of five years before they became prostitutes, and on the average they had worked as prostitutes for eight years. Another forty women began smoking crack and exchanging sex for crack almost simultaneously, with an average of four years in the life. Twenty women who were interviewed were ex-prostitutes.

Comments on Methodology

When I tell people about my research, the most frequent question I am asked is how I gained access to the women rather than what I learned from the research. For many, prostitution is an unusual topic of conversation, and many people have expressed surprise that I, as a woman, conducted the research. During my research some customers indeed thought I was a working woman, a fact that almost always amuses those who hear about my work. However, few people want to hear stories about the women's struggles and sadness. Sometimes they ask questions about the reasons why women become prostitutes. Most of the time, they are surprised when I tell them that the prostitutes as well as their customers represent all layers of society. . . .

Locating Prostitutes and Gaining Entree

One of the first challenges I faced was to identify locations where street prostitution took place. Many of these women worked on strolls, streets where prostitution activity is concentrated, or in hotels known for prostitution activity. Others, such as the crack prostitutes, worked in less public settings such as a crack house that might be someone's apartment.

I often learned of well-known public places from professional experts, such as law enforcement officials and health care providers at emergency rooms and sexually transmitted disease clinics. I gained other insights from lay experts, including taxi drivers, bartenders, and community representatives such as members of neighborhood associations. The contacts universally mentioned some strolls as the places where many women worked, where the local police focused attention, or where residents had organized protests against prostitution in their neighborhoods.

As I began visiting various locales, I continued to learn about new settings. In one sense, I was developing ethnographic maps of street prostitution. After several visits to a specific area, I also was able to expand these maps by adding information about the general atmosphere on the stroll, general characteristics of the various people present, the ways in which the women and customers connected, and the overall flow of action. In addition, my visits allowed the regular actors to notice me.

I soon learned that being an unknown woman in an area known for prostitution may cause many people to notice you, even stare at you, but it fails to yield many verbal interactions. Most of the time when I tried to make eye contact with one of the women, she quickly averted her eyes. Pimps, on the other hand, would stare at me straight on and I ended up being the one to look away. Customers would stop, blow their horn, or wave me over, frequently yelling obscenities when I ignored them. I realized that gaining entree into the prostitution world was not going to be as easy as I imagined it. Although I lacked such training in any of my qualitative methods classes, I decided to move slowly and not force any interaction. The most I said during the initial weeks in a new area was limited to "how are you" or "hi." This strategy paid off during my first visits to one of the strolls in Brooklyn, New York. After several appearances, one of the women walked up to me and sarcastically asked if I was looking for something. She caught me off guard, and all the answers I had practiced did not seem to make sense. I mumbled something about just wanting to walk around. She did not like my answer, but she did like my accent. We ended up talking about the latter and she was especially excited when I told her I came from Amsterdam. One of her friends had gone to Europe with her boyfriend, who was in the military. She understood from her that prostitution and drugs were legal in the Netherlands. While explaining to her that some of her friend's impressions were incorrect, I was able to show off some of my knowledge about prostitution. I mentioned that I was interested in prostitution and wanted to write a book about it.

Despite the fascination with my background and intentions, the prostitute immediately put me through a Streetwalker 101 test, and apparently I passed. She told me to make sure to come back. By the time I left, I not only had my first conversation but also my first connection to the scene. Variations of this entry process occurred on the other strolls. The main lesson I learned in these early efforts was the importance of having some knowledge of the lives of the people I wanted to study, while at the same time refraining from presenting myself as an expert.

Qualitative researchers often refer to their initial connections as gatekeepers and key respondents. Throughout my fieldwork I learned that some key respondents are important in providing initial access, but they become less central as the research evolves. . . .

Developing Relationships and Trust

The processes involved in developing relationships in research situations amplify those involved in developing relationships in general. Both parties need to get to know each other, become aware and accepting of each other's roles, and engage in a reciprocal relationship. Being supportive and providing practical assistance were the most visible and direct ways for me as the researcher to develop a relationship. Throughout the years, I have given countless rides, provided child care on numerous occasions, bought groceries, and listened for hours to stories that were unrelated to my initial research questions. Gradually, my role allowed me to become part of these women's lives and to build rapport with many of them.

Over time, many women also realized that I was uninterested in being a prostitute and that I genuinely was interested in learning as much as possible about their lives. Many felt flattered that someone wanted to learn from them and that they had knowledge to offer. Allowing women to tell their stories and engaging in a dialogue with them probably were the single most important techniques that allowed me to develop relationships with them. Had I only wanted to focus on the questions I had in mind, developing such relationships might have been more difficult.

At times, I was able to get to know a woman only after her pimp endorsed our contact. One of my scariest experiences occurred before I knew to work through the pimps, and one such man had some of his friends follow me on my way home one night. I will never know what plans they had in mind for me because I fortunately was able to escape with only a few bruises. Over a year later, the woman acknowledged that her pimp had gotten upset and told her he was going to teach me a lesson.

On other occasions, I first needed to be screened by owners and managers of crack houses before the research could continue. Interestingly, screenings always were done by a man even if the person who vouched for me was a man himself. While the women also were cautious, the ways in which they checked me out tended to be much more subtle. For example, one of them would tell me a story, indicating that it was a secret about another person on the stroll. Although I failed to realize this at the time, my field notes revealed that frequently after such a conversation, others would ask me questions about related topics. One woman later acknowledged that putting out such stories was a test to see if I would keep information confidential.

Learning more about the women and gaining a better understanding of their lives also raised many ethical questions. No textbook told me how to handle situations in which a pimp abused a woman, a customer forced a woman to engage in unwanted sex acts, a customer requested unprotected sex from a woman who knew she was HIV infected, or a boyfriend had unrealistic expectations regarding a woman's earnings to support his drug habit. I failed to know the proper response when asked to engage in illegal activities such as holding drugs or money a woman had stolen from a customer. In general, my response was to explain that I was there as a researcher. During those occasions when pressures became too severe, I decided to leave a scene. For example, I never returned to certain crack houses because pimps there continued to ask me to consider working for them.

Over time, I was fortunate to develop relationships with people who "watched my back." One pimp in particular intervened if he perceived other pimps, customers, or passersby harassing me. He also was the one who gave me my street name: Whitie (indicating my racial background) or Ms. Whitie for those who disrespected me. While this was my first street name, I subsequently had others. Being given a street name was a symbolic gesture of acceptance. Gradually, I developed an identity that allowed me to be both an insider and an outsider. While hanging out on the strolls and other gathering places, including crack houses, I had to deal with some of the [same] uncomfortable conditions as the prostitutes, such as cold or warm weather, lack of access to a rest room, refusals from owners for me to patronize a restaurant, and of course, harassment by customers and the police.

I participated in many informal conversations. Unless pushed to do so, I seldom divulged my opinions. I was more open with my feelings about situations and showed empathy. I learned quickly that providing an opinion can backfire. I agreed that one of the women was struggling a lot and stated that I felt sorry for her. While I meant to indicate my genuine concern for her, she heard that I felt sorry for her because she was a failure. When she finally, after several weeks, talked with me again, I was able to explain to her that I was not judging her, but rather felt concerned for her. She remained cynical and many times asked me for favors to make up for my mistake. It took me months before I felt comfortable telling her that I felt I had done enough and that it was time to let go. However, if she was not ready, she needed to know that I would no longer go along. This was one of many occasions when I learned that although I wanted to facilitate my work as a researcher, that I wanted people to like and trust me, I also needed to set boundaries.

Rainy and slow nights often provided good opportunities for me to participate in conversations with groups of women. Popular topics included how to work safely, what to do about condom use, how to make more money. I often served as a health educator and a supplier of condoms, gels, vaginal douches, and other feminine products. Many women were very worried about the AIDS epidemic. However, they also were worried about how to use a condom when a customer refused to do so. They worried particularly about condom use when they needed money badly and, consequently, did not want to propose that the customer use one for fear of rejection. While some women became experts at "making" their customers use a condom—for example by hiding it in their mouth prior to beginning oral sex—others would carry condoms to please me but never pull one out. If a woman was HIV positive and I knew she failed to use a condom, I faced the ethical dilemma of challenging her or staying out of it.

Developing trusting relationships with crack prostitutes was more difficult. Crack houses were not the right environment for informal conversations. Typically, the atmosphere was tense and everyone was suspicious of each other. The best times to talk with these women were when we bought groceries together, when I helped them clean their homes, or when we shared a meal. Often the women were very different when they were not high than they were when they were high or craving crack. In my conversations with them, I learned that while I might have observed their actions the night before, they themselves might not remember them. Once I realized this, I would be very careful to omit any detail unless I knew that the woman herself did remember the event.

In-Depth Interviews

All interviews were conducted in a private setting, including women's residences, my car or my office, a restaurant of the women's choice, or any other setting the women selected. I did not begin conducting official interviews until I developed relationships with the women. Acquiring written informed consent prior to the interview was problematic. It made me feel awkward. Here I was asking the women

to sign a form after they had begun to trust me. However, often I felt more upset about this technicality than the women themselves. As soon as they realized that the form was something the university required, they seemed to understand. Often they laughed about the official statements, and some asked if I was sure the form was to protect them and not the school.[2] None of the women refused to sign the consent form, although some refused to sign it right away and asked to be interviewed later.

In some instances the consent procedures caused the women to expect a formal interview. Some of them were disappointed when they saw I only had a few structured questions about demographic characteristics, followed by a long list of open-ended questions. When this disappointment occurred, I reminded the women that I wanted to learn from them and that the best way to do so was by engaging in a dialogue rather than interrogating them. Only by letting the women identify their salient issues and the topics they wanted to address was I able to gain an insider's perspective. By being a careful listener and probing for additional information and explanations, I as the interviewer, together with the women, was able to uncover the complexities of their lives. In addition, the nature of the interview allowed me to ask questions about contradictions in a woman's story. For example, sometimes a woman would say that she always used a condom. However, later on in the conversation she would indicate that if she needed drugs she would never use one. By asking her to elaborate on this, I was able to begin developing insights into condom use by type of partner, type of sex acts, and social context.

The interviewer becomes much more a part of the interview when the conversations are in-depth than when a structured questionnaire is used. Because I was so integral to the process, the way the women viewed me may have biased their answers. On the one hand, this bias might be reduced because of the extent to which both parties already knew each other; on the other, a woman might fail to give her true opinion and reveal her actions if she knew that these went against the interviewer's opinion. I suspected that some women played down the ways in which their pimps manipulated them once they knew that I was not too fond of these men. However, some might have taken more time to explain the relationship with their pimp in order to "correct" my image.

My background, so different from that of these women, most likely affected the nature of the interviews. I occupied a higher socioeconomic status. I had a place to live and a job. In contrast to the nonwhite women, I came from a different racial background. While I don't know to what extent these differences played a role, I acknowledge that they must have had some effect on this research.

Leaving the Field

Leaving the field was not something that occurred after completion of the fieldwork, but an event that took place daily. Although I sometimes stayed on the strolls all night or hung out for several days, I always had a home to return to. I had a house with electricity, a warm shower, a comfortable bed, and a kitchen. My house sat on a street where I had no fear of being shot on my way there and where I did not find condoms or syringes on my doorstep.

During several stages of the study, I had access to a car, which I used to give the women rides or to run errands together. However, I will never forget the cold night when everyone on the street was freezing, and I left to go home. I turned up the heat in my car, and tears streamed down my cheeks. I appreciated the heat, but I felt more guilty about that luxury than ever before. I truly felt like an outsider, or maybe even more appropriate, a betrayer.

Throughout the years of fieldwork, there were a number of times when I left the scene temporarily. For example, when so many people were dying from AIDS, I was unable to ignore the devastating impact of this disease. I needed an emotional break.

Physically removing myself from the scene was common when I experienced difficulty remaining objective. Once I became too involved in a woman's life and almost adopted her and her family. Another time I felt a true hatred for a crack house owner and was unable to adhere to the rules of courteous interactions. Still another time, I got angry with a woman whose steady partner was HIV positive when she failed to ask him to use a condom when they had sex.

I also took temporary breaks from a particular scene by shifting settings and neighborhoods. For example, I would invest most of my time in women from a particular crack house for several weeks. Then I would shift to spending more time on one of the strolls, while making shorter and less frequent visits to the crack house. By shifting scenes, I was able to tell people why I was leaving and to remind all of us of my researcher role.

While I focused on leaving the field, I became interested in women who had left the life. It seemed important to have an understanding of their past and current circumstances. I knew some of them from the days when they were working, but identifying others was a challenge. There was no gathering place for ex-prostitutes. Informal networking, advertisements in local newspapers, and local clinics and community settings allowed me to reach twenty of these women. Conducting interviews with them later in the data collection process prepared me to ask specific questions. I realized that I had learned enough about the life to know what to ask. Interviewing ex-prostitutes also prepared me for moving from the fieldwork to writing.

It is hard to determine exactly when I left the field. It seems like a process that never ends. Although I was more physically removed from the scene, I continued to be involved while analyzing the data and writing this book. I also created opportunities to go back, for example, by asking women to give me feedback on parts of the manuscript or at times when I experienced writer's block and my car seemed to automatically steer itself to one of the strolls. I also have developed other research projects in some of the same communities. For example, both a project on intergenerational drug use and a gender-specific intervention project to help women remain HIV negative have brought me back to the same population. Some of the women have become key respondents in these new projects, while others now are members of a research team. For example, Beth, one of the women who has left prostitution, works as an outreach worker on another project.

Six Themes in the Ethnography of Prostitution

The main intention of my work is to provide the reader with a perspective on street prostitution from the point of view of the women themselves. There are six fundamental aspects of the women's lives as prostitutes that must be considered. The first concerns the women's own explanations for their involvement in prostitution and their descriptions of the various circumstances that led them to become prostitutes. Their stories include justifications such as traumatic past experiences, especially sexual abuse, the lack of love they experienced as children, pressures by friends and pimps, the need for drugs, and most prominently, the economic forces that pushed them into the life. A number of women describe these justifications as excuses, as reflective explanations they have developed after becoming a prostitute.

The women describe the nature of their initial experiences, which often involved alienation from those outside the life. They also show the differences in the processes between women who work as prostitutes and use drugs and women who do not use drugs.

Although all these women work either on the street or in drug-use settings, their lives do differ. My second theme is a typology that captures these differences, looking at the women's prostitution versus drug-use identities. The typology distinguishes among (a) streetwalkers, women who work strolls and who do not use drugs; (b) hooked prostitutes, women who identify themselves mainly as prostitutes but who upon their entrance into the life also began using drugs; (c) prostituting addicts, women who view themselves mainly as drug users and who became prostitutes to support their drug habit; and (d) crack prostitutes, women who trade sex for crack.

This typology explains the differences in the women's strategies for soliciting customers, their screening of customers, pricing of sex acts, and bargaining for services. For example, the streetwalkers have the most bargaining power, while such power appears to be lacking among the crack prostitutes.

Few prostitutes work in a vacuum. The third theme is the role of pimps, a label that most women dislike and for which they prefer to substitute "old man" or "boyfriend." Among the pimps, one finds entrepreneur lovers, men who mainly employ streetwalkers and hooked prostitutes and sometimes prostituting addicts. Entrepreneur lovers engage in the life for business reasons. They treat the women as their employees or their property and view them primarily as an economic commodity. The more successful a woman is in earning them money, the more difficult it is for that woman to leave her entrepreneur pimp.

Most prostituting addicts and some hooked prostitutes work for a lover pimp, a man who is their steady partner but who also lives off their earnings. Typically, such pimps employ only one woman. The dynamics in the relationship between a prostitute and her lover pimp become more complex when both partners use drugs. Drugs often become the glue of the relationship.

For many crack prostitutes, their crack addiction serves as a pimp. Few plan to exchange sex for crack when they first begin using; often several weeks or months pass before a woman who barters sex for crack realizes that she is a prostitute.

Historically, society has blamed prostitutes for introducing sexually transmitted diseases into the general population. Similarly, it makes them scapegoats for the spread of HIV/AIDS. Yet their pimps and customers are not held accountable. The fourth theme in the anthropological study of prostitution is the impact of the AIDS epidemic on the women's lives. Although most are knowledgeable about HIV risk behaviors and the ways to reduce their risk, many misconceptions exist. The women describe the complexities of condom use, especially with steady partners but also with paying customers. Many women have mixed feelings about HIV testing, wondering how to cope with a positive test result while no cure is available. A few of the women already knew their HIV-infected status, and the discussion touches on their dilemmas as well.

The fifth theme is the violence and abuse that make common appearances in the women's lives. An ethnography of prostitution must allow the women to describe violence in their neighborhoods as well as violence in prostitution and drug-use settings. The most common violence they encounter is from customers. These men often assume that because they pay for sex they buy a woman. Apparently, casual customers pose more of a danger than those who are regulars. The types of abuse the women encounter are emotional, physical, and sexual. In addition to customers, pimps and boyfriends abuse the women. Finally, the women discuss harassment by law enforcement officers.

When I talked with the women, it often seemed that there were no opportunities to escape from the life. Yet the sixth and final theme must be the escape from prostitution. Women who have left prostitution can describe the process of their exit from prostitution. As ex-prostitutes they struggle with the stigma of their past, the challenges of developing a new identity, and the impact of their past on current intimate relationships. Those who were also drug users often view themselves as ex-prostitutes and recovering addicts, a perspective that seems to create a role conflict. Overall, most ex-prostitutes find that their past follows them like a bad hangover.

Notes

1. The names of the women who were interviewed for this study, as well as those of their pimps and customers, have been replaced by pseudonyms to protect their privacy. The use of pseudonyms is suggested by guidelines to protect the privacy of study participants (American Anthropological Association; American Sociological Association).

2. For a more extensive discussion of informed consent procedures and related ethical issues, see Bruce L. Berg, *Qualitative Research Methods for the Social Sciences*, 3rd edition, Chapter 3: "Ethical Issues" (Boston: Allyn and Bacon, 1998).

1.3 Cultural Relativism and Universal Human Rights

CAROLYN FLUEHR-LOBBAN

Cultural anthropologists have long been concerned with encouraging understanding and respect for cultural diversity. One of our guiding principles is that of cultural relativism, or the idea that cultural beliefs and practices are best understood within their own unique cultural context. A conundrum many anthropologists face, however, is this: If human values vary given different cultural, religious, and ethnic traditions, can there really be such a thing as universal human rights in a culturally diverse world? Aren't human rights culturally relative and not universal? These questions kept anthropologists from engaging in international dialogue regarding the protection of conventions concerning human rights through the better part of the twentieth century. However, in the last several decades, anthropologists have become actively engaged in human rights debates on a global scale and no longer see universal human rights and cultural relativism as diametrically opposed. In this piece, Carolyn Fluehr-Lobban draws on her own research and experiences in the Sudan surrounding female genital mutilation (FGM) to argue that anthropologists can and should offer their expertise to international debates regarding human rights. In this critical self-reflection, Fluehr-Lobban comes to terms with the "trapping" of her cultural relativist position which led her to take a neutral stance on FGM for decades until her interaction with international, cross-cultural dialogue revealed that the level of harm inflicted on women and children far outweighed any social good that might come about. In this selection, the reader will see one role an engaged and public anthropologist might play in brokering relationships between local and indigenous peoples and the international and national bodies whose policies affect their lives: that of expert witness.

Questions

1. What are the differences between human rights, human values, and human dignity? What is the role of culture their determination?
2. Fluehr-Lobban shares that for decades she found herself accepting FGM from a cultural relativist position, while at the same time criticizing Western practices that were harmful to women and children, such as breast implants or instances of domestic violence. Have you ever noticed yourself applying a double standard to critique some practices that are considered harmful and defend others? Are there circumstances where such a standard seems appropriate?
3. What are some contemporary human rights issues and debates where anthropological knowledge of cultural specificity might be useful?

Carolyn Fluehr-Lobban. "Cultural Relativism and Universal Human Rights." 1998. *AnthroNotes* 20 (2), 1–5, 16–18.

. . . Cultural relativism asserts that since each culture has its own inherent integrity with unique values and practices, value judgments should be withheld or suspended until cultural context is taken into account. What members of one culture might view as strange and bizarre in another culture (for example, polygamy, body tattooing, or strict dietary laws) can be understood best within that culture's context. Theoretically, anthropologists always should be observers and recorders not evaluators of other peoples' customs and values.

While some anthropologists would still agree with this view, others, both inside the field and outside, especially in the arena of human rights, are challenging this concept. . . .

Cultural relativism may be taken to extremes. Some argue that since cultures vary and each culture has its own unique moral system, we cannot make judgments about "right" and "wrong" in comparing one culture to another. Thus, one cannot reject any form of culturally acceptable homicide—for example, infanticide, senilicide, or "honor" killing of women in Mediterranean and Middle East societies for alleged sexual misconduct—on moral grounds because cultural acceptance or condemnation are equally valid. This extreme relativist position is actually a form of absolutism with which few anthropologists would agree. Anthropologists did not defend Nazi genocide or South African apartheid with cultural relativist arguments, and many have been critical of relativist defenses especially of Western practices they see as harmful, such as cultural institutions emphasizing violence.

The truth about our complex world of cultural difference is that moral perplexity abounds. The ability to accept that another person's or culture's position with which one disagrees is nevertheless rational or intelligible lays the basis for discussion of differences. . . .

Universal Rights Challenge Relativism: Female Circumcision

One of the most culturally and emotionally charged battlegrounds where the cultural relativist confronts the advocate of universal human rights is the issue of female circumcision or FGM (female genital mutilation). Female circumcision is the removal of all or part of the clitoris and/or labia. The issue of female circumcision has set Western feminism against African cultural traditions and Islam, and has pitted Muslim against Muslim and African against African. Despite female circumcision's prevalence in African Islamic societies, it is also found in some non-Islamic, African contexts and is rare in Islamic contexts outside Africa. There is no consensus among Muslim scholars or among African Muslims about whether female circumcision is mandated by religion. Religious interpretation in the Sudan as early as 1939 determined that female circumcision is only "desirable" (*manduh*), and not compulsory (Fluehr-Lobban 1987, 96), while in 1994 the late Grand Sheikh of Al-Azhar Islamic University in Cairo, Gad al-Haq Ali Gad al-Haq, called female circumcision "a noble practice which does honor to women." His chief rival, the Grand Mufti of the Egyptian Republic, said that female circumcision is not part of Islamic teaching and is a matter best evaluated by medical professionals (*Philadelphia Inquirer*, April 13, 1995, section A-3). . . .

For nearly 25 years, I have conducted research in the Sudan, one of the African countries where the practice of female circumcision is widespread, affecting the vast majority of females in the northern Sudan. Chronic infections are a common result, and sexual intercourse and childbirth are rendered difficult and painful. However, cultural ideology in the Sudan holds that an uncircumcised woman is not respectable, and few families would risk their daughter's chances of marrying by not having her circumcised. British colonial officials outlawed the practice in 1946, but this served only to make it surreptitious and thus more dangerous. Women found it harder to get treatment for mistakes or for side effects of the illegal surgery.

For a long time I felt trapped between my anthropological understanding of the custom and of the sensitivities about it among the people with whom I was working, on the one side, and the largely feminist campaign in the West to eradicate what critics sees as a "barbaric" custom, on the other hand. To ally myself with Western feminists and condemn female circumcision seemed to me a betrayal of the value system and culture of the Sudan which I had come to understand. But as I was asked over the years to comment on female circumcision because of my expertise in the Sudan, I came to realize how deeply I felt that the practice was harmful and wrong. In 1993, female circumcision was one of the practices deemed harmful by delegates at the International Human Rights Conference in Vienna. During their discussions, they came to view circumcision as a violation of the rights of children as well as of the women who suffer its consequences throughout life. Those discussions made me realize that there was a moral agenda larger than myself, larger than Western culture or the culture of the northern Sudan, or of my discipline. I decided to join colleagues from other disciplines and cultures in speaking out against the practice.

The Anthropologists' Dilemma

The sense of paralysis that kept me from directly opposing female circumcision (FGM) for decades was largely attributable to my anthropological training grounded in cultural relativism. From a fieldworker's standpoint, my neutralist position stemmed from the anthropologist's first hand knowledge of the local sensitivities about the practice, along with the fact that dialogue was actively underway in the Sudan leading in the direction of changes ameliorating the practice. While I would not hesitate to criticize breast implants or other Western surgical adjustments of the female body, I withheld judgment of female circumcision as though the moral considerations were fundamentally different. My socialization as an anthropology undergraduate and graduate student, along with years of anthropology teaching, conditioned a relativist reflex to almost any challenge to cultural practice on moral or philosophical grounds, especially ones that appeared to privilege the West. However, I realized that a double standard had crept into my teaching. For example, I would readily criticize rampant domestic violence in the U.S. and then attempt to rationalize the killing of wives and sisters from the Middle East to Latin America by men whose "honor" had been violated by their female relation's alleged misdeeds, from flirtation to adultery. Of course, cultural context is critical and the reading of cultural difference our stock-in-trade. One may lament the rising divorce rate and destruction of family life in the U.S. while applauding increasing rights for judicial divorce for Middle Eastern women. At times relativism may frame and enlighten the debate, but, in the end, moral judgment and human rights take precedence and choices must be made.

What changed my view away from the conditioned relativist response was the international, cross-cultural, interdisciplinary dialogue that placed female circumcision on a level of such harm that whatever social good it represents (in terms of sexual propriety and marriage norms), the harm to the more basic rights of women and girls outweighed the culturally understandable "good." Moreover, active feminist agitation against female circumcision within the Sudan has fostered the kind of indigenous response that anthropologists like, so as not to appear to join the ranks of the Western feminists who had patronizingly tried to dictate the "correct" agenda to women most directly affected by the practice. Women's and human rights associations in the Ivory Coast and Egypt, as well as the Sudan, have also called for an end to female circumcision, while the Cairo Institute for Human Rights reported in 1995 the first publicly acknowledged marriage of an uncircumcised woman. In other words, a broad spectrum of the human community has come to an agreement that genital mutilation of girls and women is wrong.

Beyond these cultural and moral considerations is a changed legal environment in the U.S. and elsewhere. The granting of political asylum by the U.S. government in 1996 to Fauziya Kasinga, a Togolese woman who argued that her return to her country would result in the forcible circumcision of her daughter and thus violate her human rights, was a turning point. Prior to this decision, articles had appeared in American law journals arguing for the U.S. to follow the examples of France and Canada and "legally protect" women and girls at risk by criminalizing female circumcision and by extending political asylum. Authors also argued against the cultural relativist or traditionalist justification for female circumcision. Typical customary cultural arguments in defense of female circumcision include: it is a deeply rooted practice; it prevents promiscuity and promotes cleanliness and aesthetics; and it enhances fertility. Defenders of the practice, female and male, African and Western, inevitably invoke cultural relativism and ethnocentrism. Opponents argue that while the morality and values of a person are certainly shaped by the culture and history of a given society, this does not negate the philosophical theory that human rights, defined as the rights to which one is entitled simply by virtue of being human, are universal by definition. So, although human behavior is necessarily culturally relative, human rights are universal entitlements that are grounded in cross culturally recognized moral values. In response to the relativist argument, Rhoda Howard writes that the "argument that different societies have different concepts of rights is based on an assumption that confuses human rights with human dignity" (1986:17). . . .

Anthropologists' Expert Testimony

I had the opportunity to offer expert testimony in an Immigration and Naturalization Service (INS) case involving application for asylum and withholding of deportation for a Nigerian family. The case revolved around the issues of Muslim persecution of Christians and the fear of female circumcision for the two young daughters of the parents, the wife having already undergone circumcision. My testimony involved responding to questions about female circumcision from the attorney for the Nigerian family and the judge. I was examined and cross-examined especially on the issue of the probability that the girls would be circumcised in their home community in northern Nigeria even if the father and mother opposed this.

Interestingly, after the 1996 Kasinga case, the U.S. State Department issued guidelines to the INS and its courts suggesting that uncircumcised girls would not be at risk if their fathers opposed the practice. I explained that on the basis of my knowledge of the practice in a comparable African Muslim context, female circumcision is the province of female kin. There is no assurance, given the influence of extended family ties, that the girls would be protected on the strength of their parents, or just their father's, opposition. The matter of the state protecting the girls was moot given its lack of interest in regulating matters of "custom" and Nigeria's poor human rights record. Even in the Sudan, where female circumcision has been illegal since 1946, there has been little or no enforcement of the law. I was not asked if I believed that female circumcision is a violation of human rights, women's rights, or the rights of the child. At a subsequent hearing, the mother, who had been circumcised as a child, testified about her fears of her daughters' forcible circumcision or, if no circumcision were performed, of their inability to be married in Nigeria as they would be socially unacceptable women. These arguments persuaded the judge in 1997 to suspend deportation and to consider a positive case for asylum for the family.

"Avoidance of Harm" Key Standard

Harm may be considered to take place when there is death, pain, disability, loss of freedom or pleasure that results from an act by one human upon another (Gert 1988, 47–49). It is the notion of harm done to individuals or groups that can be used to explore the terrain between universal rights and cultural relativism. *When reasonable persons from different cultural backgrounds agree that certain institutions or cultural practices cause harm, then the moral neutrality of cultural relativism must be suspended.* The concept of "harm" has been a driving force behind the medical, psychological, feminist, and cultural opposition to female genital mutilation. . . .

Even the most experienced anthropological field worker must negotiate the terrain between universal rights and cultural relativism with caution, to avoid the pitfalls of scientific or discipline superiority. The anthropologist is capable of hearing, recording, and incorporating the multiple voices that speak to issues of cultural specificity and universal human rights. . . . When various perspectives are taken into consideration, still in the end a judgment may have to be made when harm is a factor.

Case Study: Domestic Abuse

The concept of *darar* in the Arabic language and in Islamic family law translates as harm or abuse and is broadly applied in Islamic law (Shari`a). . . . *Darar* comes from the same root as that which is used to describe a strike or a physical blow. However, *darar* in Muslim family law as a ground for divorce has been interpreted to include both physical harm and emotional harm, the latter usually described as insulting words or behavior. It is probably most clear to make a determination between human rights and cultural practice when physical harm or abuse is taking place. It is simpler to stand against physical abuse of women within a marriage. Indeed, Western ideas of physical and mental cruelty as grounds for divorce mesh well with the concept of harm as reflected in "talaq al-darar," divorce due to harm or abuse. A woman who comes to court, alleges harm, proves it with her own testimony or that of witnesses, and is granted a divorce is probably a woman who has experienced the abuse for some time and is using the court, as women often do in Muslim settings, as a last resort.

The divorced husband often does not acknowledge the harm, as is frequently the case with abusive husbands in other countries where the "right" of a husband to discipline a wife is a cultural norm. A relativist position might attempt to split the difference here between the cultural "right" of the husband to discipline a wife and the wife's right to resist. Moreover, the relativist's position would be upheld by cultural institutions and persons in authority, judges for example, with the legitimate right to enforce the norm of "obedience" of wives. . . .

The cultural "right" of a man to discipline, slap, hit, or beat his wife (and often by extension his children) is widely recognized across a myriad of different cultures throughout the world where male dominance is an accepted fact of life. Indeed, the issue of domestic violence has only recently been added to the international human rights agenda, but it is firmly in place since the Vienna Conference of 1993 and the United Nations Beijing Women's Conference in 1995. This relatively new dialogue intersects at a point where the individual rights of the woman clash with a potential cultural defense of a man practicing harm, and is a dialogue that anthropologists could inform and enrich tremendously by their first hand knowledge of community and family life. . . .

The terrain between universal rights and cultural relativism can be puzzling and difficult to negotiate, but the use of the idea of the "avoidance of harm" can help anthropologists and others map out a course of thinking and action. We are coming to the recognition that violence against women should be an acknowledged wrong, a violation of the basic human right to be free from harm that cannot be excused or justified on cultural grounds. Likewise, children in every culture have the right to be free from harm and to be nurtured under secure and adequate conditions. Understanding the diverse cultural contexts where harm or violence may take place is valuable and important, but suspending or withholding judgment because of cultural relativism is intellectually and morally irresponsible. Anthropologists cannot be bystanders when they witness harm being practiced upon any people they study.

Anthropologists can aid the international dialogue enormously by developing approaches to universal human rights that are respectful of cultural considerations but are morally responsible. . . .

In this spirit anthropologists could be among the best brokers for inter-cultural dialogue regarding human rights. We have moved beyond the idea of a value free social science to the task of developing a moral system at the level of our shared humanity that must at certain times supersede cultural relativism. Reassessing the value of cultural relativism does not diminish the continued value of studying and valuing diversity around the globe. . . .

References

Fluehr-Lobban, Carolyn. 1987. *Islamic Law and Society in the Sudan*. London: Frank Cass, Ltd.

Gert, Bernard. 1988. *Morality, a New Justification for the Moral Rules*. New York: Oxford University Press (orig. 1966).

Howard, R. E. 1986. *Human Rights in Commonwealth Africa*. Lanham: Rowman and Littlefield.

Sipress, Alan. "Egyptian Rights Group Sues Sheik on Support of Female Circumcision."*Philadelphia Inquirer*, April 13, 1995, A-3.

1.4 Maxwell's Demons: Disenchantment in the Field

JANET MCINTOSH

Often ethnographers come to build very close relationships with their key informants and primary research assistants. These relationships may then impact the worldview of the other. In the following account, Janet McIntosh describes her own journey as an agnostic anthropologist studying religious changes among the Giriama of Kenya. The Giriama's indigenous belief system had become stigmatized by the dominant culture, but McIntosh's primary informant, Maxwell, was set on beginning a faith revival movement for young Gambini. This cause led him to work with McIntosh on her research project. Through their shared research journey, each began to doubt their own spiritual beliefs, raising questions about the influence of an anthropologist's research agenda and personal perspective on the peoples and communities they study, and vice versa. McIntosh's piece further engages questions of anthropological ethics.

Questions

1. What is the role of colonialism in changing local perspectives of Giriama customs? Give specific examples through youth perspectives of Giriama customs and beliefs in spirits.
2. What happened to McIntosh after she visited Tresea? How had her ideas about Giriama spirits shifted? Give examples.
3. How did McIntosh's anthropological training influence Maxwell? Provide specific examples of when Maxwell employed anthropological theories to explain the practices of waganga.
4. Why was McIntosh so uncomfortable when she realized she was beginning to believe in witchcraft and Giriama spirits?
5. Apply the concepts of emic and etic to understand the role of Giriama spirits. Now consider how they factor into writing ethnography.

. . . The ethical currents in anthropology clarify the importance of conscience but do not establish where the limits of the fieldworker's influence should lie. The reflexive turn gives us license to reflect on our roles as we write but does not specify how we are to navigate the differences between the ethnographer as a human being "on the ground" and the professional identity that ethnographers must at some point inhabit to succeed in the academy. And no amount of reflection can do away with the discomfiting dynamic that can arise between ethnographers and their informants when each comes at the world with a radically different epistemology, and each, through exposure, may come to change the other. Such dilemmas, I find, can be particularly acute when the agnostic, humanist ethnographer places her spyglass up against the religious convictions that make up her field assistant's world.

My account is set in a township called Malindi that extends along the Indian Ocean on the coast of Kenya. The town itself has only a few paved roads; one of these passes the stone-built quarter that houses well-to-do Arabs and Swahili, while others trace the beachfront, passing the large expatriate mansions and luxury hotels so important to an increasingly fragile

Janet McIntosh. 2004. "Maxwell's Demons: Disenchantment in the Field." Anthropology and Humanism. 29 (1): 63–77.

town economy. Unpaved routes, pitted with rocks that ruin the axles of Malindi's decrepit fleet of Toyota taxis, weave through the residential areas occupied by Giriama and members of other ethnic groups, many of them migrants in search of labor. If you make your way out of the town center to the south-west road, you pass the mud huts of outlying Giriama villages before veering down toward Mombasa.

You can learn a lot about social life in Malindi by planting yourself in the outdoor market and watching peoples' feet. The expensive sneakers usually belong to Western backpackers who bumble through the marketplace, wearing shorts and bulging money belts, looking for a cold soda and a *samosa*, a tasty fried dumpling. Swahili and Arab women are hard to mistake. Beneath their long black robes one catches glimpses of henna or red toenail polish, and many wear open-toe shoes that use straps and sparkling vinyl to declare an expensive femininity. Upwardly mobile men and women who have converted to Christianity may take advantage of the trade in secondhand clothes from the West, donning uncomfortable looking pumps or cheap loafers. And the Giriama men and women who come from rural homesteads carrying baskets of surplus mango, cassava, and bananas wear exhausted-looking flip-flops or no shoes at all.

Beyond the market, houses of Christian and Muslim worship are scattered through town. Passers-by can hear a *muezzin* intoning the call to prayer from a powerful mosque loudspeaker, or the sound of children reciting prayers in *madrasa*, or Quranic school. On Sunday morning, the church just a few doors down might resound with Christian songs accompanied by the tambourine, or the intense tumult of an entire congregation speaking in the voice of the Holy Spirit. Traditional Giriama belief and ritual, meanwhile, is more muted, its shrines tucked away in rural spaces. Yet its presence is broadcast through smaller, subtler cues: the talismans on the arms of Giriama women or the occasional sign advertising traditional healing.

I arrived in Malindi in 1998 to begin dissertation research on the ethnic, religious, and linguistic relationships between Giriama and Swahili. I knew I would need an assistant to help with interviews and translations, and I met him quite by accident while staying at a guest house on the outskirts of town. One day during my Kigiriama lesson, my instructor and I sat in the sun on rickety folding chairs just outside the main door as she tried to help me get my tongue around the language. I was learning the word for "good" when a high male voice through the wall began to correct my pronunciation with a snappy air:

"No, you don't have it yet. Say it like this: '*to-TOH-to*.'" "To-TOH-to," I said to the wall, obediently.

I ducked around the doorframe into the guest house office to find a tall man, probably in his early 20s, sitting at a table and holding a battered-looking book. He was so thin the loose end of his belt passed behind his back and dangled out again in front, but he had buttoned and linked his cuffs with panache unusual for a village youth, and he appeared to have grown out his hair a little and brushed it back with pomade. He introduced himself as Maxwell.

When I told Maxwell that I was interested in ethnic relations and changing religious practices on the coast, he processed my words quickly. "If you're looking for someone to help you see what has become of our religion," he said, "I'm the one you want." He jabbed at the table with his index finger. "Our people have been seduced by imported gods. I'm the only one in my family who still believes in the original Giriama way. I want to know everything there is to know about our traditional powers, our true nature, and when I'm done, I'm going to start a movement called 'The Revival Faith of Giriama.'"

. . . I wasn't interested in cultural purity; in fact, quite the opposite—I was interested in how locals were negotiating cultural contact and change. But Maxwell felt that his heritage was being ground away, and his wish to embark on a search for an uncontaminated religious identity seemed to be one element of the social flux I was trying to understand. He was also smart, and he talked a blue streak. I thought he might keep me company during the long days of fieldwork.

So we entered "the field" together, walking in the same direction, but with wildly mismatched lines of sight. My gaze was fixed on the human plane—the arena of ethnic and religious politics—while Maxwell's would target the supernatural world, to figure out how to harness its powers. "I'm going to see which of the diviners and healers are the most powerful," he anticipated. "I'll learn the best methods for contacting the ancestors. I'll find out who the spirits really are." Once he understood all that, he said, he would recruit the people who had the best powers, to help him bring the Giriama back to their spiritual home. Maxwell made it abundantly clear that he was collecting my wages only to empower himself and, ultimately, his followers. "I hate white people," he reminded me, and so distanced himself from the image he held most in contempt: the obsequious, disadvantaged African swallowing whole the opinions of a white employer.

***

According to customary Giriama belief and practice, the world is populated by invisible forces that cross-cut one another, each with a purpose of its own. Spirits and ancestors roam the earth, at turns mischievous, malevolent, and helpful, while an overarching deity named Mulungu controls the rains and the broader sweep of fate. Human beings can intercept these powers and steer them to their own ends, propitiating the ancestors so that they bring good fortune, soliciting the help of spirits in rituals, and harnessing evil creatures for their curses. Those who mediate best between the visible and invisible worlds are the diviners and healers called *"waganga."*

The status of waganga is heavily disparaged by many of the Muslim Swahili and Arabs who have long populated the coastal towns. In the early 19th century, Swahili and Giriama commonly intermarried and the distinction between them was fluid and indeterminate. But in the context of European colonialism and its aftermath, both groups have been politically and economically motivated to reify ever sharper boundaries between themselves and the Giriama (Cooper 1980; Willis 1993). Today, Arabs and Swahili tend to view Giriama ways as heathen and polluting, a narrative internalized by quite a few Giriama (McIntosh 2004). In the 19th century, a Giriama prophetess named Mipoho was said to have prophesied the coming of yet another threat to Giriama ways. Mipoho stood in a circle of beating drums and begin to sink, bolt upright, into the ground, as she intoned her warning. A people as pale as butterflies would come, bringing metal flying craft, vehicles that roll along the ground, and social catastrophe. Giriama youth would scorn and betray their elders, and great draughts of smoke would issue from their mouths. Soon after the earth reclaimed Mipoho, the first Western missionaries arrived, followed during the next decades by colonials and white tourists. Giriama custom was thoroughly marginalized by the colonial and postcolonial economy, while children betrayed the beliefs and practices of their elders with draughts of cigarette smoke issuing from their mouths. Today, some young Giriama pursue status however they can, through the accumulation of the boom boxes and T-shirts that might

align them with some version of modernity; through affiliation with Christianity; or, less commonly, through conversion to Islam. There are still many who engage in Giriama rituals, but they are therefore burdened by not one but two disapproving foreign gods.

The force of this disapproval was particularly evident on one field trip Maxwell and I took to a rural secondary school about forty kilometers southwest of Malindi, where we had planned to interview some students. When we arrived we found that that the headmaster had changed the terms of our appointment. We could speak to his students, but only on condition that all 50 of them were present at once. As I looked on helplessly, a crush of teenagers in crisp blue and white uniforms filed into a classroom, jamming the desks together like a blockade. I explained that I was not a missionary but had come to have a "conversation" about religion. The students tossed their pencils into the air and snickered behind their hands, while I succumbed to a sinking feeling that this conversation would never get off the ground.

"How many of you would say you are Christians?" I blushed as I asked; truly, this was fieldwork at its crudest. There was a tentative pause, then a shuffling of uprising hands from most of the students.

"How many would say you are Muslims?" Everyone else, it seemed.

"And how many of you also believe in the traditional Giriama ancestors, the spirits, and the Giriama god, Mulungu?" I heard a chair scrape across the concrete floor, and a blur of murmurs rose like steam and hung in the air for what felt like an eternity. At last the teacher raised his hand from the back of the classroom. "Madam, they are not going to answer a question like that, because they feel shy."

I leapt on his observation. "This is what I'm trying to study! If they feel shy, I want to understand why."

"Because these things are evil. The Christians have told us it is devil worship." The state, too, in fact. The colonial government of Kenya passed Witchcraft ordinances in 1909, 1918, and 1925, and since then the slippery Western category of "witchdoctor" has been used to target benign diviners and healers on an ad hoc basis. During his tenure, President Moi deflected challenges to the Christian state by setting up a special commission to eradicate "devil worship." The Swahili term *sheitani* can be translated as either "spirit" or "devil," and the national press frequently aligns any spirit belief at all with Satanic forces. I decided to take this on.

"Giriama spirits are known to be both good and bad," I ventured, "so why would you call them all devils?"

"Because it's evil to summon them or use them," the teacher replied impatiently. "In fact, it's evil to believe in them."

I nearly opened my mouth to contradict him. I had no objection to cultural change, but I did bristle at the way Giriama were shamed, even by the state itself, into renouncing their practices. Still, who was I to give them a lecture on their cultural pride? I looked at Maxwell. He was leaning against a desk with his hipbone, arms folded, his body in a tall, delicate curve. "Here, Janet, let me help," he said. He strode to the front of the classroom with preternaturally long steps, his trousers flapping like sails behind him. The students straightened and looked sharp for the first time since we had come in. Maxwell scanned the room with his eyes and began to orate as if powered by another source, some lightning bolt that touched his slender frame.

"You say you do not believe in spirits? You say you renounce your ancestors?" His upper body tilted and snapped; his long index finger targeted the boys and girls. Christ, Mohammed, and all the proselytizers who came after them became tyrants who were dismantling Africans' self-regard. The students were cowards and pawns in a great global game of exploitation. "You are following foreign gods, gods who do not love you as you are! Mulungu will love you as a Giriama! He will love you even if you smell like sweat!"

By now Maxwell had shifted out of English and Kiswahili, two languages sanctioned for classroom use, into the stigmatized Giriama mother tongue that is banned in many schools but, according to my Giriama friends, hooks into their deepest identity. His cadences began to lilt steeply. His voice dipped to a near-whisper as he described a man who worked in the tourism industry and began to neglect his ancestors—then it rose again to a shout as he recounted how the embittered, rampaging spirits immolated the man's home and struck his wife with typhoid. "Your ancestors are waiting for you to remember them! The spirits call for their palm wine, and you are out at the church wearing white people's clothes!" The students were saucer eyed with fear.

Eventually Maxwell held out his palms before him. "Now," he said, his eye brows fierce with anticipation: "Do you believe in these things? These Giriama spirits and ancestors, are they real?"

"Yes," chorused the students.

"Do these things exist?" He was triumphant, but he wanted it said again, to seal the agreement.

"Yes. Yes, they do." The students looked at him gravely.

"I am going to start a movement, something to return us to the God who loves us and the spirits and ancestors who know us and watch us every day. I am going to call it 'The Revival Faith of Giriama.' Some day I want you all to be my followers."

We walked home side by side, Maxwell striding fast and looking distant, lost in the thought of things to come.

***

After several months of working together, Maxwell and I began to focus on Giriama waganga themselves, interviewing them and sitting in on their rituals, often in a smoky corner of their mud and thatch homes. To spend so much time with this group of professionals was to invite a unique set of dilemmas. Most waganga expected a small gift or fee in exchange for our conversations—a perfectly reasonable demand, I felt. Unfortunately, many also insisted that they tell me my own fortune, a path I resisted because it unnerved me in a way I found hard to articulate. The waganga, however, found my position ungenerous. I was extracting information from them, so why shouldn't they extract it from me? Didn't I trust them? Was I hiding something, perhaps a Christian agenda?

Maxwell noticed these tensions growing during an interview with a particularly reluctant diviner, and on the way home he turned to me. "I know you don't want to have your fortune told," he said, "but I would like to have it done to myself." His relationships with certain family members had been deteriorating, and he was suffering from headaches that only seemed to get worse. He often bought a small handful of aspirins from a roadside kiosk so he could get through the day. He had suspected for some time that he had been bewitched, and now it was time to consult a specialist so he could know for sure.

The research improved after that. The diviners seemed to feel useful as they probed Maxwell's past and future, and Maxwell and I advanced our respective projects as we observed the details of ritual procedure, including the way that powerful ethnic spirits, especially Arabs and Swahili, would possess the waganga's bodies in a cloud of incense to offer diagnoses and suggest ritual remedies. Quite a few suggested Maxwell had been bewitched, but their attribution of guilt varied widely. These discrepancies hardly bothered me; my purpose was not to test the diviners but to understand their cultural roles and the ways in which they used language and responded to social change. I took notes about deftly improvised ritual content while theorizing about the fact that the diviners' spirits often spoke in tongues borrowed from prestigious social groups.

Maxwell was full of questions, eager to talk about what we witnessed. When he asked me why the spirits spoke with such an odd timbre—sometimes nasal, sometimes high pitched, sometimes stuttering—it was hard for me not to tell him about the observations of Judith Irvine (1982), whose cross-cultural survey documents the breadth of linguistic markers that can signal the presence of a spirit. Apparently almost any sound that deviates from normal talk—being slower, faster, oddly pitched, and so on—can mark the source of the sound as extra-ordinary. I told Maxell about it. "You mean she thinks the spirits themselves aren't talking? That it is just people changing their voices?" Maxwell asked, skeptically. I tried to explain that Irvine's point was not to debunk possession per se, but Maxwell suspected what kind of premise we anthropologists were starting with. He wasn't wrong. When Maxwell asked why so many spirits came from powerful or feared ethnic groups, I told him of the many ethnographies that suggest spirit possession is a human invention that can allow people creatively to process their histories and social roles and, sometimes, to exact redress from those with more power (Boddy 1989; Giles 1995; Lewis 1971; Masquelier 2001; Stoller 1984). Maxwell resisted this: "If the spirits are just inventions people use to help themselves, why do they sometimes punish people by making them sick?"

Between receiving dispatches of anthropological theory from me, Maxwell became obsessed with the diviners' veracity. I noticed that he began to apply a quasi-scientific measuring stick to evaluate them. He wondered why he got a different reading from each diviner, and his interest in finding the "most powerful" ones had expanded into a vociferous condemnation of hucksters. I assumed that he took them as an offense to Giriama tradition and a threat to his revival movement.

Drawn as Maxwell was to extremes, he was most impressed by the diviners who delivered high drama. When he was at the height of his anxiety about his own

bewitchment, we made an appointment with Tresea, who had urged us for weeks to come and see what she is capable of. Tresea and her husband eagerly led us into a small hut and offered us two wooden chairs at the edge of the room. Tresea sat close by our feet on a floor mat, her legs extending straight before her. She draped a cloth over her head and tucked a wand of incense beneath it, inhaling the smoke and rocking gently. We waited in silence for what felt like an eternity. Finally, almost imperceptibly, her rocking movements intensified like a pendulum picking up momentum, until her torso began to hurtle back and forth heavily, her head flopping as if her neck might break. It was easy to imagine that she was being pitched around by some tremendous force. After a couple of perilous minutes, Tresea's movements slowed. She seemed to gather herself and tottered to her feet, still breathing heavily. Her eyes looked strange and out of focus. She oriented towards each of us in turn, shaking our hands while offering an Arabic greeting in a protracted, eerie voice: "*Asaaaalaaaaam aleikuuum . . . Asaalaaam aleikuuum.*" Maxwell extended his hand in a sudden, rabbity motion, looking toward the doorway as if to check his escape route. Her husband, sitting next to me, offered the formulaic ritual greeting: "*Taireni!* Which spirit are you?"

In a stuttering monotone, the spirit announced itself: "*Mi-mi-kat-a-mai-niiiii . . . Mi-kat-a-mai-niiiiiii.*"

"The Liver-Cutter." I'd heard of many spirits but never this one, and I felt a small tightening in the pit of my stomach. Only a week earlier, a local doctor had told me I looked a bit jaundiced, so I had had my blood tested. It turned out my liver was off-kilter and they couldn't be sure why. Tresea's husband looked at us.

"What do you want to ask?" he said. Tresea sat and began to tilt violently to and fro again. Maxwell drew his torso back in a steep diagonal line. I glanced at his face; he looked stricken.

"Maxwell, go on! Talk to her!" I was afraid that Tresea, or Tresea's spirit, would take offense, and the momentum of her possession would dissolve.

"I'm afraid," he hissed in my direction. In an uncharacteristically timid voice, Maxwell beseeched the spirit for advice. The spirit launched into a peculiar blend of Swahili and Arabic, while wrenching Tresea's torso in circles.

"I can see you at some point in the past. You're having problems with work. There's a woman . . . she's short and fat. She loves you but you don't love her back, and now she really wants to hurt you." Maxwell would need to arrange an elaborate ritual to reverse the jilted woman's curse. It involved several expensive items, including two chickens and some rare spices. He took notes on a scrap of paper, checking and double checking the prescription until the spirit seemed to lose patience and turned its attention to me.

"You who sit in silence," it said, ominously. "You do not know me, but you will soon enough." Tresea's husband looked at me meaningfully.

"Now," the spirit added, "I ask your permission to leave." We offered our thanks and the spirit fled, leaving Tresea's body in a state of collapse. After a few seconds she heaved, spat some phlegm onto the earth, and crawled onto a bed to stretch out, eyes closed.

Later, as we walked out into the piercing sunlight, Maxwell turned to me. "Did you see how that spirit abused her body? Did you hear how it spoke? Everything it said was exactly right, exactly." Maxwell told me that several months earlier a small, rounded woman had vied for his attentions, but he told her he wasn't interested in her. As she turned to go, she remarked cryptically that he'd be sorry for rejecting her, and it had left him with a bad feeling. So it was she who had cursed him, dragging his fortunes down. He would implement the ritual antidote immediately, and things would start to improve. He seemed relieved. "If you still have doubts about whether these spirits exist, Janet, you must know by now they are real."

Did I have doubts? I thought about the house where I lived. In the late afternoon, the cool whitewashed walls provided relief from the arduous day—but by night, it became an eerie place, barricaded under the threat of armed robbery, and teeming like a miniature Jurassic Park. Gecko lizards dangled near the lights to catch giant moths; bats hung on the beams over my desk to peer at me; black millipedes as thick as my finger marched across the floor. I once opened the bathroom door to find a stick insect so large it looked like a piece of kindling with wings. In this strange crucible, sleep had taken on an unearthly quality; my antimalarial medication, notorious for neurological side-effects, converted my worst fears into exceptionally vivid nightmares. Every night a new horror visited me under my mosquito net: a river of army ants, a python, a Somali gunman. Most unnerving of all, a little Arab boy, a spirit incarnate, would come to float over my head or sit at the foot of my bed, lingering for a few seconds even after I had opened my eyes.

Some odd things had also begun to happen around the house—minor incidents, but they spooked me. One night, for example, I woke sensing that something strange had happened and turned to look at my alarm clock. It had come to a standstill five minutes earlier. How had I sensed that time had stopped, when my clock was designed to run silently? On another night, I awoke to a great crash—a cast-iron frying pan was on the kitchen floor, and there was no accounting for how it had gotten there from the counter. The missionaries next door were already convinced I was playing with fire in my research—demonic spirits were reaching me, and I needed to embrace Christ to save myself. I began to think that the membrane separating disbelief from belief was thinner than I had realized, and that my subconscious was making brief forays to the other side.

One evening, I secured the house before I went to bed in the usual way, padlocking an iron door on an outside courtyard, then a heavy wooden door at the front of the house, and finally a metal gate that shut me into the second floor. After an hour of fitful insomnia, I got up to get a glass of water from the kitchen. I flipped on the lights and went to open the gate at the top of the stairs, but when I put the key in the lock it seemed to put down roots as if possessed. It simply would not budge. I began to conjure an image of myself trapped there days later—parched, wilting, still scrabbling at the lock—when suddenly the electricity went off with a soft pop, and I was enveloped in darkness. Fear and confusion gathered in my chest and a thought ran through my mind of its own accord: "Who has bewitched me?" Could I have angered the Liver-Cutter by summoning it in bad faith, using it for research without quite believing in it? I felt a wave of queasiness before groping again for the key with jittering hands. All at once the lights sprang on and the lock released the key like a dog opening its mouth, sending me tumbling backward.

***

Shortly after meeting the Liver-Cutter, Maxwell and I went to visit Karissa, one of the few male diviners in Maxwell's village, renowned for recovering lost and stolen objects. Maxwell was feeling spent—plumbed too often and too intensely by the spirits, perhaps—so we settled on a neutral problem for Karissa to solve: The heavy rains were coming soon and I had lost my umbrella the day before. An old man with a kindly face and grizzled hair, Karissa wore a striped cloth loosely wrapped around his waist beneath his massive caramel-colored chest, scarified with the horizontal welts of a boyhood initiation ceremony. He invited us into a dark hut and seated us on low stools. Maxwell and I told him that we wanted to interview him about his work, but that we could also use his help in finding something, if he wished to take us up on it.

"Don't tell me what it is," he said. "I will do my best to tell you." He began to pile lumps of incense into a hollow coconut shell.

Maxwell whispered in my ear: "The really good ones never promise anything for sure. This man has fierce powers."

The familiar incense fumes made me heady by sheer power of association, and I had to dig my fingernails into my flesh to anchor myself. Karissa produced a solid little pouch made of something resembling shoe-leather, sewn together in thick, powerful stitches. He dangled the talisman over the curling white smoke, incanting rapidly under his breath in the Giriama language. After a short while, he looked intently at the talisman and addressed it directly.

"We want to know what has gone missing. Please tell us what has gone missing." The talisman dangled, motionless.

"Was it a radio?" Still the talisman hung without response.

"Was it clothing? A shirt? Was it a shirt? No? A dress? No?" He paused.

"Was it money?" Karissa held his breath, then made an exasperated noise, as if the talisman might be faulty, or willfully misbehaving. "Money? Money?" He paused, and tried once more. "Money?" He sighed.

"Was it a watch?" No response.

"Was it an umbrella?" The talisman started and began to whirl in rapid clockwise circles over the incense. Karissa smiled with satisfaction. Maxwell and I pushed our chairs backward in awe.

On the way home Maxwell and I conferred. Of course we knew Karissa could control the motions of the talisman, in principal. The question was why the talisman had moved when it did. Ever the fraud detector, Maxwell had long since gotten me to agree we would monitor our reactions during divination rituals, trying not to offer unconscious clues in our gaze, our body language, even our breath if we could help it. But it was far from obvious that Karissa had been attending to us for signals.

Not long after that, Maxwell and I were strolling into town when we passed an apartment building with a hand painted sign on the outside wall: "Professor Omar R. Matata: Expert treatment for ills caused by witchcraft. Unwanted spirits chased away. Drop-in Hours Sunday through Friday, 1:00 to 6:00; Saturday any time." A middle-aged man approached us, wearing a torn shirt and carrying a greasy fish wrapped in a newspaper. "Do you know this professor?" I asked, gesturing toward the sign.

"I'm his assistant," he said with pride. "My name is Mohammed." He was not a Giriama—I inferred he was Digo, a culturally related but thoroughly Muslimized people—but I had noticed that by now Maxwell had ceased to be an ethnic purist in his research. He was so riveted by supernatural mysteries, he didn't much mind where they came from, as long as they worked. I avoided reminding him of the Revival Faith of Giriama, thinking it might be a sore point.

The professor was with a client, so we persuaded Mohammed to speak to us in an empty room on the ground floor of his apartment building. "Tell us about this doctor," Maxwell demanded, without preliminaries. "How strong are his powers?"

"He trained far away, in Tanzania, where he got expert material. He can make money appear out of nowhere. And he can read your mind."

"Can you do any of this?" asked Maxwell. Mohammed thought for a moment, then gestured to my notepad with an authoritative air.

"Give me that," he said. He ripped out a thin strip of paper, about a centimeter wide and three centimeters long. "I'm going to leave the room," he said to me. "I want you to write something on that paper—anything you like. Then fold it into a square"—he demonstrated with his fingertips—"and hold onto it."

Mohammed strolled outside and inspected the hem of his shirt. I looked at the slip of paper and wrote the Swahili word for umbrella: "*mwavuli.*" Maxwell chuckled. I folded the paper and called Mohammed inside. Wordlessly, he grabbed my notebook and pen, opened to a clean page, and drew a stick figure with a circle around its midsection like a target. He held this effigy and began to incant under his breath, producing a river of strange sounds that suggested secret codes, obscure information, a window into a world of new knowledge.

Mohammed put the effigy drawing on the table. "Now, I want you to throw your folded paper at this spirit seven times." I tossed the folded square tentatively. It landed on the figure's head. "No—." He picked up the paper and threw it directly at the target area: "Like this." I obeyed, and Mohammed continued: "Now, I want you to eat that paper. Chew it well." I popped the square into my mouth and chewed.

"I'll be back," Mohammed said, and, taking a bottle of water, marched out the door. We could hear him outside, incanting and splashing.

When he reemerged, a few drops of water still clinging to his face, he took my notebook and pen out of my hands. "Look at me," he commanded. His eyes drilled into mine. This was clearly some process of reading, and I felt slightly violated. After about thirty seconds he wrenched away, turned to the notebook, and with a heavy, slow hand inscribed a row of seven digits. Then he faced the drawing of the spirit and began to incant again.

"What are you doing?"

"I'm asking the spirit to help me to translate these numbers." Ponderously, he began to write a letter beneath each number: "m"; "w"; "a"; until he had completed the word *mwavuli*. Maxwell shrieked, and we slapped each other's hands with excitement.

Mohammed refused, when we requested it, to transform paper into money, saying he needed to rest. So we walked home, racking our brains to recall when he might have had an opportunity to read the piece of paper. Mohammed had been outside when I first wrote the word, and he'd never had a chance to unwrap the square of paper before I ate it. Could some people really skirt the laws of physics to read minds and tell fortunes? The idea was disorienting, almost unthinkable, but I entertained it, turning it over and over with chills running up my neck. I was too preoccupied to write any field notes that night; in fact, I'd been distracted from my ethnographic purpose ever since encountering the Liver-Cutter. Just before going to bed, the thought crossed my mind: If Mohammed has such miraculous powers, why is his shirt so badly torn?

Somewhere in the no-man's-land between wakefulness and sleep my subconscious groped through the murk of the day and grabbed hold of something. I sat up. Mohammed had switched the folded square of paper. He had only touched it once, when showing me how to throw it, but if he had another square hidden between his fingers, he could have made a quick replacement. I dug into my bag and pulled out my notebook, opening it to the page where Mohammed

had first torn out a strip of paper and handed it to me. The torn space was now six centimeters long, not three.

William James (2002) has famously described the experience of conversion as one in which the mundane world is ruptured by an ecstatic sense of contact with the divine. What I experienced at this moment was something like a mirror image of Jamesian conversion. My growing wonder was translated suddenly into a dull, mechanical grasp of the facts, coupled with the grungy taste of having been deceived. I had to remind myself that "fakery" is not an important theoretical concept in the anthropological study of religion. Michael Lambek (1993), attending an antisorcery ritual in the Comoros Islands, once spotted a healer concealing a sac of fingernails and dirt that he subsequently "extracted" from a patient's body. On speaking to the diviner at length, Lambek realized that the diviner himself believed in sorcery and felt the planted sac had a persuasive effect important to the effect of the ritual. Even the healers who have become victims of sorcery consider this "extraction" necessary to their cure. In kind, I had seen Giriama diviners go to other diviners and healers for help, demonstrating their overarching commitment to the system, whatever their own repertoire of ritual gambits. . . . I realized with faint sadness that I was back on familiar terrain, possessing an abstract respect for the role of religion in others' lives, and a desiccated relationship to it myself.

In the morning, I set out to tell Maxwell. We were accustomed to sharing everything, and I thought he might be impressed by my resolution to Mohammed's puzzle. Instead, something seemed to drop out from under him. His anger was total, almost violent. He made scything motions of denial with his hands as he reacted, then collapsed into a contemplative stupor and announced he could not work for the rest of that day.

When we resumed our research, Maxwell had changed. It was as if the little window of skepticism that had opened in him some months earlier—back when I started to talk about anthropological theory and he started testing the waganga—had never quite closed, and in the end had been just large enough that a strong wind could blow the whole house down. We went to a famous diviner's place to watch a purification ritual: A child was missing some of his hair and his father feared a witch had snipped it off as he slept. Maxwell eyed the circular patch on the child's scalp, leaned over to me, and said flatly into my ear: "ringworm." He began to revise his past encounters with waganga: those who had divined well must have known his problems already from village gossip. . . . During our interviews he became offhand and businesslike, even mouthy, setting traps for diviners so he could spot the contradictions in their answers. He became impossibly demanding in his standards for evidence. "I won't be satisfied that they have any powers until they can do something amazing on the spot. Like change this"—he pointed to a cassette— "into a loaf of bread."

Despite his moments of humor, Maxwell seemed emptied out, and sometimes descended into a bitter anomie.

"I don't believe in spirits anymore. There is no supernatural world. There is just . . . what is."

"What about the Revival Faith of Giriama?" I asked. "What about the pride of your people in their customs?"

He thought for a minute. "Maybe," he proposed, "we could have a Revival Faith of Giriama where people still do the rituals for the spirits and the ancestors, and wear the traditional clothes, but they don't have to believe in any of it. So it wouldn't quite be religion, but it would still preserve our custom."

It occurred to me that in the practice known as cultural tourism, some Giriama families already received a hundred shillings a day for preserving their customs. All they had to do was file into a hotel dining room in traditional dress, dragging their goats on a lead and simulating ancestor propitiation with a bottle of palm wine.

***

Some time later, I left town on my own for a few weeks to do some research in a nearby area. When I returned I happened to walk past the guest house where Maxwell and I had first met, and a large white canvas sign caught my eye.

"PROFESSOR PROFESSOR," it read, "HIGHLY TRAINED TOP PROFESSIONAL DIVINER AVAILABLE FOR CONSULTATION AND HEALING." The announcement followed with a row of characters that looked like a bad approximation of Chinese. "That's funny," I said to myself. "I thought I knew all the diviners working around here." One of the maids, Taabu, approached me.

"Have you heard about Maxwell?" she asked. "What about him? Is he all right?"

"He's frightening us," she said.

"What do you mean?"

"He has become a very big diviner. Very feared."

I felt a wild flash of disorientation, and broke into confused laughter. "He's become a diviner? What do you mean? Where does he work?" Taabu gestured toward a back room.

Inside the room Maxwell had lined up the familiar accoutrements of divination and healing, with the perfect air of age and mystery. There was a stained gourd, its cork rimmed with blackened honey. There was a paper with a drawing of a bird in flight, radiating rays of some kind, flanked by two winged snakes, all presumably spirit effigies. There was a gizmo, maybe a wand, with feathers at the tip—this I hadn't even seen in our research. Maxwell was pushing the envelope. I tugged at one of the feathers and dissolved into laughter, crumpling against the wall with angry tears pricking my eyes.

Later, Maxwell demonstrated his ritual routines for me with a trickster's delight. He had gleaned almost everything directly from our research findings, and I was both bemused and horrified. If anyone in the village found out he was playing them, and playing with the powers of the spirits, they could have exiled or even killed him. But his dalliance with divination did not last very long. After a while the thrill, or maybe the anger that had propelled him, wore off. He took down his sign, and I rehired him for a couple more months to help me on a project about language that had nothing to do with spirits.

***

When I left Kenya, Maxwell used the wages I paid him as collateral for a loan to buy a taxi, which promptly broke an axle. He could not pay his debts, and fled south to Tanzania for a time. Judging from the intermittent e-mail messages he sent me, he left Kenya feeling cynical. He was fed up with his hardships, with religion, and with what he now regarded as the false hope purveyed by diviners and healers. And I would not blame him if he were also fed up with me or, perhaps, with the strange mirror I had held up to his convictions that changed them forever. In his disenchantment, Maxwell had been confronted with what he had once most feared: that a cosmos that once spoke vividly to the Giriama people was fading into the background as the generations turned over and the other forces—the Christians, the Muslims, the modernists, sometimes even the anthropologists—continued their march from over the horizon.

I was struck, though not until later, by the extent to which I had been unsettled by Maxwell's own journey into unbelief and his canny manipulation of the rituals that he now considered empty. Part of my discomfort seemed reasonable enough—even Maxwell saw himself as duping his gullible clients. Another part seemed to emerge from my quintessentially Western fixation on belief. I was vexed by the image of a Giriama going through the motions of divination without believing in it, a deep discomfort probably linked, unconsciously, to the Abrahamic assumption that "religion is (or should be) grounded in a solemn kind of faith." But most upsetting to me, I think, was that through his encounter with me Maxwell had lost his will to resist the forces that threatened to engulf a Giriama way of life still prized by some. We ethnographers are trained not to fetishize "cultural authenticity," but we are also prone to root for the underdog. I had admired Maxwell's pride and scrappiness, and his aspirations to lead a revival movement had made him a central allegorical figure (Clifford and Marcus 1986) in my ethnographic tableau about Giriama dilemmas. In abandoning his convictions, Maxwell lost his place as my figurehead of Giriama resistance—and ironically enough, my analytic approach to religion had contributed to his discouragement.

At the same time, I had complicated my own role as ethnographer by dipping my toe for a moment into an ocean of wonder, then withdrawing just as rapidly. At the beginning of fieldwork, when I resisted having my fortune told, I probably had the same ambivalence that many American agnostics might have about a Ouija board or Tarot card reading. We tell ourselves we don't believe that inert objects can prognosticate; yet disbelief is a fragile conceit, for if the wrong card turns up, then perhaps at some level in which the mind is not so tightly harnessed we might start to entertain the uncomfortable possibility of the impossible. It is that much easier to cross this line when context strips us of the social, material, and semiotic points of reference that remind us of who we are or want to be. It is hard to hold the putative self steady in an environment saturated with alternatives. I had seen spirits under my mosquito net in the realm between sleep and wakefulness, with the bats and the millipedes my silent witnesses, and no one there to talk me down. I felt assailed by mysterious health problems and fickle locks, and transported by the very scent of incense, by now so closely associated with diviners' possession.

Everyone around me talked about spirits, even implying that spirits were responsible for the peculiar events in my home, and I was close to these people. I liked and empathized with many of them, and I took seriously their commitments. And so, for a few days there, I had begun to float gingerly above all I had known to be true.

Still, context does not so quickly do away with entrenched habits of self-surveillance. I never entirely lost sight of my future reinsertion into a comfortable life in the United States with my partner, my family, my friends, my students, and my fellow academics. Ultimately, this vision reclaimed me with the inevitability of gravity. The Arab child over my bed became a side-effect of my antimalarial pills and a symptom of my suggestibility. The simultaneous failure of the lock and the lights, and the (ultimately benign) liver abnormality echoed by the name of the Liver-Cutter became coincidences. Karissa, in his remarkable detection of my missing umbrella, had revealed not the psychic ability of his talisman, but a refined sensitivity to his clients' unwitting cues.

I almost had to rewrite these stories for myself—my professional future was at stake. For however diverse anthropologists may be, a series of ideological commitments underlie ethnographic scholarship in the West today, and one of these is the notion that gods, spirits, and ancestors should be analyzed as human phenomena, bound up with local social, economic, semiotic, and political arrangements. Some ethnographers may offer the occasional nod to the mysteries of the unknown, and may even harbor deep cosmological commitments in their hearts, but to seriously entertain supernatural entities as real in one's scholarly work would be considered at best a distraction and at worst a disastrous hobbling of one's analytic abilities. Our pact as anthropologists, then, is to go "there" without ever quite leaving "here"; the emic is all very well and good, provided that the etic is close behind. This epistemological demand means that successful scholarship is most easily carried out by a particular kind of self, a self conditioned by what Katherine Ewing (1994) has identified as the powerful taboo against "going native" among those in our discipline.

No wonder my swift return to agnosticism the night after meeting Mohammed brought with it a shade of relief. I was safe again, back where I belonged, back with the assurance of a future in an elite cultural context where others would make room for me because my ontological commitments would fit neatly in. Maxwell, on the other hand, felt loosed from his mast and cast into a state of enduring liminality, left to rely on his wits, on sheer skin-of-his-teeth bricolage, while dogged by the knowledge that no matter how creative his adaptations, they would never give him the sure footing of the privileges I would go home to.

References

Boddy, Janice. 1989. Wombs and Alien Spirits: Women, Men, and the Zar Cult in Northern Sudan. Madison: University of Wisconsin Press.

Clifford, James, and George Marcus. 1986. Writing Culture: The Poetics and Politics of Ethnography. Berkeley: University of California Press.

Cooper, Frederick. 1980. From Slaves to Squatters: Plantation Labor and Agriculture in Zanzibar and Coastal Kenya 1890–1925. New Haven, CT: Yale University Press.

Ewing, Katherine. 1994. Dreams from a Saint: Anthropological Atheism and the Temptation to Believe. American Anthropologist 96(3):571–583.

Giles, Linda L. 1995. Sociocultural Change and Spirit Possession on the Swahili Coast of East Africa. Anthropological Quarterly 68(2):89–106.

Irvine, Judith. 1982. The Creation of Identity in Spirit Mediumship and Possession. *In* Semantic Anthropology. David Parkin, ed. Pp 241–260. London: Academic Press.

James, William. 2002 [1902]. The Varieties of Religious Experience: A Study in Human Nature. Amherst, NY: Prometheus Books.

Lambek, Michael. 1993. Knowledge and Practice in Mayotte: Local Discourses of Islam, Sorcery, and Spirit Possession. Toronto: University of Toronto Press.

Lewis, Ioan M. 1971. Ecstatic Religion: An Anthropological Study of Spirit Possession and Shamanism. Harmondsworth, UK: Penguin Books.

Masquelier, Adeline. 2001. Prayer Has Spoiled Everything: Possession, Power, and Identity in an Islamic Town of Niger. Durham, NC: Duke University Press.

McIntosh, Janet. 2004. Reluctant Muslims: Embodied Hegemony and Moral Resistance in a Giriama Spirit Possession Complex. Journal of the Royal Anthropological Institute 10(1):91–112.

Stoller, Paul. 1984. Horrific Comedy: Cultural Resistance and the Hauka Movement in Niger. Ethos 12(2):165–188.

Willis, Justin. 1993. Mombasa, the Swahili, and the Making of the Mijikenda. Oxford: Clarendon Press.

1.5 Is Native Anthropology Really Possible?

TAKEYUKI TSUDA

Our positionality—who we are and how we are situated as raced, ethnicized, classed, educated, et cetera, as individuals— shapes every aspect of the research process, from the questions we consider important to the people we have access to, to how informants shape their responses based on what they perceive we want to know. Some argue that the closer one is to the research population, the closer one may be to an emic, empathic, and authentic understanding of a culture. In the following account, Takeyuki Tsuda considers the benefits and potential drawbacks of "native anthropology," or ethnographies produced about a culture by a member of that cultural group. Drawing on his own experience as a Japanese American studying Japanese Americans, he demonstrates that even "natives" are not fully "native," and "othering" in fieldwork can actually be productive and essential; difference, Tsuda argues, is "good to think with."

Questions

1. What concerns have native anthropologists expressed about non-native, Western anthropologists researching and writing about natives?
2. In what ways are ethnographies written by native anthropologists seen as preferable? Does Tsuda agree that they are?
3. In what way(s) is difference "good to think with"?

The research trajectory of a number of anthropologists has followed a familiar path that begins in a foreign country and eventually "comes home" (see, e.g., Behar 1996; Motzafi-Haller 1997; Rosaldo 1989). Quite often, our first dissertation field research projects involve studying peoples in remote, foreign locations as a rite of passage that validates us as a *bona fide* anthropologist. Then, for personal or academic reasons (or out of sheer convenience), we eventually conduct research at home, often among our own people or ethnic group.

Coming Home?

I began my anthropological career as a Japan specialist and conducted fieldwork among Japanese Brazilians who have "return" migrated from Brazil to Japan as unskilled immigrants working in Japanese factories (see Tsuda 2003). My dissertation project also included extensive fieldwork among Japanese Brazilians in Brazil. During this research, I became interested in a future project comparing Japanese Brazilians in Brazil with Japanese Americans in the United States as part of the "diaspora" of Japanese descendants scattered throughout the Americas.

It was a logical extension of my dissertation research and a great opportunity to compare two ethnic minorities of the same ancestral origin who have been living for many generations in countries with different race relations and histories. In addition, being a second generation Japanese American myself, I figured there would be obvious advantages to studying my own people. After being sidetracked for quite some time with other projects, I have finally

Takeyuki Tsuda. 2015. Is Native Anthropology Really Possible? *Anthropology Today*. 31(3):14–17. By permission of John Wiley & Sons, Inc.

been able to focus my research on Japanese Americans in recent years.

Therefore, like others before me, I have experienced an ethnographic homecoming of sorts and have become a so-called "native anthropologist." However, does native anthropology really feel like coming home?

Initially, I did not think that fieldwork with my own ethnic group in my own country would be that interesting when compared with my previous dissertation research. For me, Japanese Brazilians had been an exotic "other" from a foreign, Latin American country. Even though they were also Japanese descendants, they spoke Portuguese and inhabited a different, Brazilian culture. In addition, they had migrated to Japan only to find that they had become culturally and socioeconomically marginalized, strangers in their ethnic homeland, which resulted in all sorts of novel and remarkable experiences.

Every interview and participant observation had the potential to uncover something new and fascinating. In contrast, not only were Japanese Americans familiar to me, they are well educated middle class Americans, no longer suffer from serious discrimination, and generally do not migrate. As a result, they were not "exotic" and seemed rather ordinary to me. I kept telling myself that only the comparative dimension of this project would be interesting.

However, as I began my fieldwork, I was immediately drawn to, and eventually fascinated by the experiences of Japanese Americans. They were not as familiar or ordinary as I initially expected! Although I had been acquainted with Japanese Americans my entire life, they somehow remained an anthropological "other" for me. . . .

Questioning Native Anthropology

In contrast to previous images of white (usually male) anthropologists studying the "natives" (usually darker peoples) in faraway lands, there has been considerable discussion about the apparent rise of "native anthropologists" in the last few decades. It has been repeatedly mentioned that in contrast to "non-native" anthropologists, our immediate cultural and linguistic familiarity with the people we are studying will provide us with superior access, rapport, and empathy, ultimately leading to more emic, sensitive, and authentic ethnographic portrayals that are less subject to Westernized, colonizing, and objectifying perspectives (Anae 2010, 230–232; Hayano 1979, 101–102; Kanuha 2000, 441–443; Ohnuki-Tierney 1984; Wang 2002, 166; see also Aguilar 1981 and Narayan 1993, 676–677, for summaries of such claims).

Because native anthropologists are members of the groups they study, their ethnographies are also described as more politically engaged and activist-oriented, uncovering social inequities, as well as systems of power and domination (Abu-Lughod 1991, 142–143; Anae 2010, 227–228; Hayano 1979, 101–102; Motzafi-Haller 1997, 215–217).[1] Nonetheless, native anthropologists may take certain observations for granted as insiders and apparently have more difficulty maintaining "objective" detachment from the peoples they study (Hayano 1979, 101–102; Kanuha 2000, 441–443; Ohnuki-Tierney 1984).

In addition, a number of native anthropologists have been concerned about how non-native, Western anthropologists have dominated scholarly representations and discourses about their own cultures, relegating natives to the mere status of informants or useful tools for gathering information (Kuwayama 2003; Medicine 2001, 5; Smith 2012). They have noted how the natives themselves have been highly critical of the ethnographies written about them by outsider anthropologists, which do not dialogue with them but address academic audiences (Kuwayama 2003, 10). Such ethnographies are therefore seen by certain native scholars and intellectuals as unreliable, irrelevant, and disparaging and can even reinforce Eurocentric academic and institutional power structures (Kuwayama 2003, 11–12; Medicine 2001; Smith 2012, 3; Trask 1999).

As a result, some wish to do work that is more meaningful and has a positive impact on the lives of indigenous peoples (Medicine 2001, 14; Smith 2012, 9). Native anthropologists are now challenging the past hegemony of Euro-American anthropologists and are struggling for recognition, sometimes producing a cultural power struggle between insider and outsider (see Kuwayama 2003, 12–13; Trask 1999).

Figure 1.5.1

An 1861 image expression the *Jōi* ("Expel the barbarians")
sentiment.

(Public Domain)

Although such concerns certainly have validity,
they essentialize the difference between native and
non-native anthropologists based on the simple dichotomy of insider versus outsider. Because native
anthropologists are insiders who apparently share
the cultures and concerns of those they study, it is assumed they will have a fundamentally different and
more culturally sensitive and locally relevant ethnographic perspective in contrast to the inherently
problematic representations of non-native, outsider
anthropologists.

In addition, such simple dichotomies ignore the
increasing number of "semi-native" anthropologists,
such as US-born Japanese American anthropologists
studying Japan (Tsuda 2003, 1–51; Kondo 1986) or
an American anthropologist of half Indian descent
studying India (Narayan 1993). Their complex and
constantly shifting positionality in the field cannot
be characterized by a straightforward insider versus
outsider perspective.

I suggest that we question this simple dichotomy
of native versus non-native anthropologist. Even insider anthropologists will still encounter educational,
social class, gender, generational, urban/rural, or cultural differences with the peoples they study because
all social groups (even the most homogeneous) are
fragmented by internal differences (Aguilar 1981, 25;
Jacobs-Huey 2002, 793–796; Kuwayama 2003, 9; Medicine 2001, 5–6; Motzafi-Haller 1997, 217–219; Narayan
1993, 671, 675; Nelson 1996). As a result, there are
plenty of examples of native anthropologists who are
seen as outsiders and have difficulty being accepted
by their own communities, or conversely, become
embroiled in internal conflicts (Aguilar 1981, 21;
Hayano 1979, 100; Jacobs-Huey 2002, 796–797;
Messerschmidt 1981, 8; Tsuda 2003, 32–33).

Therefore, even for those of us who study our own
ethnic group, the distance between the anthropologist
and the "natives" remains. Just like non-native
anthropologists, we must also constantly negotiate our
positionality in the field as we move along a scale of
relative distance from those we study, or what Linda
Williamson Nelson (1996) refers to as "gradations of
endogeny." All anthropologists are both partial outsiders and partial insiders who experience various
degrees of acceptance and cultural insight. Therefore,
native anthropologists do not necessarily enjoy a
privileged status compared to those who are non-
natives, nor can they really claim that their ethnographic writings have greater cultural authenticity, insight, and relevance (Hayano 1979, 102;
Jacobs-Huey 2002, 793; Motzafi-Haller 1997, 217–219;
Reed-Danahay 1997, 3–4; Wang 2002).

This simply indicates how anthropological knowledge is inherently partial and never complete because
it is always contextually situated, i.e., dependent on
how we are socially positioned in relation to our
research participants, which continuously shifts in
productive or less productive ways.

The distinction between native and non-native
anthropologists is therefore not absolute, but a relative continuum, with the former simply more likely
to be culturally and socially closer to their research
participants. Indeed, regardless of what type of anthropologist we are (native, non-native, semi-native),

the distance and differences between researcher and researched always persist and can never be completely eliminated.

Nonetheless, I argue that such cultural differences are not detrimental, but productive for fieldwork. And this is not simply because it allows us to maintain "objective" detachment or because it enables us to think about our positionality in the field and how it facilitates or restricts access to ethnographic information. Ultimately, as I will discuss [herein], difference is essential to the generation of anthropological knowledge.

How "Native" Are We? Entering the Field

As mentioned at the beginning of this article, I am a second generation Japanese American (*nisei*). However, I am what Japanese Americans call a *shin-nisei* (the "new second generation"), who are the descendants of Japanese who immigrated to the United States mainly after World War II. *Shin-nisei* therefore have experiences that are quite different from pre-war second generation *nisei*, whose Japanese parents came to the United States before 1924. They were interned in concentration camps during World War II and their descendants are either third generation *sansei* or fourth generation *yonsei*.

My father immigrated to the United States in the 1960s as a biochemistry graduate student at the University of Chicago. I grew up partly in the Japanese expatriate business community in Chicago where I attended Japanese Saturday school from fourth grade to the end of high school, primarily with children from Japan, although there were a few US-born *shin-nisei* like myself in my classes. Our parents also forced my brother and me to speak only Japanese at home and took us to Japan a number of times. As a result, like other *shin-nisei*, I became bilingual, bicultural, and transnational.

I never identified as "Japanese American" or even as a second generation "*nisei*" when I was growing up. Neither my parents nor my Japanese classmates in Saturday school ever referred to me in such a manner. Instead, I saw myself as a "Japanese" (*nihonjin*), who just happened to be born and raised in the United States. I have felt much more connected to Japan throughout my entire life than to the experiences and history of Japanese Americans in the United States. In fact, even to this day, other Americans often mistake me for a Japanese from Japan (perhaps the "1.5

generation," arriving in the US before adolescence). This is probably because my English continues to have a Japanese inflection, my demeanour may sometimes appear to be "Japanese," and I have a very distinctive, Japanese first name (in contrast to most Japanese Americans who have American first names).

Growing up in Chicago, I always regarded "Japanese Americans" as people who were descendants of Japanese who immigrated before World War II and were therefore quite different from our family. They were completely Americanized, had lost their connections to Japan, had a different history that included internment during World War II, and lived on the other side of the city. In fact, my mother had strong prejudices about Japanese Americans. She regarded them as descendants of low-class, uneducated, and poor rural Japanese who could not survive economically in pre-war Japan and had no choice but to abandon their homeland for America.

Although I did become acquainted with a number of Japanese Americans growing up, virtually all of them were other *shin-nisei* with similar bilingual and transnational Japanese backgrounds like myself. Of course, I did not think of them as "*shin-nisei*" or even "Japanese American" back then. Like me, they were American-born "Japanese." In fact, it was probably not until graduate school that I started to actively refer to myself as "Japanese American" in the ethnically diverse environment at the University of California at Berkeley.

When I went home to Chicago and called myself "Japanese American" in front of my mother, she was quite upset and tried very hard to convince me to stop using the term! However, I adamantly refused, having finally found the most appropriate ethnic label for myself. In the past, I had used "Japanese," which technically meant someone from Japan; "Asian," which lacked ethnic specificity; and "Oriental," which had been a childhood term that had long since become politically incorrect.

Given my personal background, when I first started my research on Japanese Americans, I felt like a cultural outsider. Although I was technically studying my own ethnic group, I was familiar with only the *shin-nisei*, a small sub-population that was detached from the broader Japanese American community and were not a product of the internment experience during World War II. As a result, I had never felt like an "authentic" Japanese American. Therefore, the cultural differences I experienced with most Japanese Americans were not necessarily based on educational level, professional status, social class background, or even gender, but generation.[2]

In fact, I still remember meeting my first Japanese American contact in San Diego, an elderly third generation *sansei* woman who ended up becoming one of my best informants and a good friend. After we got acquainted, the first question she asked me was: "Are you from Japan?" Great, I thought. Even the Japanese Americans think I am "Japanese" and cannot tell that I am actually a fellow Japanese American!

As I began actively attending local Japanese American community events in San Diego, I initially felt like an intruder who did not belong, although I was always openly welcomed when I met people. I had never had any contact or interest in the broader Japanese American community while growing up and was completely unfamiliar with their cultural activities, although some of them certainly resembled festivities I had seen in Japan.

Almost everyone I encountered was either a prewar *nisei* or third generation *sansei* and they were quite different from the *shin-nisei* Japanese Americans that I had known my entire life. In fact, none of the dozens of people I met through Japanese American community organizations were *shin-nisei*, as far as I could tell.

Because of my strong Japanese cultural background and lingering accent, I always felt that the people I met would wonder whether I was a real Japanese American. I was struck (actually a bit distraught) when I noticed that a few elderly Japanese American women actually *bowed* when I spoke with them! Since a Japanese American would never bow to another Japanese American, I assumed this indicated they thought that I was a Japanese foreigner from Japan. Bowing was of course a polite gesture, but for me, it meant, "We don't think you are one of us."

Apparently, the cultural and generational differences were palpable on both sides. On those occasions when Japanese Americans seemed confused about my ethnicity, I would actually say, "I'm also a Japanese American." In fact, I felt like adding, "*shin-nisei* are Japanese Americans too, you know?" Of course, once I identified myself as Japanese American, no one contested my ethnic claims, especially when I told them I was actually *shin-nisei*. Once it became clear to them that I was born in the United States, I felt accepted as a fellow Japanese American, even if I had initially appeared to them to be a Japanese

from Japan. Therefore, shared nationality became a critical factor that helped overcome cultural and generational differences.

As my fieldwork progressed, I became acquainted with many Japanese Americans and eventually became a familiar face in the local San Diego Japanese American community. In fact, when I would show up to community events, a number of people would be familiar with me and would come up to greet me. It was evident that because I am technically Japanese American, I was able to blend into the ethnic community much more than a white person. My ethnicity also probably made Japanese Americans more willing to meet for an interview and talk freely about their experiences. I was even asked to deliver a keynote speech at the annual meeting of the Japanese American Historical Society of San Diego about my research. There were hundreds of attentive Japanese Americans in the audience and the talk was well received.

Despite my progressive immersion in the field, the cultural differences between me and my research participants were never erased, as is the case with all anthropologists. The generational differences between myself and most other Japanese Americans continued to persist. It was only when I was interviewing other *shin-nisei* and sharing our similar experiences that I felt I was truly with my "own people."

Yet, it was generational differences that made Japanese Americans so inherently fascinating to me, not "ordinary" as I had initially expected.

Figure 1.5.2

Takeyuki Tsuda in the field (left): *Mochitsuki* (pounding rice to make rice cakes) at the Buddhist Temple of San Diego.

(Takeyuki [Gaku] Tsuda)

"Othering" in Fieldwork

I argue that difference is productive and essential for fieldwork. In addition to preventing boredom for "native anthropologists," I suggest that difference is also "good to think with" for both anthropologist and research participant alike in the mutual creation of social knowledge. In contrast to those who have claimed that the insider similarities of "native anthropologists" endow them with privileged, emic insight, I actually found that it was the generational differences of most Japanese Americans that led to ethnographic and even theoretical insight. This was especially true with pre-war *nisei*. Although we were both second generation offspring of Japanese immigrants, I constantly felt that our cultural, ethnic, and historical consciousness was very different, causing me to realize how different historical experiences can produce considerable variation within the same immigrant generation.

Difference was actually productive for my interviewees as well. During our conversations, I would often talk about my own experiences as a Japanese American, allowing my interviewees to use me as a sounding board to reflect on how their ethnic background was different. Many of these were generational differences. Some of the elderly pre-war *nisei* reflected upon how their internment experience as "enemy aliens" during World War II had caused them to become Americanized (in order to demonstrate their national loyalties) compared to postwar *shin-nisei* like myself who were more bicultural and transnational. Older *sansei* interviewees spoke about how their loss of heritage, culture and language, was due to their greater generational distance from their immigrant grandparents as well as their not being raised in the contemporary, multicultural environment, in contrast to myself. The *sansei*, as well as fourth generation *yonsei* youth, sometimes remarked how great it was that I spoke Japanese fluently and had maintained my cultural background—something they were not able to do.

In fact, even my knowledge of the *shin-nisei* was not absolute, and there were subtle differences in our backgrounds. For instance, most of them were college students and consider- ably younger than me, producing differences based on age. One *shin-nisei* spent part of his youth in Mexico, creating some differences in ethnic consciousness.

Therefore, "othering" is essential for fieldwork regardless of all the existential and post modernist angst the term now evokes among some anthropologists. Indeed, cultural difference has been the intellectual justification and cornerstone on which anthropology has been built. One of the hallmarks of our discipline has always been to bring the detailed, emic experiences of different (and yes, exotic) others to our audiences in a sympathetic, readable (and also unreadable) manner. No one wants to peruse a fieldwork-based account of a remote tribe living in the African bush only to hear that they are "just like us."

But more importantly, cultural difference is the foundation of knowledge for both "native" and "non-native" anthropologists alike. If our fieldwork and research simply elicits information about people with whom we are already completely familiar, it is not new knowledge, but simply confirmation of what we already know. If most Japanese Americans had in fact been very similar or even identical to me, or if I had only studied the *shin-nisei*, I would not have learned as much that was new about them. Therefore, I acquired the greatest amount of new anthropological knowledge from Japanese Americans who were from other generations. In contrast to the standard postmodernist position that the epistemological status of the "other" makes them ultimately unknowable, I argue that it is precisely this "otherness" that makes them the subject of anthropological knowledge. Even with the *shin-nisei*, there were gender, age, and regional differences[3] that made them anthropologically interesting to me. . . .

. . . [W]e must be cognizant of how the peoples we study, and their differences, are historically constituted. However, if we are to avoid the contemporary "othering" of the peoples we study in fieldwork, we threaten to undermine one of the most fundamental aspects of anthropological knowledge. While we need to be constantly wary about essentializing and exoticizing the cultural differences we encounter in the field, we should not hope to escape them.

Notes

1. It must be remembered, however, that not all "natives" are marginalized and oppressed, indicating the problematic connotations that the term has in anthropology (see also Appadurai 1988).
2. Not only are Japanese Americans in general highly educated and middle class, they completely understood the research I was conducting as a professional anthropologist. In fact, some had taken sociology and anthropology classes in college and were familiar with fieldwork.
3. I am a midwestern *shin-nisei* whereas most of my *shin-nisei* interviewees were born and raised in California.

References

Abu-Lughod, L. 1991. Writing Against Culture. In R. Fox (ed.), *Recapturing Anthropology: Working in the Present*, 137–162. Santa Fe, NM: School of American Research Press.

Aguilar, J. 1981. Insider Research: An Ethnography of a Debate. In D. Messerschmidt (ed.), *Anthropologists at Home in North America: Methods and Issues in the Study of One's Own Society*, 15–26. Cambridge: Cambridge University Press.

Anae, M. 2010. Teuleva: Toward a *Native* Anthropology. *Pacific Studies* 33(2/3): 222–240.

Appadurai, A. 1988. Putting Hierarchy in Its Place. *Cultural Anthropology* 3(1): 36–49.

Behar, R. 1996. *The Vulnerable Observer: Anthropology That Breaks Your Heart*. Boston: Beacon Press.

Hayano, D. 1979. Auto-Ethnography: Paradigms, Problems, and Prospects. *Human Organization* 38(1): 99–104.

Jacobs-Huey, L. 2002. The Natives Are Gazing and Talking Back: Reviewing the Problematics of Positionality, Voice, and Accountability Among "Native" Anthropologists. *American Anthropologist* 104(3): 791–804.

Kanuha, V. K. 2000. "'eing" Native Versus "Going Native": Conducting Social Work Research as an Insider. *Social Work: A Journal of the National Association of Social Workers* 45(5): 439–447.

Kondo, D. 1986. Dissolution and Reconstitution of Self: Implications for Anthropological Epistemology. *Cultural Anthropology* 1(1): 74–88.

Kuwayama, T. 2003. Natives as Dialogic Partners: Some Thoughts on Native Anthropology. *Anthropology Today* 19(1): 8–13.

Medicine, B. 2001. *Learning to Be an Anthropologist and Remaining "Native."* Urbana: University of Illinois Press.

Messerschmidt, D. 1981. On Anthropology "at Home."' In D. Messerschmidt (ed.), *Anthropologists at Home in North America: Methods and Issues in the Study of One's Own Society*, 3–14. Cambridge: Cambridge University Press.

Motzafi-Haller, P. 1997. Writing Birthright: On Native Anthropologists and the Politics of Representation. In D. Reed-Danahay (ed.), *Auto/Ethnography: Rewriting the Self and the Social*, 195–222. Oxford: Berg.

Narayan, K. 1993. How Native Is a "Native" Anthropologist? *American Anthropologist* 95:671–686.

Nelson, L. W. 1996. "Hands in the Chit'lins": Notes on Native Anthropological Research Among African American Women. In G. Etter-Lewis & M. Foster (eds.), *Unrelated Kin: Race and Gender in Women's Personal Narrative*, 183–199. New York: Routledge.

Ohnuki-Tierney, E. 1984. "Native" Anthropologists. *American Ethnologist* 11(3): 584–586.

Reed-Danahay, D. 1997. Introduction. In D. Reed-Danahay (ed.), *Auto/Ethnography: Rewriting the Self and the Social*, 1–17. Oxford: Berg.

Rosaldo, R. 1989. *Culture and Truth: The Remaking of Social Analysis*. Boston: Beacon Press.

Smith, L. T. 2012. *Decolonizing Methodologies: Research and Indigenous Peoples*. London: Zed Books.

Trask, H. 1999. *From a Native Daughter: Colonialism and Sovereignty in Hawai'i*. Honolulu: University of Hawaii Press.

Tsuda, T. 2003. *Strangers in the Ethnic Homeland: Japanese Brazilian Return Migration in Transnational Perspective*. New York: Columbia University Press.

Wang, M. 2002. The Third Eye: Towards a Critique of "Nativist Anthropology." *Critique of Anthropology* 22(2): 149–174.

DR. ASHRAF GHANI

Presidential Profiles

Figure 1.6.1

Ashraf Ghani. (Photo: U.S. Department of State)

On September 21, 2014, Dr. Ashraf Ghani was elected President of the Islamic Republic of Afghanistan. Ghani was trained as an anthropologist, earning both his MA and PhD in anthropology from Columbia University in the early 1980s. He spent several years in an academic career, teaching at the University of California, Berkeley (1983) and Johns Hopkins University (1983–1991) and pursuing scholarly work on state-building and social transformation. In 1991, Ghani moved to the World Bank as a lead anthropologist focusing on human dimensions of economic projects in East and South Asia. Ghani remained with the World Bank until returning to Afghanistan in the early 2000s to join their government and lead efforts to rebuild the country's economy after the collapse of the Taliban. Interviews and profiles from NPR, New Republic, BBC, and Princeton are available on www.oup.com/us/brondo.

DR. JIM YONG KIM

Presidential Profiles

Figure 1.6.2

Jim Yong Kim. (Photo: Empea1077, Creative Commons 4.0)

Jim Yong Kim became the twelfth President of the World Bank on July 1, 2012. He is a Korean American anthropologist and physician who was trained in medicine and anthropology at Harvard University, earning his MD in 1991 and PhD in 1993. During his training, he co-founded Partners in Health with Dr. Paul Farmer (see Reading 6.1

and www.oup.com/us/brondo), an organization formed to deliver community-focused health care to the world's poorest and sickest communities. Partners in Health began in 1987 with a focus on the residents of Haiti's Central Plateau region, but has since expanded throughout the world. Upon earning his degrees, Dr. Kim remained at Harvard as a lecturer and in leadership roles for several programs and centers in medicine, social science, and human rights through 2009. Between 2003 and 2009 he joined the World Health Organization, specializing in work related to HIV/AIDS in developing countries. In 2009, Dr. Kim became the President of Dartmouth College where he remained until President Barack Obama nominated him to become President of the World Bank.

 Interviews and articles from Freakanomics, the Washington Post, and the United Nations are available on www.oup.com/us/brondo.

PART 2

Communicating Culture: Language and Expressive Culture

Our ability to communicate symbolically is one of the most significant components of human culture. The importance of language in defining humanity cannot be overstated and is reflected by our discipline's dedication of an entire subfield to the study of linguistics.

Anthropologists are interested in language for several reasons, but perhaps most importantly because language is a human universal and all people use it express their experiences and to aid in their understanding of the world and interactions with others. Analyzing language, speech styles, and forms of non-verbal communication can tell us a lot about cultural beliefs and norms. Context plays a powerful role in influencing what people say, how they say it, and how that which is said is interpreted by others. This theme cuts across all of the readings, which collectively explore topics from cross-cultural miscommunication to how race, class, and gender shape what people can and cannot (or choose not to) say in conservations or joking behavior in public and private settings.

The first reading explores cross-cultural communication. In the classic piece "Shakespeare in the Bush" (Reading 2.1), Laura Bohannan tells of her attempt at sharing the story of Hamlet to a group of Tiv elders in Nigeria. While she thought its plot and the characters' motivations within the play would be universally understood, and by sharing the story she could participate in the locally respected practice of storytelling, she was met with protest by Tiv elders who felt strongly that she "misunderstood" the story. The Tiv were applying their own cultural logic to make sense of the story, revealing how our cultural categories shape meaning and interpretation.

John Hartigan's "What Are You Laughing At? Assessing the "Racial" in U.S. Public Discourse" (Reading 2.2) also explores the ways in which cultural categories shape communication and understanding. In his selection, Hartigan explores public reaction to racial remarks made by once popular radio shock jock Don Imus and comedian Michael Richards, and compares the controversy over their remarks to the lack of public critique of racially charged television ads from Geico and CareerBuilder. His piece asks readers to consider why certain jokes that contain racial descriptions are considered funny in some contexts but offensive in others.

Language ideology refers to widespread assumptions about the degree to which some languages or dialects are superior to or more sophisticated than others (Welsh and Vivanco 2014, 98). Language ideologies shape how people see themselves and how they classify others, thus working to create social difference. Thus, studying language ideology reveals how speech is "always embedded in a social world of power differences" (Schultz and Lavenda 2014, 117). Reading 2.3, "Sex, Lies, and Conversation: Why Is It So Hard for Men and Women to Talk to Each Other?" is a classic piece exploring gendered use of language; in reading the piece, students should apply their understanding of language ideologies to consider how gendered language styles are used to express power. In the article, Deborah Tannen contrasts men's and women's speech styles, arguing that men's speech styles are driven by a hierarchical social world whereby men are constantly seeking to establish and maintain their position as one up on another, whereas women are focused on building and sustaining relationships.

Shalini Shankar explores how language ideologies play out in U.S. high schools. In "Speaking Like a Minority: 'FOB' Styles, Gender, and Racial Meanings Among Desi Teens in Silicon Valley" (Reading 2.4), Shankar draws on her research with South Asian American teenagers in a Silicon Valley high school to show that linguistic styles vary by class and gender, with upper-class Desi teens adopting monolingual norms while middle-class teens speak in "FOB" (fresh off the boat) style. The importance of context in this piece cannot be overstated: FOB style is influenced by who students are talking with, who is within earshot, and whether or not they think of the school as a public or private space; their speech styles are highly gendered and classed.

Shankar's piece provokes reflection about the continuation of heritage languages upon immigration. Punjabi, of course, is in no danger of disappearing as it is the tenth most widely spoken language in the world (Wikipedia 2015). However, less common languages, with very few speakers, are indeed on the verge of disappearance as younger people stop using or never learn their native languages. Many anthropologists conduct research on or engage in language revitalization projects—that is, efforts to preserve or revive languages that are on the verge of extinction. In "Anything Can Happen on YouTube (or Can It?): Endangered Language and New Media" (Reading 2.5), Jillian Cavanaugh explores the emergence of Bergamasco, a northern Italian endangered language, on YouTube and what it means for revitalization efforts. Bergamasco has long been a language connected to place, and many people consider it something of the past, not to mention old-fashioned and unsophisticated. Yet in the 2000s, the language appeared on YouTube channels, spoken by public figures like David Beckham, Rambo, and President Obama. Cavanaugh asks, what does it mean for younger generations when they hear it spoken not just by their family members locally, but by Rambo and President Obama?

This section's "Anthropology in Practice" element also explores the topic of language revitalization. It features Dr. Bernard Perley, a linguistic anthropologist and member of the Maliseet nation from the Tobique

First Nation in Canada pursuing research on language revitalization among American Indians in the Americas. His work captures the spirit of engaged and public anthropology through his close collaboration with the Maliseet community to develop public events, such as a Maliseet prayer installation and showcase of four American Indian languages, both of which he describes in his interview.

KEY TERMS:

- Language
- Cross-cultural communication
- Linguistic relativity
- Discourse
- Dialect
- Sociolinguistics
- Genderlect
- Language ideology
- Language revitalization

2.1 Shakespeare in the Bush

LAURA BOHANNAN

Is human nature universal? Do people the world over share the same basic understandings about why people act the way they do? In this classic piece, Laura Bohannan recounts her attempt to tell the story of Hamlet to a group of Tiv elders in Nigeria. She finds that contrary to her assumption that everyone would interpret the central plot and motivations within this classic play in the same way, the Tiv understood it differently from the way she did, through their own cultural lens. In the end, the elders "explain" to Bohannan how she has misunderstood Hamlet, clarifying the story for her by applying their own cultural knowledge so that she can return home to show her own elders that they have helped her see its true meaning. This piece has become a classic because it helps students see how culture affects expectations and understanding.

Questions

1. What does Bohannan learn about the universality of human nature?
2. What were some major points of Hamlet that the Tiv elders felt important to clarify for Bohannan, and why did they think they were important?
3. What do these different interpretations reveal about cross-cultural differences?

Just before I left Oxford for the Tiv in West Africa, conversation turned to the season at Stratford. "You Americans," said a friend, "often have difficulty with Shakespeare. He was, after all, a very English poet, and one can easily misinterpret the universal by misunderstanding the particular." I protested that human nature is pretty much the same the whole world over; at least the general plot and motivation of the greater tragedies would always be clear—everywhere—although some details of custom might have to be explained and difficulties of translation might produce other slight changes. To end an argument we could not conclude, my friend gave me a copy of *Hamlet* to study in the African bush: it would, he hoped, lift my mind above its primitive surroundings, and possibly I might, by prolonged meditation, achieve the grace of correct interpretation.

It was my second field trip to that African tribe, and I thought myself ready to live in one of its remote sections—an area difficult to cross even on foot. I eventually settled on the hillock of a very knowledgeable old man, the head of a homestead of some hundred and forty people, all of whom were either his close relatives or their wives and children. Like the other elders of the vicinity, the old man spent most of his time performing ceremonies seldom seen these days in the more accessible parts of the tribe. I was delighted. Soon there would be three months of enforced isolation and leisure, between the harvest that takes place just before the rising of the swamps and the clearing of new farms when the water goes down. Then, I thought, they would have even more time to perform ceremonies and explain them to me.

I was quite mistaken. Most of the ceremonies demanded the presence of elders from several homesteads. As the swamps rose, the old men found it too difficult to walk from one homestead to the next, and the ceremonies gradually ceased. As the swamps

Laura Bohannan. "Shakespeare in the Bush." 1966. *Natural History* 75(7): 28–33. From *Natural History* August, 1966, copyright Natural History Magazine, Inc., 2015.

rose even higher, all activities but one came to an end. The women brewed beer from maize and millet. Men, women, and children sat on their hillocks and drank it.

People began to drink at dawn. By midmorning the whole homestead was singing, dancing, and drumming. When it rained, people had to sit inside their huts: there they drank and sang or they drank and told stories. In any case, by noon or before, I either had to join the party or retire to my own hut and my books. "One does not discuss serious matters when there is beer. Come, drink with us." Since I lacked their capacity for the thick native beer, I spent more and more time with *Hamlet*. Before the end of the second month, grace descended on me. I was quite sure that *Hamlet* had only one possible interpretation, and that one universally obvious.

Early every morning, in the hope of having some serious talk before the beer party, I used to call on the old man at his reception hut—a circle of posts supporting a thatched roof above a low mud wall to keep out wind and rain. One day I crawled through the low doorway and found most of the men of the homestead sitting huddled in their ragged cloths on stools, low plank beds, and reclining chairs, warming themselves against the chill of the rain around a smoky fire. In the center were three pots of beer. The party had started.

The old man greeted me cordially. "Sit down and drink." I accepted a large calabash full of beer, poured some into a small drinking gourd, and tossed it down. Then I poured some more into the same gourd for the man second in seniority to my host before I handed my calabash over to a young man for further distribution. Important people shouldn't ladle beer themselves.

"It is better like this," the old man said, looking at me approvingly and plucking at the thatch that had caught in my hair. "You should sit and drink with us more often. Your servants tell me that when you are not with us, you sit inside your hut looking at a paper."

The old man was acquainted with four kinds of "papers": tax receipts, bride price receipts, court fee receipts, and letters. The messenger who brought him letters from the chief used them mainly as a badge of office, for he always knew what was in them and told the old man. Personal letters for the few who had relatives in the government or mission stations were kept until someone went to a large market where there was a letter writer and reader. Since my arrival, letters were brought to me to be read. A few men also brought me bride price receipts, privately, with requests to change

the figures to a higher sum. I found moral arguments were of no avail, since in-laws are fair game, and the technical hazards of forgery difficult to explain to an illiterate people. I did not wish them to think me silly enough to look at any such papers for days on end, and I hastily explained that my "paper" was one of the "things of long ago" of my country.

"Ah," said the old men. "Tell us."

I protested that I was not a storyteller. Storytelling is a skilled art among them; their standards are high, and the audiences critical—and vocal in their criticism. I protested in vain. This morning they wanted to hear a story while they drank. They threatened to tell me no more stories until I told them one of mine. Finally, the old man promised that no one would criticize my style "for we know you are struggling with our language." "But," put in one of the elders, "you must explain what we do not understand, as we do when we tell you our stories." Realizing that here was my chance to prove *Hamlet* universally intelligible, I agreed.

The old man handed me some more beer to help me on with my storytelling. Men filled their long wooden pipes and knocked coals from the fire to place in the pipe bowls; then, puffing contentedly, they sat back to listen. I began in the proper style, "Not yesterday, not yesterday, but long ago, a thing occurred. One night three men were keeping watch outside the homestead of the great chief, when suddenly they saw the former chief approach them."

"Why was he no longer their chief?"

"He was dead," I explained. "That is why they were troubled and afraid when they saw him."

"Impossible," began one of the elders, handing his pipe on to his neighbor, who interrupted, "Of course it wasn't the dead chief. It was an omen sent by a witch. Go on."

Slightly shaken, I continued. "One of these three was a man who knew things"—the closest translation for scholar, but unfortunately it also meant witch. The second elder looked triumphantly at the first. "So he spoke to the dead chief, saying, 'Tell us what we must do so you may rest in your grave,' but the dead chief did not answer. He vanished, and they could see him no more. Then the man who knew things—his name was Horatio—said this event was the affair of the dead chief's son, Hamlet."

There was a general shaking of heads around the circle. "Had the dead chief no living brothers? Or was this son the chief?"

"No," I replied. 'That is, he had one living brother who became the chief when the elder brother died."

The old men muttered: such omens were matters for chiefs and elders, not for youngsters; no good could come of being behind a chief's back; clearly Horatio was not a man who knew things.

"Yes, he was," I insisted, shooing a chicken away from my beer. "In our country the son is next to the father. The dead chief's younger brother had become the great chief. He had also married his elder brother's widow only about a month after the funeral."

"He did well," the old man beamed and announced to the others, "I told you that if we knew more about Europeans, we would find they really were very like us. In our country also," he added to me, "the younger brother marries the elder brother's widow and becomes the father of his children. Now, if your uncle, who married your widowed mother, is your father's full brother, then he will be a real father to you. Did Hamlet's father and uncle have one mother?"

His question barely penetrated my mind; I was too upset and thrown too far off balance by having one of the most important elements of *Hamlet* knocked straight out of the picture. Rather uncertainly I said that I thought they had the same mother, but I wasn't sure—the story didn't say. The old man told me severely that these genealogical details made all the difference and that when I got home I must ask the elders about it. He shouted out the door to one of his younger wives to bring his goatskin bag.

Determined to save what I could of the mother motif, I took a deep breath and began again. "The son Hamlet was very sad because his mother had married again so quickly. There was no need for her to do so, and it is our custom for a widow not to go to her next husband until she has mourned for two years."

"Two years is too long," objected the wife, who had appeared with the old man's battered goatskin bag. "Who will hoe your farms for you while you have no husband?"

"Hamlet," I retorted without thinking, "was old enough to hoe his mother's farms himself. There was no need for her to remarry." No one looked convinced. I gave up. "His mother and the great chief told Hamlet not to be sad, for the great chief himself would be a father to Hamlet. Furthermore, Hamlet would be the next chief: therefore he must stay to learn the things of a chief. Hamlet agreed to remain, and all the rest went off to drink beer."

While I paused, perplexed at how to render Hamlet's disgusted soliloquy to an audience convinced that Claudius and Gertrude had behaved in the best possible manner, one of the younger men asked me who had married the other wives of the dead chief.

"He had no other wives," I told him.

"But a chief must have many wives! How else can he brew beer and prepare food for all his guests?"

I said firmly that in our country even chiefs had only one wife, that they had servants to do their work, and that they paid them from tax money.

It was better, they returned, for a chief to have many wives and sons who would help him hoe his farms and feed his people; then everyone loved the chief who gave much and took nothing—taxes were a bad thing.

I agreed with the last comment, but for the rest fell back on their favorite way of fobbing off my questions: "That is the way it is done, so that is how we do it."

I decided to skip the soliloquy. Even if Claudius was here thought quite right to marry his brother's widow, there remained the poison motif, and I knew they would disapprove of fratricide. More hopefully I resumed, "That night Hamlet kept watch with the three who had seen his dead father. The dead chief again appeared, and although the others were afraid, Hamlet followed his dead father off to one side. When they were alone, Hamlet's dead father spoke."

"Omens can't talk!" The old man was emphatic.

"Hamlet's dead father wasn't an omen. Seeing him might have been an omen, but he was not." My audience looked as confused as I sounded. "It *was* Hamlet's dead father. It was a thing we call a 'ghost.'" I had to use the English word, for unlike many of the neighboring tribes, these people didn't believe in the survival after death of any individuating part of the personality.

"What is a 'ghost'? An omen?"

"No, a 'ghost' is someone who is dead but who walks around and can talk, and people can hear him and see him but not touch him."

They objected. "One can touch zombis."

"No, no! It was not a dead body the witches had animated to sacrifice and eat. No one else made Hamlet's dead father walk. He did it himself."

"Dead men can't walk," protested my audience as one man.

I was quite willing to compromise. "A 'ghost' is a dead man's shadow."

But again they objected. "Dead men cast no shadows."

"They do in my country," I snapped.

The old man quelled the babble of disbelief that rose immediately and told me with that insincere, but courteous, agreement one extends to the fancies of the young, ignorant, and superstitious, "No doubt in your country the dead can also walk without being zombis." From the depths of his bag he produced a withered fragment of kola nut, bit off one end to show it wasn't poisoned, and handed me the rest as a peace offering.

"Anyhow," I resumed, "Hamlet's dead father said that his own brother, the one who became chief, had poisoned him. He wanted Hamlet to avenge him. Hamlet believed this in his heart, for he did not like his father's brother." I took another swallow of beer. "In the country of the great chief, living in the same homestead, for it was a very large one, was an important elder who was often with the chief to advise and help him. His name was Polonius. Hamlet was courting his daughter, but her father and her brother . . . [I cast hastily about for some tribal analogy] warned her not to let Hamlet visit her when she was alone on her farm, for he would be a great chief and so could not marry her."

"Why not?" asked the wife, who had settled down on the edge of the old man's chair. He frowned at her for asking stupid questions and growled, "They lived in the same homestead."

"That was not the reason," I informed them. "Polonius was a stranger who lived in the homestead because he helped the chief, not because he was a relative."

"Then why couldn't Hamlet marry her?"

"He could have," I explained, "but Polonius didn't think he would. After all, Hamlet was a man of great importance who ought to marry a chief's daughter, for in his country a man could have only one wife. Polonius was afraid that if Hamlet made love to his daughter, then no one else would give a high price for her."

"That might be true," remarked one of the shrewder elders, "but a chief's son would give his .mistress's father enough presents and patronage to more than make up the difference. Polonius sounds like a fool to me."

"Many people think he was," I agreed. "Meanwhile Polonius sent his son Laertes off to Paris to learn the things of that country, for it was the homestead of a very great chief indeed. Because he was afraid that Laertes might waste a lot of money on beer and women and gambling, or get into trouble by fighting, he sent one of his servants to Paris secretly, to spy out what Laertes was doing. One day Hamlet came upon Polonius's daughter Ophelia. He behaved so oddly he frightened her. Indeed"—I was fumbling for words to express the dubious quality of Hamlet's madness—"the chief and many others had also noticed that when Hamlet talked one could understand the words but not what they meant. Many people thought that he had become mad." My audience suddenly became much more attentive. "The great chief wanted to know what was wrong with Hamlet, so he sent for two of Hamlet's age mates [school friends would have taken long explanation] to talk to Hamlet and find out what troubled his heart. Hamlet, seeing that they had been bribed by the chief to betray him, told them nothing. Polonius, however, insisted that Hamlet was mad because he had been forbidden to see Ophelia, whom he loved."

"Why," inquired a bewildered voice, "should anyone bewitch Hamlet on that account?"

"Bewitch him?"

"Yes, only witchcraft can make anyone mad, unless, of course, one sees the beings that lurk in the forest."

I stopped being a storyteller, took out my notebook and demanded to be told more about these two causes of madness. Even while they spoke and I jotted notes, I tried to calculate the effect of this new factor on the plot. Hamlet had not been exposed to the beings that lurk in the forest. Only his relatives in the male line could bewitch him. Barring relatives not mentioned by Shakespeare, it had to be Claudius who was a tempting to harm him. And, of course, it was.

For the moment I staved off questions by saying that the great chief also refused to believe that Hamlet was mad for the love of Ophelia and nothing else. "He was sure that something much more important was troubling Hamlet's heart."

"Now Hamlet's age mates," I continued, "had brought with them a famous storyteller. Hamlet decided to have this man tell the chief and all his homestead a story about the man who had poisoned his brother because he desired his brother's wife and wished to be chief himself. Hamlet was sure the great chief could not hear the story without making a sign if he was indeed guilty, and then he would discover whether his dead father had told him the truth."

The old man interrupted, with deep cunning. "Why should a father lie to his son?" he asked.

I hedged: "Hamlet wasn't sure that it really was his dead father." It was impossible to say anything, in that language, about devil-inspired visions.

"You mean," he said, "it actually was an omen, and he knew witches sometimes send false ones. Hamlet was a fool not to go to one skilled in reading omens and divining the truth in the first place. A man-who-sees-the-truth could have told him how his father died, if he really had been poisoned, and if there was witchcraft in it; then Hamlet could have called the elders to settle the matter."

The shrewd elder ventured to disagree. "Because his father's brother was a great chief, one-who-sees-the-truth might therefore have been afraid to tell it. I think it was for that reason that a friend of Hamlet's father—a witch and an elder—sent an omen so his friend's son would know. Was the omen true?"

"Yes," I said, abandoning ghosts and the devil; a witch-sent omen it would have to be. "It was true, for when the storyteller was telling his tale before all the homestead, the great chief rose in fear. Afraid that Hamlet knew his secret, he planned to have him killed."

The stage set of the next bit presented some difficulties of translation. I began cautiously. "The great chief told Hamlet's mother to find out from her son what he knew. But because a woman's children are always first in her heart, he had the important elder Polonius hide behind a cloth that hung against the wall of Hamlet's mother's sleeping hut. Hamlet started to scold his mother for what she had done."

There was a shocked murmur from everyone. A man should never scold his mother.

"She called out in fear, and Polonius moved behind the cloth. Shouting 'A rat!' Hamlet took his machete and slashed through the cloth." I paused for a dramatic effect. "He had killed Polonius!"

The old men looked at each other in supreme disgust. "That Polonius truly was a fool and a man who knew nothing! What child would not know enough to shout, 'It's me!'" With a pang, I remembered that these people are ardent hunters, always armed with bow, arrow, and machete; at the first rustle in the grass an arrow is aimed and ready, and the hunter shouts "Game!" If no human voice answers immediately, the arrow speeds on its way. Like a good hunter Hamlet had shouted, "A rat!"

I rushed in to save Polonius's reputation. "Polonius did speak. Hamlet heard him. But he thought it was the chief and wished to kill him to avenge his father. He had meant to kill him earlier that evening. . . ." I broke down; unable to describe to these pagans, who

had no belief in individual afterlife, the difference between dying at one's prayers and dying "unhousell'd, disappointed, unaneled."

This time I had shocked my audience seriously. "For a man to raise his hands against his father's brother and the one who has become his father—that is a terrible thing. The elders ought to let such a man be bewitched."

I nibbled at my kola nut in some perplexity, then pointed out that after all the man had killed Hamlet's father.

"No," pronounced the old man, speaking less to me than to the young men sitting behind the elders. "If your father's brother has killed your father, you must appeal to your father's age mates; *they* may avenge him. No man may use violence against his senior relatives." Another thought struck him. "But if his father's brother had indeed been wicked enough to bewitch Hamlet and make him mad, that would be a good story indeed, for it would be his fault that Hamlet, being mad, no longer had any sense and thus was ready to kill his father's brother."

There was a murmur of applause. *Hamlet* was again a good story to them, but it no longer seemed quite the same story to me. As I thought over the coming complications of plot and motive, I lost courage and decided to skim over dangerous ground quickly.

"The great chief," I went on, "was not sorry that Hamlet had killed Polonius. It gave him a reason to send Hamlet away, with his two treacherous age mates, with letters to a chief of a far country, saying that Hamlet should be killed. But Hamlet changed the writing on their papers, so that the chief killed his age mates instead." I encountered a reproachful glare from one of the men whom I had told undetectable forgery was not merely immoral but beyond human skill. I looked the other way.

"Before Hamlet could return, Laertes came back for his father's funeral. The great chief told him Hamlet had killed Polonius. Laertes swore to kill Hamlet because of this; and because his sister Opelia, hearing her father had been killed by the man she loved, went mad and drowned in the river."

"Have you already forgotten what we told you?" The old man was reproachful. "One cannot take vengeance on a madman; Hamlet killed Polonius in his madness. As for the girl, she not only went mad, she was drowned. Only witches can make people drown.

Water itself can't hurt anything. It is merely something one drinks and bathes in."

I began to get cross. "If you don't like the story, I'll stop."

The old man made soothing noises and himself poured me some more beer. "You tell the story well, and we are listening. But it is clear that the elders of your country have never told you what the story really means. No, don't interrupt! We believe you when you say your marriage customs are different, or your clothes and weapons. But people are the same everywhere; therefore, there are always witches and it is we, the elders, who know how witches work. We told you it was the great chief who wished to kill Hamlet, and now your own words have proved us right. Who were Ophelia's male relatives?"

"There were only her father and her brother." Hamlet was clearly out of my hands.

"There must have been many more; this also you must ask of your elders when you get back to your country. From what you tell us, since Polonius was dead, it must have been Laertes who killed Ophelia, although I do not see the reason for it."

We had emptied one pot of beer, and the old men argued the point with slightly tipsy interest. Finally one of them demanded of me, "What did the servant of Polonius say on his return?"

With difficulty I recollected Reynaldo and his mission. "I don't think he did return before Polonius was killed."

"Listen," said the elder, "and I will tell you how it was and how your story will go, then you may tell me if I am right. Polonius knew his son would get into trouble, and so he did. He had many fines to pay for fighting, and debts from gambling. But he had only two ways of getting money quickly. One was to marry off his sister at once, but it is difficult to find a man who will marry a woman desired by the son of a chief. For if the chief's heir commits adultery with your wife, what can you do? Only a fool calls a case against a man who will someday be his judge. Therefore Laertes had to take the second way: he killed his sister by witchcraft, drowning her so he could secretly sell her body to the witches."

I raised an objection. "They found her body and buried it. Indeed Laertes jumped into the grave to see his sister once more—so, you see, the body was truly there. Hamlet, who had just come back, jumped in after him."

"What did I tell you?" The elder appealed to the others. "Laertes was up to no good with his sister's body. Hamlet prevented him, because the chief's heir, like a chief, does not wish any other man to grow rich and powerful. Laertes would be angry, because he would have killed his sister without benefit to himself. In our country he would try to kill Hamlet for that reason. Is this not what happened?"

"More or less," I admitted. "When the great chief found Hamlet was still alive, he encouraged Laertes to try to kill Hamlet and arranged a fight with machetes between them. In the fight both the young men were wounded to death. Hamlet's mother drank the poisoned beer that the chief meant for Hamlet in case he won the fight. When he saw his mother die of poison, Hamlet, dying, managed to kill his father's brother with his machete."

"You see, I was right!" exclaimed the elder.

"That was a very good story," added the old man, "and you told it with very few mistakes. There was just one more error, at the very end. The poison Hamlet's mother drank was obviously meant for the survivor of the fight, whichever it was. If Laertes had won, the great chief would have poisoned him, for no one would know that he arranged Hamlet's death. Then, too, he need not fear Laertes's witchcraft; it takes a strong heart to kill one's only sister by witchcraft.

"Sometime," concluded the old man, gathering his ragged toga about him, "you must tell us some more stories of your country. We, who are elders, will instruct you in their true meaning, so that when you return to your own land your elders will see that you have not been sitting in the bush, but among those who know things and who have taught you wisdom."

2.2 What Are You Laughing At? Assessing the "Racial" in U.S. Public Discourse

JOHN HARTIGAN JR.

Why do some people laugh at certain jokes that contain racial descriptions that they would not find funny in other settings? What are the cultural conventions at play in shaping racial and gender humor? Exploring speech acts can tell us a great deal about the underlying sociocultural context and norms that shape language use within a community. Like all aspects of culture, language use shifts, both over time and depending on context and who is doing the speaking. In the following article, John Hartigan analyzes public reaction to racial remarks in 2007 by shock jock Don Imus and comedian Michael Richards. Applying a cultural analytical framework, Hartigan reveals how the cultural categories of "individual" and "group" shape the boundaries of speech and inform what is and is not funny, when, and why. Hartigan compares these public remarks and the controversy that ensued to the silence and lack of criticism that television ads coded with racial significance from Geico and CareerBuilder received.

Questions

1. Cultural conventions that shape and inform "common sense" regarding racial humor have shifted over time. How and why have they changed in the United States? Give specific examples. Do the same for humor about gender and sexuality.
2. How did Richards and Imus work to distance themselves from their remarks? Discuss the role that the cultural categories of "individual" and "group" played in their attempts at boundary maintenance.
3. What racial signifiers exist in the Caveman and Office Monkey ads? Do you see these ads as racial humor? Why or why not?
4. Cultural conventions that shape and inform "common sense" regarding racial humor have shifted over time. How and why have they changed in the United States? Give specific examples. Do the same for humor about gender and sexuality.
5. Consider current popular ads. Can you think of examples that contain racial and gender signifiers? Discuss.

"I think that America has spoken." Vivian Stringer, Rutgers University women's basketball coach.

A seemingly perennial feature of American public culture is the controversial white-male-racial-remark. . . . In political forums, George Allen (former U.S. Senator from Virginia) . . . [used] the term *macaca* to label his opponent's Indian-American campaign worker; [Joseph] Biden [called] the Democratic presidential [nominee] Barack Obama . . . "the first mainstream African-American who is articulate and bright

John Hartigan Jr. 2009. What Are You Laughing At? Assessing the "Racial" in U.S. Public Discourse. *Transforming Anthropology* 17(1):4–19. Reproduced by permission of the American Anthropological Association. Not for sale or further reproduction.

and clean and a nice-looking guy."[1] . . . [Comedian and actor Michael] Richards was pilloried in the media for using the term *nigger* (among a range of offensive statements) in berating black audience members at a comedy club, and [talk show host Don] Imus' firing-saga played out over several days following his reference to the Rutgers Women's basketball team as "some nappy-headed hos."

. . .

The Richards rant became an object of intense public scrutiny because it was caught live on a video recording by cell phone, as he lashed out at black audience members for heckling his stand-up routine at the renowned Laugh Factory in West Hollywood. The video captures roughly two and a half minutes of his furious tirade, which was [preceded] by Richards' threat that, since he is rich, he could have them arrested if he felt like it. The video begins with him screaming, "Shut up! Fifty years ago we'd have had you upside down with a fucking fork up your ass," then he pointed to a black audience member, shouting, "Throw his ass out! He's a nigger," repeating, "he's a nigger" over and over again. The tape ends with Richards saying, "You interrupted me, pal. That's what you get for interrupting the white man." At that point, the audience left the club en masse.

The shocking footage quickly gained a huge national audience through its posting on http://TMZ.com and later on http://YouTube.com. The furor that followed was so intense that Richards, in quick succession, went on national television (the *Late Show with David Letterman*) to apologize for his remarks, hired a public relations expert "with deep contacts in the black community," and then undertook some unspecified form of therapy "to manage his anger."[2] He later also appeared on Reverend Jesse Jackson's nationally syndicated radio program, "Keep Hope Alive," in order to apologize further. . . . The spectacle continued, though, as a wide range of commentators, comedians, hip hop artists, and politicians largely panned his apology and engaged in a public censure of Richards' outburst. Critics focused on Richards' insistence that "anger" was the issue, instead of racism ("I'm not a racist. That's what's so insane about this."), and that the racial comments were merely ancillary to the fact that he "lost his temper on stage" (Gumbel 2006). Richards described being "shattered" and "busted up" by the incident, but, insisting that he was a "good person" at heart, consistently used remarkably passive language in describing his role in the affair. "The way this came

through me was like a freight train." . . . But fellow comedians, newspaper columnists, and other public figures assailed this disavowal emphatically.

The critical comments about both Richards' remarks quickly expanded beyond the question of Richards' racism and developed into a broad public assessments of racial speech, particularly in relation to use of the word *nigger* (Franklin 2007).[3] The commentary . . . ranged from comparative questions concerning when and by whom "nigger" is used in public to a concerted effort to ban usage of the word entirely.[4] Black comedians were most prominent in these assessments, because of the comedic context in which this incident occurred and the prevalence of the term in many comedians' repertoires (Collier 2006). Of these comics, Paul Mooney, who first gained notoriety by writing much of Richard Pryor's material, judged the remarks as primarily a comic failure. "We have the right of freedom of speech. We have the right to be funny as comedians. I believe in that, and he just *crossed the line*. It wasn't funny." He explained further, "you can do racial jokes as long as there's a funny, as long as there's an out for me" [emphasis added] (Greta Van Susteren 2006). Mooney's remarks reflect comedians' awareness of two sets of lines: those established by social conventions, which comics actively transgress in generating humor, and another set guiding what counts as "funny." This cultural activity of transgression, of crossing a line, was central to comedians' evaluations of this incident because it involved reflecting on how this differed from the inherently transgressive aspects of humor. As comedian Tony Figueroa lamented, "I fear that a Pandora's box has been opened. Instead of just dealing with the individual solely responsible for the incident, they censor everyone. They drew a line that represents acceptability and said, 'don't cross it.'; You don't do that with comedians because they will see it as a challenge and they will always have the last laugh in the end" (Tony Figueroa 2006).

. . . The commentary on Richards' remarks grew more involved as it became apparent that the crucial ground in making judgments about "context" in this case—that is, the domain of the "public," over against a presumed private sphere—was in the process of changing dramatically. . . . The increasingly widespread broadcast of "nigger," largely through the enormous popularity of hip hop music and racial comedy routines, led commentators to take stock of a host of conventions regarding race that were subsequently appearing somewhat artificial, or at least no longer simply "common sense."

Attention to these conventions was at the center of a more extensive three-part discussion, hosted by Black Entertainment Television, titled, "Hip-Hop vs. America," which featured Chuck D. and Michael Dyson arguing for recognizing and retaining the varied meanings of nigger while strictly maintaining a line against white usage of the term. Counter to this stance, Keith Boykin, author of *Beyond the Down Low* (2005), asserted that, "The problem is that you can't stop white people from using the word if we use the word. We can't tell the white community they're wrong when we're using it every damn day on the street." . . .

This cultural dimension of the issue was further highlighted by Christopher Hitchens, specifically in regards to the question of a "double standard." . . . "What we have now," with the various efforts to ban the term, "is a taboo, which is something quite different from an agreement on etiquette." A taboo, of course, is one of the most basic of cultural operations and . . . it has a host of unintended [effects]—first, of making the prohibited object more pervasive and more powerful, then positing "pollution" and "hygiene" as the primary register for addressing transgressions. . . .

"'UP NEXT, NAPPY-HEADED HOS!'" . . .

. . . Close on the heels of the media spectacle generated by Richards' wild rant came a racial comment by radio "shock jock," Don Imus, whose morning talk show (with some 2 million listeners) was a feature item for CBS Radio and MSNBC. On April 4th, on *Imus in the Morning*, Imus and the show's executive producer, Bernard McGuirk, were talking with sports announcer Sid Rosenberg about the final game of the women's NCAA basketball tournament between the University of Tennessee and Rutgers University. McGuirk referred to the women from Rutgers as "hard core hos," and Imus chimed in with "that's some nappy-headed hos there." Although similarly keyed to race, as was Richards' outburst, Imus' remark extended to gender as well. Journalist and news commentator Gwen Ifill . . . characterized this comment as "a shockingly concise sexual and racial insult, tossed out in a volley of male camaraderie by a group of amused, middle-aged white men" (Gwen Ifill 2007).

In Imus' case, his comments were posted by Media Matters for America on their website along with a video clip and a transcript that specified the racial component of additional sports references made by Imus in his remarks. Later it was posted on http://YouTube.com and received millions of hits. The next day, April 5th, the Philadelphia chapter of the NAACP issued a statement labeling the comments racist and unacceptable; MSNBC also issued a statement distancing itself from Imus' views. On April 6th the movement to critically censure Imus gained momentum with the National Association of Black Journalists condemning his comments and the presidents of Rutgers University and the National Collegiate Athletic Association characterizing the remarks as "unconscionable." Imus, in turn, offered his first apology on his show, acknowledging, "we can understand why people were offended." CBS Radio and Imus' flagship station, WFAN, also issued apologies. Over the following weekend, Reverend Al Sharpton called for Imus' resignation and Jesse Jackson organized a picket at the Chicago offices of MSNBC. On Monday, April 9th, Imus again apologized on his show and then CBS Radio and MSNBC announced that he would be suspended for 2 weeks. The next day the Rutgers team held a nationally televised news conference discussing their reactions to his remarks; as well, corporate sponsors, such as Proctor & Gamble Co., Staples Inc., and Bigelow Tea, began withdrawing their commercials from CBS Radio. On April 11th other advertiser[s] cancelled spots, including General Motors Corp., GlaxoSmithKline, American Express Co., and Sprint Nextel Corp. The following day, April 12th, CBS announced that it had fired Imus, cancelling the show that generated the company about $15 million annually.

Again, as with Richards' comments, the intense media coverage that followed this incident was framed as a "national conversation,"[5] though this time gender was a feature, as well as race. Also, as with Richards, the immediate media focus quickly shifted from whether the remarks reflected one individual's racist sensibilities to asking larger questions concerning the conventions guiding racial speech in the United States. In part, this was due to the intransigence of both Imus and Richards to considering the possibility that they might be racist or have expressed racist sentiments. . . . Both public figures took similar stances in denying that there was any "racial" aspect to their comments—Richards insisted that he was just "angry" at "hecklers" and searched for "hurtful" words; Imus insisted that he was just trying to be funny—and both depicted their role in the affair almost passively: "I think the fact I am a good person and have done good things makes it even more disturbing that something like this can come out of my mouth," Imus said in his second on-air apology.[6] Similarly, Richards also invoked the critical of "good person" in an effort to disavow any association with racism (Lynne Duke 2007). In this regard, they each fell back upon the only redemptive register available to them—invoking an authentic, inner individuality, the central locus in American culture. . . .

The "good person" defense, however, was hardly adequate in the face of the sustained critical assessment of Imus' remarks. Eugene Robinson, a columnist for the *Washington Post*, . . . wrote, "I can accept that Imus doesn't believe he is racist, but 'nappy headed hos' had to come from somewhere." In assessing that "somewhere," Robinson brought into view the larger public sphere and the way its changing verbal content was undermining long-established cultural convention.

Imus, deeply perplexed by this incident, took a similar view as he responded. . . . He insisted that his comments were meant and should be taken as a joke, albeit one that went badly, arguing that his remarks should be taken in "context," specifically in terms of "a program that makes fun of everybody, including me." Secondly, Imus gestured that the language he used came not from himself but from the "culture," generally, and "the black community," in particular. Imus articulated these points during his appearance on Sharpton's show . . . [claiming] "this phrase that I used, it originated in the black community. That didn't give me a right to use it, but that is where it originated. Who calls who that and why? We need to know that. I need to know that." These claims—that he was trying to make a joke using language he had clumsily drawn from "the black community"—received almost as much of an airing as did his original remarks. . . .

Was It Racial?

. . . When Imus asserted that he "didn't think of it as racial. I wasn't even thinking of it as racial," Sharpton replied incredulously, "Let me get this right. You call these people nappy-headed hos but you wasn't talking racial when you said nappy. 'Jigaboos and wannabees' but you didn't understand what you were saying. You just . . . what are you saying? You just blanked out?" Imus replied, "I didn't say that. I said, I wasn't thinking that . . . I'm not thinking that it's a racial insult that is being uttered at somebody at the time. I'm thinking that it's in the process of where trying to rap and be funny [*sic*]."[7] Sharpton's rebuttal was sharp and to the point. "I'm going to say what you said was racist. I'm going to say what you said was abominable. I'm going to say you should be fired for saying it." But the exchange between the two men quickly gained a larger audience, particularly for commentators who continued to ponder why and how Imus could not see his remarks as "racial." This line of questioning consistently focused on the conventions that allowed Imus and his brand of humor to operate for so long in the public sphere—conventions that, as this incident revealed, were in the process of changing.

Notably, for these commentators, the "line" that Imus so clearly transgressed concerning the racial was not as obvious in retrospective glance at his comedic career. A variety of pundits noted that Imus' style of humor has long featured insults, and his wide-ranging objects included U.S. senators and presidential candidates . . . religious and public figures . . . and even his own bosses at CBS. . . . And some of his insults were hard to categorize emphatically as "racial." Was the insult racial or not when he referred to Vice President Dick Cheney as "pork chop butt," or . . . called the New York Knicks a group of "chest-thumping pimps"? Regardless, many listeners and participants on his show were able to delineate a distinct racial strand in this history of insults, which Maxine Water highlighted in a statement calling for Imus' firing. "His show has been so audacious as to make statements such as: 'Venus and Serena Williams were better suited for National Geographic than Playboy,' 'Female soccer players are juiced-up dykes,' 'Faggots play tennis,' and . . . 'Palestinians were stinking animals'" (Maxine Waters 2007). But how had such comments, which generated such a broad, full-throated public protest, not become the focus of public outrage before?

The answer is complex and involves the changing racial and gender demographics of corporate America, the shifting contours of "mainstream" discourse in the United States, and the now apparently crumbling conventions that governed racial humor until recently. In the first regard, what comes to the fore is both the intense financial calculations that led to Imus being fired and how those calculations were shaped by African Americans and women. Quite literally, Imus' employers at CBS and the [show's] sponsors took stock, minute by minute, of the way his apologies were playing before various constituencies. "It was a cost benefit analysis, not a moral analysis," concluded Stanley Fish. . . . Strikingly, these corporate decisions were influenced by African Americans and women who work within the media. The National Association of Black Journalists was the first to call for Imus to be fired, quickly followed by the National Organization of Women's "Action Alert" encouraging members to flood CBS and NBC with protests. On April 10th, NBC News president, Steve Capus, was deluged with employee complaints concerning Imus. As a senior producer characterized the situation, "We went out and created diversity in our newsrooms and we empowered employees to say what they think. And they're telling us. It's good for us and it's good for the country."[8] These changes reflect a significant shift in the public sphere in the United States.

Such changes led University of Maryland professor Sheri Parks to conclude that "What's different about this firing compared to that of other insult jocks is that people internal to the organizations—women and African Americans at NBC and CBS—came forward and said, 'I am in this organization, and I do not want to be associated with this kind of man.'" As well, black employees at Sprint Nextel successfully lobbied the company's CEO, Gary Forsee, to withdraw the corporation's advertising. In noting particularly the role played by black business leaders, such as Kenneth Chenault, the CEO of American Express, Jannette Dates, co-editor of *Split Image: African-Americans in the Mass Media*, concluded, "This means that even though there has been this nasty hatefulness in media with comments like the ones from Imus, there has also been progress among this very group of black men and black women that has been treated so vilely. Now, we see some of them in positions of power with the means to end such hateful talk" [David Madigan and Nick Zurawik 2007]. Imus' dominance as a public figure was clearly impacted by the power of these expanding constituencies within corporate America. But this significant social change accounts for only one dimension of why so many Americans suddenly decided that Imus was no longer funny, and to grasp this we have to turn once again to the role of cultural conventions governing both what counts as humor and what people can say in public, each of which [has] been drastically impacted by recent changes in the scope and content of public discourse in the United States.

. . . [I]n cultural terms, Imus maintained a certain distance from the polluting or contaminating social charges related to race contained in his material. Imus was able to distance himself from much of his own material because it was framed in terms of a cast of characters on his show. About a half-dozen supporting cast members on "Imus in the Morning," who both wrote material and performed certain character roles on the show, worked to frame the talk show as a comedy routine. Jacques Steinberg characterized this as a division of labor in which the show's producer, Bernard McGuirk—who also was fired as a result of this incident—provided an "illusion of deniability or distance" for Imus from the show's racial content. "Only then can they express what he might want to say about blacks, Jews, gays, or women but perhaps feels he can't, given his stature as an interviewer of the famous and important" (Jacques Steinberg 2007). But the other dimension of this distance is that the supporting cast members often performed satiric roles and impersonations that allowed them to appear as "in character." These involved impersonations of very powerful figures. . . . It is exactly this type of distance provided by pretending to be a character that comedians such as Sarah Silverman and Sacha Baron Cohen mobilize when they perform their racial material.

What collapsed, then, were the conventions that let Imus—and his listeners—maintain a distinction between his words and the individual who spoke them. Comedian Larry Wilmore assessed the collapse of these conventions of distance by way of a racial formula: "I have a mathematical equation for all of this. White guys plus black slang equals comedy. But here's where the equation breaks down. White guy plus black slang minus common sense equals tragedy."[9] Wilmore's invocation of "common sense," on one hand, gestures to the type of cultural knowledge that Imus seemed to lack at that moment when he said "nappy headed hos." But his assessment can also be read as an indication that the cultural conventions that always shape and inform "common sense" had shifted in such a way that the assumed knowledge had abruptly been reconfigured. For Wilmore, this is evident in Imus' transgression of conventions as much as the verbal content of his remark: "You can't just say, 'So let's talk about what's happening to the economy this week, and up next, nappy-headed hos!' People get confused."[10] That so many people did not "get confused" for so long by such shifts reflects the conventions that allowed listeners to manage this cognitive dissonance that became disrupted when his remarks were broadcast to a much larger public. In both regards, the designation of "racial" here rests upon an extensive series of cultural assessments, which is what allows commentators to analyze so precisely where Imus failed the humor test.

But, as noted [earlier], when confronted with this focus on him personally, Imus worked desperately to shunt this attention to his use of "nappy headed hos" off onto "the black community.". . . Even before Imus raised this issue, commentators were also pointing out that a proper evaluation of his remarks required a broader assessment of U.S. public discourse. This evaluation took stock of two developments: the pervasive use of sexually derogatory terms in hip-hop and the extent to which that music and language become part of "mainstream" discourse. As T. Denean Sharpley-Whitting, author of *Pimps Up, Ho's Down: Hip Hop's Hold on Young Black Women* (2007), observed, "Hip hop gave Imus the language. He wouldn't have known what a 'ho' was if it weren't for rap records." That is largely because, as Carol Swain, a law professor at Vanderbilt University, noted, "the language from rappers and comedians has seeped into the culture to the point that Don Imus thought it was okay to call black women 'hos'" (Rob Woollard 2007). This attention to the cultural domain was amplified by Jonetta Rose Barras, who observed that, "even though it was poorly executed Imus-speak, 'nappy-headed hos' is, in fact, a progeny of black street culture. It is a culture whose symbols, idioms and fashions have not only seeped into the American mainstream over the past 20 years, but have been enthusiastically embraced."[11]

What is valuable then, in these "incidents" is not so much what they reveal about the "racial" aspects of these two white males' speech and what they, in turn, potentially reflect about American culture; but rather, how the evaluations of their remarks and the extensive commentary that followed reflect a moment when the conventions that allow certainty about what counts as racial began to shift. . . .

Laughing at Cavemen and Monkeys

. . . I turn now to a series of public cultural images and dramas that were arguably far more pervasive features of "mainstream" discourse in the United States and that featured many potentially racial aspects, but were not the subject of any kind of similar controversy or analysis. In this regard, the television ads featuring cavemen and "office monkeys" are [snugly] nestled in the cultural sphere of the mundane, "common sense," and unremarkable. . . .

Geico, an auto insurance company, first introduced the Caveman ads in 2004 and they have had an unusually long life span, running through the 2007 Super Bowl. . . . The ad campaign was initially crafted around three spots that each pivot upon a slogan/joke going bad. The first features a faux-filming of a Geico ad based on the catchphrase, "[It's] so easy even a caveman could do [it]." As the spokesman says these lines, an off-stage voice bellows, "What!?" Abruptly, the camera pans back as a boom mike crashes to the floor and the soundman—shirtless, hairy, with a densely bearded face—shouts, "Not cool!," then storms off. His presence and fury reveal, shockingly, that there are cavemen in our midst. The second spot features three cavemen in a sleek urban apartment—one is playing a grand piano, another works on his lap top while seated on a plush white sofa; large modernist paintings adorn the walls—as the ad plays on their high definition flat screen TV. "That is really condescending," one retorts, while another asks of the ad slogan, "What's that supposed to mean?" In the third installment, a flustered advertising executive takes two of the cavemen to dinner in an elegant restaurant and explains, "Seriously, we apologize. We had no idea you guys were still around." One of the cavemen then retorts, "Yeah, well next time maybe do a little research," as the other lets out a fart.

After 2 years, with the popularity of the ads increasing (as gauged by copious blog postings and YouTube chat forums), Geico and the Martin Agency expanded the series in 2006. The next wave of spots began with a [caveman] experiencing humiliation and anger at being confronted by the ads in an airport terminal. A second ad seems to spoof the very television news specials on controversial, offensive incidents, such as the ones focused on Imus and Richards' remarks, opening with a news-pundit—positioned in the screen above the banner, "So easy a caveman can do it: Offensive?"—pointedly asking, "How could it be offensive if it's true?" The caveman replies with a criticism of the anchor man's "tone" and then rattles off the accomplishments of early humans—fire, the wheel, walking upright, "laying the foundation for all mankind." But another "talking head" in the studio cracks a joke ("sounds like someone woke up on the wrong side of the rock") and the caveman is humiliated again. A third ad features the caveman in a therapy session, with a female therapist who asks, "Why does that bother you? It's just a commercial." The caveman retorts, "Well, what if it said . . . 'so easy a therapist could do it'?" She replies, "That just wouldn't make sense to me." Pressed as to why, she starts to answer, "Well therapists are . . ." and then pauses. The caveman fills in the pregnant pause with a tart, "smart?" The spot ends with his mother calling him on the phone, interrupting the session. . . .

It is not hard to find racial signifiers and structures in these ads. The racial features are materially evident in the stigmatized forms of physical difference inscribed on the bodies of the cavemen, which stand out even through their completely normative attire. Exaggerated brow ridges and eye brows, enlarged noses and cheek bones are prominent aspects of their visage—the same representational features used in the 1800s and early 1900s in making arguments about the reality, and utter distinctness, of racial groups (Lee Baker 1998). As well, this group is depicted in a "bestial" manner, in that their excessive body hair, which protrudes noticeably through their shirt collars and sleeves, while practically covering their faces, seems to symbolize fur. And, importantly, the stereotype being promoted is of their inherent ignorance—one of the enduring forms of depicting or insisting upon racial otherness. . . . In yet another regard, the forms of "difference" depicted in the ads could also easily be read in sexual terms as well, as some bloggers have noted. The effete settings in which the cavemen live—which are also apparently all-male domains—could as easily suggest the thinly veiled depiction here is of homosexuality rather than a racial other. . . .

Another consideration that weighs against a racial analysis is that, even when there is a racial dimension to invocations of "cavemen" today, it typically does not lie in a usage to disparage a minority group. Rather, it is most often invoked as a means of temporal distancing from transgressive racial comments by whites, as was evident in the controversies discussed [previously]. Imus was characterized as "cross[ing] a line, boorishly, creepily, paleolithically," and Richards was depicted as embodying "troglodytic views and behavior."[12] Imus also was dismissed as "a dinosaur in an era of political correctness,"[13] and his comments were construed as "merely another sop thrown to his

more Neanderthal fans, the kind he has been throwing for years."[14] . . .

While the racial content may be equivocal, what is apparent in any reading of the ads is that they concern a group and its stigmatized depiction by the larger society. Whether or not this campaign is designed and received as a wry commentary on current debates about the enduring forms of racial or sexual stereotyping, the overriding focus of the ads is on a group and its tenuous relation to the American "mainstream." . . .

But group, as a categorical perception is a relational entity, and its primary orientation in American culture is to the category of the individual, which is the central focus of the second set of ads. CareerBuilder.com, the largest online job site in the United States . . . launched its "Office Monkey" ads during the 2005 Super Bowl. . . . The first spot aired depicts a beleaguered white male office worker stepping out of an elevator into a corporate lobby surrounded by his chimpanzee coworkers. In rapid succession he receives a report from a colleague that "doesn't make any sense" (the chimp who hands him the report answers the phone and listens even though it hasn't rung), comes across a chimp in the copier room making photo copies of his butt, and apologies over the phone to a client, saying, "I'll correct it myself. It's just that I work with a bunch of monkeys." The camera pans back to view the array of cubicles each holding a chimpanzee at a desk playing, shrieking, or jumping around.

Two themes dominate in this ad series. The first highlights the utter incompetence of the chimpanzees in an office setting. The ads show chimps turning every material aspect of the corporate setting into some kind of toy: they play with staplers, ride around in mail carts, lick phones, toss laptops around carelessly, and rip wires out of conduits. One ad, titled the nose picker, focuses solely on a chimp in a little girl's outfit, steadily picking away at its nostrils and then meticulously eating the findings. Another spot features scene after scene of chimps drinking champagne in their cubes and in the conference room, shrieking and yowling with delight; this ad ends with the message: "Monkeys: very unreliable." The second theme, just as prominent, is of the debasing humiliation of the white male office worker, which is a central aspect of every ad and, in some sense, the key message of the series. In one, he is seen trying to tell the boss chimp in a meeting that naming their new product, "Titanic," is a bad idea; his comment is answered with flung banana peels and paper while a colleague leans over and kisses the boss's butt. In another spot, he gently berates his coworkers for ogling a female colleague as she walks past: "I don't think it's polite. So I want you to think about it. No judgments." But when he returns to his cube he sits down on a whoopee cushion they've placed in his chair and the chimps howl with laughter. In another, while the man is in the middle of a presentation, in a darkened conference room, wielding a red-beamed pointer across a screen, the demonstration collapses in riotous laughter as the monkeys in the audience fix similar red beams alternately on his crotch and his butt.

As with the caveman ads, racial signifiers abound in these spots. But are these ads "racial"? Certainly there is quite a developed history of using simians and simian-features to depict racial and ethnic difference, particularly directed to debase by creating a humorous effect. Efforts to depict African Americans as less-than-human have historically done so through a plethora of "ape-like" metaphors and figures; as well, the images of animalistic "innocence" or "foolishness" have also been staples of stereotypes of blacks (Winthrop Jordan 1974). . . .

The other dimension of racial signification in the ads involves the whiteness of the office worker. In this reading what stands out is a sense of whiteness imperiled in the brave new world of the multicultural workplace. . . . If these ads are to be read in terms of whiteness, I think they are, rather, indicative of whites' intense investment in individualism. This comes through in the basic storyline of the ads, which dramatize the emotionally fraught decision to leave a workplace in search of a better job. In cultural terms, as the ads so well depict, such a decision generally hinges upon a perception of not belonging to the company of fellow office workers. In such instances, then, whites appear quite willing to racialize—or simianize, at least—their fellow co-workers as a means of framing this existentially threatening sense of not belonging, which provides an impetus to seek out a new work situation where they do belong—an office somewhere that is not populated and run by "a bunch of monkeys."[15]

. . . I have emphasized a cultural approach here [. . .] in order to broach the compelling question of why "racial" signifiers so easily accrue to the category, group, while individuals so often are depicted as white? . . .

Conclusion

. . . [C]ulture involves the operation of conventions and categories that shape the recognition of some things as "racial" and others as not. Challenging racial thinking requires more than identifying and disparaging some statements and comments as "racist" because, as is evident in the case of both Imus and Richards, Americans so stridently believe that a "good person" does not say or think such things. Furthermore, as these ad series suggest, Americans can keep laughing at racial subjects even as they draw emphatic lines about not being entertained by racist remarks. . . . [I]t is not just racial thinking that is the problem, but a worldview dominated by categories such as good person and nice, which adhere so easily to an individual, while groups are so readily stigmatized and ridiculed. That is, it will take more than a racial framework to effectively challenge Americans' racial thinking. And, in this effort, a cultural perspective is critically important. . . .

[H]ow do we get Americans to acknowledge and assess the pervasive racial aspects of our public culture if the one thing they know they cannot be is "racist"? The stubborn refusals by both Imus and Richards—in the face of clear evidence and extensive criticisms—to even consider this possibility, indicates that an additional analytical approach is necessary. Hence, in analyzing these ads, I have emphasized the role of culture, in order to simultaneously highlight the range of racial signifiers in these images and narratives while linking them to a fundamental categorical tension of individual and group in American culture. . . .

Notes

1. For a deft dissection of the racial stereotypes at work in this one sentence, see Eugene Robinson (2007a).
2. "Michael Richards Hires PR Expert," by Solvej Schou, *Entertainment News*, November 23, 2006.
3. This public discussion is mirrored by an academic one as well. See Randall Kennedy (2003) and Jabari Asim (*The N Word: Who Can Say It, Who Shouldn't, and Why,* 2008). The title of Asim's book reflects the intense concern with establishing conventions over who can say what and how these reflect decisions about when speech is considered racial or not.
4. I examine this public debate more fully in *What Can You Say?: America's National Conversation on Race.* Stanford: Stanford University Press, 2010.

5. "The biggest cliché of the debate so far is the constant reiteration that this will be a moment for a national 'conversation' about race and sex and culture. Do people really want to have this conversation, or just talk about having it?" Frank Rich (2007).

6. Interestingly, he implicitly drew a contrast with Richards by stating, "I didn't say it out of anger. We're trying to be funny like we have for 30 years on this program."

7. Imus' pleadings that he was not being "racial" in his comments were inadvertently undermined minutes later in the interview when he lashed out at a black female caller saying, "I can't get any place with you people."

8. "The Power That Was," by Weston Kosova (2007).

9. Quoted in Kennedy, "Hey, That's (Not) Funny."

10. Ibid.

11. Jonetta Barras, "We're Our Own Worst Imuses," *Washington Post*, April 15, 2007.

12. John McWhorter, author of *Winning the Race: Beyond the Crisis in Black America* [Penguin, 2005], said, "What we really want is for Richards' *troglodytic views* and behavior to be censured publicly and that has happened. The part where we require him to apologize is really an empty ritual [emphasis added]."

13. Madigan [and Zurawik], "Dismissal May Signal Change: Women, Blacks Instrumental in Imus' Firing."

14. Kennedy, "Hey, That's (Not) Funny."

15. On similar dynamics of racialized whites, see Matt Wray (2006).

References

Baker, Lee. 1998. From Savage to Negro: Anthropology and the Construction of Race, 1896–1954. Berkeley: University of California Press.

Collier, Aldore. 2006. Black Leaders Unite in Call to End Use of the "N" Word. Jet December 11, 6.

Duke, Lynne. 2007. What Is Revealed by a Crack in the "Good Person" Facade. Washington Post, April 11, C1.

Figueroa, Tony. 2006. Thoughts on Michael Richards from a Fellow Stand-up Comic. Newstex Web Blogs, December 7.

Franklin, Marcus. 2007. Russell Simons: 3 Epithets Should Be Banned from "Clean" Rap Music. Associated Press Financial Wire, Business. April 23, sec.

Gumbel, Andrew. 2006. Kramer's Sense of Humor Failure. The Independent, November 22, 30.

[Hartigan, John. 2010. What Can You Say? America's National Conversation on Race. Palo Alto: Stanford University Press.]

Ifill, Gwen. 2007. Trash Talk Radio. New York Times, April 10.

Jordan, Winthrop. 1974. The White Man's Burden: Historical Origins of Racism in the United States. New York: Oxford University Press.

Kennedy, Randal. 2003. Nigger: The Strange Career of a Troublesome Word. New York: Vintage.

Kennedy, Randy. 2007. Hey, That's (Not) Funny. New York Times, April 15.

Kosova, Weston. 2007. The Power That Was. Newsweek, April 23, 24.

Madigan, Nick, and David Zurawik. 2007. Dismissal May Signal Change: Women, Blacks Instrumental in Imus' Firing. Baltimore Sun, April 14, 1A.

Rich, Frank. 2007. Everybody Hates Don Imus. New York Times. April 15, 2007.

Robinson, Eugene. 2007a. An Inarticulate Kickoff. Washington Post, February 2.

Sharpley-Whiting, Deanean T. 2008. Pimps UP, Ho's Down: Hip Hop's Hold on Young Black Women. New York: New York University Press.

Steinberg, Jacques. 2007. This Time, the Shock Jock's Sidekick Couldn't Shield the Boss. New York Times, April 12.

Van Susteren, Greta. 2006. Fox on the Record with Greta Van Susteren.

Waters, Maxine. 2007. Rep Waters Blasts Don Imus for His Racial Remarks. Press Release, April 10.

Woollard, Rob. 2007. Shock-Jock Racism Uproar Throws Spotlight on Rappers Yahoo News, April 16.

Wray, Matt. 2006. Not Quite White: White Trash and the Boundaries of Whiteness. Durham: Duke University Press.

2.3 Sex, Lies, and Conversation: Why Is It So Hard for Men and Women to Talk to Each Other?

DEBORAH TANNEN

Linguistic studies show that the ways in which people use language differ not only cross-culturally, but also within cultures among individuals of different ethnicities, regions, social classes, and gender identities. In this now classic piece, Tannen explores language differences, including body language and speech, among men and women in heterosexual marriages within the United States. Her research shows that high rates of divorce may be linked most closely to misunderstandings in gender-specific communication styles. Men, Tannen argues, engage in what she has described elsewhere as "report-talk," or conversations to collect and display information. Their speech styles are driven by a hierarchical social world whereby men are constantly seeking to establish and maintain their position as one up on another. Conversely, women engage in what Tannen labeled "rapport talk," or communication to build and sustain relationships, because women exist in networks of connections. Tannen discusses how these different communication styles emerge from distinct socialization processes among girls and boys in U.S. culture. In reading this piece, students might reflect on how applicable Tannen's thesis is to contemporary U.S. culture, identity, and marriage relationships.

Questions

1. According to Tannen, what are the distinct ways in which women and men communicate? Consider speech patterns, body language, and the use of silence.
2. How are gender-specific communication patterns established through childhood socialization? Provide specific examples from the reading as well as your own upbringing.
3. This article was published in 1990 and reads as if written from a heteronormative perspective. How do Tannen's conclusions play out in contemporary relationships? What about in same-sex marriages?

I was addressing a small gathering in a suburban Virginia living room—a women's group that had invited men to join them. Throughout the evening, one man had been particularly talkative, frequently offering ideas and anecdotes, while his wife sat silently beside him on the couch. Toward the end of the evening, I commented that women frequently complain that their husbands don't talk to them. This man quickly concurred. He gestured toward his wife and said, "She's the talker in our family." The room burst into laughter; the man looked puzzled and hurt. "It's true," he explained. "When I come home from work I have nothing to say. If she didn't keep the conversation going, we'd spend the whole evening in silence."

This episode crystallizes the irony that although American men tend to talk more than women in public situations, they often talk less at home. And this pattern is wreaking havoc with marriage.

The pattern was observed by political scientist Andrew Hacker in the late '70s. Sociologist Catherine Kohler Riessman reports in her [1990] book "Divorce Talk" that most of the women she interviewed—but only a few of the men—gave lack of communication as the reason for their divorces. Given the . . . divorce rate of nearly 50 percent, that amounts to millions of cases in the United States every year—a virtual epidemic of failed conversation.

In my own research, complaints from women about their husbands most often focused not on tangible inequities such as having given up the chance for a career to accompany a husband to his, or doing far more than their share of daily life-support work like cleaning, cooking, social arrangements and errands. Instead, they focused on communication: "He doesn't listen to me," "He doesn't talk to me." I found, as Hacker observed years before, that most wives want their husbands to be, first and foremost, conversational partners, but few husbands share this expectation of their wives.

In short, the image that best represents the current crisis is the stereotypical cartoon scene of a man sitting at the breakfast table with a newspaper held up in front of his face, while a woman glares at the back of it, wanting to talk.

Linguistic Battle of the Sexes

How can women and men have such different impressions of communication in marriage? Why the widespread imbalance in their interests and expectations? In the April issue of *American Psychologist*, Stanford University's Eleanor Maccoby reports the results of her own and others' research showing that children's development is most influenced by the social structure of peer interactions. Boys and girls tend to play with children of their own gender, and their sex-separate groups have different organizational structures and interactive norms.

I believe these systematic differences in childhood socialization make talk between women and men like cross-cultural communication, heir to all the attraction and pitfalls of that enticing but difficult enterprise. My research on men's and women's conversations uncovered patterns similar to those described for children's groups.

For women, as for girls, intimacy is the fabric of relationships, and talk is the thread from which it is woven. Little girls create and maintain friendships by exchanging secrets; similarly, women regard conversation as the cornerstone of friendship. So a woman expects her husband to be a new and improved version of a best friend. What is important is not the individual subjects that are discussed but the sense of closeness, of a life shared, that emerges when people tell their thoughts, feelings, and impressions.

Bonds between boys can be as intense as girls', but they are based less on talking, more on doing things together. Since they don't assume talk is the cement that binds a relationship, men don't know what kind of talk women want, and they don't miss it when it isn't there.

Boys' groups are larger, more inclusive, and more hierarchical, so boys must struggle to avoid the subordinate position in the group. This may play a role in women's complaints that men don't listen to them. Some men really don't like to listen, because being the listener makes them feel one-down, like a child listening to adults or an employee to a boss.

But often when women tell men, "You aren't listening," and the men protest, "I am," the men are right. The impression of not listening results from misalignments in the mechanics of conversation. The misalignment begins as soon as a man and a woman take physical positions. This became clear when I studied videotapes made by psychologist Bruce Dorval of children and adults talking to their same-sex best friends. I found that at every age, the girls and women faced each other directly, their eyes anchored on each other's faces. At every age, the boys and men sat at angles to each other and looked elsewhere in the room, periodically glancing at each other. They were obviously attuned to each other, often mirroring each other's movements. But the tendency of men to face away can give women the impression they aren't listening even when they are. A young woman in college was frustrated: Whenever she told her boyfriend she wanted to talk to him, he would lie down on the floor, close his eyes, and put his arm over his face. This signaled to her, "He's taking a nap." But he insisted he was listening extra hard. Normally, he looks around the room, so he is easily distracted. Lying down and covering his eyes helped him concentrate on what she was saying.

Analogous to the physical alignment that women and men take in conversation is their topical alignment. The girls in my study tended to talk at length about one topic, but the boys tended to jump from topic to topic. The second-grade girls exchanged stories about people they knew. The second-grade boys teased, told jokes, noticed things in the room and talked about finding games to play. The sixth-grade girls talked about problems with a mutual friend. The sixth grade boys talked about 55 different topics, none of which extended over more than a few turns.

Listening to Body Language

Switching topics is another habit that gives women the impression men aren't listening, especially if they switch to a topic about themselves. But the evidence of the 10th-grade boys in my study indicates otherwise. The 10th-grade boys sprawled across their chairs with bodies parallel and eyes straight ahead, rarely looking at each other. They looked as if they were riding in a car, staring out the windshield. But they were talking about their feelings. One boy was upset because a girl had told him he had a drinking problem, and the other was feeling alienated from all his friends.

Now, when a girl told a friend about a problem, the friend responded by asking probing questions and expressing agreement and understanding. But the boys dismissed each other's problems. Todd assured Richard that his drinking was "no big problem" because "sometimes you're funny when you're off your butt." And when Todd said he felt left out, Richard responded, "Why should you? You know more people than me."

Women perceive such responses as belittling and unsupportive. But the boys seemed satisfied with them. Whereas women reassure each other by implying, "You shouldn't feel bad because I've had similar experiences," men do so by implying, "You shouldn't feel bad because your problems aren't so bad."

There are even simpler reasons for women's impression that men don't listen. Linguist Lynette Hirschman found that women make more listener-noise, such as "mhm," "uhuh," and "yeah," to show "I'm with you." Men, she found, more often give silent attention. Women who expect a stream of listener noise interpret silent attention as no attention at all.

Women's conversational habits are as frustrating to men as men's are to women. Men who expect silent attention interpret a stream of listener noise as

overreaction or impatience. Also, when women talk to each other in a close, comfortable setting, they often overlap, finish each other's sentences and anticipate what the other is about to say. This practice, which I call "participatory listenership," is often perceived by men as interruption, intrusion and lack of attention.

A parallel difference caused a man to complain about his wife, "She just wants to talk about her own point of view. If I show her another view, she gets mad at me." When most women talk to each other, they assume a conversationalist's job is to express agreement and support. But many men see their conversational duty as pointing out the other side of an argument. This is heard as disloyalty by women, and refusal to offer the requisite support. It is not that women don't want to see other points of view, but that they prefer them phrased as suggestions and inquiries rather than as direct challenges.

In his book *Fighting for Life*, Walter Ong points out that men use "agonistic" or warlike, oppositional formats to do almost anything; thus discussion becomes debate, and conversation a competitive sport. In contrast, women see conversation as a ritual means of establishing rapport. If Jane tells a problem and June says she has a similar one, they walk away feeling closer to each other. But this attempt at establishing rapport can backfire when used with men. Men take too literally women's ritual "troubles talk," just as women mistake men's ritual challenges for real attack.

The Sounds of Silence

These differences begin to clarify why women and men have such different expectations about communication in marriage. For women, talk creates intimacy. Marriage is an orgy of closeness: you can tell your feelings and thoughts, and still be loved. Their greatest fear is being pushed away. But men live in a hierarchical world, where talk maintains independence and status. They are on guard to protect themselves from being put down and pushed around.

This explains the paradox of the talkative man who said of his silent wife, "She's the talker." In the public setting of a guest lecture, he felt challenged to show his intelligence and display his understanding of the lecture. But at home, where he has nothing to prove and no one to defend against, he is free to remain silent. For his wife, being home means she is free from the worry that something she says might offend someone, or spark disagreement, or appear to be showing off; at home she is free to talk.

The communication problems that endanger marriage can't be fixed by mechanical engineering. They require a new conceptual framework about the role of talk in human relationships. Many of the psychological explanations that have become second nature may not be helpful, because they tend to blame either women (for not being assertive enough) or men (for not being in touch with their feelings). A sociolinguistic approach by which male-female conversation is seen as cross-cultural communication allows us to understand the problem and forge solutions without blaming either party.

Once the problem is understood, improvement comes naturally, as it did to the young woman and her boyfriend who seemed to go to sleep when she wanted to talk. Previously, she had accused him of not listening, and he had refused to change his behavior, since that would be admitting fault. But then she learned about and explained to him the differences in women's and men's habitual ways of aligning themselves in conversation. The next time she told him she wanted to talk, he began, as usual, by lying down and covering his eyes. When the familiar negative reaction bubbled up, she reassured herself that he really was listening. But then he sat up and looked at her. Thrilled, she asked why. He said, "You like me to look at you when we talk, so I'll try to do it." Once he saw their differences as cross-cultural rather than right and wrong, he independently altered his behavior.

Women who feel abandoned and deprived when their husbands won't listen to or report daily news may be happy to discover their husbands trying to adapt once they understand the place of small talk in women's relationships. But if their husbands don't adapt, the women may still be comforted that for men, this is not a failure of intimacy. Accepting the difference, the wives may look to their friends or family for that kind of talk. And husbands who can't provide it shouldn't feel their wives have made unreasonable demands. Some couples will still decide to divorce, but at least their decisions will be based on realistic expectations.

In these times of resurgent ethnic conflicts, the world desperately needs cross-cultural understanding. Like charity, successful cross-cultural communication should begin at home.

2.4 Speaking Like a Model Minority: "FOB" Styles, Gender, and Racial Meanings Among Desi Teens in Silicon Valley

SHALINI SHANKAR

Language ideology refers to the widespread assumptions about the degree to which some languages or dialects are superior or more sophisticated than others. Language ideologies shape how people see themselves and how they classify others, thus working to create social difference. In U.S. schools and other institutional settings, English is understood to be the norm. How does this shape the way in which minority students speak and how their linguistic styles are interpreted by others? In this selection, Shalini Shankar explores what it means—linguistically—to be a "model minority." Drawing on fieldwork with Desi (South Asian American) teenagers in a Silicon Valley high school, she shows that linguistic styles vary by class and gender, with upper-class Desi teens adopting monolingual norms while middle-class teens speak in "FOB" (fresh off the boat) style, incorporating Punjabi, Desi Accented English, California slang, and hip-hop into their lexicon. Speech styles are further influenced by gendered norms within their communities and this translates into the school setting, influencing the ways in which boys and girls speak due to their understandings of schools as public or private spaces.

Questions

1. How do class and cultural capital impact the ways in which Desi teens regard school as a place to speak their heritage language? Compare middle-class and upper middle-class students.
2. Discuss the gender differences in FOB style. What is the role of community in shaping a student's understanding of school as a public or private space, and how does this influence FOB style differently for each gender?
3. When and why do FOBs use DAE, Spanish, hip-hop, and cussing in their school environment? How does this differ by gender?
4. What are the racialized implications of speech practices? How are popular Desis racially coded? What about FOBby teens?
5. How do students territorialize space at your university? What role does language play in the ways in which particular groups claim space?

In 1966, both the *US News and World Report* and *New York Times* lauded Asian Americans as a "model minority" for their high level of education, economic self-sufficiency, low crime rates, and positive social contributions. This characterization has become a stereotype that has enabled post-1965 Asian immigrants and their families' relatively easy integration into upper middle-class white society (Prashad 2000). . . . [The] strength [of this stereotype] has not diminished in the everyday lives of Asian Americans in Silicon Valley. Indeed, the prominence of Asian Americans in the high-tech industry has created an exceedingly high standard for Asian American youth in ways that not only obscure issues of racism and class inequality in schools, but also create normative expectations for teenagers with little room for variation (Shankar 2008). In this context, what does it sound like to be a model minority?

In this article I examine how everyday performances of teenage linguistic style interact with broader meanings of class, race, and gender. Beginning with the media-ascribed category of the model minority, I examine the specifics of how it shapes meanings of race for Desi (South Asian Americans) teens in a Silicon Valley high school. Ideologies of multilingualism that prevail in South Asia travel with their speakers to an increasingly monolingual California, and such an ideological clash is managed differently by upwardly mobile, well-educated Desis and by middle-class families who have prospered from the tech boom but remain in assembly line jobs. Differences in the ways Desi teens conceive of and manage these ideologies are linked to how they regard their high school, their place in it, and the ways in which school spaces are understood to be public or private. I contrast two distinct Desi teen high school styles that embody these differences: the mainstream style of teens referred to as "popular"; and a marginalized style called "FOB," or "Fresh off the Boat." I focus primarily on FOB styles to examine how FOBs are judged by Desi peers as nonnormative, how they vary according to gender, and the ways they are received at school. In so doing, I analyze how racial meaning is constructed through language use, as well as how gender differently shapes linguistic norms for these speakers.

...FOB Style

...In their multiracial, multiethnic school environment, teens who are called FOBs by popular teens for their style of speaking, dressing, and socializing are not actually brand new arrivals to the United States. Rather, FOB (pronounced as a word, not as individual letters) is a term that upper middle-class, popular Desi teens use to label second- and third-generation middle-class teens whose parents are nonskilled workers. So-called FOBs are middle-class Sikh Punjabis that

popular teens marginalize and distance themselves from based on their ways of dressing, speaking, and comportment in school. . . .

. . . FOB is commonly used by second-generation Asian American youth to distance themselves from the perceived negative attributes of first-generation or 1.5 generation youth (Jeon 2001; Loomis 1990; Rumbaut 2002; Talmy 2004; Zhou 2004). In the Desi context, FOB attributes include not adequately following fashion trends, having oily hair, speaking Punjabi at school, and speaking Desi Accented English (which I explain in detail [later]). Notably, these codes do not involve distancing oneself from everything South Asian. Cosmopolitan signs of being Desi—including wearing South Asian clothing to the prom, blasting Bollywood soundtracks from luxury automobiles, and incorporating South Asian elements into school performances—are not considered FOBby. Such choices do not mark popular teens as "whitewashed" (Pyke and Dang 2003); rather, these teens are knowledgeable and strategic about when and how they deploy aspects of their ethnicity and speak their heritage language. Such "model" ways of speaking stand in contrast to FOB styles. . . .

Although FOB styles of speaking include the use of Punjabi, English, Bollywood dialogue and song lyrics, hip-hop lyrics and lexicon, Desi Accented English, California slang, and Spanish, the stereotype that FOBs simply code switch loudly in Punjabi is what elicits negative judgment and enables popular teens to appear more model. . . . I use the terms *FOB* and *FOB style* to refer to the middle-class, marginalized Sikh Punjabi youth who engage in these marked language practices. . . .

Language Ideologies and Language Use in Silicon Valley

. . . The specific class, ethnicity, and language-based formations of Silicon Valley Desi communities have engendered different types of relationships between teens and their heritage languages. To better understand these judgments, some discussion of the status of English and Punjabi in Silicon Valley is necessary. English is ideologically favored in both South Asia and Silicon Valley, though varieties, accents, and norms of usage predictably vary between and within these locations. As the language of empire, globalization, and of diasporic locales such as the United Kingdom, Canada, Australia, and the United States, English is imbued with more power and status than other Desi languages (Kachru 2000). . . . English is a valued tool in identity-making practices for Desi teens, and they tend to use several different kinds of English, which are exemplified in transcripts [herein]. Despite English's elevated status, heritage language use plays a crucial, if not straightforward, role in shaping diasporic identity (Eisenlohr 2006). As a heritage language, Punjabi is highly valued in Silicon Valley communities. In addition to being widely spoken at family and community gatherings, Punjabi language instruction is offered at *gurdwaras* (Sikh temples) during weekend and intensive summer sessions. Many Sikh youth go to the San Jose gurdwara on a weekly or biweekly basis and participate in casual conversation in Punjabi as they wait in line for *langar*, the meal offered after prayer. This practice, along with the large and prominent Punjabi population in this area, makes Punjabi one of the most widely spoken South Asian languages in Silicon Valley. How and when it is used, however, can vary according to class.

Class is central to shaping linguistic dispositions. In these Desi communities, wealth is a topic of intense focus of conversation, but class categories are not (see Shankar 2006). Many Desi families who moved to Silicon Valley in the late 1970s and 1980s went on to experience unusually high job security until the 2001 stock market crash and can still rely on the equity of their well-appreciated homes. Adults in unskilled jobs have been able to buy property and prosper economically, but the type of cultural capital (Bourdieu 1985) they are able to instill in their children is not on par with that of upper middle-class parents. Such a rift, I argue, is important to understanding how teens regard school as a place to speak their heritage language.

At Greene High School, the diverse, overenrolled public high school where I conducted fieldwork for eighteen months . . . Desi teens were one of several racial and ethnic groups. Of the approximately 2,200 students during the 1999–2000 school year, nearly 50 percent were Asian American (about 30 percent Desi), 25 percent Latino, 12 percent white, 6 percent African American, and less than 1 percent Native American. Here, upper middle-class students are primarily Sikh Punjabi, Hindu Punjabi, and Hindu Gujaratis. They are children of well-educated, post-1965 immigrants. Their parents have upwardly mobile careers and live in wealthy areas of Silicon Valley. Upper middle-class parents who were educated in English-medium schools, whether in South Asia or elsewhere, tend to speak English far more at home. In these families, parents speak to one another and their children in their heritage language as well as in English. Their children by and large reply in English and speak English among themselves. Teens may speak their heritage language at community gatherings or with elderly relatives who are not fluent in English, but otherwise speak in English. This English-speaking norm, as well as their sophisticated understanding of school fostered through extensive parental involvement, makes English ubiquitous at home and the norm at school.

Middle-class teens are predominantly from Sikh Punjabi families. Their parents did not immigrate as professionals, and while they may have profited financially from the high-tech industry, they rarely gained more cultural capital from this windfall. Middle-class Desi teens display higher levels of spoken and comprehensive fluency in Punjabi than do upper middle-class teens. This is so because at least one middle-class teen's parents or live-in relative does not speak English fluently. Even among adults who attended high school in Yuba City or elsewhere in California, the strength of their community networks and the continuous arrival of [Sikh] relatives and spouses from South Asia keep their Punjabi in constant use, so much so that they seldom speak English to one another at home. While their children feel equally comfortable in both languages, they choose to speak Punjabi far more often than teens whose parents did not speak it at home.

Such distinctions map onto the spaces of the school campus and shape Desi teen styles. Greene's sprawling campus is filled with numerous small, one-story buildings that create multiple distinct spaces. Such a layout creates spaces to travel between buildings as well as places to socialize and "kick it," or spend routine time with friends, during morning break and lunch. Here, the seemingly private periods of social time with friends is in the same open, visible locations as other activities. . . . Although there is little that may be considered private about public high school—as student lockers, notebooks, bags, and other seemingly private spaces are all subject to seizure and search—students nonetheless territorialize the school campus during lunch and break and demarcate it into proprietary spaces that blur public and private distinctions.

The "quad" is the grassy, central . . . [space] where popular teens claim space, and the outlying regions are inhabited by socially and linguistically marginalized students. Eckert (1989) has described the ways in which popular jocks naturally claim and value school spaces as their own, while marginalized burnouts maintain that the school is not truly theirs and that school property may be used in unintended ways for illicit activities. Such differences in orientation are akin to ways in which populars and FOBs differently treat the school. In back areas of the school campus, especially behind the library and the "C" building, FOB cliques claim spaces in which they construct their own styles.

FOB Styles of Speaking

FOB styles draw on English, Punjabi, Desi Accented English, hip-hop lexicon and lyrics, as well as Spanish and California slang. The following examples are drawn from tape recordings made by students featuring teens (*M* = male, *F* = female) speaking among themselves in my absence during March–April 2001. They exemplify that what may be overheard as simply code switching between English and Punjabi is, upon closer examination, a much more complex style. FOB styles include local California slang, such as *hella* (very), and *tight* (very cool), *dude*, and *bro*. Similar to "FOB accents" (Reyes 2007), "Mock Asian" (Chun 2001), and "Stylized Asian English" (Rampton 1995), which all refer to ways of speaking that ridicule the nonstandard English associated with recent Asian immigrants, "Desi Accented English" (DAE) is a language variety I have identified through which teens index insider humor. DAE (formatted in boldface type [herein]) is not simply an accent; rather, it is a way of speaking that indexes a lack of cultural knowledge about common aspects of American life and contains atypical grammatical constructions and lexical elements that may not be shared by other speakers of South Asian English. It may seem ironic that those called FOBs are performing a "FOBby" accent, but their sophistication in doing so is a reminder that FOB styles can indeed be seen in many instances as a stylistic variable. In the following example recorded during a morning break period, Manpreet (F) offers her friend Harbans (F) some of her Pop-Tart pastry. Munching on the snack while the conversation ensues, Harbans interrupts to inquire about the Pop-Tart's flavor, and Avinash (M) offers an explanation.

Example 1: S'mores

Harbans: Hey this is good; what is it?

Manpreet: S'mores.

Harbans: S'mores?

Avinash: You know that thing with **marshmallows and chocolate? Maarrsh-mallow**, that little white thing?

By using DAE (formatted in boldface) to respond to Harbans's confusion about a flavor inspired by an American campfire treat, Avinash indexes the lack of social knowledge generally associated with FOBs. His emphatic **maarrsh-mallow** especially elicits laughter, because it is not a foodstuff available in South Asia, and makes this ordinary American flavor seem exotic to the uninitiated. Like Avinash, FOB teens readily use DAE for humorous emphasis in the midst of California accented English. In a conversation where Manpreet disclosed to Ranvir (M) that she was taping their conversation for my research, Ranvir jokingly suggested that this amounted to "sexual harassment." Manpreet smilingly replied, "**It is very-very bad!**" Ranvir laughed and echoed, "**Very-very?**" Here, not just the accent but also the construction **very-very**, a common expression in South Asian English, index their knowledge of stereotypical ways in which actual FOBs speak, and indicate that they consider themselves to be far enough from this stereotype to use it humorously.

FOB style draws heavily on Punjabi (formatted in italic type [herein]). This can include the use of expressions such as *Oh balle, balle!*, a multipurpose cheer uttered when dancing, as a rallying cry, and for surprise or exasperation, as well as *chak de fatte!* which teens translate as "let's go!" "raise the roof!" or "let's kick ass!"[1] While sometimes used literally, they are also used sarcastically, as in this exchange between Jett (M) and KB (M).

Example 2: **"Chak de fatte!" [*Kick ass!*]**.

Jett: Bend down, pick that up! All yous ready?

KB: Whaaaat?

Jett: *Chak de fatte!* [Kick ass!].

KB [sarcastically]: Thanks, bro.

In this exchange, the Punjabi phrase is used as a double entendre. In line 1, Jett tries to direct KB to pick up his bag and move along, but when KB takes his time doing so, Jett shouts, *"Chak de fatte!"* (line 3) as KB lackadaisically bends over to collect his belongings. The phrase is not just a rallying cry, but also a humorous suggestion that KB may require a swift kick in order to get moving.

Alongside Punjabi, California slang, and DAE, Spanish is also a resource for FOB style. San Jose's predominantly working-class Chicano population has exerted a visible influence on FOB styles. . . . Spanish phrases can be quite humorous when inserted into conversational exchanges. In the following excerpt from a lunchtime conversation, Kuldeep (M) uses Spanish (formatted in an underlined typeface) in an exchange with Uday (M) and Simran (F).

Example 3: *"No Habla Inglés"* [I (sic) don't speak English]

Uday: *Saleya eh* **garbage** *can vai*? [Is this a garbage can, stupid?].

Kuldeep: No habla Inglés [I (*sic*) don't speak English]. [loud round of laughter]

Kuldeep: **Don't know what you say . . .**

Simran: Throw that fuckin' shit out!

Kuldeep: *Oh balle! Hon boleya!* [Oh wow! At least you're talking to me now!].

While Uday attempts to be discreet about Kuldeep's refusal to properly dispose of trash and reprimands him in Punjabi, Kuldeep rebuffs him with two different performances of misrecognition. In the first, he feigns ignorance by saying in Spanish that he does not speak English. This is met with a round of laughter in part because it is a clever retort to Uday's directive, and in part because Uday's statement in Punjabi does not require him to know English. . . . By occasionally speaking in Spanish in a school environment where they are routinely mistaken for Latinos, FOB boys use Spanish as a way to mock faculty who cannot easily differentiate between them and Latinos. Ridiculing this misrecognition is a continual source of humor for FOBby teens. The conversation continues when Kuldeep, encouraged by the laughter of his friends, chooses DAE (formatted in bold) to tell Uday that he does not understand him. Again, it is ironic that he uses a FOBby accent to communicate this, as a true FOB would have no trouble understanding Uday's Punjabi

remark. When Simran reprimands him in English, Kuldeep responds to her sarcastically in Punjabi, and the joke has ended. While these teens studied Spanish in school and live alongside Mexican Americans in their neighborhoods, they rarely speak Spanish outside of these joking exchanges.

Similarly, FOB styles incorporate lexical elements from hip-hop without any political or social interests in black people. Blacks are concentrated in Oakland and other parts of the Bay Area but are a relatively minor presence San Jose. Desi teens listen to commercial hip-hop but do not express interest in becoming hip-hop artists or forming social alliances with blacks. In the following example, the hip-hop shout out "West Siiiiide" is used by both KB (M) and Jett (M) to mollify a tense dynamic that develops between Uday and Kuldeep about the latter's neighbor.

Example 4: "Dimag kharab hai, yaar" [*He is crazy, dude*].

Uday: Oh man, listen to the bullshit.

Kuldeep: *Dimag kharab hai, yaar. Mera neighbor, yaar* [He is crazy, dude. My neighbor, dude].

Uday: What has led you to this conclusion?

Kuldeep: *Dimag kharab hai!* [He is crazy!].

Uday: How do you know people don't say this about you?

Kuldeep: He is crazy, fool! Everybody says that, this fool really is crazy, though.

Uday: Takes one to know one?

Kuldeep: Shut up!

Uday: *Main te ude hi karda* [I'm just kidding].

Jett: West siiiiide!

Kuldeep: *Aha ki karan lag peyan tu?* [What have you started doing?]. Ain't no fuckin' California love, California thug. . . .

KB: West Siiiiide!

When Kuldeep seems genuinely annoyed at Uday's needling, Jett steps in and offers a shout out that indexes the unified front of West Coast hip-hop. Kuldeep is hardly amused and snaps at Jett with a clever use of hip-hop lyrics from the then-popular song "The Next

Episode" (line 13–14). KB reiterates Jett's shout out for unity, and the tension begins to diffuse. While such a use of hip-hop could be read as an attempt to "pass" for black or "cross" into this group (Bucholtz 1999; Cutler 2003; Lo 1999; Rampton 1995; Reyes 2005), Desi teens I observed did not use hip-hop lexicon for these purposes. FOB teens' overwhelming use of Punjabi and DAE, compared to their relatively infrequent use of hip-hop lexicon, underscores this point.

FOB styles, as I have illustrated, draw on a wide range of linguistic resources that a recent arrival could not begin to access. Some linguistic practices, including FOBs' use of California slang and ironic use of DAE, do not differ from those of popular Desi teens. What is most marked, however, is their use of Punjabi. It is significant that these teens do not use Punjabi in the classroom unless they believe they cannot be heard. They understand classroom time to be public and are careful there to maintain the monolingual school code. Lunch and break times in their corner of the school campus, however, are considered private. Indeed, the places they call their own are expected to be truly free spaces where they can say and do what they please, however loudly they please. For this reason, they are easily labeled FOBs by the rest of their Desi peers, who try to distance themselves. In turn, FOBs do not have positive opinions of popular teens—Desi and those of other ethnicities—and express their views in Punjabi to one another. . . .

Example 5: "Oh balle, balle" [*Oh, wow*].

Jett [sarcastically]: *Oh balle, balle* [Oh, wow].

Simran: Are you talking about that guy? Are you talking about that guy?

Jett: *Onu kera Punjabi andi vai!* [It's not as if he knows Punjabi!].

In such exchanges, it is evident that FOBs are well aware that popular teens ignore them or treat them with disdain. In line 1, Jett speaks caustically at a boy who is perhaps not all he thinks he is by delivering the usually upbeat chant *Oh balle, balle!* in a flat, sardonic way. Simran is curious to know if Jett is bold enough to speak about the boy in such close proximity, which Jett confirms to be the case because he does not believe he will be understood. While this boy may well understand Punjabi, Jett's assumption is that as a popular boy, he would neither understand Jett nor pay any attention to him even if he did. In this way, FOBs are able to maintain a sense of private conversation in what is otherwise a public space where they would be heard. Girls and boys differently regard the school as public and private spaces, and this shapes how they differently construct FOB styles.

Gendered Ways of Speaking

. . . While popular styles of speaking do not vary significantly according to gender, FOB language use is gendered according to topic, styles of speaking, and lexical choice. What is significant about this type of gender differentiation is that it reflects other standards of comportment that are prevalent in the lives of FOBby Desi teens. . . . Especially for FOB girls, maintaining a good reputation, or *izzat*, encourages them to minimize transgressions—be they sexual, behavioral, or disciplinary (Gillespie 1995; Hall 2002; Maira 2002). While some girls push this boundary further than others, they rarely do so to the extent that boys do.

Middle-class Sikh Punjabi girls attend Greene High School with many teens from their large community network. Here, gossip is rampant and teens are likely to spread rumors in their communities about things they witness at school. Although they can be somewhat more lax at school, girls rarely consider social time at school to occur in a private space. Even here, they are concerned about maintaining their reputation and avoiding school disciplinary measures, both things that could harm their familial and community standing. By contrast, Sikh Punjabi boys are subject to fewer social rules and tend to regard the social space of school as far more private. Treating their place in the school campus as a private space for jokes, humor, gossip, and confrontation, they criticize or choose to ignore school rules when they impede on their language styles.

Instead of quoting hip-hop lyrics, girls gravitate more toward Bollywood as their pop culture source for marking style. . . . When girls speak Punjabi in school, it is generally limited to quoting reported speech, constructing imagined utterances, and using phrases or terms, though their Punjabi speaking ability is as fluent as that of their male peers. When, for example, Raminder (F) grew tired of her friends telling her how attractive her brother is, she squealed, "Dude! He's my brother!" and recalled a humorous incident that had occurred at the gurdwara in the presence of her friends: "Remember those *budiyan* [older ladies]? There was somebody, like, at the gurdwara yesterday, some *budiya* [older lady], *keh diya, 'Meriyan bhanjiyan nursa da course kar diyan paiyan hain. Tera pra kine salan da hega? Asi Jattan da munda labdiyan hain'"* [she said to me, "My nieces are doing a nursing course. How old is your brother? We're looking for a *Jatt* (a Punjabi caste) boy]. "And [their brother is] a farmer!" added Janvi (F) and Mandeep (F) at the same time, shrieking with laughter that the prospective brides were doing a nursing course but their brother was a farmer. For effect, Raminder reiterated, "She was, like, '*Oho, nursa da course kar diyan!*'" [Oh look, they are doing a nursing course!]. I was like, 'puh-leeez!'" While Raminder could have as easily relayed the content of the older woman's utterance in English, using Punjabi enabled a much more amusing retelling. . . .

While girls spend much of their time gossiping and discussing events . . . they also use their fair share of profanity. They do not, however, stray from the "standard" English words that would elicit an FCC fine.[2] They steer clear of racial slurs and references to genitalia; the most rancorous expression I witnessed was a girl calling a boy a "bitch." Girls can get away with some linguistic transgressions if they are careful to do so only in the company of close friends. Even speaking on tape worried some girls. Raminder jokingly suggested what would happen if her friend's mother heard the recording of their conversation: "Yeah, right, you know your mom's fuckin' gonna come over here and be, like, 'what the fuck?'" Uttering such things in jest to a small group of friends is very different than shouting them in the school campus, which FOB boys do with abandon. When they "cuss" in English or even speak Punjabi, girls fear being caught by school faculty or overheard by gossiping peers, and restrain themselves.

Unlike FOB boys, FOB girls as well as other Desi girls are cautious about their language practices because using good language is part of a larger code of propriety to which girls are especially subject. Although using good language does not automatically make them good girls, using bad language can quickly earn them a bad reputation. For Desi teenage girls, using profane language is linked to improper comportment and even being sexually active in a cultural context where chastity is valued. They are subject to scrutiny from school faculty as well as peer policing. Tanya Hill, a vice principal, remarked about Desi girls

who have violated normative expectations, "These girls, if they knew the tough language they used, their parents would be absolutely floored that their kids even know these words, let alone have them come out of their mouths! In lot of cultures, girls are supposed to be more reserved. The parents would be surprised to see how uninhibited they are with the opposite sex." As Ms. Hill's comment implies, bad language is linked to what must be bad behavior. As Desi girls are expected to display levels of chastity not demanded of girls of other ethnicities, using profane language is a potentially dangerous way of tainting one's reputation. . . .

Hypermasculine FOB Style

While FOB style can be effectively used to articulate many things, for boys it centers on joking, insulting, and fighting. The use of . . . terms such as *behenchod* (sister-fucker), *gaandu* (gay; pejorative, like "faggot"), *tatti* (shit), and *tuttay* (testicles) are commonplace in boy's FOB styles. Sikh culture in San Jose, like elsewhere, is one in which Sikh boys especially take great pride. From drawing the Sikh *khanda* (religious symbol featuring the *kirpan*, or sword) on notebooks to displaying bumper stickers that say *"Jatt do it,"* these boys believe that being Sikh Punjabi is more desirable than being from any other ethnicity. In their communities, Sikh boys socialize with men at events and sit with them at the gurdwara. While Sikhism officially prohibits drinking, in families where it occurs, only males imbibe. Overall, boys are far less monitored and are not discouraged from roaming unsupervised in ways that girls are. In such a religious and social context, expressions of heightened masculinity are not uncommon. While they are not explicitly taught to be hypermasculine, many Sikh boys adopt this stance in the company of other Sikhs, especially other males. . . .

Boys use Punjabi when physically joking with one another. When Uday put KB in a headlock during morning break, KB had to shout, *"Chad de!! Oh bas kar!"* [Let me go! Oh, stop it!] over the roar of laughter to be released. Using distinct registers, such as villainous ones from Bollywood, also indexes masculinity. When, for example, Simran told Jett that only I would hear the conversation she was taping for me, he deployed evil *filmi* register to reply, *"Nahin! Main tera khoon kar dungaa!"* [No! I'm going to murder you!]. . . .

FOBby boys also enjoy using Punjabi to swear in ways that are not recognizable as transgressions by school administrators but communicate solidarity, humorous insult, and rancor among friends. By now it should come as no surprise that cussing is a cornerstone of boy's FOB style. Insults and discussions of women that could be deemed sexist usually take place out of earshot of girls. In this cultural context, it is not a norm to speak openly about such topics in the presence of the opposite sex.

On numerous occasions, boys strongly advised their female friends to leave their group as conversations headed in more illicit directions. . . . For the most part, insults are traded and boys cuss at one another, as in the following exchange in which tension arises when Kuldeep suggests that Uday might be scared to support him in an upcoming fight.

Example 8: *"Am I cussing?"*

Kuldeep: Damn, I don't give a fuck. Why you all scared, fool?

Uday: *Behenchod, tu galaan kad da?* [Sisterfucker, are you cussing at me?].

Kuldeep: Yeah, that's what really happens. *Tu galaan kad da, saleya?* [Are you cussing at me stupid?]. Uday's cussing at me!

Uday: *Mere dandi baad hoy jandi vai* [I might bite my tongue later].

Here, Kuldeep and Uday engage in a metapragmatic exchange about their own language practices. When Kuldeep implies that Uday is afraid of fighting with someone (line 1), Uday asks if Kuldeep is cussing at him to insult him (line 2). Kuldeep taunts him until Uday admits that he may indeed be cussing, and he uses an idiomatic expression (line 5) that indicates that he might feel bad about it later.

As their conversation indicates, Punjabi is the language of choice for talk about fighting, threats, and other illicit activity. When making a threat, like this one that KB jokingly made at Uday during a morning break—"*Uday nu mardena aaj! Uday nu mardena aaj!!*" [I'm going to kill Uday today! I'm going to kill Uday today!]—to recalling details of past fights, boys speak in Punjabi not only to avoid being overheard discussing illicit activity in English by school faculty, but also to convey details more graphically. . . . [U]se of

Punjabi signals a level of seriousness about fighting that English does not. In the following excerpt, Uday and Kuldeep observe a fight that has just erupted in close proximity to their spot in the back of the school campus.

Example 9: *Our Paully Vu*

Uday: What the hell? There's a fight over there. Someone got popped in the head! Oh that's Paul, isn't it? And that's our Paully Vu!

Kuldeep: No it ain't.

Uday: That's Paully Vu!

Kuldeep: It is?

Uday: Yeah, that's our Paully Vu!

Kuldeep: Well I can't see any glasses. . . .

Uday: That's Paully Vu, dude!

Kuldeep: That's not Paully Vu.

Uday: *Oy! dekh tan!* [Oh! Look at that!].

Kuldeep: Oh! It is him!

Uday: Oh, whuuut?

Kuldeep: He got popped?

Uday: Daaamn. He got popped.

Kuldeep: Well, that's embarrassing, dude.

Uday: That's fucked up!

Kuldeep: *Paul ne unu bariyan layan si* [Paul gave him a big beating].

Uday: He fought Paul Michaels—he's in our neighborhood and shit. What the fuck is going on?

Kuldeep: Neighbors fucked him up?

Uday: They probably backed him up.

Kuldeep: I want to fight that Mexican [referring to Paul].

Uday: *Oh dekh lagiyan! Oh dekh vaal kiddan khilare paya vai!* [Oh look! Oh look how his hair has been mussed up!].

During this rapid-fire exchange, Kuldeep does not even look closely at the fight until Uday signals to him to do so in Punjabi. Utterances that deal with the physicality of the fight, such as those pertaining to Paul's beating (line 17) and the postfight state of Paully (line 23), are conveyed in Punjabi. Also important here is the alliance between these FOBby boys and others from their racially diverse neighborhood. Uday repeatedly refers to Paully Vu, a Vietnamese boy, as "our" Paully, because they are from the same neighborhood. Likewise, they are surprised that Paul, a Mexican American boy also from their neighborhood, would fight with one of their own. Alliances made in neighborhoods carry over into school, especially for boys who spend time roaming around outside of school (see Eckert 1989). Such alliances are central to how FOBby boys conceive of their masculinity, and where they may fit in among lower middle-class Vietnamese Americans and Mexican Americans in San Jose. Furthermore, their interest in this fight and fighting in general can be understood as a way of asserting masculinity in the hostile company of popular students, school faculty, and the school in general.

FOB Styles and School Orientations

Using FOB styles is a source of humor and solidarity for boys and girls in an otherwise dull and alienating school environment. Unlike popular, "model" teens, FOBs do not believe that the school is working to their benefit. When discussing a report card received in the mail, Uday lamented that the school had recorded far more absences than he actually had. KB remarked, "[The] system fucked up." Kuldeep quickly added, "System is always fucking *you* up." That the system is rarely, if ever, on their side is a widespread sentiment among FOB teens. This opposition toward the school and popular teens' affinity toward it echo seminal studies of youth social categories, such as Eckert's jocks and burnouts (1989), or Paul Willis's (1977) "lads" and "earoles." In both these studies, the nonnormative group's rejection of the institutional environment makes them marginal, while the normative group's acceptance of the same fuels their popularity. The Desi situation, however, contains a third, vital element that shapes social action: their community. Both popular and FOB teens are deeply invested in their familial social circles, their reputation, and participating in these contexts. Thus, their styles in school are not performed according to the social dynamics of school alone; rather, the types of gendered identities teens construct in school are necessarily informed by those they construct in their community, and vice versa.

What is valued in their community and the dominant values of the schools can differ significantly for FOBs; it is the former that take precedence for girls and boys, in varying ways. While these youth rarely if ever have open confrontations with teachers or speak badly about them in English when they are in earshot, talking about them in Punjabi is commonplace. Boys avoid interaction with teachers outside of class while girls at the very least greet them, a move that is avoided by FOB boys. One day during lunch, Simran, Kuldeep, Uday, and Jett were perched on the railing of the library's handicap ramp when the sound of walkie-talkies grew louder. As the teacher Ms. Marie Subal approached, she announced, "Coming through, thanks!" Simran greeted her with a cheerful, "Hi Miss Subal!" Ms. Subal responded by saying "Hi" to the group and kept walking, looking at the boys who failed to greet her. As she passed, KB scowled, "**Marie** *pehri yaar. Bahut pehri yaar*" [Marie is mean, dude. She is really mean, dude]. Although Miss Subal was in earshot, KB's use of a South Asian pronunciation of her name as "MAH-ree" rather than American version "muh-REE" camouflaged the fact that she is the subject of his remark. Jett confirmed as she was walking away, "You see these teachers who are hella mean to you in class and you see them outside and they're all nice." Uday echoed this sentiment by saying "She's hella mean fool, hella fucked up." In this interaction, only Simran interacted with Ms. Subal, albeit in a brief way. By commenting about Ms. Subal in Punjabi and using DAE to pronounce her name, the boys were able to claim a private moment in an encounter that girls and faculty would regard as decidedly public.

As their use of Punjabi and English profanity illustrates, boys regard school to be a far more private space than girls do. Girls regard the school as consisting of a number of semiprivate opportunities but ultimately as a public space in which they must carefully self-regulate their speech and comportment. Girls rarely cross limits set by their communities and schools. Thus, their use of FOB style can be a stylistic variable that they control, but a status one when compared to normative standards set by popular Desi teens. Boys likewise control FOB style as a status variable, but their different conception of what is public and private makes their language use a status variable as well. Sikh Punjabi boys, who are under few constraints in community settings, are still subject to school rules. Because their reputations are not at stake, they can make any space private by using Punjabi and assuming that they will not be understood. In these ways, gendered differences in language use play an important role not only in how FOB boys express themselves differently than girls do, but also in how their language use is regarded by school faculty.

. . . Racializing Consequences

. . . In U.S. schools, as well as in other institutional settings, the ideal of English monolingualism prevails. In California schools, where bilingual education has long been a point of contention, even social uses of languages other than English have met with negative reception. . . .

. . . FOB styles stand in stark contrast to [the norm of English monolingualism]. For school faculty, such displays are immediate markers of otherness and cause for further investigation. Hearing loud displays of Punjabi is how Mr. López, a Greene High School administrator, initially noticed FOBby teens. He recalled his surprise when he realized this group is not Latino: "Where did they come from? Our population is so brown. And you were colorblind, let's say. East Indians look like Hispanics. Some of them are real dark, they may look like Afro-Americans. They come here, and it's not like they have a big flag saying 'I'm East Indian.'" Mr. López explained that in the veritable sea of brown faces at Greene, he initially mistook some Desi students for Latinos. This racial ambiguity, which is less a problem for East Asian or Southeast Asian students, was quickly clarified when he heard them speaking in "Indian" (i.e., Punjabi) as he patrolled the schoolyard. As the faculty member in charge of ESL, Mr. López is privy to assessments of each student's language abilities. As we sat in his office one morning, Mr. López scanned his list for Desi students in ELL "English Language Learners" classes as well as ESL, "English as a Second Language." . . . When he sees groups of Desi teens not speaking English, they potentially became [sic] Desi teens who may not be able to speak English well.

The monolingual ideology that values English alone conflicts with FOB styles that follow a South Asian multilingual ideology of using different varieties and registers for different purposes. On a typically sunny California morning, Mr. López offered to show me how he makes such connections and invited me to accompany him on his surveillance rounds. Gesturing toward the FOBs, Mr. López remarked, "Because of their English, they pretty much stay by themselves, which hurts, because they speak their own language and they don't speak in English and they don't get any better." Whether accurate or not, this association between being Limited English Proficient and being bilingual can be quite detrimental to FOBs. While a handful of youth actually need ESL classes, the vast majority of FOBs speak English fluently and with an American accent; many actually speak it better than Punjabi. Being called FOBs when they are second- and third-generation teens predictably does not improve this situation.

Conclusion

Language practices contribute to how some Desis remain model minorities and continue to integrate into upper middle-class white America while others share more economic, academic, and professional similarities with Latinos and other local populations. Being children of adults who hold nonskilled jobs and have far more extensive contact with extended family and new arrivals from South Asia influences linguistic aspects of FOB style in ways that marginalize them at school. . . .

. . . It has been suggested that as a model minority, Desis are poised to join white America (Prashad 2000). By engaging in normative uses of language that include speaking in English and minimizing profanity, popular Desi teens are rarely reprimanded by faculty for their styles of speaking and easily live up to the model minority stereotype. They distance themselves from FOB styles by meeting a normative standard and remaining linguistically unmarked, despite being racially marked as Asian American and brown. Popular styles can be understood as an ethnic variation on whiteness, in which a cosmopolitan, Bollywood-influenced style is showcased in performative contexts. Popular identity in school remains model in every way, including linguistically, and leaves these youth well positioned to integrate into wealthy white Californian communities.

Nonnormative use of language, combined with other unpopular speech practices such as quoting

Bollywood, exchanging insults, and talking about fights codes FOB by teens as brown rather than white. FOBs distance themselves from popular Desis and instead align with Mexican American, Vietnamese American, and other teens with whom they feel an affinity in their neighborhoods. In Silicon Valley, these populations, like Desis, are not uniformly upwardly mobile and are subject to similar types of racializing judgments. Because boys and girls differently regard the school as more or less private based on the gendered standards of propriety they are expected to achieve in their communities, boys are far less self-censoring than girls in their language use. Both are marginalized by peers, but boys tend to be more conspicuous violators of school codes. The "brownness" of Indians, as [the school Principal] Mr. López calls it, suggests that if Desis are not acting in model ways, they should be grouped with those who require reform. These social processes affect the positioning of South Asian Americans vis-à-vis other racial groups in the United States and underscore the role of language use in shaping racial meaning in diasporic communities.

Notes

1. All Punjabi-to-English translations and transliterations were done with the assistance of teenagers who made recordings and, more recently, with the assistance of a young woman in her mid-twenties whom I have known since she was a teenager in a Silicon Valley high school. My knowledge of Hindi and passive competence in Punjabi enabled me to follow much of the unspecialized conversation. Still, I relied on teens to understand specific terms as well as their norms of usage, which can vary from practices of Punjabi speakers elsewhere, as well as from those of their parents. I use their translations, as they were able to provide the contextual information about utterances as well as local, teen-specific glosses about certain terms and phrases, and have not noted deviances from "standard" Punjabi.

2. Current FCC (Federal Communications Commission) banned words still conform to George Carlin's "The Seven Words You Can't Say on Television"—*shit*, *piss*, *fuck*, *cunt*, *cocksucker*, *motherfucker*, and *tits*, although occasional exceptions are made, and girls tended to use the first three the most. Greene High School shares this list and also discourages the use of words such as *hell*, *goddamn*, and *asshole* in school contexts, which girls also used.

References

Bourdieu, Pierre. 1985. The Forms of Capital. In The Handbook of Theory and Research for the Sociology of Education. J. Richardson, ed. Pp. 241–258. New York: Greenwood.

Bucholtz, Mary. 1999. You da Man: Narrating the Racial Other in the Linguistic Production of White Masculinity. Journal of Sociolinguistics 3(4):443–460.

Chun, Elaine. 2001. The Construction of White, Black, and Korean American Identities through African American Vernacular English. Journal of Linguistic Anthropology 11(1):52–64.

Cutler, Cecelia. 2003. Keepin' It Real": White Hip-Hoppers' Discourses of Language, Race, and Authenticity. Journal of Linguistic Anthropology 13(2):211–233.

Eckert, Penelope. 1989. Jocks and Burnouts: Social Categories and Identity in High School. New York: Teachers College Press.

Eisenlohr, Patrick. 2006. Little India: Diaspora, Time and Ethnolinguistic Belonging in Hindu Mauritius. Berkeley: University of California Press.

Gillespie, Marie. 1995. Television, Ethnicity, and Cultural Change. London: Routledge.

Hall, Kathleen. 2002. Lives in Translation: Sikh Youth as British Citizens. Philadelphia: University of Pennsylvania Press.

Jeon, Mihyon. 2001. Avoiding FOBs: An Account of a Journey. Working Papers in Educational Linguistics 17(1–2):83–106.

Kachru, Braj. 2000. The Alchemy of English. In The Language and Cultural Theory Reader. LucyBurke, TonyCrowley, and AlainGirvin, eds. Pp. 29–31. London: Routledge.

Lo, Adrienne. 1999. Codeswitching, Speech Community Membership, and the Construction of Ethnic Identity. Journal of Sociolinguistics 3–4:461–479.

Loomis, Terrence. 1990. Pacific Migrant Labour, Class, and Racism in New Zealand. Alershot, UK: Avebury Publishing Ltd.

Maira, Sunaina. 2002. Desis in the House: Indian American Youth Culture in New York City. Philadelphia: Temple University Press.

Prashad, Vijay. 2000. The Karma of Brown Folk. Minneapolis: University of Minnesota Press.

Pyke, Karen, and Tran Dang. 2003. "FOB" and "Whitewashed": Identity and Internalized Racism among Second Generation Asian Americans. Qualitative Sociology 26(2):147–172.

Rampton, Ben. 1995. Crossing: Language and Ethnicity among Adolescents. New York: Longman.

Reyes, Angela. 2005. Appropriation of African American Slang by Asian American Youth. Journal of Sociolinguistics 9(4):510–533.

Reyes, Angela. 2007. Language, Identity, and Stereotype among Southeast Asian American Youth. Mahwah, NJ: Lawrence Erlbaum Associates.

Rumbaut, Ruben. 2002. Severed or Sustained Attachments? Language, Identity, and Imagined Communities in the Post-Immigrant Generation. In The Changing Face of Home: The Transnational Lives of the Second Generation. P. Levitt and M. Waters, eds. Pp. 43–95. New York: Russell Sage.

Shankar, Shalini. 2006. Metaconsumptive Practices and the Circulation of Objectifications. Journal of Material Culture 11(3):293–317.

Shankar, Shalini. 2008. Desi Land: Teen Culture, Class, and Success in Silicon Valley. Durham, NC: Duke University Press.

Talmy, Steven. 2004. Forever FOB: The Cultural Production of ESL in a High School. Pragmatics 14(2–3):149–172.

Willis, Paul. 1977. Learning to Labor: How Working Class Kids Get Working Class Jobs. New York: Columbia University Press.

Zhou, Min. 2004. Coming of Age at the Turn of the Twenty-First Century: A Demographic Profile of Asian American Youth. In Asian American Youth: Culture, Identity, and Ethnicity. Jennifer Lee and Min Zhou, eds. Pp. 33–50. New York: Routledge.

2.5 Anything Can Happen on YouTube (or Can It?): Endangered Language and New Media

JILLIAN R. CAVANAUGH

Language ideology, or widely held views about languages or dialects, including the idea that some are more sophisticated than or superior to others, influences the degree to which less common languages continue to be spoken. In the following selection, Jillian Cavanaugh explores the emergence of Bergamasco, a northern Italian endangered language, on YouTube, raising questions about how its speakers wish to be portrayed as public selves (local, national, international). Bergamasco, like other Italian local languages, has long been a language connected to place, and many people consider it something of the past, not to mention old-fashioned and unsophisticated. Yet in the 2000s, the language appeared on YouTube channels, spoken (in dubbed form) by public figures like David Beckham, Sylvester Stallone (as "Rambo"), and President Obama. Cavanaugh asks, what does it mean for younger generations when they hear it spoken not just by their family members or friends locally, but by Rambo and President Obama?

Questions

1. How are Bergamascos represented in the videos? What do these representations reveal about dominant Bergamasco language ideologies and social stereotypes? What values are they projected as holding? Provide examples.
2. How does the Bergamasco that appears on the YouTube videos compare to "pure Bergamasco"? And how do both compare to the ways in which people speak in everyday life?
3. What do the comments about these videos reveal about the connection between place and Bergamasco? In what ways is language involved in "place-making"?
4. What does the author mean when she describes "an emerging Bergamasco public"?
5. What role can—or should—social media and Internet technology play in language revitalization efforts? Are there costs and benefits to less common languages appearing on YouTube? Explain.

What do John McCain, Rambo, David Beckham, and Bill Gates have in common? Why, they all speak Bergamasco, a northern Italian local language that is in danger of being lost, of course! At least they do these days on YouTube, where numerous videos in Bergamasco have popped up over the last few years. For some, it is surprising simply to encounter Bergamasco online at all: until recently, many of the people I do ethnographic research with in Bergamo told me that Bergamasco was not suited to such environments, which they took as evidence of both its lack of modernity—it sounds so old-fashioned, they often complain—as well as what they see as its impending loss. But what is more surprising for the outsider is that when John McCain, who ran against President Obama in 2008 and lost, and the 1980s film character

Rambo are depicted as speaking Bergamasco, this is not simply a matter of translation but transformation. Instead of foreign policy or cutting taxes, McCain is lamenting the state of Bergamo's soccer stadium. Rambo is not kicking bad guys' asses or providing implicit criticism of the Vietnam War; he is describing himself as working too hard (a stereotypical Bergamasco trait) and using particularly piquant Bergamasco curses in the face of authority.

In other words, they are not just speaking Bergamasco; they are speaking *as* Bergamascos. And to comic effect: most of the commenters that respond to these videos express glee in various ways, describing themselves as laughing or depicting their laughter graphically (by writing, for instance, "ahahahahah!"). These and other comments focus on what is in the videos, as well as the language used in them. Indeed, the extent of this metalinguistic (language about language) commentary suggests that viewers are acutely tuned in to the language being used, and evaluating what they hear (and read, in the case of subtitles) in various ways.

Why does this matter? Like many languages in the world today that are in danger of being lost, Bergamasco is viewed by many people—both those who speak it and those who do not—as something of the past. Bergamasco sounds not only old-fashioned, but also rough and unsophisticated, just like the majority of those that spoke it up until the 1950s and '60s. After the Second World War, Bergamascos went from being largely poor, either peasant farmers or manual laborers, to working in factories and offices and making a decent wage. They sent their children to school and kept them there longer, where they learned Italian, the national language, and where they were discouraged from speaking Bergamasco, sometimes even punished for it. By the 1990s, fewer than half of Bergamascos still spoke their language in addition to Italian; less than 5% spoke it exclusively. The language ideologies (that is, the ideas and values that people have about their own and other people's languages) that underpin these changes depict Italian as the language of modernity, sophistication, education, and participation in the nation-state, and Bergamasco as the provincial language of the past and tradition, as a rough, peasant and male language (see Cavanaugh 2008, 2009 for further discussion). Language issues are also always tinged with politics in Italy; lately, this is due to the Northern League, a political party that champions northern local values and practices (including languages) in order to bolster its economic and political goals, which is often viewed as xenophobic and even racist for its anti-immigrant views and policies.

By the late 1990s and early 2000s, when I started my fieldwork in Bergamo, a number of Bergamascos had started to wonder: did we throw away exactly what makes us unique and sets us apart from our neighbors? Are we losing our traditions? What can we do to save them? A number of people starting writing poetry in Bergamasco, performing plays in it, compiling dictionaries and collections of old sayings and folk tales. Although these days everyday speaking in Bergamo often involves both languages, as speakers switch among them or even mix them at times, these efforts to save the language focus exclusively on purified and often archaic varieties of the language, valorizing words and phrases that are rarely used nowadays but are nonetheless viewed as "the real thing." Despite these efforts (or maybe because of them), Bergamasco sounded more and more old-fashioned and rough, just the opposite of what Bergamascos expected to find on the Internet. Italian or English are the right languages for the Internet, they told me in the early 2000s, not Bergamasco.

And yet, a few years later, Bergamasco was indeed all over the Internet, especially on social media sites like YouTube. I take all of this as evidence of an emerging Bergamasco public (Gal and Woolard 2001), that is, a site where people "by virtue of their own listening and their own reflexive awareness of others' listening to them" (Gal 2006, 166) come together in various ways to participate in a common activity or conversation. What *is* Bergamasco, this allegedly old-fashioned language, when it is used in mediated settings like the Internet, and what type of community is created through these practices? Can having an online presence thwart the ongoing decrease in use that Bergamasco is experiencing in face-to-face interactional settings? Could the entrance of Bergamasco into new mediated spheres like YouTube help to save it?

Endangered Language and New Media: Contraction or Expansion?

Endangered language activists have long advocated for increased access to technology and media as antidotes to loss. Get those languages into print, on television or the radio, and more people have more access to and reason to use them. At the same time, the language ideologies associated with those languages, many of them associated with the past, rurality, and backwardness, may be transformed so that they can be seen as modern, urban, even urbane and prestigious. While the relationship of new media like YouTube to lesser-used or endangered languages has been less often studied, the basic idea of "more media is good media"—or, what Patrick Eisenlohr calls "the valuation-enhancing effect of practices of electronic mediation" (2004, 32)—seems to be held by many minority language proponents. However, the relationship between endangered languages and media is often complex, complicated by, for example, issues of access (who is able to read or write that language?), orthography (the particular writing system used, including which letters are used to represent which sounds), standardization (when one form of a language is seen as the "real" or "best" version of it), and who has control over content and circulation. What does seem clear is that people's language ideologies play an important role in shaping the encounter between any particular endangered language and any particular form of media, new or not (Kroskrity 2000).

YouTube provides a particularly rich ground for exploring such an encounter due to its dialogic nature. On it, registered users may post video content as well as comment on this content. Comments, which range from a few to thousands, provide a relatively egalitarian context, where users work together to construct what these videos are and mean to them.[1] Video posters frame their content in various ways to signal to viewers how the videos should be approached, such as through titles and posters' descriptions. And although posters can hide comments or erase those they view as spam, viewers may comment as they wish, responding to the content of the videos, but also to each other. The meaning of any particular YouTube posting, then, is relatively undetermined until viewers, through their comments, co-construct the organizing frames and connections that contextualize that video, "placing" it relative to other videos and larger social contexts. For example, commenters may praise or criticize, thereby making something a "good" or "bad" video, or they may compare it to other videos, making it "like" or "unlike" other things one may find on YouTube or elsewhere.

Bergamasco on YouTube

There are currently around 50 videos on YouTube that contain Bergamasco and are labeled accordingly. They vary widely in terms of number of views (from just a few to hundreds of thousands) and comments (from none to hundreds), and can be divided roughly into four categories:

1. Videos taken from some other media source (usually television or film) and dubbed into Bergamasco, transforming the content such that, as I mentioned [previously], the speakers speak not only in Bergamasco but *as* Bergamascos. These include the cases I mentioned earlier—a clip from the first *Rambo* film; interviews with soccer star David Beckham and computer mogul Bill Gates, both of which took place on Italian news programs; and a clip from an Obama–McCain debate from the 2008 election.

2. Originally produced videos with spoken (and sometimes written) language in Bergamasco. These include songs with visual images tied to the lyrics; recited lists of proverbs, which often include still photographs or videos of Bergamasco locales and landscapes; as well as a pastry chef who walks viewers through a series of recipes for various sweets (none presented as typically Bergamasco).

3. Recordings of everyday usage. These include apparently normal people using Bergamasco in the course of their everyday lives, as well as video-taped recordings of various performers singing in Bergamasco, most of which display the hallmarks of spontaneous amateur recording (shaky screens, bad sound quality, lots of background noise, etc.).

4. Media clips from television and films that include speakers using Bergamasco. Many of these are short excerpts from comedy skits that revolve around 1 or more Bergamasco-speaking character and their lack of sophistication, ignorance, and willingness to undertake any construction project—in sum, these are characters that have recurred in Italy for centuries, in dramatic and poetic traditions such as the *Commedia Dell'Arte*, essentially stereotypes linked to particular places across Italy.

I focus here on translation as transformation in two examples from the first category. The first is entitled "Rambo works too much." In it, 2 characters, Rambo

General: *Scolta Rambo. E` rompich i pali.* (Listen Rambo. You really screwed up.)

Rambo: *L'èmia ira! E` capit?* (That's not ! Got it?)

E` colpa to! Me ò fai negot. (It's your fault! I didn't do anything!)

Te chel gh'ai me dicc a laura la sira con te. Rassa di Crustu! (You said that I had to work nights with you. Damn it!)

E del de torna a la ca troèr al me moèr in del lècc con unóter. (And then I come home to find my wife in bed with someone else!)

E la zèt che la usa 'vai a laura barbu!' e chi e pò chi l'e? (And people yell at me, "go to work, you bum!" and who are they [to make such a judgement]?)

Chi è per dir di tira 'zò I chei capei che sto mal issé? (and whose business is it to tell you to cuts your hair because it looks bad?)

General: *Sè Rambo. Chesto sér indò seret?* (sure Rambo. Where were you tonight?)

Rambo: *Scolta! Ch'era del vomito!* (Listen! I barfed!)

ò maiato ol brasat e la polenta e ò 'l biv fium de bira. (I ate brasato [a meat stew typical of Lombardy] and polento and I drank a river of beer)

Al sero cioche! (by evening, [I was] wasted [drunk]!)

General: *Te se prope scemo! Rembam it!* (You are ridiculous! Feeble-minded!)

Rambo: *Me laur tot ol de e fur manual!* (I work all day, and doing manual labor!)

E la siram' a dierte mai! [crying] (and at night, I never have any fun!)

E perché? Perché? (and why? Why? . . . . .)

Text (voice-over): *Povero esaurito!* (Poor exhausted one!)

Figure 2.5.1

Rambo lavora troppo (Rambo works too much).

and a military officer, the General, speak entirely in Bergamasco. As of June 26, 2015, it had 264,118 views and 99 comments. All spoken dialogue was subtitled in Italian.[2]

The next example is an excerpt from a debate between John McCain and Barack Obama during the 2008 presidential campaign. In it, McCain speaks Italian with a very strong Bergamasco accent with a few phrases of Bergamasco, and Obama speaks Italian with a "foreigner" accent (perhaps English or American) and uses one phrase—his first—in Bergamasco. As of June 26, 2015, it had 51,767 views and 20 comments.

We'll start with what these videos share in terms of content (what's in them). First of all, the figures in these videos are men. Indeed, in all the videos I have seen, male characters and voices predominate. There are virtually no women, and the few that appear are either reduced to their parts (such as their rear-ends, as in one video) or are made fun of in rather sexist ways. So, Bergamasco characters and voices on YouTube tend to be male and present an image of Bergamasco-ness as masculine.

Second, the videos share common themes: they are nearly always focused on local issues, such as the soccer stadium, or involve recurring stereotypes of Bergamascos as un- or under-educated, hard workers, and manual laborers. Even highly educated Obama is depicted as claiming to have worked in a warehouse, perhaps as an appeal to Bergamasco values. Implicit in both these videos is the depiction of Bergamascos

Transcription	English Translation
McCain: *Buona ser'a tutti.*	McCain: Good Evening to everyone.
Sta sira non ho tanta voglia di parlare di elezioni,	Tonight, I don't have much desire to talk about elections,
eeeeh, di parlare di se vincerò io o se vincerà ol me amis, Obama.	ahhh, to talk about if I will win or if my friend Obama will win.
Parliamo piuttosto della stadio nuovo a Bergamo.	Let's speak instead about the new stadium in Bergamo.
Ca le des anche se ne parla,	Which is to say also talk about it,
perche non e` possible che una squadra come Atalanta,	Because it's not possible that a team like Atalanta,[3]
che e` vinto una Coppa Italia,	Which has won the Coppa Italia,
giocato in Coppa UEFA,	Played in the Coppa UEFA,[4]
che ha sento agn de storia, eccola,	That has 100 years of history, there,
una squadra cosi bella che c'ha uno stadio brutto quasi quanto quello del Brescia.	A team this great can have a stadium almost as ugly as Brescia's.[5]
Io mi ricordo ancora che quando ho lasciato Bergamo per venire poi qui negli Stati Uniti,	I remember still when I left Bergamo to come here to the US,
mi ricordo di come allor' ho rimasto impressionato di quanto erano piu belli gli stadii anche qui nell' America.	I remember how I was hit with how many beautiful stadiums there are here in the US.
Perche non e` possible che qui da noi, che ci piace di piu` il baseball,	But how is it possible that here at home, where we like baseball more,
ci siano campi da calcio che sono addirittura piu` belli di quelli di Berghem.	There are soccer stadiums that are even nicer than that in Bergamo.
Obama: *Ah, Berghem di sura o di sota?* [audience laughter]	Obama: Ah, Upper or Lower Bergamo?[6] [audience laughter]
Non ti preoccupare, stavo solo scherzando.	No, don't worry, I was only joking.
So com'è il clima a Bergamo.	I know how it is in Bergamo.
Ci sono stato, ho fatto il magazziniero per anni.	I've been there, I was a warehouse worker there for years.
Ma credo che la costruzioni di un nuovo stadio non e` cosi importante.	But I believe that the construction of a new stadium is not that important.
Anche io frequentavo lo stadio, avevo l'abbonamento di Albino-Leffe.	I used to go to the stadium, too, I had season tickets to Albino-Leffe [another local team].
Noi potremo anche costruire un nuovo stadio,	We could in fact construct a new stadium,
potremo anche costruire un nuovo impianto,	We could in fact construct a new building,
ma se i tifosi di Atalanta rompono ogni volta la barriera dello stadio, come era successo, ad esempio, in un'Atalanta-Milan,	But if Atalanta's fans destroy the stadium's barriers every time, for example, as happened in an Atalanta-Milan [game],
noi non possiamo costruirne tutte le volte uno nuovo per loro.	We can't construct a new one for them every time.

Figure 2.5.2

Obama–McCain Debate on the stadium in Bergamo.

as poorly positioned in relation to power: Rambo is bossed around and criticized by the General, while McCain, who speaks throughout with a heavy Bergamasco accent, and his preoccupation with the stadium are dismissed by Obama as just a small part of a larger problem, as Bergamasco fans cannot be trusted to not destroy a new stadium through their excess of enthusiasm. And finally, like most of the videos I have seen, these two center on the important Bergamasco values of honesty and rough straightforwardness: this is how we think and talk, take it or leave it.

In sum, the Bergamasco world represented in these two and other videos reflects the dominant Bergamasco language ideologies and social stereotypes, in which Bergamasco is associated with male-ness, a working class or peasant socioeconomic position, roughness, straightforwardness, the value of hard work, as well as deep connections to the past. It's also slightly ridiculous, played for laughs, as Rambo laments that people make fun of his hair, and McCain seems to regard the state of a soccer stadium as more important than the election. In my research about Bergamasco and why—and if—it is being lost (Cavanaugh 2009), I found exactly these same associations and values to be what was leading fewer and fewer young people, particularly women, to choose to speak Bergamasco. Why, many young Bergamascos seem to ask themselves, speak a language that sounds—and makes me sound—old-fashioned and rough, like a hardworking, male peasant, or just silly? This alignment of how Bergamasco is depicted on YouTube with the linguistic ideological load that is contributing to a shift away from it in everyday speaking makes me worry: its presence in new media has not engendered new depictions of Bergamasco and the world in which it is used. In other words, Bergamasco has not been transformed through being used on the Internet into something new, different, and modern. Rather, it's just the same old thing, and the same old thing does not bode well for the persistence of this language.

New Language, New Possibilities?

A more complex picture emerges, however, if we focus on the language in use in these videos as well as the language that surrounds them. All of them contain Bergamasco or some mix of Bergamasco and Italian, from McCain's Bergamasco accent and switching between Bergamasco and Italian, Obama's token use of a typical Bergamasco phrase, to Rambo and the General speaking exclusively Bergamasco. This variety reflects the immense variety of everyday usage of language in Bergamo, where most speakers utilize both languages in mixed ways, running the gauntlet from Bergamasco with very few or no Italian elements (like Rambo) to Italian spoken with lots of Bergamasco elements (like McCain). To find this type of mixed language use depicted in the public sphere at all is very unusual. In the public spheres in which Bergamasco has appeared previously (local newspapers, volumes of poetry, play performances, occasionally on local television or radio stations), Bergamasco is extremely rare and Bergamasco and Italian are kept strictly apart. The Bergamasco that does appear is often archaic, full of words and phrases that are rarely used today, particularly in poetry and plays, the most popular and common public performances of it. This archaism, or tendency to use words from the past, is strongly valued, for these "old words" are often pointed to as the most authentic Bergamasco, which most clearly expresses local values and concepts. This archaism, in turn, works hand-in-hand with an ideology of purism, or the belief that pure language is the best language, which depicts the Bergamasco that is the most different from Italian (in other words, the oldest Bergamasco) as the most authentic—and therefore valuable. So, increasingly, the language that people speak in everyday life sounds and looks nothing like the language that has been held up as the best and most authentic language.

This YouTube display of different types of mixing Bergamasco and Italian is promising because it differs from the tendency to value only pure Bergamasco, which has functioned as a type of gate-keeping device, keeping out younger speakers who do not speak this older, so-called "purer" form of Bergamasco, as well as basically erasing the mixed ways in which people use language in everyday speaking. Essentially, portraying the best and most real form of Bergamasco as this pure form that very few people actually speak anymore has meant that lots of people believe that they don't speak Bergamasco, when really they do—just not this older form. All they need to do is to look at the volumes of poetry or listen to actors who perform it on stage—that is, to encounter Bergamasco in this type of public—to be told that what they speak is not "authentic." In light of this, to have a public like the one represented by these videos on YouTube, in which mixing is allowed and even routine, provides a model of language use that more closely reflects how language is used in everyday life. And if the usual "valuation-enhancing effect of practices of electronic mediation"—to use Eisenlohr's phrase again (2004, 32)—apply here, then the value of these mixed varieties should also be enhanced. People may encounter these mixed forms on YouTube and begin to view what they speak as the real thing, because, after all, it's just like what they hear online.

Comments: Mixed Language On-Line

The comments on these videos present a similar linguistic model, as they also run the gamut from pure Bergamasco (written in lots of different ways) to pure Italian and lots of mixing in between. Since writing Bergamasco has never been very common, the comments also represent a potentially promising turn for Bergamasco. A Bergamasco public in which purist language ideologies seem to impact neither speaking nor writing offers new possibilities for the language and its speakers. At the same time, comments replicate long-standing prejudices that divide Italians amongst themselves and problematize the presence of non-Italian immigrants.

In their comments, users respond to the videos but also to one another, echoing one another's praise, linking these videos to other similar ones through comparisons, and contesting the presence and participation of those they suspect of being outsiders, uniformly evidenced by their criticism of Bergamasco. Indeed, while we may echo one commentators' wonderment as to why non-Bergamascos would watch these videos in the first place, when they are clearly marked as being in Bergamasco (usually not an easy language for outsiders to understand), it seems that such boundary-crossing and boundary-making are a large part of what this public is about. When one of the commentators focuses on Obama's one utterance in Bergamasco—"*Ahah! strabello quando dice de sura oÒ de sòta!!!*" Ha ha! It's so great when he says upper or lower !!! [referring to the upper and lower sections of the town of Bergamo]—and another points out that Obama's accent appears to be English, they are both reinforcing the links between place and language that Italians commonly refer to as "*campanilismo*" (the belief that everyone who lives within sight of the same bell-tower or *campanile* shares similar tastes, language practices, and beliefs) as well as making those connections relevant and visible within a mediated sphere of interaction. Commenters do this by commenting on the language being used, saying, for example, "*Il dialetto migliore è il bergamascoooooooooooooo*" (the best dialect is Bergamascoooooo); "*Minchia, il bergamasco è allucinante,*

ci sono passaggi totalmente incomprensibili" (Dang, the Bergamasco is impressive, there are passages that are totally incomprehensible!); or even "*KE DIALETTOÒDI MERDA!!*" (What a shitty dialect!), all comments on the Rambo video. They also focus on accents or speculate on the specific origins of the speakers in the videos (who have dubbed over the original voices) within the province of Bergamo. Such attention to language and its connections to particular places helps to anchor linguistic elements to a particular social landscape; Italians often do this in everyday conversation and it appears that they are continuing to do it online. This type of attention, however, also involves evaluations, as the criticism of Bergamasco [mentioned previously] demonstrates, and *campanilismo* is often criticized in Italy for generating not only deep pride in one's own place, but also suspicions and criticism of people from other places. With no actual bell-tower in sight, it appears that one is being built using comments such as these to connect living in a place with having certain values and habits.

Other comments imbue this landscape with politics in comments such as "*non è propio così il begamasco è più veloce quando parlano questo lo capisce anche un terrone*" (Bergamasco isn't really like this it's faster when they speak this even a *terrone* [derogatory term for a southern Italian] could understand). Anti-southern attitudes such as this point to Northern League prejudices, while anti-northern attitudes, evident in the comment [mentioned earlier] criticizing Bergamasco as "*di merda*" . . ., point to resistance to the League and its politics. So, for instance, when one commenter asserted that "*IL BERGAMASCO FÀ CAGARE*" (Bergamasco makes (me/one) shit/defecate), another commenter responded: *di dove sei tu?_ Reggio Calafrica?* (where are you from? Reggio Calafrica?" that is, Reggio Calabria merged with Africa). Linking the south of Italy with Africa like this is a common anti-southern Northern League strategy, strengthened by the League's widely-known views against immigrants, large numbers of whom are from north Africa. The virtual borders between an "us" and a "them" constructed through comment such as these, then, are political as well as geographical, though the Northern League itself—or any other political party—is never explicitly mentioned.

Concluding Thoughts

The public these and other videos and comments are helping to construct is one in which the language in use is less idealized and purified than in other publics, but equally ideologized and scrutinized. Users may post what they like, but this hardly amounts to an egalitarian space in the end, as many users' participation is focused on constructing and maintaining the boundaries between us-as-Bergamascos and them-as-non-Bergamascos.

While the language used in Bergamo in everyday life seems inherently connected to the place in which it is spoken, on YouTube, such links are created out of the available materials at hand, materials which include comments that provide an interpretive frame through which these videos and that which surrounds them are made meaningful, and boundaries between insiders and outsiders are forged in various ways. Are these boundaries simply recursions of physical boundaries onto media spaces, which have long been characterized by their potential for enabling new types of circulation and value for minority languages? If so, what effect might this have on its long-term survival? Local languages like Bergamasco have long seemed—to both their speakers and to those who study them—as inherently emplaced and incapable of circulation to different locations. This emplaced quality has often been to their detriment, but it is also frequently the wellspring of their value. Looking at Bergamasco as it circulates beyond the emplaced face-to-face interactions and even publics where it has

thus far been grounded, as well as how Bergamasco may act to transform non-local figures, such as Rambo and John McCain, into locally-recognizable members of a shared moral community, shows local boundaries may be redrawn virtually to include non-geographical features such as very particular political stances. This linkage between Bergamasco and the Northern League is not (yet) complete, but it is certainly an ongoing project for some who participate in this public.

What this means for Bergamasco itself remains to be seen. Perhaps the "valuation-enhancing effects" of encountering the same type of Bergamasco they hear and use in everyday life in this emerging online public will help younger Bergamascos not only feel like what they speak is real and authentic, but also that it is valuable. On the other hand, the provincialism and politically-inflected meanings of praising one's own dialect and criticizing others' might lead other people to conclude that they (still) don't want to sound like a Bergamasco. It's too soon to tell, but what does seem clear is that local languages like Bergamasco remain powerful symbolic resources for expressing particular types of selves (local vs. national, provincial vs. cosmopolitan) but also for constructing particular publics in which speakers listen and are listened to—or argued against—in particular ways.

Notes

1. For instance, Jones and Schieffelin (2009) have shown how a series of AT&T commercials that were posted on YouTube became sites for teenagers to contribute to ongoing debates about the role and meaning of texting, explicitly, but also implicitly, as many of their posts were in "text talk."

2. In both transcripts: *italics* = Bergamasco. Italian and English translations in plain script.

3. Atalanta is Bergamo's long-suffering soccer team.
4. The Coppa Italia and Coopa UEFA are important soccer tournaments in Italy and Europe.
5. Brescia, a town about 40 kilometers away, is Bergamo's long-standing rival.
6. Bergamo is divided into an Upper and Lower City. If strangers know 1 thing about Bergamo, and 1 or 2 words in Bergamasco, it will be these.

References

Cavanaugh, Jillian R. 2008. "A Modern *Questione della Lingua*: The Incomplete Standardization of Italian in a Northern Italian Town." *Journal of the Society for the Society of the Anthropology of Europe* 8 (1): 18–31.

Cavanaugh, Jillian R. 2009. *Living Memory: The Social Aesthetics of Language in a Northern Italian Town*. Malden, MA: Wiley-Blackwell Publishing.

Eisenlohr, Patrick. 2004. "Language Revitalization and New Technologies: Cultures of Electronic Mediation and the Refiguring of Communities." *Annual Review of Anthropology* 33: 21–45.

Gal, Susan. 2006. "Contradictions of Standard Language in Europe: Implications for the Study of Practices and Publics." *Social Anthropology* 14 (2): 163–181.

Gal, Susan, and Kathryn A. Woolard, eds. 2001. *Languages and Publics: The Making of Authority*. Manchester: St. Jerome Publishing.

Jones, Graham M., and Bambi B. Schieffelin. 2009. "Talking Text and Talking Back: "My BFF Jill" from Boob Tube to YouTube." *Journal of Computer-Mediated Communication* 14: 1050–1079.

Kroskrity P. 2000. "Language Ideologies in the Expression and Representation of Arizona Tewa Ethnic Identity." In *Regimes of Language: Ideologies, Polities and Identities*, edited by Paul Kroskrity, 329–60. Santa Fe, NM: School Am. Res. Press.

DR. BERNARD PERLEY

Linguistic anthropologist and member of the Maliseet Nation from Tobique First Nation, New Brunswick, Canada.

Figure 2.6.1
Bernard Perley.

How did you become interested in the discipline of anthropology, and in language revitalization?

When I went to college, I was interested in learning about American Indian languages. I was introduced to the discipline when I took a course in anthropology to explore the variety of American Indian languages in the Americas. I spoke Maliseet as a first language and I know from personal experience what it feels like to be denied the opportunity to speak your language and participate in your cultural practices. I hope my work can reassure others who have felt the same alienation from language and culture that I have felt. I also hope that I can help others to celebrate their

languages and cultures by providing models for revitalization and long-term vitality.

Tell us about your work in storytelling and visual anthropology.

It may be a truism or an overgeneralization but everyone loves to hear good stories. My storytelling seeks alternative media for revitalizing indigenous stories to make them relevant to contemporary readers/viewers/participants. I tell stories through my oral presentations, graphic novels, art installations, and much more. The multimedia/transmedial approach seeks to innovate while respecting American Indian traditional values. I find it exciting to position visual representation as viable and vital anthropological practice.

What is the most meaningful project you've worked on over the course of your career?

It is difficult to select one project because they are interrelated to my goal for enhancing language vitality for indigenous communities. I can highlight an art installation that bridges my academic anthropology work with my indigenous language advocacy work. I view the installation piece as a construction of Maliseet sacred space in which the viewer can experience the Maliseet prayer of thanksgiving. The prayer installation became a means to rethink ethnographic representation by inviting "readers" to participate in experiential ethnography. "Readers" are not limited to the printed word; they can experience ethnographic space.

Would you classify the Maliseet prayer installation as an example of applied, engaged, or public anthropology?

All of the above. The prayer is a public event open to anyone who cares to share in the experience of entering Maliseet sacred space. It is engaged anthropology as it reflects my deliberate attempt to communicate

Figure 2.6.2

Maliseet prayer installation.

with audiences beyond the Maliseet community and the anthropology community to convey the importance of language as an integrated cultural resource. The prayer is applied anthropology because I combined the principles of ethnographic research with semiotic and linguistic analytical tools to develop the installation as an alternative ethnographic representation that invites audiences beyond anthropology to participate in ethnographic experiential space.

Who is your main audience for your research and writing, and why?

I constantly look for opportunities to expand my target audience to anyone who has interest in my research and advocacy. For example, the prayer installation was a public event where many different audiences were able to experience Maliseet sacred space. My current project integrates four American Indian languages and a local American Indian school in an effort to introduce the creative and positive work that anthropologists do on an everyday basis (see image above). My writing also broadly conceives "ethnography" to include sketches, paintings, cartoons, and graphic representations. These varieties of ethnographic representation will draw multiple audiences. The reason for my broad target audience is to introduce as many people as possible to what anthropological research is and what positive contributions anthropologists make in our communities.

What does it mean to you to be an advocate or activist anthropologist?

I am an "advocate/activist" not because I want to be one. It's because I have to be one. As an American Indian who recognizes the devastating effects of five centuries of colonialism on American Indian communities and having suffered from those ongoing pressures I realize that maintaining my language and culture is a celebration of native North America. My work is directed toward promoting such celebrations for other indigenous communities. In that context my work is more about being who I am rather being an activist/advocate. My commitment to enhancing the vitality of indigenous communities may be labeled as advocacy or activism by others and that reflects a perspective that does not necessarily undermine my work.

What are the potential ramifications of this form of scholarship?

The potential ramifications for this kind of scholarship are at least two-fold. First, what I may refer to as "celebration of indigenous worlds" and others refer to as "advocacy/activism" means that there is an opportunity to have conversations regarding the role of anthropology in promoting better understanding between the researcher and the communities where that research is developed. Second, the colonial history of anthropology has a legacy that continues to be a sensitive issue for many former colonial subjects (I do argue colonialism continues and has taken subtler forms) and the advocacy/activism is an imprecise label for the important work that contemporary anthropologists are doing to address past wrongs to redirect anthropological futures toward more ethical, respectful, and truly collaborative scholarship.

Looking towards the future, how should anthropology engage the public?

American anthropology has a long history of public engagement regarding many social and cultural issues of their respective milieus. Today we face new challenges that require anthropologists to continue to address injustices and inequalities by sharing our knowledge with the broader public audiences. For example, anthropology can be an important advocate on behalf of American Indians by condemning the current practice of professional sports teams using images of stereotypes and caricatures of American Indians and use of offensive monikers. I have been working with supportive allies in the American Anthropological Association (AAA) to encourage the AAA to issue a public statement regarding the use of Native American mascots and nicknames in professional and college sports communities. I am happy to say that the AAA did issue the public statement in March of 2015. This is just one of many initiatives that many anthropologists are pursuing to address the injustices and inequalities in our contemporary world. The statement can be found on the American Anthropological Association's website, www.americananthro.org/, and a direct link is available on brondo.oup.com.

ABOUT THE ANTHROPOLOGIST

Occupation: Associate Professor Department of Anthropology, University of Wisconsin-Milwaukee.
Hobbies: Read, read, read. I stay curious about everything around me, and often find links to other

disciplines, other perspectives, and other ways of knowing. Those perspectives continue to provide inspiration for my advocacy and scholarly activities. Because of "fun reading" I can honestly say I love my job.

CAREER ADVICE

Advice for students interested in linguistic anthropology:

Find a mentor that can guide you in your prospective research interests. An excellent mentor will be the best source for professional development throughout the student's anthropology career.

For those interested in activist anthropology:

Have passion for the kind of activism and advocacy that you are interested in pursuing but equally important, you have to be able to listen. By listening to what others have to say regarding your issues of interest, you may find allies from unexpected corners and perspectives.

PART 3
Belief Systems

Cultural anthropologists seek to undercover and explain how worldviews are constructed within the communities they study. A worldview is essentially the way someone thinks about the world, a broad philosophy of life and perspective through which one interprets the world around them. Religious belief systems are one of the most common forms of a worldview, but what sets religions apart from other worldviews is that religions assume the existence of the supernatural forces (Schultz and Lavenda 2014, 159–163).

To get at an understanding of a culture's belief system, anthropologists often focus on rituals. Rituals are repetitive social practices of a sequence of symbolic activities that are closely tied to culturally significant ideas. Through the performance of rituals, shared cultural ideas are revealed and take form. Not all rituals are of a religious nature, but all ritual action encompasses "magical" behavior (Welsh and Vivanco 2014, 346).

Magic is a set of beliefs and practices that are designed to control the world. Magic is an explanatory system that can help individuals make sense of events that fall beyond naturalistic explanations. While most anthropological accounts of magic focus on non-Western cultures, George Gmelch's classic piece, "Baseball Magic" (Reading 3.1), reveals just how common magical practices are in American life, especially in situations where people lack control over the outcome of events.

When one thinks of magic, thoughts of witchcraft are not too far behind. Witchcraft is performed by humans who are believed to have an innate, nonhuman power to do harm, sometimes intentionally and sometimes unintentionally. Belief in witchcraft is widespread across several African nations. In "No Peace in the House" (Reading 3.2), Alexandra Crampton explores witchcraft accusations and life in Ghana's "witch camps," where those accused of witchcraft flee or are sent. This piece is an example of applied and engaged anthropology, in that the author offers potential programmatic interventions for NGOs, working to reintegrate accused elderly women back into their home communities, including suggestions for culturally appropriate forms of conflict resolution and mediation.

Religious beliefs provide people with meaning and understanding and help us navigate our social worlds. Yet religious worldviews find themselves rubbing up against other ideologies, or worldviews that justify social arrangements under which people live (Schultz and Lavenda 2014, 175); for example, political parties, feminism, or racism. Readings 3.3 and 3.4 explore these tensions and the ways in which individuals navigate their world when their religious beliefs meet up with alternative ways of viewing the world. In "The Politics of Righteousness" (Reading 3.3), Judith Casselberry considers the intersections of race and gender among Apostolic-Pentecostals in New York City, in light of changing ideas about women in authority positions within the church and larger society. In "Choosing Both Faith and Fun," Lara Deeb and Mona Harb (Reading 3.4) focus on how Muslim youth negotiate morality in their leisure time in a Shi'a neighborhood in South Beirut, Lebanon, balancing advice from multiple moral authorities to make choices about what constitutes moral behavior for pious youth.

This section's "Anthropology in Practice" features Tanya Luhrmann, Professor of Anthropology at Stanford University, an award-winning author. Dr. Luhrmann's work interrogates faith from the perspective of the believer. She asks: How do people know God is real and present? Luhrmann is a public anthropologist bringing anthropology to the public realm, publishing pieces for popular audiences in venues such as *The Huffington Post*, *Psychology Today,* and *New York Times,* and has been featured on radio shows like National Public Radio's *Fresh Air* and *The Brian Lehrer Show.*

KEY TERMS:

- Religion
- Ritual
- Taboo

- Fetish
- Magic
- Witchcraft

3.1 Baseball Magic

GEORGE GMELCH

In this classic reading, Gmelch takes us into the world of baseball magic, revealing how players use ritual, taboo, and fetishes to attempt to control the outcome of their performance. Magic is an explanatory system for the cause of events that fall beyond scientific or natural explanations. Anthropologists often document the existence of magic in non-Western societies, but Gmelch turns this study back on American culture to explore the power of magic in shaping the outcome of baseball games. He applies Malinowski's early observation that magic is most frequently found in circumstances where individuals lack control over outcomes.

Questions

1. Define and distinguish between the three forms of magic: ritual, taboo, and fetish.
2. What is the role of magic in sports?
3. Why are rituals, taboos, and fetishes so prevalent among pitching and hitting, but not in fielding?
4. Share your experiences with magic in sports and other performances.

We find magic wherever the elements of chance and accident, and the emotional play between hope and fear have a wide and extensive range. We do not find magic wherever the pursuit is certain, reliable, and well under the control of rational methods.

—BRONISLAW MALINOWSKI

Professional baseball is a nearly perfect arena in which to test Malinowski's hypothesis about magic. The great anthropologist was not, of course, talking about sleight of hand but of rituals, taboos and fetishes that men resort to when they want to ensure that things go their own way. Baseball is rife with this sort of magic, but, as we shall see, the players use it in some aspects of the game far more than in others.

Everyone knows that there are three essentials of baseball—hitting, pitching and fielding. The point is, however, that the first two, hitting and pitching, involve a high degree of chance. The pitcher is the player least able to control the outcome of his own efforts. His best pitch may be hit for a bloop single while his worst pitch may be hit directly to one of his fielders for an out. He may limit the opposition to a single hit and lose, or he may give up a dozen hits and win. It is not uncommon for pitchers to perform well and lose, and vice versa; one has only to look at the frequency with which pitchers end a season with poor won-lost percentages but low earned run averages (number of runs given up per game). The opposite is equally true: some pitchers play poorly, giving up many runs, yet win many games. In brief, the pitcher, regardless of how well he performs, is dependent upon the proficiency of

George Gmelch. "Baseball Magic." 1971. *Society* 8(8), 39–41. Reprinted with kind permission from Springer Science and Business Media.

his teammates, the inefficiency of the opposition and the supernatural (luck).

But luck, as we all know, comes in two forms, and many fans assume that the pitcher's tough losses (close games in which he gave up very few runs) are eventually balanced out by his "lucky" wins. This is untrue, as a comparison of pitchers' lifetime earned run averages to their overall won-lost records shows. If the player could apply a law of averages to individual performance, there would be much less concern about chance and uncertainty in baseball. Unfortunately, he cannot and does not.

Hitting, too, is a chancy affair. Obviously, skill is required in hitting the ball hard and on a line. Once the ball is hit, however, chance plays a large role in determining where it will go, into a waiting glove or whistling past a falling stab.

With respect to fielding, the player has almost complete control over the outcome. The average fielding percentage or success rate of .975 compared to a .245 success rate for hitters (the average batting average), reflects the degree of certainty in fielding. Next to the pitcher or hitter, the fielder has little to worry about when he knows that better than 9.7 times in ten he will execute his task flawlessly.

If Malinowski's hypothesis is correct, we should find magic associated with hitting and pitching, but none with fielding. Let us take the evidence by category—ritual, taboo and fetish.

Ritual

After each pitch, ex-major leaguer Lou Skeins used to reach into his back pocket to touch a crucifix, straighten his cap and clutch his genitals. Detroit Tiger infielder Tim Maring wore the same clothes and put them on exactly in the same order each day during a batting streak. Baseball rituals are almost infinitely various. After all, the ballplayer can ritualize any activity he considers necessary for a successful performance, from the type of cereal he eats in the morning to the streets he drives home on.

Usually, rituals grow out of exceptionally good performances. When the player does well he cannot really attribute his success to skill alone. He plays with the same amount of skill one night when he gets four hits as the next night when he goes hitless. Through magic, such as ritual, the player seeks greater control over his performance, actually control over the elements of chance. The player, knowing that his ability is fairly constant, attributes the inconsistencies in his performance to some form of behavior or a particular food that he ate. When a player gets four hits in a game, especially "cheap" hits, he often believes that there must have been something he did, in addition to his ability, that shifted luck to his side. If he can attribute his good fortune to the glass of iced tea he drank before the game or the new shirt he wore to the ballpark, then by repeating the same behavior the following day he can hope to achieve similar results. (One expression of this belief is the myth that eating certain foods will give the ball "eyes," that is, a ball that seeks the gaps between fielders.) In hopes of maintaining a batting streak, I once ate fried chicken every day at 4:00 P.M., kept my eyes closed during the national anthem and changed sweat shirts at the end of the fourth inning each night for seven consecutive nights until the streak ended.

Fred Caviglia, Kansas City minor league pitcher, explained why he eats certain foods before each game: "Everything you do is important to winning. I never forget what I eat the day of a game or what I wear. If I pitch well and win I'll do it all exactly the same the next day I pitch. You'd be crazy not to. You just can't ever tell what's going to make the difference between winning and losing."

Rituals associated with hitting vary considerably in complexity from one player to the next, but they have several components in common. One of the most popular is tagging a particular base when leaving and returning to the dugout each inning. Tagging second base on the way to the outfield is habitual with some players. One informant reported that during a successful month of the season he stepped on third base on his way to the dugout after the third, sixth and ninth innings of each game. Asked if he ever purposely failed to step on the bag he replied, "Never! I wouldn't dare, it would destroy my confidence to hit." It is not uncommon for a hitter who is playing poorly to try different combinations of tagging and not tagging particular bases in an attempt to find a successful combination. Other components of a hitter's ritual may include tapping the plate with his bat a precise number of times or taking a precise number of warm-up swings with the leaded bat.

One informant described a variation of this in which he gambled for a certain hit by tapping the plate a fixed number of times. He touched the plate once with his bat for each base desired: one tap for a single, two for a double and so on. He even built in odds that prevented him from asking for a home run each time. The odds of hitting a single with one tap were one in three, while the chances of hitting a home run with four taps were one in 12.

Clothing is often considered crucial to both hitters and pitchers. They may have several athletic supporters and a number of sweat shirts with ritual significance. Nearly all players wear the same uniform and undergarments each day when playing well, and some even wear the same street clothes. In 1954, the New York Giants, during a 16-game winning streak, wore the same clothes in each game and refused to let them be cleaned for fear that their good fortune might be washed away with the dirt. The route taken to and from the stadium can also have significance; some players drive the same streets to the ballpark during a hitting streak and try different routes during slumps.

Because pitchers only play once every four days, the rituals they practice are often more complex than the hitters', and most of it, such as tugging the cap between pitches, touching the rosin bag after each bad pitch or smoothing the dirt on the mound before each new batter, takes place on the field. Many baseball fans have observed this behavior never realizing that it may be as important to the pitcher as throwing the ball.

Dennis Grossini, former Detroit farmhand, practiced the following ritual on each pitching day for the first three months of a winning season. First, he arose from bed at exactly 10:00 A.M. and not a minute earlier or later. At 1:00 P.M. he went to the nearest restaurant for two glasses of iced tea and a tuna fish sandwich. Although the afternoon was free, he observed a number of taboos such as no movies, no reading and no candy. In the clubhouse he changed into the sweat shirt and jock he wore during his last winning game, and one hour before the game he chewed a wad of Beechnut chewing tobacco. During the game he touched his letters (the team name on his uniform) after each pitch and straightened his cap after each ball. Before the start of each inning he replaced the pitcher's rosin bag next to the spot where it was the inning before. And after every inning in which he gave up a run he went to the clubhouse to wash his hands. I asked him which part of the ritual was most important. He responded: "You can't really tell what's most important so it all becomes important. I'd be afraid to change anything. As long as I'm winning I do everything the same. Even when I can't wash my hands [this would occur when he must bat] it scares me going back to the mound. . . . I don't feel quite right."

One ritual, unlike those already mentioned, is practiced to improve the power of the baseball bat. It involves sanding the bat until all the varnish is removed, a process requiring several hours of labor, then rubbing rosin into the grain of the bat before finally heating it over a flame. This ritual treatment supposedly increases the distance the ball travels after being struck. Although some North Americans prepare their bats in this fashion it is more popular among Latin Americans. One informant admitted that he was not certain of the effectiveness of the treatment. But, he added, "There may not be a God, but I go to church just the same."

Despite the wide assortment of rituals associated with pitching and hitting, I never observed any ritual related to fielding. In all my 20 interviews only one player, a shortstop with acute fielding problems, reported any ritual even remotely connected to fielding.

Taboo

Mentioning that a no-hitter is in progress and crossing baseball bats are the two most widely observed taboos. It is believed that if the pitcher hears the words "no-hitter" his spell will be broken and the no-hitter lost. As for the crossing of bats, that is sure to bring bad luck; batters are therefore extremely careful not to drop their bats on top of another. Some players elaborate this taboo even further. On one occasion a teammate became quite upset when another player tossed a bat from the batting cage and it came to rest on top of his. Later he explained that the top bat would steal hits from the lower one. For him, then, bats contain a finite number of hits, a kind of baseball "image of limited good." Honus Wagner, a member of baseball's Hall of Fame, believed that each bat was good for only 100 hits and no more. Regardless of the quality of the bat he would discard it after its 100th hit.

Besides observing the traditional taboos just mentioned, players also observe certain personal prohibitions. Personal taboos grow out of exceptionally poor performances, which a player often attributes to some particular behavior or food. During my first season of professional baseball I once ate pancakes before a game in which I struck out four times. Several weeks later I had a repeat performance, again after eating pancakes. The result was a pancake taboo in which from that day on I never ate pancakes during the season. Another personal taboo, born out of similar circumstances, was against holding a baseball during the national anthem.

Taboos are also of many kinds. One athlete was careful never to step on the chalk foul lines or the chalk lines of the batter's box. Another would never put on his cap until the game started and would not wear it at all on the days he did not pitch. Another had a movie taboo in which he refused to watch a movie the day of a game. Often certain uniform numbers become taboo. If a player has a poor spring training or a bad year, he may refuse to wear the same uniform number again. I would not wear double numbers, especially 44 and 22. On several occasions, teammates who were playing poorly requested a change of uniform during the middle of the season. Some players consider it so important that they will wear the wrong size uniform just to avoid a certain number or to obtain a good number.

Again, with respect to fielding, I never saw or heard of any taboos being observed, though of course there were some taboos, like the uniform numbers, that were concerned with overall performance and so included fielding.

Fetishes

These are standard equipment for many baseball players. They include a wide assortment of objects: horsehide covers of old baseballs, coins, bobby pins, protective cups, crucifixes and old bats. Ordinary objects are given this power in a fashion similar to the formation of taboos and rituals. The player during an exceptionally hot batting or pitching streak, especially one in which he has "gotten all the breaks," credits some unusual object, often a new possession, for his good fortune. For example, a player in a slump might find a coin or an odd stone just before he begins a hitting streak. Attributing the improvement in his performance to the new object, it becomes a fetish, embodied with supernatural power. While playing for Spokane, Dodger pitcher Alan Foster forgot his baseball shoes on a road trip and borrowed a pair from a teammate to pitch. That night he pitched a no-hitter and later, needless to say, bought the shoes from his teammate. They became his most prized possession.

Fetishes are taken so seriously by some players that their teammates will not touch them out of fear of offending the owner. I once saw a fight caused by the desecration of a fetish. Before the game, one player stole the fetish, a horsehide baseball cover, out of a teammate's back pocket. The prankster did not return the fetish until after the game, in which the owner of the fetish went hitless, breaking a batting streak. The owner, blaming his inability to hit on the loss of the fetish, lashed out at the thief when the latter tried to return it.

Rube Waddel, an old-time Philadelphia Athletic pitching great, had a hairpin fetish. However, the hairpin he possessed was only powerful as long as he won. Once he lost a game he would look for another hairpin, which had to be found on the street, and he would not pitch until he found another.

The use of fetishes follows the same pattern as ritual and taboo in that they are connected only with hitting or pitching. In nearly all cases the player expressed a specific purpose for carrying a fetish, but never did a player perceive his fetish as having any effect on his fielding.

I have said enough, I think, to show that many of the beliefs and practices of professional baseball players are magical. Any empirical connection between the ritual, taboo and fetishes and the desired event is quite absent. Indeed, in several instances the relationship between the cause and effect, such as eating tuna fish sandwiches to win a ball game, is even more remote than is characteristic of primitive magic. Note, however, that unlike many forms of primitive magic, baseball magic is usually performed to achieve one's own end and not to block someone else's. Hitters do not tap their bats on the plate to hex the pitcher but to improve their own performance.

Finally, it should be plain that nearly all the magical practices that I participated in, observed or elicited, support Malinowski's hypothesis that magic appears in situations of chance and uncertainty. The large amount of uncertainty in pitching and hitting best explains the elaborate magical practices used for these activities. Conversely, the high success rate in fielding, .975, involving much less uncertainty offers the best explanation for the absence of magic in this realm.

3.2 "No Peace in the House": Witchcraft Accusations as an "Old Woman's Problem" in Ghana

ALEXANDRA CRAMPTON

Witchcraft is a very real cultural phenomenon in Ghana and other African nations. It can be used for both good and evil and can serve as a form of social control, or can help to explain misfortune and inexplicable events. Media accounts have drawn international attention to "witches camps," places where the accused may flee or be sent. While both men and women may practice witchcraft, or be accused of practicing witchcraft, most accusations in Ghana tend to be of older, marginalized women. Crampton interrogates the value of approaching "witch camps" from a human rights–based perspective, which tends to result in educational programs about women's rights and a focus on "freeing" women from camps. If such an approach were useful, why then, Crampton wonders, would so many of the accused who were "liberated" from witch camps refuse to leave? Drawing on ethnographic work with NGOs working in elder advocacy in Ghana, Crampton offers a culturally sensitive approach to witchcraft accusation that relies on culturally appropriate forms of conflict resolution, including mediation.

Questions

1. What does the phrase "there is no peace in the house" have to do with witchcraft accusations?
2. Discuss the role structural violence plays in witchcraft accusations.
3. Who was Cramptom's key informant within Gambaga (and beyond), and what assistance did this individual provide in terms of Crampton's understanding and analysis?
4. How does the reality of witch camps contrast with how they are presented in the media?
5. Discuss the different formats that interventions into cases of witchcraft accusations take from a human rights perspective as compared to those that take a culturally sensitive approach.

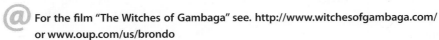 For the film "The Witches of Gambaga" see. http://www.witchesofgambaga.com/ or www.oup.com/us/brondo

Alexandra Crampton. 2013. "No Peace in the House": Witchcraft Accusations as an "Old Woman's Problem" in Ghana"
Anthropology & Aging Quarterly, Vol. 34, No. 2 (2013): 199–212. Creative Commons International Attribution License 4.0.

Witchcraft beliefs are a part of every day life in Ghana and a part of aging in Ghana as well. This is typically not a problem for older adults, in a country where the connotation of the English word "old" is more positive; a colloquial term for translating, "I am old" means "I have grown" (van der Geest [2007]). . . . On the other hand, older women marginalized within family systems are vulnerable to attack and even abuse. The national and international media have reported on horrific cases in which older women were murdered as suspected witches (e.g., Smith 2010). Follow-up reports then focused on "witches' camps," to which the accused may flee for protection where they are also effectively imprisoned if family and/or community refuse to let them return. There are no national statistics on the scope of this problem . . . [but a] general estimate of 1,000 inmates seems to be the most stable number for the six camps typically used for statistics (e.g., Whitaker 2012). The UNHCR, the United States State Department and the U.K. border control address witchcraft accusations as a human rights problem. . . . Since the 1990s, nongovernmental organizations (NGOs) have implemented projects to address witchcraft violations broadly and to "free" or assist camp inmates. The long-term impact, based on research and assessments by reporters and advocacy workers, is unclear at best, and those with sustained involvement have softened from a focus on rights violations to a more culturally sensitive approach of family conflict resolution.

The purpose of this paper is to provide anthropological analysis of witchcraft as an older woman's problem that has not been well solved using rights-based intervention. Data presented are from a larger ethnographic study of elder advocacy work by a nationally based Ghanaian NGO between 2003 [and] 2005. I call this organization Ghanaian Aging Resources (GAR). . . . Rights based intervention work attempting systemic change has not been effective but is becoming a common part of public discourse and life in at least one witches' camp. . . . What has been more effective advocacy is to work from within cultural norms through informal conflict mediation among family and community systems.

The Anthropology of Aging in Ghana

. . . A common proverb both in the literature and in conversations about aging with people in Ghana identifies the importance of interdependent relationships:

"Just as the elder helped you as you cut your first teeth, so must you help them as they lose theirs." In other words, aging is not characterized as an individual as much as a social experience very much dependent upon reciprocal relationships and demonstrated respect (van der Geest 2002a). The rights of young and old are not stressed as much as the responsibilities accorded to social roles within extended family systems. Older adults who have "done well" over the life course financially and socially have supported younger generations, and then can expect to be supported in return as they reach old age. Even as they may become weaker physically, they are valued for their wisdom accumulated through life experience. . . .

In addition to wisdom through accumulated life experience, older adults are also associated with knowledge of potentially destructive knowledge glossed as "witchcraft" in English. . . . They may use this power to curse another and bring misfortune. This attribution can also be a form of social sanction by accusers for not sufficiently sharing resources when another seems to have acted selfishly or succeeded unfairly. . . . Although both women and men may use witchcraft, the association between women and witchcraft is particularly negative in Ghana and other African contexts (Drucker-Brown 1993; Hoch-Smith 1978). Accused women include those who are unusually successful or unsuccessful. As in the media accounts of violence, those most vulnerable in witchcraft accusations are late middle aged, post-menopausal women and older women. . . .

The Anthropology of Witchcraft in Ghana

. . . Witchcraft is hard to explain and beliefs vary but it is generally believed in Ghana and across West Africa to be a term to explain how misfortune and loss are caused by one who has inflicted evil as illness, accident or death (Simmons 1980). One may acquire witchcraft intentionally as a "medicine" or may unconsciously receive it from another witch (Drucker-Brown 1993, 533). In other words, not all witches are aware they have this power or how they acquire it. . . .

Very generally, one who is accused or fear they have the witchcraft may consult a shrine. A shrine priest holds power to divine who is a witch and to "dewitch" through medicine and ritual. Typically the shrine priest is an older male who has the same witchcraft powers but uses them for different purposes (Drucker-Brown

1993, 534). In Gambaga, the village best known internationally having a "witches' camp," there is no shrine but the chief has the power to render witches harmless. He performs the divination and offers the necessary ceremony to "dewitch" if the person is guilty. He does not require the accused to remain in the camp after they pay for the dewitching but in practice lack of "peace in the house" in the home village may mean that the accused cannot return with or without a finding of guilty. Lack of peace refers to unresolved strife within a "house" that is typically several houses clustered within an extended family compound. . . . [W]itchcraft accusations are part of the "dark side of kinship" (Ciekawy and Geschiere 1998, 4), given that accusations are only among close family members. The camps then become a place of refuge if peace cannot be restored. . . . "[A]ccused women took their demolished reputations and hid themselves at the witch camps, since they knew no other remedy for the anger and violence that came with the accusation" (Palmer 2010, 216).

Witchcraft beliefs have been studied both as an explanatory theory and as a means of social organization (Stewart and Strathern 2003). . . . [T]he "witchcraft idiom" (Van der Geest 2002b, 450) is a way to answer existential questions about misfortune and loss. . . . Witchcraft accusations are a way to surface interpersonal conflicts, air grievances, and then restore social relations to a more harmonious whole (Stewart and Strathern 2003, 4). In this process, a moral order is challenged and then affirmed. . . . Social tension underlying witchcraft accusations can be linked to unequal incorporation of villages and regions into capitalist market systems (e.g., Parker 2006). Contributing factors to accusations against a family member then may require understanding what Paul Farmer refers to as the "structural violence" of poverty and social inequality (Farmer 2003). . . . Witchcraft is thus a way in which people interpret and construct modernities as well as seek to resolve tensions and misfortune within modern contexts (Sanders 2003, 339–340; Simmons 1980, 447). This is important to consider in asking why the camps are located in northern Ghana, which is a region historically deprived of development investment. . . .

. . . The famous Gambaga witches' camp was formed during precolonial (and pre-written recorded) times. . . . The local term for the camp is pwaanyankura-foango, which translates literally as, "old ladies section" (Drucker-Brown 1993, 535). . . . Some of the

accused living in the camps had been unusually successful, and some were vulnerable within family power dynamics and thus easy to attack. . . . Yaba Badoe [noted]:

> . . . those most vulnerable to witchcraft accusations were widowed women in late-middle age, who were forced to move back to their fathers' houses after the death of their husbands; successful businesswomen who headed their own households; women without children to provide them with leverage within the extended family; and women without an adult male brother from the same mother to protect their interests in the extended family. (Badoe 2011, 42)

. . . [T]ensions fueling social drama come from the vulnerability of women without male allies in extended family systems within the stress of inadequate and uneven development interventions.

Rights Discourse on Witchcraft as a Social Problem in Ghana

In contrast to a small number of academic studies on aging, gender, and witchcraft accusations, there are hundreds of articles printed and reproduced through national and international media on the plight of women, mostly older women, attacked, banished, and murdered as witches. . . . The majority of these articles were written within a rights discourse that also informs much of the advocacy work on this issue around the country. The Gambaga camp serves as the icon for representing witchcraft beliefs as a social problem and rights violation against women, particularly older women. . . . As [an] icon, the construction of the camp is one reminiscent of colonial era village studies in the 19th century. That is, the camp supposedly exists within an isolated village that seems lost in time. Here, traditional beliefs control people's lives. Few outsiders have traveled so far to discover surprising insights of how modernization has not yet reached this place. Ignorance is the source of elder women's marginalization and abuse. The camps are a national disgrace within Ghana and a global human rights violation. Demands are made to disband the camps and return the women to families. Poverty is named as the root of the problem—poverty of education, of resources, and of the ability to rise above supernatural thinking. Development is then the answer, in the form of education and development assistance. Modernity is not the problem but rather the solution. . . . [M]edia representation of witchcraft as an older woman's problem omits the more complex power dynamics and socioeconomic contexts in which accusations arise, and isolates the problem as self-evident rather than as subject to interpretation and negotiation. . . .

Lessons from GAR

I first learned of witchcraft in relation to the potential mediation program. It was in the context of helping me prepare for a mediation training as requested by GAR. . . . The example was a past case in which an adult son had accused his mother of being a witch and kept her "in a structure." GAR staff were unable to convince him to change his mind or take better care of her but they were able to negotiate to provide her with food and clothing on their own. The focus of staff attention was similar to that of professionals who intervene in elder abuse cases in the United States, in which the problem is a neglectful or abusive caregiver who is therefore both the problem and the ideal source of solution.

When I returned in 2004, GAR had secured funding for the rights program. . . . There were no witchcraft cases in this program during the study period. The observable parts of witchcraft in the legal rights program were educational materials produced for "awareness creation." For example, one had an old man as a wizard covered by a red circle and slash. The text read, "Old age is not the start of witchcrafting." When attending a community meeting in village M where the posters were distributed, the reception was muted. This reaction is probably related to how members of the village had already told the NGO that they did not need assistance. I was told that they had their own internal system of settling disputes and did not need the intervention of a rights program.

. . . Witchcraft accusations also did not seem to be a common preoccupation for older adults requesting GAR services and was not an obvious part of agency activities at the main office or in the communities where they worked. . . . In addition, of the dozens of settlement cases observed at the legal aid organization, there was [only] one case involving an older woman and witchcraft. The head of the family explained that

the woman who had owned the property was accused of being a witch by a younger family member, and that is why she left that one out of the inheritance of property and room. This statement brought a shocked reaction from the room, and the young family member's lawyer protested that this accusation was not relevant to the case, but one of the legal aid lawyers replied that it was relevant if it was related to the inheritance issue.

These brief examples suggest that witchcraft accusations happen within a context of conflict and contest. They can be quite serious, involving elder abuse and financial loss. They may also remain at the level of family rivalries and gossip. As narrated to me, each case implies a false accusation unfairly used against an older woman. While the formal program did not yield a legal case to submit in court, GAR staff used informal methods of negotiation and conflict resolution to help in cases brought to their attention. . . .

Lessons from Camps

My first trip began with Gambaga. "We get people like you all the time," was the general response I received upon arrival. This was evident from the numerous signs posted to advertise the good work of USAID and NGO projects. Gambaga was hardly an isolated village trapped in time but was rather the ongoing recipient of outsider beneficiaries and travelers.

I located an NGO guesthouse. The staff first criticized me for bringing a young man as a translator and then introduced me to a replacement. Hawa, a woman who is Mamprusi and has lived in Gambaga, became translator, guide and friend. . . .

The first step was to meet David, who ran an NGO sponsored by the Presbyterian Church called the Go-Home Project. Although David no longer works there, and the NGO project ended in 2009, the church's ministry had been the only longstanding intervention presence in the camp. This ministry to the accused witches began in the 1960s, and the Go-Home Project was established in 1994. . . . The project provided charity, such as funds for school fees, and income generating projects but the work stressed to me in 2005 was about family conflict resolution. David acted as a social worker to investigate cases, meet with families, and negotiate return. Investigation included whether the person was married, if any children were grown or not, if family came to visit, whether the relationship seemed cordial, and if there was family back home who would care for her. As David explained, he visited the families to find out if people back home were not happy and/or likely to kill her. . . . Sometimes he was successful, and reported the project had helped 300 women. . . .

David complained of how outside groups come from the capital and only stay a short time. He was particularly angry at a national women's legal organization, whom he said only came for one day and used his report. When CNN came a few days later, he refused to give them the report. When I asked about an anti-witchcraft poster David had in his office he said dismissively, "That's just awareness creation." After we talked and he gave me instructions on how to be sensitive to the chief's concern about bad press, I had dinner with Hawa. During dinner, she told me of how she was once bewitched by an aunt and the next morning, I followed the next expected step, which was to greet the chief and seek his permission to interview the women. The chief answered my questions curtly, and narrated the common origin story of how he became guardian of the witches. That is, some generations ago, people fled to a local Imam for protection from persecution and in fear of their lives. Because this matter concerned traditional beliefs, the Imam told the Gambaga chief that he should look after them. The current chief, therefore, inherited this responsibility along with the ability to detect and disarm witches of their powers.

Conversation with several women willing to meet me was awkward. My impression was that the women had a short but precise agenda to protect themselves by protecting the chief and the Go Home staff. For example, when asked about growing older, one response was, "It's good to grow old here in the camp because the chief takes care of us." And in response to asking, "Why are you here?" came the response, "Because there is no peace in the house."

The interviews were a repetition of typical responses already published in blogs and news stories. Each woman had been falsely accused through blame for an illness, accident, or death. There was enough ongoing tension in the family that they were advised by a chief or determined on their own that it was better to stay in the camp. In asking Hawa about why published stories are so uniform, she replied that most seemed to get details "from the outside." Outside in this case

both refers to people living outside the village as well as people with outside agendas, such as NGOs that are trying to establish themselves through intervention projects.

"You Can Not Believe and You Can Not Not Believe"

Hawa continued to help bridge the gap between a staged trip and what the realities might be for people living in Gambaga. . . . [W]e talk about witchcraft along with her friends and family. One person explained that witchcraft is used to "progress." Sometimes, people are merely jealous and use witchcraft to prevent progress in others. White men, however, have used witchcraft to create things like TV and cell phones. In other words, witchcraft can be positive and negative. Apparently, younger women are more likely to stay in the camps temporarily and then leave. People have more faith in rehabilitation for younger people. Sometimes younger people simply have more strength and willingness to leave the area completely and move to the capital. Whether those accused of witchcraft actually stay has a lot to do with whether they have any other place where they can go. In addition to the witches, others also come to live in the camps. Sometimes, children are sent to live with the witch and help them out. This continues a common cultural practice of fostering young children among family members. In a different example, a man followed the woman to the camp and tried to help her return with the help of David. She was not accepted but they married and eventually settled outside the camp. The popular image of total banishment and isolation turns out to be more complex in practice. Young children sent to care for the accused also benefit from funds given by the Go-Home project to pay for school fees. The local hospital no longer charges for visits. . . .

Hawa also told her story of bewitchment a few more times. The story begins with an unexplained and persistent illness. She is having panic attack. She seeks help from the hospital and was given medication for heartburn. When she returns to the hospital, she refuses the medication because it is the same as before. In one version, she [is] sent to live with the chief for a year. In most versions, she has a dream in which her aunt drives a stake into her chest, exactly where it hurts. Initially, her father resists accusing the aunt but Hawa is not getting better. In one version, the aunt has already been accused of bewitching another family member. Although the woman protests that she is not a witch, her daughters say things that indicate they know she is guilty. Five chickens are killed, and all of them indicate guilt. The woman then confesses that she has taken Hawa's spirit and turned it into a cockroach. The insect is in a jar in the garbage dump. The jar is found, proving the truth of the confession. The aunt stays for a short time in the camp, is "de-witched," and returns home. Hawa sleeps well for the first time the night after the conviction and does not have major health problems after that. As she says of her experience, "You can not believe and you can not not believe." . . .

"Our Names Have Traveled to Places We Have Not Been"

. . . I also visited two more camps. . . . Kukuo was described as more of a "clinic" for people to be cured of witchcraft and leave. Unlike Gambaga, it was not a camp that had been created for witches but over time so many additional people had come to live there that it was becoming a town that included witches who were not segregated but part of the settlement. . . .

Ngnani is a much bigger camp and has both men and women. As many as four to ten people arrive each week but many also return within a week. I was told overall numbers are hard to know since some leave "so early . . . or (stay) forever." The numbers had increased quite a bit in the wake of ethnic conflict between the Dagombas and Konkonbas in 1994. . . .

There happened to be a divination in progress when we arrived, and we were allowed to observe. The basic activities were those already described in the literature—the focal point is when a bird is pierced and everyone watches as it dies to see which way it falls. If it dies face down, the person is guilty, and if face up, the person is innocent. The first bird indicated guilt, and so the woman protested and the ritual was repeated. Unfortunately, the second one was the same. There followed a sort of pause. Everyone seemed to accept the outcome.

In these conversations with twenty women in Ngnani and one leader in Kukuo, I'm told that there is more concern about witchcraft than in the past, and

more false accusations. I also learn more about family ties, as recorded in my fieldnotes:

> The family brings you or you bring yourself. Once you are old, you need protection and seek help from the god at the shrine in Dagbon, when you become old, likely they accuse you, you don't have to wait and go for protection and some stay and beat them. . . . Once they are here, they are under the protection of the shrine. You go here and take medicine at the shrine. If your family is strong, you are sent back to the community. Otherwise, find an old lady for you to stay with and you move in. The family collaborates with community members to put up the house (where you live). The family provides material, the people around help to build it. The family might come with a child and prepare food and help. . . . There is still a link (to family). Especially if you came here voluntarily, the family will follow up.

Some of the women were there because they had followed when their mothers were accused of witchcraft. Over time, it was easier for them to stay. . . .

When asked about NGO work, replies were that groups and individuals sometimes come. They usually only come once, donate some things, and then leave. . . . Although most were not aware of media stories, one translated response was, "Some time ago, they came and shot pictures and later those on radio heard stories and voices of colleagues and they were happy, realized their names have gone far—even to where they had not gone."

The camps are a complicated site for ethnographic work given the range of interlocutors and familiarity with the iconic representation of witches camps as a rights violation. However, even a brief visit revealed how there is more variation in accusations and aftermath than the simple politicized story of an old woman wrongfully accused of loss or misfortune, who is then permanently banished by ignorant family. There is a disproportionate number of older women [but] . . . [t]his does not mean that only old women are accused but rather older women who are unable to resist accusations are also unlikely to have resources to leave if the family will not take them back. The women may first arrive as daughters or grandchildren expected to support the accused relative, and then have to stay.

"Awareness Creation" Versus "Bringing Peace in the House"

The camps are attractive as a human rights problem to tackle and yet sustained engagement is rare. Awareness creation takes place in conferences held far from the camps, and through sporadic public presentations that are unlikely to change deeply ingrained beliefs that seem to explain otherwise unexplainable loss. Political struggle over resources, whether at the micro level of families or the more macro level of communities, are unlikely to be resolved through lectures or brochures. Existential questions of why one person succeeds while another fails or falls ill are not really answered by rational or scientific explanations. The "dark side" of kinship is not simply eradicated by passionate speeches against ageism or sexism. These explanations could be reasons why a women's legal aid organization raised funds to "free" the witches in 1998 but most of the women refused to leave. One who did return had her ear cut off and came back to the Gambaga camp with a warning that the other ear would be cut off if she attempted to return again (Ameyibor 1998). Bringing peace to ensure a safer return requires greater engagement, time, and persistence.

The few examples of successful intervention learned through GAR and through the Go-Home project were examples of informal conflict resolution. This requires direct engagement with perpetrators of accusation and abuse that might result in partial rather than total victory. . . .[T]his requires working with those who caused harm and who may feel they are victims rather than perpetrators. GAR staff, for example, were not able to convince the son that his mother was not a witch but they were able to provide her with food and clothing.

Accepting spiritual beliefs while trying to address dimensions of abuse is also consistent with culturally sensitive gerontological and social work practice. Another culturally sensitive dimension to this intervention is to use mediation. That is, a common response to interpersonal conflict in Ghana is to seek a third party who can fairly assess the situation and advise but not impose a solution (Lowy 1973). The mediator role is to convene meetings for communication and reconciliation. GAR staff and David became mediators when asked, and also negotiated to play that role in seeking to bring peace in families and communities. . . .

Conclusion

. . . In their intervention work, Ghanaian rights advocates are keen to highlight problems not of witchcraft beliefs but of false accusation. In fact, what seems like rallying against superstition can be interpreted as a means of upholding cultural values that respect older adults. Rather than focus on witchcraft accusations as an older woman's rights problem, a more useful approach may be to address harmful accusations as a form of elder abuse that disproportionately impacts women. One parallel between witchcraft accusations and elder abuse as studied in the U.S. and globally is that elder abuse is not a typical part of aging for most older adults, and neglect by caregivers is a far more common problem than outright physical attack (Statistic Brain 2013). In other words, attention to the camps is important but may miss more commonly experienced marginalization and neglect. Another is that abusers are most commonly family members, and thus elder abuse is another example of "the dark side of kinship" (Anetzberger 2012, Statistic Brain 2013). A third parallel is in risk factors. That is, one identifying risk factor identified in elder abuse is caregiver dependency upon older adults for housing and money (Anetzberger 2012; Phelan 2013, 14–22), which is reminiscent of the man who accused his mother when he was "struggling in life." Another risk factor is marginalized status within family systems. The story of the man who kept his mother in a structure reminds me of a legal case in the U.S. portion of my study. An older woman was dependent on a son who severely neglected her and provided only chips and soda for food. Successful prosecution would have also removed the primary caregiver. If this case were in Ghana, the informal solution of family conflict mediation would be likely.

. . . [E]lder advocacy [should be viewed] as culturally mediated intervention work. Within rights based discourse, the moral boundaries of witchcraft violations appear far more clear than they may to those who genuinely fear witches. Whether one believes or not, the reduction of witchcraft to a problem of violence against women of whatever age misses a larger social context of ambiguity, contingency, and negotiation. More importantly, the solution to simply banish beliefs or force change has been resisted in the camps and does not seem to be taking root in the country as a whole. As in studies of advice on AIDS and substance abuse intervention, one moral (or scientific) system cannot simply replace another as an explanatory framework or means of resolving social drama (Farmer 1990; Roy et al. 2011). However, more modest intervention goals seem to have been possible. . . . [I]t seems that GAR and the Go-Home Project have achieved some success by working from within cultural systems and negotiating with abusive accusers. . . .

References

Ameyibor, Edward. 1998. "CULTURE-GHANA: 'Witches' Refuse to Go Home." Inter Press Service (IPS). http://www.ipsnews. net/1998/07/culture-ghana-witches-refuse-to-go-home/.

Anetzberger, Georgia. 2012. "An Update on the Nature and Scope on Elder Abuse." GENERATIONS: Journal of the American Society on Aging 36(3):12-20.

Badoe, Yaba. 2011. "The Witches of Gambaga: What it Means to be a Witch in the Northern Region of Ghana." Jenda 19.

Ciekawy, Diane, and Peter Geschiere. 1998. "Containing Witchcraft: Conflicting Scenarios in Postcolonial Africa." African Studies Review 41(3):1–14.

Drucker-Brown, Susan. 1993. "Mamprusi Witchcraft, Subversion and Changing Gender Relations." Africa 63(4): 531–549.

Farmer, Paul. 1990. "Sending Sickness: Sorcery, Politics, and Changing Concepts of AIDS in Rural Haiti." Medical Anthropology Quarterly 4(1): 6–27.

Hoch-Smith, Judith. 1978. "The Witch and the Prostitute." In Women in Ritual and Symbolic Roles, edited by Judith Hoch-Smith and Anita Spring, 245–267. New York: Plenum Press.

Lowy, Michael. 1973. "Modernizing the American Legal System: An Example of the Peaceful use of Anthropology." Human Organization 32(2):205–209.

Palmer, Karen. 2010. Spellbound: Inside West Africa's Witches Camps. New York: Free Press.

Parker, John. 2006. "Northern Gothic: Witches, Ghosts and Werewolves in the Savanna Hinterland of the Gold Coast 1900s–1950s." Africa 76(3): 352–380.

Phelan, Amanda. 2013. "Elder Abuse: An Introduction." In International Perspectives on Elder Abuse, edited by Amanda Phelan, 1–23. London: Routledge.

Roy, Elise, Nelson Arruda, and Phillipe Bourgois. 2011. "The Growing Popularity of Prescription Opioid Injection in Downtown Montreal: New Challenges for Harm Reduction." Substance Use & Misuse 46: 1142–1150.

Sanders, Todd. 2003. Reconsidering Witchcraft: Postcolonial Africa and Analytic (Un)Certainties. American Anthropologist 105.2: 338–352.

Simmons, William. 1980. "Powerlessness, Exploitation, and the Soul-Eating Witch: An Analysis of Bedyaranke Witchcraft." American Ethnologist 7(3): 447–465.

Smith, David. 2010. "Ghanaian Woman Burned to Death for being a 'Witch.'" The Guardian, November 29. Accessed October 7, 2013. http://www.theguardian.com/world/2010/nov/29/ghanaian-woman-burned-death-witch Statistic Brain. 2013. "Elderly Abuse Statistics." Research Date: June 18, 2013. Accessed October 18, 2013. http://www.statisticbrain.com/elderly-abuse-statistics/.

Stewart, Pamela, and Andrew Strathern. 2003. Witchcraft, Sorcery, Rumors, and Gossip. Cambridge: Cambridge University Press.

Van der Geest, Sjaak. 2002a. "Respect and Reciprocity: Care of Elderly People in Rural Ghana." Journal of Cross-Cultural Gerontology 17: 3–31.

Van der Geest, Sjaak. 2002b. "From Wisdom to Witchcraft: Ambivalence towards Old Age in Rural Ghana." Africa 72 (3): 437–463.

Van der Geest, Sjaak. 2007. "Complaining and Not Complaining: Social Strategies of Older People in Kwahu, Ghana." Global Ageing 4, no. 3.

Whitaker, Kati. 2012. "Hundreds of Women Trapped in Ghana's 'Witch Camps'; Up to a Thousand Elderly Women in Ghana have been Banished to Remote Camps as Alleged Witches." Telegraph (UK), 30 August 2012. Accessed October 7 2013. http://www.telegraph.co.uk/ news/worldnews/africaandindian ocean/ghana/9509493/ Hundreds-of-women-trapped-in-Ghanas-witch-camps.html

3.3 The Politics of Righteousness: Race and Gender in Apostolic Pentecostalism

JUDITH CASSELBERRY

Religious ideas provide believers with meaning and understanding to navigate their social worlds. In the following selection, Casselberry explores the ways in which black women negotiate power through the teachings and practice of Apostolic Pentecostalism. The author draws on fieldwork in a New York–based Holiness-Pentecostal denomination to examine the ways in which women incorporate doctrines of female submission in ways that at once observe an obedience to God and male church authority, while also providing them with an authority to "lead from the background" or practice "acceptable disobedience" in intra-racial and inter-gender relationships in the home, workplace, and church.

Questions

1. What was Robert Lawson's purpose in recalling African contributions in antiquity and early Christianity in The Anthropology of Jesus?
2. Discuss what Casselberry means by saying that Lawson's theology placed Black women in the body of Christ. What are the implications of this for women's ability to negotiate power and for their strategies for negotiation of power?
3. Provide examples of how women in Casselberry's case study "lead from the background."
4. Provide examples of how women in Casselberry's case study engage in "acceptable disobedience"?
5. Discuss public stances about women's submission. Do spiritual leaders' statements about women's position vary by gender? If so, how?
6. In what ways do the themes Casselberry raises resonate with your own spiritual beliefs and doctrines?

The obstacles and the challenges that you face in a corporation as a Black female[,] . . . that glass ceiling. . . . I mean, when I got to where I was, I should have been there like ten years ago actually. But[,] . . . being a Black female, forget it. . . . [E]very door was closing. . . . God, He keeps you focused. That's [because of daily] six o'clock [morning] prayer [services]. Prayer works. You cannot bend from God in the life of Jesus.

—MOTHER REEVES, TRUE DELIVERANCE
CHURCH OF THE APOSTOLIC FAITH, INC.

Caseselberry, Judith. 2013. The Politics of Righteousness: Race and Gender in Apostolic Pentecostalism. *Transforming Anthropology*, 21: 72-86.

Mother Reeves recently retired as an assistant vice-president of sales with Chase Corporation where she handled private clients' multi-million dollar portfolios. According to her testimony, divine intervention mediates intersecting systemic forces of racism and sexism in a personalized manner, and her own career advances came as a direct result of rigorous religious practices. Mother Reeves is an Apostolic Pentecostal and member of Queens, New York–based True Deliverance Church (TDC). True Deliverance is part of the Church of Our Lord Jesus Christ of the Apostolic Faith, Inc. (COOLJC), arguably the most orthodox denomination within African American Holiness-Pentecostalism.

At the heart of Apostolic doctrine and identity is a system that privileges spiritual authority and a church polity that excludes women by prohibiting their ordination. Male-headed church hierarchy operates in concert with doctrine that espouses submission and obedience as central tenets. Women are required to submit and be obedient to God, male church authority, and their husbands, while men's acquiescence is to God and men of higher rank. . . . [W]omen cannot serve as deacons and cannot be ordained as elders and ministers. Moreover, stringent dogma regarding appearance and comportment is codified most rigorously on women's bodies, thereby positioning women at the center of discourses of power, submission, and obedience. Nevertheless, spiritual power is available to women and men alike through conversion, evidenced by speaking in tongues and more fully developed by adhering to doctrine—"righteous living." . . .

"Women of Color in the Ancestry of Jesus Christ"

. . . Early in my fieldwork, Mother Thomas directed me to an extra-biblical source for interpreting COOLJC women's holy identities: the theological writings of the organization's founder, Robert C. Lawson. "If you want to understand more about the women in the church you have to read Lawson," she advised. . . .

Robert C. Lawson (1883–1961) founded the Church of Our Lord Jesus Christ of the Apostolic Faith, Inc. (COOLJC) in 1919, in Harlem, New York. As a theologian, he operated both at the center and on the margins of early 20th century Pan-African discourse. . . .

Lawson identified with Africa as a source of Black political and religious consciousness. . . .

As participants in (or a thorn in the side of) American civil society, Black theologians, church leaders, and congregants were part and parcel of national discourses on race. Lawson's church emerged at a time when the eugenics movement had insinuated itself into science, social policy, popular culture, and education. Churches, key organizations within the Black public sphere, brought people together in religious settings while sustaining the quest for black liberation and "respectability" (E. B. Brown 1994; Higginbotham 1993). Holiness-Pentecostal churches operated within the mainstream of the Black religious milieu of liberation and respectability, yet simultaneously on the margins by forwarding distinctive theologies (Taylor 1994). To this end, in 1925 Lawson published *The Anthropology of Jesus Our Kinsman (Dedicated to the Glory of God and to the Help of Solving the Race Problem)*, which espoused an "afro-biblical" analysis, linking early African civilization, biblical history, and theology.

. . . Lawson wanted to establish an anti-racist theology for Christians in America, as well as eradicate racist attitudes of White Christian missionaries outside of America—a hindrance to "soul saving." . . .

Lawson had at least two purposes in recalling African contributions in antiquity, and thus to early Christianity. First, he wanted to instill in Black Christians, specifically Pentecostals, entitlement to full religious participation. Lawson's central argument in this regard states that God had deliberately created Jesus' mixed bloodline, Hamitic, Semitic, and Japhetic. If all three races contributed to the ethnic lineage of Jesus then the atonement was for all, giving equal access to his salvation and blessings. Tracing Jesus' Hamitic genealogy in Biblical scripture, he argued that Mary, the progeny of David and the tribe of Judah, descended in part from "two Negro [Canaanite] women," Shuar and Tamar. "Thus," he maintained, ". . . [i]f any race have whereof to boast as touching things of the flesh, relative to our Lord Jesus Christ, the colored race has more, for they gave to the world the two mothers of the tribe of Judah, out of which Christ came. . . . The fact that Christ had Negro blood in him is vitally connected with our redemption through Calvary" (Lawson 1969 [1925]: 24–26, 30).

Second, Lawson looked to combat religious segregationists' racist interpretation of biblical scripture, as they aimed to exclude Black people from full religious, societal, and political belonging. "Our brethren of the white race are laboring under a handicap," he asserted. "[T]heir spiritual condition is deplorable. To see them laboring under the two ideals, once [sic] racial and the other spiritual, trying to adjust themselves according to two different principles, makes them cowards in one sense and hypocritical in another" (Lawson 1969 [1925]: 1). In concert with many Black theologians and adherents, Lawson identified racism as a moral issue at odds with Christian ethics.

Placing his theology at the center of the contemporary race mixing debate, Lawson read Christ's body as divinely multiracial. His claim struck a blow at fears of miscegenation, which had become pervasive within popular culture, social science, and law (Baker 1998). Through deliberate intermarriage, he argued, God "intensified" the strong "psychic and spiritual" traits of Abraham, "the Semitic contribution to the anthropological development of Jesus Christ." While Hamitic women contributed their "warm, loving, peaceful, sympathetic, and moral" nature to Christ's lineage.

Ascribing human qualities on the basis of race and gender is fundamentally flawed. Nevertheless, Lawson's theology undoubtedly had a profound impact on his predominately Black female following. He conveyed ideal female attributes that holy women should aspire toward, indicating they were qualities of the Christ—at once human and divine. Not only did Christ arrive via a woman's body but also by racial and gendered association, Lawson's theology placed Black women *in* the body of Christ. Jesus' "Negro blood" flowed by way of women's veins. More than having access to salvation, the blood Jesus shed on the cross *was* their blood, placing them at the center of the atonement.

In 1949, Lawson printed an open letter in the organization-wide journal, *Contender for the Faith*, summarizing his theology. "Is it a surprise to you to know," he began, "that a 'Colored' woman was the first mother of the Tribe of Judah?" His reiteration two decades after the original publication ensured that new generations of Apostolics understood vital elements of founding theology. Over fifty years later and thirty-four years after Lawson's passing, church leadership issued yet another reprint. The Fall 2000 issue of *Contender* carried Lawson's 1949 letter in an article entitled, "Remembering Words from Our Founder, Bishop R. C. Lawson: Women of Color in the Ancestry of Jesus Christ" (2000: 32). These two reprints, 1949 and 2000,

show that Lawson's theology is not just archival but carried forward into late 20th and early 21st century Apostolic hermeneutics and identity. . . .

Lawson's ideology regarding gendered characteristics informed his position on church women's formal leadership. . . . Although, according to Lawson, "Negro" women's blood runs through Christ, church polity belongs to men.

Men's official leadership pathway is brother, deacon, minister, (officially ordained) elder, bishop, and apostle. . . .

The assumption that all men will rise to a titled position carries complex consequences for both women and men. Many young adult women assert that boys and young men receive formal mentoring, while girls and young women do not. Yet, as majority, women hold most positions within auxiliaries, which effectively creates unique female space within a male hierarchical structure. At the same time, patriarchal structure may negatively impact male membership, contributing to the church's gender imbalance. Pressure to rise to leadership contributes to men leaving once they reach young adulthood. . . .

Men's titles become markers of identity beyond young adulthood. Marking progress through public naming does not exist for women over the course of their church life. Women are not considered eligible to rise to Mother until their senior years. "See, all the brothers need to become deacons or ministers eventually," said Sister James, a single woman in her late-twenties. "As a woman, you're just a sister." Bishop Lawson's bifurcated gender ideology *politically* fixes men to church while *spiritually* fastening women. At the same time, as we will see, Lawson's unambiguous stance against racial oppression remains foundational to COOLJC members' identity, which women carry along with spiritual authority into the world.

"[You're] Supposed to be Successful in Life. . . . [You're] Holy Ghost Filled!"

Apostolic women neither shun public titles nor carry the doctrine of submission into their professional lives. Many have advanced degrees and careers that place them in supervisory positions over male workers. Black American women's advances in education, occupation, and professionalization are mirrored across Holiness-Pentecostal denominations. . . . Cheryl Townsend Gilkes notes that, "Even among those women who sincerely believe that preaching is a man's province (and sometimes even more among such women) there is a tradition of a militant assertion of personhood and a sincere belief in their own competence and capabilities in the larger society" (2001:108–109).

This rings true within COOLJC. Mother Reeves, a minister's wife, supports tenets of male hierarchy within church polity, and her "belief in [her] own competence and capabilities in the larger society" was crucial in the journey from agrarian life to urban corporate culture at Chase Bank. In 1970, while in her mid-twenties, she moved from rural North Carolina to New York City with her husband and four young sons. The daughter of sharecroppers, after the age of ten years she spent school breaks working the fields, mostly picking cotton ("I had to get that 200 pounds of cotton per day") and sometimes vegetables and fruits. Reeves always thrived in school, yet she gave up two full-tuition college scholarships to marry. She had completed some college and worked as a substitute teacher when the family ventured north. Once in New York, she secured a secretarial position at Chase Bank. She described the climate to me:

> Blacks had just began to . . . become tellers. [Management] didn't trust 'em with the money and stuff. [Most Black people] had the background, cleaning the mailroom, all that kind of good stuff. . . . I found out there was a book that I could read that would teach me anything that I wanted to know in banking. So that became my lunch every day, every day. . . . I found out that nobody was gonna teach me anything because I was Black.

Through diligence, by 1988 she ascended the ranks of the corporation to assistant vice-president, which entailed her surpassing (primarily White) male managers and negotiating peer relationships that changed as she advanced into supervisory positions. Mother Reeves understands her goals and achievements in the context of holiness. "God, He makes that possible," she told me, referring to her corporate success, "because He keeps you, to break the chains that hold you and binds you up. Because not only do you have the White managers that don't want you to be there, you got your everyday co-workers. . . . [Y]ou become their manager and you have to stay humble.

God keeps you humble." She explained how staying in God's humility through prayer guided her management strategies, style, and ethics. Going out of her way to teach coworkers all she had learned, she helped them to advance in their careers. Even though managers disapproved of her style, she persisted. She rejected the idea of adopting strategies "not of God." So while she drew strength from her practices of faith, incorporating management strategies aligned with holiness principles proved to be a source of contention with her superiors. She explained:

> [M]y manager is saying to me, . . . "You're not rigid enough." I'm not cold-hearted enough. . . . They want me to do the wrong thing. When with God I can't just tell you lies. . . . So that held me back from accomplishing my goals long ago. [But,] God brought me the best of clients, and I managed the best of monies. I had a portfolio of $163 million [and] a client base of 685 souls or clients, households that I managed. . . . [There were] fifty-seven branches in Manhattan and I always ranked in the top five. . . . If you're a White male and I'm a Black female, . . . if you want to feel that [you're superior], that's fine. But what brings me there is what I do. . . . God will make me the head and never the tail. . . . I always told them that. Woe unto you! You might as well have a millstone around your neck as to hurt me, because you really don't know what you're doing! I've seen God move all the managers, just move them away from me. Turn it all around. That's through prayer and supplication.

By her analysis, Mother Reeves' promotions were delayed by oppression operating at the intersections of religion, race, and gender. Bringing lived holiness into her work ethic compounded her already fraught political position as an African American woman in the corporate world. Yet ultimately, by her testimony, it assured her success.

According to Bishop Cook, the 82-year-old pastor of TDC, righteous living, spiritual empowerment, and racial achievement are inextricably linked. During one Sunday's sermon, he instructed, "[We have to] fight against the system that thinks a Black man can't be successful in the Lord. . . . [You're] supposed to be successful in life because God is blessing you. [You're]

Holy Ghost filled!" Bishop Cook's charge to, "fight against the system that thinks a Black man can't be successful in the Lord," is meant and understood as both specific to Black manhood and general to "the race." After a Monday night's Bible study, he used an announcement as an opportunity to encourage women and men to "move higher." "The Building Committee met with the lawyer[,] . . . a young smart Apostolic woman," he told the congregation. "It's good that women are really going someplace." . . .

A holy woman's educational and career advances translate into racial progress in general, "fight[ing] against the system" while exemplifying the successful "Holy Ghost-filled" church member. Bishop Cook holds individuals responsible for maintaining the proper relationship with God, which allows them to set and reach their goals. Nonetheless, he instructs women to use spiritual leadership to improve the conditions of Black men in their lives. On the one hand, this calls into question women's position as submissive. On the other hand, he is seeking to bring/return men to their "natural" position as head of women. On Mother's Day the sermon topic was "The Wisdom of Mothers," wherein "mother" carried a dual meaning—natural mothers and spiritual Mothers. He told the congregation, "There is a conspiracy against the Black man. A wedge has been driven, but the mother can break that yoke. Help your son to be successful in life. Teach your son how to be a man, not a weakling! . . . Many Black women have been successful. . . . [T]each [men] that they can have leadership. . . . It's gonna take the Mothers, the women, to bring the men out."

Bishop Cook's directives highlight expectations and experiences of churchwomen. Women thwart the "conspiracy against the Black man" by teaching men "leadership," "how to be successful in life," and "how to be a man." The underlying assumption that women possess these qualities, or have sufficient insight to pass them on, elevates them to distinctive positions of authority—with the added responsibility of elevating the "race." COOLJC members grapple with secular racial politics and the struggle for full societal inclusion within the context of holiness. Bishop Cook calls on women as spiritual leaders to mitigate the impact of systemic oppression. This is the same authority and race consciousness Mother Reeves carried into Chase Corporation's Manhattan offices. . . .

"I Might Be Disobedient, But God Forgive Me"

One morning in Adult Sunday school class, Mother Pea, the 92-year-old "Church Mother" of TDC, expounded on "the proper place of women." She told the women, "Let the man lead. Don't push ahead. Stay in the background. God made woman a great thing. A lot of women don't know how great they are. God made man first. Let him be first. Let him know he can make it." As senior Mother of the church, Mother Pea instructs women in the ways of holiness. Directives to her Sunday school students indicate that women allow men to lead. And they must consciously work at doing it. Taken in conjunction with Bishop Cook's Mother's Day sermon, women let men lead after they have taught them how to lead. . . . Successfully following Mother Pea's dictates to not "push ahead" and "stay in the background" demonstrates "struggle, effort, exertion, and achievement" (Mahmood 2005:29). Moreover, "stay[ing] in the background," just as choosing to lead, is a choice, exhibiting agency.

. . . Apostolic adherents employ the language of submission and obedience—men in relation to God and women in relation to God and men. . . . Women are required to submit to formal male leadership within the church polity and to their husbands. Both arenas of submission, however, are quite nuanced. . . . In relationships with men in the church community and their husbands, women's strategies include negotiated submission, leading from the background, and acceptable disobedience.

Within church operations, "letting men lead" sometimes requires that women lead from the background. I was unwittingly involved in one such incident. Over the course of my two years in TDC, I participated in the "New Converts" Sunday school class. The name is somewhat misleading; the class is for any adult newcomer, whether converted or not, and is team-taught by Minister Lee and Mother England. . . . During one Sunday's class, Minister Anderson, Superintendent of Sunday School, approached me during the lesson. "Next week I want you to move to the Young Adults class," he told me. "Monica and Jeffrey both work on Sundays now so, they need more people over there." I nodded in agreement, of course, and he walked off. Immediately pausing her lesson, Mother England told me, "You're staying here," then continued teaching. I nodded in agreement, of course, thinking, "How is this going to work?" Aside from concern about my perceived dilemma, I found Mother England's semi-public override of Minister Anderson instructive. She did not seem concerned that the other ten class attendees, including Minister Lee, heard the exchange.

After the lesson, I was standing next to Mother England with Minister Lee a few feet away when Minister Anderson returned. "Be sure to go over to the Young Adults next week," he reiterated. Not knowing how to respond, I gave him a slight smile. As he walked off, Mother England said, "Don't worry about that. You come back here next week. I'll let him know." In a mildly exasperated tone she continued, "You don't belong over there. He should know that." Minister Lee remained silent throughout but nodded in agreement with Mother England's last statement.

At issue was prioritizing administrative business over spiritual business. As administrator of Sunday school, Minister Anderson's concerns included keeping all the classes adequately populated. As a spiritual leader, Mother England knew I was not "saved" and, according to church protocol, should remain in New Converts until after I had received the Holy Ghost and moved to a new level of spiritual maturity. Traditionally, she "graduated" students out by letting them know it was time to move on to the Young Adult or Adult class (depending on their age).

At the time of this exchange, I had been attending TDC services for a year. Six months earlier, Bishop Cook told the congregation I was an anthropologist conducting fieldwork. It was common knowledge that I was not saved, thus Mother England's exasperation with Minister Anderson's directive. Her spiritual leadership did not, in Mahmood's terms, "disrupt the existing power relations." She was not challenging his official position; she was exerting her own spiritual authority. I was not privy to any subsequent exchange between them, so the details of their negotiation remain unclear. However, the next week I returned to the New Converts class and my relationship with Minister Anderson stayed intact; he had no expectation of me following his directive.

Outside of church, tenets of submission do not necessarily carry into women's social relationships with male church leadership. One Sunday evening after services, I accompanied Sister Holmes and her three children to Minister and Sister Clark's home. He is in his early forties and Sister Clark in her late thirties. They tend to have an open door policy (in fact, it is rarely locked) and young people frequently gather in their Queens home. They have three young sons, so the house is always a whirlwind of activity. On this evening, Camille Roland and Anna Highland, both in their mid-twenties, and sixteen-year-old Tamara Jones were there. Minister Clark was holding court in his recliner. Stocky and strong from years of construction work, he is a gregarious and opinionated man who loves to "witness" about Jesus.

Minister Clark had not given the sermon at services; the younger Minister Thomas had preached. Thomas has a fiery style and, as one of the young boys told me, "He keeps it real," meaning his messages are direct. On this day, he preached about temptation and staying holy, specifically "keeping your body," and his message became the topic of conversation. Minister Clark was not pleased with Thomas' detailed personal example, as he had used a situation in his own life to explicate his message. Thomas was attracted to a female coworker and she to him. By his testimony, it was an intense physical pull that he fought hard to resist. Camille, Anna, and Sister Holmes all vehemently disagreed with Minister Clark, arguing that transparency in the pulpit had a greater impact on the congregation.

. . . . I was struck by the way the young women debated with the minister. They had no qualms about raising their voices or interrupting him to make their points. They never backed down from their position. Nor did he seem to expect they would. Given the rhetoric of female submission, I was surprised by the level playing field of the debate.

As evidenced by Mother England's strategy with Minister Anderson, in church, women exercise prudence when disagreeing with leadership. Yet, the women in Minister Clark's home were outspoken and direct. This is understandable in the context of a few variables. First, the women challenged Minister Clark's opinion, not a decision, and being outside the church building may have provided more leeway in communication. Second, they all enjoy social familiarity and closeness to Clark. Sister Holmes, also in her early forties, has known Minister Clark since they were teens, and he is like an uncle to the younger women. Last, the women's achievements in the world imbue them with "a sincere belief in their own competence and capabilities," which includes debating effective preaching strategies with a minister (Gilkes 2001:109). Sister Holmes holds a master's degree and has occupied various leadership positions with New York's Board of Education, both paid and volunteer, at local school and citywide levels. Anna is a graduate student, and Camille enjoys a successful career in corporate management. Like Mother England, each woman claims life-long active membership in COOLJC (attending multiple weekly services) and dedication to the ways of holiness. The women's assertiveness exemplifies a refusal to be submissive that is acceptable, not only to them, but to Minister Clark as well.

Studies extending the reach of tenets of submission into nearly all areas of Black religious women's lives fail to appreciate the nuances of women's interpretive strategies (A. L. Brown 1994). While adhering to the doctrine and rhetoric of submission, women in COOLJC do not view themselves as subordinate to men and by extension do not see themselves as inherently lower than their husbands in status, or secondary in importance. During a service on "Family Relationships," Mother Reeves spoke about the biblical ideal of spousal relationships. "Marriage. . . is designed by God, not man," she instructed. "God gave [Adam] woman to be [a] helpmeet . . . not a slave, not a housekeeper, not someone subservient, but equal partners." At the same time, she emphasized man's duty as provider. "Don't marry someone who's gonna lay on your mama's couch," she warned. "It's solely man's responsibility to take care of his wife and family, but a wife can decide to work if she has the desire to work." At the culmination of service, Bishop Cook addressed the congregation. "I'm from the old school," he asserted. "Man should work and the wife shouldn't. My wife wanted to work. So, she did."

Clearly, women's submission to husbands occurs on negotiated terrain that both men and women acknowledge. Public exchanges, like the one between Mother Reeves and Bishop Cook, inform members' ideas concerning acceptable parameters of marital relations. . . .

Sister Lee, the wife of Minister Lee (the New Converts Sunday school teacher), described one example of the balance of power within the church. In her mid-forties, she was baptized in the Holy Spirit at the extraordinarily young age of five and has remained deeply entrenched in the church ever since. The Lees have been married for over twenty-five years and have two children. Sister Lee spoke to me about an exchange she had with Bishop Cook prior to her husband being appointed deacon:

> You see the wife has a big role. [Bishop Cook] came to me and said, these are not his exact words, but, is your husband ready to be a deacon? Is your husband deacon material? That's not exactly what he said, but that's what he meant. What is he doing in the home? I was able to say, "He's a good husband. I want him to go to church more." He didn't go to church like I did. When we first got married, although he was saved, he didn't have that zeal that I had.

Sister Lee and women like her are spiritual gatekeepers to institutional leadership. Her husband's formal elevation was partially, possibly primarily, dependent on her assessment of his readiness. They are both fully aware of the impact any dissatisfaction with the partnership would have had on his ability to advance within the church structure. This type of leadership from the background remains critical to church operations. Yet, Sister Lee maintains an admittedly submissive role in their relationship, operating in a religious world with fairly fixed notions of the meanings and parameters of male and female. By her explanation gender relations are based in the Bible and biology. She told me:

> Even though the woman was made from that man and came out of that man, but it takes a strong woman, a strong mother, a strong wife to really help that man, help that husband, help that son. . . . But it does say in the Bible that women are the weaker vessel, but we're the weaker *stronger* vessel! We're strong in that we can take more. That's why a woman bears children and the man doesn't. We can take more and be under rule more.

"The weaker stronger vessel" who "can take more," is the same woman who, following Mother Pea's teachings, "let[s] men lead." Within this framework, however, men are also responsible to live holy lives. Women do not submit to their husbands if they believe their mates' wishes counter the will of God. . . . In other words, if spouses are not in agreement, the wife's assessment of her spouse's righteous living factors into the extent of her compliance.

Many women in TDC, however, are married to men who are not in the church. Some spouses have never belonged; others are "backsliders"—converted individuals who have left the church and no longer adhere to the doctrine. Women married to and living with nonbelievers navigate a wide range of circumstances. Sister Allen was born in 1944 into a South Carolina sharecropping community and raised in Holiness. She moved to New York with her twin sister at the age of seventeen. Like Sister Lee, she has always been in the church. She has been married for nearly forty years to a husband who left the church. Her situation is particularly poignant.

> My husband and I . . . were always in church together until he [backslid]. . . . [Then he would say,] "you only go to church when I say go to church." I said, "No. . . . I go to work every day, so why should I listen to you?" And my uncle that raised me [and was also pastor of the family church] said, "If your husband tell you that you can't go to church, you stay home." . . . I said, "I'm sorry, [but] . . . I want to go to church. I might be disobedient, but God forgive me."

I asked if she felt her uncle was saying obedience to her husband was more important than her obedience to God. She responded with a scriptural reference. "Like the Bible said, 'wives be obedient,' you know, 'obey your husband in the Lord,' which is right. But then also [the Bible said] 'husbands must treat your wife right.'" Referencing this scripture was also a way for her to introduce her husband's physical abuse into our conversation. I was first made aware of her brutal situation when she spoke at a Wednesday night Missionary Service some months earlier. Between disobedience to doctrine that discourages divorce and disobedience to an abusive husband, Sister Allen chose the latter, which held dire consequences. She explained:

> Every time [I] would go home [from church] my husband would treat me so bad, kick me, bite me, beat me, put a water hose on me and everything. Someone said, "If you stay home then you won't get this treatment." I said, "Well, Devil, you're a liar. I'm going to church . . . and when I get home, if I get beat up or whatever, I had a good time with the Lord." And that's why I started going [in spite of the abuse].

Her response to being advised by "someone" to stay home prompted me to ask, "Are you saying that you

didn't believe that [staying home from church] would make a difference in how he treated you?" "No," she replied. "[If I stayed home] He'd pick another reason [to be abusive,] . . . any reason. So if the dinner wasn't right, I didn't iron his shirt right, he would you know, do anything. So you know. . . . "

She trailed off and we sat in silence for a moment. Then she continued, "I said, 'Well I would be disobedient. I'm going to church.' I said, 'God have to forgive me because I feel as if, as a wife I do the wifely duty . . . why should I be penalized and stay home when I go to work every day and do my housework and take care of my family?'" Notably, in addition to performing her "wifely duty," Sister Allen predicates her authority on the fact that she "go[es] to work everyday." Participation in the workforce and her position of co-provider reinforce her self-assertion. Sister Allen is living holy and fulfilling her responsibilities, while her husband is not. She, therefore, operates from a position of acceptable disobedience, complicated by her repetitions of, "God forgive me."

Sister Allen is still with her husband. As his health declined, and their sons got older and increasingly intolerant of his abusiveness, he became less violent. . . . Sister Allen's interpretation of church doctrine, which frowns on divorce and prohibits remarriage, has been instrumental in keeping her bound in such an appalling state of affairs. I say her interpretation because, at the end of that Missionary service in which Sister Allen testified about her circumstance, Mother Pea, in concluding remarks, emphatically told Sister Allen, and in essence the entire congregation, "If you had gotten a pan and slapped him upside his head he would have backed up off you! You was too easy, but thank God. He delivered you and kept you." Mother Peas' public stance, to fight back, like Mother Reeves' and Bishop Cook's earlier statements, serve notice to the membership that women can stipulate parameters of submission and obedience. . . .

Black holy women's adherence to tenets of submission and obedience operate across a spectrum. Women avow doctrinal observance yet maintain authority to decide when it is appropriate to negotiate, lead from the background, or practice acceptable disobedience in intra-racial, inter-gender relationships. In formal interviews and casual conversations, women explained their rejection of various tenets, telling me, "*That's* not my conviction," meaning God had not yet "placed it on their heart" to adhere to a particular rule. "God is still working with me" is another explanation. There are no single or fixed definitions of submission and obedience; they are defined in context. Moreover, couching gendered resistance in religious terms—"conviction" and "God is still working"—imbues women with assurances of righteousness. . . .

References

Baker, Lee D. 1998. From Savage to Negro: Anthropology and the Construction of Race, 1896–1954. Berkeley: University of California Press.

Brown, Audrey Lawson. 1994. Afro-Baptist Women's Church and Family Roles: Transmitting Afrocentric Cultural Values. Anthropological Quarterly 67(4):173–186.

Brown, Elsa Barkley. 1994. Negotiating and Transforming the Public Sphere: African American Political Life in Transition from Slavery to Freedom. Imprint Public Culture 7:107–146.

Gilkes, Cheryl Townsend. 2001. "If It Wasn't for the Women . . .": Black Women's Experience and Womanist Culture in Church and Community. Maryknoll: Orbis Books.

Higginbotham, Evelyn Brooks. 1993. Righteous Discontent: The Women's Movement in the Black Baptist Church, 1880–1920. Cambridge: Harvard University Press.

Lawson, Robert C. 1969 [1925]. The Anthropology of Jesus Christ Our Kinsman. New York: The Church of Christ Publishing Co.

Lawson, Robert C. 2000. Women of Color in the Ancestry of Jesus Christ. In The Contender for the Faith, Fall: New York: The Church of Our Lord Jesus Christ of the Apostolic Faith, Inc.

Mahmood, Saba. 2005. Politics of Piety: The Islamic Revival and the Feminist Subject. Princeton: Princeton University Press.

Taylor, Clarence. 1994. The Black Churches of Brooklyn. New York: Columbia University Press.

3.4 Choosing Both Faith and Fun: Youth Negotiations of Moral Norms in South Beirut

LARA DEEB AND MONA HARB

How do Muslim youth negotiate morality in times of leisure? What factors influence their decisions about when and where to go out? This selection explores the moral worlds of youth in a Shi'a neighborhood of South Beirut, Lebanon. South Beirut is known globally to be a popular leisure destination catering to the young, fashionable, and pious. In what follows, Deeb and Harb illustrate how the new generation of Shi'a youth seek to have fun in ways that do not violate moral norms. Youth have a range of moral rubrics, including religious and social, to draw upon in making individual decisions about what is morally appropriate behavior. The authors illustrate that, for youth, the rules of piety are flexible, especially with respect to ideas about leisure.

Questions

1. How are the categories of "religious" and "social" valuable for analyzing morality among Shi'a Lebanese youth?
2. In what ways does moral behavior rely on the individual? Provide examples from the reading.
3. When might individuals make moral compromises? What are examples of times when pious youth might make moral compromises?
4. How are Shi'a youth different from the vanguard generation? Why? How is your own generation different from that of your parents?
5. What role do changes in religious interpretations play in generational differences in what youth find to be morally acceptable? Give examples of shifts from your own culture and faith backgrounds.

Beirut is known as a polarized city, images of cosmopolitan club-hopping youth vying with those of bearded young men toting Kalashnikovs. . . . Whether this binary opposes youth as radicals against youth as targets for development or youth as shallow consumers against youth as easily co-opted by Islamic movements, overall Muslim youth are viewed as either a challenge to development, democracy, and regional stability, or as carefree consumers at the vanguard of cultural trends.[1]

Such polarizations leave out many, including those young people who want to have fun while striving to follow moral norms in their recreation. Just as Christian youth in the USA attend dances along with bible study, many youth in the Shi'i community in the southern suburb of Beirut (Dahiya) seek to have fun that does not violate moral norms. Yet they do not do so blindly. Rather, youth often redefine those norms through their practices, interpreting injunctions in ways that may open moral codes to broader definition or limit them more stridently. . . .

"Choosing Faith and Fun: Youth Negotiations of Moral Norms in South Beirut." 2013. *Ethnos* 78 (1), 1–22. Reprinted by permission of Taylor & Francis Ltd, www.tandfonline.com.

Flexible Moral Rubrics

. . . Moral rubrics . . . are the different sets of ideals and values that are revealed and produced through discourses and actions. In some cases, they take the form of prohibitions and in other cases the form of what one "ought" to do. The dominant religious rubric at work for many Shi'i Lebanese is based on a set of values that emerge from histories of interpretations of religious texts . . . but with continual temporal manifestations through jurisprudents and innovations related to individual judgment and responsibility. The social rubric is based on values of social obligation, propriety, hierarchy, manners, and reciprocity; values shared across Lebanese society. Of course, the "religious" and the "social" are not natural categories. They are, however, categories used by many of our interlocutors and a useful heuristic for teasing apart this moral landscape. For example, without this analytic separation, we would not be able to describe why wedding invitations in particular cause such anxiety in this context. On the one hand, the religious and social are co-constructed and overlap, such that youth are able to argue that maintaining good social relations is *mu'amalat*, a value within the Islamic discursive tradition. On the other hand, clear distinctions between religious and social rubrics of morality are seen in admonishments when people violate norms: a transgression within the religious rubric (say, drinking alcohol) is described as *haram*, using the normative theological value-reference, while a transgression within the social rubric (say, failing to attend a relative's funeral) is described as *'ayb*, a commonly invoked word that means "shameful" and can be used to refer to a wide range of inappropriate behavior. What is *'ayb* is not necessarily haram and vice versa, as the former describes a violation affecting one's relationship with other people and the latter a violation affecting one's relationship with God.

In the end, what this all boils down to is that in many situations, there are multiple paths available through which one can make a moral choice, a choice understood to be good by accepted standards of behavior. And sometimes those paths converge and sometimes they conflict. From this context of multiple moral rubrics, we argue that youth practices and discourses of morality are multiple and flexible in their deployments, perhaps especially when it comes to ideas about leisure. This interpretive flexibility may also be working to redefine ideas about leisure within both the social and religious rubrics of morality. . . .

Generational Change

Why have youth negotiations of moral norms concerning leisure proliferated in the past decade? . . . We suggest that youth discussions of appropriate practice around leisure represent the continuation of a trajectory that began with the Lebanese Shi'i Islamic mobilization in the late 1960s. This resulted in two changes significant to understanding the contemporary context. First, there are today numerous Shi'i social and political institutions that serve as moral authorities, including Hizbullah and the institutions of the late Sayyid Muhammad Husayn Fadlallah.[2] Second, a lifestyle based on specific religious ideas and practices has become both part of commonsense knowledge and desire for many in Dahiya, and a social norm to which people are often expected to conform. This social landscape includes a critical mass of youth who view a religious rubric of morality as a key element with which they are concerned as they strive to live lives that they understand as "good." We suggest that this critical mass of youth and their genuine concern for their souls reflects one of the major successes of the grassroots Islamic mobilization in Lebanon. . . .

[P]ious Shi'i youth in Lebanon represent a significant generational shift away from the "Islamic vanguard" generation: those whose efforts in the 1960s, 1970s, and 1980s produced and institutionalized the Lebanese Shi'i Islamic movement. That generation had to fight existing notions of morality in order to enact their new understandings of religious commitment (Deeb 2006).

This experience contrasts sharply with that of our interlocutors, who were born and raised in the 1980s, may have attended Islamic schools established by the vanguard, and came of age in an environment where norms of public piety were taken for granted and Hizbullah was already a popular political party. Vanguard parents sometimes expressed concerns that their children are not adequately pious. . . . [T]hey were concerned that pious practice had become normative and routinized, and that this might facilitate the dilution or insincerity of piety among youth. These parental concerns highlight how Shi'i youth have begun to question moral boundaries related to leisure. While many youth embrace a pious lifestyle, they may define the details and moral valuations of practices in that lifestyle differently.

Multiple Moral Authorities

The diversity of youth opinion on matters of leisure is itself facilitated by the existence of multiple sources of moral authority in the Lebanese Shi'i community. Piety and morality in this context are defined in relation to, in the context of, and in dialog with, but not exclusively by formal sources of moral authority. Young pious Muslims are often well-versed in multiple jurisprudents' interpretations and tend to view moral rubrics with greater flexibility than did the vanguard. This is facilitated by the ease of access to authoritative opinions youth enjoy, through media produced by the offices of religious leaders and Hizbullah. Sermons, fatwas, and advice are distributed through books, pamphlets, audiotapes, and CDs, and broadcast via websites, television, and radio.[3] Youth also obtain knowledge and advice from religious leaders through private meetings and telephone and website consultations, and discuss these opinions, passing information around that may or may not be accurate.

Hizbullah is a key voice in defining the boundaries of moral behavior within Dahiya. The party does not formally enforce most norms, though there are certain limits that differentiate Dahiya from other Beirut neighborhoods—most obviously the absence of alcohol in cafes and restaurants.[4] Many youth attend party-affiliated schools or camps, and support the party and especially the Resistance, but political support does not necessarily translate into moral conformity.

Another important voice in defining moral behavior is the late, popular jurisprudent Sayyid Muhammad Husayn Fadlallah. Since the 1990s, Fadlallah has been a *marja' al-taqlid*, ("source of emulation"), meaning that he may be "followed" by practicing Shi'i Muslims in religious matters. Fadlallah is among the most popular *marja*'s in Lebanon,[5] due to his clarity, pragmatism, and insistence that Islam should adapt to the contemporary world and that interpretation should facilitate youth lifestyles whenever possible. He tends to be viewed as more progressive than others on many issues, including gender and sexuality.

Fadlallah also explicitly encourages followers to use their judgment in interpreting situations. As his son and representative Sayyid Ja'far explained to us, Fadlallah is concerned with advising people on what is *haram* and *halal* (religiously prohibited and permitted), and proscriptions on alcohol and adultery fall into this realm. But, he continued, "There is another level related to life in general, and that is the level of *akhlaq* (morals) or *qiyam* (values). And this level rests on the choice of the individual himself . . . depending on his mood, environment, culture, and perspective on his role in life". The key point here is that Fadlallah clearly delineates religious tenets from morality, separating religiously determined moral norms from a broader moral framework. And when it comes to the broader framework, responsibility for implementing (and determining) morals rests on the individual.

While young people often highlight this emphasis on individual responsibility, they also indirectly pressure jurisprudents to rethink their opinions, especially by asking questions. . . . Increasing questions about a topic may lead a *marja'* to reconsider it. Because jurisprudence is often produced in direct response to questions, young people may prompt flexibility, direct a *marja*'s attention to specific matters, or indirectly suggest that something should be reconsidered.

This is the case even in relation to what might be considered unimportant topics, for example nail polish. Most Shi'i jurisprudents state that if a person wants to pray with polished nails, she must complete her ablutions prior to applying polish (essentially making the continual wearing of polish incompatible with regular prayer). Fadlallah's opinion shifted recently in response to questions asked by young women who found this stipulation problematic. We learned of this shift after observing the strange prevalence of young women wearing polish on only four fingers of each hand in summer 2008. When we asked where this apparent fashion had originated, we were told that Fadlallah had stated that if one nail of each hand and foot remained clear, ablutions could be completed while wearing polish (and we confirmed this with his office). By spring 2009, another young woman told us that his opinion had changed again. To check, we asked the question via his website, and indeed, received a response in April 2009 confirming that nail polish does not interfere with ablutions even if worn on all fingers and toes.

Like these young women, today's youth in Dahiya are educated, literate, expectant, and media-savvy, able to access, select, and consume a wide-range of information. We refer to them as "more-or-less pious" to emphasize the flexibility with which they tend to approach most moral norms. While for the most part, young people do not spontaneously cite jurisprudents, they do occasionally argue about what a particular *marja'* stated, or suggest that one is better than another. Most commonly youth seem to depend on secondary knowledge of this information, as well as on websites and call-in radio shows. Indeed, one of us inadvertently contributed to secondary knowledge when she described the new nail polish fatwa to a young interviewee who changed her polish practices accordingly. . . .

Music and Alcohol

Many factors enter into decisions about where to go out, including concerns about security, expense, location, transportation, dress, time of year, type of music, presence of alcohol or hookah, with whom one is going, and one's mood that evening. Here we focus on two that are of especial concern for our young interlocutors in relation to the religious rubric of morality: the presence of music and alcohol.

Music is not officially regulated in Lebanon, and its acceptability is interpreted widely by youth. Most agree with the vanguard generation, Hizbullah, and Fadlallah that music conducive to dancing is *haram*. Some also believe that jurisprudents forbid all songs. Fadlallah actually emphasizes the content of lyrics, suggesting that listeners be alert to the difference between acceptable *shawq* (longing or desire) and unacceptable *ghara'iz* (sexual instincts).

Among the 55 young people we interviewed, 31% listened to songs freely in all contexts, 29% did not listen to songs and avoid cafes that play them, 18% did not listen on their own, but went to such cafes, explaining that songs could be ignored, 7% insisted that lyrical content matters, and 6% noted that musical volume was their primary concern. Only 3% (two young women) said that they listened in secret to songs. This variety reflects what we have observed among young people we know in Dahiya, as does the malleability of views on music, with people commonly changing their minds and practices at different points in their lives.

Youth who listen to songs are divided between those who think this is morally acceptable and those who view it as a "small sin". Twenty-three-year-old Amer, a college student studying engineering, is among the latter:

> I listen to songs. I don't consider myself 100 percent committed, but you know, normal. From a young age I pray and fast. . . . But I do have some things that are red lines I don't cross, you know, big sins we don't do. Like alcohol, for example. I would never go to a place where there is alcohol, and I would never drink.

Amer's statement reminds us of the two aspects of moral flexibility in our argument: flexible practice within clear-cut rules versus flexibility of the rules themselves. Listening to songs exemplifies both: there can be a great deal of flexibility as to whether or not it is immoral to listen to songs, as well as flexibility as to whether or not one abides by that prescription if one believes it to exist. Amer also illustrates the ideas of processual piety and "degrees of sin" as ways of understanding moral flexibility, with listening to songs, drinking alcohol and being around alcohol, representing different levels of sinful or *haram* behavior.

Drinking alcohol is the most significant "red-line" among more-or-less pious youth. No one we interviewed admitted to drinking. But while all agreed with Amer that drinking is a non-negotiable "big sin", they disagreed about what relationship a non-drinker could have to a place serving alcohol. Can you purchase things from places that sell alcohol or sit there with friends? Only 13% of our interlocutors refused to purchase anything where alcohol was sold. This is relatively low compared with our experience with older pious people who tend to ask about the separation of cash registers if alcohol is present. This suggests that for youth, the issue is less about permissible uses of money and more about being in the presence of sinful behavior. Approximately half our interlocutors stated that they would categorically refuse to enter a place with alcohol and leave if they discovered it after entering, and the other half said they would go, but simply not drink themselves. Of the latter group, several differentiated between cafes that serve beer and "bars with whiskey" and others explained that they would ask their friends not to drink, highlighting the visibility and proximity of alcohol and drunkenness as deciding factors. People who firmly stated that they would not enter alcohol-serving establishments often told stories later in our interviews about times when they had in fact hung out in such pubs and cafes. The higher moral stakes of alcohol consumption and the greater agreement on its status as *haram* led to greater incongruities between initial statements about behavior and stories about "exceptional" situations.

Exceptional situations were most commonly explained with "I had no choice." These moral compromises usually transpired when the religious prohibition of alcohol came into direct conflict with the social rubric for morality. For example, many who believed it was *haram* to be near alcohol also believed that it was *'ayb* to neglect family or friends visiting from outside Lebanon. High rates of emigration and labor migration ensure that most Lebanese have friends or family visiting during summers. Those living "at home" are expected to "host" visitors, sharing their knowledge of the newest hangouts, including those with alcohol. Fulfilling such social expectations is also a measure of one's morality. As Amer explained, "Sometimes people visit for five days, you need to show them more than one place. You cannot take them just to Dahiya, they'll get bored." For him, this moral contradiction was stressful: "In any place that has alcohol, it is impossible for me to be comfortable. I feel something bothering me; I feel I am doing something wrong; I feel guilty."

Deeply felt conflict between moral rubrics also emerges in social situations among resident Lebanese, especially college students who mix with peers from different backgrounds. Many students shared situations where non-pious or Christian friends asked them out for a beer. Responses varied from directly explaining why they do not drink to fabricating excuses. Muhammad and Ali disagreed about whether lying or suggesting that you are better than someone else is the more immoral act:

> Ali: Sometimes my Christian friends ask me to go out and have a beer. . . . I say I have studies. Or they ask me to a nightclub, I tell them I can't, I'm busy. I don't show them I don't want to hang out, but I get away in a different way.
>
> Muhammad: But that's *haram*, you're lying to them.
>
> Ali: No it's not, because I'm not saying that I'm better. It's *haram* to say I'm better or he's worse.

In both examples, youth express a strong desire to live in a way they understand as moral. When different moral rubrics clash, those caught in the middle express feeling conflicted about their choices, experiencing guilt, or otherwise making a concerted effort to navigate this complex terrain.

We see a significant generational difference in willingness to compromise or cross "red lines" during these navigations. This was exemplified in a group interview that included two colleagues who work in media: Rabi', in his late 20s, and Mahmoud, in his mid-30s. We asked them whether they would go to places that serve alcohol. Rabi' began, "In principle no. . . . But frankly, it has happened with me. Once we were invited out and there were Christians there and they wanted to drink."

What did you do?

I generally try to avoid going with them to cafes and to restaurants, so I don't embarrass them (*aHrujhum*) and they don't embarrass me (*yiHrijuni*). That time, I waited a short while and then left quietly and it wasn't noticed. I didn't hurt anyone's feelings. There was another time we were invited to a birthday party and the plan was to have it at their home. We accepted, and later they changed the place to a nightclub. The idea here is clear, it was too much to accept. Of course you can say no with your pride and without worrying about it. It doesn't need much thought.

Mahmoud chimed in, "On this point, I don't want to go to a place and be embarrassed (*iniHrij*). If I am sitting at a table, and someone orders alcohol and wants to drink, I'll leave."

You don't do what Rabi' did?

No, I'd leave immediately.

Even if it upsets the people with you?

Yistiflu! ["Let them do what they want!" or "Tough, they can deal!"] Just as he has the freedom to drink alcohol, I have the freedom to leave. Even if this is a relative of mine. My uncle (father's brother), for example, drinks alcohol. We were at my sister's wedding, and he wanted to trick us, to hide it; he mixed it with Pepsi. I heard that my uncle did this, and I went to him, [and said] "if you please." Of course he may have thought I wasn't respectful enough, but I explained, ". . . this is a wedding, and we don't want to have sins here."

> So if I were with someone [drinking], I would
> leave. . . . I am not going to stay at the same table.
> I want to show him that he should respect me, and
> respect my presence. Ok, he drinks, but respect
> me! How should I respect him when he doesn't
> respect me?

While both Rabi' and Mahmoud avoid being in the presence of alcohol, there is a striking difference in their attitudes and approaches to situations where friends or family members are drinking. Rabi' is worried about not hurting his friends' feelings and does what he can to maintain good relationships with them, although going to a nightclub is plainly beyond his limits. Mahmoud instead privileges his religious values over his social relationships. He goes so far as to explicitly correct the behavior of his father's brother, who according to the social rubric of morality is due his respect. Respect is in fact a key idiom in Mahmoud's response, as he prioritizes a claim for respect for religious values over respect for social values supporting patriarchal age hierarchies. . . .

Weddings are perhaps the best example of these difficult moral navigations. Many activities that some people consider *haram* take place at weddings, among them drinking, dancing, and listening to songs. Pious youth rarely confront alcohol at family weddings. Dancing and songs, however, continue to create dilemmas for those who believe these activities are immoral. Some families play only classical music and others only music for *dabkeh*, a Lebanese folk dance that men and women can dance separately, making it more acceptable. When confronted with an invitation to a wedding that would violate the religious rubric for morality, most people attended anyway, indicating that they "had no choice", and reframing the situation by downplaying the importance of the violated rule. Only two people did not attend weddings at all. One young woman refused to attend her brother's wedding. And Rami, an undergraduate in his early twenties, declined the wedding invitation of a childhood friend because there would be a DJ. "He invited me, I didn't ask him to go. . . . I said to him, 'I can't do that.'" His classmate and co-interviewee Qasim frowned on this, and disapprovingly related a story about acquaintances that spent only 5 min at their own brother's wedding. "Look how far it will go, it's their brother, and they will not sit there for his sake!" Qasim goes to friends' weddings no matter what,

and goes for a walk outside if he needs a break from the environment.

Many pious youth who avoid songs drew on the strategy Qasim found distasteful, arriving early at weddings so that they could depart before music and dancing commenced. This allowed them to make an appearance, fulfilling their social obligations, without violating their morals. Twenty-six-year-old Hadi explained:

> When I was invited to my friend's sister's wedding,
> I had to go. First he is from the neighborhood and
> also they invited me four times.

They don't know that you don't listen to songs?

> Yes they do, but people invite you. So, in the end
> I had to go. I went early. Like ten minutes earlier
> just to show myself. I sat, and they played classical
> music. They served food; I ate till I was full. I told
> the D.J., "before you start the music, tell me." So
> before he started the songs I left.

Hadi's story also highlights the intensity of social pressure around weddings, such that declining an invitation makes a significant statement. Family members may even pressure pious youth to include activities at their own weddings or engagement parties that they generally try to avoid. Zaynab was struggling with this issue when we interviewed her along with two of her friends. She avoids mixed weddings if there is any dancing at all, even *dabkeh*, because she does not dance in front of guys but also does not "like to sit at the table like an idiot." She explained the exceptions to her efforts:

> . . . unless it's in the family and I can't [avoid it].
> For example, I am having an engagement party
> soon. I want to have music for *dabkeh*, not for any-
> thing else, but it is going to have to be mixed-sex.
> I know that this is *haram*, but this is a compromise
> solution [with her parents].

> Fatima chimed in, "For me, it depends on the
> person. . . . I try as much as I can to avoid going to
> mixed-sex weddings. But, for Zaynab, she is my
> friend, I have to be there."

With the exception of drinking alcohol, youth are open with one another about their differing standards, opinions, and behaviors. Again and again in our group interviews, among friends, peers, spouses, and strangers, young people shared that they listen to songs or go to places with alcohol. And while certainly some feel pressure to cease these activities, most reported that the prevailing understanding is that moral behavior is something that every individual determines and develops in her own way. As long as red lines are not crossed, there remains space for negotiation, movement, moods, and even day-to-day changes in activities without accusations of hypocrisy or immorality. This does not mean that these negotiations are easy or discussions are devoid of critique. Youth often feel guilty as they try to navigate social norms while avoiding sin. Indeed, for someone who wants to be a moral person according to both religious and social rubrics, the notion that individuals are responsible both for moral action and for deciding what counts as moral in the first place raises the stakes of everyday decisions significantly.

Conclusion: Inhabiting the Space Between Morality and Not-Immorality

The youth we describe negotiate a world in which understandings of "how to be Muslim" include individual choice. In their view, piety does not narrow faith to a theocratic understanding, but rather, emerges in their senses of themselves as good according to a religious rubric of morality that may or may not align with other equally important moral rubrics, including a social one. In Lebanon, it is more-or-less pious Shi'i youth who view practices and discourses of morality as flexible, whether negotiating among different rubrics or disagreeing about a particular rule. In our research experience, it is less common for those over 30 to assert such flexibility. In answering the question of why youth are more morally flexible, we suggest . . . [a] key component is generational difference in context. Today's youth may take the status quo for granted in a way that the vanguard generation did and does not. The world in which they came of age is one where morality was assessed in terms of specific religious tenets as well as social norms; one where actions spoke loudly about piety (Deeb 2006), and where consulting a religious leader like Fadlallah was both normal and easy. This is a world that the vanguard generation struggled against social convention to produce. It is also a (for the most part) post-war world, one of relative security where youth *can* go out and interact more frequently with others.

In addition, it is difficult to underestimate the importance of a context where the existence of *multiple* moral authorities is the norm and where pious youth interact regularly with youth who live very different lifestyles in Lebanon's pluralist society. Much is left up to the individual believer. The existence of these differing perspectives and of the flexibility to choose from multiple interpretations and authorities—even within one faith—allows youth to search for interpretations and opinions that most closely reflect their own desires and ideas.

Another factor is Fadlallah's influence, whether explicit or merely as a dominant aspect of the social environment. Fadlallah himself modeled flexibility by changing his opinion readily through rethinking his opinions, sometimes in response to the availability of new information on an issue (Clarke 2009). . . .

Fadlallah's teachings about individual moral responsibility are often echoed by youth as they insist on their authority to choose for themselves and display a "to each his own" attitude about moral behavior. Our interviews and group interviews highlighted the diversity of youth opinion about the presence of alcohol and songs, and their acceptance of that diversity among their friends and peers. . . .

. . . The ease of access to authoritative opinion on moral matters signifies another aspect of the world in which our interlocutors came of age. Technology is a key contributor to youth's ability to navigate multiple moral rubrics simultaneously.[6] . . .

In sum, the context of contemporary Lebanon and south Beirut facilitates moral flexibility through the existence of multiple moral rubrics and authorities, the prevalence of consumerist and technologically connected sensibilities, and the quiet dominance of Fadlallah's ideas about individual moral responsibility, ideas that mesh perfectly with notions of a liberal individual choosing from among moral options. In this context, youth are able to produce numerous possibilities for living a good life. . . .

. . . Many in this generation believe that they can and should individually assess their behavior and that they can read and listen and demand answers to questions and then choose which ones to apply in their lives. They frequently inhabit the more colorful spaces between "being moral" and "not being immoral." In their day-to-day negotiations of a complex moral terrain, they may at times know themselves to be doing something wrong and do it anyway with varying levels of guilt, believe that what they are doing is not very wrong, or believe that it is not wrong at all. And these ideas may change from year to year, mood to mood, and moment to moment.

As part of this process, many youth in Dahiya express a strong desire to live a moral life that includes the right to appropriate leisure. This is not a top-down imposition of norms, but a ground-up desire to rework the terms of morality in ways that make sense to young people both socially and for their own senses of themselves as good people. . . .

Notes

1. The focus on youth as naturally transgressive dominates recent work on Iranian youth resisting the Islamic regime (Khosravi 2008; Mahdavi 2009). Bayat (2010) is more nuanced, highlighting the specificity of youth rebellion in Iran. The idea of youth as easily co-opted dominates US policy and media.

2. For more on this history and Hizbullah, see Deeb 2006, Harb 2010, Norton (1987, 2007).

3. Dorothea Schulz (2003) highlights the effect media have on the "growing emphasis on individual opinion-making" (152) by facilitating access to knowledge.

4. This has been achieved through social and economic pressure. Alcohol is available for purchase at several supermarkets in Dahiya.

5. The other popular jurisprudents here are Khamenei and Sistani. Khamenei is the formal marja'for Hizbullah, though party members may follow a different jurisprudent. Sistani's popularity has risen since the US invaded Iraq.

6. Melki's (2010) survey of Arab youth confirmed high rates of media consumption. See also Bayat and Herrera (2010).

References

Bayat, Asef. 2010. Muslim Youth and the Claim of Youthfulness. In *Being Young and Muslim: New Cultural Politics in the Global South and North*, edited by Linda Herrera & Asef Bayat, pp. 26–47. Oxford: Oxford University Press.

Bayat, Asef, & Linda Herrera. 2010. Introduction: Being Young and Muslim in Neoliberal Times. In *Being Young and Muslim: New Cultural Politics in the Global South and North*, edited by Linda Herrera & Asef Bayat, pp. 3–24. Oxford: Oxford University Press.

Clarke, Morgan. 2009. *Islam and New Kinship: Reproductive Technology and the Shariah in Lebanon*. London: Berghahn Books.

Deeb, Lara. 2006. *An Enchanted Modern: Gender and Public Piety in Shi'i Lebanon*. Princeton: Princeton University Press.

Harb, Mona. 2010. *Hezbollah: De la Banlieue a` la Ville*. Paris-Beirut: Karthala-IFPO.

Khosravi, Shahram. 2008. *Young and Defiant in Tehran*. Philadelphia: University of Pennsylvania Press.

Mahdavi, Pardis. 2009. *Passionate Uprisings: Iran's Sexual Revolution*. Stanford: Stanford University Press.

Melki, Jad. 2010. Media Habits of MENA Youth: A Three-Country Survey. Youth in the Arab World Working Paper Series #2 (July 2010). Beirut, Lebanon: Issam Fares Institute for Public Policy and International Affairs. American University of Beirut.

Norton, Augustus Richard. 1987. *Amal and the Shi'a: Struggle for the Soul of Lebanon*. Austin: University of Texas Press.

Norton, Augustus Richard. 1987. *Hezbollah*. Princeton: Princeton University Press.

Schulz, Dorothea E. 2003. Charisma and Brotherhood' Revisited: Mass-Mediated Forms of Spirituality in Urban Mali. *Journal of Religion in Africa*, 33(2):146–71.

DR. TANYA MARIE LUHRMANN

Psychological anthropologist specializing in prayer, spiritual experience, and psychiatric illness.

Figure 3.5.1

Tanya Luhrmann.

How did you become interested in the discipline of anthropology?

I've always thought that myths and folklore and stories in general were important in shaping the way people experience their world. That's really what anthropology studies—the way shared stories and ideas shape how people think and feel and act.

You've written extensively on prayer, spirituality, morality, and psychiatry. What central anthropological concepts cut across all of your work?

You could say that all these topics are about how people judge what's real, particularly when something someone judges to be real conflicts in some ways with the concrete, everyday world. After all, gods and spirits are "super" natural. They can't be seen in ordinary ways, and they don't behave the way people do. How do people come to be confident that they are there? How do they think about the difference between being "crazy" and being religious? Of course there is a difference—but how much do local

expectations play a role in the way that people make that judgment about other people? What about for themselves?

The central anthropological concept here is "social construction," which is that our social worlds shape what we take to be true. I'm interested in how deeply our social ideas shape what we take to be real, and where the limits of social construction are. So, for example, when people say that they hear God speak in their minds, do they use the same cues to distinguish God's words from their own thoughts everywhere in the world? Can people learn to hear God speak? How?

How did you come to be interested in spirituality and morality?

I became interested in these topics because I grew up as a spiritual in-between, and as the daughter of a psychiatrist. My cousins were very conservative Christians. My parents were not. We lived in an Orthodox Jewish neighborhood. So I knew good, sensible people who had very different ideas about what's real. And I knew, because of my father, that there were good people who had ideas about reality that were judged just wrong—rather than different. So I became fascinated by what became real to people and how.

What is the most meaningful project you've worked on over the course of your career and why?

I don't think there's any one project. But I was most changed by my work on magic and on religion, because when I began that work, I thought that what was different between groups of people were just the stories and ideas they held. As I began to study these different practices more deeply, I learned that people actually sensed what they called the supernatural differently. In some sense, people who were religious and people who were not religious really did live in different worlds because they learned to experience the world so distinctly. When I discovered this, I began to think very differently about religion. I began to think of religion as a practice, not as a set of ideas. My work has focused on how these practices change people's direct experience of their senses.

Who is your main audience for your research and writing, and why?

I think of myself as having three audiences: anthropological, psychological and psychiatric, and popular. There is the anthropological audience of scholars, whom I reach through books and anthropological articles. I write more scientific journal articles for psychologists and psychiatrists. I also write more accessible pieces for the broader public.

Do you identify as an applied, engaged, or public anthropologist? What do these titles mean to you?

I think of myself as an engaged anthropologist. I see myself not so much as critiquing medicine or religion in order to show their inevitable limitations, but thinking about how my research can make the world a better place.

What do you see as the future for anthropology and religion?

I don't think religion will ever disappear. I think people need it. The question is how religion will change as people become more and more aware of different kinds of faiths. Anthropology I am less confident about. Academic disciplines do shift and change over time. But I think there will always be a role for thoughtful exploration of the way people make meaning in their lives, and that fundamentally is what anthropology is about. For more information on Dr. Luhrmann and links to her books and interviews see: http://luhrmann.net/.

ABOUT THE PROFESSOR

Occupation: Professor, Stanford University
Education: Ph.D. in Social Anthropology, Cambridge University
Hobbies: "I work in the garden with my dog, who likes to help me to dig."

CAREER ADVICE

Advice for students interested in a career in anthropology of religion:

- Learn how to observe and learn how to write.
- Be patient with people who seem different.
- Remain generous.
- Seek to understand before you judge.

PART 4

Marriage, Family, Gender and Sexuality

Humans are social beings. We need one another to survive, as well as to reproduce. While sociality is a human universal, cultures vary in the ways in which they create and maintain their social ties with one another. The readings in this section take up questions about the universality of what some readers may think are "natural" categories, showing instead that even some things that many may take for granted—like mother love, the definition of marriage, or sex and gender identities—are culturally constructed.

The first two selections are classics, each working to illustrate cross-cultural variation in kin ties. Kinship refers to the social relationships that are publicly recognized and based on descent and marriage. Marriage is a socially approved institution that formalizes relationships—economic, political, and sexual—between adult partners within a family. This anthropological definition of marriage makes room for various partnership compositions, regardless of gender, and includes polygamous unions. While monogamy, or the practice of having only one spouse at one time, is the norm in the Western world, a vast number of world cultures do not agree that this is the most preferable arrangement. Polygamy, or plural marriage, was widely practiced throughout much of the world and continues to be a preferential form of marriage in many cultures. The classic piece by Melvyn Goldstein, "When Brothers Take a Wife" (Reading 4.1) describes the Tibetan practice of fraternal polyandry, a form of plural marriage where a woman marries two or more brothers at one time.

Descent refers to socially recognized kinship connections traced through the generations, including parent-child relationships. Many readers may hold the belief that parent-child relationships are immediately sacred and cherished, and a parent will do anything to keep their child alive from the moment they emerge from the womb. In "Death Without Weeping" (Reading 4.2), Nancy-Scheper-Hughes asks: Is mother love for an infant an innate human universal? Tracing more than twenty-five years of research on mother-infant relationships in the Alto de Curzeiro, a shantytown in Northeast Brazil, Scheper-Hughes explores the reasons why mothers engage in passive infanticide for infants they consider to be "angels" born "wanting to die," while they nurture those they consider to be "survivors."

Just as there are no "natural" feelings that can be universally applied to parent-child relationships, cross-cultural studies demonstrate that there are also no "natural" sex and gender categories. The term *sex* is used to describe sex organs and reproductive functions of the body, while *gender* captures culturally recognized expectations about how males and females should behave. *Intersex* refers to individuals who exhibit sexual organs somewhere between male and female elements, and the ways in which people classify intersex individuals into gender categories also varies cross-culturally. Anthropological studies of sex and gender systems reveal variation in the total number of sex/gender categories acknowledged across the globe, with some societies recognizing "third genders." Serena Nanda's classic piece, "Hijra and Sādhin: Neither Man nor Woman in India" (Reading 4.3) offers examples of a "third gender" from India. Hijras are "neither man nor woman" because they lack male genitals due to being born intersex or undergoing castration but embrace superficial aspects of femininity. The sādhin is a female gender variant who renounces marriage and sexuality and becomes viewed as asexual. Both are culturally accepted and supported by Hinduism.

Discussions of third genders often become enmeshed in debates about sexuality, even though sexual preferences and practices do not map neatly onto gender or sex categories, as is clearly illustrated in Nanda's piece. In addition to societies trying to capture and control sexual behavior by creating cultural frameworks that box some sexes or genders into homosexual or heterosexual relationships, society also attempts to limit sexuality by developing formal and informal mechanisms of monitoring and enforcement. From "sodomy" laws that prohibit same-sex intercourse to family planning programs to virginity testing, governments and communities attempt to enact control over people's bodies. In "Virginity Testing as a Local Public Health Initiative: A 'Preventative Ritual' More Than a 'Diagnostic Measure'" (Reading 4.4) Annette Wickström describes the long-standing Zulu tradition of testing girls' virginity. It turns out that this ritual is less about "outing" sexually active girls and more about collectively celebrating virginity as a community. Wickström also considers how informal sexual education has changed over time as Zulu traditions encountered Western ideas about sexual decision-making and sex education.

This section's "In the News" element returns to the definition of marriage, covering the 2015 Supreme Court ruling declaring the constitutional protection of same-sex marriage and anthropological evidence in support of a flexible definition of marriage.

The section closes with the profile of Megan E. Springate, Prime Consultant for the National Park Service's (NPS) LGBTQ Heritage Initiative. Springate, a historical archaeologist, describes her work with the NPS to document and provide historic context about American LGBTQ communities in order to facilitate their nomination into the National Register of Historic Places. In addition to describing her work in applied public anthropology/archaeology, Springate also reflects on the future of queer anthropology in her interview.

KEY TERMS:

- Marriage
- Motherhood
- Passive infanticide
- Lifeboat ethics
- Sex
- Gender
- Intersex
- Sexuality
- Polygamy
- Polyandry
- Virginity testing
- Marriage equality
- LGBTQ

4.1 When Brothers Take a Wife

MELVYN C. GOLDSTEIN

Polygamy (plural marriage), while becoming less common, does continue to be practiced among many cultures of the world. Polygyny, where a man marries more than one woman, is far more common than polyandry, the marriage of one woman to more than one man at the same time. In this classic contribution, Melvyn Goldstein describes the Tibetan practice of fraternal polyandry, where sets of brothers marry one woman. He explores the reasons behind the preference for this form of marriage, showing that it enables a family to retain their wealth, economic security, and social prestige.

Questions

1. What are the advantages to fraternal polyandry? What are the drawbacks?
2. Compare the common explanations offered for the continuation of fraternal polyandry to those offered by Goldstein.
3. Consider the relationship between marital practices, social prestige, and the control of family wealth in your own culture. Does maintaining the wealth and prestige of a family factor into marital practices in the United States?

Eager to reach home, Dorje drives his yaks hard over the seventeen-thousand-foot mountain pass, stopping only once to rest. He and his two older brothers, Pema and Sonam, are jointly marrying a woman from the next village in a few weeks, and he has to help with the preparations.

Dorje, Pema, and Sonam are Tibetans living in Limi, a two-hundredsquare-mile area in the northwest corner of Nepal, across the border from Tibet. The form of marriage they are about to enter—fraternal polyandry in anthropological parlance—is one of the world's rarest forms of marriage but is not uncommon in Tibetan society, where it has been practiced from time immemorial. For many Tibetan social strata, it traditionally represented the ideal form of marriage and family.

The mechanics of fraternal polyandry are simple. Two, three, four, or more brothers jointly take a wife, who leaves her home to come and live with them. Traditionally, marriage was arranged by parents, with children, particularly females, having little or no say. This is changing somewhat nowadays, but it is still unusual for children to marry without their parents' consent. Marriage ceremonies vary by income and region and range from all the brothers sitting together as grooms to only the eldest one formally doing so. The age of the brothers plays an important role in determining this: very young brothers almost never participate in actual marriage ceremonies, although they typically join the marriage when they reach their midteens.

The eldest brother is normally dominant in terms of authority, that is, in managing the household, but all the brothers share the work and participate as sexual partners. Tibetan males and females do not find the sexual aspect of sharing a spouse the least bit unusual, repulsive, or scandalous, and the norm is for the wife to treat all the brothers the same.

Offspring are treated similarly. There is no attempt to link children biologically to particular brothers, and

Melvyn C. Goldstein. "When Brothers Share a Wife." 1987. *Natural History* 96(3), 109–112. From *Natural History* March 1987, copyright Natural History Magazine, Inc., 2015.

a brother shows no favoritism toward his child even if he knows he is the real father because, for example, his other brothers were away at the time the wife became pregnant. The children, in turn, consider all of the brothers as their fathers and treat them equally, even if they also know who is their real father. In some regions children use the term "father" for the eldest brother and "father's brother" for the others, while in other areas they call all the brothers by one term, modifying this by the use of "elder" and "younger."

Unlike our own society, where monogamy is the only form of marriage permitted, Tibetan society allows a variety of marriage types, including monogamy, fraternal polyandry, and polygyny. Fraternal polyandry and monogamy are the most common forms of marriage, while polygyny typically occurs in cases where the first wife is barren. The widespread practice of fraternal polyandry, therefore, is not the outcome of a law requiring brothers to marry jointly. There is choice, and in fact, divorce traditionally was relatively simple in Tibetan society. If a brother in a polyandrous marriage became dissatisfied and wanted to separate, he simply left the main house and set up his own household. In such cases, all the children stayed in the main household with the remaining brother(s), even if the departing brother was known to be the real father of one or more of the children.

The Tibetans' own explanation for choosing fraternal polyandry is materialistic. For example, when I asked Dorje why he decided to marry with his two brothers rather than take his own wife, he thought for a moment, then said it prevented the division of his family's farm (and animals) and thus facilitated all of them achieving a higher standard of living. And when I later asked Dorje's bride whether it wasn't difficult for her to cope with three brothers as husbands, she laughed and echoed the rationale of avoiding fragmentation of the family and land, adding that she expected to be better off economically, since she would have three husbands working for her and her children.

Exotic as it may seem to Westerners, Tibetan fraternal polyandry is thus in many ways analogous to the way primogeniture functioned in nineteenth-century England. Primogeniture dictated that the eldest son inherited the family estate, while younger sons had to leave home and seek their own employment—for example, in the military or the clergy. Primogeniture maintained family estates intact over generations by permitting only one heir per generation. Fraternal polyandry also accomplishes this but does so by keeping all the brothers together with just one wife so that there is only one *set* of heirs per generation.

While Tibetans believe that in this way fraternal polyandry reduces the risk of family fission, monogamous marriages among brothers need not necessarily precipitate the division of the family estate: brothers could continue to live together, and the family land could continue to be worked jointly. When I asked Tibetans about this, however, they invariably responded that such joint families are unstable because each wife is primarily oriented to her own children and interested in their success and well-being over that of the children of the other wives. For example, if the youngest brother's wife had three sons while the eldest brother's wife had only one daughter, the wife of the youngest brother might begin to demand more resources for her children since, as males, they represent the future of the family. Thus, the children from different wives in the same generation are competing sets of heirs, and this makes such families inherently unstable. Tibetans perceive that conflict will spread from the wives to their husbands and consider this likely to cause family fission. Consequently, it is almost never done.

Although Tibetans see an economic advantage to fraternal polyandry, they do not value the sharing of a wife as an end in itself. On the contrary, they articulate a number of problems inherent in the practice. For example, because authority is customarily exercised by the eldest brother, his younger male siblings have to subordinate themselves with little hope of changing their status within the family. When these younger brothers are aggressive and individualistic, tensions and difficulties often occur despite there being only one set of heirs.

In addition, tension and conflict may arise in polyandrous families because of sexual favoritism. The bride normally sleeps with the eldest brother, and the two have the responsibility to see to it that the other males have opportunities for sexual access. Since the Tibetan subsistence economy requires males to travel a lot, the temporary absence of one or more brothers facilitates this, but there are also other rotation practices. The cultural ideal unambiguously calls for the wife to show equal affection and sexuality to each of the brothers (and vice versa), but deviations from this ideal occur, especially when there is a sizable difference in age between the partners in the marriage.

Dorje's family represents just such a potential situation. He is fifteen years old and his two older brothers are twenty-five and twenty-two years old. The new bride is twenty-three years old, eight years Dorje's senior. Sometimes such a bride finds the youngest husband immature and adolescent and does not treat him with equal affection; alternatively, she may find his youth attractive and lavish special attention on him. Apart from that consideration, when a younger male like Dorje grows up, he may consider his wife "ancient" and prefer the company of a woman his own age or younger. Consequently, although men and women do not find the idea of sharing a bride or a bridegroom repulsive, individual likes and dislikes can cause familial discord.

Two reasons have commonly been offered for the perpetuation of fraternal polyandry in Tibet: that Tibetans practice female infanticide and therefore have to marry polyandrously, owing to a shortage of females; and that Tibet, lying at extremely high altitudes, is so barren and bleak that Tibetans would starve without resort to this mechanism. A Jesuit who lived in Tibet during the eighteenth century articulated this second view: "One reason for this most odious custom is the sterility of the soil, and the small amount of land that can be cultivated owing to the lack of water. The crops may suffice if the brothers all live together, but if they form separate families they would be reduced to beggary."

Both explanations are wrong however. Not only has there never been institutionalized female infanticide in Tibet, but Tibetan society gives females considerable rights, including inheriting the family estate in the absence of brothers. In such cases, the woman takes a bridegroom who comes to live in her family and adopts her family's name and identity. Moreover, there is no demographic evidence of a shortage of females. In Limi, for example, there were (in 1974) sixty females and fifty-three males in the fifteen- to thirty-five-year age category, and many adult females were unmarried.

The second reason is also incorrect. The climate in Tibet is extremely harsh, and ecological factors do play a major role in perpetuating polyandry, but polyandry is not a means of preventing starvation. It is characteristic, not of the poorest segments of the society, but rather of the peasant landowning families.

In the old society, the landless poor could not realistically aspire to prosperity, but they did not fear starvation. There was a persistent labor shortage throughout Tibet, and very poor families with little or no land and few animals could subsist through agricultural labor, tenant farming, craft occupations such as carpentry, or by working as servants. Although the per-person family income could increase somewhat if brothers married polyandrously and pooled their wages, in the absence of inheritable land, the advantage of fraternal polyandry was not generally sufficient to prevent them from setting up their own households. A more skilled or energetic younger brother could do as well or better alone, since he would completely control his income and would not have to share it with his siblings. Consequently, while there was and is some polyandry among the poor, it is much less frequent and more prone to result in divorce and family fission.

An alternative reason for the persistence of fraternal polyandry is that it reduces population growth (and thereby reduces the pressure on resources) by relegating some females to lifetime spinsterhood (see Figure 4.1.1). Fraternal polyandrous marriages in Limi (in 1974) averaged 2.35 men per woman, and not surprisingly, 31 percent of the females of child-bearing age (twenty to forty-nine) were unmarried. These spinsters either continued to live at home, set up their own households, or worked as servants for other families. They could also become Buddhist nuns. Being unmarried is not synonymous with exclusion from the reproductive pool. Discreet extramarital relationships are tolerated, and actually half of the adult unmarried women in Limi had one or more children. They raised these children as single mothers, working for wages or weaving cloth and blankets for sale. As a group, however, the unmarried women had far fewer offspring than the married women, averaging only 0.7 children per woman, compared with 3.3 for married women, whether polyandrous, monogamous, or polygynous. While polyandry helps regulate population, this function of polyandry is not consciously perceived by Tibetans and is not the reason they consistently choose it.

If neither a shortage of females nor the fear of starvation perpetuates fraternal polyandry, what motivates brothers, particularly younger brothers, to opt for this system of marriage? From the perspective of the younger brother in a landholding family, the main incentive is the attainment or maintenance of the good life. With polyandry, he can expect a more secure and higher standard of living, with access not only to his family's land and animals but also to its inherited collection of clothes, jewelry, rugs, saddles, and horses.

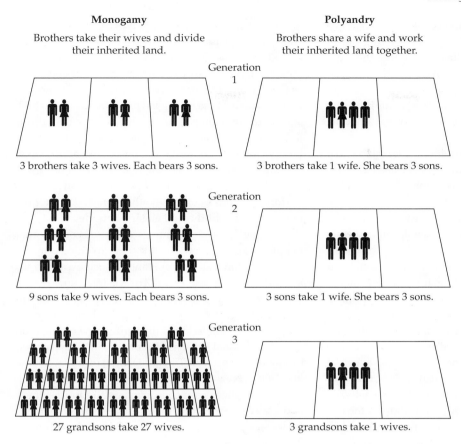

Monogamy	Polyandry
Brothers take their wives and divide their inherited land.	Brothers share a wife and work their inherited land together.

Figure 4.1.1

Family planning in Tibet.

Generation 1

3 brothers take 3 wives. Each bears 3 sons.

3 brothers take 1 wife. She bears 3 sons.

Generation 2

9 sons take 9 wives. Each bears 3 sons.

3 sons take 1 wife. She bears 3 sons.

Generation 3

27 grandsons take 27 wives.

3 grandsons take 1 wives.

In addition, he will experience less work pressure and much greater security because all responsibility does not fall on one "father." For Tibetan brothers, the question is whether to trade off the greater personal freedom inherent in monogamy for the real or potential economic security, affluence, and social prestige associated with life in a larger, labor-rich polyandrous family.

A brother thinking of separating from his polyandrous marriage and taking his own wife would face various disadvantages. Although in the majority of Tibetan regions all brothers theoretically have rights to their family's estate, in reality Tibetans are reluctant to divide their land into small fragments. Generally, a younger brother who insists on leaving the family will receive only a small plot of land, if that. Because of its power and wealth, the rest of the family usually can block any attempt of the younger brother to increase his share of land through litigation. Moreover, a younger brother may not even get a house and cannot expect to receive much above the minimum in terms of movable possessions, such as furniture, pots, and pans. Thus, a brother contemplating going it on his own must plan on achieving economic security and the good life not through inheritance but through his own work.

The obvious solution for younger brothers—creating new fields from virgin land—is generally not a feasible option. Most Tibetan populations live at high altitudes (above 12,000 feet), where arable land is extremely scarce. For example, in Dorje's village, agriculture ranges only from about 12,900 feet, the lowest point in the area, to 13,300 feet. Above that altitude, early frost and snow destroy the staple barley crop. Furthermore, because of the low rainfall caused by the Himalayan rain shadow, many areas in Tibet and northern Nepal that are within the appropriate altitude range for agriculture have no reliable sources of irrigation. In the end, although there is plenty of unused land in such areas, most of it is either too high or too arid.

Even where unused land capable of being farmed exists, clearing the land and building the substantial terraces necessary for irrigation constitute a great undertaking. Each plot has to be completely dug out to a depth of two to two and a half feet so that the large rocks and boulders can be removed. At best, a man might be able to bring a few new fields under cultivation in the first years after separating from his brothers, but he could not expect to acquire substantial amounts of arable land this way.

In addition, because of the limited farmland, the Tibetan subsistence economy characteristically includes a strong emphasis on animal husbandry. Tibetan farmers regularly maintain cattle, yaks, goats, and sheep, grazing them in the areas too high for agriculture. These herds produce wool, milk, cheese, butter, meat, and skins. To obtain these resources, however, shepherds must accompany the animals on a daily basis. When first setting up a monogamous household, a younger brother like Dorje would find it difficult to both farm and manage animals.

In traditional Tibetan society, there was an even more critical factor that operated to perpetuate fraternal polyandry—a form of hereditary servitude somewhat analogous to serfdom in Europe. Peasants were tied to large estates held by aristocrats, monasteries, and the Lhasa government. They were allowed the use of some farmland to produce their own subsistence but were required to provide taxes in kind and corvée (free labor) to their lords. The corvée was a substantial hardship, since a peasant household was in many cases required to furnish the lord with one laborer daily for most of the year and more on specific occasions such as the harvest. This enforced labor, along with the lack of new land and the ecological pressure to pursue both agriculture and animal husbandry, made polyandrous families particularly beneficial. The polyandrous family allowed an internal division of adult labor, maximizing economic advantage. For example, while the wife worked the family fields, one brother could perform the lord's corvée, another could look after the animals, and a third could engage in trade.

Although social scientists often discount other people's explanations of why they do things, in the case of Tibetan fraternal polyandry, such explanations are very close to the truth. The custom, however, is very sensitive to changes in its political and economic milieu and, not surprisingly, is in decline in most Tibetan areas. Made less important by the elimination of the traditional serf-based economy, it is disparaged by the dominant non-Tibetan leaders of India, China, and Nepal. New opportunities for economic and social mobility in these countries, such as the tourist trade and government employment, are also eroding the rationale for polyandry, and so it may vanish within the next generation.

4.2 Death Without Weeping

NANCY SCHEPER-HUGHES

Is mother love an innate human universal? Does the bond between mother and infant look the same across all cultures? This classic selection, from medical anthropologist Nancy Scheper-Hughes, traces twenty-five years of research on the question of mother-infant love in the Alto de Curzeiro, a shantytown in Northeast Brazil. In 1965, Scheper-Hughes witnessed more than 350 babies die during a drought in a town of approximately just 5,000 people. After witnessing mother indifference to babies who "died off," Scheper-Hughes began to explore the underlying reasons that led to different patterns of nurturing for infants considered to be "survivors" and the "angels" born "wanting to die." For the latter, mothers engage in "mortal selective neglect," or what other anthropologists have called passive infanticide, stepping back to let nature take its course. Scheper-Hughes likens this strategy to "lifeboat ethics," biologist Garrett Hardin's triage model that compared the poor to overcrowded vessels. As in battlefield military medicine, you don't invest in those who will die no matter what, but only those who show they have the ability to survive. In a context of extreme poverty, hunger, and economic exploitation, withholding emotional attachment to infants until it is clear they will survive, is a survival strategy for women living in harsh conditions. The author also illustrates how what appears to be indifference of mothers to infant death reflects an official indifference of the state and the church to the plight of the poor. This piece illustrates the holistic nature of culture, revealing how other factors and institutions (economic, religious) influence cultural behaviors and attitudes.

Questions

1. What does mother love mean to the women of Bom Jesus da Mata?
2. Discuss the position of the Church on infant death.
3. Discuss the socioeconomic transitions in Bom Jesus da Mata and how these changes have impacted households and family structure. What do these changes have to do with mother love?
4. Is mother love a human universal? Is it innate or learned? How does it vary cross-culturally?

> *I have seen death without weeping*
> *The destiny of the Northeast is death*
> *Cattle they kill*
> *To the people they do something worse*
>
> —ANONYMOUS BRAZILIAN SINGER (1965)

 For an update on the status of "angel babies" in Brazil, see www.oup.com/us/brondo.

Nancy Scheper-Hughes. 1989. Death Without Weeping. 1989, *Natural History* 98(10):8–16. Updated 2011, 2016.

"Why do the church bells ring so often?" I asked Nailza de Arruda soon after I moved into a corner of her tiny mud-walled hut near the top of the shantytown called the Alto do Cruzeiro (Crucifix Hill). I was then a Peace Corps volunteer and a community development/health worker. It was the dry and blazing hot summer of 1965, the months following the military coup in Brazil, and save for the rusty, clanging bells of N. S. das Dores Church, an eerie quiet had settled over the market town that I call Bom Jesus da Mata. Beneath the quiet, however, there was chaos and panic. "It's nothing," replied Nailza, 'just another little angel gone to heaven."

Nailza had sent more than her share of little angels to heaven, and sometimes at night I could hear her engaged in a muffled but passionate discourse with one of them, two-year-old Joana. Joana's photograph, taken as she lay propped up in her tiny cardboard coffin, her eyes open, hung on a wall next to one of Nailza and Ze Antonio taken on the day they eloped.

Nailza could barely remember the other infants and babies who came and went in close succession. Most had died unnamed and were hastily baptized in their coffins. Few lived more than a month or two. Only Joana, properly baptized in church at the close of her first year and placed under the protection of a powerful saint, Joan of Arc, had been expected to live. And Nailza had dangerously allowed herself to love the little girl.

In addressing the dead child, Nailza's voice would range from tearful imploring to angry recrimination: "Why did you leave me? Was your patron saint so greedy that she could not allow me one child on this earth?" Ze Antonio advised me to ignore Nailza's odd behavior, which he understood as a kind of madness that, like the birth and death of children, came and went. Indeed, the premature birth of a stillborn son some months later "cured" Nailza of her "inappropriate" grief, and the day came when she removed Joana's photo and carefully packed it away.

More than fifteen years elapsed before I returned to the Alto do Cruzeiro, and it was anthropology that provided the vehicle of my return. Since 1982 I have returned several times in order to pursue a problem that first attracted my attention in the 1960s. My involvement with the people of the Alto do Cruzeiro now spans a quarter of a century and three generations of parenting in a community where mothers and daughters are often simultaneously pregnant.

The Alto do Cruzeiro is one of three shantytowns surrounding the large market town of Bom Jesus in the sugar plantation zone of Pernambuco in Northeast Brazil, one of the many zones of neglect that have emerged in the shadow of the now tarnished economic miracle of Brazil. For the women and children of the Alto do Cruzeiro the only miracle is that some of them have managed to stay alive at all.

The Northeast is a region of vast proportions (approximately twice the size of Texas) and of equally vast social and developmental problems. The nine states that make up the region are the poorest in the country and are representative of the Third World within a dynamic and rapidly industrializing nation. Despite waves of migrations from the interior to the teeming shantytowns of coastal cities, the majority still live in rural areas on farms and ranches, sugar plantations and mills.

Life expectancy in the Northeast is only forty years, largely because of the appallingly high rate of infant and child mortality. Approximately one million children in Brazil under the age of five die each year. The children of the Northeast, especially those born in shantytowns on the periphery of urban life, are at a very high risk of death. In these areas, children are born without the traditional protection of breast-feeding, subsistence gardens, stable marriages, and multiple adult caretakers that exists in the interior. In the hillside shantytowns that spring up around cities or, in this case, interior market towns, marriages are brittle, single parenting is the norm, and women are frequently forced into the shadow economy of domestic work in the homes of the rich or into unprotected and oftentimes "scab" wage labor on the surrounding sugar plantations, where they clear land for planting and weed for a pittance, sometimes less than a dollar a day. The women of the Alto may not bring their babies with them into the homes of the wealthy, where the often sick infants are considered sources of contamination, and they cannot carry the little ones to the riverbanks where they wash clothes because the river is heavily infested with schistosomes and other deadly parasites. Nor can they carry their young children to the plantations, which are often several miles away. At wages of a dollar a day, the women of the Alto cannot hire baby sitters. Older children who are not in school will sometimes serve as somewhat indifferent caretakers. But any child not in school is also expected to find wage work. In most cases, babies are simply left at home alone, the door securely fastened. And so many also die alone and unattended.

Bom Jesus da Mata, centrally located in the plantation zone of Pernambuco, is within commuting distance of several sugar plantations and mills. Consequently, Bom Jesus has been a magnet for rural workers forced off their small subsistence plots by large landowners wanting to use every available piece of land for sugar cultivation. Initially, the rural migrants to Bom Jesus were squatters who were given tacit approval by the mayor to put up temporary straw huts on each of the three hills overlooking the town. The Alto do Cruzeiro is the oldest, the largest, and the poorest of the shantytowns. Over the past three decades many of the original migrants have become permanent residents, and the primitive and temporary straw huts have been replaced by small homes (usually of two rooms) made of wattle and daub, sometimes covered with plaster. The more affluent residents use bricks and tiles. In most Alto homes, dangerous kerosene lamps have been replaced by light bulbs. The once tattered rural garb, often fashioned from used sugar sacking, has likewise been replaced by store-bought clothes, often castoffs from a wealthy *patrao* (boss). The trappings are modern, but the hunger, sickness, and death that they conceal are traditional, deeply rooted in a history of feudalism, exploitation, and institutionalized dependency.

My research agenda never wavered. The questions I addressed first crystallized during a veritable "die-off" of Alto babies during a severe drought in 1965. The food and water shortages and the political and economic chaos occasioned by the military coup were reflected in the handwritten entries of births and deaths in the dusty, yellowed pages of the ledger books kept at the public registry office in Bom Jesus. More than 350 babies died in the Alto during 1965 alone—this from a shantytown population of little more than 5,000. But that wasn't what surprised me. There were reasons enough for the deaths in the miserable conditions of shantytown life. What puzzled me was the seeming indifference of Alto women to the death of their infants, and their willingness to attribute to their own tiny offspring an aversion to life that made their death seem wholly natural, indeed all but anticipated.

Although I found that it was possible, and hardly difficult, to rescue infants and toddlers from death by diarrhea and dehydration with a simple sugar, salt, and water solution (even bottled Coca Cola worked fine), it was more difficult to enlist a mother herself in the rescue of a child she perceived as ill-fated for life or better off dead, or to convince her to take back into her threatened and besieged home a baby she had already come to think of as an angel rather than as a son or daughter.

I learned that the high expectancy of death, and the ability to face child death with stoicism and equanimity, produced patterns of nurturing that differentiated between those infants thought of as thrivers and survivors and those thought of as born already "wanting to die." The survivors were nurtured, while stigmatized, doomed infants were left to die, as mothers say, *a mingua*, "of neglect." Mothers stepped back and allowed nature to take its course. This pattern, which I call mortal selective neglect, is called passive infanticide by anthropologist Marvin Harris. The Alto situation, although culturally specific in the form that it takes, is not unique to Third World shantytown communities and may have its correlates in our own impoverished urban communities in some cases of "failure to thrive" infants.

I use as an example the story of Zezinho, the thirteen-month-old toddler of one of my neighbors, Lourdes. I became involved with Zezinho when I was called in to help Lourdes in the delivery of another child, this one a fair and robust little tyke with a lusty cry. I noted that while Lourdes showed great interest in the newborn, she totally ignored Zezinho who, wasted and severely malnourished, was curled up in a fetal position on a piece of urine- and feces-soaked cardboard placed under his mother's hammock. Eyes open and vacant, mouth slack, the little boy seemed doomed.

When I carried Zezinho up to the community daycare center at the top of the hill, the Alto women who took turns caring for one another's children (in order to free themselves for part-time work in the cane fields or washing clothes) laughed at my efforts to save Ze, agreeing with Lourdes that here was a baby without a ghost of a chance. Leave him alone, they cautioned. It makes no sense to fight with death. But I did do battle with Ze, and after several weeks of force-feeding (malnourished babies lose their interest in food), Ze began to succumb to my ministrations. He acquired some flesh across his taut chest bones, learned to sit up, and even tried to smile. When he seemed well enough, I returned him to Lourdes in her miserable scrap material lean-to, but not without guilt about what

I had done. I wondered whether returning Ze was at all fair to Lourdes and to his little brother. But I was busy and washed my hands of the matter. And Lourdes did seem more interested in Ze now that he was looking more human.

When I returned in 1982, there was Lourdes among the women who formed my sample of Alto mothers— still struggling to put together some semblance of life for a now grown Ze and her five other surviving children. Much was made of my reunion with Ze in 1982, and everyone enjoyed retelling the story of Ze's rescue and of how his mother had given him up for dead. Ze would laugh the loudest when told how I had had to force-feed him like a fiesta turkey. There was no hint of guilt on the part of Lourdes and no resentment on the part of Ze. In fact, when questioned in private as to who was the best friend he ever had in life, Ze took a long drag on his cigarette and answered without a trace of irony, "Why my mother, of course." "But of course," I replied.

Part of learning how to mother in the Alto do Cruzeiro is learning when to let go of a child who shows that it "wants" to die or that it has no "knack" or no "taste" for life. Another part is learning when it is safe to let oneself love a child. Frequent child death remains a powerful shaper of maternal thinking and practice. In the absence of firm expectation that a child will survive, mother love as we conceptualize it (whether in popular terms or in the psychobiological notion of maternal bonding) is attenuated and delayed with consequences for infant survival. In an environment already precarious to young life, the emotional detachment of mothers toward some of their babies contributes even further to the spiral of high mortality—high fertility in a kind of macabre lock-step dance of death.

The average woman of the Alto experiences 9.5 pregnancies, 3.5 child deaths, and 1.5 stillbirths. Seventy percent of all child deaths in the Alto occur in the first six months of life, and 82 percent by the end of the first year. Of all deaths in the community each year, about 45 percent are of children under the age of five.

Women of the Alto distinguish between child deaths understood as natural (caused by diarrhea and communicable diseases) and those resulting from sorcery, the evil eye, or other magical or supernatural afflictions. They also recognize a large category of infant deaths seen as fated and inevitable. These hopeless cases are classified by mothers under the folk terminology "child sickness" or "child attack." Women say that there are at least fourteen different types of hopeless child sickness, but most can be subsumed under two categories: chronic and acute. The chronic cases refer to infants who are born small and wasted. They are deathly pale, mothers say, as well as weak and passive. They demonstrate no vital force, no liveliness. They do not suck vigorously; they hardly cry. Such babies can be this way at birth or they can be born sound but soon show no resistance, no "fight" against the common crises of infancy: diarrhea, respiratory infections, tropical fevers.

The acute cases are those doomed infants who die suddenly and violently. They are taken by stealth overnight, often following convulsions that bring on head banging, shaking, grimacing, and shrieking. Women say it is horrible to look at such a baby. If the infant begins to foam at the mouth or gnash its teeth or go rigid with its eyes turned back inside its head, there is absolutely no hope. The infant is "put aside"—left alone—often on the floor in a back room, and allowed to die. These symptoms (which accompany high fevers, dehydration, third-stage malnutrition, and encephalitis) are equated by Alto women with madness, epilepsy, and worst of all, rabies, which is greatly feared and highly stigmatized.

Most of the infants presented to me as suffering from chronic child sickness were tiny, wasted famine victims, while those labeled as victims of acute child attack seemed to be infants suffering from the deliriums of high fever or the convulsions that can accompany electrolyte imbalance in dehydrated babies.

Local midwives and traditional healers, praying women, as they are called, advise Alto women on when to allow a baby to die. One midwife explained: "If I can see that a baby was born unfortuitously, I tell the mother that she need not wash the infant or give it a cleansing tea. I tell her just to dust the infant with baby powder and wait for it to die." Allowing nature to take its course is not seen as sinful by these often very devout Catholic women. Rather, it is understood as cooperating with God's plan.

Often I have been asked how consciously women of the Alto behave in this regard. I would have to say that consciousness is always shifting between allowed and disallowed levels of awareness. For example, I was awakened early one morning in 1987 by two neighborhood children who had been sent to fetch me to a hastily organized wake for a two-month-old infant whose mother I had unsuccessfully urged to breast-feed.

The infant was being sustained on sugar water, which the mother referred to as *soro* (serum), using a medical term for the infant's starvation regime in light of his chronic diarrhea. I had cautioned the mother that an infant could not live on *soro* forever.

The two girls urged me to console the young mother by telling her that it was "too bad" that her infant was so weak that Jesus had to take him. They were coaching me in proper Alto etiquette. I agreed, of course, but asked, "And what do *you* think?" Xoxa, the eleven-year-old, looked down at her dusty flip-flops and blurted out, "Oh, Dona Nanci, that baby never got enough to eat, but you must never say that!" And so the death of hungry babies remains one of the best kept secrets of life in Bom Jesus da Mata.

Most victims are waked quickly and with a minimum of ceremony. No tears are shed, and the neighborhood children form a tiny procession, carrying the baby to the town graveyard where it will join a multitude of others. Although a few fresh flowers may be scattered over the tiny grave, no stone or wooden cross will mark the place, and the same spot will be reused within a few months' time. The mother will never visit the grave, which soon becomes an anonymous one.

What, then, can be said of these women? What emotions, what sentiments motivate them? How are they able to do what, in fact, must be done? What does mother love mean in this inhospitable context? Are grief, mourning, and melancholia present, although deeply repressed? If so, where shall we look for them? And if not, how are we to understand the moral visions and moral sensibilities that guide their actions?

I have been criticized more than once for presenting an unflattering portrait of poor Brazilian women, women who are, after all, themselves the victims of severe social and institutional neglect. I have described these women as allowing some of their children to die, as if this were an unnatural and inhuman act rather than, as I would assert, the way any one of us might act, reasonably and rationally, under similarly desperate conditions. Perhaps I have not emphasized enough the real pathogens in this environment of high risk: poverty, deprivation, sexism, chronic hunger, and economic exploitation. If mother love is, as many psychologists and some feminists believe, a seemingly natural and universal maternal script, what does it mean to women for whom scarcity, loss, sickness, and deprivation have made that love frantic and robbed them of their grief, seeming to turn their hearts to stone?

Throughout much of human history—as in a great deal of the impoverished Third World today—women have had to give birth and to nurture children under ecological conditions and social arrangements hostile to child survival, as well as to their own well-being. Under circumstances of high childhood mortality, patterns of selective neglect and passive infanticide may be seen as active survival strategies.

They also seem to be fairly common practices historically and across cultures. In societies characterized by high childhood mortality and by a correspondingly high (replacement) fertility, cultural practices of infant and child care tend to be organized primarily around survival goals. But what this means is a pragmatic recognition that not all of one's children can be expected to live. The nervousness about child survival in areas of northeast Brazil, northern India, or Bangladesh, where a 30 percent or 40 percent mortality rate in the first years of life is common, can lead to forms of delayed attachment and a casual or benign neglect that serves to weed out the worst bets so as to enhance the life chances of healthier siblings, including those yet to be born. Practices similar to those that I am describing have been recorded for parts of Africa, India, and Central America.

Life in the Alto do Cruzeiro resembles nothing so much as a battlefield or an emergency room in an overcrowded inner-city public hospital. Consequently, morality is guided by a kind of "lifeboat ethics," the morality of triage. The seemingly studied indifference toward the suffering of some of their infants, conveyed in such sayings as "little critters have no feelings," is understandable in light of these women's obligation to carry on with their reproductive and nurturing lives.

In their slowness to anthropomorphize and personalize their infants, everything is mobilized so as to prevent maternal over-attachment and, therefore, grief at death. The bereaved mother is told not to cry, that her tears will dampen the wings of her little angel so that she cannot fly up to her heavenly home. Grief at the death of an angel is not only inappropriate, it is a symptom of madness and of a profound lack of faith.

Infant death becomes routine in an environment in which death is anticipated and bets are hedged. While the routinization of death in the context of shantytown life is not hard to understand, and quite possible to empathize with, its routinization in the formal institutions of public life in Bom Jesus is not as easy to accept uncritically. Here the social production of indifference takes on a different, even a malevolent, cast.

In a society where triplicates of every form are required for the most banal events (registering a car, for example), the registration of infant and child death is informal, incomplete, and rapid. It requires no documentation, takes less than five minutes, and demands no witnesses other than office clerks. No questions are asked concerning the circumstances of the death, and the cause of death is left blank, unquestioned and unexamined. A neighbor, grandmother, older sibling, or common-law husband may register the death. Since most infants die at home, there is no question of a medical record.

From the registry office, the parent proceeds to the town hall, where the mayor will give him or her a voucher for a free baby coffin. The fulltime municipal coffinmaker cannot tell you exactly how many baby coffins are dispatched each week. It varies, he says, with the seasons. There are more needed during the drought months and during the big festivals of Carnaval and Christmas and Sao Joao's Day because people are too busy, he supposes, to take their babies to the clinic. Record keeping is sloppy.

Similarly, there is a failure on the part of city-employed doctors working at two free clinics to recognize the malnutrition of babies who are weighed, measured, and immunized without comment and as if they were not, in fact, anemic, stunted, fussy, and irritated starvation babies. At best the mothers are told to pick up free vitamins or a health "tonic" at the municipal chambers. At worst, clinic personnel will give tranquilizers and sleeping pills to quiet the hungry cries of "sickto-death" Alto babies.

The church, too, contributes to the routinization of, and indifference toward, child death. Traditionally, the local Catholic church taught patience and resignation to domestic tragedies that were said to reveal the imponderable workings of God's will. If an infant died suddenly, it was because a particular saint had claimed the child. The infant would be an angel in the service of his or her heavenly patron. It would be wrong, a sign of a lack of faith, to weep for a child with such good fortune. The infant funeral was, in the past, an event celebrated with joy. Today, however, under the new regime of "liberation theology," the bells of N.S. das Dores parish church no longer peal for the death of Alto babies, and no priest accompanies the procession of angels to the cemetery where their bodies are disposed of casually and without ceremony. Children bury children in Bom Jesus da Mata. In this most Catholic of communities, the coffin is handed to the disabled and irritable municipal gravedigger, who often chides the children for one reason or another. It may be that the coffin is larger than expected and the gravedigger can find no appropriate space. The children do not wait for the gravedigger to complete his task. No prayers are recited and no sign of the cross made as the tiny coffin goes into its shallow grave.

When I asked the local priest, Padre Marcos, about the lack of church ceremony surrounding infant and childhood death today in Bom Jesus, he replied: "In the old days, child death was richly celebrated. But those were the baroque customs of a conservative church that wallowed in death and misery. The new church is a church of hope and joy. We no longer celebrate the death of child angels. We try to tell mothers that Jesus doesn't want all the dead babies they send him." Similarly, the new church has changed its baptismal customs, now often refusing to baptize dying babies brought to the back door of a church or rectory. The mothers are scolded by the church attendants and told to go home and take care of their sick babies. Baptism, they are told, is for the living; it is not to be confused with the sacrament of extreme unction, which is the anointing of the dying. And so it appears to the women of the Alto that even the church has turned away from them, denying the traditional comfort of folk Catholicism.

The contemporary Catholic church is caught in the clutches of a double bind. The new theology of liberation imagines a kingdom of God on earth based on justice and equality, a world without hunger, sickness, or childhood mortality. At the same time, the church has not changed its official position on sexuality and reproduction, including its sanctions against birth control, abortion, and sterilization. The padre of Bom Jesus da Mata recognizes this contradiction intuitively, although he shies away from discussions on the topic, saying that he prefers to leave questions of family planning to the discretion and the "good consciences" of his impoverished parishioners. But this, of course, sidesteps the extent to which those good consciences have been shaped by traditional church teachings in Bom Jesus, especially by his recent predecessors. Hence, we can begin to see that the seeming indifference of Alto mothers toward the death of some of their infants is but a pale reflection of the official indifference of church and state to the plight of poor women and children.

Nonetheless, the women of Bom Jesus are survivors. One woman, Biu, told me her life history, returning again and again to the themes of child death, her first husband's suicide, abandonment by her father and later by her second husband, and all the other losses and disappointments she has suffered in her long forty-five years. She concluded with great force, reflecting on the days of Carnaval '88 that were fast approaching:

> No, Dona Nanci, I won't cry, and I won't waste my life thinking about it from morning to night . . . Can I argue with God for the state that I'm in? No! And so I'll dance and I'll jump and I'll play Carnaval! And yes, I'll laugh and people will wonder at a *pobre* like me who can have such a good time.

And no one did blame Biu for dancing in the streets during the four days of Carnaval—not even on Ash Wednesday, the day following Carnaval '88 when we all assembled hurriedly to assist in the burial of Mercea, Biu's beloved *casula*, her lastborn daughter who had died at home of pneumonia during the festivities. The rest of the family barely had time to change out of their costumes. Severino, the child's uncle and godfather, sprinkled holy water over the little angel while he prayed: "Mercea, I don't know whether you were called, taken, or thrown out of this world. But look down at us from your heavenly home with tenderness, with pity, and with mercy." So be it.

Epilogue: The Afterlife of "Death Without Weeping"

Many students write to me after reading this article asking whether the situationhas changed in the Alto do Cruzeiro. Is life better or worse for mothers and newborn babies? One of the advantages of traditional, long-term ethnographic research is that one gets to see history in the making. I began my engagements with the people of the Alto in 1964 at the start of twenty years of military rule, a ruthless political-economic regime that produced widespread impoverishment among those excluded populations living in deep urban slums (favelas) and in peripheral rural

communities. The scarcities and insecurities of that era contributed to the death of infants and small babies. By the time I completed my study of mother love and child death in the early 1990s Brazil was well on its way to full democratization which ushered in many important changes, most notably a national health care system (SUS) which guaranteed poor women adequate pre-natal care, hospital delivery and basic maternal infant care during the first years of life.

The decade of the 1990s witnessed in Brazil what population experts call the demographic or epidemiologic transition. Both births and infant deaths declined which radically transformed the way newborns were perceived and received by Alto mothers. The old hesitant stance of maternal "watchful waiting" that was accompanied by "letting go" of infants viewed as having no "taste" or "talent" for life, was replaced by a new maternal ethos of "holding on" and "holding dear" each infant seen as capable of survival.

Today, young women of the Alto can expect to give birth to three or fewer infants and to see all of them live to adolescence. Many factors came together in producing this reproductive transition. The new teachings of liberation theology did eventually dislodge a baroque folk Catholicism that saw God and the saints as "authorizing" infant death by "calling" the infants to themselves. Women began to think of themselves as able to determine how many pregnancies they would have. The availability of the drug Cytotec used "off label" as a risky "morning after" pill provided, for all its risks, the possibility of birth spacing that had not previously existed. President Fernando Henrique Cardoso (1995–2003) and his wife, the anthropologist Ruth Vilaça Correia Leite Cardoso, worked hard to fortify the national health care system (Serviço Único de Saúde) with a program of local "health agents," "barefoot doctors," who visit poor households door to door, identifying those at risk and rescuing a great many vulnerable infants, toddlers and old people from premature death. However, the primary cause of the decline in infant mortality on the Alto do Cruzeiro was the result of a state supported municipal program to install pipes reaching almost all the homes in the shantytown with sufficient and clean water. Water = life! One can actually see how maternal sentiments and practices closely follow and reflect changes in the basic material conditions and therefore the possibilities of everyday life.

Motherhood is not only a social and a cultural construction but a constellation of embodied practices responding to the requirements and limitations of the political economy that determines the food people eat or don't eat, the water they drink or don't drink, the shoes they wear or don't wear, the books they read or cannot read, the homes made of mud and sticks or of brick and tiles.

There are new problems faced by the people of the Alto do Cruzeiro today. Since the publication of "Death Without Weeping" drugs and gangs have made their ugly mark on the community as have new disease epidemics. Death squads and "extermination groups" sprang up to minister a kind of vigilante justice before they were interrupted by the justice system. Those new features of anti-social life in "Bom Jesus da Mata" take a bit of the pleasure away, as I had to take note of so many children of the Alto do Cruzeiro who survived that dangerous first year of life only to be cut down by bullets and knives at the age of 15 or 17 by local gangs, "strong men," *bandidos, pistoleiro* (hired guns) and local police in near equal measure.

But that story, and its resolution, awaits a much longer telling in my forthcoming book, *Longing for Brazil: The Afterlife of "Death Without Weeping"* (UC Press).

4.3 Hijra and Sādhin: Neither Man nor Woman in India

SERENA NANDA

Cross-cultural studies of sex and gender systems demonstrate that there are no "natural" categories; both sex and gender are artificial and constructed. The hijra and sādhin in India are examples of a "third gender," a term that reflects societies that recognize three or more categories of sex/gender. Hijras are neither man nor woman, but "man minus man" because they lack male genitals due to being born intersex or undergoing castration, and "man plus woman" because they embrace superficial aspects of femininity. Hijras are highly valued in society, for their spiritual connection to important Hindu deities, and hold special roles at birthing rituals. While respected, they also may face ridicule due to their work in prostitution and because they exist beyond normal caste and kinship relationships. The sādhin is a female gender variant, who renounces marriage and sexuality, and becomes viewed as asexual. Sādhins live "as if" men and can perform masculine productive and social activities, however, they do not hold a spiritual role like hijras. The cultural recognition of hijras and sādhins is supported by Hinduism and provides social meaning and power to anatomical sex/gender ambiguity. While this piece appears in the gender, sex, and sexuality section, it is also particularly useful for discussions surrounding the social functions and symbolism found within birthing rituals.

Questions:

1. How are hijras regarded within Hindu culture?
2. How do hijras and sādhins challenge the Western assumption that sex and gender are "natural" categories?
3. What is the relationship between sex/gender systems and religious doctrine?

. . . Gender diversity in India is set within a basically binary sex/gender system that is hierarchical and patriarchal rather than one that is egalitarian.

In Hindu India, male and female / man and woman are viewed as natural categories in complementary opposition. This binary construction incorporates—and conflates—biological qualities (sex) and cultural qualities (gender). Males and females are born with different sexual characteristics and reproductive organs, have different sexual natures, and take different and complementary roles in marriage, sexual behavior, and reproduction. The biological or "essential" nature of the differences between male and female, man and woman, is amply demonstrated in the medical and ritual texts of classical Hinduism, in which body fluids and sexual organs are presented as both the major sources of the sex/gender dichotomy and its major symbols (O'Flaherty 1980).

In Hinduism, in contrast to Western culture, the female principle is the more active, animating the male principle, which is more inert and latent. This active female principle has an erotic, creative, life-giving aspect and a destructive, life-destroying aspect. The erotic aspect of female power is dangerous unless it is controlled by the male principle. Powerful women, whether deities or humans, must be restrained by male authority. Thus, the Hindu Mother Goddess is kind and helpful when subordinated to her male consort, but when dominant, the goddess is aggressive, devouring, and destructive. The view that unrestrained female sexuality is dangerous characterizes a more down-to-earth sexual ideology as well. In India, both in Hinduism and in Islam, women are believed to be more sexually voracious than men; in order to prevent their sexual appetites from causing social chaos and distracting men from their higher spiritual duties, women must be controlled.

The Religious Context of Gender Diversity

. . . Unlike Western cultures and religions, which try to resolve, repress, or dismiss sexual contradictions and ambiguities as jokes or trivia, Hinduism has a great capacity to allow opposites to confront each other without necessarily resolving the opposition, "celebrating the idea that the universe is boundlessly various, and . . . that all possibilities may exist without excluding each other" (O' Flaherty 1973, 318). The presence of alternative genders and gender transformations in Hinduism gives positive meaning to the lives of many individuals with a variety of alternative gender identifications, physical conditions, and erotic preferences. Despite the criminalization of many kinds of transgender behavior under British rule and even by the Indian government after independence, Indian society has not yet permitted cultural anxiety about transgenderism to express itself in culturally institutionalized phobias and repressions.

Ancient Hindu origin myths often feature androgynous or hermaphroditic ancestors. The Rg Veda (a classical Hindu religious text), for example, says that before creation the world lacked all distinctions, including those of sex and gender. Ancient poets often expressed this concept with androgynous or hermaphroditic images, such as a male with a womb, a male deity with breasts, or a pregnant male (Zwilling and Sweet 2000, 101). . . . Individuals who do not fit into society's major sex/gender categories may be stigmatized but may also find, within Hinduism, meaningful and valued gender identifications.

. . . Within the Hindu sex/gender system, the interchange of male and female qualities, transformations of sex and gender, the incorporation of male and female within one person, and alternative sex and gender roles among deities and humans are meaningful and positive themes in mythology, ritual and art. Among the many kinds of male and female sex/gender variants, the most visible and culturally institutionalized are the *hijras.*

Hijras are culturally defined as "neither man nor woman." They are born as males and through a ritual surgical transformation become an alternative, third sex/gender category (Nanda 1999). . . . Their traditional employment is to perform at marriages and after a child (especially a son) has been born. They sing and dance and bless the child and the family for increased fertility and prosperity in the name of the goddess. They then receive traditional payments of money, sweets, and cloth in return.

Hijras as Not-Men . . .

The recognition of more than two sex/genders is recorded in India as early as the eighth century BCE; like the hijras, alternative or third sex/gendered persons were primarily considered to be defective males. The core of their deficiency centered on their sexual impotence, or inability to procreate (Zwilling and Sweet 1996, 361). In India today, the term hijra is most commonly translated as "eunuch" or intersexed, and emphasizes sexual impotence. Hijras are culturally defined as persons who are born as males but who adopt the clothing, behavior and occupations of women, and who are neither male nor female, neither man nor woman.

Hijra sexual impotence is popularly understood as *a physical* defect impairing the male sexual function in intercourse (in the inserter role) and in reproduction. This is the major way in which hijras are "not-men." Hijras attribute their impotence to a defective male sexual organ. A child who at birth is classified as male but whose genitals are subsequently noticed to be ambiguous, culturally would be defined as a hijra, or as potentially a hijra (though in fact not all such individuals become hijras). Like their counterparts in native North America, hijras (as receptors) frequently have sexual relationships with men. While hijras are not defined by their sexual practices, they often define themselves as "men who have no desire for women." Linguistically and culturally, hijras are distinguished from other men who take the receptor role in sex and are identified by their same-sex sexual orientation (Cohen 1995). It is the hijras' sexual impotence and in-between sex/gender status that is at the core of their cultural definition. A male who is not biologically intersexed who wishes to become a hijra must transform his sex/gender through the emasculation operation. . . .

Although all hijras explain their deficient masculinity by saying, "I was born this way," this statement is not factually true. Rather, it expresses the Hindu view that qualities of both sex and gender are inborn, and is also consistent with the Hindu view that fate is important in shaping one's life chances and experiences.

Hirjras as Women and Not-Men

While hijras are "man minus man," they are also "man plus woman." Hijras adopt many aspects of the feminine gender role. They wear women's dress, hairstyle, and accessories; they imitate women's walk, gestures, voice, facial expressions and language; they have only male sexual partners and they experience themselves positively as sexual objects of men's desires. Hijras take feminine names as part of their gender transformation and use female kinship terms for many of their relationships with each other, such as sister, aunty, and grandmother (Hall 1995). They request "ladies only" seating in public transportation and they periodically demand to be counted as women (rather than men) in the census. Being a hijra means not only divesting oneself of one's masculine identity, but also taking on a feminine one.

Although hijras are "like" women, they are also "not-women." Their feminine dress and manners are often exaggerations and their aggressive female sexuality contrasts strongly with the normatively submissive demeanor of ordinary women. Hijra performances do not attempt a realistic imitation of women but rather a burlesque, and the very act of dancing in public violates norms of feminine behavior. Hijras also use coarse and abusive speech, both among themselves and to their audiences, which is also deviant for Indian women. . . .

Because hijras are defined as neither men nor women they were sometimes prohibited from wearing women's clothing exclusively: some Indian rulers in the eighteenth century required that hijras distinguish themselves by wearing a man's turban with their female clothing. A century later, hijras were reported as wearing "a medley of male and female clothing," with a female sari under a male coat-like, outer garment (Preston 1987, 373). This seems similar to North American gender variant transvestism, though hijras today for the most part do not wear gendermixed clothing.

The major reason why hijras are considered—by themselves and others—as not-woman is that they do not have female reproductive organs and therefore cannot have children. The hijras tell a story about a hijra who prayed to god to bear a child. God granted her wish, but since she had not specifically prayed for the child to be born, she could not give birth. She remained pregnant until she could not stand the weight any more and slit her stomach open to deliver the baby. Both the hijra and the baby died. This story illustrates that it is against the nature of hijras to reproduce like women do, thereby denying them full identification as women.

Religious Identifications

An important sex/gender identification of hijras is with Arjun, hero of the great Hindu epic, the Mahabharata. In one episode Arjun is exiled and lives for a year in the disguise of a eunuch-transvestite, wearing women's dress and bracelets, braiding his hair like a woman, and teaching singing and dancing to the women of the king's court. In this role he also participates in weddings and childbirths, a clear point of identification with the hijras (Hiltelbeital 1980).

The hijras' identification with Arjun is visually reinforced by Arjun's representation in popular drama as a vertically divided halfman/half-woman. In this form Arjun is identified with the sexually ambivalent deity, Shiva, who is also frequently represented as a vertically divided half-man/half-woman, symbolizing his union with his female energy.

Shiva is particularly associated with the concept of creative asceticism, which is the core of hijra identity and power. In Hinduism, sexual impotence can be transformed into procreative power through the practice of asceticism, or the renunciation of sex. The power that results from sexual abstinence (called *tapas*) paradoxically becomes an essential feature in the process of creation.

In one Hindu creation myth, Shiva was asked to create the world, but took so long to do so that the power of creation was given to another deity, Brahma (The Creator). When Shiva was finally ready to begin creation he saw that the universe was already created and got so angry, he broke off his phallus saying "there is no use for this," and threw it into the earth. Paradoxically, as soon as Shiva's phallus ceased to be a source of individual fertility, it became a source of universal fertility (O'Flaherty 1973). This paradox expresses the power of the hijras who as emasculated men are individually impotent but nevertheless are able to confer blessings for fertility on others. As creative ascetics hijras are considered auspicious and powerful, and this underlies their ritual performances at marriages and childbirth.

While at one level the hijras' claim to power is through Shiva's ritual sacrifice of the phallus, at a more conscious and culturally elaborated level, the power of the hijras is based on their identification with the Mother Goddess. In Hindu India, salvation and success are equated with submission, particularly in regard to the Mother Goddess. The Mother Goddess must offer help when confronted with complete surrender of the devotee, but those who deny her wishes put themselves in danger. Thus, underlying the surrender is fear. . . . [T]he Hindu Mother Goddess is singularly intense in her destructive aspects, which, nevertheless, contain the seeds of salvation. . . . Popular Hindu mythology (and its hijra versions) abounds in images of the aggressive Mother Goddess as she devours, beheads, and castrates—destructive acts that nevertheless contain the possibility of rebirth, as in the hijra emasculation ritual. This dual nature of the goddess provides the powerful symbolic and psychological context in which the hijras become culturally meaningful as an alternative sex/gender.

Deficient masculinity by itself does not make a hijra. Hijras are deficient men who receive a call from their goddess—which they ignore at the peril of being born impotent for seven future rebirths—to undergo a sex and gender change, wear their hair long, and dress in women's clothes. The sex change, which involves surgical removal of the genitals, is called "the operation" (even by hijras who do not otherwise speak English). For hijras, the operation is a form of rebirth and it contains many of the symbolic elements of childbirth. Only after the operation do hijras become vehicles of the power of the Mother Goddess whose blessings they bestow at weddings and childbirth. For hijras not born intersexed, the operation transforms an impotent, "useless" male into a hijra, and a vehicle of the procreative power of the Mother Goddess. . . .

The surgery is (ideally) performed by a hijra, called a "midwife." The client is seated in front of a picture of the goddess and repeats Bahuchara's name over and over, which induces a trancelike state. The midwife then severs all or part of the genitals (penis and testicles) from the body with two diagonal cuts with a sharp knife. The blood from the operation, which is considered part of the male identity, is allowed to flow freely; this rids the person of their maleness. The resulting wound is healed by traditional medical practices and a small hole is left open for urination. After the operation the new hijra is subject to many of the same restrictions as a woman after childbirth and is supervised and taken care of by hijra elders. In the final stage of the ritual, the hijra is dressed as a bride, signifying the active sexuality potential in marriage, and is taken through the streets in procession. This completes the ritual and the sex/ gender transformation. Although emasculation is prohibited by Indian law, hijras continue to practice it secretly (Ranade 1983).

Hijras as Ascetics

In India, gender is an important part of being a full social person. Through marriage, men are expected to produce children, especially sons, in order to continue the family line. An individual who dies without being married, an impotent man, or a woman who does not menstruate is considered an incomplete person. However, the individual who is not capable of reproduction, as either a man or a woman, or who does not wish to marry, is not necessarily excluded from society. . . . In India, a meaningful role that transcends the categories of (married) man and (married) woman is that of the ascetic, or renouncer, a person both outside society yet also part of it. In identifying with the ascetic role, individuals who are sexually "betwixt and between" for any number of biological reasons or personal choices are able to transform an incomplete personhood into a transcendent one. Within the Hindu religion, the life path of an ascetic is one of the many diverse paths that an individual may take to achieve salvation.

Hijras identify themselves as ascetics in their renunciation of sexual desire, in abandoning their family and kinship ties, and in their dependence on alms (religiously inspired charity) for their livelihood. As ascetics, hijras transcend the stigma of their sex/ gender deficiencies.

An important Hindu belief, called *dharma*, is that every individual has a life path of his/her own that he/she must follow, because every individual has different innate essences, moral qualities, and special abilities. This leads to an acceptance of many different occupations, behaviors, and personal styles as legitimate life paths. . . . Hinduism thus affords the individual personality wide latitude in behavior, including that which Euro-American cultures might label criminal or pathological and attempt to punish or cure. This Hindu concept of the legitimacy of many different life paths applies to hijras and to other sex/gender variants as well.

Ritual Roles and Social Acceptance

In India, the birth of a son is viewed as a major purpose of marriage. As auspicious and powerful ritual figures, on this occasion hijras bless the child and the family and provide entertainment for friends, relatives, and neighbors. . . .

At some point in the performance, one hijra inspects the genitals of the newborn to ascertain its sex. Hijras claim that any baby born intersexed belongs to their community and it is widely believed in India that this claim cannot be resisted. The hijras then confer the power of the Mother Goddess to bless the child for what they themselves do not possess—the power of creating new life, of having many sons, and of carrying on the continuity of a family line. When the performance is completed, the hijras claim their traditional payment.

Hijras also perform after a marriage, when the new bride has come to her husband's home (traditionally, and even today ideally, the couple lives with the groom's parents). The hijras bless the couple so that they will have many sons, which is not only the desire of the family, but also means more work for the hijras. These performances contain flamboyant sexual displays and references to sexuality, which break all the rules of normal social intercourse in gender-mixed company and on this occasion are a source of humor. The hijras' skits and songs refer to potentially conflicting relationships in Indian marriages, for example between mother-in-law and daughter-in-law, or between sisters-in-law. As outsiders to the social structure because of their ambiguous sex/gender status, the hijras are uniquely able to expose the points of tension in a culture where sex, gender, and reproduction are involved. In humorously expressing this tension, the hijras defuse it, yet at the same time, their very

ambiguity of sex and gender keep the tension surrounding sex, gender, and fertility.

Hijras are generally regarded with ambivalence; social attitudes include a combination of mockery, fear, respect, contempt, and even compassion. Fear of the hijras is related to the "virility complex" in India, which has an ancient history and which is also part of contemporary culture. This complex identifies manhood with semen and sexual potency, both of central concern in India's patriarchal culture (Zwilling and Sweet [2000], 6). Hijras have the power to curse as well as to bless, and if they are not paid their due, they will insult a family publicly and curse it with a loss of virility. The ultimate weapon of a hijra is to raise her skirt and display her mutilated genitals; this is both a source of shame and a contamination of the family's reproductive potential.

Hijras are also feared for another reason. Having renounced normal family life, hijras are outside the social roles and relationships of caste and kinship, which define the social person in Hindu culture and which are the main sources of social control of an individual (Ostor, Fruzzetti, and Barnett 1982). Hijras (and other ascetics) are thus an implicit threat to the social order (Lannoy 1975; O'Flaherty 1973). The hijras use their sexual and social marginality to manipulate and exploit the public to their own advantage. Hijras themselves say that because they are marginal to the social rules that govern the behavior of men and women, they are a people without "shame" (Hall 1995; 1997, 445). Hijra audiences know this and feel vulnerable to economic extortion, as they weigh the financial cost of giving in to the hijras' coercive demands for payment against the likelihood that if they do not pay, they will be publicly abused, humiliated, and cursed.

Nevertheless, if hijras challenge their audiences, their audiences also challenge the hijras. Sometimes a member of the hijras' audience will challenge the performers' authenticity by lifting their skirts to see whether they are emasculated and thus "real" hijras or "fake" hijras, men who have male genitals and are thus only impersonating hijras. If hijra performers are found to be "fakes" they arc insulted and chased away without payment.

Hijra Sexuality

Part of the ambivalence surrounding hijras focuses on their sexuality. Sexuality is also a source of conflict within the hijra community. . . . [T]he term hijra translates as eunuch not homosexual; the power of the hijra role resides in their renunciation of sexuality and the transformation of sexual desire into sacred power. In reality, however, many hijras do engage in sexual activities, exclusively in the receptor role with men and frequently as prostitutes. . . .

In addition to the exchange of money for sex with a variety of male clients, hijras also have long-term sexual relationships with men they call their "husbands." These relationships may be one-sided and exploitative, as when the "husband" lives off his hijra "wife," but they may also be affectionate and involve some economic reciprocity. Most hijras prefer having a husband to prostitution and many speak of their husbands in very loving terms, as indeed husbands sometimes do of their hijra wives. For many hijras, joining the hjira community provides an opportunity to engage in sexual relations with men in a safer, more organized and orderly environment than is afforded by street prostitution.

Hijra sexual relationships cause conflict within the hijra community, however. Because active sexuality runs counter to the cultural definition of hijras as ascetics, knowledge of hijra prostitution and sexuality undermines their respect in society. In cities where the hijra population is large, hijra prostitutes are not permitted to live with hijra ritual performers. . . .

The Sādhin: A Female Gender Variant

. . . As noted [previously], marriage and reproduction are essential to recognition as a social person in Hindu India, and "spinsters" rarely exist in rural areas. Among the Gaddis, a numerically small pastoral people of the Himalayan foothills, a female gender variant role called sādhin emerged in the latenineteenth century. Sādhins renounce marriage (and thus, sexuality), though they otherwise live in the material world. They are committed to celibacy for life. Sādhins do not wear women's clothing, but rather the everyday clothing of men, and they wear their hair close cropped (Phillimore 1991).

A girl voluntarily decides to become a sādhin. She usually makes this decision around puberty, before her menarche, though in one reported case, the parents of a six-year-old girl interpreted her preference to dress in boy's clothing and cut her hair like a boy, as an indication of her choice to be a sādhin. For most

sādhins, this role choice, which is considered irreversible, is related to their determined rejection of marriage. A sādhin must be a virgin; she is viewed, however, not just as a celibate woman but as a female asexual. Although the transition from presexual child to an asexual sādhin denies a girl's sexual identity, the girl is not considered to have changed her gender, so much as transcended it. Entering the sādhin role is not marked by ritual, but it is publicly acknowledged when the sādhin adopts men's clothing and has her hair cut in a tonsure, like a boy for his initiation rite into adulthood. Despite her male appearance, however, a sādhin remains socially a woman in many ways, and she retains the female name given to her when she was a child. Sādhins may (but are not obliged to) engage in masculine productive tasks from which women are normally excluded, for example, ploughing, sowing crops, sheep herding, and processing wool. They also, however, do women's work. On gender-segregated ceremonial occasions, adult sādhins may sit with the men as well as smoke the water cigarettes, definitely masculine behaviors. Yet sādhins do not generally attend funerals, a specifically male prerogative.

Ethnographer Peter Phillimore characterizes the role of the sādhin as an "as if" male (1991, 337). A sādhin's gender is not in question, but she can nevertheless operate in many social contexts "like a man." A sādhin can, for example, make the necessary offerings for her father's spirit and the ancestors, a ceremony otherwise performed only by a son. Unlike hijras, though, sādhins have no special ritual or performance roles in society, nor are they considered to have any special sacred powers. Sādhins, like hijras, are ascetics in their renunciation of sexuality, although sādhins are only ambiguous ascetics because they do not renounce other aspects of the material world.

Hindu asceticism is primarily identified with males so that female ascetics behave in significant respects like men; this maleness makes visible and legitimates female asceticism, though it is different from male asceticism in important ways (Humes 1996; Phillimore 1991, 341). Unlike male ascetics, who transcend sex/gender classification and who can renounce the world at any age or stage of life, the sādhin's asceticism must begin before puberty and her lifelong chastity, or purity, is essential to the public acceptance of her status. These differences suggest that within orthodox Hinduism, the sādhin role is a way of controlling female sexuality and providing a social niche for the woman who rejects the only legitimate female roles in traditional Hindu India, those of wife and mother.

. . . When Gaddi migration in the late-nineteenth century brought them into contact with more orthodox Hindus, Gaddis came under increasing cultural pressure to curtail the relative equality and freedom of their women. However, because a woman's decision to reject marriage is an unacceptable challenge to gender conventions among the orthodox Hindus, the sādhin role, defined as an asexual female gender variant, acts as a constraint on the potential, unacceptable, sexuality of unmarried women. The definition of sādhin as asexual transforms "the negative associations of spinsterhood" into the "positive associations of sādhin-hood" (Phillimore 1991, 347).

The sādhin role provides one kind of response to the cultural challenge of adult female virginity in a society where marriage and motherhood are the dominant feminine ideals, while the hijra role, despite its many contradictions, gives meaning and even power to male sex/gender ambiguity in a highly patriarchal culture. While all cultures must deal with those whose anatomy or behavior leaves them outside the classification of male and female, man and woman, it is the genius of Hinduism that allows for so many different ways of being human.

References

Cohen, Lawrence. 1995. The Pleasures of Castration: The Postoperative Status of Hijras, Jankhas, and Academics. *In* Sexual Nature, Sexual Culture. Paul R. Abramson and Steven D. Pinkerton, eds. Pp. 276–304. Chicago: University of Chicago Press.

Hall, Kira. 1995. Hijra/Hijrin: Language and Gender Identity. Unpublished doctoral dissertation in Linguistics, University of California, Berkeley. Ann Arbor, MI: UMI dissertation Services.

Hall, Kira. 1997. Go Suck Your Husband's Sugarcane!: Hijras and the Use of Sexual Insult. *In* Queerly Phrased: Language, Gender, and Sexuality. Anna Livia and Kira Hall, eds. Pp. 430–60. New York: Oxford.

Hiltelbeital, Alf. 1980. Siva, the Goddess, and the Disguises of the Pandavas and Draupadi. History of Religions 20(1-2):147–74.

Humes, Cynthia Ann. 1996. Becoming Male: Salvation through Gender Modification in Hinduism and Buddhism. *In* Gender Reversals and Gender Cultures: Anthropological and Historical Perspectives. Sabrina Petra Ramet, ed. Pp. 123–37. London: Routledge.

Lannoy, Richard. 1975. The Speaking Tree. New York: Oxford University Press.

Nanda, Serena. 1999. The Hijras of India: Neither Man nor Woman, 2nd ed. Belmont, CA: Wadsworth.

O'Flaherty, Wendy Doniger. 1973. Siva: The Erotic Ascetic. New York: Oxford.

O'Flaherty, Wendy Doniger. 1980. Women, Androgynes, and Other Mythical Beasts. Chicago: University of Chicago Press.

Oster, Askos, Lina Fruzetti, and Steve Barnett, eds. 1982. Concepts of Person: Kinship, Caste, and Marriage in India. Cambridge, MA: Harvard University Press.

Phillimore, Peter. 1991. Unmarried Women of the Dhaula Dhar: Celibacy and Social Control in Northwest India. Journal of Anthropological Research 47(3):331–50.

Preston, Lawrence W. 1987. A Right to Exist: Eunuchs and the State in Nineteenth Century India. Modern Asian Studies. 21 (2): 371–387.

Ranade, S.N. 1983. A study of Eunuchs in Delhi. Unpublished Manuscript. Government of India, Delhi.

Zwilling, L. and M. Sweet. 1996. Like a City Ablaze: The Third Sex and the Creation of Sexuality in Jain Religious Literature. Journal of the History of Sexuality 6(3):359–84.

Zwilling, L. and M. Sweet. 2000. The Evolution of Third Sex Constructs in Ancient India: A Study in Ambiguity. *In* Constructing Ideologies: Religion, Gender, and Social Definition in India. Julia Leslie, ed. Delhi: Oxford University Press.

4.4 Virginity Testing as a Local Public Health Initiative: A "Preventative Ritual" More Than a "Diagnostic Measure"

ANNETTE WICKSTRÖM

Virginity testing is a long-standing Zulu tradition that has come to hold an important place as a collective ritual to address the AIDS epidemic. Drawing on fieldwork in Nkolokotho, South Africa, Annette Wickström describes how from the perspective of the women and girls who practice it, virginity testing is not about the individual girl (not about "outing" sexually active girls), but rather about celebrating virginity as a community. It is a collective ritual that serves to reinforce local understandings of morality, and community responsibility for delaying sexual intercourse. The ritual is especially important given changing and contrasting notions of personhood and responsibility, as Zulu traditions clash with Western ideas both about who is responsible for sexual decision-making and sex education. Traditionally, Zulu youth would be taught by their peers to engage in non-penetrating "thigh sex"; with colonialism came educational systems that placed responsibility for sexual relations on the individual and education on parents, contrasting with cultural norms, and the teaching of this form of sexual activity declined. In addition to presenting a cultural mechanism for controlling life-threatening health epidemics, this piece provides case study fuel for a lively debate surrounding universal human rights versus cultural relativism, and invites a critical gender perspective. Why should boys have their "right to choose" to practice circumcision be protected through legislation but girls have their rights upheld by protecting against virginity testing?

Questions

1. Compare and contrast Western and Zulu perspectives on sexuality, personhood, integrity, and responsibility.
2. Discuss the changes to Zulu moral codes and sexual practices that were brought about by post-colonialism and with Christian missionaries.
3. Apply what you learned about cultural relativism and human rights perspectives from Fleur-Lobban (Reading 1.3) to this case study, and argue for and against virginity testing and circumcision from each perspective.
4. What are advantages and disadvantages of sexual education and AIDS campaigns that focus on women?

In the simple stone school below the mountain slope, some women had pushed the school desks aside in one of the classrooms. At the very back of the hall the tester had seated herself on a mat on the floor, her legs wide apart. Between her legs was a cushion with a blanket spread over it. She was putting on plastic gloves when I entered. A woman by her side, wearing the traditional Zulu hat for married women, was tearing off pieces of

Wickström, Annette. "Virginity Testing as a Local Public Health Initiative: A 'Preventative Ritual' More Than a 'Diagnostic Measure.'" 2010. *Journal of the Royal Anthropological Institute* 16(3), 532–550.

toilet paper and folding them. The woman who had asked me to come inside offered me a chair close to the tester, while another woman sat nearby on the floor. Then she returned to a table just inside the entrance, where she and another woman were checking the lists that had been filled in by the girls outside the door. After a while, the same woman opened the door a little, and the first girl, who seemed to be about 17 years old and wore a short skirt and colourful t-shirt, ran inside. She quickly let her underpants drop to the floor and hurried over to the tester. She was a bit confused before she understood how to lie down, with her bottom between the tester's legs. The tester took two pieces of folded toilet paper and drew from the thighs downwards and out, to uncover the hymen. She gave the girl a rough but encouraging tap on her thigh and said "muhle," which means "beautiful." Then the tester asked me to come and see what a virgin looks like inside. I felt that looking would violate the integrity of the girl, but it seemed to be unproblematic for all the others in the room, including the girl herself. The girl then dressed, and one of the women by the table painted a white round mark on her forehead. Full of happiness, she hurried outside and was met by shouts of joy from her peers, who were waiting in the queue on the stairs outside the classroom, and by the characteristic ululation from some adult Zulu women who were present.

In KwaZulu Natal, groups of Zulu have carried out virginity testing campaigns since the mid-1990s, both in the form of large movements including celebrations for several days with the Zulu King at the centre, and in the form of smaller-scale local initiatives, where girls are tested under simple and everyday circumstances. The initiator is often the headman for a community or a female *isangoma* (traditional healer) in different parts of KwaZulu Natal. Some women, practised in examining girls' hymens, have been engaged as examiners, while local women and men have arranged the events.

The Commission on Gender Equality and the Human Rights Commission have condemned the activities. The testing is seen as encroaching on young women's private lives and as humiliating (Scorgie 2002). . . . Organizers and local people have hurried to take a stand in support of the practice. In August 2000, Zulu girls and some middle-aged women who perform the testing demonstrated on the streets of Pietermaritzburg, the administrative centre of KwaZulu Natal. Handwritten posters announced "We are not

being forced!" and "Down with the Gender Commission!" (Scorgie 2002: 55). However, in June 2005, the South African Parliament banned virginity testing for girls under the age of 16 (Children's Act 2005). Two months later, the newspapers reported that nearly 20,000 young women had visited the Zulu King's palace in Nongoma for the reed dance, to be tested and celebrate virginity for three days (cf. Mthethwa 2005).

In the present article, I wish to present virginity testing as the local people in Nkolokotho see it, as an urgent and vital necessity. In the face of a life-threatening epidemic [AIDS], they are organizing something that is both a kind of local public health initiative and a collective ritual. . . . [T]hey see virginity testing as the best possible way to try to change behaviour, in the context of possessing limited means through which to influence their circumstances. Forced to live with inadequate health facilities, no drainage, and a substandard water supply—sometimes without sufficient nutrition to be able to tolerate medications—and with the breakdown of family structures alongside exclusion from the advantages of "modern" society, people are left with little recourse but to try to protect themselves. Virginity testing serves the purpose of addressing human distress and gathering the political body around what is perceived to be a collective moral effort.

The article draws on ethnographic data gathered in 2004 in a former homeland in northeastern rural KwaZulu Natal, an area where the vast majority of households are poor and where the rates of unemployment and illness are high. . . .

Panic Measures Against AIDS

Female virginity inspection has been carried out in Natal and Zululand long before the contemporary campaigns. In the early twentieth century, and probably earlier, young girls in a specific area were tested by a local elderly woman (Scorgie 2002, 16) or individually by their mothers or grandmothers in the homesteads (Krige 1950 [1936]; van der Vliet 1974). The hymenal inspection was a precaution against childbearing out of wedlock. . . .

Today, for the inhabitants of Nkolokotho, the starting point for taking the initiative to arrange virginity testing is the devastation created by HIV/AIDS in their community. However, from a biomedical perspective, virginity judgements are difficult to make. First, the hymen is more like a wrinkle than a veil, which means that it does not automatically look like a covering (Christianson & Eriksson 2004). Second, the hymen heals rapidly, so that sexual intercourse does not necessarily affect it permanently. It has been observed that the majority of victims of sexual assault have no hymenal tears (e.g., Adams, Girardin & Faugno 2001). The certified Zulu testers, however, have long lay experience of studying hymens and assert that they can determine where in the menstrual cycle a girl is and also whether she has had intercourse only once or is involved in a continuous sexual relationship. I do not intend to judge the validity of the testers' accounts or of the testing I observed. What I want to do instead is to shift the focus from a discussion of scientific validity to an understanding of why many people support the practice. I suggest that even if the individual girl is the focus of the testing, it is mainly about reinstating and reinforcing morality, not only in individual girls, but also in the community as a whole. By making virginity a matter of public concern, the thinking goes, people can help girls delay their sexual debut and encourage men to respect girls' sexual integrity.

On the day of the testing, about a hundred exhilarated girls assembled outside the school building. The examiner emphasized that the testing was aimed at confirming virginity; she asked everybody who had a boyfriend to go home. She also showed a certificate they could buy if they passed. The girls who flocked together around the woman were in high spirits and full of expectations. One of the girls in the crowd told me that she was tested for the first time when she was 12 years old. Now she was 14 and in grade 11. She came because her mother wished it, and she really enjoyed it herself. Underneath her black quilted jacket she wore her traditional skirt for virgin girls, which is mostly seen on ceremonial occasions. Other teenage girls I had got to know did not turn up. One of them told me that she did not want to be examined. She suggested a similar joyful event for young girls to me, a chance to celebrate virginity but without testing. Yet another told me that she had enjoyed being tested over the years, but she quit when she got a boyfriend. Virginity testing is more of a preventive than a diagnostic event, an effort to celebrate, defend, and promote virginity, and thus, in the long run, to prevent young girls from contracting HIV.

By the end of the day, I had counted that 100 girls had been examined and that 89 had passed, but I seemed to be the only one interested in the numbers.

Eleven girls went home disappointed. Two of them seemed shocked. They sat in their chairs, not wanting to leave the classroom. One of them was very young and told the tester that she had not had sex, that perhaps she had destroyed the hymen herself. The tester asked her to speak to her mother and to go and see a social worker. She told the other women that perhaps she had been assaulted by someone at home without telling anyone. The other girl had brought her mother, who was asked to come in. The mother was upset and the tester tried to determine whether the girl had a boyfriend without telling anyone or whether she had been raped. The tester later told me that when she suspected rape, she referred the girl to a social worker, medical doctor, or perhaps to the police, for further investigation. . . .

The organizers try to involve parents in protecting girls and encouraging them to accept the consequences of sexual activity, such as HIV testing and counselling. Claiming that one is HIV negative has become a common aspect of courtship. Some families follow prospective sons-in-law to the clinic for an HIV blood test. Living with daily personal experiences of the AIDS epidemic, it seems natural to people to work together towards a common cause as well as to intensify care for the individual body in order to reduce the threat. . . .

Urgent Call for Women

My observations in Nkolokotho suggest that this local initiative is an attempt to strengthen women and protect them from unsafe sexual relationships. Painfully aware of the consequences of the AIDS epidemic, mothers and fathers encourage their daughters to be careful, patient, and proud, to not allow themselves to be forced into sexual relationships, and to make sure that boys take responsibility for sexual relationships and any consequences that may arise.

Irene is a 57-year-old woman who mostly sat rather quietly when I visited her beautiful homestead by the hillside. However, when I came to ask about the virginity testing in which her daughter, Lindiwe, aged 20, had participated, she became enlivened and engaged in a way I had not seen earlier. Her oldest daughter, Nokuphiwe, was severely ill at times, and I took it that she had HIV. That seemed to be the most painful thing in Irene's life. "She nearly died last week," she told me one day when we met on the road. Irene knew that there is no cure for AIDS and that everyone infected will ultimately die as a result of the disease. On this occasion, Nokuphiwe was better and Irene was anxious to tell me about the meaning of the testing:

> [Virginity testing] started because of this disease [HIV/AIDS]. Then it was said that the girls should be tested because this disease finishes people. . . . I think it is very important because girls die because of diseases and if they get tested they will be afraid of doing as they please . . . Except for the girls testing, girls should be told that they are not allowed to sleep with any man before they get married. If they are in love already they should go for the blood test so that they can know their status. Men are irritating because they do not want to do the blood test. So if he refuses the girl must tell him that it is over because you do not know the reason for him to refuse. The problem is that it takes time for the men to die whereas the women they just get sick fast.

Irene . . . states that young women are dying very quickly, which has been painfully obvious to every family in Nkolokotho. Virginity testing is an effort to fight a problem that has beset the whole community in a tangible way.

However, when campaigns are aimed at strengthening women, they also put the responsibility on women. Perhaps that is an inevitable effect of empowerment. Women all over the world are often the targets of campaigns aimed at helping young people make good choices in relation to life-style. . . . When I saw advertising for sexual abstinence on state television in Nkolokotho, I was struck by the fact that it sometimes only addressed women. "If you can abstain, he can too," was one final slogan. The responsibility for sexual negotiation was placed on the woman. South African and internationally sponsored AIDS campaigns such as Love Life and Soul City have been criticized for targeting women more than men in their extensive work towards positive life-style changes (Juelson 2008). . . .

Still, people in Nkolokotho see the need for targeting women and they hope that it will have positive effects for the women themselves. Both individuals and the entire society are facing a catastrophe. . . . By instituting the physical examination of girls' hymens to determine whether they are virgins, people are trying to protect them from engaging in sexual activities too

early, to increase individual responsibility via collective pressure and support. The testing entails an urgent call for women to assert themselves and for men to respect women.

Virginity in Combination with Sexual Experience

Zulu concepts of virginity have historically been a challenge to Western thought. In contrast to the Victorian concept of chastity, virginity among Zulus has not previously been associated with abstinence. The important thing was to avoid penetrative sex, defloration, and thus pregnancy. Thus, it was bad to destroy someone's virginity, but it was also bad not to "play at all" (Gaitskell 1982, 341). Courtship was, and still is, socially desirable. Thus, virginity is not connected to chastity; both virginity and sexual experience are of great importance.

Up to the 1970s, young girls were educated by older girls who already had boyfriends, but were still virgins. They looked after the younger ones and arranged meetings between boys and girls. To prevent penetration, they learned to practise "thigh sex," which meant that the girl laid on her right side with her legs strongly crossed, and the boy who laid on his left side could break in between her thighs to the mons Veneris, but without reaching inside the labia (Krige 1968, 174). The boys, on their part, went to initiation schools where they learned not to penetrate a girl (Krige 1950 [1936], 93). When Axel-Ivar Berglund did his field study on Zulu symbolism in the 1970s, he could hear mothers telling their daughters to have thigh sex with different men so that they could compare the men's skills. He also heard young girls discuss different boys and how they satisfied them. The time when a woman was a virgin was also the time when she gained experiences and prepared herself for choosing one of her suitors.

The practice of thigh sex has survived to some extent, though it has been subjected to changes since colonial time. . . . During the 1920s, missionaries tried to shift the responsibility for young girls' sexuality and courtship from older girls to mothers. Initiation rites and education on thigh sex were forbidden. . . . The young girls were supposed to find new attitudes towards their sexuality and the family. Their mothers . . . were supposed to take responsibility for sexual education, which they had never been in charge of before, and which seemed strange because a young Zulu girl was supposed to respect her mother and not speak about sex in front of her (Gaitskell 1982, 340). In a seeming paradox, measures that were intended to "civilize" people caused the breakdown of existing institutions and people's "moral" culture. . . .

When I asked Mphile, a 45-year-old woman, about her adolescence, I got an exhaustive answer on the difference between individual and collective control:

> People are more into Christianity now and this Christianity is the one that made people forget about their culture. You find that people are growing up without knowing who they are. The boy will talk to you and if you feel that you love him you will tell him that, before asking old people about it. You have to ask your sisters what to do if you are in love with a boy, because there are ways that things were done before.

I wondered what Mphile meant and asked what Christianity taught young people.

> They didn't teach them anything, it's just that the Zulu wasn't there anymore. We were just like white people and I don't think they do things like Zulu people. They were controlling themselves because Christianity came with the notion that people must control themselves.

Mphile asserts that blacks are not like whites, who control themselves. To Mphile and the other interviewees, the family and social relations are the basic elements of a person's personality, and thus it seems difficult to understand what the right thing is if you only control yourself. Life is fundamentally seen as a state of continuous collective dependence.

Sexuality has changed from something that was under social control between peer groups to something that is a private affair under pressure from different moral regimes and contradictory messages. . . .

Today, being a virgin is mostly connected with abstinence, as non-penetrative sex seems to be disappearing, according to my interviewees. Mphile explained what thigh sex meant and why it is difficult today:

> They tried to protect themselves because condoms were not there before. Their condom was the way they had sex [thigh sex] until they got married. . . . [Condoms] are acceptable because

they [young people] cannot go back to their culture. They don't know their culture so who will teach them? Even if we can talk about it as we are talking now, they won't understand because you'll have to show them exactly what to do [how to have thigh sex].

Thigh sex was a sort of contraceptive. The older girls' education and control were the means by which the sexual practice was kept up, at the same time preserving virginity. Because peer education no longer exists, and because abstinence is hard to maintain, even people who promote virginity testing are sceptical about it. . . .

Integrity as Being in Harmony with Others

. . . One day, some girls happened to enter the room I was sitting in and they showed up topless. Immediately they hurried to explain that it was natural for them to show their breasts because they did not go out with someone and were still virgins. They thought that I, as a white woman, would feel offended and want them to dress. But for many young Zulu girls, nakedness is accepted and even desired, a sign that one is not pregnant and a sign of respectability (cf. Berglund 1976, 71; Krige 1968, 180). Virgins are called "the flowers of the nation." For the girls I met, nakedness implied pride and prestige, a special time in life and role in society. A married woman, on the contrary, is not supposed to show her body to anyone other than her husband. Young girls show moral uprightness through exposing themselves, while a sexually experienced woman may bring misfortune if doing the same. . . . One day I told Mphile that my husband wanted me to look beautiful to others. She looked shocked, and I understood that I had put my husband in a bad light. How could he want others to see my beauty, Mphile wondered, and perhaps try to entice me closer to them? The body always has sexual meanings, and for many married Zulu women, this entails covering it to protect oneself and one's relationship.

The woman who was the examiner when I visited the virginity testing was careful to ask girls who were not virgins to go home before the test started. She did not wish to examine someone who was not a virgin. A virgin is supposed to show up, but someone who has had her sexual debut is supposed to dress and not even show herself to a tester. As I said in the introduction, I was asked to come closer and look at hymens during the testing. The examiner described some hymens as the veil, the covering or the shining eye. To me they looked like the surface of a bubble-gum bubble. They were beautiful, she explained. She also told me that the hymen appears when a girl is about 10 years old. When a girl is to have her menstrual period, the hymen becomes sharper than during other periods in the menstrual cycle. Other hymens she described as destroyed, and there I could not see anything like a veil. The examiner seemed to be embarrassed when she saw these, as if she was looking at something she was not supposed to see. In contrast to other sorts of hymenal inspection—such as that performed on prostitutes and the psychologically unstable in Europe in the nineteenth century and right up to 1918 (Svanström 2006) or in present-day suggestions for gynaecological control of immigrant girls in Sweden to see whether they have been subjected to circumcision—virginity testing is not about inspecting the deviant, but about finding and accentuating the desired and the beautiful.

How are we to understand this relationship to the human body? . . . What does it mean in terms of integrity? . . . In many cases, integrity is associated with individual freedom. That view is built on an understanding of the individual as mainly an independent unit. When I asked individual girls about their experiences of virginity testing, their answers included showing respect for your parents, not causing them pain, and being proud of yourself. The girls see themselves as being in a continuous interplay with others and as part of a larger whole, not in opposition to independence but as a fundamental ground for being someone.

If we consider the definition of the Latin word *integritas*, we find a concept that means wholeness, interplay, connection, and harmony. . . . Harmony and interplay may be achieved and experienced in different ways based on how people view the relationship between the individual, the group, and the society. In a society where the kinship group is of great importance, integrity is not connected to independence in the same way as Western ideology implies. . . . In Zulu the word for integrity stems from *qotho*, which means genuine or reliable, and from *phelela*, which means entire or complete. The individual's body is part of a collective whole, though this does not entail violation of the integrity of the individual. It is more of an understanding of the ground for being a person.

For almost all Zulu people to whom I spoke, belonging is of such great importance that it influences how they view themselves. Every individual is part of a web of social relations (Wickström 2008). The concept of *umuntu, ngumuntu, ngabantu*, means a person is a person through persons. . . . Social relations are as important a determinant of people's well-being as are individual behaviour and actions. Even if individual failures or infectious agents are recognized as the proximate cause of disease, the ultimate cause is almost always thought to be a breakdown of social relationships.

In a submission to the South African Parliament, the Commission for Gender Equality described virginity testing as "an invasion of bodily and physical integrity, and an invasion of privacy" (Grobler 2005). Instead, I assert that girls who voluntarily participate in virginity testing have a different understanding of the concept of integrity than that used by the Commission in their statement. To them, integrity means showing respect and living in harmonious relationships with those close to them, listening to one's elders, and not getting involved in relationships without security, which means without any agreement between families. . . .

Even Boys Lose Their Virginity

A young man's transition from virginity to manhood is not biologically striking, and thus it is not used as a social symbol to the same extent as is female virginity (cf. Hastrup 1993 [1978]). . . . However, the AIDS epidemic and its devastating effect on the families I came to know have widened the concept of virginity. The expressions "to get one's virginity destroyed" or "to be damaged" were often applied to boys, and the interviewees were eager to start testing for boys too. Mphile, who had two sons, explained:

> What makes boys to love this [testing] is this
> disease. They also need to learn to take good
> care of themselves, both the male and female.
> Because people are dying. And this disease
> that is not curable. They don't have the pills
> or injection to get rid of it. I think that is what
> made them want this testing. Before boys didn't
> care because they knew that they didn't get
> destroyed. The only one who got destroyed

was the woman. So now they know that they get destroyed both of them by getting this disease and also losing the virginity. They don't know where and who they both have been with before they met each other. That's why they are scared of this disease. . . . I will teach them [the sons] that they should wait until the right time comes and that they mustn't use girls because girls will use them also after a short time. Because girls cannot be trusted. You can tell yourself that the girl is fine without any diseases and later find that she is sick. Then that same girl will come here to infect my child with this disease.

. . . Mphile asserts that boys also lose their virginity because of this disease. They too need to take care of themselves, and understand that they are being destroyed.

The community is planning to start testing for boys by reinventing an old initiation rite. A boy's frenulum, the wrinkle that runs from underneath the glans to the foreskin, is thought to bleed at the first coitus, and inspection of it is supposed to reveal if he has had sex or not. During the rite, an incision is made in the boys' frenulum, where a piece of horsehair is tied. The pain is supposed to show that losing one's virginity is painful. The aim of the rite is to teach boys "how you grow and become a man" and how to learn to be "patient" and "faithful," as the examiner for the girls explained. The testing is thought to promote preferred sexual behaviour. In 2004, 70 per cent of the men in Nkolokotho voted for the proposal, so the decision was postponed until they might reach consensus. The practice is controversial because now and then newspapers in South Africa report that a boy has died after getting infections caused by circumcision. . . . During the reed dance in Nongoma in 2005, the Zulu King Goodwill Zwelithini announced that he planned to start testing for boys and that examiners had been chosen (Mthethwa 2005). . . .

A Local Public Health Initiative

The control of girls' virginity is only partly about the status of individuals' hymens. The controls have a primarily social purpose. They are not only about the

individual body of a girl, but about reinstating and reinforcing morality in society as a whole. . . . Virginity testing is a public health strategy in which joint societal pressure is put on the individual as well as the collective, as opposed to the pressure brought about by individual self-control. . . .

In combination with virginity testing, some parents insist that men take a blood test and prove that they are HIV negative before starting a sexual relationship with their daughter. The woman who was the examiner at the testing had two daughters in their twenties who were supposed to marry in 2005. Both the husbands-to-be had taken the HIV blood test. "The person that you are going to marry, you have to go with him and do the blood test so that you can be sure that you are both alive. After that you can allow him to go and see your parents, if he is alive," she explained. A certificate of virginity is a sign for the girl, the family, and others, a proof that renders her respect. The certificate is also an economic document that may be used in negotiations on *ilobolo* or bridewealth. Organizers and parents incorporate phenomena such as HIV tests and documents into the testing. Virginity testing in Nkolokotho is a question not of resorting to tradition, but of re-tooling culturally familiar technologies as new means for new ends (Comaroff & Comaroff 1997). People try to rescue and reinvent something useful and down-to-earth from the olden days, to transform their specific understandings to meet today's needs and conditions.

Conclusion

. . . Collective healing and public rituals are sometimes incomprehensible to Western thinking (cf. Feierman 1999, 204). That may be one of the reasons why the liberal South African state has banned virginity testing. . . . [T]he initiative of virginity testing challenges AIDS prevention programmes' focus on the individual and their emphasis on human mastery over the self. The main characters of Western preventive and treatment programmes are human discipline and personal responsibility. This conception does not take into consideration people's insight that the collective and the family need to be involved in changing behaviours. In contrast to virginity testing, male circumcision is not banned in the Children's Act. Instead, it is stated that "every male child has the right to refuse circumcision" (Vincent 2006: 19), thus giving boys the agency and autonomy not granted to teenage girls, who are forbidden by the state from undergoing virginity testing. Thus the question arises:

Why does a young woman not have the right to choose to participate or refrain from virginity testing? If she chooses to participate, she is seen as being in need of protection from both herself and her own people. . . .

References

Adams, J. A., B. Girardin, & D. Faugno. 2001. Adolescent sexual assault: documentation of acute injuries using photo-colposcopy. Journal of Pediatric and Adolescent Gynecology 14: 175–80.

Berglund, A.-I. 1976. Zulu thought-patterns and symbolism. Bloomington: Indiana University Press.

Children's Act No. 38 of 2005. Republic of South Africa. Available online: http://ci.org.za/depts/ci/plr/pdf/bills/ChildrensAct38-2005.pdf (accessed 21 May, 2010).

Christianson, M., & C. Eriksson. 2004. Myter om mödomshinnan—en genusteoretisk betraktelse av mödomshinnans natur och kultur (Myths about the hymen: a gender-theoretical reflection of the nature and culture of the hymen). *In* Kropp och genus i medicinen (Body and gender in medicine). B. Hovelius & E. E. Johansson, eds. Lund: Studenlitteratur.

Comaroff, J. L., & J. Comaroff. 1997. Occult economies and the violence of abstraction: notes from the South African postcolony. American Ethnologist 26: 279–303.

Feierman, S. 1999. Colonizers, scholars, and the creation of invisible histories. In *Beyond the cultural turn: new directions in the study of society and culture* (eds) V.E. Bonnell & L. Hunt, 182-216. London: University of California Press.

Gaitskell, D. 1982."Wailing for purity": prayer unions, African mothers and adolescent daughters 1912–1940. *In* Industrialisation and social change in South Africa: African class formation, culture, and consciousness, 1870–1930. S. Marks & R. Rathbone, eds. Pp. 338–57. London: Longman.

Grobler, F. 2005. Virginity testing may soon be banned custom. Mail & Guardian, 13 December. Available on-line: http://www.mg.co.za/article/2005-12-13-virginity-testing-may-soon-be-banned-custom (accessed 21 May, 2010).

Hastrup, K. 1993 [1978]. The semantics of biology: virginity. In *Defining females: the nature of women in society. Cross-cultural perspectives on women*, vol. 4 S. Ardener, ed. Pp. 34–50. Oxford: Berg.

Juelson, K. 2008. The struggles of youth in a time of HIV/AIDS awareness and prevention programs. Master's thesis, Linköping University.

Krige, E. J. 1950 [1936]. The social system of the Zulus. Pietermaritzburg: Shuter & Shooter.

Krige, E. J. 1968. Girls' puberty songs and their relation to fertility, health, morality and religion among the Zulu. Africa 38: 173–85.

Mthethwa, B. 2005. Male virgin testing now a royal decree. Sunday Times, September 11.

Scorgie, F. 2002. Virginity testing and the politics of sexual responsibility: implications for AIDS intervention. African Studies 61: 55–75.

Svanström, Y. 2006. Prostitution in Sweden: debates and policies 1980–2004. *In* International approaches to prostitution: law and policy in Europe and Asia. G. Gangoli & N. Westmarland, eds. Pp. 67–90. Bristol: The Policy Press.

van der Vliet, V. 1974. Growing up in traditional society. *In* The Bantu-speaking peoples of Southern Africa. W. D. Hammond-Tooke, ed. Pp. 211–47. London: Routledge & Kegan Paul.

Vincent, L. 2006. Virginity testing in South Africa: re-traditioning the postcolony. Culture Health & Sexuality 8: 17–30.

Wickström, A. 2008. Love as action: managing relationships, sickness and medicine in a Zulu society. Medische Antropologie 20: 47–68.

IN THE NEWS Same Sex Marriage

On June 26, 2015, the U.S. Supreme Court recognized the constitutional right to marriage for same-sex couples. The ruling was a historic victory ending one of the major civil rights fights of the era. Anthropologists have been writing for public audiences in support of same-sex marriage since the earliest days of the discipline, with Margaret Mead offering an early progressive lens on marriage and sexuality, informed by cross-cultural examples from across the globe. The articles "Same-Sex Marriage from an Anthropological View" by Terry McFadden and "Defending 'Traditional' Marriage? Whose Definition?" by Richard Feinberg, both written before the historic ruling, provide cross-cultural evidence in favor of a flexible definition of marriage.

The 2015 decision was won after a long and arduous struggle. Just as recently as 2004, then U.S. President George W. Bush had called for a constitutional amendment to ban gay marriage as a "threat to civilization." The American Anthropological Association responded strongly and publicly at the time, issuing a Statement on Marriage and Family, available alongside the McFadden and Feinberg articles on www.oup.com/us/brondo.

 Visit www.oup.com/us/brondo for weblinks.

MEGAN E. SPRINGATE, MA

Historical Archaeologist and PhD Candidate in Anthropology at the University of Maryland, College Park

Figure 4.6.1

Megan Springate.

Figure 4.6.2

Aerial view of excavations behind caretaker's residence at Wiawaka Center for Women, Lake George, New York.

How did you become interested in the discipline of anthropology?

I have always been interested in people and their stories. I discovered archaeology quite by accident while in high school, when my mom came home with information about a three week field school that could substitute as a senior social science credit. I jumped at the chance to take high school credit outside the classroom, and fell in love with archaeology during those three weeks. We were excavating a mid-1500s Iroquoian Village just outside Toronto. As a result, I pursued archaeology at university, and was exposed to the other fields of anthropology, including cultural anthropology, medical anthropology, biological anthropology, and a touch of linguistics. Being a student of anthropology has deeply informed how I understand and relate to the world; by teaching anthropology— both in the classroom and in public engagement settings—I hope to impart some of the understanding and skills that I learned.

What is the LGBTQ initiative and what does your day-to-day work look like in working for the NPS on this initiative?

The LGBTQ Heritage Initiative is one of several National Park Service projects exploring ways in which the legacy of underrepresented groups can be recognized, preserved, and interpreted for future generations. My primary tasks focus around the completion of the associated theme study, a document that provides historic context about American LGBTQ communities and sites to facilitate their nomination to the National Register of Historic Places and National Historic Landmarks programs, both of which are managed by the National Park Service. This includes identifying and working with authors and peer reviewers for the theme study, writing an introduction to the study, as well as a couple of other chapters, editing, and compiling the work. Other tasks associated with the Heritage Initiative include: responding to public comments; reaching out to partners and communities; maintaining a mapped list of sites across the United States that have LGBTQ history and heritage associated with them; preparing materials to support the Initiative (like a FAQ, website text and layout, a how you can get involved document, community outreach materials, etc.); and providing technical assistance to parks and those looking to recognize or share LGBTQ history and heritage. More information can be found at: http://www.nps.gov/history/heritageinitiatives/LGBThistory/

How do you put anthropology to use in your work?

One of the things I like best about what I do, is that no two days are the same. In archaeology, I could be preparing an excavation plan, talking to landowners and other stakeholders, doing historical research, digging small test pits, excavating large areas of a site, teaching others how to dig and "see" archaeologically, washing artifacts, cataloging, filling out paperwork, doing analysis, writing reports, presenting to the public, explaining the importance of the archaeological record, preparing maps, working in Geographic Information Systems, collaborating with other archaeologists and historians . . . the list is almost endless. And then there are all of the activities I do for the LGBTQ Heritage Initiative, which I already described.

Anthropology has definitely shaped how I think about the world, which in turn influences my work. Two of the most important things that I have taken from my anthropology training are to value cultures on their own terms and to look at things from a holistic and intersectional perspective. To value cultures on their own terms to me means not judging or imposing my own cultural norms onto other groups. In archaeology, this means in part, trying not to make assumptions about family structures, gender identities, or cultural norms in the past and instead having research questions that will allow the data to provide

that information. In the context of the LGBTQ Heritage Initiative, it means actively listening and responding to community feedback about the project, including naming, organization of the theme study, and providing space for many of the different communities under the LGBTQ umbrella, including those often excluded, to be represented. These many voices taken together, form the basis for a rich, diverse, and intersectional LGBTQ context.

What do you see as the future for queer anthropology (i.e., most pressing issues)?

One of the main strengths I see of queer anthropology is the challenge it makes of all assumptions and its demands to support our conclusions. For example, a queer anthropological approach challenges interpretations that assume that households consist of families and that families are by default heterosexual; it challenges assumptions of chrononormativity, or the idea that the past and present are necessarily distinct; and it challenges ideas that identities, like gender and race, are fixed. Challenges to these assumptions force us to think differently about things; opening up the possibilities of other ways of being; and provide a means of getting out of our own ways when we try to understand people, cultures, and societies both past and present.

The two biggest challenges that I see for queer anthropology are (1) to engage beyond the discipline and (2) to be deeply incorporated into anthropology, rather than relegated as a separate chapter or an upper-level specialty course. In engaging beyond the discipline, I am thinking both in terms of being interdisciplinary in the theories and methods used, but also in being published or presented in forums and language and venues such that other disciplines also find the work done in queer anthropology to be useful. If we truly believe that queer anthropology (and its predecessors and close relatives, gender anthropology and feminist anthropology) is important and transformative to the discipline, then we must incorporate it throughout the curriculum, including introductory classes, and not have it relegated to a separate chapter at the end of the book or confined to a specific lecture.

You are also working on your doctoral degree in anthropology. What is your focus?

My dissertation is about the making of the modern American woman at the beginning of the twentieth century, using women's holiday houses as locations. These holiday houses were places where working women could vacation for free or low cost in rural or natural settings away from urban factories. While they all appear very similar, there were actually several different types, each with their own ideological underpinnings. Some were operated by unions, like the teachers' holiday house in Massachusetts; some, like the one run by General Electric in New York, by corporations as part of their anti-union strategies; and some, like my dissertation site on Lake George, New York, were run by church or moral reform groups in part as a way of keeping working women off the streets and teaching them values.

In your opinion, how should anthropology engage the public?

I think it is important to, as much as possible, include the public as collaborators or co-investigators in anthropological research, not as subjects, annoyances, or add-ons to projects. I don't for an instant claim that I am the paragon of this approach; in fact, I have more often not met these goals than I have met them, but it is something I consider and think about . . . a lot.

What does it mean to you to be a publically engaged archaeologist?

Being publicly engaged means working with communities when planning projects; it means being accessible to answer questions; it means being able to explain clearly what the decision-making processes were when planning and implementing a project (my research needs; needs of the communities; needs of funders; etc.). It means taking the time to answer questions while working and to not use jargon.

It means, that when digging with community members, that they are given the information they need to do the work and are treated as collaborators and not just "free labor." It means that I need to shut up and listen when members of communities I am not a part of have something to say, I need to hear what they are saying and treat it seriously. It means not talking *at* people, but talking *with* people. It means needing to give up tight control of projects and be willing to compromise, adapt, and even sometimes let go. It means that (hopefully) these projects are places of meaningful conversation, learning, and relationship-building.

ABOUT THE ANTHROPOLOGIST

Occupation: Prime Consultant for the National Park Service's LGBTQ Heritage Initiative
Hobbies: Contra dance (especially queer/gender free!), laugh at the antics of my two cats, visit with friends, and unwind with too much TV and video games

CAREER ADVICE

Advice for students interested in LGBTQ anthropology:

While LGBTQ still carries with it some stigma, and homophobia and discrimination are still very real around the world (including in the United States), the world has changed significantly and it is less of a risk now than ever to pursue anthropological work on LGBTQ issues.

I urge students to not ignore the risks of pursuing LGBTQ research, but there is fantastic work being done. I also urge students to broaden their reading outside of anthropology and take advantage of some of the great thinking about LGBTQ issues that is being done in departments and fields including American Studies, English, Queer Studies, Gender Studies, History, Performance Studies, Public Health, and Sociology. And always remember our pioneers who made the work we do possible.

PART 5
Race, Ethnicity, Class, and Inequality

Is race real? Is it genetically based? Is it just another word for ethnicity? And what do race and ethnicity have to do with class? Race is a social and cultural construct that reflects categorizations of people into groups based on specific physical traits, whereas ethnicity—also a social construct—refers to membership in a group due to shared history, ancestry, or social status.

Race is a social invention rooted in colonialism. In the second part of the nineteenth century, European thinkers, including early anthropologists, developed ranking systems to classify the "races of Mankind" from lowest to highest, placing the "white" Northern Europeans (i.e., those who invented the system) at the highest spot in the social hierarchy. Darker-skinned individuals, such as native populations in Africa, Asia, and the Americas, were all ranked lower within the classification system, a hierarchy that justified slavery and oppression (Schultz and Lavenda 2014, 321). Over time, racial categories changed, and some populations previously classified as "inferior races" were absorbed into other, higher ranked racial categories. For instance, during the 1840s and 1850s, Irish immigrants to the United States were considered closely related, both positioned in an inferior and separate race from settlers who descended from the English. But by the close of the nineteenth century, they became "white," welcomed into the category and distanced from the "black race" (Welsh and Vivanco 2014, 265–6). Thus, race is not real or static, but rather is a culturally constructed concept that was invented to serve the interests of specific populations.

Many people believe that racial identities result from unchanging biological differences, but there is no scientific evidence to support this claim. Biological anthropologists take care to contrast genotype, one's genetic inheritance, with phenotype, one's physical appearance, which is shaped by environmental factors as well as genetic influences. Racial categories are based on phenotypic differences which vary widely within a singular "race." That is, there is more variation within a race than between races. The first reading in this section, "Can White Men Jump? Ethnicity, Genes, Culture, and Success" by David Shenk (Reading 5.1), explores the relationship between race and genetics, upending the common belief that some races are genetically gifted, and biologically advantaged with superior genes to excel in certain activities. In this selection focused on sports success, Shenk shows that genetic features do not correspond neatly to "racial categories" and cannot explain athleticism on their own; culture and environment prove to be a much stronger influence on success in sports.

Racism, or systematic oppression through unequal and repressive practices and beliefs of one or more socially defined race by another race, is an outgrowth of the invention of race. And as a result, "race" seems very real indeed. Race is real because it is a social construct and a lived experience, and racism and racial discrimination are felt in a myriad of ways by those who are not seen as "white." "Whiteness" is an unmarked racial category, one that does not involve value judgments linked to skin color and other physical traits. White is considered the "norm" and all other racial groups are measured against it. Reading 5.2, "Maintaining Whiteness: The Fear of Others and Niceness" by Setha Low, takes up the advantages of being associated with white skin, otherwise known as "white privilege." Discussing her research with people who live within urban gated communities, Low unpacks the hidden meaning of "niceness," showing that this construct shrouds racist assumptions about urban landscapes and rationalizes a choice to live in exclusionary spaces which serve as a strategy for regulating and patrolling poor Latino and Black minorities.

Reading 5.3, "Intimate Apartheid and Drug Consumption Among Racialized Bodies," also explores racialized geography. In it, Philippe Bourgois and Jeff Schonberg analyze the racialized micro-geography and hostile social relationships that emerge among white, black, and Latino homeless heroin addicts in the streets of San Francisco who are forced to live in close proximity. Through their rich ethnographic discussion of a range of individuals, the authors explore the structural and economic forces at play that lead people to "misrecognize" racial inequality as the "natural order of things." This piece is a selection from their book *Righteous Dopefiend*, a strong example of critically applied public anthropology.

Race and class are deeply intertwined, and just as with race, class—"the hierarchical distinctions between social groups in society based on wealth, occupation and social standing" (Welsch and Vivcano 2014, 278)—is also socially constructed. In "Birthdays, Basketball, and Breaking Bread: Negotiating with Class in Contemporary Black America," (Reading 5.4), John Jackson interrogates the relationship between race and class, undoing popular beliefs that there are "two black Americas"— an underclass and a middle-class—and that individuals from one class do not live or socialize with members of the other. Drawing on fieldwork in Harlem, Jackson shows that while class-stratified relationships with friends, family, and co-workers are varied and complicated, they nonetheless exist. Shalini Shankar's discussion of how class and race intersect among Asian Americans (Reading 2.4) pairs well with this piece.

Popular discussion of a black "underclass" emerged in the aftermath of the shooting and killing of unarmed teenager Michael Brown in Ferguson, Missouri. The events surrounding his death, police brutality, and public protests are featured in this section's "In the News," with several citations to anthropologists' public response and connections to the discipline. The American Anthropological Association's (AAA) "Race: Are

We So Different?" public education project, a traveling exhibition that explores the history, science, and lived experience of race and racism, accompanies these articles.

The section closes with a profile of Dr. Raymond Codrington, who has been a public voice on racialized police brutality, serving as Co-Chair of the AAA's Task Force on Race and Racism, Chair of the AAA's Committee on Minority Issues, and Member of the Working Group on Racialized Police Brutality and Extrajudicial Violence. Dr. Codrington is a practicing anthropologist working on applied and public research projects with the New York Hall of Science Innovation Institute and is a senior research fellow at the City University of New York's Graduate Center.

One final note: While the selections in this part focus to a great extent on U.S. racial classification systems, the general points about race, ethnicity, and class apply cross-culturally. All are socially constructed and thus all cultures have their own classification systems and ideas about who belongs in what "box." Classification systems vary significantly from one place to another, informed by cultural context.

KEY TERMS:

- Race
- Ethnicity
- Whiteness
- White privilege
- Racism
- Genotype
- Phenotype
- Racialized geography
- Class
- Class stratification
- Black underclass
- Cultural capital
- Habitus
- Colorblindness
- Ferguson, Missouri
- Police brutality

5.1 Can White Men Jump? Ethnicity, Genes, Culture, and Success

DAVID SHENK

Why do so many Kenyans win marathons? Why are Jamaicans so fast? Do genes determine athletic prowess? Does ethnicity have anything to do with athleticism? Through a discussion of cultural and psychological factors influencing success in sprinting and long-distance running, Shenk upends the "gene-gift" paradigm in two ways: first, unraveling the notion that genetic features correspond neatly to "racial" categories, and second, showing that genes do not act in isolation and cannot explain anything on their own. Instead, genes are just one of several agents in a complex and dynamic set of factors influencing our life trajectories.

Questions

1. What is sports geography?
2. How does culture shape success in long-distance running among the Kalenjin tribe of western Kenya? What is the role of culture in Jamaican sprinting success?
3. What does it mean to say that genes are "probabilistic rather than deterministic"?
4. Why would Jamaica be one of the last places in the region expected to excel in running according to a gene-gift paradigm?

Clusters of ethnic and geographical athletic success prompt suspicions of hidden genetic advantages. The real advantages are far more nuanced—and less hidden.

At the 2008 Summer Olympics in Beijing, the world watched in astonishment as the tiny island of Jamaica captured six gold medals in track and field and eleven overall. Usain Bolt won (and set world records in) both the men's 100-meter and the men's 200-meter races. Jamaican women took the top three spots in the 100-meter and won the 200-meter as well. "They brought their A game. I don't know where we left ours," lamented American relay runner Lauryn Williams.

A poor, underdeveloped nation of 2.8 million people—one-hundredth the size of the United States—had somehow managed to produce the fastest humans alive.

How?

Within hours, geneticists and science journalists rushed in with reports of a "secret weapon": biologically, it turned out that almost all Jamaicans are flush with alpha-actinin-3, a protein that drives forceful, speedy muscle contractions. The powerful protein is produced by a special gene variant called *ACTN3*, at least one copy of which can be found in 98 percent of Jamaicans—far higher than in many other ethnic populations.

An impressive fact, but no one stopped to do the math. Eighty percent of Americans also have at least one copy of *ACTN3*—that amounts to 240 million people. Eighty-two percent of Europeans have it as well—that tacks on another 597 million potential sprinters. "There's simply no clear relationship between the frequency of this variant in a population and its capacity to produce sprinting superstars," concluded geneticist Daniel MacArthur.

What, then, is the Jamaicans' secret sauce?

This is the same question people asked about champion long-distance runners from Finland in the 1920s and about great Jewish basketball players from the ghettos of Philadelphia and New York in the 1930s. Today, we wonder how tiny South Korea turns out as many great female golfers as the United States—and how the Dominican Republic has become a factory for male baseball players.

The list goes on and on. It turns out that sports excellence commonly emerges in geographic clusters—so commonly, in fact, that a small academic discipline called "sports geography" has developed over the years to help understand it. What they've discovered is that there's never a single cause for a sports cluster. Rather, the success comes from many contributions of climate, media, demographics, nutrition, politics, training, spirituality, education, economics, and folklore. In short, athletic clusters are not genetic, but systemic.

Unsatisfied with this multifaceted explanation, some sports geographers have also transformed themselves into sports geneticists. In his book *Taboo: Why Black Athletes Dominate Sports and Why We're Afraid to Talk About It*, journalist Jon Entine insists that today's phenomenal black athletes—Jamaican sprinters, Kenyan marathoners, African American basketball players, etc.—are propelled by "high performance genes" inherited from their West and East African ancestors. Caucasians and Asians don't do as well, he says, because they don't share these advantages. "White athletes appear to have a physique between central West Africans and East Africans," Entine writes. "They have more endurance but less explosive running and jumping ability than West Africans; they tend to be quicker than East Africans but have less endurance."

In the finer print, Entine acknowledges that these are all grosser-than-gross generalizations. He understands that there are extraordinary Asian and Caucasian athletes in basketball, running, swimming, jumping, and cycling. (In fact, blacks [did] not even dominate the latter three of these sports as of 2008.) In his own book, Entine quotes geneticist Claude Bouchard: "The key point is that these biological characteristics *are not unique* to either West or East African blacks. These characteristics are seen in all populations, including whites." (Italics mine.) (Entine also acknowledges that we haven't in fact found the actual genes he's alluding to. "These genes will likely be identified early in the [twenty-first century]," he predicts.)

Actual proof for his argument is startlingly thin. But Entine's message of superior genes seems irresistible to a world steeped in gene-giftedness—and where other influences and dynamics are nearly invisible.

Take the running Kenyans. Relatively new to international competition, Kenyans have in recent years become overwhelmingly dominant in middle- and long-distance races. "It's pointless for me to run on the pro circuit," complained American 10,000-meter champion Mike Mykytok to the *New York Times* in 1998. "With all the Kenyans, I could set a personal best time, still only place 12th and win $200."

Ninety percent of the top-performing Kenyans come from the Kalenjin tribe in the Great Rift Valley region of western Kenya, where they have a centuries-old tradition of long-distance running. Where did this tradition come from? Kenyan-born journalist John Manners suggests it came from cattle raiding. Further, he proposes how a few basic economic incentives became a powerful evolutionary force. "The better a young man was at raiding [cattle]—in large part a function of his speed and endurance—the more cattle he accumulated," Manners says. "And since cattle were what a prospective husband needed to pay for a bride, the more a young man had, the more wives he could buy, and the more children he was likely to father. It is not hard to imagine that such a reproductive advantage might cause a significant shift in a group's genetic makeup over the course of a few centuries."

Whatever the precise origin, it is true that the Kalenjin have long had a fierce dedication to running. But it wasn't until the 1968 Olympics that they became internationally renowned for their prowess, thanks to the extraordinary runner Kipchoge Keino.

The son of a farmer and ambitious long-distance runner, Keino caught the running bug early in life. He wasn't the most precocious or "natural" athlete among his peers, but running was simply woven into the fabric of his life: along with his schoolmates, Keino ran many miles per day as a part of his routine. "I used to run from the farm to school and back," he recalled. "We didn't have a water tap in the house, so you run to the river, take your shower, run home, change, [run] to school . . . Everything is running." Slowly, Keino emerged as a serious competitor. He built himself a running track on the farm where his family worked and by his late teens was showing signs of international-level performance. After some success in the early 1960s, he competed admirably in the 1964 Olympics and became the leader of the Kenyan running team for the 1968 games in Mexico City. It was Kenya's fourth Olympics.

In Mexico City, things did not begin well for Keino. After nearly collapsing in pain during his first race, the 10,000 meters, he was diagnosed with gallstones and ordered by doctors not to continue. At the last minute, though, he stubbornly decided to race the 1,500 meters and hopped in a cab to Mexico City's Aztec Stadium. Caught in terrible traffic, Keino did the only thing he could do, the thing he'd been training his whole life for: he jumped out of the cab and ran the last mile to the event, arriving on the track only moments before the start of the race, winded and very sick. Still, when the gun sounded, Keino was off, and his performance that day shattered the world record and left his rival, American Jim Ryun, in the dust.

The dramatic victory made Keino one of the most celebrated men in all Africa and helped catalyze a new interest in world-class competition. Athletic halls and other venues all over Kenya were named after him. World-class coaches like Fred Hardy and Colm O'Connell were recruited to nurture other Kenyan aspirants. In the decades that followed, the long-standing but profitless Kalenjin running tradition became a well-oiled economic-athletic engine. Sports geographers point to many crucial ingredients in Kenya's competitive surge but no single overriding factor. High-altitude training and mild year-round climate are critical, but equally important is a deeply ingrained culture of asceticism—the postponement of gratification—and an overriding preference for individual over team sports. (Soccer, the overwhelming Kenyan favorite, is all but ignored among the Kalenjin; running is all.) In testing, psychologists discovered a particularly strong cultural "achievement orientation," defined as the inclination to seek new challenges, attain competence, and strive to outdo others. And then there was the built-in necessity as virtue: as Keino

mentioned, Kalenjin kids tend to run long distances as a practical matter, an average of eight to twelve kilometers per day from age seven.

> *Joke among elite athletes: How can the rest of the world defuse Kenyan running superiority? Answer: Buy them school buses.*

With the prospect of international prize money, running in Kenya has also become a rare economic opportunity to catapult oneself into Western-level education and wealth. Five thousand dollars in prize money is a very nice perk for an American; for a Kenyan, it is instant life-changing wealth. Over time, a strong culture of success has also bred even more success. The high-performance benchmark has stoked higher and higher levels of achievement—a positive feedback loop analogous to technological innovation in Silicon Valley, combat skills among Navy SEALs, and talents in other highly successful microcultures. In any competitive arena, the single best way to inspire better performance is to be surrounded by the fiercest possible competitors and a culture of extreme excellence. Success begets success.

There is also an apparent sacrificial quality particular to Kenyan training, wherein coaches can afford to push their athletes to extreme limits in a way that coaches in other parts of the world cannot. *Sports Illustrated'*s Alexander Wolff writes that with a million Kenyan schoolboys running so enthusiastically, "coaches in Kenya can train their athletes to the outer limits of endurance—up to 150 miles a week—without worrying that their pool of talent will be meaningfully depleted. Even if four out of every five runners break down, the fifth will convert that training into performance."

And what of genetics? Are Kenyans the possessors of rare endurance genes, as some insist? No one can yet know for sure, but the new understanding of G×E and some emergent truths in genetic testing strongly suggest otherwise, in two important ways.

1. DESPITE APPEARANCES TO THE CONTRARY, RACIAL AND ETHNIC GROUPS ARE NOT GENETICALLY DISCRETE.

Skin color is a great deceiver; actual genetic differences between ethnic and geographic groups are very, very limited. All human beings are descended from the same

African ancestors, and it is well established among geneticists that there is roughly ten times more genetic variation within large populations than there is between populations. "While ancestry is a useful way to classify species (because species are isolated gene pools, most of the time)," explains University of Queensland philosopher of biology John Wilkins, "it is rarely a good way to classify populations within species . . . [and definitely not] in humans. We move about too much." By no stretch of the imagination, then, does any ethnicity or region have an exclusive lock on a particular body type or secret high-performance gene. Body shapes, muscle fiber types, etc., are actually quite varied and scattered, and true athletic potential is widespread and plentiful.

2. GENES DON'T DIRECTLY CAUSE TRAITS; THEY ONLY INFLUENCE THE SYSTEM.

Consistent with other lessons of G×E, the surprising finding of the $3 billion Human Genome Project is that only in rare instances do specific gene variants directly cause specific traits or diseases. Far more commonly, they merely increase or decrease the likelihood of those traits/diseases. In the words of King's College developmental psychopathologist Michael Rutter, genes are "probabilistic rather than deterministic." As the search for athletic genes continues, therefore, the overwhelming evidence suggests that researchers will instead locate genes prone to certain types of interactions: gene variant *A* in combination with gene variant *B*, provoked into expression by *X* amount of training + *Y* altitude + *Z* will to win + a hundred other life variables (coaching, injury rate, etc.), will produce some specific result *R*. What this means, of course, is that we need to dispense rhetorically with the thick firewall between biology (nature) and training (nurture). The reality of G×E assures that each person's genes interact with his climate, altitude, culture, meals, language, customs, and spirituality—everything—to produce unique life trajectories. Genes play a critical role, but as dynamic instruments, not a fixed blueprint. A seven—or fourteen—or twenty-eight-year-old outfitted with a certain height, shape, muscle-fiber proportion, and so on is not that way because of genetic instruction.

***

As for John Manners's depiction of cattle-raiding Kenyans becoming genetically selected to be better and better runners over the generations, it's an entertaining theory that fits well with the popular gene-centric view of natural selection. But developmental biologists would point out that you could take exactly the same story line and flip the conclusion on its head: the fastest man earns the most wives and has the most kids—but rather than passing on quickness genes, he passes on crucial external ingredients, such as the knowledge and means to attain maximal nutrition, inspiring stories, the most propitious attitude and habits, access to the best trainers, the most leisure time to pursue training, and so on. This nongenetic aspect of inheritance is often overlooked by genetic determinists: culture, knowledge, attitudes, and environments are also passed on in many different ways.

The case for the hidden performance gene is even further diminished in the matter of Jamaican sprinters, who turn out to be a quite heterogeneous genetic group—nothing like the genetic "island" that some might imagine. On average, Jamaican genetic heritage is about the same as African American heritage, with roughly the same mix of West African, European, and Native American ancestry. That's on average; individually, the percentage of West African origin varies widely, from 46.8 to 97.0 percent. Jamaicans are therefore *less* genetically African and *more* European and Native American than their neighboring Barbadians and Virgin Islanders. "Jamaica . . . may represent a 'crossroads' within the Caribbean," conclude the authors of one DNA study. Jamaica was used as a "transit point by colonists between Central and South America and Europe [which] may have served to make Jamaica more cosmopolitan and thus provided more opportunities for [genetic] admixture to occur. *The large variance in both the global and individual admixture estimates in Jamaica attests to the cosmopolitan nature of the island.*"

In other words, Jamaica would be one of the very last places in the region expected to excel, according to a gene-gift paradigm.

Meanwhile, specific cultural explanations abound for the island's sprinting success—and for its recent competitive surge. In Jamaica, track events are beloved. The annual high school Boys' and Girls' Athletic Championships is as important to Jamaicans as the Super Bowl is to Americans. "Think Notre Dame football," write *Sports Illustrated's* Tim Layden and David Epstein. "Names like Donald Quarrie and Merlene Ottey are holy on the island. In the United States, track and field is a marginal, niche sport that pops its head out of the sand every four years and occasionally produces a superstar. In Jamaica . . . it's a major sport. When *Sports Illustrated* [recently] visited the island . . . dozens of small children showed up for a Saturday morning youth track practice. That was impressive. That they were all wearing spikes was stunning."

With that level of intensity baked right into the culture, it's no surprise that Jamaicans have for many decades produced a wealth of aggressive, ambitious young sprinters. Their problem, though, was that for a long time they didn't have adequate college-level training resources for these promising teenagers. Routinely, the very best athletes would leave the country for Britain (Linford Christie) or Canada (Ben Johnson) and often never return.

Then, in the 1970s, former champion sprinter Dennis Johnson did come back to Jamaica to create a college athletic program based on what he'd experienced in the United States. That program, now at the University of Technology in Kingston, became the new core of Jamaican elite training. After a critical number of ramp-up years, the medals started to pour in. It was the final piece in the systemic machinery driven by national pride and an ingrained sprinting culture.

Psychology was obviously a critical part of the mix. "We genuinely believe that we'll conquer," says Jamaican coach Fitz Coleman. "It's a mind-set. We're small and we're poor, but we believe in ourselves." On its own, it might seem laughable that self-confidence can turn a tiny island into a breeding ground for champion sprinters. But taken in context of the developmental dynamic, psychology and motivation become vital. Science has demonstrated unequivocally that a person's mind-set has the power to dramatically affect both short-term capabilities and the long-term dynamic of achievement. In Jamaica, sprinting is a part of the national identity. Kids who sprint well are admired and praised; their heroes are sprinters; sprinting well

provides economic benefits and ego gratification and is even considered a form of public service.

All things considered, it seems obvious that the mind is the most athletic part of any Jamaican athlete's body.

The notion that the mind is of such paramount importance to athletic success is something that we all have to accept and embrace if we're going to advance the culture of success in human society. Within mere weeks of British runner Roger Bannister becoming the first human being to crack the four-minute mile several other runners also broke through. Bannister himself later remarked that while biology sets ultimate limits to performance it is the mind that plainly determines how close individuals come to those absolute limits.

And we keep coming closer and closer to them. "The past century has witnessed a progressive, indeed remorseless improvement in human athletic performance," writes South African sports scientist Timothy David Noakes. The record speed for the mile, for example, was cut from 4:36 in 1865 to 3:43 in 1999. The one-hour cycling distance record increased from 26 kilometers in 1876 to 49 kilometers in 2005. The 200-meter freestyle swimming record decreased from 2:31 in 1908 to 1:43 in 2007. Technology and aerodynamics are a part of the story, but the rest of it has to do with training intensity, training methods, and sheer competitiveness and desire. It used to be that 67 kilometers per week was considered an aggressive level of training. Today's serious Kenyan runners, Noakes points out, will cover 230 kilometers per week (at 6,000 feet in altitude).

These are not superhumans with rare super-genes. They are participants in a culture of the extreme, willing to devote more, to ache more, and to risk more in order to do better. Most of us will understandably want nothing to do with that culture of the extreme. But that is our choice.

References

Bouchard, T. J. and M. McGue. "Familial studies of intelligence: a review." *Science* 212, no. 4498 (1981): 1055–59.

Layden, Tim and David Epstein. "Why the Jamaicans Are Running Away with Spirit Golds in Beijing." *Sports Illustrated* Website, August 21, 2008.

Manners, John. "Kenya's running tribe." *The Sports Historian* 17, no. 2 (November 1997): 14–27.

Noakes, Timothy David. "Improving Athletic Performance or Promoting Health Through Physical Activity." World Congress on Medicine and Health, July 21-August 31, 2000.

Wilkins, John. "Races, Geography, and Genetic Clusters." Posted on the Evolving Thoughts blog, April 22, 2006.

Wolff, Alexander. "No Finish Line." *Sports Illustrated*, November 5, 2007.

5.2 Maintaining Whiteness: The Fear of Others and Niceness

SETHA LOW

White privilege is an unearned advantage associated with having white skin. It provides special privileges unavailable to people of color, such as being able to dress how one pleases or walk freely at night and not be harassed by police. Whiteness is not just linked to skin color, but is an achieved category that is associated with middle-class values and practices, and often represented through a discourse of "niceness." Drawing on her research with residents of gated communities in New York City and San Antonio, Texas, Low unpacks the hidden meaning of "niceness," showing how it can shroud racist assumptions about urban landscapes. Low argues that discourses of "niceness" combine with the fear of others to maintain white privilege within these built communities.

Questions

1. How is whiteness culturally constructed? What is the role of "cultural capital" in producing and maintaining whiteness?
2. How do the people Low spoke to rationalize their choices to live in gated communities? What are they trying to hold onto and why?
3. How does the growth of gated communities link to changes in the urban landscape and social control mechanisms produced by neoliberalism?

In this article, I link two ways of maintaining whiteness and white privilege employed by gated communities residents in the surrounding suburbs of New York City and San Antonio, Texas. The first, [is] the fear of others . . . [and] [t]he second, the desire for "niceness." . . .

. . . [T]he fear of others, when combined with niceness, inscribes racist assumptions on the landscape. This inscription of whiteness is seen as natural, normative, taken-for-granted, and most importantly out of residents' everyday awareness. Thus, gated communities with private governance and a homeowners' association are creating and maintaining white spaces. . . . [The] addition of the concept of niceness to our understanding of how gated communities work as racist and exclusionary places begins the unraveling of how "nice" people, who say "nice" things, and have "nice" or liberal values, participate in maintaining whiteness in their built environment. . . .

The Context of Gating in the USA

The gated community is a response to transformations in the political economy of late-20th-century urban America. The increasing mobility of capital, marginalization of the labor force, and dismantling of the welfare state began with the change in labor practices and deindustrialization of the 1970s, and accelerated with the "Reaganomics" of the 1980s. . . .

The shift to the right during the Reagan years intensified an ideological focus on free market capitalism. Power, wealth, and income all tilted toward the richest portions of the population. While the income share of the upper 20 percent of Americans rose from 41.6 percent to 44 percent from 1980 to 1988, the period of the greatest expansion in gating, the average after-tax income of the lowest ten percent dropped 10.5 percent from 1977 to 1987, producing an increasingly bifurcated class system (Phillips 1991). These economic and political changes intensified already existing inequalities of neighborhood resources and services, while escalating housing prices left more families homeless and without health care.

Globalization and economic restructuring also weakened existing social relations and contributed to the breakdown of traditional ways of maintaining social order. Social control mechanisms and their associated institutions, such as the police and schools, were no longer seen as effective. This breakdown in local control threatened middle-class neighborhood residents, and the gated residential community became a viable and socially acceptable option.

The creation of gated communities . . . is a strategy for regulating and patrolling the urban poor comprising predominantly Latino and Black minorities. Gating is only one example of this new form of social ordering that displaces and regulates people or activities rather than eliminating them. . . . A safe environment excludes all those who are considered dangerous, who consequently become increasingly defined by their isolation and indices of race and class (Low 2008).

. . . Cities continue to experience high levels of residential segregation based on discriminatory real estate practices, zoning ordinances, and mortgage structures designed to insulate Whites from Blacks. Blacks are less likely to move to the suburbs in the first place, and then more likely to return to the city (Massey and Denton 1988). Residential proximity to Blacks intensifies Whites' fear of crime, and Whites who are racially prejudiced are even more fearful (Skogan 1995).

Residents of middle-class and upper middle-class neighborhoods often cordon themselves off as a class by building fences, cutting off relationships with neighbors, and moving out in response to problems and conflicts. At the same time, governments have expanded their regulatory role through zoning laws, local police patrols, restrictive ordinances for dogs, quiet laws, and laws against domestic and interpersonal violence that narrow the range of accepted behavioral norms. Indirect economic strategies that limit the minimum lot or house size, policing policies that target nonconforming uses of the environment, and social ordinances that enforce middle-class rules of civility further segregate family and neighborhood life (Merry 1993, 1990, 1981). . . .

The evolution of "pod," "enclave," and "cul-de-sac" suburban designs further refined the ability of land use planners and designers to develop suburban subdivisions where people of different income groups would have little to no contact with one another. Regulated resident behavior, house type, and "taste culture" are moresubtle means of control. Even landscape aesthetics function as a suburban politics of exclusion, often referred to as making everything "nice" (Government by the Nice, for the Nice 1992). . . .

. . . Walls can provide a refuge from people who are deviant or unusual, but they require patrolling the border to be sure no one gets in. The resulting vigilance necessary to maintain these "purified communities" actually heightens residents' anxiety and sense of isolation, rather than making them feel safer. These interlocking processes depict a world with increasing reliance on urban fortification, policing, and segregation to maintain whiteness. . . .

Definitions and the Mechanics of Whiteness

. . . [W]hiteness is not only about race, but is an historical and cultural construct actively produced and reproduced to further and/or improve an individual or social group's position within the power dynamics of the neighborhood, region and/or nation/state. . . .

Whiteness and the privileges accrued are viewed as middle-class privileges and are not restricted to access by color, but also by class, gender, sexual orientation, and place of origin. Karen Brodkin (2000) writes that many groups now considered White were not originally and illustrates how Italians, Irish, and Jewish immigrants became White only when assimilated economically and culturally into the middle class. This transformation based on the taking on of middle-class, so-called American, values is an important aspect of whiteness within the gated community in that residents confound whiteness and middle-class attributes in such a way that one can be substituted for the other.

Whiteness also refers to the privileges of being a member of a socially unmarked category (Carter 1997; Fine 2004, 2009). Blacks and Hispanics, as well as other members of minority or immigrant populations within the USA, are racially and ethnically identified by socially constructed notions of phenotypic traits; these "traits" are used to mark groups as different from being White. Whiteness, on the other hand, is the assumed norm, socially, physically, and even politically, and dominates national ideas of beauty, social class, and goodness. . . .

Maintaining whiteness in the context of the suburban USA and particularly within gated communities,

thus, is not only about race and racializing, but is a middle-class and normative concept. Whiteness is defined by a person's "cultural capital," that is, the ability to have access to and make use of things like higher education and social graces, vocabulary, and demeanor that allow one to prosper or at least compete within the dominant culture. It is a sense of entitlement to certain privileges that are out of the reach of others. Thus "middle-class whiteness" is defined as much by mainstream acceptance of norms, values, and life expectations as by race or ethnicity (Kenny 2000). . . .

Fear of Others

. . . But it is not just in Texas and California that residents of gated communities stigmatize immigrants as a source of fear. In New York as well, residents identify "ethnic changes" and a changing socioeconomic environment as potentially threatening.

VIGNETTE 1   VISITING MY SISTER IN HER GATED COMMUNITY

My husband and I have reservations about going to a Fourth of July party, but my sister coaxes us with the promise of margaritas and sinful desserts, finally winning us over. Dressed in New York chic, we cross the street to enter an imposing Santa Fe style house decorated with Mexican furniture and colorful textiles, full of people talking, children racing about, and our hosts serving drinks and dishing out enormous quantities of food. My husband wanders out to the pool, while I stay inside where it is air-conditioned. My choices are watching television with the older men, or sitting with our hosts' teenage son and his friends. I sit down at their table, and am soon involved in a spirited discussion.

"Should we go downtown after dinner to see the fireworks along Riverwalk?" the host's son asks. Riverwalk is the commercially successful development that revitalized the center of San Antonio.

"Will there be many Mexicans there?" a tall, gangly boy in a Nike tee shirt and nylon running shorts asks.

"It'll be mobbed with Mexicans, I'm not sure I want to go," a girl with heavy blond bangs responds.

I am struck with how they used the word "Mexican." Yesterday I toured the local missions where the complex history of Spanish conquest and resettlement of indigenous peoples is inscribed in the protective walls of the church compounds. Surely, these young people learn about Texas history in school.

I interrupt the flow of conversation and ask them what they mean by "Mexican"? A young man in baggy khakis and a baseball hat worn backwards looks at me curiously:

"Why, the Mexicans who live downtown, on the south side of the city."

"What makes you think they are Mexican," I reply, frowning a bit. "Because they speak Spanish?"

"They are dangerous," a young woman in a tennis skirt asserts, "packing knives and guns. Our parents don't allow us to go downtown at night."

They decide to stay and watch the fireworks from the golf course, at least they would not be with their parents, and wander off to find their other friends.

I remain at the table, my mind racing to bring together scattered bits of the history and culture of the region. Texas was originally part of Mexico, colonized by the Spanish. The majority of people who live in Texas identify themselves as descendants of the Spanish and/or Mexicans who settled the area. "Mexicans" can refer to the founding families of San Antonio, hacienda owners and other landholders, who make up a significant part of the political elite and upper class. "Mexicans" also can mean visiting Mexican nationals who maintain summer houses in the region and this neighborhood. There are people who legally immigrated to Texas, but retain strong ties to their native birthplace, and call themselves "Mexicans." Finally, there are the "Mexicans" that the teenagers mentioned, a stereotyped group of what some locals think of as poor, undocumented workers who speak Spanish, but who in fact come from all over Latin America.

VIGNETTE 2 CAROL AND TED IN A GATED COMMUNITY IN SUBURBAN LONG ISLAND

Carol and Ted Corral have been living at their gated community for eight months and had previously lived in Great Neck for the past twenty-eight years. Prior to Great Neck, they had lived in Brooklyn.

I ask about their life in Great Neck. Ted replies that it's a great community socially, and the children had a good school. It's an affluent community and offers lots of benefits. Carol adds that most of her friends were made there when her children were small. Ted describes the community as "very, very educated. . . . You know so everyone goes on to college, and it stressed the role of family, and you know, it's just a wonderful community. But it's changing, it's undergoing internal transformations."

Carol says, "It's ethnic changes."

And Ted repeats "It's ethnic changes, that's a very good way of putting it."

Carol agrees and adds that it started to happen "in the last, probably, seven to eight years."

The changing composition of the neighborhood made them so uncomfortable they decided to move.

I ask about their prior residence in Brooklyn. Ted shrugs his shoulders. I say that I would like to know about why they left for comparison, and finally Carol answers. She tells me they had moved from Brooklyn to bring up their children in a better environment. The school system was changing, and they did not want their children to go to school with children from lower socioeconomic backgrounds who were being bused into their Brooklyn neighborhood.

"Those kids were wild," she says, "and had a different upbringing." She wanted to protect her children from exposure to the kinds of problems these kids might cause. The neighborhood was still comfortable, but the school system was not "desirable," as she put it. They had both grown up in Brooklyn, but the neighborhood changed, so they decided to build their own home in the suburbs.

I ask how they decided to move here, and Ted answers that they were looking for something that would suit their lifestyle better. He adds that they chose a gated community because they wanted a secure lifestyle with no hassles and no responsibilities.

The psychological underpinnings of this fear of others discourse is "dualistic thinking," a form of social splitting used to cope with anxiety and fear. It oversimplifies and dichotomizes cultural definitions and social expectations to differentiate the self from the other regardless of whether it is a contrast of Anglos and "Mexicans," Whites and illegal immigrants, or Whites and "ethnic others." . . .

Psychological splitting can be used as a form of denial and resistance, providing a means of distancing oneself from an undesirable self-image and projecting it onto another. Social splitting . . . helps to explain the kind of "us" versus "them" thinking employed by the gated community residents to rationalize their fears of those outside the gates.

During periods of economic decline and social stress, middle-class people become anxious about maintaining their social status and seek to identify the reasons that their environment and social world is deteriorating. Social splitting offers a strategy that is reinforced by cultural stereotypes and media distortions, allowing people to psychologically separate from people who are threatening their tranquility and neighborhood stability. The walls and gates of the community reflect this splitting physically as well as metaphorically, with "good" people (the good part of us) inside, and the "bad" remaining outside. . . .

Neoliberal practices of the shrinking state and the reinscription of responsibility on individuals and communities provide the structural substrate for these psychological processes. Individuals and communities in cities are encouraged to protect themselves from perceived threats, thus contributing to the emergence of a new pattern of civic militancy even at home. . . .

. . . [T]he psychological underpinning of social splitting and the structural analysis of neoliberalism, become part of a defense of whiteness through what

[John] Fiske (1998) calls "nonracist racism," a racism that is encoded in race-neutral discourses, such as law, economics, health, education, and particularly housing and capital accumulation. . . .

. . . [C]ompared with most large cities, the suburbs do not have many public places where strangers intermingle, and the relative isolation and homogeneity of the suburbs discourages interaction with people who are identified as the "other." Baumgartner's (1988) study of an upper middle-class suburban town outside of New York City documents how local residents are upset by outsiders appearing on residential streets. Strangers by virtue of their race or unconventionality are singled out as "suspicious" even if merely walking down the street. The physical organization of the street pattern, cul-de-sacs and dead-end streets, enables residents to monitor their neighborhoods and to spot outsiders who linger.

Residents explain their monitoring behavior by citing their "fear of crime," by which they mean "predatory behavior by strangers." They voice concerns about poor Blacks and Hispanics from New York City or San Antonio entering their town and preying upon residents. Despite the low rate of crime in the gated area, residents are overly concerned about people who seem out of place. . . .

Gating exacerbates this ability to monitor and be concerned about "marked" intruders by creating a kind of "pure space" for residents. The more "purified" the environment, the more homogeneous and controlled, the greater residents' ability to identify any deviant individuals who should not be there (Sibley 1995). "Pure spaces" expose differences and have clear boundaries that facilitate policing. . . . Gating only makes the boundaries more visible and psychologically salient.

. . . Helen and Ralph offer a vivid description of their "nonracist racism" and how the desire for a pure white space occurs.

VIGNETTE 3 # HELEN AND RALPH IN SUBURBAN SAN ANTONIO, TEXAS

Helen and Ralph were one of the first families to move into the gated community. They originally moved to Sun Meadow for the golf course but now would only consider living in a gated community. When I ask her why, she replies:

Because after seeing that there are so may beautiful neighborhoods that are not [in] a secure area, [and] that's where burglaries and murders take place. It's an open door [saying] to people, come on in. Why should they try anything here when they can go somewhere else first. It's a strong deterrent, needless to say.

She feels that there is less crime in gated developments than in San Antonio in general. She knows people living in . . . equally nice nongated neighborhoods who have had their homes broken into and who have been assaulted with weapons. The worst that has happened is a few cars have come through and "messed things up." She thinks that it was probably kids.

Only a few families have been robbed or burglarized.

Helen feels her community is different because it is secured. Without the gates, she thinks, anybody could come knocking on your door and put you in compromising situation. She illustrates her point by telling me what happened to a friend who lives "in a lovely community" outside of Washington, D.C.: She said this fellow came to the door, and she was very intimidated because she was white, and he was black, and you didn't get many blacks in her neighborhood. She only bought it [what he was selling] just to hurry and quick get him away from the door, because she was scared as hell. That's terrible to be put in that situation. I like the idea of having security.

Helen and Ralph put on their burglar alarm every time they leave, although she thinks they may be overly cautious. She also keeps her doors locked, because she has had people walk in her front door thinking her house was for sale.

I ask her if she is concerned about crime in her gated community. She answers, "no, not here, but in San Antonio." She goes on to explain that San Antonio, like any major city, has problems:

There are gangs. People are overworked, they have families, they are underpaid, the stress is out of control, and they abuse their children. The children go out because they don't like their home life. There's too much violence everywhere. It starts in the city, but then the kids get smart enough and say "oh, gee, I need money for x, y or z, but it's really hot in the city, let's go out and get it someplace else." We're the natural target for it. So being in a secure area, I don't have to worry as much as another neighborhood that doesn't have security.

Ironically, Helen's concern with crime developed after she moved into her gated community, but living there reinforces the importance of having gates and guards for personal security. She is more concerned about someone walking into her house than with crime in general. Yet she is one of the few residents who specifically cites an example where racial difference triggers a sense of fear. Like Ted and Carol Corral, who moved because of "ethnic changes," Helen alludes to her friend's experience as the kind of thing that she is frightened of. "She was scared as hell," Helen comments. Her story, although displaced on her friend, suggests how Helen would feel if a Black person came to her door. . . .

Niceness

. . . [T]here are "very powerful cultural categories in the USA, such as 'nice,' 'friendly,' and 'comfortable' which Americans operate in exclusionary manners

on a variety of fronts that include, but are certainly not limited to race" (Hartigan 2009). In my research, "niceness" emerged as an important moral and aesthetic judgment for gated community residents. Gating, in fact, has been called "government by the nice," referring to the CC&Rs (covenants, contracts and restrictions) written into deeds dictating even the colors a house can be painted, the weight of family dogs, the type of furniture or curtains that can be seen in one's picture window, and the color (white), number and type of Christmas tree lights (Government by the Nice, for the Nice 1992). Some homeowners associations even regulate behavior; a woman caught kissing her boyfriend in her driveway in the evening was fined and threatened with expulsion. . . .

Niceness is about keeping things clean, orderly, homogeneous, and controlled so that housing values remain stable, but it is also a way of maintaining whiteness. Whiteness provides access to education, elite taste cultures and behaviors, and allows a group to prosper within the dominant culture. In places like Long Island, New York, and San Antonio, Texas, being "middle class" and being "White" overlap such that one social status can be taken for another.

. . . The CC&Rs and the rulings of the homeowners association board are strategies for making sure that the gated community will remain a "nice" environment, separated from others and the city, thus retaining its whiteness and privilege.

VIGNETTE 4 REBECCA IN A SUBURBAN SAN ANTONIO GATED COMMUNITY

Rebecca's reasons for moving in[to] a gated community were simple, she wanted safety and no hassles. Property value and choosing a good location were her other major concerns. . . .

She had her heart set on this gated community because of the convenient location, and because it was "nice, nicer than any other community." She wanted to be the first one in, to get a prime piece of land, and picked the best lot right across from the clubhouse. She now has everything: newness, luxury, safety, scenery, and value.

Rebecca and her husband are relieved they know what the houses will look like beforehand, and that the architect uses only traditional styles. There are no modern houses . . . they are all the "New England line" using only four colors: soft beige, yellow, gray, and white.

One great thing about Manor House is that she will be able to sell her two-story, colonial style home easily and move in[to] another model.

"Well, I don't think this will be our final home," she adds. "Maybe we can talk again."

"I thought you said it was perfect?"

"It's nice in many ways, but it won't be my permanent home."

. . . [I]t is important for neighbors to maintain a firm line between the value of money, and resale value of their home, and neighborly love. The reason for such concern is that about 64 percent of American households put "just about everything they have into buying a house," and the maintenance and appreciation of house value is dependent on how well everyone else keeps up their house and landscape (Ross et al. 1996).

Based on this reality, it is not difficult to understand why most gated community residents accept the extensive set of covenants and restrictions that they think will bolster the value of their house and property. Residents cannot change the exteriors of their houses or the landscape, thus insuring a certain level of quality and consistency. Even though residents complain about the restrictions and inconvenience, the CC&Rs provide an extra measure of safety and security, socially and financially. . . .

Another way that a discourse of niceness appears is when "offenders" or "outsiders" violate the public

order by ignoring or challenging local standards of cleanliness and aesthetics. Residents may become annoyed, for example, by poorly kept buildings, run-down yards and gardens, and rusting automobiles parked outside a home. . . . Cleanliness and orderliness indicate the "type of people" who live in a place and establish a norm of middle-class civility, masking the imposition of whiteness.

. . . Residents perceive and read ecological changes in their local environment as part of an ongoing assessment of their social worth as well as the stability of their housing market. It is therefore not surprising that subtle visual cues are closely attended to. . . . [T]he changing physical conditions are conflated with what is perceived as a changing social environment. As one New York City resident explained, she moved to a gated community, "when Bloomingdale's moved out and Kmart moved in."

. . . [T]he "niceness" and "cleanliness" required for "safety" works as a coded way to talk about and take action against racial difference and a loss of white privilege.

"Niceness" is one way of maintaining social control of the neighborhood and becomes particularly powerful when linked to "changes in the neighborhood" that justify the reasons that a person or family decides to move to a gated community, a "safer" and more secure environment. . . .

VIGNETTE 5 | LAUREL AND HENRY IN A SUBURBAN LONG ISLAND GATED COMMUNITY

Laurel moved in eight months ago. She did not feel safe in her previous Long Island neighborhood. Her husband travels and keeps late hours, so an alarm system was installed after a neighbor was robbed.

When I ask whether there is anything the family misses about their previous home, the conversation takes a sudden turn. The one thing I don't like about condominium living is that everything has to be cleared [by the homeowners' association board]. One of the first things we realized is that we didn't have a storm door on the front door.

I said, "That's crazy," especially when we let our dog out she jumps on the door and you can hear her when she's ready to come in. "We've got to get a storm door. Henry, go out and buy a storm door."

And he said, "I can't go out and buy a storm door." We just had the storm door put in this week, and that was eight months ago. It had to pass the committee. . . . You can't buy the strong wood one either. They choose the storm door and you pay for what they choose. And if you don't like it, tough.

Laurel continues talking about the restrictions imposed by what she calls "the committee." Laurel continues:

If I want to put in planting, especially in front, it has to meet community standards. . . . That's the part I don't like. But I've decided to accept it.

. . . Laughing I ask: "so what do they do, come and look at your backyard, at your tulips?" Laurel looks at me.

I don't know. I was speaking to the man who is the landscaper and told him about our concerns on our property, on making changes. I asked, 'Why can't I just plant? I have to plant my bulbs now, or I won't have anything in the spring." This was last fall.

He said, "Well, you know, we have a committee, and you have to tell them what you want to do, and I'm sure they'll let you do it, but. . . . ."

. . . The committee even gave them trouble about putting up a television satellite when they moved in.

. . . Unfortunately, new owners often are not aware of the extent of CC&R restrictions at the time of purchase. Nor are they cognizant that they have agreed to abide by an arbitration panel appointed by the community association industry, rather than having legal recourse for litigation of disputes in the public court system. New residents do not understand that they have waived many of their free speech rights, because they are living in a private space controlled by a corporation, much like a mall or office complex. . . .

. . . In other words, residents are trading many of their basic civil rights in order to be sure that their community is "nice." . . .

One explanation for why some residents are willing to accept these apparently excessive restrictions can be attributed to their anxiety about maintaining their middle-class lifestyle and socioeconomic position. Baby boomers across the nation are worried that the advantages of a middle-class life, the so-called cultural capital, that families pass on, knowledge, contacts, and inherent privileges, are being lost. For the middle class, and especially the lower middle class, downward mobility during the 1980s and 1990s due to economic restructuring and shrinking job opportunities meant that their children face diminished expectations, including living in less affluent communities with fewer amenities. The deterioration of middle-class suburban neighborhoods, escalating housing prices, a flat job market, and limited job advancement enhances the fear that the economic future is not as secure as it was for the previous generation when there were expanding employment and housing opportunities. This anxiety about losing one's social position translated into an expression of a loss of white privilege.

One of the ways that previous generations heralded their arrival into the middle class was to buy a home in the suburbs. Now, this symbolic arrival is not enough because many of traditional middle-class suburbs are situated in areas with decaying physical environments, increasing heterogeneity, and in some cases, rising crime. Gated communities, with their increased security to keep "others" out, and strict enforcement of rules and regulations, are an attempt to bolster resident's middle-class status. By regimenting the environment, keeping it "nice" and filled with "nice" people, maintaining the resale value of one's home, and putting up with increasing privatization and restrictions, residents hope to keep the threat of economic decline, and loss of class position at bay. . . .

Niceness reinforces this defense of whiteness by adding an aesthetic and moral dimension to the justification for closing others out. Wanting to live in a nice house, with nice neighbors, in a nice neighborhood where your home values and environment are stable [is] simply another way of rationalizing the desire to maintain whiteness. . . .

References

Baumgartner, M. P. 1988. The Moral Order of a Suburb. Oxford: Oxford University Press.

Brodkin, Karen. 2000. How Jews Became White Folks and What That Says About Race in America. New Brunswick, NJ: Rutgers University Press.

Carter, Robert T. 1997. Is White a Race? Expressions of White Racial Identity. In Off White: Readings on Race, Power, and Society. 1st ed. Michelle Fine, Lois Weis, Linda Powell and L. Mun Wong, eds. Pp. 198–209. New York: Routledge.

Fine, Michelle. 2004. Witnessing Whiteness/Gathering Intelligence. *In* Off White: Readings on Race, Power, and Society. M. Fine, L. Weis, L. Powell Pruitt and A. Burns, eds. Pp. 245–256. New York and London: Routledge.

Fine, Michelle. 2009. Circuits and Consequences of Dispossession: The Racialized Realignment of the Public Sphere for U.S. Youth. Transforming Anthropology 17(1):20–33.

Fiske, John. 1998. Surveilling the City: Whiteness, the Black Man and Democratic Totalitarianism. Theory, Culture and Society 15(2):67–88.

Government by the Nice, for the Nice. Economist 324 (7769): 25, 26.

Hartigan, John. 2009. What Are You Laughing at? Assessing the "Racial" in U.S. Public Discourse. Transforming Anthropology 17(1):4–19.

Kenny, Lorraine Delia. 2000. Daughters of Suburbia. New Brunswick, NJ: Rutgers University Press.

Low, Setha. 2008. Fortification of Residential Neighbourhoods and the New Emotions of Home. Housing, Theory and Society 25(1): 47–65.

Massey, D. S., and Nancy Denton. 1988. Surbanization and Segregation. American Journal of Sociology 94(3):592–626.

Merry, Sally. 1990. Getting Justice and Getting Even. Chicago: University of Chicago Press.

Merry, Sally. 1993. Mending Walls and Building Fences: Constructing the Private Neighborhood. Journal of Legal Pluralism 33:71–90.

Merry, Sally Engle. 1981. Urban Danger: Life in a Neighborhood of Strangers. Philadelphia: Temple Press.

Phillips, Kevin. 1991. The Politics of Rich and Poor. New York: HarperCollins.

Ross, Mary Massaron, Larry J. Smith, and Robert D. Pritt. 1996. The Zoning Process: Private Land-Use Controls and Gated Communities. Urban Lawyer 28(4):801–7.

Sibley, D. 1995. Geographies of Exclusion. London: Routledge.

Skogan, Wesley G. 1995. The Impact of Victimization of Fear. Crime and Delinquency 33:135–154.

5.3 Intimate Apartheid and Drug Consumption Among Racialized Bodies

PHILIPPE BOURGOIS AND JEFF SCHONBERG

The following piece is from a photoethnography in "critically applied public anthropology" that explores the everyday lives and suffering of homeless heroin injectors and crack smokers in San Franscico. It picks up with an introduction to the central figures of the book, describing a core homeless encampment and the "intimate apartheid" that marks its territory. Bourgois and Schnoberg use the phrase "intimate apartheid" to capture the racialized micro-geography and accompanying hostile social relationships that arise among diverse individuals living in close proximity and forced to rely on one another. This selection also covers distinct "techniques of the body" that inscribe ethnic distinctions onto the bodies of heroin users and then become associated with racial characteristics. The authors apply Bourdieu's concept of "habitus"—our personal dispositions, both conscious and unconscious likes, dislikes—throughout to show how structural power becomes encoded into everyday practices that work to legitimize social inequality.

Questions

1. What are the ethnic hierarchies of the street? How do they mirror mainstream ethnic hierarchies and social realities?
2. What is "intimate apartheid" and how does it manifest itself? What do the authors mean when they say that intimate apartheid reinforces distinctions between people and that people end up "misrecognizing" them as "natural" racial attributes?
3. How does the relationship between Sonny and Al violate the patterns of intimate apartheid? What does it show you about cultural variation?
4. What are "techniques of the body" and how are they racialized among the Edgewater homeless?
5. Discuss the difference between the outlaw and outcast habitus. How is this ethnicized and racialized? How are these habituses produced? What is the role of structural political-economic forces (that are at work "invisibly") in shaping habituses?

If you notice, it's real racial. Whites in one camp, blacks in another camp. And I live right in the middle, by myself. They're all a bunch of racist motherfuckers—both the niggers and the whites.

The whites ain't no better than the blacks. They will rip you off too. I don't trust either group. So I'm alone. The only Latino . . . I don't have nothin' here.

—FELIX

 Visit www.oup.com/us/brondo for an interview with Philippe Bourgois.

Philippe Bourgois and Jeff Schonberg. "Chapter 1: Intimate Apartheid." 2000. *Righteous Dopefiend*. Berkeley: University of California Press, 26–45, 85–93.

Toward the middle of the first year of our fieldwork, a lull in law enforcement allowed a central camp to emerge that was larger and somewhat drier than the other, more precarious encampments we had been visiting in the alleys behind Edgewater Boulevard. This new camp was protected from the rain by a supersize I-beam retrofitted in the decade following the 1989 Loma Prieta earthquake to support a double-decker, eight-lane freeway. The site was also camouflaged by garbage and a canopy of scrub oaks and eucalyptus branches. A tangle of access and exit ramps further isolated the spot, which became its own mini-universe, despite the thousands of commuters speeding by on the freeway above and the steady flow of pedestrians on the boulevard a half dozen yards away. At rush hour, the dull white noise of traffic made the camp feel almost safe, although it reeked of urine and rotting detritus and was wet and cold. . . .

Max was the first to settle the spot, followed by running partners Felix and Frank, who moved there after they were evicted from a more exposed site at the foot of the freeway embankment. Petey and Scotty, two inseparable running partners newly arrived from Southern California, were the next to move in. They slept together on a twin-size mattress laid out on the bare ground. At night they spooned for warmth under a thin blanket given to them by a church soup kitchen in the residential neighborhood up the hill from the boulevard. Felix nicknamed Scotty and Petey "the Island Boys" because they spent most of their daylight hours panhandling and selling heroin on the surrounding traffic islands. Felix maintained the more profitable and safer sales spot in front of the A&C corner store. The heavy flow of anonymous pedestrian traffic heading to the three catty-corner bus stops surrounding the corner store allowed Felix to camouflage his dealing as panhandling.

Al, a toothless, forty-year-old man, moved into the encampment soon after the Island Boys. He built a shack out of loading pallets that was just wide enough to fit a full-size double bed, which he shared with his "girlfriend," Rosie. She visited once a month, on the day he received his Social Security Insurance (SSI) disability payments for alcoholism, and enough to help him spend his entire check on crack, leaving him, dopesick, within hours. Felix and Frank resented Rosie's exclusive access to Al's crack and eventually persuaded him to kick her out. Al's only comment was, "She never even let me fuck her! She's got something against sex. Seems like her stepfather raped her when she was a kid." Al was exceptionally easy-going, and after Rosie left, he allowed "no-hustle" Hogan to sleep at the entrance to his shack under a makeshift tarp.

Hank, an old-timer in his mid-fifties, was the last to establish himself as a regular inhabitant of the camp. He slept in a bright red pup tent, having just been thrown out of a housing project apartment in the residential neighborhood up the hill, where he had been living for the past year. According to Felix, the apartment belonged to "an old dopefiend lesbian bitch" whom they had all known since adolescence. The night he first arrived, Hank had a fresh "stab wound" under his right armpit, but Felix dismissed it: "Probably just an abscess they cut out of him at the county hospital. Don't ever believe a word Hank says." Nevertheless, Felix and everyone else treated Hank well because he was exceptionally generous, sharing heroin and fortified wine. Like Al, Hank was also energetic, constantly building and cleaning when high. On weekends, he would scavenge overripe vegetables from the dumpsters at the farmers market half a mile down the boulevard and cook stew for everyone in the camp. . . .

Besides Al's crack-smoking ex-girlfriend, Rosie, only two other women occasionally stayed overnight in the camp during our first year on Edgewater Boulevard. One, an acquaintance of Felix, worked at San Francisco's lowest-budget, sex-for-crack prostitute stroll on Capp Street, some twenty blocks away. The other woman was Nickie, who lived with her eight-year-old son in a project apartment a half mile down the boulevard, near the farmers market. Welfare paid her rent directly to the Housing Authority through the Aid to Families with Dependent Children program. Nickie supported her heroin habit by combining odd jobs cleaning houses with panhandling and shoplifting from liquor stores. She also let some of the Edgewater homeless use her apartment to shower, wash their laundry, and inject in return for shares of their heroin and alcohol. Life on the street was more dangerous for women than for men (Bourgois, Prince, and Moss 2004). . . .

Ethnic Hierarchies on the Street

During our first year, all the homeless in the central encampment were white, except Felix, whose parents were from Central America. We rarely saw

African-Americans, Asians, or Latinos visit the encampments. In the immediate neighborhood, however, the daytime and early evening population was a kaleidoscope of San Francisco's ethnic diversity. . . .

On a typical warm summer evening, the main corner where the homeless spent a great deal of their time, in front of the A&C convenience store, attracted a half dozen very diverse groups of people. Most visible were the middle-aged African-American men who, on their way home from work, congregated and drank beer by a barbecue at the entrance to the alley behind the store. By nightfall, younger African-American crack dealers arrived. They camouflaged their sales by mingling with the barbecue crowd and by circulating among the Latino and Asian commuters around the corner who were waiting at the bus stops. . . .

In this mix, two or three of the white homeless leaned against a wall at the edge of the African-American barbecue scene or inside one of the bus shelters nodding in deep heroin sedation. Latino and Filipino youths, mostly high school age, in the latest hip-hop outfits, passed by to ask the Edgewater homeless to buy beer, cigarettes, and cigars for them. They would hollow out the cigars to prepare "blunts" of marijuana, but they rarely stopped to smoke on the corner.

The homeless, middle-aged, white heroin injectors we befriended were at the bottom of the corner's social hierarchy and often displayed their low status by begging in tattered clothing. An early set of fieldnotes reveals how rapidly we had to learn the meaning of our skin color in this scene. Even though we looked healthy and dressed in clean clothes, we were lumped by default with the low-status "stanky white dopefiends."

Philippe's Fieldnotes

While accompanying Al and Hogan back to the main encampment, I slow down as we pass the barbecue scene in the alley, hoping to initiate a passing conversation with one of the younger African-American crack dealers. My attempt at friendly eye contact is dismissed with a wave of the arm and a gruff "Keep moving, keep moving." When I smile and nod hello, the young man shouts, "I said keep moving!" I overhear him telling his partner in a lower voice, "Damn! Do those motherfuckers smell bad!" Embarrassed, I hurry to catch up with Al and Hogan, noticing that Hogan has

brown stains in the rear of his pants, presumably from having lost control of his bowels this morning as a result of dopesickness.

The ethnic hierarchies of street culture in San Francisco are not exclusive to drug culture and homelessness. The hegemony of African-American style extends throughout the United States and through much of global popular culture. It is historically inscribed in slang (from jive to hip-hop), in music (from blues and jazz to rap), in clothing (from zoot suits to sagging jeans), and in body posture (from handshakes to gait and facial expressions).

But the "coolness" of African-American street culture does not translate into economic and political power in the United States. On the contrary, blackness and expressions of hip-hop or working-class street culture exclude individuals from access to upward mobility in the corporate economy. Despite their clear subordination within the local street-hustler hierarchy and their exclusion from mainstream white society, the durability of racism in the United States allowed the homeless whites on Edgewater Boulevard to hold on to an ideology of white supremacy. Among themselves, for example, they used the word *nigger* routinely. When African-Americans were in earshot, however, they practiced deference, fearing violence or humiliation. At first, it did not occur to the whites that we might not share their racism. They treated racialized distinctions as self-evident common sense and often used the cliches of middle-class society when we asked them about race relations.

Philippe: Why is this scene so white?

Hank: I've never really thought about it. We keep amongst ourselves. The black with the black and the white with the white. That's about it, you know. Basically, blacks stay to themselves.

Philippe: But where are the black dopefiends? I never see any here.

Hank: Well, they're around, but they don't hang out. Everybody buys from everybody, but for actually sitting there and actually using together? They don't do that. I've got a lot of black connections, but if I was to sit there and use with them. . . . I won't use with them.

Matter of fact, you'll see very few black people homeless . . . because they're knocking out kids on welfare.

Philippe: [surprised] 'Cause what?

Hank: You know, having kids. Every one of those black guys over there [pointing toward the barbecue grill in the alley] has three or four kids, and an old lady at home. They're all collecting welfare.

Have you ever seen a black guy really walk?

Philippe: [confused] Really what?

Hank: Walk. Just about every black guy I know owns a car, either a Cadillac or something new.

Yeah, they pretty much stay to themselves. I've never really got in to find out where they go or what they do, you know. Hell, they don't bother me, I don't bother them, you know. Keep the peace that way.

But when you start mixing the races, especially the blacks down there [pointing to the alley and rolling his eyes], everybody's kind of semi-prejudiced. So we don't really exchange information. We say hello-just general things.

Felix: [interrupting] Blacks are into crack . . . scandalous crack monsters. You can't trust niggers.

Hank: Yeah.

Felix: They'll rob you. They'll steal from their own mother. None of the blacks want to work.

Hank: Can't trust niggers.

Felix: I hate selling to them. They'll come back and mug you.

The irony of the assertion by the whites that they were the victims of black violence and theft emerged years later when we coded our fieldnotes and transcripts. We discovered that during our first year none of the whites in our Edgewater homeless scene had been robbed by an African-American. In fact, their most generous patron was an elderly African-American man who was an evangelical Christian. When it rained heavily, he allowed several of them to sleep under an old camper shell in a storage lot he owned on the boulevard. Furthermore, the only case of black-on-white violence we recorded that first year occurred when one of the whites peripheral to our social network stole thirty dollars' worth of crack from an African-American dealer for whom he was supposed to be selling on consignment. He was beaten "as a warning" for "smoking up the product," and when he

"came up short" again the next week, he fled from the boulevard and never returned.

. . .

The Arrival of African-Americans

During the second year of our fieldwork, an African-American heroin injector named Carter James became a regular in our homeless scene. He had grown up on the same block as Felix, in the neighborhood up the hill, and Hank also knew him, having used heroin with Carter's older brother during his adolescence. Directly contradicting everything Hank had previously told us about "never mingling with blacks," all the white heroin injectors welcomed Carter onto Edgewater Boulevard, referring to him by his nickname, C. J. He worked as a parking attendant for a Jaguar auto dealership and contributed generously in the moral economy of sharing. Every day, he came directly from work to the A&C corner store to buy heroin from Felix with the money he earned from tips.

As Carter spent more and more of his free time on the corner after work, his heroin habit and alcohol consumption escalated. At the time, he was living with his eldest sister, Beverly, in Hunters Point, sleeping on her living room couch. His trajectory into full-time homelessness took only six weeks. It began when he stopped contributing his share of rent and food to his sister's household. . . . Finally, early one morning, Carter arrived with his army duffle bag full of clothes. He was not on his way to work, and he no longer had money to rent a room. Felix and his running partner, Frank, the sign painter, made room for Carter next to them under the I-beam, and he laid out a mattress of scavenged carpet remnants. . . .

Racial Disequilibrium

Within a week, Carter went from being an employed, housed, and a high-status giver in the moral economy to a quarrelsome taker. Having suddenly lost his steady source of legal income, he had not yet established an effective street hustle. He considered begging from strangers demeaning. Instead, he coerced money out of friends and acquaintances and intimidated campmates to give him the leftover cottons from their injections. He gave up buying vodka and began bumming slugs of Cisco Berry. The whites now dismissed him as "nothin' but a fuckin' nigger peon."

Carter's full-time presence in the main encampment and in front of the corner store attracted three additional African-Americans into the core group of regulars on Edgewater Boulevard: Stretch, Sonny, and Tina. Stretch, in his mid-thirties, was the youngest, and he was only beginning to use heroin. . . . Stretch still did not know how to inject himself, and he exchanged puffs from his glass crack pipe with Felix and Carter in return for assistance with administering shots of heroin. They were happy to help him, since his physical tolerance for opiates was still low, and they did not have to give him much heroin in exchange for his shares of crack. Tina, a woman in her early forties, never injected heroin. She drank large quantities of whatever sixteen-ounce can of malt liquor was on sale at the corner store and smoked crack. Sonny, in his late forties, had just "left" his girlfriend's apartment in the housing project on the far side of the residential neighborhood up the hill, following a stint in county jail for selling crack.

Stretch and Sonny placed their mattresses next to Carter's in the dry corner of the camp where Felix and Frank slept. Tina did not sleep in the camp because she still had access to a couch in a cousin's project apartment down the boulevard. Sometimes, however, she stayed up all night in the main encampment binging on crack with Carter, Sonny, and Stretch. Several additional African-American men, who had more stable housing, began visiting the encampment regularly to inject heroin, smoke crack, and hang out. . . .

The ethnic transformation of the main hang-out scene in front of the A&C corner store was most dramatic. Reggie, dressed in a black leather suit, would call out loudly to passersby, "I need ya!" His smile would turn into a curse if no money was forthcoming. When white pedestrians failed to acknowledge eye contact, he accused them of racism. No one dared to cross Reggie except for Felix, who resented losing control of this optimal panhandling and heroin selling spot. . . .

White Flight

Hogan was the first to move out of the encampment "to escape from the niggers." Carter had repeatedly threatened to beat him up unless he took a shower, changed his clothes, and cleaned out his half dozen abscesses. Hogan exemplified the low status of the whites in the scene, and everyone scorned him. . . . His especially unhygienic injection practices resulted in multiple foul-smelling chronic abscesses. Furthermore, in contrast to the other homeless, who were skinny to the point of emaciation, Hogan was obese, straining from the weight of his oversized body and constantly sweating as he hobbled with an uncoordinated gait on swollen feet.

Hogan set up camp three blocks away in a gully along the freeway embankment behind an all-night diner and bar, the Dockside Bar & Grill. . . .

Isolated in his new camp, Hogan tearfully told anyone who would listen that his festering multiple abscesses were the result of AIDS. His formerly scornful companions expressed sympathy and stopped by to give him wet cottons. Even the hardened storekeepers along the boulevard started giving him money and food. We too brought him clothes, food, blankets, and petty cash and began tape-recording his life story. There was not yet any effective treatment for HIV at the time. . . .

Meanwhile back at the main camp, ethnic tensions were deepening with complaints by the whites that the "scandalous niggers" were attracting too much attention from the police. Scotty and Petey, the Island Boys, who had emerged as the steadiest retail heroin sellers on the boulevard, moved to Hogan's camp. . . . Hank was the next white to leave. He obtained a beat-up motor home and parked it up the hill, on the same block where he had lived as a teenager. Al also left, but not out of antipathy to the African-Americans; he was simply taking advantage of an invitation from his parents to help renovate their garage in San Francisco's southern suburbs. Max, meanwhile, was hospitalized for several weeks for an abscess on his upper arm that required complicated muscle transfer surgery. Upon his release, he took "one look at the nigger camp" and joined Hogan in the gully behind the Dockside Bar & Grill.

A Latino Interlude

Felix was the only member of our original social network to maintain friendly relations with Carter and the newly arrived African-Americans, sharing crack and heroin with them regularly. Frank, who had been Felix's running partner for years, was furious about this. He blamed Felix for having "turned our camp into a niggers' shooting gallery." Formerly, Felix had been the only Latino in the scene and had been treated as an "honorary white." The arrival of the African-Americans allowed him to establish a new ethnic space for himself, and he began referring to his former companions as "lame whites."

Felix asserted his Latino identity by befriending a Puerto Rican injector named Victor, who drove a forklift at a corrugated cardboard factory in South San Francisco. A barrel of glue had fallen on Victor at work, fracturing two disks in his lower back, and he was placed on disability payments for three months to recover. During those months, he spent most of his time with Felix. Shortly after returning to work, Victor was arrested while purchasing a ten-dollar bag of heroin during his lunch break. He claimed he needed the heroin to treat his ongoing lower back pain, but he spent three days dopesick in the county jail before the charges were dismissed. His supervisor immediately fired him for absenteeism, and he began hanging out full time on Edgewater Boulevard.

A few weeks later, Victor's twenty-four-year-old son, Little Vic, just released from two years in San Quentin prison for crack selling, drove up to the corner in a brand-new Mitsubishi Montero SUV looking for his father. Little Vic stayed with his grandmother in the housing project up the hill. . . .

Like most of the under-thirty-year-olds who passed through our scene, Little Vic spurned heroin and needle use, but he wanted to spend time with his father and treated him to a prolonged crack binge. Felix joined them, and soon Little Vic was calling him "uncle." Little Vic's mother was white, but he presented himself proudly as "Puerto Rican one hundred percent, just like my father." Maintaining a perennially angry expression on his face, he began harassing the whites. He referred to Felix's running partner, Frank, as "that white trash motherfucker." In contrast, he curried favor with the African-Americans and spent most of his time hanging out with the younger crack sellers by the barbecue grill and at the bus stops. . . .

. . . Little Vic, now grown up, bonded with his father through crack smoking and aggression against the whites. He "beat down" Jim, a newly arrived heroin injector from San Francisco's white, formerly working-class suburb of Brisbane, chasing him permanently out of the scene. Little Vic also regularly bullied Hogan, the weakest man in the group, taxing his panhandling earnings. He also mugged Frank, and, to our surprise, Felix helped him. . . .

Scared and depressed after this betrayal by his long-term running partner, Frank entered a twenty-one-day methadone detox facility. He abandoned his mattress and all his possessions under the overpass, declaring, "Felix didn't stab me in the back. He stabbed me right here [patting his heart]." Frank lasted for a week in detox before dropping out and settling into the new encampment of whites behind the Dockside Bar & Grill. He became Max's running partner. Felix, meanwhile, felt guilty: "I wish Frank knew what really happened. I was trying to help him. I was just trying to push him aside, and now he blames me for beating him up. Oh, man! Frank has left me forever."

Shortly after mugging Frank, Little Vic drove off in his girlfriend's SUV with another woman and disappeared on an extended crack binge across town. Before leaving, Little Vic ordered his girlfriend to stay with Felix under the I-beam. To enforce his mandate, he took her shoes, leaving her barefoot in the mud. Little Vic's girlfriend remained semi-catatonic next to Felix's mattress, ignoring our offers to help. At first, she did not touch any alcohol or drugs, but Tina reached out to her and, in a gesture of feminine solidarity, shared food with her. Soon they were smoking crack together and drinking malt liquor. . . .

Victor Senior reduced his presence on the boulevard following his son's reincarceration. He persuaded his mother to pay for him to enter a methadone maintenance program, and she invited him to move into her housing project apartment. We occasionally saw him in the neighborhood up the hill, carrying his mother's grocery bags in the supermarket or walking her to the Senior Services Center.

Victor's exit from Edgewater Boulevard left Felix isolated. He claimed that Victor refused to recognize him when he chanced upon him up the hill, where Felix scavenged for aluminum cans with his shopping cart. Felix now had no running partner and was sandwiched between the African-Americans and the whites. The one other Latino in the scene, Sal, a Chicano, was a successful heroin dealer who had moved his operations to the neighborhood months earlier to escape a law enforcement offensive in the Mission District. He snubbed Felix as "a knucklehead." . . .

Unable to compete with Reggie and Tina (who now maintained a full-time presence on the boulevard) for space in front of the store, Felix stopped panhandling at the corner. "You can't make money out there when there's five blacks in front of the store. It scares away the customers!" Instead, he scavenged full time for cans and bottles to recycle and began selling clean syringes for two dollars each. Syringe selling proved to be an excellent business. He would exchange "one clean one for two dirties" and was able to double his supply of clean syringes by regularly visiting the once-a-week needle exchange across town. He was also able to increase his heroin consumption because, in lieu of payment, he let customers come back to his camp to inject so long as they gave him a taste.

Felix began accusing his African-American campmates of stealing from his supply of used needles. He started carrying the syringes with him at all times in an overflowing fanny pack, sometimes confusing the clean ones with the dirty. This increased his risk of arrest for "possession of controlled paraphernalia with intent to sell." The epithet "nigger" returned to his everyday lexicon and he reduced his crack smoking. Soon he was routinely referring to the African-Americans as "crack monster motherfuckers" and blaming them for attracting the police. He responded defensively when we asked him about his change in attitude:

> I might be racist, but hell! It's the niggers that are making me this way. They're power tripping. . . . Trying to take over the entire show. They didn't used to be like that with me, but once a nigger, always a nigger.

> That Carter is the fuckin' ringleader. He's the biggest nigger of them all. The big, black nigger. I'm gonna move down with Frank and the whites. I gotta get away from the niggers.

As a first step toward rapprochement with the whites, Felix began parking his shopping cart at their camp overnight, to keep his cans and bottles "safe from the niggers." A week later, he moved into the white camp full time and slid back into his former honorary white status.

Ethnicity and Habitus

In everyday interaction, the Edgewater homeless were forced to commingle intensely across ethnic lines. African-Americans, whites, and Latinos shared and competed for the same limited resources—public space, income, and drugs. It might seem reasonable to suppose that physical addiction to drugs to the point of indigence would override the social distinctions that drive ordinary life and reduce people to a common human denominator. But the homeless on Edgewater Boulevard were deeply divided along racialized lines, and their hostility was exacerbated by their physical proximity.

In the 1990s and 2000s, San Francisco was an ethnically diverse city by U.S. standards. Its visible multiculturalism, however, was shallow. We developed the term intimate apartheid to convey the involuntary and predictable manner in which sharply delineated segregation and conflict impose themselves at the level of the everyday practices driven by habitus (Bourgois and Schonberg 2007). Intimate apartheid manifests itself explicitly in the special demarcations the Edgewater homeless drew between blacks and whites in their encampments. It also operates at the preconscious level, expressing itself as embodied emotions, attitudes, and ways of acting that reinforce distinctions, which in turn become misrecognized as natural racial attributes. . . .

In everyday practice . . . individuals do not consistently behave in racially dichotomous ways. Segregation is frequently violated, and many individuals purposefully transgress ethnic practices. Al, for example, did not move into the camp when he returned to Edgewater Boulevard after renovating his parents' house in the suburbs. Instead, he slept under the I-beam, curled up between Sonny, Carter, Tina, a conspicuous white body in a now all-black scene. He also traveled regularly to Third, the main thoroughfare in the African-American neighborhood of Hunters Point, where crack was cheaper. His behavior was considered unusual by the African-Americans; for the most part, they welcomed him. He was dismissed by all the whites as a bizarre and embarrassing person. . . . Al referred to himself as having "black friends" but continued to treat racism against African-Americans as self-evident and acceptable. On one occasion, he used the epithet "nigger" in front of Sonny, provoking an awkward silence rather than the violent response we expected.

Early childhood socialization processes tend to generate many of the most durable dimensions of habitus. Al had grown up in the Potrero housing projects, a dozen blocks east of Edgewater Boulevard. "We were the only white family in the whole place, surrounded by niggers. I ran with the Medallions [a local African-American gang]." This background may have been the reason why he violated intimate apartheid with such ease. Sonny had belonged to another teenage gang, which fought with the Medallions. He would reminisce with Al about their famous childhood acquaintance in the Potrero projects, retired football star O. J. Simpson, whose prolonged televised trial for the murder of his ex-wife and her friend took place during the early months of our fieldwork. The reactions of the Edgewater homeless to Simpson's acquittal underlined the racialized divisions that existed all across the United States. National surveys revealed that whites were convinced that 0. J. was guilty, whereas most African-Americans declared him innocent (CNN 1995). Significantly, Al defended 0. J., claiming that "he was framed." This assertion did not stop Al from quipping, however, that Simpson's murdered ex-wife deserved her fate: "She's nothin' but white trash! After all, she married a nigger, didn't she?"

Al purchased a dilapidated 1979 Volvo station wagon with the money he earned renovating his parents' garage and invited Sonny to "move in" with him. They slept side by side on the folded-down bucket seats and became inseparable running partners. They eventually upgraded to a late 1970s Ford pickup truck outfitted with a camper shell, which was given to Al by a racist white construction worker, who told him, "I been watching you because I been wanting to give this camper to a good, hardworking white man. We white guys gotta stick together out here." At the time Al had been alone, pushing a shopping cart full of aluminum cans in front of the tool rental outlet on Edgewater Boulevard where he and Sonny sometimes stole tools from the backs of customers' pickup trucks. When recounting the story in front of Sonny, Al joked that he had responded, "Thanks. That's mighty white of you." . . .

Like all running partners in the gray zone of Edgewater Boulevard, Al and Sonny frequently traded accusations of injecting heroin "on the sneak-tip [secretly]." . . .

Despite their bickering, Al and Sonny enjoyed one another's company and were often openly affectionate. Sonny took great pleasure in his heroin highs and was prone to overdosing. Immediately after injecting, he often fell into a heavy nod of euphoric relaxation or else became hyperenergized and "tweaked" in eccentric ways, such as shadowboxing furiously until collapsing, or twirling himself around a signpost, oblivious to the world around him. Al indulged Sonny's ecstatic displays by watching over him carefully to prevent Sonny from injuring himself. . . .

Al and Sonny could not, of course, escape the logic of the gray zone and frequently betrayed one another. Nevertheless, by Edgewater Boulevard standards, they maintained a friendship of exceptional solidarity that violated the patterns of intimate apartheid, to everyone's discomfort and surprise. . . .

Drug Consumption as Racialized Habitus

Heroin injectors often brag about the size of their habit, exaggerating how many "grams of dope" they inject per day. Like many of the identity and micropower relations along Edgewater Boulevard, competition over who had the biggest heroin habit often became racialized:

> Felix: Man, none of these niggers is real dope-fiends. They're crackheads. These guys can't shoot dope like I do. I don't have their kind of habit. They ain't even in my league. Give 'em a half a gram . . . and they'll die. Carter would die for sure.

Polydrug preferences also followed ethnic patterns. The whites, for example, referred to crack as "a nigger drug," even though most of them also smoked crack themselves. With the notable exception of Al, however, they were ashamed to admit it. Even those whites who smoked large quantities of crack would pretend shamefacedly, as they lit their pipes, that they only smoked opportunistically: "I never buy it. But if someone has it—sure, I'll take a hit." A few of the whites, such as Nickie and Max, never smoked crack, even when it was offered to them, claiming that it ruined their heroin highs. Everyone on Edgewater Boulevard, black and white, agreed that "crack makes you sicker quicker."

Virtually all the African-Americans devoted significant effort to raising money to buy crack once they had satisfied their daily physical need for heroin. When successful, they often stayed up all night on binges. The whites generally hustled less money than the African-Americans, and when they did obtain a sudden windfall, they usually purchased fortified wine or extra heroin rather than more crack. As a result, many of the whites had larger heroin habits and tended to fall asleep at sunset, unless they were dopesick or belligerently drunk.

On special occasions, the African-Americans injected speedballs to propel themselves onto a roller-coaster high and mesh the sedative effects of heroin with the wide-awake exhilaration of cocaine. They would sometimes celebrate their speedball sessions by "booting-and-jacking" their injections—that is, repeatedly flushing blood in and out of their syringes to provide multiple rushes of pleasure. When we were filming a speedball session on one occasion, Sonny chuckled, "Lady in red give daddy some head," as a plume of red blood flooded into the barrel of his syringe, indicating that his needle tip was safely inside a vein. He then pushed the plunger halfway into the barrel, only to follow it with, "Come back, Little Sheba," as he pulled the plunger back to reflood the barrel with blood. On the final flush, he sang, "Hit the road, Jack, and don't come back." All of the whites dismissed booting-and jacking as "a nigger thing." In all our years on Edgewater Boulevard, Al was the only white we saw inject a speedball on purpose.

The whole crack package—the rapid spending, the celebratory binges, and the stimulating physiological effect—meshed with the racialized late-twentieth-century persona of the enterprising black "outlaw," which, on Edgewater Boulevard, was mobilized in opposition to the persona of the broken-down white "bum." Most of the homeless in the scene, of course, fell somewhere in between these two stereotyped ways of being in the world, but the African-Americans in our social network strove more consistently to maintain the public appearance of being in control of their lives and having fun. In sustaining a sense of self-worth, they embraced an ecstatic commitment to getting high. Most of the whites, in contrast, considered themselves to be depressed and, indeed, most of the time looked and acted dejected. Furthermore, even though we often observed Frank, Hank, Hogan, Max, Petey, and Scotty nodding after they injected, they usually claimed with stoic boredom that they no longer enjoyed shooting and that they were merely staving off withdrawal symptoms: "I get well. I don't nod no more."

Everyone in our scene had severely scarred the veins in their arms as a consequence of long careers of injection. It was difficult for them to "direct deposit" heroin into a vein. By the midpoint of our fieldwork, most of the whites had given up searching for operable veins and skin-popped. They sank their needles perfunctorily, often through their clothing, into their fatty tissue.

In contrast, the African-Americans, even in the final years of our fieldwork, rarely skin popped their injections. Instead, they often spent up to forty-five minutes searching for a functional vein. This could become a bloody process as they made a half dozen or more punctures, pulling back on the plunger each time in order to register a vein. An intravenous injection, though difficult, provides an instantaneous rush of pleasure. Rejecting the aura of failure and depression associated with the whites, even the oldest African-Americans continued to pursue this kind of exhilarating high. They also expressed their pleasure openly in public sessions of deep nodding immediately after injecting. Some individuals, such as Carter, Sonny, and Vernon, performed their highs dramatically, collapsing into full-bodied relaxation and moaning with pleasure or jumping hyperenergetically to their feet. The white addicts, however, usually tried to nod discreetly, their chins slowly dipping onto their chests as if they were merely cat-napping. When energized, they might, at most, talk enthusiastically, scratch their noses compulsively, or clean up their camp.

These distinct injection methods and manners of experiencing and expressing the heroin high become physically inscribed on the body. The whites, for example, suffered from more abscesses, because skin-popping traps impurities in the soft tissue under the skin (picked up from dirty fingers, cookers, water, lint, or whatever adheres to a needle point when it is pushed through filthy clothing and unwashed skin) (Bourgois et al. 2006; Ciccarone et al. 2001). In an intravenous injection, these same impurities are usually safely filtered out by the body's vascular system. The disadvantage of an intravenous injection, however, is that it increases the risks of fatal overdose and also of hepatitis C and HIV infection because of the greater potential for blood-to-blood contact when syringes are shared (Rich et al. 1998). Significantly, the Centers for Disease Control and Prevention documented that the rate of AIDS in the United States in 2005 was ten times higher among African-Americans than among whites (Centers for Disease Control and Prevention 2007).

The HIV prevention mandate that was part of our National Institutes of Health (NIH) funding motivated us to document hundreds of injection episodes in our fieldnotes. The ethnic differences became evident when we began coding these detailed (and often repetitive) descriptions of the ostensibly trivial acts of preparing, injecting, and savoring heroin. The following excerpt from Jeff's notes is merely one of hundreds of descriptions that reveal ethnically patterned contrasts.

Jeff's Fieldnotes

Felix opens the door of Frank's van when I knock. They are in the midst of fixing. Felix pulls down his pants and, with a polite "Excuse my ass," pushes the needle of his syringe three-quarters of the way into his right butt cheek.

The radio is tuned as usual to an AM talk show. The right-wing host is attacking President Bill Clinton over the war in Kosovo. While debating the pros and cons of deploying U.S. troops in the Balkans, Felix pushes forcefully on the plunger. It barely moves, however, because it has struck scar tissue. He leaves the syringe hanging unattended from his rear for a few minutes to let the liquid heroin seep around the brittle tissue. When he pushes on the plunger again, it slides forward a few millimeters but starts to bend under the pressure, so he leaves it dangling again for a few more minutes to allow more liquid to seep out. He repeats this push-and-dangle sequence five or six more times until the syringe is finally empty, arguing the whole time with Frank about the war in the Balkans.

Frank meanwhile has jabbed his needle directly through his filthy t-shirt into the flesh of his upper arm, just over his right shoulder. He flushes his heroin solution in one rapid motion. I offer him an alcohol wipe, but he politely declines. Within a few minutes he starts to nod. He periodically tries to lift his chin and open his eyes to pretend that he is listening intently to Felix's commentary, but his chin keeps dropping back down, his eyes fluttering in evident relaxation.

I walk to where Sonny is currently "staying" inside the Discount Grocery's garbage storage shed. He is with Carter and they too are about to fix. Carter taps with his fingertips along the left side of Sonny's neck to increase blood flow while Sonny sucks on his thumb to swell his jugular. Grimacing anxiously, Sonny looks uncharacteristically passive and vulnerable, like an overgrown toddler sucking his thumb. Carter completes the injection into Sonny's jugular smoothly and pats him on the back. "You'll be feelin' better real soon."

Sonny smiles, "That's my doctor." Carter begins to explain to me that it takes longer for heroin to affect you when you are dopesick and "have nothing for it to piggyback onto." Sonny's dope, however, takes immediate effect. His eyes clear up; his voice drops an octave and becomes gravelly. He drapes his arm affectionately over Carter's shoulder to keep from slumping over.

Carter turns his back on Sonny and probes his needle into his own biceps, holding his breath as he concentrates on finding a vein. Unable to register blood after half a dozen attempts, he jerks the syringe out of his arm, cursing.

He plunges the needle deeper into his biceps several more times, reaching almost under his armpit and changing the angle each time while wiggling the point. He tugs the skin in all directions as he repeatedly pulls back on his plunger to check for blood. Suddenly he starts jabbing violently, as if trying to spear a miniature fish in his bloodstream. Unsuccessful, he yanks the syringe out again.

He sits back and holds the syringe chamber in the window light with the needle pointing up. Air bubbles marble into the mixture of red blood and black heroin in the chamber. He mutters another curse and, with several abrupt chops of his wrist, forces the air bubbles to the top of the chamber. He then slowly pushes the plunger upward until the bubbles surface one by one through the point of the needle. He licks it so as not to waste a drop.

He pokes again into the same awkwardly located biceps muscle in his armpit. After fifteen more minutes of jabbing, poking, and pulling, he finally manages to register a vein and quickly flushes the heroin directly into his bloodstream. He drops the used needle on the ground, and I can see visible traces of blood inside the empty syringe. I suggest that he rinse it, but he is already nodding and moaning with pleasure.

Carter tries to give Sonny a cigarette but nods abruptly in the middle of handing it to him and mumbles, "Love you brother . . . hmmm . . . done my good deed for the day . . . hmmm." Sonny, who is also nodding, lets the precious cigarette fall to the ground in mid-grab. The conversation comes to an abrupt halt; they have both suddenly fallen into heavy nods.

I open the door of the garbage shed to leave, and the noise snaps both of them out of their postinjection heroin bliss. They immediately stand up to follow me—energetic and ready to go, as if their deep nodding moments earlier had occurred hours ago. Carter pops the cotton lying in the bottom of the cooker into his mouth and we walk out.

Techniques of the Body

Bourdieu, following Mauss, would have called these distinct ways of injecting and experiencing heroin "techniques of the body" (Bourdieu 2002:110–126; Mauss 1936). They are complex, historically grounded sets of innumerable cultural practices that contribute to the perception of radical ethnic difference. Countless other routine interactions and markers naturalize such ethnic distinctions into an everyday "common sense" that casts them as genetico-cultural differences infused with moral judgment. In the very same encampment or on the same streetcorner, the African-Americans were usually dressed stylishly in the latest hip-hop fashions, while the whites often wore ripped t-shirts, dirty jeans, and disintegrating sneakers: Frank would never tilt his baseball hat cockily to the side.

Patterns of cultural diversity are a banal fact of social organization and are not necessarily significant in and of themselves. What is significant about the ethnic distinctions in behaviors that we describe among the homeless is that they are "misrecognized" by most people as the "natural order of things" (Bourdieu 1990, 2004). Most dramatically, as seen in the injection process, ethnic distinctions become inscribed onto bodies as scars and infections and are acted out in postures that become associated with racial characteristics. For example, after we made a presentation on ethnic patterns in injection techniques and abscess prevalence at the medical school where we worked, a laboratory-based scientist expressed his interest in obtaining a grant for research to discover the "black gene" for resilient veins.

The down-and-out way of being in the world common to most of the whites was reinforced by the absence of a culturally celebrated model for performing outlaw masculinity on the street among middle-aged white men. The white street culture—the leather-clad biker riding a Harley Davidson and sporting a graying ponytail, or the prison-based Aryan Brotherhood gang member—did not carry mass appeal. In contrast, fashionable hip-hop youth culture in the 1990s and 2000s had created a positively inflected linguistic term for over-forty-year-olds, O.G. *(Original Gangsta)*, with which African-American and Latino homeless injectors could self-identify. Whites, however, could not pass as streetwise hustlers or former gang members even when they tried. . . .

The middle-aged whites sought to mitigate their pariah status as public masculine failures by presenting themselves as traumatized Vietnam veterans. This identity was predicated on their victimization and the pity they elicited for suffering from a psychiatric disability labeled posttraumatic stress disorder (PTSD). When Hogan's multiple abscesses made him limp, he blamed it on "that round in my hip from 'Nam." He reminisced about "Hamburger Hill 84 in the Aishon Valley, south of Bon Son, Pol Point, not too far from Dan Lok," where he received "three Silvers, two Bronzes, an MOH [Medal of Honor] . . . and two Purples." When drunk and angry, he would call out for "my baby," the name he gave to the M-16 that he claimed to have buried in the brush by the freeway. Similarly, Hank spoke in detail of how he had been demoted from captain to sergeant for "conduct unbecoming an officer." He claimed that "two black soldiers" in his squad reported him when he commandeered a helicopter to rescue wounded comrades trapped in a firefight. During our first year, when Felix was still an honorary white, he told us about "stuffing body bags with body parts" in Vietnam as a "phlebotomist-medic."

Some of the blacks also claimed to be Vietnam veterans. Almost immediately after we met him, Carter spoke with visible trauma of being sent on a covert mission deep inside the Mekong Delta:

There was no honoring of the Geneva Conventions or nothin'. That shit about cutting off penises and sewing the mouths and de-legging and de-heading people was true. My partner,

Hughes, his brains was splattered all over my neck and on the side of my face. . . . [shaking at the memory] "Oh, my mother! Please don't let me die over here!"

We obtained everyone's military records and found that only Vernon, Carter, and Petey had actually been in the military. None of the three was sent to Southeast Asia; in fact, both Carter and Petey had served after the end of the Vietnam War. According to Hank's sister, "Hank was classified 4F, unfit for military duty. He didn't want to go in the army. He fixed into both his

hands right before going in for the interview. . . . They looked like balloons." Nevertheless, thirty years later, Hank regularly evoked full-blown Vietnam War PTSD symptoms: "I lived and died in 'Nam. I wanna live and die here, on the street, too." Like Hogan and Carter, Hank interrupted his gory stories with bouts of sobbing and shaking—sometimes even ducking for cover when cars backfired. Arguably, these men did in fact suffer from what could be diagnosed as PTSD, but it had been induced by the continuum of violence in the gray zones of their childhood homes and of their ongoing lives on the street. . . .

References

Bourdieu, Pierre. 1990. *The Logic of Practice*. Translated by Richard Nice. Cambridge: Polity Press.

Bourdieu, Pierre. 2002. *Le bal des célibataires: Crise de la société paysanne en Béarn* [The bachelors' ball: The crisis of peasant society in Béarn]. Paris: Éditions du Seuil.

Bourgois, Philippe, Alexis Martinez, Alex Kral, Brian R. Edlin, Jeff Schonberg, and Dan Ciccarone. 2006. "Reinterpreting Ethnic Patterns among White and African American Men Who Inject Heroin: A Social Science of Medicine Approach." *PLoS Medicine* 3(10): 1805–1815.

Bourgois Philippe, Bridget Prince, and Andrew Moss. 2004. "Everyday Violence and the Gender of Hepatitis C among Young Women Who Inject Drugs in San Francisco." *Human Organization* 64(3): 253–264.

Bourgois, Philippe, and Jeff Schonberg. 2007. "Intimate Apratheid: Ethnic Dimensions of Habitus among Homeless Heroin Injectors." *Ethnography* 8(1): 7–31.

Centers for Disease Control and Prevention. 2007. "Racial/Ethnic Disparities in Diagnoses of HIV/ AIDS: 33 States, 2001–2005." *Morbidity and Mortality Weekly Report* 56(9): 189–193.

Ciccarone, Dan, Josh Bamberger, Alex Kral, Brian Edlin, Chris Hobart, A. Moon, E. L. Murphy, Philippe Bourgois, Hobart W. Harris, and D. M. Young. 2001. "Soft Tissue Infections among Injection Drug Users: San Francisco, California, 1996–2000." *Morbidity and Mortality Weekly Report* 50(19): 381–384.

CNN. 1995. "Races Disagree on Impact of Simpson Trail—CNN/Time Magazine Poll." www.cnn.com/ US/OJ/daily/9510/10-06/poll_race/oj_poll_txt.html (accessed February 15, 2005).

Mauss, Marcel. 1936. "Les techniques du corps." *Journal de psychologie* 32 (3-4): 365–386.

Rich, Josiah D., Brian P. Dickinson, John M. Carney, Alvan Fisher, and Robert Heimer. 1998. "Detection of HIV-1 Nucleic Acid and HIV-1 Antibodies in Needles and Syringes Used for Non-Intravenous Injection." *AIDS* 12(17): 2345–2350.

5.4 Birthdays, Basketball, and Breaking Bread: Negotiating with Class in Contemporary Black America

JOHN L. JACKSON JR.

Race and class are deeply intertwined. They are also hotly contested social constructs. What is curious, though, is the persistence of the popular narrative that two black Americas exist—an underclass and a middle-class—and never shall they meet. This popular notion assumes that black Americans live geographically and socially segregated lives. The following excerpt, taken from John Jackson's ethnography Harlemworld, undoes this proposition. Through engaging ethnographic accounts that reveal the biographical details and lived experiences of some Harlemites that Jackson got to know well, we see clearly that social relationships can and do exist across class lines. These class-stratified relationships with childhood friends, family, or work peers are complicated and take many forms, but to deny their existence, Jackson argues, does little to move social science explanations from "easy explanatory models for perpetual poverty" toward a more nuanced understanding of how people negotiate their lives as raced and classed individuals.

Questions

1. How does Jackson capture common social science explanations of the black middle class? How do those explanations compare to popular beliefs about class mobility?
2. How do the people in Jackson's study describe their class-varied relationships? What opportunities arise from these relationships? What are the challenges associated with maintaining these relationships?
3. Do you have class-stratified friendships? Why or why not? Do they create any problems for social navigation in your world?

Party Politics, or the Two-Party System

On a particularly hot and humid summer day, Paul, an African American architect living and working in New York City, celebrated his thirty-first birthday with an extravagant party. In fact, he had two of them: the first with old friends and family members in his mother's Bedford-Stuyvesant apartment that afternoon; the second inside his friend Wilson's plush Harlem brownstone and lasting well into the wee hours of the morning. Paul scheduled these two separate parties (replete with distinct guest lists) because, as he puts it, "it's really like I have two lives." Today, he is an up-and-coming professional who hobnobs with other six-figure salaried black Americans from across the country and jet-sets to Caribbean Islands for occasional attempts at rest and relaxation. However, before his five-year sojourn at a southern university and his

John L. Jackson Jr. "Birthdays, Basketball, and Breaking Bread: Negotiating with Class in Contemporary Black America." 2003. *Harlemworld: Doing Race and Class in Contemporary Black America*. Chicago: The University of Chicago Press, 88–122.

well-paying position in a small architectural firm, Paul was born in a lower-income housing project, attended city public schools through twelfth grade, and spent most of his teenage years with a single mother, older sister, and younger brother in a one-bedroom apartment not more than twenty minutes away from the block where he was born and raised.

Paul's life story could easily make sense as a rags-to-riches tale of upward social mobility, one of those tales that continue to keep Americans dreaming. But what stands out about Paul's story is its interesting concretization into two separate birthday fetes—along with his specific explanations for that double bash: "It's like I have to be two different people," he offers, shaking his head as he briskly rakes five short, stubby fingers over and through his recently trimmed, tightly curled black hair. The fingers of his other hand steady a cigarette between his lips. We're sitting across a dining room table in his girlfriend Laura's place, a nicely furnished condo just outside of the city, one of those relatively close parts of New Jersey that just seem to get more and more expensive every housing market year. Paul sits up purposefully as he speaks, checking his watch periodically for Laura's imminent return from the store.

> Paul: So, it can just be easier to let my two
> parts stay apart, you know. I don't want people
> feeling uncomfortable around other people
> because they don't talk the same language, or
> do the same things or anything like that, so I'd
> just as soon keep them apart. That cuts down
> on the drama. It cuts down on the drama for
> everybody—especially myself. . . . I got my
> peers from work and that environment, business
> and professional, the movers and the shakers,
> and my peops from way back when I used to
> run around in the streets like a wild man. Now
> and then.

Paul's is an almost proverbial tale of the black middle class, ever positioned betwixt and between seemingly discrete and easily separable social worlds: the rich and the poor, the black and the white. . . .

The black middle-class experience has received a great deal of critical attention lately. . . . Even with the growing interest in black middle-class lives, a good deal of important information is sometimes left out of discussions about how class affects the daily experiences of black citizens. Many people give the same party line, arguing that with affirmative action and 1960s anti-discrimination legislation, the contemporary black middle class has exercised an unprecedented residential freedom, leaving the black poor behind to fend for themselves—with little or no social interaction between the two groups. Studies based on this premise downplay the black middle class's continued relationships with lower-classed African Americans, foregrounding their estrangement as one of the major reasons for many poor blacks' inability to escape poverty. . . . Harlem residents not only have life histories that transcend the discrete categories of "black underclass" and "black middle-class," they not only live in close proximity to other residents with markedly different socioeconomic realities, they also have social interactions that cut across many class lines. In Paul's case, he recognizes and negotiates class-inflected differences within his familial and friendship networks by carving kith and kin into two discrete social groupings for his birthday celebration. He has one party for his professional friends, "the black movers and shakers . . . my peers," and another for his "peops,"[1] the people who know him from when he hung out in the street "like a wild man." Paul thus sets the parameters for an important distinction between "peers" and "peops" that meshes with and foregrounds class-based concerns. Peers and peops stand in as proxies for different members of his multi-classed world:

> Paul: I mean, I don't know how different they are.
> Just makes me feel more comfortable. Because
> people have very, very different kinds of lives.
> So they won't like the same things, talk about the
> same kind of things, even talk the same way, and it
> just, I don't know, we'll see. But people like differ-
> ent things. Some have Masters degrees and these
> kinds of things. Big deal jobs. My mom hasn't been
> to college. Most of my family hasn't been. This is
> the truth.

Of course, Paul's dualistic approach to class differences among the people he knows is hardly the only way to go about dealing with disparities in education, occupation, interests and lifestyle, tastes, speech patterns, behavior, and social experiences. These are all areas that Paul slices in half and connects to the "very, very different" attendees of his two parties. These people are almost all African American; race doesn't distinguish the groups, but class-inflected differences most certainly do. Paul invokes these class-marked differences to justify the need for two separate social gatherings in celebration of his one birthday.[2] . . .

"The Peops" Versus "the Peers"

Many of the folks who attended Paul's two get-togethers didn't even live in Harlem. The second party's attendees, "the peers," were from places like Greenwich Village, different parts of New Jersey and even California—a friend in town for the weekend. Most of the people in his first party, "the peops," lived in Brooklyn—where many of them have always lived. They grew up with Paul—a few (like his Uncle Ronny and Cousin Dee) in the same low-income housing complex that was his social world for a good portion of his life. The rest of the peops at the first party either knew Paul's family very well or were his extended family: Aunt Leslie from Brownsville, cousins from different parts of Brooklyn and the Bronx, and, especially, his sixty-two-year-old mother, sitting like a proud matriarch on her living room sofa. Some of Paul's "running buddies" from "back then" attended as well. Jimmy, thirty-three, is living in the same apartment he lived in when they were kids. Still with his mother, Jimmy's been unemployed for the past two years. Another old friend, Tim, also in his early thirties, talks longingly about wanting to be a firefighter, but he's currently selling "warm" electronics on the street and off the books. Devon, late thirties, was like a mentor to Paul and his other buddies when they were younger; now he's a bus driver for the city and doing "pretty damn well," in Paul's estimation, especially relative to what some of the people from their old neighborhood are doing for a living. Tim, Jimmy, Paul, and Devon don't get together often these days, at least not as much as they claim they'd like to, but whenever they do, as at his early birthday party, they still talk as if they "never missed a day," with a familiarity that belies their brief and infrequent encounters. During the peops party, the guys ended up in a kind of ad hoc rap session in the back bedroom over a foldout table and a game of cards:

Jimmy: There ain't no way we could ever, I don't think, not be tight. That just ain't possible to me. It

Paul [interrupting]: We are brothers, we are brothers, we are family, you don't speak, you do speak,

but you always thinking about family, and they know you thinking about them. You don't have to see each other every day or nothing like that to know that.

Jimmy: That's what I'm trying to say.

Devon: Man, but it ain't like old times. I mean, we used to run tight. All day and night like that.

Jimmy: True. True. True.

Paul: Brother's gotta work and get that paper together.

Jimmy: Make it happen.

Devon: You gotta grow up and do your thing, no doubt, I just know we used to roll hard.

Curlicues of smoke filled the room as the men enjoyed one another's company and memories. They all talked about how close they felt to one another, but with a slight tinge of loss since their friendship's childhood dynamics (which, they claim, were more "tight" than they are now) have changed, as if the bonds that once bound them together have loosened just a bit—in ways that can't easily or fully be restored.

Paul's mother lives by herself most of the time, even though relatives from out of town, or just crashing overnight from other boroughs, often stay in this second room, where Paul, Devon, Jimmy, and Tim played cards. The hallway and living room areas, where most of the attendees mingled, glittered with party decorations taped up to the ceiling, cursive "happy birthdays" accordioned across the walls. The lights were dim; the place was dark. A record player pumped out mostly old 1960s Motown tunes and 1980s soul music. The younger kids danced enthusiastically but eventually managed to get a tape from the rap group De La Soul into a cassette deck over quite a few adult objections. Paul surveyed his well-wishers and shouted to me over a hip-hop tune's extra-heavy bass line: "I could go broke tomorrow, and they would still be there for me. They would still love me. They would still say 'that is Paul.' All the other stuff is extra."

Although three people who were at the first party also attended the second one (Paul's girlfriend, his uncle, and me), most of his family only took part in the first. When Paul got himself ready to leave for his second engagement, everyone simply kissed him, congratulated him, and offered him their best wishes.

Some didn't even know that he had another party brewing for later on. Paul's aunt Mary, an elementary school cook or custodian ("or both"—Paul's not sure), offered this response to my passing query about the other party: "Paul is a grown man. He don't have time to just be hanging with us all day. He got his own life and his own business. I'm just glad I get a chance to see him. I'm too proud." Paul's mother smilingly puts that second party in perspective: "This is where his family is. He'll tell you that. He'll tell you that himself. If you ask him, he'll tell you that." . . .

Paul conceptualizes some of the difference between the two parties in terms of business relationships versus nonbusiness relationships, a line that is not easily crossed. He thinks Laura makes the move better than most:

> Paul: The second one [party] we were gonna talk business, talking about making money, getting things done. It was more business. I knew we would have a good time, don't get me wrong, but we are going to be making moves as well. Wil[son] had made sure some really interesting people were gonna come. That is why Laura is so bad. That is what is so cool about her. She can roll anywhere. We can be at a hip-hop concert, at a, a play, at a business meeting, what have you, and she is perfect in all those places. That's the kind of woman you need. Someone who is just comfortable in all kinds of circles and arenas. She does that better than me.

Laura is able to bridge the peers-peops, business-nonbusiness divide rather skillfully, a talent Paul admittedly finds essential.

By the time we left the first party, the place looked well spent. It had started slowly that afternoon at about 3:00 and lasted until 9:00-—at which point Paul, Laura, and I traveled to Paul's house so that he could change clothes before we took off for round two. Rudy caught up with us there. Wilson's place was larger and several folks milled about on both floors. A soft and mellow instrumental jazz tune massaged our eardrums. Wilson, the official host, had only invited the black professionals with whom he and Paul often hang out, imposing their own brand of self-selected, self-enforced two-worldliness on Paul's social universe, a two-worldliness analogous to many social scientists' understandings of black America as bifurcated into two estranged and mutually isolated halves. However, this bifurcation isn't a function of Paul's having no access to poorer, less successful blacks. It is contingent on the

fact that he does have such contact, and unavoidably so. Despite his big-digit salary and his postbaccalaureate success, Paul still has relationships with differently classed African Americans that he must think about and negotiate. That summer, those interactions had the seemingly trivial effect of forcing him to throw two separate parties for at least two "very, very different" parts of his social network. Other Harlemites' social networks show some of the same socioeconomic variety that Paul's does. I want to look at a few of these class-varied relationships to see how people describe them. Where and when were they formed? Do they create particular problems for social navigation? What do they mean to and for the people involved?

No Friends

Some of the class-stratified relationships that I found in Harlem cut across friendships, others through family ties. Some people are able to negotiate class differences while maintaining the vibrancy of the relationships in question; other people recognize class differences as an insurmountable chasm across which meaningful and substantive relationships have difficulty thriving. Sometimes, when I tried to get at the issue of friendship networks head-on, specifically querying Harlemites about their friends, many adamantly maintained that they did not have any friendships with differently classed people at all. It seemed evident, however, that some of these folks did have powerfully class-stratified social relationships—even if they were not willing to call them friendships during formal, tape-recorded interviews. Zelda was one of the first people to exemplify this very split in conspicuous ways:

> John: Do you know any people who are really doing well?
>
> Zelda: You mean like money and stuff?
>
> John: Yeah, or whatever you think doing well means.
>
> Zelda: I know people that are happy. Not making a lot of money, maybe, but they happy. That are doing good. I think there is a lady down the hall who works for the Board of Ed. I don't really know her. We ain't really, like, close. We speak from time to time, but I don't really know her. I try to stay out of people's business. . . . I figure, I don't need that aggravation.

Several months later, I first met Kate, one of Zelda's co-workers. The two hang out and "go clubbing" periodically, about "once every couple weeks or so." Kate has both a B.A. and an M.A., and she works higher up the occupational food chain at the center where Zelda works. "She's up there with the bigwigs," Zelda offers. The two women get together fairly often outside of work and have very different socioeconomic realities, but Zelda didn't initially point to Kate as an example of a friend of with a markedly different socioeconomic reality—or even as a friend at all—in some of our conversations. . . .

Dexter prides himself on being able to talk to anybody, but even he can make a case for his substantial relationships being class homogenous:

Dexter: It's hectic, son. We all just wanna make it, you know what I'm saying. Living. Just living. I know people who are living what I'm living. Trying to get that paper. Paying rent and trying to keep it moving. I don't run in million dollar circles like that. Not everybody is like you, bruh.

Dexter jokes, but he is also serious . . . when he maintains that he doesn't really have friends of different class positions. Even Paul . . . made a case, during one of our more formal interview sessions early in my fieldwork, for the fact that he only had friendships with people in the same socioeconomic position he occupies:

John: Tell me more about your friends. Who are they, and what do they do?

Paul: I hang out with people at work. People at the gym where I work out. People who do what I do or go places where I go, and they are mostly pretty well-off, I guess. We can relate to each other.

John: Why do you think that is? That you hang out with people from work?

Paul: We relate. You share things with people that have experienced some of the same things. You know what I'm talking about? That is important. You won't agree on everything, but you have things in common.

John: Things like what?

Paul: The job for one. Things you like to do. They'll be people you went to school with. You have those things in common. Or you just happen to do the same work.

The first time I ever met Paul face to face, I conducted the interview from which the [preceding] is excerpted. I can almost remember him saying the words. They seemed clear, precise, measured, and sensible. However, half a year later, after the birthday parties, after going back through some of this material, it stood out as problematic. Paul did have friends that he called "friends" who were not colleagues from the job, who did not share the same occupation, and who weren't even working full-time. I was able to revisit these earlier responses after the birthday parties had come and gone, asking him again about the class stratification he did not mention earlier:

John: What about your boys, the ones from the party? Jimmy and those guys.

Paul: Dev and Jimmy and those guys. I guess that is true. It's definitely true. Yeah, but I don't see them that often. I'm usually busy working.

John: How often do you see them?

Paul: Maybe once a month, but they are definitely my boys. I can't forget them.

There was a kind of pattern with respect to class and friendship networks among many of the Harlem folks with whom I spoke. Like Paul and Zelda, several other Harlemites at different points in time tended to dismiss or "forget" their contacts with people from different rungs of the socioeconomic ladder. Many people found it easy to minimize all nonfamilial relationships, often going so far as to say that they have no close friendships whatsoever— not with anybody, regardless of class differences or similarities; that it is too "dangerous" and leads to "bullshit" or "drama." . . .

Even if he doesn't consider them his "friends," Dexter knows just about everybody he passes on the street. . . . But they aren't friends, he says, they are just "people you know." According to Cynthia, thirty-two, a college graduate and office manager at a Harlem-based educational institution, a woman named Karen "used to be" a friend back when they were in high school but now is "not really" a friend. When I first met Karen, wiry and tall, she was hanging out on the corner of 133rd Street and Seventh Avenue. It was early in the afternoon, and she had on dark and dirty clothes. I had stopped there to meet Cynthia, who was connecting up with me for a visit to the Studio Museum of Harlem. . . . Karen spotted Cynthia as soon as we passed by and immediately smiled.

The two women exchanged pleasantries: what was going on with families; who had seen whom; details about Cynthia's Aunt Rita moving to Atlanta with some doctor she recently married. After about three minutes, Cynthia and I took our leave of Karen and headed down the block toward 125th Street. As we walked, Cynthia and I discussed Karen a bit. Cynthia is particularly clean-cut, well-groomed, and professional looking if one's standards are creased pant suits and beauty salon hair. And Cynthia's well-groomed look made Karen's disheveled appearance that much more noticeable. In spite of their obvious history (a history I, as yet, knew nothing about, but could sense even from their brief conversation in the street that day), Cynthia seemed a bit cold and aloof toward Karen—even a bit rude, which wasn't like her at all. I'm not sure if Karen recognized it, but I most certainly thought that I did. Cynthia was cordial and polite enough, I guess, but she kept Karen at something of a distance. . . . Even with Cynthia's purposeful social distance vis-a-vis Karen, I wanted to think that I could still glimpse, hidden beneath all of that nonchalance and indifference, a closeness and affection that Cynthia held for this woman who looked old enough to be Cynthia's mother:

Cynthia: She's my age. Drugs and stuff done that to her. Because she is not that old. I know she looks it though.

John: That's awful.

Cynthia: Oh yeah. She and I used to be girls. We still cool, but I mean we used to hang hard. We were always together. She got pregnant and got hooked on smoke. . . . She is still my girl, I guess, we do go back, but she's on some other tip now. Off the hook, you know. She's done some stupid shit too, and all that is, she needs to try to get help.

John: Does she work?

Cynthia: No. On the street. Selling her body for a smoke. And I am like, girl, are you crazy. Her apartment is in a shambles. She has a pretty baby, Shannon. I feel so bad for that baby sometimes. That's who I feel bad for. Sometimes I'll watch her [the baby] for a bit. . . . [S]ome people don't have money, but that is not the same thing as living in a pig pen. We never had money when I was growing up, but we still had a nice home. Clean, you know. With nice stuff. Being broke ain't the same thing as being nasty and dirty.

Cynthia voices a popular perception about the difference between being "a deserving" poor person who still has American values and being one of those freeloading, lazy, shiftless, dirty, and pig-pen-dwelling poor people who are poor because they refuse to do anything positive with their lives. At the time, Cynthia had a full-time job and a well-kept apartment. Karen was on welfare and hadn't worked full-time in years. That was especially terrible, in Cynthia's opinion, because the two women started out on the same road. . . .

. . . We ran into Karen again on another day, this time on 5th Street. Cynthia seemed a bit more comfortable as they talked and laughed at length about that crazy boy who got their other high school friend, Liz, pregnant at fourteen—and about when and if Cynthia's Aunt Rita would ever move back to New York City. The conversation ended with Cynthia sliding Karen a few dollars and a hug. Once we [were] out of earshot, Cynthia, unsolicited, seemed to feel the need to justify her generosity.

"At first I wouldn't give her shit," she admitted, "'cause I knew what she was doing with it, but then I said you know what. I'm just gonna pray on it and ask God to step in and just do what I can."

When I accompanied Cynthia to Karen's apartment for the first time several weeks later, any reservations Cynthia held about their closeness seemed to dissolve in the warm heat of their laughter and stories. The two joked and reminisced with one another—and were even joined in their merriment later on by Liz, the woman who had grown up with them and gotten pregnant very young. I don't know what the three women talked about that night. I only walked Cynthia over to Karen's apartment, was introduced to Liz, chatted for a minute, and then left. In those few moments, I could see that these women shared a great deal and still, despite what I had interpreted as Cynthia's attempts at downplaying their relationship, gained tremendous amounts of pleasure and enjoyment from one another. A few days later, in another discussion I had with Cynthia about her relationship with Liz and Karen, the weight of the two other women's difficult lives almost brought her to tears:

Cynthia: I don't know what happened. But it's fucked up. [Pause.] They used to be my girls. I mean that was it and a bag of chips. You don't know. I feel like now that is all fucked up. They are still cool, but they are so fucked up now with all of this shit.

And not just the welfare. Shit happens like that sometimes, I guess. Fine. But they are like just not trying to get out of that, they are just like accepting it and getting deeper down the hole.

When Cynthia offers that Karen and Liz "used to be my girls," she's still placing the friendship in the distant past as opposed to the very real present of, say, that joy-filled get-together where the three of them were able to catch up with one another. . . . Cynthia is just as quick to help them out as she is to downplay the importance of such assistance and to argue against the significance of the relationships in general:

John: Are they good examples of the people you grew up with? I mean, are most of your friends in the same boat that those two are in?

Cynthia: No. I don't have a lot of friends. They aren't really my friends, I mean, Liz used to be, and I'm not nasty to her, I feel sorry for her, but she isn't my friend. I can't do anything with her, unless I wanted to do something stupid.

One Sunday morning, I spied Cynthia and Karen through the window of a local eatery. Karen was finishing off a breakfast that Cynthia had paid for. It was only the fourth time Karen had seen me over a two-month period, but she treated me like an old friend. And I appreciated her warmth.

Weeks later, Cynthia again downplayed her relationship with Karen, describing buying Karen a meal on Sunday morning as "nothing really, I'm just like, I got some time, she is, she needs food in her belly, what? I can do that." However, Cynthia did admit that she wanted to try making their weekend breakfasts a more regular thing. She thinks that's the least she can do, especially since Karen "used to be" such a good friend.

Paul and Tim (one of Paul's "peops" from that first birthday party) are basketball buddies. They meet up at least every few weekends or so during the summer and fall months to play a little ball, usually back in the neighborhood where they grew up, and where Tim lives to this day. It's a very self-conscious thing for Paul. "I know I'm not rich," he said, swerving down Kings

Highway toward the above-ground subway's rusting trestlework, "but I do see that Tim is, like, really getting his ass busted. I don't want to roll out on him just 'cause he doesn't have it all straight and narrow." Tim, about three inches taller and twenty pounds heavier than Paul, lives frugally with the mother of his third child. According to Paul, he's unemployed and "trying hard to be lazy."

. . . I watched the two men attack one another with drives and jump shots at the netless basket. Every shot was contested, every point celebrated. . . .

After dropping Tim off at his home, Paul explained how the two men use basketball as a means of keeping their relationship viable. After a game, they'll usually get something to eat and just talk a bit. "I'm not trying to change the man," Paul insisted, his car idling anxiously in front of my West Harlem building, "just play some ball with my boy." Paul feels that Tim's main problem is simple: he needs a job. If he got one and stuck with it, Paul believes that Tim would be on the right track. Paul even once tried using his peer contacts to get both Tim and Jimmy a job about a year earlier. He called in a favor, and "they fucked it up." After that fiasco, Paul believes that his buddies aren't really ready for his help.

Paul: I tried to push it on them, you know, big brother style. Let me hook you up, that kind of thing. They were just not there. They came late, got into shit that was just awful. If they tell me they are ready, if they come to me like, put me on, that is one thing. But that is not the same thing as trying to force someone who isn't ready. . . . But we'll call and touch base for a second or two. Play some ball sometimes over here by my place, 'cause he has no beef down here with anybody, sometimes Brooklyn, just working up a sweat.

Jordan, Zelda's "fly" social worker acquaintance, the one she thinks might possibly be just "trying to get a piece," often deals with decidedly poorer African Americans as a function of his occupation. Thus he has clear opinions about the nature of the differences that separate him from the poorer blacks in need of his professional assistance:

Jordan: I see poor black people, poor people, all the time. I mean I could tell you stories. People who are barely holding on, and I respect that. But sometimes, I get so frustrated, they get on the white man, but really they just aren't doing what they need to do. Not the white man. Some people are just not taking care of what they have to take care of. It's as simple as that.

Jordan's been called a "house nigger" and an "Uncle Tom" many times on the job, usually when he fails to fulfill the expectations of black people sitting on the other side of his desk. In that context, he's pretty leery of dealing with blacks as a function of the work he does. Sometimes, he even claims he wants to leave social work altogether, because "it's like they hate you for having what they don't have. Not everyone, but enough." Until he finally does decide to actually leave, though, and until he finds that new job, Jordan often tries to avoid any extended contact across class lines with the black people coming in for help:

> Jordan: People will take advantage of you. And if you don't give them what they want they are quick to call you out your name and all that kind of shit. I just want to stay away from folks who aren't about anything. And focus on what I need for me and not what other people think of me and put on me that is really about them and not me.

Jordan's is another argument about class-based avoidance, similar in some ways to the kind that Paul used to explain why he needed to keep his two sets of guests separated. And it's also akin to Dexter's thoughts about certain kinds of people he tries to avoid every now and then. For instance, the last time Dexter had an encounter with the police, he got harassed just because he was hanging with one of his boys, Dupree, a twenty-two-year-old whom he describes as "knee-deep in all kinds of shit." The police questioned Dexter because he was standing on the corner and just talking with Dupree. Dexter admits to feeling a little on edge even when he's just walking alongside Dupree, because "when people want to settle they score they do that irregardless of who is there in the way. I don't want to catch a stray or something, some stupid-ass way to go out." Therefore, Dexter watches his back when he walks down the street. He calls himself paranoid, but that's because he knows a few people who are living a more underground lifestyle, "living kind of foul." Dexter has a job and responsibilities on the home front, and he doesn't want to get pulled down into any street confrontations.

Consequently, he tries to be careful about when and where he hangs out with Dupree. . . . Even Paul will play basketball with Tim only in some parks—and only on certain days.

. . .

Paul believes that weekdays or "real, real early" on weekends are the safest times for the two of them to play. As for Cynthia, she can pay for Karen's meals every once in a while and give her some change, but she doesn't bandy the term *friend* about in describing that relationship, at least not very easily, distrusting the term's application to a relationship that links her to a woman she grew up with who is now not doing very well. Cynthia is clear about not wanting to spend too much of her time with Karen, at least not every day. She feels that that could put her in compromising and dangerous social settings. . . .

Cynthia . . . and Paul are not the only individuals with agency and intentionality in these social relationships. Karen . . . and Tim also have thoughts about these same interactions. And sometimes it means that they jostle over how to define the most common aspects of the lives they share. . . .

Karen is quick to call Cynthia a friend, even her "ace," and she is much more likely to place that friendship in the present tense than Cynthia sometimes is. . . . The two jostle over what definition seems most applicable for describing their lives together. They use the labels they affix to their relationship as a way of tugging on the interpersonal boundaries between them. . . . These kinds of moves are more than semantic double-talk; they provide people with the tools they use to identify their social worlds in personally acceptable ways. . . .

Conclusion

. . . Many African Americans have family members, friends, former friends, acquaintances, colleagues, bosses, social workers, and case managers who occupy various class positions. Often, the significance of these interactions is downplayed (by both the people themselves and the social scientists who analyze them), but they exist nonetheless. Class isolation is not the only possible narrative model for discussing how blacks of various socioeconomic positions experience their social worlds. Surely, it is a convincing enough argument to make if one wants to offer that isolation as an explanation for transgenerational poverty and inequality. However, if you look at the relationships people actually have . . . these relationships often push and pull at the boundaries of belonging in several different directions at once. Class-stratified interactions don't always translate into occupational opportunities for the poorer partners (it might only mean a free meal on an occasional Sunday or a ride to church where class "ain't got nothing to do with it"), but these exchanges are important nonetheless—if for no other reason than the fact that they don't let social scientists off the hook with easy explanatory models for perpetual poverty.

Social scientists offer truncated social networks and inadequate social skills as an important part of the explanation for perpetual poverty. Surely, social networks can translate into gainful employment and other opportunities more easily for the rich than the poor.[3] And maybe some people who have interactions across class lines are unwilling . . . to extend an extra hand once they've been burned after offering such hospitality in the past. My argument is not that

class-stratified interactions always or necessarily lead to socioeconomic advancement, but only that the lack of such advancement is not reducible to the idea that there are no such networks at all. People often do have relationships across class lines—even when they might hastily offer that they do not or question the term used (friend, acquaintance, former friend) to define such persons. They often have relationships that reach up and down the class ladder. Sometimes such relationships land people jobs. Other times, as in Paul's case, they can mean little more than semiregular pick-up basketball games where the class-stratified social world is left out of bounds and out of play, if only for a few sweat filled hours. Or, it might mean a free breakfast for one person and the sense, for the other, that one is "just doing the right thing" for someone who "used to be" a friend. Whatever the case, Harlemites are constantly dealing with the socioeconomic stratification inherent in their social networks—even if that just means attempting to impose class isolation and trying, with different degrees of success, to keep purportedly "very, very different worlds" apart.

Notes

1. *Peops* is a derivative of *peop(l)e,* meaning very close friends and relatives. It's a commonly used term among many of the folks I spoke with in Harlem.

2. It is also important to note that a binary model of class difference within black America . . . rears its dichotomous head here. This time, however, it is not an "etic" analytical category that social scientists impose from above. Instead, it is an "emic" articulation of the social world based on Paul's own subjective understandings of class differences within his

social networks. One cannot simply rail against Paul's conception as wrongheaded and mistaken; one must understand why this binary folk-analysis exists as categorization in the first place—and try to understand the cultural work it achieves.

3. See Mark Granovetter, *Getting a Job* (Chicago: University of Chicago Press, 1995), for a discussion about the importance of "weak ties" in the transformation of social capital into more than just lateral occupational movement.

IN THE NEWS Race, Racism, Police Brutality, and Social Injustice

On August 9, 2014, Michael Brown, an unarmed eighteen-year-old, was shot and killed by Officer Darren Wilson in the streets of Ferguson, Missouri. Protesters filled the streets and stayed for months, while police descended on them with tanks and tear gas. Every major media outlet covered the events, and social media commentary exploded. Americans watched the trial of Darren Wilson closely, and the grand jury decision not to indict him for the killing of Michael Brown incited passionate debate and discussion about justice, racism, and "colorblindness."

The articles from *Savage Minds* provide reaction from anthropologists to the grand jury ruling, shedding light on the linkages between our discipline and police brutality against black Americans. Together they treat the role of privilege in our legal system, resulting in structures that do not warrant social justice for all. Authors describe the effects of racism and racist institutions on the socialization processes for black children who must learn to navigate being black in "colorblind" America.

Students can also read about the die-in at the 2014 American Anthropological Association (AAA) annual meetings in which hundreds of anthropologists participated, laying lifeless on the ground for 4.5 minutes, symbolizing the four and a half hours that Michael Brown's body was left in the streets before it was covered and carried away. The articles also show other actions by the AAA including the "Statement Against Police Violence and Anti-Black Practices" issued by the Association of Black Anthropologists and the creation of an AAA Committee on Minority Issues in Anthropology Working Group on Racialized Police Brutality and Extrajudicial Violence, set up to support and track instances of brutality and violence and develop resources for applying anthropological knowledge to public debate and efforts to reduce and mitigate such violence and its impacts.

The discussions surrounding Ferguson that have ensued on social media and in news outlets incite expanded publicity for the American Anthropological Association's "Race: Are We So Different?" project, an example of public anthropology at its finest.

 Visit www.oup.com/us/brondo for weblinks.

DR. RAYMOND CODRINGTON

Cultural Anthropologist and Senior Research Fellow at the Advanced Research Collaborative at the Graduate Center, City University of New York

Figure 5.6.1
Raymond Codrington.

How did you become interested in the discipline of anthropology?

After finishing the requirements for my undergraduate government degree I had a few elective credits to use. I took an Introduction to Cultural Anthropology class. The course left a lot to be desired. It was a basic survey of "primitive" peoples that gave a tired version of culture. While the discussion around "others" and "primitive" people made me uncomfortable, the approach around cultural relativism (even though we did not practice this in the class) resonated with me.

I made it out of the class and looked for other anthropology courses to take. I came across two, one dealing with African-American males in American society and the other with the black diaspora. The classes were pivotal in pointing me towards studying anthropology at the graduate level. As the child of Jamaican immigrants born in England and moving to the U.S. at the age of nine, a course on the black diaspora was extremely relevant while connecting me to a broader history of race, culture, labor and immigration. While I was growing up I travelled regularly between the UK, U.S. and Jamaica. I was able to place myself alongside people who had similar experiences and notions around how blackness is created through large social, economic, and political processes. After that, I was sold on anthropology.

What do you do on a day-to-day basis at the Advanced Research Collaborative?

Documentary, archival, and ethnographic research, and identifying emerging and established individuals and organizations working on issues related to anti-racism. We are also conducting rapid ethnography at sites where there have been significant ruptures or events around race to find out more about the context of these events, responses, sustained activity and treatment of the issues on the ground and links to broader movements in the US and abroad. In addition, we are attending events that address race and racism to understand how the issues are being collectively framed in and through public discourse. Our first rapid ethnographic activity took place recently in Cleveland where I attended a national conference called the Movement for Black Lives which encompassed much of the dialogue addressed the issues that Black Lives Matter and related groups are concerned with.

What is the most meaningful project you've worked on over the course of your career? Why?

While I was the Sandy Boyd Postdoctoral Fellow at the Field Museum's Center for Cultural Understanding and Change, I organized the Hip-Hop and Social Change conference which took place at the Field Museum. This project brought my work in museums together with my research in global Hip Hop. It was great to see Hip-Hop being discussed from a global and comparative perspective in a museum setting. We brought in artists, activists, and academics from Brazil, Tanzania, Chile, South Africa and across the U.S. to participate on panel discussions, facilitate workshops and screen films. Every participant was great. So for example we had a boying/girling (dance) being taught right next to the Western Mammals diorama. Zephyr, a very well respected graffiti writer, gave a talk in the education department and it was phenomenal. Activists from all over talked about the impact Hip-Hop had at the local and global level. That's about the most diverse I'd ever seen the museum's visitorship. It's a good feeling when you can invert the demographic of an institution, or should I say, supplement it through several days of programming. This event showed me the potential of both Hip-Hop and museums to engage a broader public.

You're a member of the AAA's Working Group on Racialized Police Brutality and Extrajudicial Violence. Can you share a little about the work you are doing?

I consider the work of the Working Group to be a response to the murders of black children and adults both men and women at the hands of the state and private citizens. The cases are well known so I won't recite the long list of names that unfortunately continues to grow. The working group provides a dedicated space to unpack the structural issues around racism and violence against communities of color that allow these murders to continue. The Working Group also provides anthropologists the opportunity to dialogue with each other to develop responses to this. It is great to see tangible outcomes of the work we do and it is good to see anthropology directly engage the issue of racism and violence in a head on way.

Please share your experiences in public anthropology.

The first example of public anthropology in my work is in my race and policy work. At the Aspen Institute I was responsible for bringing together people across sectors (nonprofit, government, private sector) to talk about race and help them develop policy analyses and implementation plans to address race in their

spheres of influence. We organized convenings and working groups in an effort to develop projects that would address these issues. I constantly used my ethnographic expertise to better understand organizations and civic dynamics in which project participants were involved. I also had to think about ways to communicate very complex topics and analytical approaches to extremely broad audiences.

The second example is as anthropologist in residence at the New York Hall of Science's (NYSCI) Innovation Institute. Here, I build the capacity of staff, high school and college students to use qualitative research methods such as observation, interviewing, and asset mapping to develop prototypes of products that are responsive to community needs in Corona, Queens. We collect data in Corona and use that data to design and make products that are of value and use to the broader community. This is a new initiative at NYSCI that is part of a broader approach that considers the role of designing, making and playing alongside ethnography in creating products that encourage learning in non-linear ways.

Who is your main audience for your research and writing, and why?

Policy makers, academics and community members. Because my work usually is geared towards those audiences in various forms whether that has been through publications, exhibits or civic engagement projects.

What do you see as the future for anthropology of race?

I think what's going on with the Black Lives Movement where you have politics, identity and organizing strategies being simultaneously rethought represents an interesting moment. The presence and participation of "young" people under the age of 35 (yes, I am slightly stretching the notion of youth here) in this movement gives these efforts a different feel and look. The open presence of queer and trans people also feels different than in the past as is the prominence of women. The social media component of this work also gives this movement some uniqueness. So we will see where this movement takes the discourse around race, identity and organizing. Otherwise, the intersectional analysis seems to gaining a second wind. My hope is that comparative work between racialized minorities in different parts of the world continues to gain traction. There is strong work being done around this and it would be great to see this increase as we see similar processes of racialization occur that produce similar forms of economic, social, and political marginalization across the globe.

We are also going to have work through the postracial moment that was and is effectively an analytical and practical debacle. We are nowhere close to being a postracial nation and judging by recent poll data race relations are the worst they have been in decades. As such, understanding and documenting what the implications of this are from a social and policy perspective will definitely provide analytical, theoretical, and applied opportunities to further engage issues related to race, racism, and racialization.

What advice do you have for students?

It's a good time to be working in engaged spaces. I think for the health of the discipline it has to strive to be more relevant. As cuts to academic anthropology are proposed and what looks like some pretty strong attempts at dismantling tenure, the post graduate school tenure track model may not be as accessible as it was once was. The increasing space given to applied anthropology and the core concepts and approaches of applied anthropology at the meetings and the discipline more generally seems to signal that anthropology is changing and is more open to these approaches. I think that this bodes well for the discipline. I would say to students, do not be intimidated by working in applied spaces within and outside the academy. The boundaries between applied and non-applied work can be relatively porous. As such, it is a good time to find and make professional opportunities in applied, public and engaged spaces.

ABOUT THE ANTHROPOLOGIST

Areas of Focus: Race, popular culture, museums, and policy
Education: Ph.D., Anthropology, The Graduate Center, City University of New York
Hobbies: Collecting vinyl records, movies/film, bicycling around Brooklyn and NYC.

CAREER ADVICE

Advice for students interested in anthropology of policy:

- Recognize that your skills are marketable; think about ways to translate your skills into non-academic settings. In many cases, you will have to rationalize your worth and make the case for the use of anthropology on projects.
- Places to consider looking for work include: research institutes, think tanks, nonprofits, NGOs. With this in mind, attempt to network in those spaces.
- Stay in touch with those who supported your work. Developing and maintaining strong relationships with people who support your work can present some very interesting opportunities.

PART 6

Medical Anthropology

Medical anthropologists explore the relationship between culture and human health, considering factors that contribute to disease or illness and how different populations adjust, adapt, respond, or cope with disease and illness. Medical anthropologists have long been critical of Western biomedicine for its emphasis on Western forms of scientific knowledge and inability to capture non-Western health systems and beliefs. Rather than speaking of "disease" (i.e., forms of biological impairment explained by biomedicine), anthropologists use the terms "suffering" to refer to the physical, mental, and emotional distress recognized by members of a particular culture and "sickness" to capture local constructions and classifications of that distress (Schultz and Lavenda 2014, 342).

Critical medical anthropologists highlight the linkages between social, political, and economic processes to human health and illness. Scholars, who identify within this tradition, pay close attention to how social inequalities create barriers to healthcare and make some people more vulnerable to disease and suffering than others (Schultz and Lavenda 2014, 16). Several researchers undertaking a critical medical approach have been influenced by Paul Farmer's work on structural violence (Reading 6.1). Structural violence refers to the systematic ways in which the political and economic organization of our social world harms or disadvantages certain individuals or populations. In "An Anthropology of Structural Violence," Farmer applies this framework to understand the causes of Haiti's tuberculosis and AIDS epidemics. Further discussion of structural barriers can be found in "Bad Biocitizens? Latinos and the U.S. 'Obesity Epidemic'" (Reading 6.2) by Susan Greenlaugh and Megan Carney. Here the authors point out how obesity in the United States is framed in the media, in health policy, and in programmatic interventions as something caused by individual behavior and thus ultimately solved by individuals. Greenlaugh and Carney's research with Latino immigrants reveals that high rates of obesity among Latinos is not due to "ignorance" or "laziness" but rather from deep structural barriers associated with migration and assimilation.

One area that has generated a lot of attention from medical anthropologists is women's reproductive health. Anthropological research in the area of reproductive health includes cross-cultural studies of childbearing, population control, assisted reproduction, and midwifery, among other topics. The final two article selections fall within this realm, focusing on pregnancy and birth, reproductive rights, and reproductive justice. In "Democracy as Social Action: Home Birth, Midwives, and the Push for State Licensure" (Reading 6.3), Tara Hefferan, an anthropologist-advocate for midwifery and mother to several home-birthed children, explores efforts to bring home birth back into the U.S. "mainstream." This discussion is followed by Dana-Ain Davis' "The Politics of Reproduction: The Troubling Case of Nadya Suleman and Assisted Reproductive Technology" (Reading 6.4), which draws a distinction between reproductive rights and reproductive justice. The former tends to be framed in a neoliberal discourse of choice, while the latter is an approach that emphasizes reproductive health alongside social, economic, and political equality and power enabling individuals to make healthy decisions about their own bodies, sexuality, and reproduction. Dana-Ain Davis applies critical medical anthropological insights about "stratified reproduction" (Ginsburg and Rapp 1995) to show how certain social strata are supported in their efforts to reproduce while those in marginalized social strata are actively discouraged from doing so (Schulz and Lavenda 2014, 356).

The subfield of medical anthropology is one of the fastest growing branches of our discipline and an expanding area of employment for applied anthropologists interested in work outside of university settings. This section's "In the News" and "Anthropology in Practice" pieces offer examples of how anthropologists are helping to improve healthcare for marginalized populations throughout the globe. "In the News" describes the role of anthropologists in stopping the spread of Ebola. This discussion is followed by a profile of Dr. Robert Hahn, a leading figure in the anthropology of public health and coordinating scientist at the Centers for Disease Control and Prevention. Dr. Hahn was a central voice in global discussions of the Ebola epidemic and has spent decades pursuing work that demonstrates the importance of anthropological insights to successful public health interventions. The second "Anthropology in Practice" highlights the work of Dr. Ippolytos Kalofonos, a medical doctor and medical anthropologist with experience working on global AIDS treatment interventions in Mozambique and inpatient hospitalization for psychiatric crises.

KEY TERMS:

- Disease
- Illness
- Biomedicine
- Suffering
- Critical medical anthropology
- Structural violence
- Biocitizenship
- Obesity

- Reproductive health
- Reproductive justice
- Assisted reproductive technologies
- Stratified reproduction
- Midwifery
- AIDS
- Ebola

6.1 **An Anthropology of Structural Violence**

PAUL FARMER

Structural violence refers to the systematic ways in which the political and economic organization of our social world harms or otherwise disadvantages individuals and populations. These forces are often not ethnographically visible, but, Farmer argues, they are essential to understanding that which is apparent to the ethnographer's eye. Drawing on his experience as an anthropologist-physician, Farmer illustrates the profound violence Haiti's history of slavery and debt has inflicted on the bodies of the world's vulnerable, resulting in tuberculosis and AIDS epidemics of a grand scale. These leading causes of young adult death in Haiti, Farmer argues, are outcomes of European expansion in the New World, and the slavery and racism that accompanied it. This ethnographically rich piece also provides students with an example of an illness narrative. An illness narrative is an explanatory model of what is happening to a patient's body, covering the psychological and social experience that a patient encounters. Illness is distinct from disease, which refers to the physiological conditions that doctors tend to focus on. Through Farmer's narration of Anite, a patient he encountered with a large, fungating breast mass and her search for explanation and cure, one can see the tensions that arise at the interface of biomedical traditional and biomedical health systems.

Questions

1. What is important about Anite's illness narrative? What does it reveal about Haitian ideas about biomedicine and about the social nature of illness? How does her narration—its content and the context of her telling it—differ from Western biomedical interactions between doctors and patients and the settings in which they interact?
2. What is the relationship between debt, trade, and HIV and tuberculosis?
3. Discuss the importance of situating what is ethnographically visible within that which is not visible. Apply the concept of structural violence in this response, using examples from the reading.

*T*he ethnographically visible, central Haiti, September 2000: Most hospitals in the region are empty. This is not because of a local lack of treatable pathology; rather, patients have no money to pay for such care. One hospital—situated in a squatter settlement just 8 kilometers from a hydroelectric dam that decades ago flooded a fertile valley—is crowded.... Every bed is filled, and the courtyard in front of the clinic is mobbed with patients waiting to be seen. Over a hundred have slept on the grounds the night before and are struggling to smooth out wrinkles in hand-me-down dresses or pants or shirts; hats are being adjusted, and some are massaging painful cricks in the neck. The queue of those waiting to have a new medical record created is long, snaking toward the infectious disease clinic I am hoping to reach. First, however, it is better to scan the crowd for those who should be seen immediately.

Paul Farmer. "An Anthropology of Structural Violence." 2004. *Current Anthropology* 45 (3), 305–325. By permission of The University of Chicago Press.

Less ethnographically visible is the fact that Haiti is under democratic rule. For the first time in almost two centuries, democratic elections are planned and could result in a historic precedent: President Ren Prval, elected some years earlier, could actually survive his presidency to transfer power to another democratically elected president. If Prval succeeds, he will be the first president in Haitian history ever to serve out his mandate, not a day more, not a day less. To local eyes, the prospect of this victory (which later did indeed come to pass) is overwhelmed by the vivid poverty seeping into the very seams of Haitian society. For the rural poor, most of them peasants, this means erosion and lower crop yields; it means hunger and sickness. And every morning the crowd in front of the clinic seems to grow.

To foreign eyes, the Haitian story has become a confused skein of tragedies, most of them seen as local. Poverty, crime, accidents, disease, death—and more often than not their causes—are also seen as problems locally derived. The transnational tale of slavery and debt and turmoil is lost in the vivid poverty, the understanding of which seems to defeat the analyses of journalists and even many anthropologists, focused as we are on the ethnographically visible—what is there in front of us.

Making my way through this crowd has become a daily chore and triage—seeking out the sickest—a ritual in the years since I became medical director of the clinic. . . .

I see two patients on makeshift stretchers; both are being examined by auxiliary nurses armed with stethoscopes and blood-pressure cuffs. Perhaps this morning it will take less than an hour to cross the 600 or so yards that separate me from another crowd of patients already diagnosed with tuberculosis or AIDS. . . .

A young woman takes my arm in a common enough gesture in rural Haiti. "Look at this, doctor." She lifts a left breast mass. The tumor is not at all like the ones I was taught to search for during my medical training in Boston. This lesion started as an occult lump, perhaps, but by this September day has almost completely replaced the normal breast. It is a "fungating mass," in medical jargon, and clear yellow fluid weeps down the front of a light blue dress. Flies are drawn to the diseased tissue, and the woman waves them away mechanically. On either side of her, a man and a woman help her with this task, but they are not kin, simply other patients waiting in the line.

"Good morning," I say, although I know that she is expecting me to say next to nothing and wants to be the speaker. She lifts the tumor toward me and begins speaking rapidly. "It's hard and painful," she says. "Touch it and see how hard it is." Instead, I lift my hand to her axilla and find large, hard lymph nodes there—likely advanced and metastatic cancer—and I interrupt her as politely as I can. If only this were a neglected infection, I think. Not impossible, only very unlikely. I need to know how long this woman has been ill.

But the woman, whose name is Anite, will have none of it. She is going to tell the story properly, and I will have to listen. We are surrounded by hundreds, and at least 40 can hear every word of the exchange. I think to pull her from the line, but she wants to talk in front of her fellow sufferers. . . . There is so much to complain about. Now I have time only to see patients as a physician and precious little time for interviewing them. I miss this part of my work, but although I want to hear Anite's story, I want even more to attend to her illness. And to do that properly will require a surgeon, unless she has come with a diagnosis made elsewhere. I look away from the tumor. She carries, in addition to a hat and a small bundle of oddments, a white vinyl purse. Please, I think, let there be useful information in there. Surely she has seen other doctors for a disease process that is, at a minimum, months along?

I interrupt again to ask her where she has come from and if she has sought care elsewhere. We do not have a surgeon on staff just now. We have been promised, a weary functionary at the Ministry of Health has told me, that the Cuban government will soon be sending us a surgeon and a pediatrician. But for this woman, Anite, time has run out.

"I was about to tell you that, doctor." She has let go of my arm to lift the mass, but now she grips it again. "I am from near Jrmie," she says, referring to a small city on the tip of Haiti's southern peninsula—about as far from our clinic as one could be and still be in Haiti. To reach us, Anite must have passed through Port au Prince, with its private clinics, surgeons, and oncologists.

"I first noticed a lump in my breast after falling down. I was carrying a basket of millet on my head. It was not heavy, but it was large, and I had packed it poorly, perhaps. The path was steep, but it had not rained on that day, so I don't know why I fell. It makes you wonder, though." At least a dozen heads in line nod in assent, and some of Anite's fellow patients make noises encouraging her to continue.

"How long ago was that?" I ask again.

"I went to many clinics," she says in front of dozens of people she has met only that morning or perhaps the night before. "I went to 14 clinics." Again, many nod assent. The woman to her left says "Adj!" meaning something along the lines of "You poor thing!" and lifts a finger to her cheek. This crowd response seems to please Anite, who continues her narrative with gathering tempo. She still has not let me know how long she has been ill.

"Fourteen clinics," I respond. "What did they say was wrong with you? Did you have an operation or a biopsy?" The mass is now large and has completely destroyed the normal architecture of her breast; it is impossible to tell if she has had a procedure, as there is no skin left to scar.

"No," replies Anite. "Many told me I needed an operation, but the specialist who could do this was in the city, and it costs $700 to see him. In any case, I had learned in a dream that it was not necessary to go to the city." ("The city" means Port au Prince, Haiti's capital.)

More of the crowd turns to listen; the shape of the line changes subtly, beginning to resemble more of a circle. I think uncomfortably of the privacy of a U.S. examination room and of the fact that I have never seen there a breast mass consume so much flesh without ever having been biopsied. But I have seen many in Haiti, and almost all have proven malignant.

Anite continues her narrative. She repeats that on the day of the fall, she discovered the mass. "It was small and hard," she says. "An abscess, I thought, for I was breastfeeding and had an infection while breastfeeding once before." This is about as clinical as the story is to get, for Anite returns to the real tale. She hurt her back in the fall. How was she to care for her children and for her mother, who was sick and lived with her? "They all depend on me. There was no time."

And so the mass grew slowly and "worked its way under my arm." I give up trying to establish chronology. I know it had to be months or even years ago that she first discovered this "small" mass. She had gone to clinic after clinic, she says, "spending our very last little money. No one told me what I had. I took many pills."

"What kind of pills?" I ask.

Anite continues. "Pills. I don't know what kind." She had given biomedicine its proper shot, she seems to say, but it had failed her. Perhaps her illness had more mysterious origins? "Maybe someone sent this my way," she says. "But I'm a poor woman—why would someone wish me ill?"

"Unlikely," says an older man in line. "It's Gods sickness." Anite had assumed as much—"God's sickness" being shorthand for natural illness rather than illness associated with sorcery—but had gone to a local temple, a *houmfor*, to make sure. "The reason I went was because I'd had a dream. The mass was growing, and there were three other small masses growing under my arm. I had a dream in which a voice told me to stop taking medicines and to travel far away for treatment of this illness."

She had gone to a voodoo priest for help in interpreting this dream. Each of the lumps had significance, said the priest. They represented "the three mysteries," and to be cured she would have to travel to a clinic where doctors "worked with both hands" (this term suggesting that they would have to understand both natural and supernatural illness).

The story would have been absurd if it were not so painful. I know, and once knew more, about some of the cultural referents; I am familiar with the style of illness narrative dictating some of the contours of her story and the responses of those in line. But Anite has, I am almost sure, metastatic breast cancer. What she needs is surgery and chemotherapy if she is lucky (to my knowledge, there is no radiation therapy in Haiti at this time). She does not need, I think, to tell her story publicly for at least the fifteenth time.

Anite seems to gather strength from the now rapt crowd, all with their own stories to tell the harried doctors and nurses once they get into the clinic. The semicircle continues to grow. Some of the patients are straining, I can tell, for a chance to tell their own stories, but no one interrupts Anite. "In order to cure this illness, he told me, I would have to travel far north and east."

It has taken Anite over a week to reach our clinic. A diagnosis of metastatic breast cancer is later confirmed.

. . . I will be talking about Haiti and about tuberculosis and AIDS. I'm not sure I would know how *not* to talk about these diseases, which each day claim almost 15,000 lives worldwide, most of them adults in their prime. I hope less to take on grand theory than to ask how the concept of *structural violence* might come to figure in work in anthropology and other disciplines seeking to understand modern social life. Standing on the shoulders of those who have studied slavery, racism, and other forms of institutionalized violence, a growing number of anthropologists now devote their attention to structural violence.

. . . Structural violence is violence exerted systematically, that is, indirectly by everyone who belongs to a certain social order: hence the discomfort these ideas provoke in a moral economy still geared to pinning praise or blame on individual actors. In short, the concept of structural violence is intended to inform the study of the social machinery of oppression. Oppression is a result of many conditions, not the least of which reside in consciousness. We will therefore need to examine, as well, the roles played by the erasure of historical memory and other forms of desocialization as enabling conditions of structures that are both "sinful" and ostensibly "nobody's fault." . . .

. . . An honest account of who wins, who loses, and what weapons are used is an important safeguard against the romantic illusions of those who, like us, are usually shielded from the sharp edges of structural violence. I find it helpful to think of the "materiality of the social," a term that underlines my conviction that social life in general and structural violence in particular will not be understood without a deeply materialist approach to whatever surfaces in the participant-observer's field of vision—the ethnographically visible.

By "materialist" I do not mean "economic" as if economic structures were not socially constructed. I do not mean biological as if biology were likewise somehow immune from social construction. . . . The adverse outcomes associated with structural violence—death, injury, illness, subjugation, stigmatization, and even psychological terror—come to have their final common pathway in the material. . . .

An anthropology of structural violence necessarily draws on history and biology, just as it necessarily draws on political economy. To tally body counts correctly requires epidemiology, forensic and clinical medicine, and demography. . . .

. . . Erasing history is perhaps the most common explanatory sleight-of-hand relied upon by the architects of structural violence. Erasure or distortion of history is part of the process of desocialization necessary for the emergence of hegemonic accounts of what happened and why. . . .

"Modern" Haiti: Resocializing History and Biology

. . . [In Haiti] I learned a good deal about the selective erasure of history and the force, often less readily hidden, of biology, but these erasures had not so much taken place within Haiti. In Haiti, the past was present—in proverbs, in the very language spoken, itself a product of the slave colony, and in popular Haitian readings of its present-day misfortune. In Haiti structural violence continues to play itself out in the daily lives and deaths of the part of the population living in poverty. People know about the body count because they bury their kin.

. . . The biggest problem, of course, is unimaginable poverty, as a long succession of dictatorial governments has been more concerned with pillaging than with protecting the rights of workers, even on paper. . . . While the dictatorships may be gone, the transnational political and economic structures that maintained them are still in place and still inflicting their harm. An ethnographic study of modern Haiti may or may not discuss the ways in which West Africans were moved to Haiti. It may or may not discuss tuberculosis, smallpox, measles, or yellow fever. A modern ethnographer may not mention the former colony having been forced to repay a debt to the French supposedly incurred by the loss of the world's most profitable slave colony. . . . [T]heir absence makes a fully socialized accounting of the present nearly unthinkable. Allow me to sum up the post-independence history of Haiti:

The Haitian revolution began in 1791. France's refusal to accept the loss of so "efficient" and profitable a colony led, ultimately, to the expedition of the largest armada ever to cross the Atlantic. After the 1803 Battle of Vertires, in which Napoleon's troops were defeated, Haiti was declared an independent nation. But its infrastructure lay in ruins: some estimate that more than half of the island's population perished in the war. The land was still fertile, if less so than when the Europeans began mono cropping it, and so the new republic's leadership, desperate to revive the economy, fought to restore the plantations without overt slavery. . . .

Even if there were other ways of growing these products—and coffee, unlike sugar, was clearly a product that could be grown on small homesteads— who would buy them? The Europeans and the only other republic in the Western Hemisphere, the United States, were the only likely customers, and they mostly followed a French-led embargo on Haiti. How many people in France remember that, in order to obtain diplomatic recognition, Haiti was required to indemnify France to the tune of 150 million francs to the government of Charles X beginning in 1825? One hundred fifty million francs in reparations *to the slave owners,* a social and economic fact redolent with meaning then and today and one with grave material consequences for the Haitians. . . .

This set the tone for the new century: trade concessions for European and U.S. partners and indirect taxes for the peasants who grew the produce, their backs bent under the weight of a hostile world. Especially hostile was the United States to the north, the slave-owning republic (Lawless 1992: 56).

> The United States blocked Haiti's invitation to the famous Western Hemisphere Panama Conference of 1825 and refused to recognize Haitian independent until 1862. This isolation was imposed on Haiti by a frightened white world, and Haiti became a test case, first for those arguing about emancipation and then, after the end of slavery, for those arguing about the capacity of blacks for self-government.

In the years following independence, the United States and allied European powers helped France orchestrate a diplomatic quarantine of Haiti, and the new republic soon became the outcast of the international community. . . .

But the isolation was largely diplomatic and rhetorical. . . . The United States was increasingly present as a trading partner and policeman. . . . Continuous U.S. naval presence led, eventually, to an armed occupation of Haiti in 1915. This occupation, another chapter of U.S. history now almost completely forgotten by the occupiers, was to last 20 years. . . .

Since 1915, at the latest, the United States has been the dominant force in Haitian politics. The modern Haitian army was created, in 1916, by an act of the U.S. Congress. From the time of troop withdrawal in 1934 until 1990, no Haitian administration has risen to power without the blessing of the U.S. government. . . . Indeed, there have been no major political discontinuities until perhaps 1990, with the result that the template of colony—a slave colony—continued to shape life in Haiti. Just as the wealthy were socialized for excess, the Haitian poor were socialized for scarcity. . . .

This is the framework I had in mind when I began studying specific infectious diseases—one old, one new—in rural Haiti. In anthropology a version of this framework has been called "world systems theory" (Wallerstein 1974). . . . It is an approach that is committed to ethnographically embedding evidence within the historically given social and economic structures that shape life so dramatically on the edge of life and death. These structures are transnational, and therefore not even their modern vestiges are really ethnographically visible. . . .

How on earth could one rebuild such a broken place? Haiti has no roads to speak of and poor telecommunications. Agriculture has faltered, perhaps irreparably, and no industry promises to replace it. . . .

The public health infrastructure is of special concern to me. In the past decade I have witnessed two related processes in central Haiti: the collapse of the public health sector and the overwhelming of the hospital of which I am the medical director. Even if our hospital were uninterested in seeking foreign aid in the conventional sense, we would desperately be awaiting the rebuilding of the Haitian health system. . . . We have read the Durban declaration, which calls for reparations to postslavery societies. We agree that this hemisphere's poorest country is also and not coincidentally its largest postslavery society. Cuba would be in second place. Guess which two Western Hemisphere republics are under an aid embargo? Does anyone think that Haitians, at least the ones I live with, do not see the continuity between the current and previous embargoes?

"What embargo?" one may well ask. "Imposed on Haiti? By whom?" Since the Haitian elections of 2000, the U.S. government has used its influence with international lending institutions such as the Inter-American Development Bank to withhold already approved loans earmarked for development and improving health, education, and water quality in Haiti. . . .

. . . Take as an example Inter-American Development Bank (IDB) Loan No. 1009/SFHA, Reorganization of the National Health System. On July 21, 1998, the Haitian government and the IDB signed a $22.5-million loan for phase 1 of a project to decentralize and reorganize the Haitian health care system. The need to improve the health care system was and remains urgent: there are 1.2 doctors, 1.3 nurses, and 0.04 dentists per 10,000 Haitians; 40% of the population is without access to any form of primary health care. HIV and tuberculosis rates are by far the highest in the hemisphere, as are infant, juvenile, and maternal mortality. To use the bank's jargon, the project was to target 80% of the population for access to primary health care through the construction of low cost clinics and local health dispensaries, the training of community health agents, and the purchase of medical equipment and essential medicines. . . . [1]

Ratification of the loan agreement was initially held up by Haiti's famously obstructionist 46th Legislature, whose goal was clear enough within Haiti to paralyze all social services, including health care, in order to undermine every effort of the executive branch . . . to improve the living conditions of the poor majority that had elected him by a landslide. . . .

In October 2000, after the installation of the more representative 47th Legislature, the new parliament voted immediately to ratify the health project along with the three other vital IDB loan agreements. Nevertheless, by early March 2001, the IDB had not yet disbursed the loan but announced that it fully intended to work with the new Aristide government and to finance projects already in the pipeline. It demanded, however, that a number of conditions be met, requiring the poorest nation in the hemisphere to pay back millions of dollars of outstanding debts racked up by the previous U.S.-supported dictatorships, as well as "credit commissions" and interest on undisbursed funds. For example, as of March 31, 2001, Haiti already owed the IDB $185,239.75 as a commission fee on a loan it had never received. The total amount of fees owed on five development loans from the IDB was $2,311,422. Whereas in the nineteenth century Haiti had had to pay reparations to slave owners, at the start of the twenty-first century a different sort of extortion was being practiced to ensure that Haiti not become too independent. The health loan has still not been disbursed and thus the embargo on international aid to Haiti continues, despite the fact that the Haitian government has followed all the stipulations set down for resolving the disputed elections. In the meantime, the courtyard around our hospital remains overflowing—that is the ethnographically visible part.

These details about loans and such may seem pedestrian to an academic audience. They certainly would hold no great interest for me were it not for their direct and profound impact on the bodies of the vulnerable (Farmer 2003). Trust me, they are of life-and-death significance.

For those reluctant to trust a physician-anthropologist on this score, one has only to consider the case of Anite, dying of metastatic breast cancer. She inhabits a world in which it is possible to visit 14 clinics without receiving a diagnosis or even palliative care. The contours of this world, a world in which her options and even her dreams are constrained sharply, have been shaped by the historical and economic processes described in this paper. . . .

Creating Mirages: Erasing Biology

. . . I am convinced that a robust medical anthropology could be critical to our understanding of how structural violence comes to harvest its victims. Tuberculosis and AIDS cause millions of premature deaths every year. These two pathogens are, in fact, the leading infectious causes of adult death in the world today. Everyone interested in structural violence should have a particular interest in these diseases and in the social structures that perpetuate them. . . .

. . . When AIDS was first recognized, in the early eighties, it was soon apparent that it was an infectious disease, even though other, more exotic interpretations abounded at the time. Well before Luc Montagner discovered HIV, many believed that the etiologic agent was a never-before described virus, and people wanted to know, as they so often do, where this new sickness came from. During the eighties the hypotheses circulating in the United States suggested that HIV came to the United States from Haiti. Newspaper articles, television reports, and even scholarly publications confidently posited a scenario in which Haitian professionals who had fled the Duvalier regime ended up in western Africa and later brought the new virus back to Haiti, which introduced it to the Americas. AIDS was said to proliferate in Haiti because of strange practices involving voodoo blood rituals and animal sacrifice.

These theories are ethnographically absurd, but they are wrong in other ways, too. First, they happened to be incorrect epidemiologically. AIDS in Haiti had nothing to do with voodoo or Africa. Second, they had an adverse effect on Haiti—the tourism industry collapse in the mid-eighties was due in large part to rumors about HIV, and on Haitians living in North America and Europe. The perception that "Haitian" was almost synonymous with "HIV-infected" in the minds of many U.S. citizens, has been well documented. . . .

How, then, was HIV introduced to the island nation of Haiti? An intracellular organism must necessarily cross water in a human host. It was clear from the outset that HIV did not come to Haiti from Africa. None of the first Haitians diagnosed with the new syndrome had ever been to Africa; most had never met an African. But many did have histories of sexual contact with North Americans. In a 1984 paper published in a scholarly journal, the Haitian physician Jean Gurin and colleagues revealed that 17% of their patients reported a history of sexual contact with tourists from North America (Gurin, Malebranche, and Elie et al. 1984). These exchanges involved the exchange of money, too, and so sexual tourism—which inevitably takes place across steep grades of economic inequality—was a critical first step in the introduction of HIV to Haiti. . . .

There is more, of course, to the hidden history of AIDS in Haiti. By the time HIV was circulating in the Americas, Haiti was economically dependent not on France, as in previous centuries, but on the United States. From the time of the U.S. military occupation through the Duvalier dictatorships (1957–86), the United States had come to occupy the role of chief arbiter of Haitian affairs. After the withdrawal of troops in 1934, U.S. influence in Haiti grew rather than waned. U.S.-Haitian agribusiness projects may have failed, deepening social inequalities throughout Haiti as the rural peasantry became poorer, but U.S.-Haitian ties did not. Haiti became a leading recipient of U.S. aid, and the United States and the "international financial institutions" were the Duvalier family's most reliable source of foreign currency. Haiti became, in turn, the ninth largest assembler of U.S. goods in the world and bought almost all of its imports from the United States. Tourism and *soustraitance* (offshore assembly) replaced coffee and other agricultural products as the chief sources of foreign revenue in Haiti.

Haiti is the extreme example of a general pattern. If one uses trade data to assess the degree of Caribbean basin countries' dependency on the United States at the time HIV appeared in the region, one sees that the five countries with the tightest ties to the United States were the five countries with the highest HIV prevalence. ". . . AIDS in Haiti is a tale of ties to the United States, rather than to Africa; it is a story of unemployment rates greater than 70 percent. AIDS in Haiti has far more to do with the pursuit of trade and tourism in a dirt poor country than with, to cite Alfred Mtraux . . ., dark saturnalia celebrated by 'blood-maddened, sex-maddened, god-maddened' negroes" (Farmer 1992, 264).

But this was merely the beginning of a biosocial story of the virus. The Haitian men who had been the partners of North Americans were by and large poor men; they were trading sex for money. The Haitians in turn transmitted HIV to their wives and girlfriends. Through affective and economic connections, HIV rapidly became entrenched in Haiti's urban slums and then spread to smaller cities, towns, and, finally, villages like the one in which I work. Haiti is now the most HIV-affected country in the Americas, but the introduction and spread of the new virus has a history—a biosocial history that some would like to hide away.

Like many anthropologists, I was not always careful to avoid stripping away the social from the material. But HIV, though hastened forward by many social forces, is as material as any other microbe. Once in the body, its impact is profound both biologically and socially. As cell-mediated immunity is destroyed, poor people living with HIV are felled more often than not by tuberculosis. Last year, HIV was said to surpass tuberculosis as the leading infectious cause of adult death, but in truth these two epidemics are tightly linked. . . .

All this is both interesting and horrible. What might have been done to avert the deaths caused by these two pathogens? What might be done right now? One would think that the tuberculosis question, at least, could be solved. Because there is no nonhuman host, simply detecting and treating promptly all active cases would eventually result in an end to deaths from this disease. Money and political will are what is missing—which brings us back to structural violence and its supporting hegemonies: the materiality of the social.

AIDS, one could argue, is thornier. There is no cure, but current therapies have had a profound impact on mortality among favored populations in the United States and Europe. The trick is to get therapy to those who need it most. Although this will require significant resources, the projected cost over the next few years is less than the monies allocated in a single day for rescuing the U.S. airlines industry (see Swoboda and McNeil [Hamilton] 2001). But the supporting hegemonies have already decreed AIDS an unmanageable problem. The justifications are often byzantine.

For example, a high-ranking official within the U.S. Department of the Treasury (who wisely declined to be named) has argued that Africans have "a different concept of time" and would therefore be unable to take their medications on schedule; hence, no investment in AIDS therapy for Africa. The head of the U.S. Agency for International Development later identified a lack of wristwatches as the primary stumbling block. Cheap wristwatches are not unheard of, but, as I have said, the primary problem is a matter of political will. . . .

The distribution of AIDS and tuberculosis—like that of slavery in earlier times—is historically given and economically driven. What common features underpin the afflictions of past and present centuries? Social inequalities are at the heart of structural violence. . . .

Notes

1. This article is a published version of the lecture Paul Farmer gave for the 2001 Sidney W. Mintz Lecture in Anthropology on November 27, 2001 and thus the data he reports is from that time period.

References

Farmer, Paul. 1992. *AIDS and accusation: Haiti and the geography of blame.* Berkeley: University of California Press.

Farmer, Paul. 2003. Unjust embargo of aid for Haiti. *The Lancet* 361:42023.

Gurin, J., R. Malebranche, A. Elie, et al. 1984. Acquired immune deficiency syndrome: Specific aspects of the disease in Haiti. *Annals of the New York Academy of Sciences* 437:25461.

Lawless, Robert. 1992. *Haiti's bad press.* Rochester, Vt.: Schenkman Books.

Swoboda, Frank, and Martha Mc Neil Hamilton. 2001. Congress passes $15 billion airline bailout. *Washington Post*, September 22.

Wallerstein, Immanuel. 1974. *The modern world system: Capitalist agriculture and the origins of the European world economy in the sixteenth century.* San Diego: Academic Press.

6.2 Bad Biocitizens? Latinos and the U.S. "Obesity Epidemic"

SUSAN GREENHALGH AND MEGAN CARNEY

As stated in the book's introductory chapter, much contemporary policy and programs are influenced by a neoliberal philosophy that privileges individual responsibility, both citing individuals for causing contemporary social and environmental problems and calling upon individuals to take personal responsibility for finding solutions to the world's problems. Obesity and public health interventions to address growing obesity are no different. In this case study, Greenhalgh and Carney reveal how high rates of obesity among Latinos is not something caused by misinformed, lazy, or "ignorant" individuals who simply need more knowledge about the link between a healthy diet and exercise and maintaining a normal weight. Rather, there exist deep structural barriers associated with migration and assimilation. Public health interventions focused on "healthy education" will continue to miss their mark unless they address these structural issues.

Questions

1. How is obesity among the Latino population the result of structural factors? Why don't public health intervention programs take these structural factors into consideration?
2. What is "biocitizenship"? Have you observed examples of "biopedagogy" and "bioabuse" in your own life?
3. What does Greenhalgh and Carney's ethnographic research illustrate about the idea that Latinos are unaware of the importance of diet and exercise in maintaining a normal weight?
4. Discuss the role of social marginalization associated with immigration. What role does it play in diet and obesity? How are experiences gendered?
5. Consider this question raised by the authors: "What wider effects does the assumption of ignorance—which gets embedded in programmatic interventions as well as the ubiquitous media messages about minority responsibility for the obesity epidemic—produce?"

Obesity: "The Latino Threat"

For over a decade, America has faced an obesity epidemic that, according to the narrative of government, public health, and media sources, is threatening the nation by worsening the burden of disease, raising health care costs, and lowering productivity. . . .

Public health messages about the obesity epidemic invariably mention ethnic differences, in particular, the finding that African-Americans and Latinos consistently have higher prevalence of obesity than Whites. In its latest report, the Centers for Disease Control (CDC) notes that Hispanics are 1.2 times more likely to be obese than non-Hispanic Whites (the CDC

Susan Greenhalgh and Megan Carney. "Bad Biocitizens? Latinos and the US 'Obesity Epidemic'." 2014. *Human Organization*. 73 (3) 267–276.

uses United States Census racial/ethnic terms), and they have the second highest rates of obesity in the United States (Flegal et al. 2012; Ogden et al. 2010). Although Blacks have higher obesity rates, Latino obesity is deeply worrying to the public health community because of demographic forecasts that predict rapid growth of the United States-based Latino population. Indeed, by 2060, one-third of Americans will be of Hispanic origin, up from one-sixth in 2012 (United States Census Bureau 2012). Read through the lens of cultural hysteria about the alleged "threats" to the United States posed by Latino immigration (Chavez 2007, 2008), these projections signal not only a likely expansion of the Latino obesity problem but also a new perceived Latino "threat" to the nation. . . .

When these ethnic differences were first uncovered, the public health literature tended to attribute the higher rates of obesity among minorities to cultural differences in health knowledge and body ideals. Minorities were said to have limited knowledge about healthful eating and exercising. . . . Latinos were also subject to the general stereotypes that apply to all fat people in the United States: they were widely seen as lazy, irresponsible, and a drain on social services (Chavez 2008, 2012).

More recently, however, researchers have begun to underscore the role of structural factors in producing higher weights among Latinos. The *American Journal of Preventative Medicine* published a special issue in March 2013 reporting findings from the Salud America! Campaign—a national initiative to curtail Latino childhood obesity—that attributed overweight and obesity among Latinos to nutrient-poor food environments, poor exercise environments, and unregulated marketing of unhealthy foods to children (Ramirez and Ayala 2013).

If structural factors bear significant responsibility for the heavier weights of Latinos, then an effective response would entail programs that improve job opportunities, raise wages, enhance food environments, ensure safer neighborhoods for exercise, and so on. Yet . . . efforts to reduce and prevent obesity continue to put the onus on individuals and families, calling on them to learn to eat better and exercise more so as to achieve normal weight. Notably, First Lady Michelle Obama has been promoting her Let's Move! campaign to eliminate childhood obesity with Latino audiences. At the 2013 annual conference of the National Council of La Raza (NCLR), the nation's largest Latino advocacy group, she placed responsibility for obesity on beliefs and behaviors in the Latino community and called on her listeners to "own this as a serious problem":

> Right now, nearly 40 percent of Hispanic children in this country are overweight or obese. Nearly 50 percent are on track for diabetes. . . . We all know that the food industry has some serious work to do when it comes to how they market food to our kids, but here's the thing, ultimately, we all have the power to decide whether or not to actually buy those foods. We need to step up. We need to own this as a serious problem in our communities. We need to admit that what we're doing simply isn't working anymore, and we need to start questioning the behaviors and beliefs that are making our kids sick (Satchfield 2013).

Explaining the First Lady's message, Jorge Plasencia, the Board Chairman of NCLR, said, "We have over 5,000 people [here] and each one of them can become delegates of sorts to promote healthy eating in their community. . . . Now when you all go back home . . . make sure to go back and tell folks in your communities that they gotta eat healthy" (Satchfield 2013). The implication here, conveyed through the messages of both First Lady Obama and NCLR's Board Chairman, is that Latinos have not questioned their own dietary practices.

This emphasis on the individual responsibility of Latino families and communities is evident in a wide range of anti-obesity campaigns. For instance, the California-based Champions for Change program, coordinated by Network for a Healthy California, frequently disseminates dietary information in the form of healthy-recipe books at grocery stores, health fairs, and public schools. According to the program website, "Champions for change are people who are committed to helping their families eat more fruits and vegetables and be more physically active. They are also involved in making healthy changes in their neighborhoods" (Champions for Change 2013). Promotional images of moms in the grocery store buying veggies and using a TV remote to turn off the television underscore the point that parents, especially moms, are responsible for their families' healthy practices. Since 2007, Champions for Change (2011) has been California's major anti-obesity program; in 2008, it conducted outreach with 1.6 million low-income, Latino adults. All of these messages imply that Latinos are less knowledgeable than other groups and that this lack of knowledge is what accounts for their higher weights.

Will the approach championed by the First Lady work? Do Latino families need more education about the health risks of consuming a high-calorie, low-nutrient diet with minimal to no exercise? Does the root of the problem lie in a lack of knowledge about healthy eating and failure of Latinos to "step up" and question their own behaviors and beliefs? What wider effects does the assumption of ignorance—which gets embedded in programmatic interventions as well as the ubiquitous media messages about minority responsibility for the obesity epidemic—produce? What political work might it do?

Elsewhere, Greenhalgh (2012, 2015) has argued that the political dynamics of the American obesity epidemic constitute a morally laden project in which an individual's deservingness of citizenship is perpetually held in question. The almost 15-year-old "war on fat" works by creating a "biocitizenship society" in which, to be deemed a worthy, responsible American, each of us must become a virtuous biocitizen. A good biocitizen is one who devotes large amounts of time to dieting and exercising in order to maintain a medically "normal" weight and who takes responsibility for ensuring that others in his social environment also become good biocitizens (Halse 2009; also Rose 2007). Although both men and women are expected to become thin, fit biocitizens, because of cultural norms making appearance more central to women's identities and gendered norms making mothers responsible for health within the family, the burdens of biocitizenship—both achieving the slender, toned body oneself and ensuring others do likewise—fall more heavily on women. The main mechanism for the spread of biocitizenship culture is "fat-talk," both biopedagogical (serving to inform) and bioabusive (serving to induce change through shaming). As a moral discourse, biocitizenship grants membership based on success in endeavors of personal health while excluding those who fail from the community of good Americans. Latinos thus now face yet a new, even more insuperable barrier to becoming "real" or "valued Americans": they must become good biocitizens who eat a certain way, move a certain amount, and maintain a certain weight, all the while ensuring that other Latinos do the same. Extensive research shows that in the United States today, the benefits to thin bodies and successful biocitizenship are economic, social, political, and cultural. Proper-bodied Americans are rewarded with better jobs and higher incomes, more friends and romantic prospects, superior access to state employment and benefits, and more positive representation in the media and other cultural venues (Fikkan and Rothblum 2012; Puhl and Heuer 2009). Weight-centered biocitizenship thus affects belonging in the widest sense. The findings from our research suggest that virtually all institutions and actors in our society—from families and communities to doctors, schools, political officials, and corporations—actively manage and promote the terms of biocitizenship. Biocitizenship is so pervasive a feature of our culture and society that it seems that everyone everywhere is lecturing everyone else about being a good biocitizen.

. . . Our data will show that regardless of immigrant status or age/parental status, all Latinos we worked with were deeply affected by the biopolitics of fat in the United States. . . .

"We Know about Healthy Eating, Exercise, and Weight"

In Greenhalgh's research, Latinos were indistinguishable from the young people of other ethnic groups: regardless of cultural background, virtually everyone was knowledgeable about the necessity of eating well and exercising regularly to reach a healthy weight. This relatively high level of knowledge is illustrated by Angela, a Mexican-American woman who wanted to lose weight: "[She] eats very healthy and watches the amount of food she eats and won't even have a bite of a cookie or a scoop of ice cream. She counts every single calorie, only eats 1,000–1,500 calories a day, reads nutritional facts, and goes to the gym at least three times a week."

Young Latinos were so knowledgeable about weight and health because their social worlds were full of dutiful biocitizens who readily informed them of their weight problem if they carried extra pounds and what they must do to fix it. . . . Messages about diet, weight, and exercise pervaded [their] everyday experiences. Parents hearing these messages were concerned not only about their children's health, but also about their ability to fit in, be happy, and eventually find a partner in life. These concerns often started early in a child's life. Allison's case is typical: "My entire life

I have always been chubby at the least. . . . In third grade my mom put me on my first diet. My mom was always sure to let me know when I was eating the wrong things or if she thought I should go exercise instead of sitting and watching TV. . . . In the sixth grade, my mom took me to Weight Watchers for the first time." Diet, exercise, and weight are such fundamental features of American culture today that even recent immigrants were keenly aware of the importance of thinness to belonging. Sofia's parents, recent immigrants from Guatemala, insisted that their two daughters be thin because they wanted the girls to assimilate into mainstream Orange County culture and be accepted. So keen were they to guarantee their daughters' thinness that they gave them water pills to spur weight loss.

If parents taught kids healthful practices, knowledge of the BMI scale and the consequences of a bad BMI came primarily from interactions with health professionals. In roughly half the cases in Greenhalgh's research, young people learned their BMIs from doctors during a routine health examination or from nurses conducting school fitness tests, which in California are required of all fifth, seventh, and ninth graders. This was often the first time young people learned that their bodies were "abnormal"; for many it was a traumatic experience that precipitated a dramatic change in which they suddenly began to perceive themselves as bad and defective and in need of remediation. Ignacio described the experience this way:

> I remember going to the doctor's office as she told my mother and me that I was considered overweight and a few pounds from being obese. I found this concept absurd . . . nonetheless it put the idea of obesity in my head. The doctor pulled out a BMI chart and told me what my ideal weight should be. As soon as my mother heard this, she became concerned for my health. . . . It was at this point that I made a conscious decision to try to control my eating habits.

Lauren's encounter with her physician trampled her self-esteem:

> When I was 10 years old, I went to the doctor's office for a routine check-up. . . . I knew I had a weight problem, but no one had ever called me fat directly. This doctor told my mom that if she

did not do anything soon I would be in danger of contracting diseases like high blood pressure, diabetes, and hypertension. . . . I did not realize it at that time, but [that diagnosis] caused traumas in my life. My self-confidence was shot down.

. . . Pedro learned the essentials of good biocitizenship not only from his doctor but also from school health classes:

> When I was little I was overweight. I was like really big. I was like 160 in fourth grade. When my mom used to take my sister and me to the doctor, he would say, "You're fat, you know." Almost literally, he said in Spanish, gordo. . . . Our weight was a big part of what we always talked about. . . . In middle school and high school health ed classes, there was always someone to tell you what a nutritious diet is. But you hear it and hear it; I heard it often enough that I was like, "Eh, I know what it is."

If parents and medical professionals provided these young people with concrete knowledge about diet, exercise, and the BMI, interactions with their peers and popular culture made it more real, more personal, and often more uncomfortable, goading them into action. [Young Latinos' in Greenhalgh's study] . . . evoked memories of being ridiculed by peers, underperforming in school sports, and feeling inadequate in comparison to popular media images of the ideal body. Ignacio recalled being routinely bullied by kids on the playground at the age of 12: "Other students would find it funny to pick on the fat kid. I would often be last to be picked for pick-up basketball games because I was fat and couldn't run as fast as the other skinnier guys." Lucia learned at an early age that her body size would keep her from being socially accepted:

> I didn't need to be told by my doctor that there was something wrong with me; all I had to do was just look around and realize that society looked down upon overweight individuals such as myself. . . . The last years of elementary school were when I experienced the most fat discrimination. . . . I remember not being chosen for team activities, the cool kids never giving

me more than a glance, and how I did not fit into the cultural obsession of slenderness evident in the fashion industry, on television, and in other types of media.

The ubiquitous media images of thin, fit bodies and the biobullying and social exclusion of peers are equally effective in conveying the message that heavier bodies merit scrutiny and criticism and must be rectified through dieting and exercise. If these cases are typical—and we surmise that they are in important ways—the notion that Latinos are unaware of the importance of diet, exercise, and maintaining medically normal weight has scant basis in social fact.

Trying but Always Failing: The Insuperability of Structural Barriers

. . . In Carney's research, the circumstances of migration intersected with other structural barriers that contributed to poor health and obstructed efforts to maintain a healthy body size. . . . Women in Carney's research ascribed certain aspects of post-migration life to this weight gain. These included: the convenience and affordability of unhealthy foods; isolation from social networks to support the retention of healthful behaviors; and stress from low-wages, multiple responsibilities in the home, and lack of time between jobs. Juliana (late 30s, from Guerrero), for instance, noted how demanding work schedules prevented immigrant mothers from preparing and sharing in nutritious foods: "Women don't have time, for the reason that they work. So they go buying something quick, perhaps for the reason of work. Because many times they eat this way, in large part, this is what does them harm, makes them gain weight." Malena (late 30s, from Guerrero) assigned herself to this category of working mothers; as the sole provider for her children, she would regularly arrive home late from her job as a hotel maid with no time or wherewithal to prepare a meal: "[We get] McDonald's or pizza [instead], because it is cheap."

Similar to the descriptions of these women, the child of an immigrant family in Greenhalgh's research recalled how the move from Guatemala to the United States made everyone in her family gain weight: "In Guatemala . . . portions are much smaller than they are here in America. It is customary to eat at home every

night for dinner, and it is rare that a family eats out. It is also much more uncommon to eat fast food. However, making the move here changed my and my family's customs drastically. Since we began eating out more and consuming more fast food, everyone's weight shifted [i.e., rose]."

Luisa (early 40s, from Michoacán) recalled drastic changes to her diet upon arriving to the United States: "When I got here, when one arrives here from Mexico, you see so much variety and you say 'in Mexico we never ate like this.' The truth is that [at first] I ate a lot. Because I was hungry for everything. I was longing for sweets, everything that we did not have in Mexico." This type of binge eating, as noted by Luisa, pervaded women's accounts of adjusting to the harsher conditions of life that they encountered in the United States, which included a sense of social isolation. As Dolores (late 30s, from Guerrero) explained: "One suffers when they come here because they do not know anyone. Everything is different. When one arrives, one feels sad and alone, not knowing what to do."

The experience of social marginalization associated with the process of immigration also had effects for the Latino youth in Greenhalgh's research. In these cases, exposure to social trauma and life disruptions led them to turn to compulsive over-eating as a coping strategy, resulting in weight gain. Perhaps because of the higher level of poverty, Latino kids were more likely than children of other ethnic groups to suffer individual and family traumas that were beyond their control. In one case, it was the trauma of immigration, followed by a parental breakup, and the subsequent reappearance of a father who had been jailed, that led a young woman to quit her diet and exercise routine and to start eating more to calm her nerves. In a second case, a family medical emergency and the fear of losing a mother forced a young boy to become his father's right-hand man; with no control over his life circumstances, he overate and gained weight. In a third case, a young woman ate more compulsively to dull the pain of fat abuse. Ridiculed by a boy on the school playground who yelled, "Why do you want the ball, you are so fat, I'm sure you can't even shoot!" Lauren was crushed: "That day is one I will never forget, he broke me down. For years after that I felt ugly, fat, disgusting, not good enough. . . . So I began to eat. Food was delicious and it made me feel good. . . . slowly but surely I gained more and more weight until the point where I was borderline obese."

Although women in Carney's research desired to establish healthier diets within their families, the ubiquity of certain comida chatarra (junk) and comida rapida (fast foods, i.e., burgers, pizza, processed bread, and fast food) frequently undermined these women's efforts. Natalia (early 50s, from Oaxaca), a mother of four, expressed dismay with the meals served at her son's school: "I don't like junk food. I fight with [my son] because I prefer that he'd eat a plate of lentils rather than a burger. Because, for example, burgers are eaten in school or the children are given pizza. So I prefer that in my house, [he eats] rice with chicken. Lentils. A bit of fish with salad." In addition to school lunches, which often contained items—such as pizza and hamburgers—perceived as chatarra by the mothers, children also acquired snacks in the form of chatarra from local street vendors who carted around items for sale in women's neighborhoods. Some women even blamed their husbands—the occasional purveyors of fast food—as undermining their efforts to ensure comida saludable (healthy meals). Juliana, for example, relayed an incident on Mother's Day when her husband arrived home with pizza after she had prepared a healthy meal. Referring to his actions, she said, "Sometimes these barriers exist in your own home."

In reporting on the undesirable changes to their bodies that they observed since arriving to the United States, immigrant mothers in Carney's research complained of feeling helpless and depressed. Marisol, a single mother in her early 30s, struggled to manage her weight while being the sole financial provider for her three daughters. She related high levels of stress from working multiple part-time jobs: "I have gained a lot of weight, and I feel that I can't change my body. I feel really tired, really stressed." Linda (late 30s, from Michoacán) reported problems with weight in her entire family. She expressed concern for the weights of her son and husband; meanwhile, she framed her own weight gain in terms of stress from work, managing her household, and coping with her husband's alcoholism:

I think I'm a bit overweight because of my husband being fat. He keeps putting on [weight]. But he drinks, and I think this makes him fat. He likes to drink a lot, a lot, everyday. I've gained eight pounds, and I think it is because I'm not eating well, because I'm

not keeping to a schedule. My son is also overweight but he's been this way since he was really little. I think that now my weight is really affecting me, because I have back pain. I'm stressed because my back hurts me so much—three months ago I was at a normal weight. I was always 138 pounds and now I'm 142, no, 146. I feel bad. I need to lose weight. I think [maybe] stress makes one gain weight? Because I'm really stressed. I stress all the time, and I think that is what this is. I get nervous but in the form of hunger. Anything I put into my mouth, bread, a cookie, makes me gain weight when I'm stressed. The stress also comes from driving without a license all the way to my job. It comes from needing to pick up my kids quickly, to get home to make the meals. Now my husband is getting home from work very late, like at eight o'clock at night, so every responsibility falls on me: go to work, leave kids at school, return, get them from school, make dinner, do the laundry, everything is for me to do. For these reasons, I feel so much stress. But I can't stop working because when I do, I feel stressed again because there is no money to pay the rent, the bills, for things we need. If it is not one thing, it is another.

As Linda articulates that it is she, rather than her husband, who is charged with overseeing so many aspects of the household, her case suggests that the changes associated with adjusting to life in the United States and translating to negative health outcomes, including increased anxiety, affect women disproportionately (for further discussion of this gendered suffering, see Carney 2014a, 2014b, 2015).

In terms of gender differences, there was also some evidence from our research that Latinas felt more pressure than men to conform to gendered body ideals. For instance, one woman from Carney's research pursued somewhat extreme measures in attempting to control her weight. As the accumulated result of many years of compulsive eating since migrating to the United States, Brenda (mid-50s, from Mexico City) decided to address her weight problem by electing to undergo gastric band surgery. However, since her doctors in the United States would not approve her for the procedure, she drove across the border to a clinic in Tijuana.

Although the surgery enabled her to lose weight, her desired results proved only temporary. . . .

Arguably, Brenda's efforts to lose weight vis-á-vis elective surgery were not successful because they did nothing to address her tendency toward compulsive eating, a behavior she had developed since living estranged from most of her children (who were still in Mexico) and spending much of her time alone. While Brenda's experience perhaps edges on the extreme, many women in Carney's study cited how structural factors such as financial constraints and social isolation steered them toward gain weight or prevented them from losing it, despite attempts at dieting and exercise.

For United States–born Latinos raised in low-income communities, these same forces made it difficult to keep their weight down. Pedro knew the diet-and-exercise mantra, but a lack of money undermined his efforts to put it into effect:

> In the past year and a half, I've gained 70 pounds, . . . I had knee surgery—to repair a meniscus that I tore at the gym. . . . I had the surgery like six months later because I didn't have the insurance. I was in bed and depressed because I couldn't work out. . . . I've [had to] put the whole working-out thing on the backburner for now. . . . The week my son was born, my girlfriend and I had Jack in the Box three times a day for a week. There was no time to cook. . . . Everyone knows that fruits and veggies are good for you. But you don't always have fruits [available to eat]. We don't buy fruits a lot because they expire and we forget about them. Or it's hard to buy enough fruit for every day because it's not that cheap. We're getting food stamps— actually, free food from WIC—right now, and it's a limited amount. . . . We just [had] a really big expense that we weren't expecting, so come November or December, we're like, eh, we don't know where our money will be coming from. We just stocked up on Costco foods; we filled our fridge really bad. . . . We don't know if we'll have money later on. At least we will have food.

When financial constraints are so severe that urgent surgery must be postponed and having any food to eat

is a worry, following the dietary and exercise rules of good biocitizenship is an impossible dream.

Feeling "Irresponsible" and "Unworthy": Bad Biocitizens and Bad Moms

[As stated earlier in this chapter], for heavyset Latino youth, feelings of being inadequate often started in childhood with the receipt of a non-normal BMI score. Such feelings persisted into young adulthood. The young people in Greenhalgh's research internalized the shame associated with being overweight in our society and took on the identity of the "bad biocitizen" who is "lazy," "irresponsible," and therefore undeserving of full inclusion in the political community. In high school, AnneMarie's bad BMI—in the high 20s, marking her as unhealthy and overweight—"warped the image of my existence in society," making her feel guilty and inadequate. After gaining back 15 pounds she had lost, Lucia:

> began to feel guilty about the unhealthy foods I ate. I began thinking about my weight every day. . . . Feeling "fat" when I didn't exercise three times a week is something I considered lazy and due to my lack of focus. Not going out shopping . . . on "fat" weeks is something that I started then . . . if I had been naughty and over-ate with larger portions. . . . This constant thinking of weight also affects the way I perceived my acceptance into society.

Pedro defended himself from the common view that people like him who fail at good biocitizenship are "lazy." Deep down, however, he felt that there was something very wrong with him and that his fatness and his failed efforts marked him as undeserving of the respect shown to those who succeed:

> [Two years ago] I was not eating too well, so in a few months I went down [from 230] to 200.1 felt really good and tried to maintain that weight. I have pictures here [in my phone] because I need to know what I can look like—my potential. Because if [I don't have the photos], I'm just like, I feel bad a lot of the time. . . . I hate it, you know, because I've seen what I can do. . . . I've tried—I try eating healthy, I try

eating small portions, you know. . . . I made an effort, it's not that I'm lazy. That's a misconception a lot of people have—that overweight people are just lazy. But they're not. I've tried, you know. I've been 70 pounds lighter, and I've lost weight. And I have other things to do. But then you have other people who have the same stuff to do, but they weigh less. You think, you know, that something's wrong with you. You think you're not—I don't know—I think I'm doing something wrong. I think when I diet alone, I can control my weight at least to a more reasonable level. Like maybe 220 or 230, instead of [my current] 270 or 260. . . . But it's hard. I just don't know how to do it.

In addition to feeling like "bad citizens," women from Carney's research feared the possibility of being perceived as "bad mothers." Many of the messages stemming from the field of public health reinforce the notion that Latina moms are not taking proper care of their progeny. Campaigns for preventing childhood obesity such as Salud America!, for instance, gesture to changes in dietary behaviors that assume a mother's oversight. Thus, particularly blameworthy in the anti-obesity rhetoric is the Latina mother, who is yet again being portrayed as incompetent in overseeing her own health as well as that of her children (Horton and Barker 2009; Inda 2007; Molina 2006).

Aside from desiring to evade social scrutiny around their own bodies, immigrant women in Carney's research strived to distinguish themselves from so-called "bad mothers" by denigrating other women they knew who apparently worked too much and were not available to prepare healthy meals for their children. Olivia (late 20s, from Guerrero), for instance, described working mothers as too unconcerned about their children's diets: "The problem that children eat junk food is the problem of [a mother]. . . . We have to find options to buy better food or to make food at home. Because here, in this country, as mothers work, it is easier to buy prepared food or to take your kids to McDonald's. But it depends on how you, as a mother, provide them with healthy food." Statements such as Olivia's reproduced negative depictions of single mothers and operated as a form of symbolic violence against those who were already struggling with both limited financial resources and social capital.

. . .

The Obesity Epidemic as a New Source of Structural Vulnerability: Concluding Thoughts

Our research reveals that both Latino immigrants and United States–born Latinos feel increasingly anxious and troubled about their bodies, anticipating the onset of an acute sense of exclusion from society. The impossible demands of biocitizenship operating alongside public sentiment that blames Latinos for harming the nation, conspire in yielding this sense of exclusion and in delineating the parameters of inclusion. Thus, Latinos are effectively blocked from exhibiting good biocitizenship and subsequently from enjoying the privileges of social belonging. Among the younger generation of United States–raised Latinos, both men and women, subject to pervasive pressures in their social worlds, were anxious about achieving the proper, thin, trim body. In the older immigrant generation of parents, women bore a much greater responsibility for following biocitizenship norms. Even as they tried to keep their own weight down, they were charged with ensuring that their children were raised in healthful environments, a project their husbands, apparently less concerned about weight, sometimes undermined.

Consistent with a rhetoric stressing the economic burden that obesity imposes on United States society, it seems clear that the public concern about the girths of Latinos serves larger political-economic interests. As Latinos strive—and generally fail—to embody the principles of good biocitizenship, barriers to this effort become increasingly internalized and normalized so that the emotional angst around one's body size, or other feelings of inadequacy (Gonzales and Chavez 2012; Horton and Barker 2010), are viewed as natural and deserved. Relegating Latinos and other minorities to a position of marginality in this way allows for their continued exploitation as workers in the lower rungs of the United States labor economy (Guthman 2011; Holmes 2013).

. . . Rather than enabling Latinos and other minority groups to overcome the oppressive social, economic, and political conditions that systematically ostracize them as "lesser" bodies that produce less value for society, anti-obesity programs frame their agency as "destructive" (Berlant 2007), leading them to feel further ashamed, responsible, and bad about themselves. . . . Thus, the always-already failing biocitizen is one who also comes to accept the view of him[self] or herself as less deserving of dignity and belonging.

Although the relatively high levels of Latino obesity pose health risks that are worrying and need to be addressed, current public health interventions into "overweight" individual bodies caused by "Latino ignorance" have little chance of working. Their failure to address some of the most fundamental sources of higher weights in the Latino community can be seen as compounding the health problems, as the education-focused programs, in place now for many years, fail to miss their mark. Their limited success adds to the urgency of finding more effective solutions. Even as we search for more effective ways to address the health problems, we need also to redress the general malaise that has emerged from a practice of shaming and blaming minorities for dragging the nation down with their higher weights.

References

Berlant, Lauren. 2007. Slow Death (Sovereignty, Obesity, Lateral Agency). Critical Inquiry 33(4):754-780.

Carney, Megan A. 2014a. The Biopolitics of 'Food Insecurity': Towards a Critical Political Ecology of the Body in Studies of Women's Transnational Migration. Journal of Political Ecology 21:1-18.

Carney, Megan A. 2014b. "La Lucha Diaria": Migrant Women in the Fight for Healthy Food. In Off the Edge of the Table: Women Redefining the Limits of the Food System and the Experience of Food Insecurity. Janet Page-Reeves, ed. Pp. 127–144. Lanham, Md.: Lexington Press.

Carney, Megan A. 2015. The Unending Hunger: Tracing Women and Food Insecurity Across Borders. Berkeley: University of California Press.

Champions for Change. 2011. Achieving Statewide Success in Nutrition Education and Outreach. http://www.cdph.ca.gov/programs/cpns/Documents/BRO-210_SEPT_2011.pdf (accessed September 20, 2013).

Champions for Change. 2013. Champions for Change. http://www. cachampionsforchange.cdph.ca.gov/en/index.php (accessed September 18, 2013).

Chavez, Leo R. 2007. A Glass Half Empty: Latina Reproduction and Public Discourse. In Women and Migration in the US-Mexico Borderlands: A Reader. Patricia Zavella and Denise A. Segura, eds. Pp. 67–91. Durham, N.C.: Duke University Press.

Chavez, Leo R. 2008. The Latino Threat: Constructing Immigrants, Citizens, and the Nation. Stanford, Calif.: Stanford University Press.

Chavez, Leo R. 2012. Undocumented Immigrants and Their Use of Medical Services in Orange County, California. Social Science and Medicine 74(6):887–893.

Fikkan, Janna L., and Esther D. Rothblum. 2012. Is Fat a Feminist Issue? Exploring the Gendered Nature of Weight Bias. Sex Roles: A Journal of Research 66(9):575–592.

Flegal, Katherine M., Margaret D. Carroll, Cynthia L. Ogden, and Lester R. Curtin. 2012. Prevalence of Obesity and Trends in the Distribution of Body Mass Index among US Adults, 1999-2010. Journal of the American Medical Association 307(5):491-497.

Gonzales, Roberto G., and Leo R. Chavez. 2012. "Awakening to a Nightmare": Abjectivity and Illegality in the Lives of Undocumented 1.5-Generation Latino Immigrants in the United States. Current Anthropology 53(3):255–281.

Greenhalgh, Susan. 2012. Weighty Subjects: The Biopolitics of the US War on Fat. American Ethnologist 39(3):471–487.

Greenhalgh, Susan. 2015. Making War on Fat: The Human Story of America's AntiObesity Campaign. Ithaca, NY: Cornell University Press.

Guthman, Julie. 2011. Weighing In: Obesity, Food Justice, and the Limits of Capitalism. Berkeley: University of California Press.

Halse, Christine. 2009. Bio-Citizenship: Virtue Discourses and the Birth of the BioCitizen. In Biopolitics and the "Obesity Epidemic." J. Wright and V. Harwood, eds. Pp. 45–59. New York: Routledge.

Holmes, Seth M. 2013. Fresh Fruit, Broken Bodies: Migrant Farmworkers in the United States. Berkeley: University of California Press.

Horton, Sarah, and Judith C. Barker. 2009. "Stains" on their Self-Discipline: Public Health, Hygiene, and the Disciplining of Undocumented Immigrant Parents in the Nation's Internal Borderlands. American Ethnologist 36(4):784–798.

Horton, Sarah, and Judith C. Barker. 2010. Stigmatized Biologies: Examining the Cumulative Effects of Oral Health Disparities for Mexican American Farmworker Children. Medical Anthropology Quarterly 24(2):199–219.

Inda, Jonathan X. 2007. The Value of Immigrant Life. In Women and Migration in the US-Mexico Borderlands. Patricia Zavella and Denise Segura, eds. Pp. 134–157. Durham, N.C.: Duke University Press.

Molina, Natalia. 2006. Fit to Be Citizens? Public Health and Race in Los Angeles, 1879–1939. Berkeley: University of California Press.

Ogden, Cynthia L., Margaret D. Carroll, Lester R. Curtin, Molly M. Lamb, and Katherine M. Flegal. 2010. Prevalence of High Body Mass Index in US Children and Adolescents, 2007–2008. Journal of the American Medical Association 303(3):242–249.

Puhl, Rebecca M., and Chelsea A. Heuer. 2009. The Stigma of Obesity: A Review and Update. Obesity 17(5): 1–24.

Ramirez, Amelie G., and Guadalupe X. Ayala. 2013. An Introduction to Salud America! A Research Network to Prevent Obesity among Latino Children. American Journal of Preventative Medicine 44(3S3): 175–177.

Rose, Nikolas. 2007. The Politics of Life Itself: Biomedicine, Power, and Subjectivity in the Twenty-First Century. Princeton, N.J.: Princeton University Press.

Satchfield, Scott. 2013. Michelle Obama Speaks Out about Childhood Obesity during N.O. Visit. http://www.fox81ive.com (accessed August 26, 2013).

United States Census Bureau. 2012. US Census Bureau Projections Show a Slower Growing, Older, More Diverse Nation a Half Century from Now. Washington, D.C.: United States Census Bureau.

6.3 Democracy as Social Action: Home Birth, Midwives, and the Push for State Licensure

TARA HEFFERAN

The act of giving birth is a universal experience, yet the circumstances and strategies of childbirth vary cross-culturally and within cultures. In the United States, pregnancy and childbirth tend to be pathologized and medicalized, with the vast majority of children born in hospitals under the supervision of medical personnel. This isn't the case everywhere, nor was it always the case in the United States. This selection, written by an anthropologist-advocate for midwifery and mother to several home-birthed children, explores efforts to bring home birth back into the "mainstream." The experimental style of the piece reflects contemporary ethnographic approaches—to writing and research—where past lines between researcher and the subject of study have become permeable and interactive.

Questions

1. Compare and contrast the dominant "technocratic" model of pregnancy and birth with the approach of direct-entry midwives.
2. What is the role of power in shaping birthing options for women in the United States?
3. How might the licensure of direct-entry midwives benefit poor and marginalized women?
4. Why do so few women give birth at home in the United States? What does the limited number of home births suggest about American culture?
5. How is this case study an example of engaged and public anthropology?

"Some women give birth at home," I say. "Would you ever consider having a home birth?" The students in my cultural anthropology class are quick to say "no," shaking their heads in vigorous disapproval. They speak animatedly. "Home birth is not safe—what if there was a problem during labor?" "Who would clean up the mess?" "Would the doctor come to the house?"

That today home birth is largely an unthinkable option for many demonstrates the power of culture to shape our views, to mold our realities. In the United States, more than 98% of all births take place in the hospital, but until the turn of the 20th century, almost all births happened at home with midwives (MacDorman

et al. 2014). This rapid shift from home to hospital was not natural or inevitable. Rather, it was the strategic outcome of medical and political actors consciously transforming where and with whom birth happens. Through public relations campaigns to discredit midwives, the rewriting of laws to define physician control of the birth process, and broader cultural beliefs associating hospitals with "progress," home birth midwifery was virtually eliminated in the United States by the 1950s (Craven 2007). In recent decades, however, there has been a push among home birth midwives and their supporters to once again bring home birth into the "mainstream," in part by formalizing it within state-level legal structures (Craven 2010; Davis-Floyd and Johnson 2006). Here I explore this movement through the lens of "biography and history," alternating my own experiences of home birth with the larger politics of home birth in Michigan (Mills 2000, 6).

Home Birth

It is 2:00 AM and the contractions are starting to come with some force. A tightening of the abdomen, cramps from deep within, a full-body flexing that stops me from any other movement. Better call the midwife, before it is too late. She missed the last birth; the baby came too quickly. Thirty minutes of active labor and the surprise urge to push meant the baby arrived before the midwife. We were not prepared for that. Had we not planned a home birth, we would have been the nightly news's sensational headline: "Dad delivers baby in car on way to hospital!" But, this time, things would be different. My husband calmly calls the midwife and lets her know that she's needed at our house.

Home birth in the U.S. follows a logic different from hospital birth. Most home births are attended not by physicians but instead by "direct entry" midwives, who are sometimes called "independent," "lay," or "traditional" midwives. Direct-entry midwives enter the profession through apprenticeship or midwifery training programs, without first passing through nursing or medical school. Thus, their knowledge systems often are grounded in experience and their competency in practice. Moreover, many direct-entry midwives hold a "holistic" model of birth that runs counter to the dominant "technocratic" model, which frames pregnancy and birth as inherently risky, a kind of pathology best managed by medical experts using technological tools (Davis-Floyd 1993, 1992; Jordan 1992; Martin 1987). By contrast, the midwifery model understands pregnancy and birth as normal processes (see Figure 6.3.1). It often includes space for recognizing instinct and intuition as knowledge, with a privileging of a mother's own self-knowledge (Lay 2000; Davis-Floyd and Davis 1996). Such beliefs encourage direct-entry midwives to take supportive, non-technological rather than managerial roles vis-à-vis pregnancy and birth.

The midwife and her two assistants are here. They enter quietly. I'm in the living room, talking with my mom, wondering why this labor seems to be taking so much longer than the last. Maybe this

The Midwives Model of Care includes:

- Monitoring the physical, psychological, and social well-being of the mother throughout the childbearing cycle
- Providing the mother with individualized education, counseling, and prenatal care, continuous hands-on assistance during labor and delivery, and postpartum support
- Minimizing technological interventions
- Identifying and referring women who require obstetrical attention

The application of this woman-centered model of care has been proven to reduce the incidence of birth injury, trauma, and cesarean section.

(Midwifery Task Force 2001)

Figure 6.3.1 Midwives Model of Care.

time I called the midwife too early. They ask how I am, inquire about the frequency and intensity of the contractions, listen to the baby's heart through a handheld Doppler instrument. Each birth is different, they assure me. No need to worry that this one isn't as fast as the last. Do I need anything? Am I thirsty? Want a heating pad? They slip softly away, gathering around the kitchen table as I prepare to walk around the block in hopes of jumpstarting "serious" labor.

Certified Professional Midwives

While many direct-entry midwives practice without certification, some 2,000 direct-entry midwives are credentialed as Certified Professional Midwives (CPMs) (NARM 2014). The CPM credential recognizes that a midwife has the "entry-level knowledge, skills, and abilities necessary to practice competently" according to the Midwives Model of Care, primarily attending women in non-hospital settings (NARM 2014). This competency is demonstrated through successfully passing a written exam and a skills assessment, after which the CPM credential is conferred.

The legal status of direct-entry midwives varies from state to state, ranging from legal to illegal (Devries 1996; Reed and Roberts 2000). State governments have the power to decide whether direct-entry midwifery is permitted or prohibited. In some states, including Michigan, home birth midwifery operates in a gray zone, for the most part "tolerated," though neither prohibited nor regulated, and generally understood to exist in a space "outside the scope of the prohibition against the unlicensed practice of medicine" (Pope and Fisch 2013, 297). Since 2008, there has been a national campaign—called the Big Push for Midwives—to promote the CPM as the basis for state regulation and licensure. Currently, 28 states use the CPM as the credential for licensure, though the Big Push is providing guidance and support to another 17 states—including Michigan—working toward CPM legislative recognition (Big Push 2014).

> As I walk toward the door, I feel it: the kind of contraction that brings you to your knees. I can't stroll around the block; the baby is on the way NOW. The midwives are at the table chatting, and I send my husband to tell them that I'm getting into the birth tub to push out the baby. They are a bit surprised, since I haven't given any hint of being so close to pushing. But, birth happens on its own schedule. As I slip into the water, I feel some relief. I'm buoyant, my heavy belly supported by the warm water. The midwife listens to the baby's heartbeat while I contract. The pain is deep and raw. My bones feel like they're grinding against one another, a painful yet satisfying contortion that signals the baby will be here soon.

Michigan Democracy in Action

Responding to this sense of legal ambiguity and drawing energy from successful licensure campaigns in other states, some Michigan midwives and their supporters have come together to lobby the Michigan legislature for legal recognition and licensing standards for direct-entry midwifery. This activism has been ongoing since 2009, and despite the introduction of two bills to the Michigan legislature, no legislation has yet to pass out of committee and into law. The Chair of the Health Policy Committee is a known ally of physician groups, and the hope is that now that she has been term-limited out of office, a new and friendlier Chair will be installed.

The direct-entry midwives and their supporters who are advancing this Michigan legislation are not the power elite. They do not hold tremendous wealth, nor do they have notable political clout. Rather, they are "every day" women (nearly all are women) who hope that recognition and licensure will lead to greater access to care for marginalized women in underserved areas, particularly those who cannot afford to have a home birth, which is not covered by Medicaid and is rarely covered by insurance in Michigan. They hope it will offer greater integration in and collaboration with the conventional medical system, that it will free them from the threat of prosecution, the fear of being accused of practicing medicine without a license.

> "Try not to push. Just breathe," she says. I'm squatting, and the midwife is supporting my tissues with her hands, protecting me from tearing while the baby exits. Slow, gentle. "The head is born. Lots of hair!" she coos. My husband smiles in anticipation. There is relief, but I want to keep pushing. After more than 41 weeks, the baby is almost here. I try to relax. No rush right? As another contraction builds, I focus on maintaining control, but I push hard instead. It's okay. Yes, it's okay. I feel suddenly light. A sweet baby, covered in waxy white vernix, is pulled out of the water and put into my arms.

The System

Childbirth is not merely a biological event. Like all aspects of health, birth weaves together complex cultural and social threads, shaped by and shaping the political and economic dimensions of a society. For direct-entry midwives in Michigan, birth is shaped by the legal recognition of physicians as the privileged caretakers of pregnancy and birth, and by the insurance industry's lack of coverage for the costs associated with home birth. Midwives are pushing back, though, through demands for legal recognition and licensure, to demand respect for their work and provide a framework for expanding its reach. As an anthropologist, I have supported these efforts by sharing scholarly work that helps to situate the Michigan campaign within the larger licensure movement, by offering meeting space to the decentralized network of midwives to carry out face-to-face meetings, and by developing and carrying out research in collaboration with the midwife community. Indeed, the research focus on licensure emerged at the suggestion of one of the lead activists in the pro-licensure movement.

In her ethnography examining economic development in rural Haiti, Jennie M. Smith (2001) suggests that Haitian peasants have a deep understanding of democracy, one that moves past simple notions of voting to incorporate elements of social justice, equity, and dignity. "Real democracy," they suggest, is when everyone has a bed to sleep in, a chance for an education, and enough to eat. I would argue that campaigns like those headed by home birth midwives in Michigan likewise expand popular U.S. notions of democracy. Democracy is when everyday people become intimately involved in the inner-workings of government, its power structures, its culture. It is when they act to overturn policies and practices that further disadvantage the already marginalized. Rather than assuming the system is fixed and unchangeable, they see it as malleable, given the right conditions, sets of relationships, and pressures.

Home birth midwives working for licensure cast the state as an identifiable set of actors, who can be lobbied and persuaded to support a midwife-friendly bill. Individual legislators are specifically linked to notions of health, access to care, and women's rights to birth as they see fit. State actors are transient, though, as elections shift potential allies and enemies in and out of positions of power; as such, forging relationships and "educating" lawmakers about the importance of home birth midwifery is important and ongoing work.

The state does not stand apart from—or above—its citizens in this framing. It is not a monolith of preexisting forms working in lockstep only with powerful interests. While certain lobbies, including state and national medical societies, can exert disproportionate influence in the political arena, they are understood to be just one set of players on the field, rather than the game itself. The sense that licensure will move midwives toward a better future suggests a certain faith in the legislative process and a belief that the state is a potential force for good rather than repression. Indeed, in Michigan, licensure advocates frame their efforts as proactive attempts to both shape the future of the profession and assure their own personal security.

Yet, licensure supporters are not naïve about the realities that regulation can move in the other direction, too. Indeed, direct-entry midwives in Michigan (and elsewhere) have found licensure to be a particularly divisive issue, as the community itself wrestles with licensure's costs versus benefits (Erikson and Colo 2006; Hough 2006; May and Davis-Floyd 2006). Gaining formal recognition for the work they do means that midwives might need to sacrifice their autonomy and current scope of practice, and that not all currently practicing midwives will meet the newly instituted requirements; some will be locked out. That is, licensure will have uneven effects among direct-entry midwives, with some benefiting and some losing. As such, not all direct-entry midwives think that licensure is worth the compromises it will require. Indeed, the push for licensure has created tremendous divisions between pro- and anti-licensure advocates. As an anthropologist, this means I must tread carefully in advocacy efforts, mindful that "the midwife community" itself is a shifting, amorphous collection of individuals and networks with competing goals and interests. I did not have this awareness when I first began working with the pro-licensure movement in 2009.

My daughter. My daughter stares at me. She is so alert, her eyes wide, gazing up at me. We are in the pool, the umbilical cord still pulsing, linking us. The midwife has examined her briefly but doesn't take her from my arms. Instead, we are left to embrace one another, peacefully, relaxed in the dim glow of the night light. Welcome to your new home, baby girl.

References

Big Push. 2014. "Benefits of Licensing Certified Professional Midwives."

Craven, Christa. 2010. *Pushing for Midwives: Homebirth Mothers and the Reproductive Rights Movement.* Philadelphia: Temple University Press.

Craven, Christa. 2007. "A 'Consumers Right' to Choose a Midwife: Shifting Meanings of Reproductive Rights under Neoliberalism." *American Anthropologist* 109(4):701–712.

Davis-Floyd, Robbie. 1992. *Birth as an American Rite of Passage.* Berkeley: University of California Press.

Davis-Floyd, Robbie. 1993. "The Technocratic Model of Birth" In *Feminist Theory in the Study of Folklore*, edited by Susan Tower Hollis, Linda Pershing, and M. Jane Young, 297–326. Champaign: University of Illinois Press.

Davis-Floyd, Robbie, and Elizabeth Davis. 1996. "Intuition as Authoritative Knowledge in Midwifery and Homebirth." *Medical Anthropology Quarterly* 10(2):237–269.

Davis-Floyd, Robbie, and Christina Barbara Johnson, eds. 2006. *Mainstreaming Midwifery: The Politics of Change.* New York: Routledge.

Devries, Raymond. 1996. *Making Midwives Legal: Childbirth, Medicine and the Law.* 2nd Edition. Columbus: Ohio State University Press.

Erikson, Susan, with Amy Colo. 2006. "Risks, Costs, and Effects of Homebirth Midwifery Legislation in Colorado." In *Mainstreaming Midwifery,* edited by Robbie Davis-Floyd and Barbara Johnson, 289–309. New York: Routledge.

Hough, Carolyn A. 2006. "'I'm Living My Politics': Legalizing and Licensing Direct-Entry Midwives in Iowa" In *Mainstreaming Midwifery,* edited by Robbie Davis-Floyd and Barbara Johnson, 347–374. New York: Routledge.

Jordan, Brigitte. 1992. *Birth in Four Cultures: A Cross-Cultural Investigation of Childbirth in Yucatan, Holland, Sweden, and the United States.* Longrove, IL: Waveland Press.

Lay, Mary M. 2000. *The Rhetoric of Midwifery: Gender, Knowledge, and Power.* New Brunswick, NJ: Rutgers University Press.

MacDorman, Marian F., T. J. Mathews, and Eugene Declercq. 2014. "Trends in Out-of-Hospital Births in the United States 1990–2012." *NCHS Data Brief,* No. 144. March. http://www.cdc.gov/nchs/data/databriefs/db144.htm

Martin, Emily. 1987. *The Woman in the Body: A Cultural Analysis of Reproduction.* Boston: Beacon Press.

May, Maureen, and Robbie-Davis Floyd. 2006. "Idealism and Pragmatism in the Creation of the Certified Midwife: The Development Midwifery in New York and the New York Midwifery Practice Act of 1992." In *Mainstreaming Midwifery: The Politics of Change,* edited by Davis-Floyd and Johnson, 81–158. New York: Routledge.

Mills, C. Wright. 2000 (1959). *The Sociological Imagination.* New York: Oxford University Press.

NARM. 2014. "How to Become a CPM." http://narm.org/certification/how-to-become-a-cpm/.

Pope, Thaddeus, and Deborah Fisch. 2013. "Legal Briefing: Home Birth and Midwifery." *The Journal of Clinical Ethics* 24(3):293–308.

Reed, Alyson, and Joyce E. Roberts. 2000. "State Regulation of Midwives: Issues and Options." *Journal of Midwifery and Women's Health* 45(2):130–149.

Smith, Jennie M. 2001. *When the Hands Are Many: Community Organization and Social Change in Rural Haiti.* Ithaca, NY: Cornell University Press.

6.4 The Politics of Reproduction: The Troubling Case of Nadya Suleman and Assisted Reproductive Technology

DANA-AIN DAVIS

In 2009, the United States' second set of octuplets was born to Nadya Suleman as a result of assisted reproductive technologies (ART). Public commentary quickly moved from celebration to criticism when more information about the mother's race, ethnicity, class, and marital status came to light. Through text analysis of public dialogue surrounding Suleman's decision to use in vitro fertilization after already having six children, Davis reveals the hidden social script that ART is sanctioned and legitimized for White heterosexual, middle and upper class women, and not for women of color, poor or low-income women, lesbians, or disabled women. Davis herself is a long-time activist in the field of reproductive justice. She draws on this experience to further interrogate the absence of mainstream reproductive rights groups from the public debate surrounding Suleman. Through this case, students will learn the core distinction between reproductive rights, as framed at times in a neoliberal discourse of choice, and reproductive justice.

Questions

1. How has the fertility of people of color been regulated throughout history?
2. Davis argues that one imagined social script in the United States is that ART is only for people in sanctioned heterosexual relationships. Do you agree or disagree? Why? What other imagined social scripts exist in our culture?
3. How did public discourse change once details about Suleman's race, ethnicity, marital status, and class were revealed?
4. Davis mentions the popular reality shows Jon & Kate Plus Eight and 18 Kids and Counting where rights to use ART were not questioned in the way that Suleman's rights were questioned. What is different about these families that appears to make them "legitimate"?
5. What is the distinction between reproductive rights and reproductive justice?
6. Why were reproductive rights groups silent about Suleman? What does their silence reveal about the focus of this movement?

The USA's first set of octuplets was born in Houston, Texas, in December 1998 to Nkem and Iyke Chukwu. The Nigerian-born couple, who were US citizens, had used fertility drugs to achieve the pregnancy, and all but one of the children survived (Lyman 1998). Just as with the Chukwu octuplets, the global media trumpeted the arrival of another high-order multiple birth on January 26, 2009, when Nadya Suleman gave birth to the nation's second set of octuplets in Bell-flower, California, at Kaiser Permanente Hospital. Following the delivery the mother and the children were doing well—despite the infants being two and a half months premature. Initially the story possessed all the elements of a mediagenic success. . . . [But] [i]t seemed that what interested most people was: Who were the parents of these children?

. . . In unpacking the story I found that the blogging public viewed the event as a joyous miracle. Simultaneously, medical and bioethical professionals' appearance on news programs tempered the public's elation by conjecturing how Suleman became pregnant. Embryologists thought it unlikely that the octuplets were the result of natural conception, but rather the product of assisted reproductive technology (ART). The range of ART options that might have been used included in vitro fertilization (IVF) or intrauterine insemination (IUI), with partner or donor sperm. As answers to various questions unfolded, there was a rising tide of sentiment against Suleman, and as the din of chastisement grew louder, I began to wonder why so few mainstream reproductive rights groups weighed in on the discussions. My interest was piqued since Suleman's utilization of ART quite clearly reflects the reproductive rights movement's goals of access and choice. But there was more to this story than meets the eye. . . .

. . . I use Suleman's story to trouble the implications of her choice as this choice relates to the broader reproductive concerns of women of color, low-income women, and others whose reproduction is organized hierarchically in relation to White heterosexual women and those who can afford to pay for health services. . . .

The Landscape of Art

. . . From the low-tech strategies of artificial insemination (using turkey basters) to surrogate mothers as the solution for mostly White middle-class infertility, the breadth of the reproductive technology landscape has proliferated over the last 30 years. The technologies hold both promise and challenge. . . . Domestically analyses of ART encompasses, among other issues, ethics, health-related concerns, equitable access, and regulatory matters. From an ethical standpoint one central focus is to assess the meaning of life when money is involved in its creation (Spar 2006). As ART has developed into an industry many scholars have

centered their work on the sometimes problematic role that biotechnologies play in facilitating the exchange and consumption of human tissues, organs, and biological information (see, e.g., Franklin and Lock 2003).

. . . With regard to equity issues a major question that ART raises is its inaccessibility to all women given the often-high costs that can run into and beyond tens of thousands of dollars. And finally, there are regulatory issues. . . . While ART guidelines have been developed by the fertility industry in the USA, it is not illegal to not follow the standards. Consequently some have called this lack of regulatory oversight the "Wild West" of assisted reproduction (Spar 2009).

Not surprisingly the phrase *Wild West* in many ways illustrates the startlingly biased representations of Ms. Suleman that circulated. The media, blogging public, and fertility professionals used Ms. Suleman to police reproductive boundaries similarly to how marginalized women have been scrutinized, at almost every stage of their reproductive lives. The ways in which Suleman was cast, as unfit, and the possible policies that may be implemented as a consequence reflect a striking resemblance to the racial and class discourses controlling the "untamed" reproduction of marginalized or unqualified women in the past. Going back to 1939, for example, the Birth Control Federation developed the Negro Project, which sought to restrain Black women's fertility and childbearing based on the racist assumption that "Negroes" might outpopulate Whites. Moreover, it was argued that control was necessary to prevent those less intelligent and less fit from having and rearing children (Ross 1993). Clearly fecundity continues to echo earlier tensions at the intersection of race, class and reproduction. Paradoxically that angst, deepened by ART, encompasses both the fertility and infertility of Black and other women of color, poor and single women. This point is clarified by such comments as one made by Spar (2009) who wrote, "as reproductive technologies continue to expand, they are bringing us options that push the notion of personal choice to terrifying limits. Do we really want single, unemployed mothers of six (or anyone, really) to produce eight more babies?" . . .

Nadya Suleman's story cannot and should not be separated from interrogating ART and the reproductive rights movement, since Ms. Suleman ostensibly actualized the movements' stated goals of choice. What is of concern though is the apparent silence of mainstream reproductive rights groups from public debates about Suleman. Their omission or self-imposed exile from commenting on the issue left it to the media, fertility specialists, and the blogging public to shape Suleman's denigration. My critique of their absence is influenced by my participation with reproductive issues since 1974, as an activist, as Coordinator of the Reproductive Rights Education Project at Hunter College, working with the National Network of Abortion Funds (The Network), and as the former co-Chair of NARAL Pro-Choice New York. I left NARAL somewhat jaded because there seemed to be resistance to embracing a broad reproductive justice approach in favor of a reproductive choice perspective. While the latter centers on legal protections for women to obtain abortions, the former includes addressing housing and employment, among other issues. A reproductive justice approach emphasizes reproductive health, as well as the social, economic, and political power to make healthy decisions about one's body, sexuality, and reproduction. . . .

Let me make clear from the outset that I refer to this story to neither justify nor condemn Ms. Suleman's use of ART, nor to speculate on the logic of her maternal impulses. However, Suleman's scathing public treatment elucidates some of the broader implications of who ART is intended for, as well as the meaning of choice, which is inflected with race and class reproductive normativity.

Stratified Reproduction

On the day the octuplets were born, the *LA Times* reported in an update that the "event" was unbelievably rare. One medical professional claimed that the arrival of the eight infants, if it had been achieved by ART, was not a medical triumph but rather a serious complication. While the first blog responses on January 26 were positive, by 10:54 am on January 27—just one day after the birth—suspicions surfaced regarding the mother's intentions. Questions arose about why she would want so many children. By the 28th bloggers inquired if the woman had plotted to have that many children for monetary gain—a la Angelina Jolie or Jennifer Lopez; suggesting that she may have wanted to be paid for magazine exclusives which come with substantial compensation. Because the process by which Suleman had conceived was still unconfirmed

through January 28, newspaper reports increasingly incorporated medical professionals' assessment of the risks associated with high-order multiple births, with many emphasizing how unethical it would be for an IVF specialist to implant a large number of embryos—if in fact that was what happened. . . .

Then on January 29, the mother, Nadya, was "outed"—she already had six children at home being cared for by her mother while she was at the hospital. Upon this revelation, one blogger wrote: "Who know who the *dads* are?" [of the other six]. Another wrote, "Now she brings a [liter] litter of eight kids into an already over populated world. Those babies will cost taxpayers millions. I think this is criminal" (Posted by Joe 1/29/09 6:13 pm—LA *Times* Blog). But still there was too little information about who the parents were, allowing Ms. Suleman to escape the full denunciation based on her marital status. On February 9 Suleman's mother Angela confirmed that her daughter had undergone IVF. Professionals asked such questions as: Had she been appropriately counseled regarding reductive abortion of some of the fetuses since she already had six children? Which doctor might have assisted her? Medical professionals' concerns about the conception process and the medical risks continued to center on the questionable ethics of any fertility clinic that did not follow industry standards which limit implantation to two embryos. However, this discussion only lasted as long as it was assumed Suleman was married; an assumption based on the imagined social script that ART is only for people in sanctioned heterosexual relationships. When it was discovered Suleman was a single mother (although previously married) criticism against her crystallized. Initially, the fact that Suleman had a large number of children did not necessarily define her as an imperfect mother in the eyes of medical professionals. But trajectory of their questions revealed a sea change. It was only after the accrual of Suleman's nonnormative statuses came to light, that her childbearing decisions constituted bad judgment and bad mothering. In thinking about the children's birth and health, the potential cause of harm was redirected away from the ethics of the fertility clinic and directed toward Ms. Suleman for her irresponsibility and moral ineptitude.

As for some members of the blogging public "the miracle" turned into disgust, which seemed to be fueled in part by an inability to "profile" the woman who gave birth. On February 5, for example, in a *Good Morning America* interview Suleman's newly hired publicist Joanne Killeen was asked by Diane Sawyer, "Who is this woman? We know nothing about her." Since no pictures of Suleman had been released, newscasters had no idea what she looked like, making it difficult to use visual cues to determine class status, educational achievements and race or ethnic categories. Seemingly, her unknown identity frustrated attempts to establish the legitimacy of both her maternal aspirations and her use of ART.

Interestingly, for bloggers, the missing information about Suleman's class and race resulted in indexing her citizenship status and then her race. It was her fertility that became the marker identifying Suleman as an illegal alien evidenced by this blog entry "Does anyone know if the mother is 'Legal'? I still remember the last story the *Los Angeles Times* ran about the illegal alien mom who used fertility drugs and ended up with 10 kids, all at California [T]axpayer expense" (Posted by Skip 1/27/09 at 11:29 am). Shortly thereafter another blogger claimed that Suleman was African American. Cumulatively the inferences were that "illegal" and African American women are hyperreproductive. Another blogger hoped that the Superbowl would overshadow the "welfare baby momma" news. From there it did not take long for an ideological default to be asserted: she was on welfare. In fact, Ms. Suleman received $460 a month in food stamps and disability payments for two of her six children. It should be pointed out that welfare includes government programs that provide benefits and economic supports to no- and low-income people. But the negative shroud of welfare, erroneously associated as it is with people of color and single mothers who presumably take advantage of the system by having more children, overrode any possibility that Suleman might have just wanted to be a mother. By using the welfare card to justify denigrating Suleman's decision to have children using IVF, what was also accomplished was that the right to use ART was inextricably linked to White middle-class normativity in the construction of family making.

. . . Once it became clear that she had been a stay-at-home mom with an unknown source of income, Suleman "achieved" a level of toxicity replicating a decades-old stereotype that single and low-income or poor women are bad mothers (Ladd-Taylor and Umansky 1997). This logic led to the view that she should be punished, and Suleman even received death threats. Thus it was no surprise when bloggers and media personalities such as Bill O'Reilly and radio host Dr. Carole

Lieberman demanded either Suleman's arrest or that she have her children removed based on the argument that although having 14 children was not abuse, there is bound to be some form of neglect in the future.

Essentially Suleman, vis-à-vis her childbearing, was vilified in much the same way that low-income and women of color have been in the past for their reproductive acts. As is so often the case, assessments of women's childbearing is related to race and class. For example in a response to a Salon.com inquiry about Suleman, Lynn Paltrow, Executive Director of National Advocates for Pregnant Women, remarked that when a pregnant woman is not brown or black and the drugs/technologies are provided by big pharmaceutical the discussion (of reproduction) focuses on questions of ethics. She went on to say that when drugs/technologies are related to low income, and women of color and their reproduction, the focus is on punishment through the criminal justice or child welfare system. Take as one example the rising arrests of pregnant women who test positive for drugs and are then charged with child abuse (reinterpreted as fetal abuse) for delivering drugs to a minor either through the umbilical cord or breast milk. In some cases women are charged with homicide if the baby is stillborn or is born and then dies. Yet there is differential treatment of mothers at the intersection of race and the drugs used. Campbell (2000) concludes that the type of drugs White women use (such as methamphetamine) does not register the same portrayal or castigation as mothers of color who use such drugs as crack. Legal scholar Dorothy Roberts (1997) also points out that most of the women arrested while pregnant and criminally charged are poor and Black. These observations are clearly congruent with the reproductive control, stigmatization and criminalization of what I call "particular others"—those who are valued differentially based on race, ethnicity, citizenship, class, nationality, sexuality and gender (Silliman et al. 2004, 4).

Backlash against "particular other" women and their reproductive desires [is] evident in the representational and linguistic repertoires often used to describe them. One example is when they are referenced in nonhuman terms such as . . . [the] moniker "octo-mom" . . . to describe the fact that she had eight children and to summon up an image of the notorious invertebrate with eight arms. Deploying the term *octo-mom* generated images of Suleman's supposedly questionable subhuman qualities making it easier to condemn her reproductive decisions. . . .

Technologies associated with infertility, according to Quiroga (2007), are often directed to creating families that reproduce the heteropatriarchal norm. . . . Ms. Suleman's Iraqi–Latvian background, although identified later during the media blitz, came too late to rescue her from being maligned relative to the dominant racial privilege associated with ART. She had already been "marked," if you will, as a "particular other" despite her ethnicity. . . .

One might even argue that her marital status, the number of children she had, and her Middle Eastern / Eastern European parentage conspired to "primitivize" her as against the celebrated White middle-class standard of motherhood, making her culturally ineligible for IVF.

Further, in terms of kinship, Ms. Suleman, as a single woman, was not viewed as having a "real" family. . . . Nadya Suleman may be seen as a casualty in the process of stratified reproduction, whereby her right to reproduce and nurture was denounced because she was single, had no verifiable source of income, and was an inadequate representative of whiteness. This, despite Ms. Suleman's constant claim of wanting a large family and saying that all she wanted in life was to be [a] mother (Garrison and Yoshino 2009). In the court of public, medical professional, and elite media opinion, Suleman violated the stratified privileges associated with ART and maternalism, leading to calls for measures to circumscribe the choice she made. How is choice recast in this case? . . .

Neoliberal Consumption and Reproductive Choice

. . . [R]eproductive rights and choices operate in a marketplace characterized by consumption, marketing, and commercialization geared to White women (Craven 2007). To illustrate this point a recent Newsweek.com article titled "Have Another Fertilitini" (Kalb 2009) is accompanied by a photo of a young White woman wearing a belt with a clock for a buckle. The article reports on the Fertility Association's launch of a series titled "Manicures and Martinis" at the upscale Dashing Diva Nail Salons in New York City. It is hoped that the program will go national and is being billed as a series of 1-hour conversations about reproductive health targeting women in their 20s and 30s. Participants will learn from leading fertility experts about the reality of the biological clock and other risk factors for infertility. Narrow in scope, the informational series on reproductive health is limited to infertility issues, obscuring other reproductive justice concerns, such as childcare, that might also be germane in one's reproductive health decision making. But this focus makes a highly probable bet that the target audience will in fact only need to make decisions about delaying pregnancy as a result of prioritizing their careers, and how they might be able to address that problem later on.

Given the location of the salons and the content of the workshops, the women attending the "Fertilitini" events are likely to be White with either earnings or potential earnings that will enable them to afford fertility treatments, which routinely cost $10–15,000. Such costly treatments almost guarantee stratification in the direction of those with "means," the definition of which coalesces around race and affluence. For those without the means, ART, specifically IVF, can be prohibitively expensive. And, since there are 35 states that do not provide insurance coverage for ART, there is geographic stratification as well. These very facts prompt a falsity about participating in the marketplace of reproductive services. Touted as an open market accessible to all, ART is in fact highly restricted both economically and geographically. Here again, Ms. Suleman's story is instructive. She took advantage of a reproductive option using a portion of a $165,000 settlement received after a work-related injury, to pay to have six embryos implanted—two of which split. Ironically, while she complied with two constructed ideologies, that of maternalism and consumption, some saw Ms. Suleman's choice to participate in the reproductive marketplace to actualize her maternalist impulse (whatever the reasons) as an abomination of science and morality. . . .

Ms. Suleman's choice and her access to ART generated ire which was fueled by questioning her judgment and denaturalizing her, a project in which her mother and to a lesser degree her father participated. Her mother commented that instead of "becoming a kindergarten teacher or something, she started having them, but not the normal way" (Associated Press 2009). There were further insinuations that Ms. Suleman had mental health issues, and some television broadcasters made provocative comments saying that Suleman would not be able to love 14 children; she has an Angelina Jolie fetish; and that her priorities were mixed up because she got her nails done after the delivery and release from the hospital. . . .

Interest in restricting Suleman's choice represents a clumsy backlash against the valorization of individualism and the coherency of choice. How was this achieved? By constructing a neurotic profile of Suleman. It was suggested that she was psychologically and economically incapable of raising children and should therefore be prevented from actualizing the choice she made. Inadequacy as the rationale for controlling reproduction sits in contradistinction to neoliberal assumptions of free choice and the role that race plays therein. To get the relationship between the two one must ask: Are questions about using ART and the possibility of having to raise large families being asked of married White middle-class women? Evidently race, marital status, and class results in varying degrees of acceptance with regard to having large families especially when they are formed through reproductive technology. We see this in the more positive depiction bestowed upon two large families, the first being Jon and Kate Gosselin, a married couple with eight children and the stars of their own TLC show, *Jon & Kate Plus Eight*. Kate underwent fertility treatments, first having twins, followed by more treatments which resulted in the birth of sextuplets. For several years the public has watched this reality TV show with great interest, and although the tides of public support have turned somewhat against the Gosselins due to infidelity and other issues, questions about their rights to have used ART have not been as virulent as against Suleman (see Stelter 2009). A second example of a circumstance in which large families are deemed acceptable, even valorized, rests with Michelle and Jim Bob Duggar who have 18 children and are also the subjects of a TLC program, *18 Kids and Counting*. In the Duggars' case, their religious beliefs justify the number of children they have. At the same time their source of income, primarily from rental property, helps solidify the construction of White heteronormative families achieved through marital and class status. . . .

The Reproductive Choice Conundrum

. . . In the context of the broad themes that emerged from Nadya Suleman's story, it is curious that no mainstream reproductive rights organization participated in the debates. . . . [T]he silence rendered despite how the story was represented in the media and on blogs is disturbing because the conclusions that circulated in the public sphere included Suleman being marginalized, symbolically criminalized, and castigated for her maternalism and her reproductive decisions and process.

These conclusions speak to some of the ideological and political incongruences surrounding the politics of reproduction. . . . "[C]hoice," as I have argued earlier, can be conditional. It is "choice" that is of concern to the mainstream reproductive rights organizations, and the problem is that the lure of "choice" obscures the legitimate needs and concerns of women who do not have any. . . . "[C]hoice" rests on the availability of resources and sanctioned status; without resources and status some women are unable to actualize "choice" in the same way that others might. Prochoice language has framed the work of mainstream reproductive rights organizations, which have historically engaged in single issue organizing: Abortion. My reading of prochoice groups . . . is they focus on the moral culpability of people who have children but may not have the power to protect the life of their children. This is why pro-choice groups for example have not challenged the criminalization of pregnant women of color, discussed earlier.

Further the "choice" framework rests on consumerist ideas of free choice that operates neatly with the neoliberal stance of individualism. In the Suleman case, it was her right not as a citizen but as a consumer of goods and services that was challenged. Challenging her decision to use IVF and then to carry all of the implanted eggs to come to term illustrates one [problem] of neoliberalism. It creates a hierarchy among women based on who is capable of making "legitimate" choices (. . . Solinger 2002, 6). In the marketplace of reproductive services, then, "choice" serves in the interest of those with access and the privilege of legitimacy, trumping the "choices" of those in need. Because choices can be reined in, it is consistent to withdraw reproductive options from any number of categorically marginalized women including poor women who, for example, have experienced the consequences of restrictive reproductive policy in the form of the Hyde Amendment, which eliminated federal funding for abortion (Smith 2005, 128).

This is where reproductive justice is more efficacious because it is concerned with rights that are accessible regardless of the woman's resources. The justice approach is organized around the particular understanding that women of color have of their reproductive needs and operates within a political agenda that seeks to make linkages between all women's oppression, their agency, and reproductive rights. . . . A reproductive justice approach does not condemn Suleman for her choice but asks what supports does she have a right to as a person raising 14 children?

In the absence of principles and politics guided by reproductive justice, few mainstream groups opposed Suleman's public condemnation, and few challenged the harmful discourse, which was the very same discourse that has dominated marginalized women's reproductive rights. This left an awkward opening to undermine political projects seeking to secure the full articulation of rights to information, birth control, economic resources, and the multitude of supports needed to control fertility, activate fertility, raise children, select birthing options, and live in fundamentally good housing, among other concerns. With too few critiques for example, of the call for state regulatory agencies to investigate and remove Suleman's children, other women—poor and low-income, women of color, disabled women and lesbians—were put at risk for being subjected to similar punitive demands. . . .

. . . [T]he Nadya Suleman story . . . demonstrates the fragility of the choice framework and complicates the implications of ART, where race, class, marital status, and family formation intersect. . . . [I]n terms of underlying assumptions about the achievement of perfect motherhood, Suleman was portrayed as a "bad" mother. In contradistinction to Suleman, a "good" mother would not choose to have a child if she were poor or low-income, and/or single. As well no "good" mother would choose to have a child if she were not White, or White enough. Using this logic, poor, low-income, single and non-White women should not seek to have children.

Suleman's case also reveals two crises, both imagined. One is that White middle-class women have fertility problems that should be addressed. The other is that women of color, or women marked as being of color, poor or low-income women, and single women do not have fertility problems that should be addressed. While arguing for the "choice" to use ART by deserving White middle-class women, this construct simultaneously limits the understanding of reproductive justice issues for "particular other" women as one of having to control their reproduction in terms of preventing conception or birth. But also the fact remains that illegible women are subjected to a discursive failure in the domain of choice. They neither possess legitimate claims to the choice to have children through ART nor legitimate claims to not have children (specifically abortions).

References

Associated Press. 2009. Grandma: Octuplets Mom Obsessed with Kids. MSNBC.com, January 31. http://www.msnbc.msn.com/id/28948599 (accessed January 31, 2009).

Campbell, Nancy. 2000. Using Women: Gender, Drug Policy, and Social Justice. New York: Routledge.

Craven, Christa. 2007. A Consumer's Right to Choose a Midwife: Shifting Meanings for Reproductive Rights Under Neoliberalism. American Anthropologist 109(4):701–712.

Franklin, Sarah, and Margaret Lock. 2003. Rethinking Life and Death: Toward Anthropology of the Biosciences. Santa Fe, NM: SAR Press.

Garrison, Jessica, and Kimi Yoshino. 2009. Octuplets' Mother Obsessed with Children. LA Times, January 30. http://latimesblogs.latimes.com/lanow/2009/01/nadya-sulemans.html (accessed April 28, 2009).

Kalb, Claudia. 2009. Have Another Fertilitini. Newsweek. January 27. http://www.newsweek.com/id/181840 (accessed January 30, 2009).

Ladd-Taylor, Molly, and Lauri Umansky, eds. 1997. "Bad" Mothers: The Politics of Blame in Twentieth-Century America. New York: NYU Press.

Lyman, Rick. 1998. Mother of the Octuplets Goes Home to Recover. New York Times, December 31.

Quiroga, Seline Szkupinski. 2007. Blood Is Thicker than Water: Policing Donor Insemination and the Reproduction of Whiteness. Hypatia 22(2): 143–161.

Roberts, Dorothy. 1997. Killing the Black Body: Race, Reproduction, and the Meaning of Liberty. New York: Pantheon Books.

Ross, Loretta J. 1993. African-American Women and Abortion: 1800–1970. In Theorizing Black Feminisms: The Visionary Pragmatism of Black Women. Stanlie Myrise James and Abena P. A. Busia, eds. Pp. 141–169. New York: Routledge.

Silliman, Jael, Marlene Gerber Fried, Loretta Ross, and Elena R. Gutierrez. 2004. Undivided Rights: Women of Color Organize for Reproductive Justice. Boston, MA: South End Press.

Smith, Andrea. 2005. Beyond Pro-Choice Versus Pro-Life: Women of Color and Reproductive Justice. NWSA Journal (Spring) 17(1):119–140.

Solinger, Rickie. 2002. Beggars and Choosers. New York: Hill and Wang.

Spar, Debora. 2006. The Baby Business: How Money, Science, and Politics Drive the Commerce of Conception. Boston, MA: Harvard Business Press.

Spar, Debora. 2009. "Taming the Wild West of Assisted Reproduction." Columbia Spectator Online Edition. February 26. http://www.columbiaspectator. com/2009/02/26/taming-wild-west-assisted- reproduction (accessed February 27, 2009).

Stelter, Brian. 2009. "Jon & Kate 'Are a Business at This Point,' Magazine Editor Says." May 27, 2009. http:// mediadecoder.blogs.nytimes.com/2009/05/27/ jon-kate-are-a-business-at-this-point-magazine- editor-says/ (accessed June 14, 2009).

IN THE NEWS The 2014 Ebola Response and Anthropology

When the 2014 Ebola outbreak occurred, teams of medical professionals from the World Health Organization (WHO), Doctors Without Borders, and other relief agencies arrived in Guinea, Liberia, and Sierra Leone to help fight the deadly virus and to treat and contain those who were affected. Anthropologists were critical to helping foreign aid personnel understand the sociocultural context that contributed to the spread of the virus. The epidemic—and its initial treatment by medical professionals—highlights the illness vs. disease distinction. Diseases are considered within the biomedical realm, whereas illnesses take culture and social relations into consideration.

The points of transmission for Ebola are, at their very core, social. Yet medical professionals were alienating local peoples by not paying attention to local cultural, behavioral, and social issues that surround transmission and care. Nor did they demonstrate cultural understanding by respecting local burial beliefs and practices. For instance, local beliefs and traditions surrounding death include rituals that require people to touch the corpse as they prepare them for burial. In "How Anthropologists Help Medics Fight Ebola in Guinea," Amazath Fassassi describes anthropologist Sylvain Landry Faye's work with WHO to facilitate an understanding between local populations and medical teams. For instance, among the Kissi ethnic group in southern Guinea, it is forbidden to bury a woman with a baby inside her. However, when it is impossible to extract the fetus through an operation, the Kissi will hold a reparation ritual. Applying knowledge of Kissi cultural belief systems, Faye's team found an acceptable solution for the Kissi burial, and WHO paid for the ritual.

There are several resources available online that describe initial missteps by medical teams and the significance that anthropologists made in addressing the epidemic. Explore the online articles as well as the American Anthropological Association's Emergency Ebola Response workshop report, "Strengthening West African Health Care System to Stop Ebola: Anthropologists Offer Insights," which resulted from a November 5–7, 2014, workshop of leading anthropologists with expertise in the subject matter and region.

 Visit www.oup.com/us/brondo for weblinks.

DR. ROBERT HAHN

Medical Anthropologist and Coordinating Scientist at the Centers for Disease Control and Prevention

Figure 6.6.1

Robert Hahn (photo by Carolyn Beeker)

How did you get interested in anthropology?

I am the son of German immigrants who fled injustice and were committed to social justice and to education. In college, I could not decide what to study, so I chose anthropology because it was described as "the science of man," and I thought that with this background, I could probably do anything I wanted. I was fascinated by cultural relativity and the notion that culture and society made sense as a system.

How did you gain employment at the CDC?

After completing my PhD and dabbling in academia without much success or satisfaction, I decided to put my anthropology to use for the solution of human problems. I was particularly drawn to the intersection between mind, body, and society, so my decision to turn first to medical anthropology and then public health was fairly straightforward. I participated in several programs related to medical anthropology and then got a Masters in Public Health at the University of Washington. In 1986, I joined the Epidemic Intelligence Service at the US Centers for Disease Control where I was assigned to conduct research on sexually transmitted diseases. I then secured a regular CDC position in which I have since worked on a wide variety of topics, including how the government classifies "race" and "ethnicity," and how this process affects our health statistics. I have also worked on projects in Hungary, Brazil, the Cameroon, and Niger—often on focusing on how to improve data systems to advance public health.

What do you do on a day-to-day basis in your job? How do you put anthropology to use in your work?

Since the fall of 1999, I have been part of a terrific project at the CDC called "The Guide to Community Preventive Services" (www.thecommunityguide.org) whose goal is to evaluate the state of knowledge on interventions in the major fields of public health. We synthesize all available scientific evidence on interventions such as tobacco taxes, automobile safety laws, immunization programs, and cancer screening to determine what works, what might be harmful, and what lacks sufficient evidence to draw conclusions. I have led teams looking at (1) the prevention of violence by and against juveniles, (2) the reduction of excessive alcohol consumption, and(3) for the past 6 years, the promotion of long-term health among low-income and minority populations in the U.S. The goal of the current project is referred to as "health equity." Anthropology always informs my work as I consider how social organization and culture affect institutions, behavior, and change.

How did your training in anthropology prepare you for the work that you do?

I believed that there are good and harmful aspects of anthropological training, at least as I experienced and observed it. The anthropological habit of listening and seeking the perspectives of others is invaluable. But, paradoxically, I think that anthropologists are often trained to communicate in a language that is impenetrable to others. I have trouble understanding what I wrote in my early days. I spent my early years at CDC relearning how to write in plain English. While anthropologists should be optimally able to communicate across cultural and disciplinary boundaries, we often fail in this to the detriment of our field, its understanding, and uptake.

Do you identify as an applied, engaged, or public anthropologist? What do these titles mean to you?

If forced to choose, I would choose "applied," but I don't see much difference among these. What they have in common is a rejection of ivory tower purism which mistakenly professes that the solution of social problems is not the proper work of the scholar and contaminates scholarly efforts. Inaction is passive endorsement of the status quo and its many problems.

You spent some time working as a Capitol Hill Fellow. How and why did this come about? What does an Anthropologist - Congressional fellow do?

The CDC provides long-term training opportunities to its employees. I was fortunate to participate in a

Government Affairs Fellowship in which I worked in the U.S. House of Representatives in 1999. I first worked for the House Veterans Committee where I was asked to evaluate an extensive program to help veterans infected with Hepatitis C. I then worked with Congresswoman Louise Slaughter on her genetic information privacy bill. Congress was a fascinating field site where my focus was the use (and non-use) of science in decision making. This place was as exotic as the indigenous Amazon where I did my dissertation research.

You've written several influential books and articles on anthropology and public health. Who is your main audience and why?

One of my basic goals in public health has been to persuade this traditionally infectious-disease, medically oriented occupation to recognize the importance of anthropology and other social sciences and to use these disciplines. Anthropologists can easily figure this out, but it is critical and more challenging to persuade practitioners of public health.

What do you see as the future for anthropology and public health?

Anthropology should be a major player in the future of public health, along with medicine, laboratory science, and epidemiology. Understanding public health issues, solving public health problems, designing, implementing, and evaluating public health programs—success in these activities NEEDS anthropology. The public health community may not know it yet, which is why we have to learn their language and communicate with them in clear, jargon-free language, to demonstrate these needs. In the early 1990s, I was asked to start up the Behavioral and Social Science Working Group at CDC to foster the development of these disciplines as part of public health. I led a team that launched this group which thrives today. Communication by academic anthropologists remains a challenge.

ABOUT THE ANTHROPOLOGIST

Occupation: Coordinating Scientist, Community Guide Branch; Division of Public Health Information and Dissemination; Center for Surveillance, Epidemiology, and Laboratory Services, Office of Public Health Scientific Services at the Centers for Disease Control
Education: PhD (Harvard) and MPH (University of Washington)
Hobbies: I like to design and make things. I have been making wire sculptures for more than a decade now, and I also make light fixtures.

CAREER ADVICE

Advice for students interested in a career in medical anthropology at the CDC:

- Learn basic epidemiology, and get experience in a public health setting.
- It's a great field, rich in learning and powerful in benefiting lives.

DR. IPPOLYTOS KALOFONOS

Medical Anthropologist and Psychiatrist

Figure 6.7.1

Ippolytos Kalofonos.

How did you become interested in pursuing both training as a medical doctor and as a PhD in anthropology?

I was an undergraduate premed at UCSD. I began as a biochemistry major and started working in a molecular biology research lab during my second year. I was soon drawn to life on a different scale. I became interested in the broader issues relating to local, state-wide, national, and global forms of inequality that were swirling around me. Affirmative action was repealed while I was a student and I participated in UCSD and UC-wide activism to advocate for continued attention to racial and economic disparities in California public education. The infamous Proposition 187, a legislative initiative denying prenatal and emergency care to undocumented immigrants also passed in California while I was a student. I began volunteering in a Red Cross emergency room in Tijuana on the weekends, and was really struck by differences and similarities on either sides of the border.

I discovered anthropology when I heard Lola Romanucci-Ross give an introductory talk on the anthropology of medicine as a guest lecturer in an undergraduate study skills seminar. I was inspired as it seemed to be the place where my interest in health, medicine and social context came together. That lecture sparked an exploration that in many ways is ongoing. I decided to study abroad in Oaxaca, Mexico, because I wanted to improve my Spanish and learn about traditional healing. The program I chose happened to focus on critical development studies, and my eyes were opened to much more than traditional medicine.

When I returned from studying abroad, I changed my major to anthropology. As I prepared for life after graduation and considered my interest in anthropology and medicine, my undergraduate mentor advised me to choose between one or the other. After I graduated, I attended the Joint Medical Program at University of California, San Francisco CSF & Berkeley that included a master's in health sciences degree integrated with the medical school curriculum. I spent a year off from school studying leptospirosis epidemics in Salvador, Brazil, as an epidemiologist. It was that experience, of showing up to people's homes, listening to their rich stories about their daily lives that made me realize I really wanted to be an anthropologist and to delve into the complexities of everyday life.

When I returned to medical school, I met some medical students who were pursuing PhDs in medical anthropology and I felt like I had met my people. I applied for the joint PhD program in medical anthropology at UCSF and Berkeley after completing my preclinical coursework, the first half of medical school, and I entered the MD/PhD track. For my dissertation research, rather than returning to Brazil as I had planned to, I went to another Portuguese-speaking country, Mozambique, where AIDS testing and treatment programs were just being initiated, and I looked at how these global health interventions became a part of everyday life, and how people individually and collectively responded to AIDS treatment programs. After I finished my PhD in 2008 I completed medical school and decided to pursue residency training in psychiatry. In residency I became interested in the diverse ways mental illness is understood and responded to, both within and outside of psychiatry.

Tell us a little about your research.

My research examines how social, cultural, and political-economic contexts shape the distribution and experience of illness and health care. I am particularly interested in how health, illness, and therapeutic systems shape subjectivity and sociality.

I have a book manuscript in progress with the University of California Press Public Anthropology series that is entitled *All I Eat Is ARVs: Surviving the AIDS Economy in Central Mozambique*. It is an ethnography of the scale-up of AIDS testing, treatment, and care in Mozambique. The tale of the AIDS treatment scale-up, focused on providing antiretroviral medication (ARVs), is often told as a remarkable story of contemporary humanitarian intervention on a grand scale, of the potential of technology and innovation to save lives in out-of-the-way places.

My ethnography looks at how the scale-up actually played out in ordinary people's lives, those positioned as the "target population." I argue that AIDS treatment interventions have important impacts beyond saving and extending lives. Even while antiretroviral medication saved millions of lives in Mozambique, AIDS treatment both exposed and exacerbated the precarious circumstances that allowed to epidemic to flourish in the first place—hunger, food insecurity, poverty, underemployment, and inequality. The influx of resources for AIDS treatment into one of the poorest countries in the world turned HIV into a resource and contributed to the emergence of an AIDS economy. New opportunities opened up—free medical services for those testing positive, the potential for other material benefits, such as food aid and employment, and support for community organizations mobilizing to address AIDS. There was hope and movement around AIDS. As people's health returned, their focus shifted from surviving their illness to securing a sufficient livelihood and regaining full social participation, with reciprocity, respect, and recognition. The biological focus of the treatment effort, of getting drugs into bodies, was ultimately seen as falling short of the care many Mozambicans sought. This was articulated by a phrase I heard repeated by people

receiving treatment for AIDS—"All I eat is ARVs." This phrase served as a clarion critique of an intervention that exacerbated hunger without adequately addressing it, even as it saved lives. From the perspective of people being treated for AIDS in Mozambique, hunger infected and altered the therapeutic experience. This hunger expressed both a painful embodied reality and a powerful moral metaphor for antisocial accumulation. These dynamics highlight the narrow scope of the vision of care of this global health intervention, a vision structured by notions of scarcity and sustainability.

I am currently interested in how notions of the self and the social are conceptualized in contemporary forms of psychiatric knowledge production and treatment. I am currently involved in a project looking at how individuals and their families understand and respond to symptoms of psychosis. I am also interested the ways mental illness can shape the life courses of individuals and social groups, and in the moral economies of social security disability insurance in the contemporary United States.

What is the most meaningful project you've worked on over the course of your career? Why?

All of the projects I've worked on have been meaningful for different reasons. My first project was my undergraduate thesis that looked at access to prenatal care for Latina immigrants in the wake of the passage of legislation restricting access to medical care for undocumented immigrants in San Diego. It was very meaningful because I had a chance to examine the impacts of public policy and the surrounding discourses on individual lives in my own community.

My work in Mozambique has been meaningful as well, for several reasons. For one, I have been able to contribute to a discussion that closely examined the impact of an intervention that was deemed by many as an unassailable good. At the time I started my research, there seemed to be a reluctance to critique aspects of the global expansion of AIDS treatment, and that has changed, particularly in terms of the role of hunger and food insecurity in AIDS treatment.

My current interest in severe mental illness comes out of my clinical work with this marginalized and extremely vulnerable population. People with severe mental illness in the United States have a life expectancy on the average 20 years less than the general population without severe mental illness, and globally, including in the United States, these people are more often the victims of violence than the recipients of care. Ideas of what constitutes care, however, are contested. Anthropology has a lot to bring to this discussion with nuanced and sophisticated perspectives of subjectivity and social relations.

In all this work, the challenge is to take the stories people tell me and to find ways to bring those into discussions about care, justice, equity, and ultimately, what it means to be human.

Do you identify as an applied, engaged, or public anthropologist? What do these titles mean to you?

To some extent, all of the above, though I would add I identify as a social medicine practitioner and researcher. I see my task as engaging anthropological theory and methods with health services and public policy, identifying, redefining, and understanding particular sets of concerns in ways that are understandable and accessible, but still are true to the complexity of everyday life.

Who is your main audience for your research and writing, and why?

The publics I have most consistently addressed in my work would include researchers, policy-makers, clinicians, patients and families of patients; an interdisciplinary audience concerned with health—anthropologists, epidemiologists, physicians, nurses; policy makers, students. I also see my work as using health as a lens to understand broader social dynamics, so understanding contemporary Mozambique through the lens of global AIDS interventions, while at the same time understanding health through the experiences of particular people in particular places, so understanding global AIDS interventions through the lens of contemporary Mozambique.

ABOUT THE ANTHROPOLOGIST

Occupation: Fellow, Robert Wood Johnson Foundation Clinical Scholars Program, UCLA/VA
Education: PhD & MD University of California, San Francisco; BA University of California, San Diego
Hobbies: Rock-climbing; spending time with family.

CAREER ADVICE

Advice for students interested in medical anthropology and global mental health:

- Be comfortable working collaboratively and across disciplines.
- Don't be afraid to ask the big questions: How do people survive? What is care? What is psychosis? What is mental health?

PART 7

Taste, Food, and Foodways

Anthropologists who study food and culture recognize that there is much more to food than it being a source of nutrition. Food is central to understanding culture. We organize our lives around food, from how we produce it to how we connect to others through sharing meals or define our tastes and preferences in contrast to others. The selections in this section begin with an anthropological classic, "Eating Christmas in the Kalahari" by Richard Borshay Lee (Reading 7.1). In it, Lee describes the reaction of his Ju/'hoansi hosts when he purchases the largest ox he can find for a Christmas meal as a way to thank the community for participating in his research project. Confused by the way in which his informants mocked and insulted his food gift, Lee's account reveals how different cultures have their own unique customs for giving and receiving food. This piece introduces us to the idea that food sharing communicates and solidifies social relations.

In addition to communicating social relationships, food preferences also communicate identities. In considering how food preferences communicate identity, anthropologists focus their attention on "taste." Taste not only refers to the sense that allows people to detect flavor, but it is also a concept that captures the social distinction associated with particular foods. One's "taste" or food preferences communicate their status, prestige, and overall location within their society's social hierarchy. Consider how members of the upper class are associated with preferences for particular foodstuffs, or how different genders are associated with distinct preferences for food.

Taste is something that is explored in both Richard Wilk's "Real Belizean Food: Building Local Identity in the Transnational Caribbean"

(Reading 7.2) and Paige West's "Making the Market: Specialty Coffee, Generational Pitches, and Papua New Guinea" (Reading 7.3). Drawing on decades of research on foodways in Belize, Richard Wilk explores how taste hierarchies are dynamic and shaped by transnational flows. In this piece, we consider how taste hierarchies change as more and more people connect across the globe, and individuals adopt new tastes to assert "modern" or "cultured" identities. While Wilk considers the identities that people adopt by choosing to eat particular foods, West asks us to think about the stories that marketers sell when advertising particular foods and whether they are truth or fantasy. Her focus is on fair trade, organic coffees, which are marketed to buyers in ways that appeal to their desire to "help" indigenous coffee farmers out of poverty while consuming an environmentally sustainable and socially just product. West concludes that the "fantasy" specialty coffee marketers peddle obscures the social reality of extreme inequality that defines the coffee industry.

West's piece shares an analytical frame with the remaining pieces. West's work is grounded in a theoretical approach called "political ecology," which analyzes the ways in which the environmental arena reflects the structured relations of power and inequality. As such, her work uncovers the role that 1980s neoliberal development policies played in creating the inequalities that pervade the lives of coffee farmers in New Guinea. Similarly, in "Migrant Farmworkers and the Pain of Picking" (Reading 7.4), Seth Holmes uncovers the structural causes that create physical and emotional suffering and undermine healthcare access for migrant farmworkers in the fresh fruit industry. Like Jim Yong Kim (Anthropology in Action, Part 1) and Paul Farmer (Reading 6.1), Holmes is a physician-anthropologist whose work focuses on understanding and alleviating health inequalities among the world's most vulnerable populations. His selection reveals the pain and suffering associated with work on berry farms in the United States through the stories of three indigenous migrants from Oaxaca, Mexico, unveiling the structural, symbolic, and political violence that workers face in the global food market.

Like Holmes, Donald D. Stull's work focuses on the lived realities of immigrant farmworkers in the United States. In "American Meat" (Reading 7.5), a piece written exclusively for this book, Stull echoes West and Holmes in inciting readers to consider first the people behind their food production, and not just the food itself. His selection draws on decades of applied ethnographic research on the meatpacking industry, sadly showing that little has changed to make packinghouses safer or more sustainable and socially just places of employment. The selection closes with some suggestions for readers who are interested in adopting alternatives to the dominant food system.

The "Anthropology in Practice" feature dovetails well with Stull's call for viable alternative food systems. This section features Dr. Micah Trapp, a food anthropologist who was trained in public anthropology at American University, and is currently an assistant professor of anthropology at the University of Memphis. Dr. Trapp is an engaged anthropologist working in collaboration with several Memphis-based nonprofits and schools to build capacity for sustainable local food systems through urban agriculture. In addition to her collaborative local work, Dr. Trapp continues to have a research agenda on humanitarianism and food aid among Liberian refugees in Ghana.

This section's "In the News" feature considers urban foraging, including dumpster-diving and the gathering of edibles in public parks and other public spaces. It dovetails well with Stull's and Trapp's discussion of alternative sustainable food systems.

KEY TERMS:

- Foodways
- Gift-giving
- Food preferences
- Taste hierarchies
- Political ecology
- Indigeneity
- Neoliberal economic development
- Migrant farmwork

- Structural violence
- Meatpacking
- Community-supported agriculture (CSA)
- Farmers markets
- Urban agriculture
- School gardens
- Urban foraging

7.1 Eating Christmas in the Kalahari

RICHARD BORSHAY LEE

Anthropologists who study food and culture recognize that there is much more to food than it being a source of nutrition. Food, and the cultural practices surrounding its distribution and consumption, also reinforces and stabilizes social relationships. In this classic selection, Richard Lee tells a story of his choice to purchase and share the largest and must succulent ox he could find for a Christmas meal among the Ju/'hoansi (who at that time were referred to by outsiders as !Kung Bushman). This gift, Lee's way of saying thank you to the community for participating in his study, was met with mockery and criticism as community members belittled and insulted his choice. This example of cross-cultural misunderstanding reveals different customs and social attitudes surrounding gift giving and food sharing.

Questions

1. How do the Ju/'hoansi typically respond to one another after a hunt? Why? What mistakes did Lee make by boasting about the black ox?
2. Why was Lee the perfect target for the charge of arrogance?
3. What does this story show about conducting fieldwork?

The !Kung Bushmen's knowledge of Christmas is third-hand. The London Missionary Society brought the holiday to the southern Tswana tribes in the early nineteenth century. Later, native catechists spread the idea far and wide among the Bantu-speaking pastoralists, even in the remotest corners of the Kalahari Desert. The Bushmen's idea of the Christmas story, stripped to its essentials, is "praise the birth of white man's god-chief"; what keeps their interest in the holiday high is the Tswana-Herero custom of slaughtering an ox for his Bushmen neighbors as an annual goodwill gesture. Since the 1930s, part of the Bushmen's annual round of activities has included a December congregation at the cattle posts for trading, marriage brokering, and several days of trance-dance feasting at which the local Tswana headman is host.

As a social anthropologist working with !Kung Bushmen, I found that the Christmas ox custom suited my purposes. I had come to the Kalahari to study the hunting and gathering subsistence economy of the !Kung, and to accomplish this it was essential not to provide them with food, share my own food, or interfere in any way with their foodgathering activities. While liberal handouts of tobacco and medical supplies were appreciated, they were scarcely adequate to erase the glaring disparity in wealth between the anthropologist, who maintained a two-month inventory of canned goods, and the Bushmen, who rarely had a day's supply of food on hand. My approach, while paying off in terms of data, left me open to frequent accusations of stinginess and hard-heartedness. By their lights, I was a miser.

Richard Borshay Lee. "Eating Christmas in the Kalahari." December 1969. *Natural History*, 14–22, 60–64. From *Natural History* December, 1969, copyright Natural History Magazine, Inc., 2015.

The Christmas ox was to be my way of saying thank you for the cooperation of the past year; and since it was to be our last Christmas in the field, I determined to slaughter the largest, meatiest ox that money could buy, insuring that the feast and trance dance would be a success.

Through December I kept my eyes open at the wells as the cattle were brought down for watering. Several animals were offered, but none had quite the grossness that I had in mind. Then, ten days before the holiday, a Herero friend led an ox of astonishing size and mass up to our camp. It was solid black, stood five feet high at the shoulder, had a five-foot span of horns, and must have weighed 1,200 pounds on the hoof. Food consumption calculations are my specialty, and I quickly figured that bones and viscera aside, there was enough meat—at least four pounds—for every man, woman, and child of the 150 Bushmen in the vicinity of /ai/ai who were expected at the feast.

Having found the right animal at last, I paid the Herero £20 ($56) and asked him to keep the beast with his herd until Christmas day. The next morning word spread among the people that the big solid black one was the ox chosen by /ontah (my Bushman name; it means, roughly, "whitey") for the Christmas feast. That afternoon I received the first delegation. Ben!a, an outspoken sixty-year-old mother of five, came to the point slowly.

"Where were you planning to eat Christmas?"

"Right here at /ai/ai," I replied.

"Alone or with others?"

"I expect to invite all the people to eat Christmas with me."

"Eat what?"

"I have purchased Yehave's black ox, and I am going to slaughter and cook it."

"That's what we were told at the well but refused to believe it until we heard it from yourself."

"Well, it's the black one," I replied expansively, although wondering what she was driving at.

"Oh, no!" Ben!a groaned, turning to her group. "They were right." Turning back to me she asked, "Do you expect us to eat that bag of bones?"

"Bag of bones! It's the biggest ox at /ai/ai."

"Big, yes, but old. And thin. Everybody knows there's no meat on that old ox. What did you expect us to eat off it, the horns?"

Everybody chuckled at Ben!a's one-liner as they walked away, but all I could manage was a weak grin.

That evening it was the turn of the young men. They came to sit at our evening fire. /gaugo, about my age, spoke to me man-to-man. "/ontah, you have always been square with us," he lied. "What has happened to change your heart? That sack of guts and bones of Yehave's will hardly feed one camp, let alone all the Bushmen around /ai/ai." And he proceeded to enumerate the seven camps in the /ai/ai vicinity, family by family. "Perhaps you have forgotten that we are not few, but many. Or are you too blind to tell the difference between a proper cow and an old wreck? That ox is thin to the point of death."

"Look, you guys," I retorted, "that is a beautiful animal, and I'm sure you will eat it with pleasure at Christmas."

"Of course we will eat it; it's food. But it won't fill us up to the point where we will have enough strength to dance. We will eat and go home to bed with stomachs rumbling."

That night as we turned in, I asked my wife, Nancy: "What did you think of the black ox?"

"It looked enormous to me. Why?"

"Well, about eight different people have told me I got gypped; that the ox is nothing but bones."

"What's the angle?" Nancy asked. "Did they have a better one to sell?"

"No, they just said that it was going to be a grim Christmas because there won't be enough meat to go around. Maybe I'll get an independent judge to look at the beast in the morning."

Bright and early, Halingisi, a Tswana cattle owner, appeared at our camp. But before I could ask him to give me his opinion on Yehave's black ox, he gave me the eye signal that indicated a confidential chat. We left the camp and sat down.

"/ontah, I'm surprised at you; you've lived here for three years and still haven't learned anything about cattle."

"But what else can a person do but choose the biggest, strongest animal one can find?" I retorted.

"Look, just because an animal is big doesn't mean that it has plenty of meat on it. The black one was a beauty when it was younger, but now it is thin to the point of death."

"Well, I've already bought it. What can I do at this stage?"

"Bought it already? I thought you were just considering it. Well, you'll have to kill it and serve it, I suppose. But don't expect much of a dance to follow."

My spirits dropped rapidly. I could believe that Ben!a and /gaugo just might be putting me on about the black ox, but Halingisi seemed to be an impartial critic. I went around that day feeling as though I had bought a lemon of a used car.

In the afternoon it was Tomazo's turn. Tomazo is a fine hunter, a top trance performer, and one of my most reliable informants. He approached the subject of the Christmas cow as part of my continuing Bushman education.

"My friend, the way it is with us Bushmen," he began, "is that we love meat. And even more than that, we love fat. When we hunt we always search for the fat ones, the ones dripping with layers of white fat: fat that turns into a clear, thick oil in the cooking pot, fat that slides down your gullet, fills your stomach and gives you a roaring diarrhea," he rhapsodized.

"So, feeling as we do," he continued, "it gives us pain to be served such a scrawny thing as Yehave's black ox. It is big, yes, and no doubt its giant bones are good for soup, but fat is what we really crave and so we will eat Christmas this year with a heavy heart."

The prospect of a gloomy Christmas now had me worried, so I asked Tomazo what I could do about it.

"Look for a fat one, a young one . . . smaller, but fat. Fat enough to make us //gom ('evacuate the bowels'), then we will be happy."

My suspicions were aroused when Tomazo said that he happened to know of a young, fat, barren cow that the owner was willing to part with. Was Toma working on commission, I wondered? But I dispelled this unworthy thought when we approached the Herero owner of the cow in question and found that he had decided not to sell.

The scrawny wreck of a Christmas ox now became the talk of the /ai/ai water hole and was the first news told to the outlying groups as they began to come in from the bush for the feast. What finally convinced me that real trouble might be brewing was the visit from u!au, an old conservative with a reputation for fierceness. His nickname meant spear and referred to an incident thirty years ago in which he had speared a man to death. He had an intense manner; fixing me with his eyes, he said in clipped tones:

"I have only just heard about the black ox today, or else I would have come here earlier. /ontah, do you honestly think you can serve meat like that to people and avoid a fight?" He paused, letting the implications sink in. "I don't mean fight you, /ontah; you are a white man. I mean a fight between Bushmen. There are many fierce ones here, and with such a small quantity of meat to distribute, how can you give everybody a fair share? Someone is sure to accuse another of taking too much or hogging all the choice pieces. Then you will see what happens when some go hungry while others eat."

The possibility of at least a serious argument struck me as all too real. I had witnessed the tension that surrounds the distribution of meat from a kudu or gemsbok kill, and had documented many arguments that sprang up from a real or imagined slight in meat distribution. The owners of a kill may spend up to two hours arranging and rearranging the piles of meat under the gaze of a circle of recipients before handing them out. And I also knew that the Christmas feast at /ai/ai would be bringing together groups that had feuded in the past.

Convinced now of the gravity of the situation, I went in earnest to search for a second cow; but all my inquiries failed to turn one up.

The Christmas feast was evidently going to be a disaster, and the incessant complaints about the meagerness of the ox had already taken the fun out of it for me. Moreover, I was getting bored with the wisecracks, and after losing my temper a few times, I resolved to serve the beast anyway. If the meat fell short, the hell with it. In the Bushmen idiom, I announced to all who would listen:

"I am a poor man and blind. If I have chosen one that is too old and too thin, we will eat it anyway and see if there is enough meat there to quiet the rumbling of our stomachs."

On hearing this speech, Ben!a offered me a rare word of comfort. "It's thin," she said philosophically, "but the bones will make a good soup."

At dawn Christmas morning, instinct told me to turn over the butchering and cooking to a friend and take off with Nancy to spend Christmas alone in the bush. But curiosity kept me from retreating. I wanted to see what such a scrawny ox looked like on butchering, and if there *was* going to be a fight, I wanted to catch every word of it. Anthropologists are incurable that way.

The great beast was driven up to our dancing ground, and a shot in the forehead dropped it in its tracks. Then, freshly cut branches were heaped around the fallen carcass to receive the meat. Ten men volunteered to help with the cutting. I asked /gaugo to make the breast bone cut. This cut, which begins the butchering process for most large game, offers easy access for removal of the viscera. But it also allows the hunter to spot check the amount of fat on the animal. A fat game animal carries a white layer up to an inch thick on the chest, while in a thin one, the knife will quickly cut to bone. All eyes fixed on his hand as /gaugo, dwarfed by the great carcass, knelt to the breast. The first cut opened a pool of solid white in the black skin. The second and third cut widened and deepened the creamy white. Still no bone. It was pure fat; it must have been two inches thick.

"Hey /gau," I burst out, "that ox is loaded with fat. What's this about the ox being too thin to bother eating? Are you out of your mind?"

"Fat?" /gau shot back, "You call that fat? This wreck is thin, sick, dead!" And he broke out laughing. So did everyone else. They rolled on the ground, paralyzed with laughter. Everybody laughed except me; I was thinking.

I ran back to the tent and burst in just as Nancy was getting up. "Hey, the black ox. It's fat as hell! They were kidding about it being too thin to eat. It was a joke or something. A put-on. Everyone is really delighted with it!"

"Some joke," my wife replied. "It was so funny that you were ready to pack up and leave /ai/ai."

If it had indeed been a joke, it had been an extraordinarily convincing one, and tinged, I thought, with more than a touch of malice as many jokes are. Nevertheless, that it was a joke lifted my spirits considerably, and I returned to the butchering site where the shape of the ox was rapidly disappearing under the axes and knives of the butchers. The atmosphere had become festive. Grinning broadly, their arms covered with blood well past the elbow, men packed chunks of meat into the big cast-iron cooking pots, fifty pounds to the load, and muttered and chuckled all the while about the thinness and worthlessness of the animal and /ontah's poor judgment.

We danced and ate that ox two days and two nights; we cooked and distributed fourteen potfuls of meat and no one went home hungry and no fights broke out.

But the "joke" stayed in my mind. I had a growing feeling that something important had happened in my relationship with the Bushmen and that the clue lay in the meaning of the joke. Several days later, when most of the people had dispersed back to the bush camps, I raised the question with Hakekgose, a Tswana man who had grown up among the !Kung, married a !Kung girl, and who probably knew their culture better than any other non-Bushman.

"With us whites," I began, "Christmas is supposed to be the day of friendship and brotherly love. What I can't figure out is why the Bushmen went to such lengths to criticize and belittle the ox I had bought for the feast. The animal was perfectly good and their jokes and wisecracks practically ruined the holiday for me."

"So it really did bother you," said Hakekgose. "Well, that's the way they always talk. When I take my rifle and go hunting with them, if I miss, they laugh at me for the rest of the day. But even if I hit and bring one down, it's no better. To them, the kill is always too small or too old or too thin; and as we sit down on the kill site to cook and eat the liver, they keep grumbling, even with their mouths full of meat. They say things like, 'Oh this is awful! What a worthless animal! Whatever made me think that this Tswana rascal could hunt!'"

"Is this the way outsiders are treated?" I asked.

"No, it is their custom; they talk that way to each other too. Go and ask them."

/gaugo had been one of the most enthusiastic in making me feel bad about the merit of the Christmas ox. I sought him out first.

"Why did you tell me the black ox was worthless, when you could see that it was loaded with fat and meat?"

"It is our way," he said smiling. "We always like to fool people about that. Say there is a Bushman who has been hunting. He must not come home and announce like a braggart, 'I have killed a big one in the bush!' He must first sit down in silence until I or someone else comes up to his fire and asks, 'What did you see today?' He replies quietly, 'Ah, I'm no good for hunting. I saw nothing at all [pause] just a little tiny one.' Then I smile to myself," /gaugo continued, "because I know he has killed something big.

"In the morning we make up a party of four or five people to cut up and carry the meat back to the camp. When we arrive at the kill we examine it and cry out, 'You mean to say you have dragged us all the way out here in order to make us cart home your pile of bones? Oh, if I had known it was this thin I wouldn't have come.' Another one pipes up, 'People, to think I gave up a nice day in the shade for this. At home we may be hungry but at least we have nice cool water to drink.' If the horns are big, someone says, 'Did you think that somehow you were going to boil down the horns for soup?'

"To all this you must respond in kind. 'I agree,' you say, 'this one is not worth the effort; let's just cook the liver for strength and leave the rest for the hyenas. It is not too late to hunt today and even a duiker or a steenbok would be better than this mess.'

"Then you set to work nevertheless; butcher the animal, carry the meat back to the camp and everyone eats," /gaugo concluded.

Things were beginning to make sense. Next, I went to Tomazo. He corroborated /gaugo's story of the obligatory insults over a kill and added a few details of his own.

"But," I asked, "why insult a man after he has gone to all that trouble to track and kill an animal and when he is going to share the meat with you so that your children will have something to eat?"

"Arrogance," was his cryptic answer.

"Arrogance?"

"Yes, when a young man kills much meat he comes to think of himself as a chief or a big man, and he thinks of the rest of us as his servants or inferiors. We can't accept this. We refuse one who boasts, for someday his pride will make him kill somebody. So we always speak of his meat as worthless. This way we cool his heart and make him gentle. "But why didn't you tell me this before?" I asked Tomazo with some heat.

"Because you never asked me," said Tomazo, echoing the refrain that has come to haunt every field ethnographer.

The pieces now fell into place. I had known for a long time that in situations of social conflict with Bushmen I held all the cards. I was the only source of tobacco in a thousand square miles, and I was not incapable of cutting an individual off for non-cooperation. Though my boycott never lasted longer than a few days, it was an indication of my strength. People resented my presence at the water hole, yet simultaneously dreaded my leaving. In short I was a perfect target for the charge of arrogance and for the Bushmen tactic of enforcing humility.

I had been taught an object lesson by the Bushmen; it had come from an unexpected corner and had hurt me in a vulnerable area. For the big black ox was to be the one totally generous, unstinting act of my year at /ai/ai, and I was quite unprepared for the reaction I received.

As I read it, their message was this: There are no totally generous acts. All "acts" have an element of calculation. One black ox slaughtered at Christmas does not wipe out a year of careful manipulation of gifts given to serve your own ends. After all, to kill an animal and share the meat with people is really no more than Bushmen do for each other every day and with far less fanfare. . . .

7.2 "Real Belizean Food": Building Local Identity in the Transnational Caribbean

RICHARD WILK

Food and food preferences are closely tied to cultural identity and social status. While food prefer-ences may be culturally constructed, they are certainly not static. Drawing on decades of research on foodways in Belize, Richard Wilk demonstrates the transnational flows that shape local cuisines and taste hierarchies. Wilk describes the role cuisine plays in nation-building projects in post-colonial Belize. Further, he illustrates a breakdown in colonial taste hierarchies as greater numbers of Belizeans encounter foreign people and products and adopt new tastes to assert particular identities associated with knowledge and modernity.

Questions

1. Discuss the role of the "other" in the making of Belizean national cuisine.
2. What does consumption of foreign products symbolize for Belizeans?
3. Is there a hierarchical taste order in Western culture? Can you think of an example of a "stratified taste sandwich" in your culture?
4. How has taste been used in political projects in Belize, from colonial times through independence?

... [F]ood is both substance and symbol, providing physical nourishment and a key mode of communi-cation that carries many kinds of meaning (Couni-han and Van Esterik 1997). Many studies have dem-onstrated that food is a particularly potent symbol of personal and group identity, forming one of the foundations of both individuality and a sense of common membership in a larger, bounded group. What is much less well understood is how such a stable pillar of identity can also be so fluid and changeable. . . .

... Belize is a wonderful place to study the relationship between food and national identity be-cause nationhood is such a recent construct there. Belize only attained independence in 1981, and . . . [s]ince that time foreign media, tourism, and migration have spread a broad awareness that Belize needs a national culture, cuisine, and identity to flesh out the bare institutional bones of nationhood provided by the British. . . .

. . . Many, but not all, Belizeans identify with a lan-guage or ethnic group. . . . The "Creole" category was once applied to local Europeans, then was extended to those of mixed European and African ancestry, and now it has become a general term for people with multiple or overlapping ethnic backgrounds (see Stone 1994). Diverse groups of migrants from neighboring Spanish-speaking countries are usually labeled "Spanish," though many are of Amerindian origins. In addition there are relatively bounded ethnic groups defined by language, residence, and livelihood, including Mopan, Kekchi, East Indians, Mennonites, Chinese, and Garifuna. . . .

. . . To show how rapidly Belize has been transformed, and to argue for the crucial importance of foreign influence in the growth of local culture, I begin with a contrast between two meals, separated by 17 years.

Eating Culture: A Tale of Two Meals

Meal One: Tea with the Gentles. May 1973, Orange Walk Town (a predominantly Hispanic community in the northern sugar zone)

Henry and Alva Gentle, both schoolteachers in the Creole lower middle class, invited a 19-year-old archaeology student to their home for a meal. I showed up one evening about 5 p.m., just as the family sat down to the evening meal. "Dinner" at midday was the main meal of the day in Belize; evening "Tea" was usually leftovers from dinner, with some bread or buns and coffee or tea.

Everyone was excited about having a foreign visitor in the house and stopped eating when I entered. I was ushered into the uninhabited and unused front "parlor" for a few minutes while furious activity took place in the kitchen, and children were sent running out of the back door to the local shops. Then we all went back to the kitchen table to finish tea. Everyone sat before small plates of fish and plantain dumplings simmered in coconut milk, with homemade coconut bread, and either fresh fruit juice or tea. After six weeks on archaeological camp food (most of which had been sent out in a large crate from England), my mouth watered at the prospect of tasting something authentically Belizean. Instead, as an honored guest I was treated to the best food the house could afford, food they thought I would be comfortable with: a plate of greasy fried canned corned beef (packed, as I later found out, in Zimbabwe), accompanied by six slices of stale Mexican "Pan Bimbo" white bread, a small tin of sardines in tomato sauce, and a cool Seven-up with a straw. When this was presented, the whole family paused in their own meal to smile shyly and expectantly, waiting for my pleased reaction. I did as well as I could, given that I dislike both sardines and canned meat.

Despite the food, the meal was relaxed and fun, with a lot of joking between family members. There was no formal beginning or end to the meal; late arrivals were seated and served. People got up and went to

the kitchen to fill their plates when they wanted more food. Gradually people drifted out to the verandah to sit and discuss the day, and see who was walking by on the street.

Meal Two: Dinner with the Lambeys. August 1990, Belmopan (a small town of about 3,000, also the nation's capital, with a mixed population)

Lisbeth and Mike Lambey lived across the street from us in a nice part of town, populated mostly by middle-rank civil servants. Mike worked in the refugee office, and Lisbeth was an assistant to a permanent secretary. A bit more educated than the Gentles and better paid, they still belonged to the same salaried middle class. Lisbeth was born into an old Creole family in Belize City, while Mike's family included Creole and East Indians from the southern part of Belize. All of Mike's family live in various parts of Belize, but all of Lisbeth's seven siblings have emigrated to the United States.

When Mike invited us to dinner, over the front wall of his yard one morning, he said, "I want you to taste some good local food." By 1990, many younger Belizeans, especially those with both spouses working for wages, had shifted to what was seen as an "American" practice of eating a light lunch and the main family meal in the evening.

When my wife and I arrived, we were seated in front of the TV, handed large glasses of rum & Coke (made with local rum and "local" Coke), and were shown a videotape about the refugee situation in Belize, produced by the United Nations. Then we sat down to a formal set table; all the food was laid out on platters, and it was passed from hand to hand. Everything we ate, both Mike and Lisbeth said, was produced in Belize and cooked to Belizean recipes. We had tortillas (from the Guatemalan-owned factory down the road), stewed beans (which I later found were imported from the United States, but sold without labeling), stewed chicken (from nearby Mennonite farms), salad (some of the lettuce was from Mexico) with bottled French dressing (Kraft from England), and an avocado with sliced white cheese (made locally by Salvadoran refugees). We drank an "old-fashioned" homemade pineapple wine.

The meal was formal, with a single common conversation about local politics to which each of us contributed. When everyone was finished, Lisbeth circulated a small dish of imported chocolate candies, and we all rose together and went back to the TV. Mike proudly produced a videocassette on which a friend had taped Eddie Murphy's "Coming to America" from a satellite broadcast. . . .

That same week Radio Belize carried advertisements for the grand opening of the first self-proclaimed "Belizean Restaurant." Owned by a Belize-born couple who had recently returned from a 20-year sojourn in the United States, the advertisement asked customers to "Treat yourself to a Belizean Feast. Authentic Belizean dishes—Gamachas, Tamales, Rice and Beans, Stew Chicken, Fried Chicken." All these foods were already served in numerous restaurants all over the country; the only other kind of food available in most places is Chinese. But this was the first time they had been granted the public distinction of being the national cuisine.

In the next two years the notion of Belizean restaurants and Belizean cuisine became commonplace, and most people accepted that there was indeed a national and traditional lexicon of recipes. . . . How is it that British and Mexican dishes, and global standards like stewed and fried chicken, emerged so quickly as an emblematic Belizean cuisine? This is a clear example of nation building. . . .

. . . National cuisine explicitly incorporates and crosscuts local traditions, which are simultaneously codified as each local group finds a significant contrastive "other" in neighboring areas and in the superordinate national melange. In Belizean cuisine the internal contention over how different ethnic and regional groups will be incorporated in the national has been quite muted. Instead, Belizean cooking has emerged through an explicit contrast with an externalized "other." The crucible of Belizean national cooking has been the *transnational* arena: the flow of migrants, sojourners, tourists, and media that increasingly links the Caribbean with the United States. . . .

Belizean National Culture

. . . Just twenty years ago, the concept of "Belizean Culture" was no more than politicians' rhetoric and a project for a small group of foreign-trained intellectuals. Official national dance troupes, endless patriotic speeches, history textbooks, and border disputes with neighboring Guatemala have helped establish the existence of a category of "Belizean Culture," but they have not filled it with meaning. . . . Contrasts between

the local and the foreign are on everyone's lips, though there are many shades of opinion about which is good or bad, and about where it will all end up. People constantly talk about authenticity and tradition, contrasting the old "befo' time" with everything new, foreign, and "modan."

Popular ideas about how the foreign is affecting "little Belize" are dramatized in jokes and stories about Belizeans who mimic or affect foreign ways. The traveler who returns after a few weeks in the States with an American accent is a common figure of fun. So is the returned cook who no longer recognizes a catfish, and the shopper who buys pepper sauce from an American supermarket to bring home, and pays a hefty import duty before looking at the label and seeing that it was made in Belize.

Opportunities for drawing contrasts appear often. Estimates of the number of Belizeans living in the United States range widely, but 60,000 seems a reasonable low estimate, or 30% of the total living in Belize (Vernon 1990). . . . There is constant flow of people, goods, and money between domestic and foreign communities (Wilk and Miller 1997). At the same time, more than 140,000 foreign tourists visit Belize every year. Belize is flooded with American media, from books and magazines to a barrage of cable and satellite television.

. . . During colonial times, foreign culture was received indirectly, with the expatriate and local colonial elite acting as selective agents and gatekeepers. Now all classes have direct access to foreign culture, and the foreign is no longer as closely associated with wealth and power (Wilk 1990).

This suggests an important way of reading the differences between the two meals I discussed [earlier in the chapter]. While class differences between my two hosts account for some of the variation, the most dramatic differences between the Gentles and the Lambeys have little to do with changes in the content of Belizean culture or identity. Instead, they result from changing knowledge about foreigners and increased consciousness of culture itself. The Gentles, despite (or maybe even because of) their education, really knew very little about Americans or American culture. Travelers were rare; personal contact with foreigners was sought for the very purpose of learning. The Gentles wanted to please me—they just did not know how Americans were different from the British. They could not know that young Americans wanted something "local," "cultural," and "authentic"—the very things they knew educated and rich people looked down upon. . . .

Seventeen years later, the Lambeys know how to play this game properly. They are Belizean nationalists who know that they are supposed to have something authentic. . . .

[A newspaper editor] . . . related that even recently Belizeans were relatively unsophisticated consumers and were "easy marks" for advertising—bad loans and credit terms and shoddy goods—because they lacked the experience and sophistication of Americans. As an ardent and radical nationalist, he decried the effects of television on local culture, but in the same breath praised the way TV has "raised Belizeans' consciousness," making them knowledgeable and aware of the rest of the world. No longer were they blinded by surface appearances. . . .

. . . They have been abroad and have learned to perceive and categorize differences as "national" and "cultural." They have learned that foreigners expect them to be Belizean, and they know how to do the job. They are as busy creating traditions and national culture as the itinerant Belizean woodcarvers who now tell tourists that their craft was handed down from their African ancestors (rather than taught by Peace Corps volunteers). Serving an authentic Belizean meal, for the Lambeys, is a performance of modernity and sophistication. The emotion it evokes for them is closer to pride or defiance than to nostalgia, the warmth of memory, or the comfort of repeated family habits. On the contrary, the meal expresses a sense of distance. . . .

To sneer at this accomplishment, at the Lambeys' dinner, by laughing at its shallowness or inauthenticity, is to miss its point (Friedman 1992). Mastering the performance and the role asserts a claim to categorical equality, to knowledge and power . . .

. . . By putting this knowledge into play in their everyday consuming lives, by performing and enacting and using unfamiliar goods, Belizean consumers transform abstract images, words, and names into the familiar appliances of life in Belize. Through consumption the foreign is made part of local existence, and it therefore comes under the same sorts of (albeit limited) control. . . .

. . . In the process, a colonial-era hierarchical discourse that opposed the backward local against the modern and foreign has begun to crumble. . . .

The Colonial Taste for Imports

During the nineteenth century Belize was a logging colony . . . [and] dependent on imported foods of all kinds. While scattered rural subsistence farmers produced most of their own food, the standard diet of mahogany cutters and working-class urban dwellers was imported flour and salt meat. A weekly ration for workers was four pounds of pork and seven of flour, eaten as dishes like "pork and doughboys." The managerial and mercantile European and Creole middle and upper classes consumed a wide variety of imported foods and drink and limited amounts of a few local vegetables, fish, poultry, and game. Given the very uneven quality of imported goods, consumers who could afford packaged and branded foodstuffs became highly "brand loyal" to established lines and companies. Brands were ranked according to both price and quality, with the highest ranks from Britain and lower ranks from the United States and Latin America. Access to the best brands was tightly controlled both through price and a strict system of exclusive distributorships that kept them in only the "best" shops. Branding was a key element of cultural capital, and it came to connote quality. . . . The poor bought generic goods, often dipped out of barrels, and had little choice when compelled to purchase in company stores through various forms of debt-servitude and payments of wages in goods.

Diet was highly class stratified. A single scale of values placed local products at the bottom and increasingly expensive and rare imports at the top. Imports were available to anyone who had the money, but in practice people did not usually consume above their class, whatever their economic resources. . . . Among the laboring class, almost any kind of store-bought food was considered superior to the rural diet based on root crops, rice, game, fruits, and vegetables.

This relatively simple hierarchy put the greatest pressure on the thin middle class of local petty merchants, low-level officials, tradespeople, and clerical workers. They did not have the resources for an exclusively imported diet but had to work hard to distance themselves from the kind of cheap and local foods that were the rural and working-class staple. One consequence was that they shunned local foods like fresh fish and game meat. These were common fare for the rural poor (for whom they were part of a subsistence lifestyle) and the upper elite (for whom selected varieties were considered exotic delicacies as long as they were prepared according to European recipes and smothered with imported sauces).

While the middle class depended most heavily on imports, menus from elite ceremonial meals included local snapper fillets in fish courses, garnished with oysters imported fresh from New Orleans. Venison, duck, and a few other local game animals with European analogs also appeared on the tables of the local gentry. Lobster is a good example of a stratified taste "sandwich": eaten by the poor because it was cheap, by the elite because it was prized in Europe, but shunned by the middle class as a "trash fish." . . .

The middle class built dietary diversity by borrowing foods from the Hispanic mercantile and managerial elites in the northern part of the country. "Spanish" food, especially festive dishes like tamales, relleno (a stuffed chicken stew), and tacos, entered the middle-class diet as a safely exotic option—associated neither with the class below nor the class above. "Spanish" food quickly became naturalized as part of the middle-class Creole diet. In this case, the "foreign" quickly became "local" and authentic.

There was some local resistance to or evasion of colonial food hierarchy. Foreign dishes were often localized or made affordable by substituting ingredients, renaming, and recombination. Kin ties cut across class and ethnic boundaries, and local produce therefore circulated between classes through networks of extended kin. Certain kinds of rare "country foods," especially wild game, honey, hearts of palm and the like, came to carry a connotation of familism and embeddedness, of belonging to place, even for the urban middle class. Some rustic dishes were enjoyed only in privacy, or on special occasions or during visits to country relatives. Festivals and celebrations also provided sites for the legitimate consumption of local products as holiday foods. . . .

The colonial regime of consumption in Belize, therefore, was similar to that seen by Bourdieu in modern France (1984). A relatively stable social hierarchy was defined by differential access to economic and cultural capital, which takes the form of "taste" and thoroughly naturalized predisposition and preference. Goods were positional markers within the hierarchy, both the means by which culture is internalized as taste and an external symbolic field through which groups identify boundaries and define differences among classes. There was a slow flow downward, as

lower ranks emulated the elite and the elite found new markers. There was also a stable degree of resistance, as some local products and practices were regenerated and adopted upwards through kin ties.

. . . Boundaries with lower classes were policed through many forms of class and racial discrimination. Up until the 1970s there were racially exclusive clubs, and working-class people were not welcome and [were] subject to humiliation in the few shops that catered to the elite (Conroy 1997).

Elite power was embodied in practices of consumption, and through roles as cultural gatekeepers the elite were arbiters of taste in everything. The choices of the middle and working classes were limited to accepting or rejecting what was offered. They could not find alternative sources of goods, information, or taste, except in the immediately neighboring Hispanic republics.

Pupsi and Crana; The Beginning of the End

This hierarchy of taste remained remarkably stable until the early 1960s. An incident, where food entered national political debate, illustrates one of the ways the colonial order began to unravel. In 1963 the British finally granted Belize limited local self-government. The anticolonial Peoples United Party was promptly elected, led by George Price, who had been imprisoned for nationalist activity in the 1950s (Shoman 1985). With limited legislative power, Price began to make symbolic changes in flags, official dress, and the names of towns and landmarks. He chose to de-emphasize some colonial holidays and changed the name of the country from British Honduras to Belize. There was a lot of popular support for most of these measures.

Then he gave a speech about the local economy, which exposed the country's ambivalence about the depth of the decolonizing project. In the speech he suggested that it was time to stop aping the food standards of the colonial masters. Belizeans would have to become self-sufficient in food and value the "traditional" local foods instead of copying foreign models and continuing to depend on imported foodstuff. He told his audience they should eat less imported wheat bread and more of their own products, drinking fevergrass tea and sweet potato wine, and eating pupsi and crana (abundant local river fish) instead of imported sardines. Like a number of colonial agricultural officers, he argued that it was unreasonable for a country rich in fertile soil, surrounded by abundant sea life, to import grain and fish from Europe.

The pro-British opposition, which had unsuccessfully fought Price's other cultural initiatives, now found an issue that aroused popular support that threatened Price's whole nationalist project.

> When the PUP started they promised you ham and eggs, etc., if you put them in power. They also promised you self government. But today when they get Self Government, they tell you to boil fever grass and eat pupsi and other river fishes. What will they tell you to eat when they get independence? [Belize Billboard, January 5, 1964]

> The human body is like a machine, and it must have fuel to keep it running. And the fuel of the human machine is food, protective and sustaining foods such as milk and other dairy products, eggs, vegetables, fruits, whole grain and enriched bread and other cereals, just to name a few. Food must supply the vitamins needed, along with other essential nutrients such as proteins to keep the body running in high gear. . . . It is obvious that pupsie and crana, which live mostly in polluted swamps[,] cannot replace, as our premier advises, our sources of vitamin rich food and proteins, the most important ingredients in our diet. Conditions such as pellagra and aribotlavinosis (disease dues [sic] to lack of vitamin B) occur in people who live continuously on restricted diets such as com and salt pork only. [Belize Billboard, January 11, 1964]

While the PUP's previous nationalist program challenged British political authority, the suggestion about diet turned the entire edifice of colonial cultural values and hierarchy literally upside-down. The words *pupsi* and *crana* became a rallying point for the formation of an opposition party. Price's suggestion was also unpopular among working- and middle-class people, who felt that they were being told to be satisfied with poverty instead of "improving" their lot. Many who had supported Price had seen his goal in terms of equity—a society where everyone would eat "high table" imported foods, sardines, and wine, not one where even the elite would be eating "bush food." Surprised by the reaction, Price moderated his position to one of import substitution, particularly supporting local rice and bean production, and he never publicly again called for a change in the national diet. The violent reaction to his speech shows just how resistant to change the cultural order of colonial taste had become. It brought home to Belizeans the realization that the end of colonialism would mean more than a new flag and new street names. The "Pupsi and Crana" speech was the point where the colonial regime of taste was no longer part of the taken-for-granted of everyday life.

The Royal Rat

Queen Elizabeth's 1985 visit to Belize marked a major symbolic recognition of Belize's independence, at a time when Belizeans were increasingly worried about the veracity of British defense guarantees against Guatemalan aggression (the result of a long-standing border dispute). A major event during the visit, the first by a reigning Monarch, was a state banquet at the residence of the British High Commissioner in Belmopan, the new capital city built by the British. A selection of Belizean delicacies was prepared for the royal party by the best local cooks.

One of the tastiest wild mammals of the Belizean rain forest is a large rodent called a *gibnut* or *paca* (*Agouti paca*). Highly prized in the rural diet, it was never widely eaten by the urban middle class. At the suggestion of local cooks and officials, but with the approval of the High Commissioner, roast gibnut was given the place of national honor as a main meat course at the Queen's banquet. She did not eat very much of it, but as a graceful veteran of hundreds of inedible feasts of local specialties, she still praised it to the cook. There the story would have ended, but for the British tabloid press. *The Sun* and other British newspapers produced a slew of outraged headlines, variations on the theme of "Queen Served Rat by Wogs." Angry letters were printed in the British press by citizens who were enraged by this assault on HRH's dignity.

The press reports were quickly transmitted back to Belize, where they provoked outrage and widespread anger, even among those who had never eaten gibnut. A few conciliatory conservative writers tried to explain to the British that the gibnut was *not* a rat and suggested that the incident was merely a misunderstanding. But most Belizeans saw this as an example of British arrogance and racism. For the first time, a Belizean dish became a matter of public pride. Nationalist chefs and nutritionists defended the Belizean gibnut as tasty, healthful, and nutritious. Reinterpreted as a national delicacy, today it often appears on restaurant menus as "Royal Rat," and its high price and legitimacy in national cuisine place heavy hunting pressure on remaining populations.

The incident of the royal rat came at a crucial time, just after political independence was granted in 1981. A legitimate category of Belizean food was beginning to emerge. The government, interested in cutting down food imports, had halfheartedly sponsored several campaigns through the Ministry of Education aimed at promoting production and consumption of local foods with help from CARE and the Peace Corps. During the 1970s the thrust was one of substituting local products for imports in familiar recipes: making bread with plantain flour, jams with local fruits. During the eighties the emphasis shifted to rediscovering (or reinventing) traditional foods; eating pupsi and crana was no longer unthinkable.

Belizean restaurants in the United States, cookbooks, public festivities where food is served, and the expensive dining rooms of foreign-owned luxury hotels were all crucial stages where ideas about Belizean food were tried out. By 1990, many dishes that were once markers of rural poverty had been converted into national cuisine. Others had quietly disappeared. Foreigners, expatriates, tourists, and emigrants were crucial agents in formulating and valuing the local.

Taste and Hierarchy Today

Colonial Belize had a clear hierarchy of social and economic strata, marked by their food practices and preferences....

... Under the colonial regime, diversity was managed and regulated through the flows of fashion and taste, which entered through the gatekeepers at the top who were legitimate models for emulation or resistance. Today this hierarchy has been drastically undercut by new flows of information and goods. Travel, once the province of the privileged elite, is now practical for most Belizeans. My survey shows that 73% of Belizean adults have traveled out of their country, while 34% have lived abroad for three months or more.

Variation by class is not high. For example, 45% of skilled manual workers have lived abroad, compared to 54% of business managers. The average Belizean has 2.6 immediate consanguineal relatives living abroad, again with little difference broken down by class, education, or wealth....

Similarly, tourists who once concentrated in a few oceanside resorts are now diffusing through the countryside and cities as ecotourists in search of unspoiled nature, ancient ruins, and authentic folk culture. A growing portion of the population has direct contact with foreigners....

Finally, greater access to electronic and print media has vastly broadened the images that Belizeans have of the world and has destroyed much of the gatekeeping role of the elite. Satellite-fed cable television had reached 35% of the urban population by1990, and broadcast stations served almost all of the rest.... Belizeans now have a diversity of models, fantasies, and dramas to choose from.... People are now faced with the need to contrast, weigh, and choose. What seems to be emerging is both a clearer definition of the national and local, and a less hierarchical diversification of lifestyles.

In one survey I asked 389 Belizeans to rate 21 main course dishes on a four-point scale from love to hate (Wilk 1997). Eight were clearly Belizean Creole food, and the other 13 were foreign in varying ways (Hispanic, Chinese, and Indian dishes represented Belizean minority ethnic groups, while dishes like macaroni and cheese or pizza have no local constituency). The responses were striking in their lack of clear order or hierarchy; tastes did not cluster together, nor did they help disaggregate the population by class or education.... Ethnicity was a surprisingly weak variable in explaining differences in taste, especially so among the young. All ethnic, age, and income groups showed a high degree of agreement in their preferences for basic nationalized dishes like rice and beans or tamales....

The neat orderings of taste that Bourdieu found in France are absent from the Belizean data on food or other kinds of preferences for art, clothing, and music.... There was no consensus on "highbrow," "middlebrow," and "lowbrow" that was more pronounced than the differences based on basic demographic categories like age and gender. Belize is a mosaic when it comes to consumer preferences, not a simple hierarchy....

Conclusion: Cultural Capital Revisited

. . . Today knowledge of the foreign is no longer the monopoly of either the economic or cultural elite; it is accessible to many people directly through travel and indirectly through television and the movement of relatives back and forth. . . .

. . . [T]he educated middle class have now adopted local, "Caribbean" or pan-African styles and practices that are self-consciously similar to workingclass fashions (though not dangerously similar). They can eat "roots food," listen to Caribbean music, and wear dreadlocks, but they are neat and clean dreadlocks. The hierarchy of power and capital is not gone, but it is no longer mirrored by simple hierarchies of taste.

Tastes and preferences are therefore always polysemic in Belize; there is no overwhelming order imposed by a strict hierarchy of capital. Fashion exists not in Bourdieu's two-dimensional space, linked to underlying variation in class, but in a multidimensional space tied to a series of different sources of power inside and outside of Belizean society. These other kinds of power include access to foreign culture through relatives, visits, tourism, or temporary emigration. As Basch et al. (1994) point out, transnational migration is now at least partially motivated by what the emigrant can *bring* and *send home.* Foreign goods create local identity on a global stage. . . .

References

Basch, Linda, Nina Schiller, and Cristina Blanc. 1994. Nations Unbound. Langhorne, PA: Gordon & Breach.

Bourdieu, P. 1984. Distinction: A Social Critique of the Judgment of Taste. Cambridge, MA: Harvard University Press.

Conroy, Richard. 1997. Our Man in Belize: A Memoir. New York: St. Martin's Press.

Counihan, C., and P. Van Esterik. 1997 Introduction. *In* Food and Culture: A Reader. C. Counihan and P. Van Esterik, eds. Pp. 1–7. New York: Routledge.

Friedman, Jonathan. 1992. The Past in the Future: History and the Politics of Identity. American Anthropologist 94(4):837–859.

Shoman, Assad. 1985. Party Politics in Belize. Benque Viejo, Belize: Cubola.

Stone, Michael. 1994. Caribbean Nation, Central American State: Ethnicity, Race, and National Formation in Belize, 1798–1990. Ph.D. dissertation, University of Texas, Austin.

Vernon, Dylan. 1990. Belizean Exodus to the United States: For Better or Worse. *In* Speareport 4, Society for the Promotion of Education and Research, Belize City. Pp. 6–28.

Wilk, Richard. 1990. Consumer Goods as Dialogue About Development: Research in Progress in Belize. Culture and History 7: 79–100.

Wilk, Richard. 1997 A Critique of Desire: Distaste and Dislike in Consumer Behavior. Consumption, Markets and Culture 1(2):175–196.

Wilk, Richard, and Stephen Miller. 1997. Some Methodological Issues in Counting Communities and Households. Human Organization 56(1):64–71.

7.3 Making the Market: Specialty Coffee, Generational Pitches, and Papua New Guinea

PAIGE WEST

What really is behind that $6 fair-trade, 100% organic macchiato made from specialty beans harvested in Papua New Guinea? Is it just a drink or is it also a story, a fantasy? Grounded in political ecology, a theoretical approach that centers on understanding the ways in which the environmental arena reflects the structured relations of power and inequality, the following selection from Paige West's book "From Modern Production to Imagined Primitive: The Social World of Coffee from Papua New Guinea" (Duke University Press, 2012) explores the creation of "fictitious political ecology narratives" in the coffee industry. The narratives created by specialty coffee marketers have been carefully crafted and packaged in the marketing and advertising world to tap into consumer fantasies about indigeneity, primitivism, and poverty. Yet these fantasies are misrepresentations that obscure the inequalities produced by structural changes brought about with neoliberal economic development policies from the 1980s forward. In reading this piece, students should consider how their tastes take shape – what stories are behind the food and drink you consume, and what do you know of the social lives of producers?

Questions

1. How does Mr. Nebraska's generational stories fit your reality? What is the purpose of capturing an entire generation in a thumbnail sketch?
2. How are Papua New Guineans represented in the popular media, and how does this link to the specialty coffee market and consumer purchasing decisions?
3. How are consumers "produced," and how are producers "produced"? Where are the overlaps and where are the points of tension?
4. What does West mean when she says that the process of marketing special coffee "makes consumers who do not enact real politics"

Consumer Production

The tall blond man from Nebraska wears the clip-on microphone like a professional. He towers above us, the participants in his seminar on marketing at the Specialty Coffee Association of America's annual meeting, and smiles a radiant row of perfect white teeth. He breaks the ice by revving up the fairly caffeinated crowd when he says, "Okay. OKAY. We are here to sell coffee! YEAH." People in the audience cheer enthusiastically.

We are all (coffee shop owners and an anthropologist who studies coffee consumption) here in this conference room in our attempt to understand why people buy specialty coffees. Our first task, before we begin any discussion of coffee, consumption, or anything

Paige West. 2012. *From Modern Production to Imagined Primitive: The Social World of Coffee from Papua New Guinea*. Durham: Duke University Press. Pp. 33–42;47;59–60;64–67. Published in an earlier form as "Making the Market: Specialty Coffee, Generational Pitches, and Papua New Guinea" in *Antipode* 42(3):690–718. Reproduced here by permission of John Wiley and Sons, Inc.

really, is to break into groups and come up with a list of the "essential qualities" (I know, too perfect for an anthropologist, right?) of our own "generation." I am put into the Generation X group. We were all born between 1964 and 1982 and although I momentarily hope that we will bond over our great love for the music of The Replacements, powerful memories of anti-apartheid protests and divestment campaigns, and our ability to quote long bits of the movie *Point Break*, we don't, as a group, seem to have much in common. So we get to our task and try to make a list of essentialisms. We have trouble because we don't seem to agree on any of them.

After a break, Mr. Nebraska smiles us back to our seats and we get started. People yell out the answers to his questions.

Mr. Nebraska (MN): "Okay, so you Silent Generation folks [those born between 1927 and 1944], give us your qualities."

"We are loyal and dependable," says one man in the front.

"We built and defended this country," says another who seems to be wearing a hat with a battleship's name on it.

MN: "Okay, now for the Baby Boomers [those born between 1945 and 1963], what do you have to contribute as a generation?"

"We are tenacious and idealistic," says a woman wearing a perky little red suit.

"We are free thinkers!" shout several people at the same time.

MN: "What about the Xers?"

Several people from my seemingly stoic group now perk up and yell, "We are individuals," "We question authority," and "We are fast technology!"

MN: "Now, what about you Millennials? Hello, Millennials? Where are my Millennials?"

Two young guys shyly raise their hands. They appear to be just out of college and sort of out of place in this older business-suited crowd. One of them says, "We are *much* faster technology."

Everyone laughs. Then Mr. Nebraska begins his lecture.

For the next hour he talks about different American generations and how they hold the key to marketing.

He begins with his analysis of the essential characteristics of each generation. "The Silent Generation" is "defined by World War II and the Korean War." They are hardworking-loyal-sacrificing-dedicated-conformist-never- questioning-authority-respectful-patient-delayed-gratification-duty-before-pleasure kinds of folks. Mr. Nebraska smiles broadly when he talks about these people, calling them "folks" at several points and mentioning his grandparents. Then he tells us that we won't talk about them anymore because as a generation they don't have any purchasing power in the retail world so they are a waste of time for the seminar.

He then moves on to the Baby Boomers. They are "all about civil rights, Vietnam, and Woodstock" and they can be summed up as essentially full of "optimism," "team-oriented," dedicated to "personal growth" and "personal-gratification." They work long hours and have a "hard core" work ethic but a "youthful mindset" which they keep up with "health and fitness."

He says, "GUYS, come ON. There are some values going on here, right? VALUES." He says this meaningfully, pacing the stage and smiling at his own insight.

It turns out that my generation, Generation X, is defined by "Three-Mile Island," "the fall of the Berlin wall," and "Rodney King," and that we are "liquid." We have "liquid value" and "a liquid mindset." We can "adjust to anything" because we are independent-individualist-selfish- latchkey kids who are "all about experience" and who have "no loyalty to anyone or anything." We are hard to work with because we have a "totally flat view of organization," which means we have "no respect for authority."

Finally, he moves on to the Millennials, prefacing his discussion by saying, with no hint of insight into his role in the creation of this marketing fetish, "Isn't it just weird? It is just weird that generations are getting shorter. Isn't it?"

For Mr. Nebraska, Millennials are defined by the Oklahoma City bombing, the Clinton–Lewinsky affair, 9/11, and the Columbine shootings. They want "achievement" but are "not driven." They value "globalism" but are "community focused" and think that by "looking inward" they can "change the world." They are also apparently "teetotalers" who "don't want drugs or alcohol."

When he is finished with his description of the Millennials, Mr. Nebraska looks at us thoughtfully, pauses, and says meaningfully, "This, THIS, is at the very core of people, it is who they are."

Next we move onto how to market to the different generations. Mr. Nebraska says, "The logo, product, service and atmosphere, or CULTURE of a business," is "key" to making your "generational pitch." And he cautions the audience, "You want to listen to this, the cultures I'm talking about, they are in people's DNA."

Baby Boomers' DNA is apparently encoded with the deep and abiding desire for iconic logos that symbolize gratification, indulgence, and the "unyielding" defiance of age and aging. Their DNA forces them to desire lots of choices among products, quick and thoughtful professional services, and "upscale" consumer-comes-first type "retail culture."

My "Generation X" "cultural DNA" makes me skeptical of logos and desirous of multiple, similar products with a unique story behind each of them and service that is "authentic," and during which I can "make a connection" and "share a story." Culturally, I desire casual, flexible, liquid space where I can read the paper, check my e-mail, and chat with friends. I "can't abide" images of control.

Millennials are "encoded" with the desire for brands and logos. They "value the symbols of products" more than anything else "about the retail world." They want "global products" that are "political" and "environmentally friendly," things that allow them to "express" their "self-knowledge" and "politics." When buying services they want to "be coddled" and "made to feel important." They want to "see people who know, really know, how to work the equipment." And culturally, they desire and can find "a meaning-filled experience" during "retail time."

After the description of the generations, their "DNA," and the sort of "retail culture" that appeals to them, Mr. Nebraska begins to talk about specialty coffee and its emerging market. He focuses on the "stories" behind the coffee and the ways it can be made to appeal to different generations. The stories exist on two scales: that of the coffee shop and that of the coffee producer.

Mr. Nebraska's Baby Boomers, constructed against a social mirror of the 1960s (the civil rights movement, protests against the war in Vietnam) and the constrained, restrained rebellion of going to a music festival (Woodstock), who are produced as deeply desirous of validating their continued youth even in the face of their sixtieth birthdays and deeply connected to the idea that they have spent their lives working harder than others, can easily be sold specialty coffees and specialty coffee venues that appeal to their ideas of work and activism. He discusses their work ethic, how they "worked long hours themselves" when they were young and "understand" labor. Because of this, stories about coffee shops will appeal to the Boomers. He says that they "love Starbucks" because it started out as one shop and is now, "the biggest and the best." They like a story of success that somewhere along the way meanders through a sense of helping "the downtrodden." If small coffee shops and roasters can tell a story of having "fought hard" for their market share and "made hard choices" along the way, the Boomers will flock to them. If people selling coffee can write stories about producers that appeal to the convictions they formed in the 1960s that rights must be defended and war ended, they can win consumers. He suggests that Boomers are more likely to buy coffee grown by people who live in a war-torn country ("Guatemala really appeals to their sense of postwar hardships"). Since they are health-conscious and "really wrote the first book on organics" they are particularly interested in organic-certified coffee, in that its story is one of a "more healthy" drink than regular coffee. He also argues that Boomers want the standardization of a chain retail outlet but the "feel" of an "upscale," personalized experience. This is why they especially like chains that are meant to feel like local coffee shops (e.g., Peets, Caribou, and Starbucks).

Since Generation X is defined against depressing events of the Reagan era, and since we are "liquid," we are hard to sell to. We are "cynical" when it comes to retail and want "diverse venues" for standard consumer products. We don't want the same experience over and over again (the aforementioned chain coffee shops). We want a coffee shop that has an authentic story that we can connect with. We like alternative venues that might have been begun as anti-establishment shops. We like the "Seattle connection" to be articulated in the shop stories. We want to know the story of the shop and the stories of the people who work there. We also want stories behind each of the products, all similar but marketed to us as "unique." We like the idea of authenticity when it comes to the people who grow the coffee. And we like the idea of experiencing some aspect of their lives by drinking the coffee. We want to connect to the authenticity of others in some way, and that way can easily be through buying product. We also like the idea of supporting people whose story shows that they are "bucking" the establishment in some way.

The people that Mr. Nebraska called millennials are for him the "driving force" behind the "globalism" that is emerging in the specialty coffee market. While Boomers and Generation Xers appreciate certain aspects of the stories behind origin-marketed, fair-trade, and organic coffees, it is the millennials who "thrive" on these stories. "They want to change the world and they know that they can do it through coffee." They also "know that the politics of their parents are not their politics" and that their politics "can change the world one village at a time." They are much less concerned with the shop and its story and much more concerned with the ways coffee can connect them with "people all over the world" and allow them to "participate in" the grower's struggles. They define self through their consumption, seeing themselves as politically active through their connection with "these stories about growers and the environment."

The marketing seminar is wrapped up by Mr. Nebraska with a long discussion about how each generation wants a particular story about the products that it buys. He talks about the process of creating a story for a business and how coffee works to "sell itself in today's market universe" because of the stories of growers that can be associated with it. He is passionate about the reality that he has just laid out for us—he repeatedly talks about how the "DNA" of the consumer is set along generational lines and how these generations want to "know and experience" stories about their coffee.

Producer Production

The following blog entry, entitled, "Papua New Guinea—Back to the Future," is one example of how coffees from Papua New Guinea are given a story by marketers and roasters and how that story is conveyed to consumers. It was written by an employee of Dean's Beans and placed on the company's website—a form of media with increasing power both in terms of number of consumers reached and the reach of what is inspired by the media. The company is a small, extremely successful specialty coffee-roasting company in Massachusetts that specializes in organic and fair trade-certified coffee. It sells only certified specialty organic and fair-trade coffees and associates each of its coffees with certain origins. The Dean's Beans employee who

visited the Eastern and Western Highlands of Papua New Guinea in 2005 writes:

Chiseled warriors in Bird of Paradise headdresses and spears, impassable mountain roads, stunning vistas, abundant gardens of coffee and vegetables. Papua-New Guinea is the final frontier of dreams, of images from the pre-colonial past. Yet here I am, the first American anyone can remember coming into these Highlands, many say the first white guy. I have dreamed of this land since I was a child, looking at National Geographic (yeah, those photos!), reading about its wildness in my Golden Book Encyclopedia.

There are no roads connecting the capital, Port Moresby, with the rest of this island, which is the size of New England. We have to fly to the interior, and I am glued to the window of the small plane, knowing that below me are anacondas and pythons, tree kangaroos and Birds of Paradise, wild rivers and still uncontacted tribes.

There is also coffee, introduced to the Highlands only in the 1950's from rootstock taken from the famed Jamaican Blue Mountains. Coffee is the only cash crop in the Highlands. The people grow all of their own food, using the coffee money to buy cooking oil, sugar, used clothes and other necessaries. They depulp the cherries by hand using round rocks. This is the only place in the world where coffee is depulped this way. It is a family affair, and I visit with several families singing and depulping by the river. After sun drying the beans, the villagers have to carry the sixty pound sacks on their backs for up to twenty miles, over mountains, through rivers via rocky paths.

Historically, they would sell their beans to a number of middlemen who wait by the only road, giving the farmers pennies for their labor. But we are here to change that. We are here to work with several farmer associations to create legally recognized cooperatives, and to create more direct trade relationships that should increase the farmer's income fourfold, as well as increase sales.

As I am the first coffee buyer to come into this area, the farmers organize a Coffee Cultural Show. I thought that meant a few dancing and singing groups, a feast and a gift exchange. Wrong! As we rolled into a distant village after three hours over rivers, boulders, mudpits and bridges that shook beneath the land rover, we were greeted by ten thousand people! It was the largest gathering ever seen in these parts. Traditional warrior societies, women's clans, singing groups, hunters and every possible combination of feathers, noses pierced with tusks, and painted bodies festooned with coffee branches and berries greeted us riotously. I was hoisted into the air and carried almost a mile by joyful men, while the women called a welcoming chant. There were speeches by every village's elders, by coffee farmers and of course by me.

For two days the festivities roared on, segued together by an all-night discussion around a fire about coffee techniques, trade justice, the role of women and every imaginable subject for people who have never met an American or a Fair Trader. Wild pigs were cooked on hot stones in pits, covered with banana leaves. Huge plates of yams (they laughed when I told them about research which links yam consumption to twin births—and they have a lot of twins there!). Of course, we brewed up lots of Dean's Beans Papuan coffee (Ring of Fire). It was the first time these farmers had ever had their own coffee, and they loved the taste almost as much as they loved seeing their own tribal names on the coffee bags, tee-shirts and hats I had made for the visit. As we passed through the Highlands, we had to stop at each tribal boundary for permission to enter the territory.

Considering that there are over eight hundred tribes in PNG, we were crossing boundaries every ten miles or so. At each boundary we were greeted by warriors in full dress, with welcoming chants and speeches, and invited to feast and speak. Needless to say, it took a long time to get a short distance, but we were well fed and made hundreds of new friends every day.

Back in the capital, we went on the radio (four million listeners nightly, as there is no electricity in the villages, only battery powered radios) and talked about making strong cooperatives and quality coffee to insure vibrant communities. Our meeting with the Prime Minister didn't happen, so we spent a day on an island of fisherman and their families, cooking the bounty of the sea and playing with the kids. My kinda day. Papua-New Guinea. A life-long dream come true. It was a profound honor to be able to go as an emissary of peace and positive social change. If you ever get to go, DO IT! You can be assured of a warm welcome and a great cup of coffee. Just tell them you're a friend of mine.[1]

This blog entry is a good example of what Mr. Nebraska suggested that roasters, importers, and marketers do to create a story for specialty coffees.[2] It is representative of many of the narratives one finds today about specialty coffee from Papua New Guinea. . . .

The narratives created by Mr. Nebraska and the Dean's Beans employee are what Bryant and Goodman (2004, 344) have called "political ecology narratives." These marketing narratives engage a set of representational practices that seem to show clear connections between "alternative forms of consumption in the North" and social and environmental justice in the South (345). However, they show a fictitious version of political ecology. In addition, they craft producers and consumers in ways that are equally fictitious. These moments, the moment of consumer production, the moment of producer production, and the moment of fictitious political ecology, would not be possible were it not for the neoliberal changes in the global economy that have taken place over the past fifty years. Nor would they be possible without the growth of the specialty coffee industry.

Specialty Coffee

In the late 1980s the popular media in the United States began to carry stories about the relationship between coffee production and environmental sustainability, and by the mid-1990s "sustainable" coffee production was being directly linked to "saving" tropical rainforests ("The Greening of Giving" 1993; Hull 1999; Pennypacker 1997). . . . Today the coffee-related popular narrative around the world encompasses not only an environmental message but also a message about how growing particular kinds of coffee can help rural peoples pursue small-scale economic development in ways that allow them access to their fair share of the global circulation of cash, without destroying the natural environment in which many of them live (Alsever 2006; Pascual 2006). In addition, the purchasing of coffee and other commodities that have been cast as embedding "ecological, social, and/or place-based values" into market transactions has come to be thought of as a potential "form of resistance" to globalization that individual consumers can practice (Guthman 2007, 456; see also Bryant and Goodman 2004). The kinds of coffee that are linked to environmental and social sustainability, economic justice, and resistance to neoliberalization are known as specialty coffees. These coffees include single-origin-marketed coffee, organic coffee, fair-trade coffee, flavored coffee, bird-friendly coffee, and other coffees that are seemingly socially responsible. . . .

. . .

People who had not been coffee drinkers in the past were targeted through the creation of stories and images that were designed to appeal to them along generational, political, and class lines. Certain types of specialty coffee were marketed to appeal to people's ideas about their own refined tastes and their unique position as a certain type of consumer, while others were marketed to appeal to people with particular political beliefs. Marketers wanted coffee consumption to be seen as a way to distinguish oneself in terms of class and to express one's political ideas. To this end they worked to create consumers' desire right along with the growth of the new specialty industry. . . .

Natural Stone Age Natives Marching Toward Modernity

Over five hundred articles in the popular media are accessible through the search engine Lexis Nexis by means of the search terms "New Guinea" and "Stone Age." This image of New Guinea and its inhabitants—the inhabitants of both West Papua and Papua New Guinea—as somehow located close to or directly linked to something called the "Stone Age" is deeply embedded in the fantasy lives of Europeans, Americans, and Australians. . . . Many visitors to Papua New Guinea fantasize about and desire "authentic" natives who live in an "authentic" and "untouched" nature. They want these natives to conform to the stereotypes of "indigenous,"

"native," and "tribal" peoples that they have been exposed to through undergraduate anthropology classes, television programs, magazines, and movies. When the real residents of Papua New Guinea do not fit these stereotypes, they are considered not only less authentic but also less deserving of the rights to their traditional lands and livelihood strategies (West 2006, 167). . . .

. . . For example, rural landholders who participate in the cash economy are seen as less authentic than rural landholders who do not have access to the cash economy; if people have houses made of "traditional" materials they are seen as more authentic than people who have houses made of store-bought materials; and if people attend missionary inspired churches they are assumed to be less authentic than those who do not. After rural people are measured and understood through this process, they are accorded rights and responsibilities according to a set of rhetorical devices that locate them on a scale that assumes a linear progression from indigeneity to modernity.

The rhetorical devices used include discourses of parental relations that liken rural peoples to "children" who must be helped to understand the modern world by well-meaning outsiders, and discourses of threat and danger that characterize rural peoples who are not "indigenous enough" as overpopulating, tree-cutting, over-harvesting resource users. The assumed linear progression locates authentic indigeneity as a prior condition for modernization and fixes authentic relations with the biophysical world directly to indigeneity. . . .

These . . . fantasies are grafted onto coffee from Papua New Guinea by the likes of Mr. Nebraska, Dean's Beans, and other people and organizations engaged in specialty marketing. The images and fantasies discussed previously also endure in, and are perpetuated by, coffee marketing and certification, through the physical and ideological layout of coffee shops across the world, through the discursive production of "middlemen" who are out to rob authentic natives of their income, and in the rhetoric about saving the lifestyles of indigenous peoples living in "stone age" conditions through the helping hand of capitalism (even though it is capital's evils that are forcing the inevitable march toward modernity).

. . . Papua New Guineans are rarely in control of the images used to sell the coffee they produce. It is much more the case that the commodification of the coffee results in the production of images of ethnicity (see Comaroff and Comaroff 2009, 67). It is the politics of these images that I am concerned with.

The Politics of Neoliberal Consumer and Producer Production

Two questions related to coffee grow out of all this work: How are the commercial possibilities for coffee in the United States and other northern nations tied to particular narratives about indigenous peoples, savagery, pristine nature and culture, and development in places like Papua New Guinea (Bryant and Goodman 2004)? And what are the material effects of these narratives on the people portrayed by them?

The coffee growers constructed by the Dean's Beans narrative seem to possess the same values as the virtual consumers for which the narrative was constructed. These growers seem to want to maintain tradition and maintain benign ecological relations with their forests. But at the same time they seem to wish to become incorporated more fully into the market economy as it is represented by Dean's Beans and its emissaries for coffee based sustainability. They want to understand modernity but not lose their souls to it; they are ecologically noble savages who are fallen from grace but deeply want to maintain the ecological stability of their pristine forested lands. . . . [T]hese images penetrate deeply into the Euro-American psyche and are a reflection of Euro-American fantasies about indigenous peoples.

When businesses tell stories like this one about virtual producers, they also want consumers to see natives as poor, third-world agricultural laborers who value and contribute to the ecological sustainability of the earth, while at the same time making just enough money to maintain their coffee-producing ways of life without wanting to gain access to all the things that consumers have, including the feeling of having the right to overconsume the world's resources. They want to provide consumers with an aura of social responsibility, political action, exotic locality, environmental sustainability, and social status through a capitalist marketing version of a Geertzian "being there" narrative. The idea is to market meaningfulness without actually going .all the way down the road of consumer education. Coffee companies like Dean's Beans add value to their products

by going halfway, by creating virtual producers and hoping that their narratives appeal to the virtual consumers who have been made for them by the likes of Mr. Nebraska.

This process makes consumers who do not enact real politics. The marketers recommend that retailers create a particular narrative, and retailers create stories which coffee drinkers consume. Not only do they reproduce troubling stereotypical images, they occlude the real history and political economic position of the real producers and both the social benefits and consequences of coffee production. Under the regulatory system in place from the end of the Second World War to the 1980s, the coffee industry in Papua New Guinea had a stable market. There was a place—set and standard—for the coffee grown there, and growers could expect a certain price for their coffee. Today, with a deregulated coffee market, Papua New Guinea coffee has to compete in a different way. This has caused a particular sort of marketing—marketing that rests on images of nature and culture in Papua New Guinea that may or may not be offensive, racist, and inaccurate. These images now create a location within the global market for the coffee. My argument is that these images have bled into coffee from other sites and are bleeding out of coffee, with real political and economic consequences.

Narratives like the one presented by Dean's Beans also attempt to repackage poverty as uniqueness and primitivism as a form of scarcity. Scarce things have value, and by producing a fantasy of Papua New Guinea's coffee industry as primitive and of primitivism as scarce, this narrative adds value to the coffee at the expense of people from Papua New Guinea by turning them into virtual producers. The virtual producers created by Dean's Beans are poor farmers yearning for a benevolent and right-thinking American ·businessman to come in and create economic equality through the softer side of capitalism. They are also crafted as if the coffee industry in Papua New Guinea had no history and as if the rural smallholders who grow coffee there were the only people whose lives depended on coffee production.

By fixing these images and fantasies onto the people who grow coffee in Papua New Guinea and the places where it is grown, these agents of neoliberalization work to erase history and society. By erasing history and society and replacing it with fantasy, they set the stage for dispossession.

Notes

1. http://www.deansbeans.com/coffee/deans_zine
   .html?blogid=829, first accessed for this book on 13
   November 2006, accessed again on 1 November 2010.
2. It is an unsettling example to be sure, one that locates
   Papua New Guinea in a morass of colonial nostalgia,
   the self-aggrandizing travel narrative bravado of
   white exploration, inaccurate information (e.g., the
   description of middlemen and the claim that cooperatives would "increase the farmer's income fourfold"),
   and outright falsehoods (e.g., references to anacondas
   and uncontacted tribes, which do not exist in Papua
   New Guinea, and the absurd claim that the writer was
   the "first coffee buyer" to enter places in the Western
   and Eastern Highlands).

References

Alsever, Jennifer. 2006. "Fair Prices for Farmers: Simple
   Idea, Complex Reality." *New York Times*, 19 March, 5.

Bryant, Raymond L., and Michael K. Goodman. 2004.
   "Consuming Narratives: The Political Ecology of 'Al-
   ternative' Consumption." *Transactions of the Institute of
   British Geographers* 29, no. 3, 344–66.

Comaroff, Jean, and John Comaroff. 2009. *Ethnicity, Inc.*
   Chicago: University of Chicago Press.

"The Greening of Giving." 1993. *Economist*, 25 December, 53.

Guthman, J. 2007. "The Polanyian Way? Voluntary Food
   Labels as Neoliberal Governance." *Antipode* 39, no. 3,
   456–78.

Hull, Jennifer Bingham. 1999. "Can Coffee Drinkers
   Save the Rain Forest?" *Atlantic Monthly*, August,
   19–21.

Pascual, Aixa M. 2006. "Peace, Love and Coffee;
   Woodstock Coffeehouse Opens Third Store."
   Atlanta Journal-Constitution, 17 December, 18ZH.

Pennypacker, Mindy. 1997. "Habitat-Saving Habit:
   Shaded Coffee Plantations Help Preserve Tropical
   Rainforests." *Sierra Journal* 82, no. 2.

West, Paige. 2006. *Conservation Is Our Government Now:
   The Politics of Ecology in Papua New Guinea.* Durham:
   Duke University Press.

7.4 Migrant Farmworkers and the Pain of Picking

SETH HOLMES

What does it feel like to pick the fresh fruit most college students are so fortunate to be able to consume? For most of the world's population, the fresh strawberries that mainstream U.S. college students take for granted are unobtainable, even for the families of those who are doing the picking. Not only are food choices limited due to global inequalities, but global inequality also leads to physical and emotional suffering for the structurally vulnerable who work within the fresh fruit market. In the following selection, physician-anthropologist Seth Holmes explores sickness as an embodiment of violence among Triqui farmworkers on a berry farm in Washington. Through the stories of three migrants from the indigenous communities of Oaxaca, Mexico, Holmes reveals that pain and suffering that these workers experience are manifestations of structural, symbolic, and political violence.

Questions

1. What was the social and political genesis of Abelino's knee pain? What does his knee pain have to do with this position within the farm's ethnicity–citizenship–labor hierarchy?
2. What do Crescencio's headaches reveal about his position within the labor hierarchy? Apply the concept of symbolic violence to understand and explain his experiences of suffering, both physical and emotional.
3. Discuss and assess the linkages between migrant health status and their labor and living conditions.
4. To what degree are migrant workers able to access healthcare services? How does this compare with the popular American narrative regarding undocumented immigrants and the stability of the American healthcare system?
5. Compare and contrast the health fair run by the Evangelical Christian missionary to the exchanges Holmes had with migrant farmworkers. What is the role of anthropology in public health initiatives with migrant workers?
6. How does this selection parallel the selections by Scheper-Hughes (Reading 4.2), Bourgois and Schonberg (Reading 5.3), and Farmer (Reading 6.1)?

During both of my summers of fieldwork on the Tanaka Brothers Farm, I picked berries once or twice a week and experienced several forms of pay for days afterward. I often felt sick to my stomach the night before picking, due to the stress about picking the minimum weight. As I picked, my knees continually hurt; I tried different position, sometimes squatting, sometimes kneeling, sometimes propped up on just one knee. Each time I stood up to take my berries to be weighed, it felt as if a warm liquid like my own blood was running down my pants and into my shoes. All day, I leaned forward to see the strawberries below the leaves, and my neck and back began to hurt by late morning. For two or three days after picking,

Seth Holmes. "Fresh Fruit, Broken Bodies: Migrant Farmworkers in the United States." 2013. *Migrant Farmworkers and the Pain of Picking*. University of California Press. Pp. 89–115.

I took ibuprofen and sometimes used the hot tub in a local private gym to ease the aches, all too aware of the inequality of having access to such amenities.

After the first week of picking on the farm, I asked two young female pickers how their knees and backs felt. One replied that she could no longer feel anything ("*Mi cuerpo ya no puede sentir nada*"), though her knees still hurt sometimes. The other said that her knees, back, and hips are always hurting ("*Siempre me duelen*"). Later that same afternoon, one of the young Triqui men I saw playing basketball every day the week before the harvest told me that he and his friends could no longer run because their bodies hurt so much ("*Ya no corremos; no aguantamos*"). In fact, even the vistas that were so sublime and beautiful to me had come to mean ugliness, pain, and work to the pickers. On multiple occasions, my Triqui companions responded with confusion to my exclamations about the area's beauty and explained that the fields were "pure work" (*puro trabajo*).

Knee, back, and hip pain are only a few of the ways in which the social context of migrant farmwork—especially living and working conditions—affects the bodies of my Triqui companions. These pains are examples of the structural violence of social hierarchies becoming embodied in the form of suffering and sickness. The shacks in which the Triqui pickers live, the grueling conditions in which they work, and the danger they face in the border desert function as mechanisms through which structural violence produces suffering. I use the word *suffering* to indicate not only physical sickness but also mental, existential, and interpersonal anguish.

Scheper-Hughes and Bourgois propose understanding violence as a continuum, including not only direct political violence but also structural, symbolic, and everyday violence.[1] They suggest that these wartime and peacetime expressions of violence potentiate, produce, conceal, and legitimate one another. Bourgois defines direct political violence as "targeted physical violence and terror administered by official authorities and those opposing [them]."[2] Structural violence is manifested as social inequalities and hierarchies, often along social categories of class, race, gender, and sexuality.[3] Symbolic violence, as defined by Bourdieu, is the internalization and legitimation of hierarchy, "exercised through cognition and misrecognition, knowledge and sentiment, with the unwitting consent of the dominated."[4] . . .

This chapter focuses ethnographic attention on "how the poor suffer," in this case the poorest of the poor on the farm, the Triqui strawberry pickers. . . . During my fieldwork, many Triqui people experienced notable health problems affecting their ability to function in their work and families. I discuss . . . the experiences of three Triqui migrants whom I came to know well, Abelino, Crescencio, and Bernardo. While the suffering of Triqui berry pickers in general is determined by their position at the bottom of various hierarchies, each of these three vignettes serves to underscore the embodiment of a different expression of the violence continuum. Abelino's knee injury highlights the physical and mental suffering caused by the structural violence of segregated labor. Crescencio's headache brings to light the embodied effects of the verbal and symbolic violence of racist insult and stereotype. Finally, Bernardo's stomach pains underline the health effects of the direct political violence of military repression. . . .

Abelino and the Pain of Picking

The first Triqui picker whom I met when I visited the Skagit Valley was Abelino, a thirty-five-year-old father of four. He, his wife, Abelina, and their children lived together in a small shack near me in the labor camp farthest from the main road. During one conversation over homemade tacos in his shack, Abelino explained in Spanish why Triqui people have to leave their hometowns in Mexico.

> In Oaxaca, there's no work for us. There's no work. There's nothing. When there's no money, you don't know what to do. And shoes, you can't get any. A shoe like this [*pointing to his tennis shoes*] costs about 300 Mexican pesos. You have to work two weeks to buy a pair of shoes. A pair of pants costs 300. It's difficult. We come here and it is a little better, but you still suffer in the work. Moving to another place is also difficult. Coming here with the family and moving around to different places, we suffer. The children miss their classes and don't learn well. Because of this, we want to stay here only for a season with [legal immigration] permission and let the children study in Mexico. Do we have to migrate to survive? Yes, we do.

The economic situation in the Triqui Zone of Oaxaca is both depressed and depressing. To keep their homes and support their families in Oaxaca, they must leave to work. Oaxaca's economic depression is linked to discriminatory international policies—such as NAFTA—originating in the United States as well as unequal economic practices with colonialist roots in Mexico. Abelino describes some of the ways in which the transitory nature of migration leads to suffering on many levels. Moving from place to place allows for the most earnings to be saved toward whichever goal each worker may have as well as to be sent back to family members in Oaxaca. At the same time, this ongoing movement leads to periods of homelessness, fear of apprehension and deportation, uprooting of connections and relationships outside of the migration circuit, and loss of productive studies and continuity for children. Moving from state to state also functionally disqualifies workers, including pregnant women and recent mothers, from social and health services for which they would otherwise be eligible.

Later that same night, Abelino explained the difficulty of entering the United States without official documents: "We have to migrate to survive. And we have to cross the border, suffering and walking two days and two nights, sometimes five days, to get here to work and support the American people. Because they don't work like we do. They just get rich working a light job like the shops, the offices, but they don't work in the field. We Mexicans from many Mexican states come here to maintain our families. We want to get permission to enter just for a harvest season and then return to our country."

Crossing the border from Mexico to the United States involves incredible financial, physical, and emotional suffering for Triqui migrants. Each migrant pays approximately $1,500 to $2,500 to various people along the way for rides and guidance. They walk hurriedly in physically impossible conditions, getting speared by cactus spines, attempting to avoid rattlesnakes, climbing and jumping over numerous barbed-wire fences—all the while using no flashlights in order to avoid being seen by the Border Patrol and vigilante groups. As a rule, they do not bring enough food or water because of the weight. Every step of the way carries a fearful awareness that at any moment one might be apprehended and deported by the Border Patrol, which would entail beginning the nightmarish trek all over again after figuring out a way to scrape together enough money for another attempt.

The suffering Abelino talked about most, however, related to picking berries on the farm. After arriving in the Skagit Valley, many Triqui people attempt to obtain various types of jobs, including in construction or in the farm's processing plant, but the only job they are offered is the harvest of berries. . . . Abelino explained to me the experience of picking: "You pick with your hands, bent over, kneeling like this [*demonstrating with both knees fully bent and his head bowed forward*]. Your back hurts; you get knee pains and pain here [*touching his hip*]. When it rains, you get pretty mad and you have to keep picking. They don't give lunch breaks. You have to work every day like that to make anything. You suffer a lot in work." . . .

One day in the middle of my first summer on the farm, like the other mornings I picked, I followed Abelino, his wife, and their oldest daughter as they led the way to the field we were to pick that morning. It was pitch black before the sun rose, and we wore heavy clothes in layers to take off as the sun came up. We walked through a line, and our picking cards for the day were marked with our beginning time, though, as we came to expect, the cards were marked as though we had arrived thirty minutes later. We were assigned rows next to each other and began picking into our individual buckets without saying a word. As usual, I was quickly left behind in the row, though I had learned to pick relatively quickly using both hands at once. We picked as fast as we could while squatting, alternating back and forth from right to left to pick both rows of berries next to us.

In the middle of one of the rows, while picking, Abelino experienced acute, intense pain in his right knee during one of the countless times he pivoted from the right to the left. At the end of the day, he told me about the incident. He said it felt like his foot would not move, and then the pain suddenly began. The pain was most intense on the inside of the knee just behind the kneecap. He also felt like there was something loose moving around within his knee. He attempted to keep working for the rest of the day in the vain hope that the pain would go away. He tried picking with his knees straightened while he bent at the hips, but this hurt almost as intensely and slowed him down significantly, and he almost missed the minimum weight. At the end of the day, as we approached our cars to drive back to the camp, Abelino told our supervisor about the incident. The supervisor said simply, "OK," and drove away in his white farm pickup without any follow-up. Unsure of what to do, Abelino tried to pick again the next day in great pain and once again barely picked the minimum. Abelino ended up seeing four doctors, a physical therapist, and a Triqui healer, as well as attempting to go through the bureaucracy of worker's compensation. In the end, his pain was diagnosed by a rehabilitation medicine physician as patellar tendonitis, or inflammation of the tendons behind the kneecap.

The social and political genesis of Abelino's knee pain could not have been clearer. His pain was caused unequivocally by the fact that he, as an undocumented Triqui man, had been excluded by both international market inequalities and local discriminatory practices from all but one narrow and particularly traumatic labor position. This occupation required him to bend over seven days a week, turning back and forth, in all kinds of weather, picking strawberries as fast as he possibly could. Tendonitis is understood biomedically to be inflammation caused by repetitive strain and stress on a particular tendon. The inflammation can be brought on over years of overwork and worsened by individual straining events. Abelino's position at the bottom of the farm's ethnicity-citizenship-labor hierarchy meant that he, like hundreds of other Triqui pickers with knee, back, and hip pain, was forced into the precise conditions ripe for the harvesting of chronic joint inflammation and deterioration. Furthermore, his suffering was compounded by the fact that he, like other Triqui people from Oaxaca, had been driven by the results of international economic policies and the expansion of multinational corporations to cross a mortally dangerous border and then live in fear and remain transient wherever he worked, despondently reproducing the same situation for his children, who could not stay in school to seek a better future. In this way, his body was victim to multiple layers of structural violence. . . .

Suffering the Hierarchy

On the Tanaka farm, the hierarchies of perceived ethnicity and citizenship correlate closely with the labor and housing pecking order. . . . Attending to the body in an analysis of the violence continuum in U.S.-Mexico migration allows deeper understanding of the links among class, ethnicity, citizenship, health, and sickness. In many ways, employees of the berry farm . . . come to embody power differentials and prejudice. The working and living conditions, degree of respect received, and access to political power of each of the groups within the labor hierarchy lead to different forms of suffering from top to bottom. . . .

In general in U.S. agriculture, the more Mexican and the more "indigenous" one is perceived to be, the more psychologically stressful, physically strenuous, and dangerous one's job. Thus where a migrant body falls on the dual ethnic-labor hierarchy shapes how much and what kind of suffering must be endured. The farther down the ladder from AngloAmerican U.S. citizen to undocumented indigenous Mexican one is positioned, the more degrading the treatment by supervisors, the more physically taxing the work, the more exposure to weather and pesticides, the more fear of the government, the less comfortable one's housing, and the less control over one's own time.

Of course, the people on every level of the hierarchy suffer. Yet suffering is also roughly cumulative from top to bottom. Some of the social and mental forms of suffering are described as anxieties over profitability and increasing competition by the farm executives, over farm profitability and disrespect from supervisors by the administrative assistants, and over racist insult from supervisors and familial economic survival by the berry pickers. On the more strictly physical level of suffering, this rough accumulation continues to hold. For example, the farm executives worry most about what are sometimes called the diseases of the upper middle class, like heart disease and breast cancer. The administrative assistants worry about these sicknesses, as well as repetitive stress injury like carpal tunnel syndrome. The strawberry pickers are at risk for heart disease and many cancers but worry most about pesticide poisoning, musculoskeletal injury, and chronic pain.

The Triqui people inhabit the bottom rung of the pecking order in the Skagit. They live in the coldest and wettest shacks in the most hidden labor camp with no insulation, no heat, and no wooden ceiling under the tin roof. They hold the most stressful, humiliating, and physically strenuous jobs working seven days a week without breaks while exposed to pesticides and weather. Accordingly, the Triqui pickers bear an unequal share of sickness and pain.

Crescencio and the Anguish of Insult

After a full day of picking strawberries near the end of my first summer of fieldwork, I returned to my shack to find the local migrant clinic preparing a health fair in the labor camp. The health fair involved a retired Evangelical Christian missionary formerly stationed in South America arriving in a large RV that had been converted into a mobile dental clinic, as well as a dentist, a few nurses, a few health educators, and several medical students coming in their private cars. As the pickers showered, changed out of their berry-stained clothing, and did laundry, the nurses and health educators walked the dusty dirt road around the camp letting people know about the fair being set up on the basketball court. The fair began with the nurses and health educators rounding up the children who lived in the camp and demonstrating how they should brush and floss their teeth. After handing out toothbrushes and toothpaste to the children present, they brought out a large rectangular cake with brightly colored frosting, cut it into small pieces, and handed it out to the long line of excited children. Next, they showed a video in which a Mexican subsistence farming single mother contracted HIV from her boyfriend after her husband died. The nurse who led the question-and-answer session afterward made the point several times that "it is not just faggots [*jotos*] who get HIV; it is also women subsistence farmers [*campesinas*], mothers, and girlfriends." The young men with whom I was standing snickered every time she said *joto*. The dozen medical students, all but two of whom spoke no Spanish, came from a nearby medical school and spent the three hours of the health fair alternately watching, chitchatting among themselves, and throwing used clothing up in the air above a bustling crowd of migrant workers.

As the health fair was winding down and the staff from the local migrant clinic packed up, a Triqui man approached me. Crescencio was living with his wife, two daughters aged five and eight, and a son aged twelve in a shack near mine in the camp. Having heard from the camp manager that I was a student doctor, he asked if I had any medicine for headaches. When I asked for more information, he explained that he had had a debilitating headache for almost seven years, approximately the same length of time he had been migrating for work. He described the headache as located on top of his head near the center, sometimes behind one or the other eye. The pain was so excruciating that he could no longer focus on anything until it dissipated. Like any good medical student, I asked far too many questions. I found out that the headache was not made better or worse by eating, resting, sitting,

standing, exercising, drinking water, or taking Tylenol or ibuprofen. Crescencio patiently explained to me that every time a farm supervisor called him names on the job, made fun of him, or reprimanded him unfairly, he developed one of these severe headaches. The most common triggers included being called "stupid Oaxacan" or being told in a deprecating or angry manner to "hurry up" when he was already picking as fast as possible. He explained to me that he was concerned because whenever he developed the headaches, any unpleasant noise or annoyance could upset him, and thus he felt more prone to anger with his wife and children. His primary reason for seeking help with the headache was so that he would not get angry with his family. He wanted to take care of this problem before it could evolve into anything serious, specifically, violence against his wife or children.

After the first few seasons of migration to other states within Mexico, Crescencio went to see doctors at the government clinic in San Miguel who tried different pills and injections. Some of the medicines produced short-term relief, but the headaches kept coming back. After years of migrating within Mexico, Crescencio began coming to work on the Tanaka farm in Washington and the headaches continued. In the labor camp as well as back in Oaxaca when he returned in the winters, he met with a Triqui healer who performed the traditional reading of his future as well as a cleansing meant to draw bad spirits away from his body. These interventions alleviated the headaches for a time. After every biomedical or traditional treatment, however, the headaches returned when triggered by mistreatment on the job. The only treatment Crescencio had found that made his headache go away was drinking twenty to twenty-four beers. He told me matter-of-factly that when he drank this amount of beer, he could relax and the pain would be gone the next morning when he woke up. He had to use this remedy a few times in an average workweek.

Crescencio's headaches present a complicated cycle of linkages between suffering and the social and symbolic forces structuring his life. To start the series off, like Abelino and other Triqui migrants, Crescencio is victim to the social forces obliging him to live and work in damaging conditions at the bottom of a labor hierarchy. Next, some of the individuals positioned above him in the hierarchy insult him with racist slurs and impossible demands. In turn, the contempt with which Crescencio is treated leads to his excruciating headaches. These socially structured headaches lead him to get angry with his family and to get drunk, thus involuntarily embodying the stereotype of Mexican migrants as misogynists and alcoholics. This stereotype then serves to legitimate the ethnic-citizenship hierarchy on the farm as well as the racist treatment the migrant workers receive. This symbolic violence, embodied so precisely by Crescencio, works to make invisible the racism and xenophobia underlying the disrespect that he and other Mexican migrants are seen to deserve. Finally, this disrespect is added to the forces positioning migrant berry pickers at the bottom of the farm hierarchy.

Migrant Farmwork and Health Disparities in Context

Nationwide, migrant farmworkers are sicker than other groups. . . . [T]he National Agricultural Worker Survey indicates that 81 percent of farmworkers are immigrants, 95 percent of whom were born in Mexico[5] and 52 percent of whom are undocumented.[6] Researchers estimate that there are one million indigenous Oaxacans in the United States, mostly Mixtec, Zapotec, and Triqui.[7] The average age of agricultural workers is twentynine, and very few are over sixty.[8] However, health statistics for migrant farmworkers are inexact given the impossibility of an accurate census. . . . In addition, most morbidity and mortality data are skewed down due to undocumented workers' fear of reporting health problems, poor enforcement of labor and health policies in agriculture, and the fact that many Latin American migrants return to their home countries as they age or become disabled, leading to a "healthy worker bias."[9] . . .

. . . Triqui strawberry pickers belong to the disadvantaged category of immigrants in the United States. . . . [T]he health status of immigrants declines with increasing time in the United States. Such health indicators as obesity, serum cholesterol, tobacco smoking, alcohol use, illicit drug use, mental illness, suicide, and death by homicide increase between first and second-generation Mexican immigrants in this country.[10] Nutritional value of the diet of immigrants also decreases significantly during the first year in the United States.[11] . . . Undocumented status further increases "allostatic load"—understood biomedically as the accumulation of health risk associated with chronic stress—due to traumatic experiences crossing the border and fear of deportation.[12]

In addition, Mexican migrant farmworkers suffer poor health due to their class position. Agricultural workers have a fatality rate five times that of all workers.[13] Moreover, agricultural workers have increased rates of nonfatal injuries, musculoskeletal pain, heart disease, and many types of cancer.[14] There is also an increased risk of stillbirth and congenital birth defects in children born near farms.[15] Furthermore, research indicates that approximately one-third to one-half of agricultural workers report chronic symptoms associated with pesticide exposure such as headache, skin and eye irritation, and flu-like syndromes.[16]

To further specify class position, migrant and seasonal farmworkers suffer the poorest health status in the agriculture industry. The vast majority of these individuals and families live below the poverty line.[17] They have increased rates of many chronic conditions, such as malnutrition, anemia, hypertension, diabetes, dermatitis, fatigue, headaches, sleep disturbances, anxiety, memory problems, sterility, blood disorders, dental problems, and abnormalities in liver and kidney function.[18] Migrant farmworkers have increased pulmonary problems to such a degree that farmwork has an effect on lung health comparable to smoking.[19] They have increased incidence of acute sicknesses such as urinary tract and kidney infections, heat stroke, anthrax, ascariasis, encephalitis, leptospirosis, rabies, salmonellosis, tetanus, and coccidioidomycosis, most of which are believed to be caused in large part by poor living and working conditions and lack of sanitary bathrooms.[20] Tuberculosis prevalence, also related to poor living conditions, is six times higher among migrant workers than in the general U.S. population,[21] and HIV infection is three times more common than in the overall U.S. and Mexican populations.[22] Finally, children of migrant farmworkers show high rates of malnutrition, vision problems, dental problems, anemia, and blood lead poisoning.[23]

Despite worse health status and a resulting need for increased health and social services, migrant farmworkers have many obstacles to accessing these services. Farmworkers are entirely or partially excluded from worker's compensation benefits in all but fifteen states.[24] The Fair Labor Standards Act of 1938 guaranteed minimum wage, time and a half wage for overtime, and restricted child labor, but it did not apply to agricultural workers. . . . The 1974 amendments retained the previous exclusions. Most farmworkers were excluded also by the Social Security Act and its later amendments from benefits related to unemployment, which in any case are not available to undocumented immigrants. In addition, even though migrant housing conditions are addressed in the Housing Act of 1949 and the Occupational Safety and Health Act of 1970, living conditions in labor camps continue to fall below the requirements. Finally, agricultural workers were denied the right to collective bargaining under the Wagner Act of 1935. They have gained the right to bargain only in the state of California under the Agricultural Labor Relations Act of 1975 after strong organizing by and a heavy toll of violence against the United Farm Workers (UFW). While this win led to labor improvements, the agriculture system in California for workers on farms without UFW contracts remains extremely exploitative. Furthermore, we must remember that even existing provisions for farmworkers are violated regularly because of vast power differentials and threats by employers to have undocumented migrants deported if they report violations.

Although there is a federal Migrant Health Program, it is estimated that it serves only 13 percent of the intended population of migrant workers.[25] . . . Researchers estimate that less than 30 percent of migrant laborers have health insurance, in contrast to an estimated 84 percent of U.S. residents overall.[26] . . . Furthermore, it is estimated in California that less than 10 percent of indigenous Mexican farmworkers have health insurance, in contrast to 30 percent of their mestizo counterparts.[27] In part due to these obstacles, migrant laborers are less likely than other people to obtain preventive care, with 27 percent never receiving a routine physical exam, 25 percent never having a dental checkup, and 43 percent never receiving an eye exam.[28] In fact, many migrant workers in the United States go through significant hardships to return to Mexico for health care and cite economic, cultural, and linguistic reasons for this choice.[29] Importantly, these statistics directly contradict the popular American complaint that undocumented immigrants are the cause of the demise of the American health care system through overuse.

Bernardo and the Damage of Torture

During my time on the farm in Washington State, I met one Triqui family who lived outside the labor camp in an apartment in town. The twenty-seven-year-old father in this family, Martin, had been able to gain U.S. residency through his father, Bernardo, who became a U.S. resident in the 1986 amnesty for farmworkers under the Bracero Program. Martin no longer works on the Tanaka farm but at a chicken packing plant, along with his wife. Bernardo was one of the first Triqui people to come to Washington. When he gained U.S. residency, he stopped working on the farm and moved back to Oaxaca. Each summer since the 1980s Bernardo has spent five months working in a fish processing plant in Alaska to support himself, his wife, and his sister. This family is from San Pedro, a Triqui town in the mountains of Oaxaca near San Miguel, the hometown of the rest of the Triqui people I knew in Washington. While the whole Triqui Zone in Oaxaca is reputed to be violent, San Pedro is most notorious. It is also home to the Unified Movement for Triqui Liberation (MULT), which, at the time of my fieldwork, was in the process of transforming from a rebel movement to an official political party. . . .

In the middle of winter, Martin called and invited me to go with him on a road trip to Oaxaca. We left two days later and drove straight to Oaxaca without stopping to sleep. There were five people in my Honda Civic hatchback for the three-thousand-mile trip in each direction: me, Martin, his four-year-old daughter, and his six-year-old and seven-yearold sons. The only stops we made were for oil changes in Arizona on the way down and the way back up, to buy food quickly once or twice daily, and to fix a flat tire once in rural Oaxaca. Otherwise, Martin and I took turns driving, napping, entertaining the children, and cleaning up after Martin's daughter got food poisoning, leading to diarrhea and vomiting on the drive south.

I spent my first week in the state of Oaxaca in Bernardo's house in the city of Juxtlahuaca. Though this family was originally from San Pedro, their land was on the edge of town, next to a mestizo village, and they were under frequent armed attack from their neighbors and frequently attacked those neighbors as well. The ongoing attacks were related primarily to landownership and political affiliations; most people in San Pedro support the MULT, whereas the neighboring town overall supported the Institutional Revolutionary Party (PRI), which had been in power in most of Mexico for over seventy years. Bernardo described the situation in broken Spanish, his second language.

> There have been many deaths. Oh! Many deaths! There was a fourteenyear-old girl there [*pointing toward the mountains where most Triqui people live*], just a girl. They got her before she went up the hill. Many raped her. They raped her, many! Then she was killed, very violent, many knife cuts. Then a teacher was killed there, where we went [*pointing toward San Pedro*]. Oh! The son of Miguel [one of the leaders of the MULT], remember? I gave him soda? I was here [*gesturing with his hand*], and you were there next to Martin. They shot his son. Then over there [*gesturing different directions with his hand*] and there and there. Oh, many deaths. Maybe eight, maybe ten in the last two months. Evil people, very evil. They kill between political parties.
>
> There is a lot of danger here. If you say something and don't realize someone heard you and they are hidden, all of a sudden, "pow!" or a knife, and you are dead. I can't go out at night, even if we need something. Not at night, no! A lot of danger; there is a lot of danger here. During the day is fine. I go to the market to see the doctor. But not at night. I have fear. A lot of danger, yes, yes.

Bernardo and Martin's family, along with many others, moved from San Pedro to the nearby small city of Juxtlahuaca to escape the violence. Many such land wars are still going on in La Mixteca region of Oaxaca. With the money Bernardo made migrating to the United States, the family was able to build a house in Juxtlahuaca and start a small store in one room of their house.

At night, after we drove back on the steep dirt roads from visiting San Pedro, Bernardo asked me if I knew of any good medicine for his stomach. He explained that his stomach had been hurting for eight years. He said, "My stomach does not like food any more. I don't have the desire [*ganas*] to eat. It hurts to eat." Before he goes to Alaska to work each spring, his

doctor in Juxtlahuaca gives him a long series of "vitamin shots" and "shots to give [him] hunger" so that he has enough energy to work in the processing plant. When he returns from Alaska, he is weak and thin and receives another long series of the same shots to recover his strength in order to tend the family cornfields just outside Juxtlahuaca. The following description of his stomach pain was punctuated by frequent groans and moans.

> It gives me such a pain! Right here [*pointing to his lower abdomen*], such a pain, and it goes up. It jumps and jumps like chords jumping, like this, like this [*rapidly opening and closing his hands*]. I wake up and my stomach hurts, ay! It gets hard like this bench is hard [*touching the wooden bench on which he sits*]. So I mash my stomach with a soda bottle. I mash, mash, mash here, mash here [*pushing his fist slowly into his abdomen*]. And it helps a little. But, ay! I can't stand it. I can't eat! Nothing! Each time I eat it hurts, but it hurts. But I hold out [*me aguanto*]. I hold out until work is over.

Bernardo had lost weight over the past several years and felt weak each morning when he left at 5:00 to work the family cornfields before I woke up. His wife told me that he had to force himself to eat a tortilla and an egg before working in the fields.

When I asked him why his stomach hurt, he first explained that it was because he had worked so hard all his life.

> I have my pains because of so much work. Ay; so much work. I left for Veracruz to cut cane when I was eight. So much work all my life. Veracruz, Baja California, Washington, Oregon, California, Norte Carolina, ay! And now, 'laska. And here, the cornfield and the house, too. All my life I work a lot, and one gets tired, tired, and the body hurts. In 'laska, we work 16 hours, no! Seven days a week. No rest for 2 months. Then maybe 10 hours or 8 hours a day 7 days a week for 2 more months. Ay! So much work!

"So much working [*tanto trabajar*] wears out a body," he said with a weak smile. He continued, "All I have is from my work. I harvest the corn, cut the *zacate* [corn plants], bind it, all alone, alone. I am sixty-two or maybe eighty; I don't know.[30] This house, the land, it is all from my work. Who will feed me and my family if I don't work? No one. There is nothing here."

When I asked him why the pain started eight years ago, he added another important fact: "Also, the soldiers. You know what soldiers [*soldados*] are, right? Yes, the soldiers punched and kicked me many, many times. Punched like this [*making a fist and punching into the air*], here in my stomach. Ah! But many beatings [*chingadazos*] until there was blood all over. Because of the Movement [MULT]. People said rumors against us and the soldiers, the blue soldiers, came and beat me up."

Eight years before, Bernardo was kidnapped and tortured by the Mexican federal police in charge of narcotics enforcement, whom he calls "the blue soldiers" because of the color of their uniforms. This branch of the Mexican military is funded by the U.S. Drug Enforcement Agency, officially in order to stop drug smuggling between Mexico and the United States. Bernardo was beaten several times by these soldiers and put in prison. There, despite several requests, he was denied medical help such that he resorted to drinking his own urine as a remedy to help his abdomen heal. Furthermore, he was refused food many of the days he was in captivity. The "blue soldiers" told him that he had been kidnapped under suspicion that he was part of the MULT, even though the movement had no links with the drug trade. After several months of petitions by Bernardo and his family, the mayor of Juxtlahuaca signed and stamped an official paper—which Bernardo proudly showed me—stating that Bernardo had done no wrong, and he was finally released from prison.

Like Abelino and Crescencio, Bernardo endures a form of suffering determined directly by social and political forces. The contemporary system of neoliberal corporate capitalism has built global inequalities, leading southern Mexico into a deepening economic depression. This poverty is one of the primary factors producing the local land wars as well as the survival-seeking out-migration of able-bodied workers. The political alliances of the Mexican military, with its ties to U.S. federal financing, have translated into a repression of the movements seeking redistribution of power and resources in a more equitable fashion. The political violence against suspected members of indigenous rights movements is not only embodied as sickness, as

in Bernardo's case, but also reinforces the neoliberal economic project and thus deepens the poverty and suffering of millions of marginalized people. The logic behind this violence affirms that the poorest of the poor must not assert themselves or be allowed political economic power. . . .

The suffering of Triqui migrant laborers is an embodiment of multiple forms of violence. The political violence of land wars has pushed them to live in inhospitable climates without easy access to water for crops. The structural violence of global neoliberal capitalism forces them to leave home and family members, suffer through a long and deadly desert border crossing, and search for a means to survive in a new land. The structural violence of labor hierarchies in the United States organized around ethnicity and citizenship positions them at the bottom, with the most dangerous and backbreaking occupations and the worst accommodations. Due to their location at the bottom of the pecking order, the undocumented Triqui migrant workers endure disproportionate injury and sickness.

Abelino's knee pain is a direct result of structural violence, particularly as it drives him into jobs requiring repetitive, harmful movements that all but guarantee physical deterioration, inflammation, and pain. He is not given the option of other forms of work, like the "light jobs" in which he sees U.S. citizens engaged. National and local prejudices and stereotypes further shape the hierarchy of labor such that Triqui workers are often treated with disrespect and racist insult. For the vast majority, their undocumented status leads to fear of authority and fear of demanding the redress of wrongs. These external and internalized forms of symbolic violence not only shore up unequal labor hierarchies through normalization but also lead to various forms of suffering, such as Crescencio's intractable headaches. These headaches, in turn, lead back to the symbolic violence of stereotypes of Mexican migrant men as alcoholic and *machista*. Simultaneously, the Mexican military enacts violence in response to the fear of the economic elite at the prospect of disenfranchised people organizing for economic, health, education, and political rights. Bernardo's debilitating stomach pain began with the direct political violence of several well-placed fist and boot blows to his stomach and evolved through the structural violence requiring him to work long, difficult days in Alaska and Oaxaca in order for his family to survive. . . .

Notes

1. Scheper-Hughes, Nancy and Philippe Bourgois.2004.; Bourgois, Philippe. 2001. The Power of Violence in War and Peace: Post-Cold War Lessons from El Salvador." *Ethnography* 2(1): 5–34.

2. Bourgois 2001:8.

3. Galtung, John. 1969 "Violence, Peace, and Peace Research." *Journal of Peace Research* 6: 167–91.; Farmer, Paul. 1997. "On Suffering and Structural Violence: A View from Below." In *Social Suffering,* ed. Arthur Kleinman, Veena Das, and Margaret Lock, 261–83. Berkeley: University of California Press.

4. Bourdieu, Pierre. 2001. *Masculine Domination.* Stanford, CA: Stanford University Press.

5. Kandula,Namratha, Margaret Kersey, and Nicole Lurie. 2004. "Assuring the Health Immigrants: What the Leading Health Indicators Tell Us." *Annual Review of Public Health* 25: 357–76.

6. Villarejo, Don. 2003. "The Health of U.S. Hired Farm Workers." *Annual Review of Public Health.* 24: 175–93.

7. McGurie, Sharon Sr., and Jane Georges. 2003. "Undocumentedness and Liminality as Health Variables." *Advances in Nursing Science* 26(3): 185–96.

8. Frank et al. 2004; Slesinger, Doris. 1992. "Health Status and Needs of Migrant Farm Workers in the United States: A Literature Review," *Journal of Rural Health* 8(3): 227–34.

9. Villarejo 2003.

10. Bourdieu, Pierre. 1997. *Pascalian Meditations.* Stanford, CA: Stanford University Press..; Villarejo 2003.

11. Villarejo 2003.

12. McGuire and Georges 2003.

13. Frank, Arthur, Robert McKnight, Steven Kirkhorn, and Paul Gunderson. 2004. "Issues of Agricultural Safety and Health." *Annual Review of Public Health* 24:224–45.

14. Ibid.

15. Ibid.; Mobed, Ketty, Ellen Gold, and Marc Schenker. 1992. "Occupational Health Problems among Migrant and Seasonal Farm Workers." *Western Journal of Medicine* 157(3): 367–85.

16. Frank et al. 2004.

17. Rust 1990; Slesinger 1992; Villarejo 2003.

18. Slesigner 1992; Mobed, Gold, and Schenker 1992.

19. Mobed, Gold, and Shenker 1992.

20. Ibid.; Sakala, Carol. 1987. "Migrant and Seasonal Farmworkers in the United States: A Review of Health Hazards, Status, and Policy." *International Migration Review* 21(3): 659–87.

21. Villarejo 2003.

22. *Rural Migration News.* 2005. "Health and Insurance." 11(1): www.migration.ucdavis.edu/rmn.

23. Mobed, Gold, and Schenker 1992.

24. Sakala 1987.

25. Villarejo 2003.

26. Health Outreach Partners. 2010. *Breaking Down the Barriers: A National Needs Assessment on Farmworker Health Outreach.* 4th ed. Oakland, CA: Health Outreach Partners; Villarejo 2003; *Migration News* 2004.

27. Mines, Richard, Sandra Nichols, and David Runsten. 2010. "California's Indigenous Farmworkers." www.indigenousfarmworkers.org; See also Bade, Bonnie. 1999. *"Is There a Doctor in the Field?" Underlying Conditions Affecting Access to Health Care for California Farmworkers and Their Families.* CPRC Report. [Berkeley]: California Policy Research Center, University of California.

28. Slesinger 1992.

29. Kauffold, Andrea, Edward Zuroweste, Deliana Garcia, Carmel T. Drewes. 2004. "Assuring the Health of Immigrants: What the Leading Health Indicators Tell Us." *Annual Review of Public Health* 25: 357–76.

30. Several elderly Triqui people in Oaxaca did not know their ages and often said "sixty or eighty," which seemed to mean simply, "I am considered old."

7.5 **American Meat**[1]

DONALD D. STULL

Widespread concern about the health and environmental consequences of industrial agriculture has led to growing interest in rethinking foodways in more sustainable and just manners. While you may be familiar with alternative food markets in your communities, when you think about alternative markets, do you think first of the food or first of the people behind food production? Reflecting on decades of applied ethnographic research on the impact of the meatpacking industry, Don Stull asks us to confront the fact that the American public appears to care more about the animals farmed than the people who put their food on the table. In what follows, Stull reveals that hardships faced by today's meatpacking workers are all too similar to those described in The Jungle, *Upton Sinclair's damning exposé of Chicago packinghouses, first published in 1906.*

Questions:

1. What were the applied outcomes from the team's research in Garden City? How was their work put to use?
2. Discuss the disconnect between the rhetoric of "safety first" and the practice of "safety second." What social, political, and economic factors contribute to the rift between this ideal and real behavior?
3. Stull states that "the public is far more concerned about the welfare of farmed animals than the welfare of those who turn them into meat for our tables." Do you agree or disagree? Why?
4. Consider Stull's advice for creating change to the contemporary foodways. How likely are you to engage in some of these activities? Are there barriers to your participation?
5. Draw on the outcomes of the Garden City work to brainstorm how applied anthropological research on contemporary food production can help inform future changes to American foodways.

and thou shalt say, I will eat flesh, because thy soul longeth to eat flesh; . . . then thou shalt kill of thy herd and of thy flock, which the Lord hath given thee. . . . Ye shall not eat of any thing that dieth of itself . . . .

—DEUTERONOMY 12:20, –21; 14:21

Most of us encounter meat only at the grocery store or the restaurant. But meat must be made, and it can only be made by the slaughter of animals. In fact Jewish, Christian, and Islamic traditions forbid the eating of animals that die by other than human hands. Slaughter, evisceration, and dismemberment are essential in transforming living creatures into food, but most of us prefer to remain ignorant of where our meat comes from. But that process and its consequences for livestock producers, packinghouse workers, and the communities that host the industry's giant meat factories have been my professional passion for three decades.

I came to the study of meat in a round-about way. After the opening of two massive beef plants in the early 1980s, the population of Garden City, Kansas, jumped by one-third to become the state's fastest growing community. Most of the newcomers who flocked to jobs in these plants were refugees from Southeast Asia and immigrants from Mexico and Central America. Beginning in the summer of 1987, I led five anthropologists and a geographer in an investigation of changing ethnic relations in Garden City, as part of the Ford Foundation's national study of what was then called the new immigration. Overwhelmingly Anglo and agrarian at the beginning of the 1980s, by the time we arrived, Garden City was in the midst of a dramatic social and cultural transformation that foreshadowed a tide of economic and demographic change that was to sweep across rural North America in the coming decades. We submitted our final report to the Ford Foundation in February 1990. It concluded with a series of recommendations to the people of Garden City on education, housing, health care, day care, and social services. In conjunction with the school district, we organized an advisory board representing public school teachers, city government, Garden City's three main ethnic groups, and service organizations. We worked with this committee to fine tune our recommendations and present them to appropriate institutions and agencies.

Our report was soon put to local use: social service agencies used our findings to obtain external funds; the school district used our recommendations to revise policies and procedures on curriculum, bilingual and English as a second language (ESL) instruction, extracurricular activities, community outreach, personnel training, evaluation, and retention; the city commission established a cultural relations board with representation from its main ethnic groups; and local law enforcement sought to increase its minority personnel.

What we did not know as we concluded more than two years of fieldwork was whether the changes we witnessed in Garden City also confronted other packinghouse towns. Over the next decade, social geographer Michael Broadway and I studied Lexington, Nebraska, where a beef plant opened in 1990, and Guymon, Oklahoma, which attracted a pork plant. Broadway also launched a study of the city of Brooks, located in Alberta, Canada, which became home to a plant owned by the largest beef-processing company in the United States. I turned my attention to my birth community in western Kentucky, which in the mid-1990s began sprouting the commonwealth's newest cash crop—chickens—and the plants to process them.

Like Garden City, each of these places faced rural industrialization and rapid growth, creating an array of problems common to so-called boomtowns: population mobility, severe housing shortages, soaring school enrollments, rising rates of crime and social ills, inadequate medical services, strains on infrastructure and social services, dramatic increases in cultural and linguistic diversity, and environmental concerns.

Packinghouses at the turn of the 21st century are a far cry from those Upton Sinclair described in *The Jungle* at the turn of the 20th. But for all their computerization and laser technology, their robotics and ergonomics, the knife, the meat hook, and the steel are still the basic tools of the trade. And today's plants remain, like the ones they replaced, rigidly organized, labor-intensive factories that turn animals into meat. Workers remain on their feet most of the day and perform the same repetitive motions thousands of times during their shift, whether it's halving beef carcasses with a hydraulic splitting saw, "dropping tongues," or artfully cutting meat into retail portions which will be vacuum packed and sent directly to a supermarket's meat counter.

Work in a meatpacking plant has always been dangerous. In 1917, eleven years after *The Jungle* was published, and long before the federal government required companies to report worker injuries or illnesses, the welfare director of Chicago's Armour plant reported that 50 percent of the company's workers became ill at work or were injured over the course of the year. Historian James Barrett attributes this high injury rate to sharp knives, damp and cold working conditions, and the speed of the work.

By the time I began studying meatpacking in the 1980s, workers were required to wear hardhats, safety glasses, earplugs, steel-toed and rubber-soled boots, and an amazing array of additional gear intended to protect them from injury. Even so, meatpacking was among the most dangerous industries in America for the last quarter of the 20th century. It still is. After all, sharp knives, damp and cold working conditions, and the pace of the work remain the same.

Meatpacking is one of North America's few remaining manufacturing industries where a high school diploma, previous work experience, and the ability to speak English are not necessary for employment. These characteristics help explain why today's meat and poultry industry relies heavily on immigrants and refugees. Typical of the industry overall, two-thirds of employees in a meatpacking plant I studied a few years ago were Hispanic, one-fourth were white, and one-tenth Asian. But overall figures are misleading: three-quarters of the plant's officials and managers were white males (7 percent were white females, 11 percent were Hispanic men, and 2 percent Hispanic women). Out on the floor, six of ten workers classified as unskilled were Hispanic men (61 percent) (followed by Hispanic women [13 percent] and white men [12 percent]). Today, Mexicans and Guatemalans might stand beside workers from Somalia, Myanmar, and the Marshall Islands on the line at this and similar plants.

Its employee handbook said the company "is dedicated to quality and safety." "Safety first" appeared on bulletin boards and walls throughout the plant. Safety was highlighted and reinforced in celebrations and rituals. It was prominent in corporate and plant competitions, awards, training meetings, and paperwork. Supervisors who failed to turn in their safety-meeting records were rebuked on bulletin boards and in company memoranda. Injured employees could be called into upper management's morning meeting to explain how they were hurt and suggest what the plant might do to prevent such occurrences.

"Safety" was always written first on maintenance supervisors' "to-do" lists. But as they went to and from their office and the plant floors, they discussed work priorities, allocation of time and effort, and strategies to solve pressing problems. They didn't talk about safety, except to laugh and say "safety second!" They knew that "hitting the numbers" is what matters most.

"Nothing gets fixed until someone gets hurt," was the most prevalent and bitter complaint heard from line workers. Part of the problem was that many in positions of authority "pass the buck" to avoid being held accountable. That "they only fix it after someone gets hurt" was borne out by management's regular discussion of problems after, rather than before, they resulted in physical harm to an employee.

Work on the line is tedious, monotonous, and risky—it wears workers down, and sooner or later most get fired, get hurt, or quit. Take Marcial, a line worker at a different plant. He gave his two weeks' notice and worked his last day at the plant eight years and one day after he started. When he began working on the killfloor, he was Number 500 on the seniority list, when he quit he was Number 75. The woman who administered his exit interview asked why he was quitting, and he replied, "The lines go too fast, the supervisors are too mean, they push their workers too hard, and I don't like anything about working there." Startled at his candor, she looked blankly at him as he laughed. She left the space on the form for why he quit empty.

Despite the protestations of industry spokespersons, turnover is tacitly encouraged because it helps keep wages and workers' compensation costs down. It also mitigates against union organizing. Meat and poultry companies depend on vulnerable classes of laborers to work on their lines—minorities, women, immigrants, and especially refugees. They can be paid less. Industry executives also believe they will work harder, put up with worse working conditions, and be less likely to organize or assert their rights (even if they know them). And the very presence of immigrants on the line serves as a warning to native-born workers that they can always be replaced.

The impact of the meat and poultry industry on host communities and packinghouse workers has concerned me for many years. The general public cares more about other issues.

The industry's negative impact on water and air quality was first to garner serious public concern. Concentrated animal feeding operations, commonly known as CAFOs, have become the norm in livestock production. For example, hog operations with 5,000 or more animals accounted for 62 percent of U.S. production in 2009, up from just 18 percent in 1993. Problems arise from the excessive size of these operations and their density. Twenty percent of the 1.2 billion broilers produced in Arkansas every year come from just two counties in the northeast corner of the state—Benton and Washington. The biggest problem created by CAFOs is manure disposal.

Feedlot steers eat about 30 pounds of feed and produce about 27 pounds of waste each day. The average hog produces 3,000 pounds of solid manure and over 5,000 gallons of liquid manure each year—2.5 times the production of the average human. For every pound of gain, a chicken produces half a pound of dry waste. This waste, combined with the rice hulls or wood chips used to line the floors of chicken houses, is called litter. The average broiler house is one-and-a-half times the length of a football field (460 feet or 510 feet) and one-fourth its width (43 feet). Broiler houses hold between 25,000 and 27,000 birds at a time, and ideally each house produces seven flocks in a year (10 weeks from egg to finish; 7 weeks from hatch to slaughter). At this rate, each broiler house produces as much as 200 tons of litter a year. All this waste must go somewhere. Someday it may be converted into alternative power, but for now virtually all of it gets sprayed or spread on cropland as fertilizer. And if applied at levels above the nutrient absorption rates of soils and crops, runoff and subsequent ground and surface water pollution will occur.

Manure and litter aren't the only pollutants produced by CAFOs. Each chicken house produces about 5 tons of ammonia annually. Up to one-third of workers in swine CAFOs experience occupationally related health problems, especially respiratory problems. Matched control studies show that people who live near hog CAFOs suffer ailments similar to those who work in the facilities: elevated rates of nausea, diarrhea, headaches, depression, anger, fatigue. CAFOs foul the air for workers and neighbors alike. But their harmful effects do not stop there. Antimicrobials are used to promote animal weight gain and protect against infections likely to result from confinement. As much as three-fourths of the antimicrobial agents given to confined livestock and poultry are excreted, thereby entering the environment as organic fertilizer which may contaminate water supplies through runoff and infiltration. A study published in the April 2015 issue of *Environmental Health Perspectives* found tetracycline and other antibiotics both downwind and upwind for at least 100 yards from feedyards in the Texas Panhandle. Recent studies suggest they may combine with bacterial organisms in the environment to contaminate the food chain.

In 2012, according to the Food and Drug Administration (FDA), 19.6 million pounds of antibiotics considered medically important for human health were sold for use in farmed animals, and this is an increase of 1.5 million pounds from the amount used in each of the previous two years. In March of 2015 McDonald's USA announced "new menu sourcing initiatives including only sourcing chicken raised without antibiotics that are important to human medicine."

CAFOs are bad for water and air quality. What about for farmers? In 1976, the typical Corn Belt hog farm averaged 320 acres, met 75 percent of its own feed requirements, and produced 650 slaughter hogs. The farmer and his family provided most of the necessary labor, collected animal waste on site, and spread it as fertilizer on his crops and pasture. Nineteen out of 20 of those hogs were sold on the open market. Four decades later, most of those farms have disappeared, to be replaced by large confinement operations. And 9 of 10 hogs are directly owned by transnational processing firms or raised under contract to them. Hog farming has spread out from the Corn Belt to North Carolina, Utah, Oklahoma, and Kansas.

The displacement of family hog farms by confinement operations has had a disastrous impact on rural economies. Agricultural economist John Ikerd found that a $5 million investment in contract hog production in Missouri created 40–50 new jobs, but it displaced almost three times that number of independent hog producers. Having fewer farmers translates into fewer people to support local businesses and a decline in local tax receipts. Studies in Illinois, Iowa, Michigan, and Wisconsin confirmed his findings.

The radical transformation of hog production is most evident in North Carolina. Between 1982 and 1997, North Carolina's hog production skyrocketed from 2 million to 9.6 million, putting it in second place behind Iowa. This fivefold increase in hog output was accompanied by a fourfold drop in the number of hog farmers, from 11,400 to about 3,000. In 2007, more than 99 percent of North Carolina's 10 million hogs were produced on just 1,600 farms—almost half came from just two counties.

The poultry industry pioneered vertical integration, and in so doing destroyed the market for chickens. Virtually all chickens are owned from the genetics to the grocer's meat counter by one of a handful of firms: Tyson, JBS, Perdue. The market for hogs all but disappeared by the turn of the 21st century. It is seriously threatened for beef cattle as well. A 2010 study by David Domina and Robert Taylor found that half, and perhaps as much as 80 percent, of the cattle now slaughtered in the United States are procured through what is called captive supply: they are owned by the packers, they are raised on contract to the packers, or they are finished at feedyards that have only one viable buyer.

The Humane Society of the United States (HSUS) and PETA (People for the Ethical Treatment of Animals) have fostered public awareness and outrage over how farmed animals are raised and slaughtered. Visit PETA's Web site and you will find a documentary narrated by Alec Baldwin entitled "Meet Your Meat."

The video consists of a series of clips of workers inside factory farms mistreating chickens, turkeys, pigs, and cows, as well as animals living in confined quarters such as gestation and veal crates where they are unable to turn around. Such videos make big food processing corporations very nervous; so nervous that they have successfully lobbied state legislatures to implement "ag gag" laws, which criminalize undercover photography or video inside animal farms. Ag gag laws currently exist in seven states—Idaho, Iowa, Missouri, Montana, North Dakota, Utah, and Kansas. Enacted in 1990, the Kansas Farm Animal and Field Crop and Research Facilities Act was the first such law. It makes it a crime to "enter an animal facility to take pictures by photograph, video camera or by any other means" with the intent of causing harm to the enterprise.

Public outcry has pushed the industry toward more humane treatment of animals. Veal crates, for example, where young calves are kept in strict confinement, have been banned after voter referendums in Arizona and California. Burger King reached an agreement with the HSUS to switch completely to so-called cage-free eggs by 2017. In 2012, McDonald's announced that by 2022 it will no longer buy pork from producers who use gestation stalls to house their pregnant sows. Safeway, the nation's second largest supermarket chain, followed suit soon thereafter.

Complaints by workers and unions against packinghouse working conditions have largely fallen on deaf ears, however. Indeed the federal government has made it harder to document such complaints. One of the most common work-related injuries in a packing plant is carpal tunnel syndrome, a musculoskeletal disorder caused by repetitive motions that can lead to a crippling of the hand or wrist and the inability to grip or even pick up objects. In 2002, the federal government's Occupational Safety and Health Administration stopped requiring employers to report such injuries. And so, as if by magic, the rates for repeated trauma disorders went from 8.1/100 workers in 2000 to who knows what today? The American Meat Institute, the meatpackers' lobby arm, brags that given the drop in work-related injuries, work safety is "a noncompetitive issue in the meat and poultry industry."

Despite the many detailed exposés of miserable working conditions in packinghouses and factory farms in books such as Eric Schlosser's *Fast Food Nation* and my own *Slaughterhouse Blues* (written with Michael Broadway, published by Wadsworth, 2004, 2013)—the public is far more concerned about the welfare of farmed animals than the welfare of those who turn them into meat for our tables. In a 2010 national survey by Context Marketing, 69 percent of respondents said they would willingly pay more for "ethically produced" food. When asked what they meant by "ethical food," more than 90 percent identified three main qualities: "protects the environment, meets high quality and safety standards, and treats animals humanely." Working conditions and wages of food processing workers were not among the criteria for "ethical" food!

The typical American grocery store is stocked with 50,000 items, triple what it was 30 years ago. In 2010 alone, more than 15,000 new foods and beverages came to market in the United. States. With so much to choose from, it's no wonder we usually come home with stuff that wasn't on our shopping list.

But how much choice do we really have? Just five companies account for almost half of supermarket food sales in the United States. And what about the food those companies offer us? Let's take meat. Just four companies provide us with 79 percent of our beef, 65 percent of our pork, and 57 percent of our poultry. So, no matter what kind of meat we have for dinner, most likely it comes from the same handful of companies: Tyson, JBS, Cargill, Smithfield. What, you say, you can never decide which bacon to bring home: Armour, Eckrich, Farmland, Gwaltney, John Morrell, or Smithfield? All are owned by Smithfield.—which is now owned by China's biggest pork producer— Shuanghui.

OK, so market power is consolidated in the hands of a few multinational corporations. What does this mean for the food we eat and the people who produce it? Since 1980, 4 out of 10 farmers who raise cattle and 9 out of 10 who raise hogs have gone out of business. But farmers still raise cows, and pigs, and chickens, don't they? Well, yes they do, but most of them don't really own the animals they raise. Virtually all the chickens sold in the United States are grown under production contracts to a handful of companies, who own the birds from egg to supermarket. Tyson Foods, the largest U.S. poultry company, contracts with about 6,000 of what it calls family farmers to raise its chickens. They are expected to grow birds to slaughter weight under strict company guidelines as quickly and as cheaply as possible. If Tyson is not satisfied, it may cancel their contracts with little notice and even less recourse, leaving them under a mountain of debt for their otherwise useless chicken houses.

Our food system is an hourglass. In one chamber are tens of thousands of farmers and ranchers, but their sands are steadily receding. In the other are hundreds of millions of eaters, whose sands continue to swell. In the narrow middle between growers and eaters sit a handful of giant corporations, what economists call an oligopoly. Those who grow the animals that become our meat are more and more likely to face a monopsony—only one buyer for their animals. Eaters would seem to have unlimited choice as they cruise the supermarket aisles, but those myriad choices are presented to them by a few companies, who use monopolistic practices to expand their product lines and increase their market share. The results: lower prices for farmers and higher prices for eaters. Over the last decade retail meat prices have risen more than 40 percent! But during that same time, gross farm income for small- and medium-sized hog and cattle farmers fell by 32 percent. Seventy-one percent of chicken farmers live below the federal poverty line.

Choice. More and more farmers are going broke for lack of it. In his first term, President Obama promised to reform American agriculture through vigorous antitrust enforcement. We are still waiting. In the 2008 farm bill, Congress instructed the Department of Agriculture to write regulations to restore fairness and competition in livestock and poultry production, but under pressure from interests that dominate industrial agriculture, it has refused to either approve or fund enforcement of almost all the proposed reforms.

Each of us chooses the food we eat, and those choices help shape prevailing systems of food production, processing, and packaging. Our food choices have economic implications; they have moral ones too.

The National Catholic Rural Life Conference has proclaimed an Eaters' Bill of Rights. Each of us has the right to know how our food is grown and processed. We have a right to food that is safe, nutritious, and produced under socially just circumstances, without harming air, water, land—or people. We also have a right to know the country of origin of our food and whether it has been genetically modified. The conference advocates policies that "uphold the dignity of family farmers," and opposes the contract-grower system of agricultural production, which makes "serfs of family farmers."

Do we want a food system built on the illusion of variety, abundance, and choice, while systematically monopolizing and exploiting both those who provide its raw products and those who purchase the foods made from them? Since the U.S. government has turned a deaf ear to concerns about monopolistic practices of the giant corporations that control our food, what can we do?

We do not have the political influence of multinational corporations, but we are not without power, especially if we join with other concerned citizens in common cause. Legislators can be influenced by campaigns in the public interest—country-of-origin labeling is a case in point, not only in what can be done, but also about how hard it is to achieve basic reform. And how easily that reform can be undone. Country of origin labeling (COOL) for meats was repealed in 2015 after the World Trade Organization upheld complaints from Canada and Mexico that COOL was hurting their meat producers.

Another example comes from Kansas where, in 2013, a bill was introduced in the state senate to repeal the ban on corporate ownership of farmland. If enacted it would have allowed any agricultural business entity to establish agricultural operations anywhere in the state. It would also have eliminated the requirement that new corporate swine and dairy operations be subject to approval by county commissioners or public vote. Thanks to public opposition and testimony, this bill did not make it out of committee.

Land use regulations dictate agricultural policy and practice. Zoning ordinances are enacted by local governments, and private citizens shape such decisions. The most effective means available to private citizens and local communities to regulate animal agriculture is to support stronger rural zoning to limit the number and size of CAFOs, ensure adequate setbacks from neighbors, and protect air and water quality. Paradoxically, in cities and suburbs, citizens may wish to rescind or revise local ordinances that prohibit or restrict modest forms of animal agriculture.

Legislation is not the only means by which food giants can be convinced to alter their corporate practices. Under pressure from consumers, fast food giants like McDonald's and grocery chains like Whole Foods are insisting on more humane treatment and slaughter of animals. More and more chain restaurants—Arby's,

Chipotle, Chick-fil-A, Panera—are responding to public demand for hormone- and antibiotic-free meats. And thanks to sustained protests, McDonald's and Walmart are raising hourly wages.

Multinational corporations have been pushed and prodded into making modest reforms in how animals are raised and slaughtered and how much some of their workers are paid. But tweaking the industrial food system can get us only so far and only so fast. In the short term, we will be better served to look for viable alternatives to the dominant food system. And viable alternatives do exist. A growing number of producers and providers do offer something different. We can patronize farmers' markets, local food co-ops, community-supported agriculture (CSA) or box schemes, which offer in-season fruits and vegetables, meat and dairy products from local farms. You can also ask your supermarket manager to stock and label local

and regional foods and sell natural, grass-fed, free-range, and antibiotic-free meat.

You can grow some of your own food. Why not give backyard gardens or even backyard chickens a try? You don't need to be a farmer or a master gardener to plant, harvest, and enjoy delicious and nutritious fruits and vegetables. Nor do you need a "back 40" to grow them—a sunny spot in the backyard, some pots on the deck or patio, a plot in the community garden; some good soil, compost, and a few simple tools are all you need to get started. Sure, these options may not be as convenient. And they may not be cheap. But they will be fresher, tastier, and safer. And they will come from food systems that are, in the long run, far more sustainable—and just. Isn't that worth a few cents more at the cash register? It's your choice. And your choices have significant consequences for the food security, safety, and quality of all of us.

Notes:

1. Sources for most of the statistics in this chapter can be found in Donald D. Stull and Michael J. Broadway. 2013 . Slaughterhouse Blues: The Meat and Poultry Industry in North American. Second Edition. Belmont, Calif.: Wadsworth.

IN THE NEWS Forged Food

Foraging refers to obtaining food by searching for it, as opposed to growing crops or raising livestock. Anthropologists have long studied hunter-gatherers in small-scale societies, who subsist through foraging. More recently anthropologists are turning their attention to foragers in urban settings, including "dumpster-diving" and the foraging of mushrooms, roots, fruits, berries, and other edibles.

The audio story "Foraged Lunch: Harvesting Urban Food Crops as a Hedge Against Food Insecurity" follows forager Melissa Vorass Herrera in Seattle, Washington. Herrera was part of anthropologist Melissa Poe's research project designed to address the gap in our understanding of food foraging practices in urban, post-industrial spaces. After listening to the story, readers can find a fuller description of the anthropological insights offered through this study by exploring Poe's research project description on the University of Washington's Department of Anthropology website in the article "Foraging Wild Foods in Urban Spaces."

In the article "Eat Like a Queen for Free—Dumpster Diving and Wasteful Consumer Culture," anthropologist Maria Grewe explores waste as a social construct, showing how dumpster-divers transform what some consider "waste" into meals while protesting a growing consumerist society.

Both studies discuss the symbolic meanings attached to food, and in these cases, to free, foraged food. Studies like these challenge the notion that "urban" and "nature" are diametrically opposed, as well as work to counter consumerism and address food insecurity.

 Visit www.oup.com/us/brondo for weblinks.

ANTHROPOLOGY IN PRACTICE

DR. MICAH TRAPP

Food Anthropologist and Assistant Professor at the University of Memphis

Figure 7.6.1
Micah Trapp.

How did you become interested in the anthropology of food?

As an undergraduate majoring in anthropology, I wrote an honors thesis, "Chopsticks and Chicken Wine," that looked at the relationship between food and identity as a means of perpetuating discrimination through the production of disgust. This project emerged after spending some time in the Guangdong province in Southern China, where I absolutely loved eating. Of all the delicious meals I enjoyed, it

was one particularly unpleasant gustatory moment that stood out: I was presented with a bowl of wine, covered in a glistening layer of chicken fat. The alcohol was so strong that I felt intoxicated simply from smelling it. My hosts described the esteemed status of the wine soup that emerged from the elaborate process of aging the wine in a barrel with chicken. Despite protestations from my stomach, I took a small sip to avoid offending my gracious hosts. After this, I was keenly aware of the relationships between food and social relationships and studied identity construction and discrimination among Chinese-Americans.

What is the most meaningful project you've worked on over the course of your career? Why?

In 2008 and 2009, I conducted research on humanitarianism and food aid at the Buduburam Liberian refugee camp in Ghana. At the time, the camp had been in existence for 19 years, but the Ghanaian government and UNHCR were on the verge of closing the camp. This project has been really important to me because I've struggled with finding a way to critically challenge the simultaneity of protection and violence in humanitarian aid. I'm currently working on a piece about the role of taste in the refugee camp that explores the contradictions between the deliciousness of the Liberian food and the expectation that refugees subsist upon the bare essentials.

Do you identify as an applied, engaged, or public anthropologist? What do these titles mean to you?

All three. I was trained in public anthropology at American University and have written about humanitarian aid for public policy audiences, but have also worked in a variety of applied capacities, including a brief stint as a Food and Nutrition Outreach Program Officer at the U.S. Committee for Refugees and

Figure 7.6.2

Market Entrance, Buduburam Refugee Camp, Ghana.

Immigrants. At the University of Memphis, my work focuses on engaged scholarship and the intersections between the academy, community organizations, and student learning.

Can you tell me more about the collaborative work you do in Memphis?

As co-chair of the School Gardening, Education, and Policy Working Group of the Memphis and Shelby County Food Advisory Council (FAC), I am working on a collaborative project with the FAC, GrowMemphis, and Aspire Hanley Elementary School to build the capacity of school gardening programs.

How did this partnership develop, and what does the work entail?

GrowMemphis, a non-profit organization committed to the development of local, sustainable food systems through urban agriculture, maintains an ongoing relationship with the University of Memphis and has partnered with several anthropologists to conduct research to support and evaluate its programs. For example, students in my Food, Culture, and Power course collaborated on a lunch plate analysis and stakeholder interviews at the Aspire Hanley Elementary School in Memphis to learn about student tastes and behavior in the cafeteria. We are using this exploratory research to start a community dialogue about a school garden program.

What do you see as the future for anthropology of food?

When I wrote the prospectus for my undergraduate thesis, my advisor commented that my use of food as a site for anthropological inquiry was unexpected and unique. That is certainly no longer the case! The anthropology of food has exploded in the last decade and it is hard to imagine how the anthropology of food might continue to develop and grow. I think it is crucial that the public be willing to grapple with deep questions about value in our food system. My most recent research has focused on how grocery auctions—as a place where food that would otherwise be destined for the landfill regains value—reflects upon value and values in the industrialized food system. I am very interested to explore the transformative potential of art as an effective means of building social awareness and change. Performance artist Alison Knowles has constructed an enormous salad numerous times—wouldn't it be great if a similarly spectacular production could be used not simply as a convivial celebration, but to spark dialogue on the gastro-politics of food waste in the industrialized food system?

ANTHROPOLOGY IN PRACTICE

Research Areas: Food and Taste, Humanitarianism, Refugees, West Africa
Education: Ph.D. in Anthropology, American University
Hobbies: Cooking. Baking. Eating. Right now I am cooking my way through Yotam Ottolenghi's "Plenty More: Vibrant Vegetable Cooking." Try the Cauliflower Cake.
I'm also an avid contact improviser—an improvisational dance form that draws on principles of aikido, the law of gravity, and partnering.

CAREER ADVICE

Advice for students interested in anthropology of food:

My community partner and Executive Director at GrowMemphis, Carole Colter and I encourage students to get involved in a community project that focuses on an issue that they feel connected to and passionate about.

- Volunteer or work as an intern with an organization to develop hands-on learning experience with food systems issues.

- Check out your local food pantries, nonprofit organizations, community gardens, healthcare institutions, farmers markets, and food policy councils.
- Don't forget to reflect on your own food practices and ask questions about the food system!

PART 8
Environmental Anthropology

Environmental anthropologists study the relationship between culture and the natural world. Broad questions include, for example, how non-Western knowledge of nature is similar to or different from science, why it seems some societies have more sustainable relationships to natural resources, and what sociocultural factors lead to environmental destruction (Welsh and Vivanco 2014, 186).

Understandings of the natural environment are culturally based. This means that even definitions of nature or the environment vary cross-culturally, including science-based understandings. Most Westerners think of nature as void of human activity. Natural and protected areas, therefore, should be conserved and protected, separate from humans who are seen as threats to biodiversity. Jim Igoe's "Seeing Conservation Through a Global Lens" (Reading 8.1) offers a counter-narrative. In his study of national parks in East Africa, Igoe shows how instead of helping to protect and conserve natural resources in East Africa, the creation of national parks negatively transformed the landscape for the local indigenous population, destroying their traditional livelihood practices and forcing them out of their homeland.

Igoe's piece shares both a topical focus on land rights and a theoretical approach with Michael Walker's "Negotiating Land and Authority in Central Mozambique" (Reading 8.2). Both Igoe and Walker are grounded in political ecology, a theory that focuses on the linkages between political and economic power, social inequality, and environmental issues. Both pieces ask questions like "Who has access and control over land resources, and why?" and "How do people legitimate their claims to land?" Walker's piece explores these dimensions in post-colonial Mozambique, paying attention to the ways in which avenues to claim land are impacted by gender and social relations.

Keisha-Khan Perry continues our focus on land rights, but within an urban setting and through the lens of environmental justice. The environmental justice movement is concerned with addressing the linkages between racial discrimination, social justice, and access to environmental quality. Environmental justice activists are not concerned with conservation or the protection of biodiversity, but are focused on everyday living and the right to live, work, and play in a healthy community. In "'If We Didn't Have Water': Black Women's Struggle for Urban Land Rights in Brazil" (Reading 8.3), Perry explores connections between environmental justice activism and Afro-Brazilian religious traditions, demonstrating how religious traditions shape connections to the sea and rights to land alongside it, and are thus intimately connected to land rights mobilization.

Environmental anthropology is a rapidly growing subfield, swelling, not coincidentally, just as we enter a new historical epoch, one marked by ecological crisis. The 2000s and beyond are now widely known among scholars as the Anthropocene, a term used to denote the period in which human activities have profoundly altered geological conditions and processes, serving as the primary driver of global ecological change. Environmental anthropologists are deeply concerned with understanding both the causes and impacts of the contemporary ecological crisis. Collectively, scholars in this area focus on uncovering unequal access to resources and patterns of injustice, but also on discovering and documenting sustainable solutions. The last two readings look at these two ends of the spectrum.

In **"Gone the Bull of Winter? Contemplating Climate Change's Cultural Implications in Northeastern Siberia, Russia"** (Reading 8.4), Susan Crate explores the global threat that climate change brings, especially to marginalized communities. Crate's selection is an example of "climate ethnography"; in it she discusses the significance of climate change for the Sakha horse and cattle breeders of northeastern Siberia, sharing Sakha observations and understandings about the changing climate and its impacts on their culture.

In "On the Mundane Significance of Bike Lanes . . . And the Pursuit of Anthropology in the Here and Now" (Reading 8.5), Luis Vivanco explores a symbol of sustainable living: the bicycle. The bicycle and urban infrastructure to support cycling and pedestrian traffic have emerged as representations of ecologically aware sustainable lifestyles, yet Vivanco's study of urban bicycle culture and politics in Bogotá, Colombia, counters this popular narrative. Many advocates of cycling argue that "if you build them [bike lanes], they will come." However, Vivanco's work illustrates that this technological determinism is not universal. Culture plays a significant role in shaping bicycling practices—rather than seeing bicycling as unequivocally a decision to act "sustainably," Vivanco's study shows that a fuller cultural analysis pays attention to the structural dynamics that create connectivity and security for some bike riders and disconnection and insecurity for others, which inevitably impact both the ability and choice to use Bogata's *cicloruta* infrastructure. Vivanco's piece serves as this section's example of an engaged case study. Here he pushes readers beyond the labels of practicing, applied, activist, public, or even engaged, toward an anthropology of the "here and now" where ethnographic research is brought to bear on the most pressing issues confronting people in the Anthropocene.

This section's "In the News" and "Anthropology in Practice" pieces feature topics of critical concern in the Anthropocene and examples of anthropologists working at the helms of resource extraction, fisheries management, climate change, and environmental disaster. The "In the News" selection covers the 2010 Deepwater Horizon oil spill—the largest accidental marine oil spill in history—and its sociocultural impacts on surrounding communities. The news coverage includes applied environmental anthropologist Dr. Diane Austin's testimony in the U.S. government's case against BP which revealed that those impacted the most were among the area's poorest families, businesses, and communities. The profile of Dr. Shirley Fiske covers the career of a very "public" environmental anthropologist. Dr. Fiske is a former Research Program Manager for the federal agency National Oceanic and Atmospheric Administration (NOAA) and served as an U.S. Senate Legislative Advisor on Climate, Energy, and Natural Resources. Students interested in pursuing a career in government work related to environmental issues will appreciate learning how Dr. Fiske carved her path, and will value the advice she has for those interested in pursuing similar lines of work. The second profile features Dr. Fabiana Li, Associate Professor of Anthropology at the University of Manitoba in Winnipeg, Canada. The area in which Dr. Li works—mineral extraction and corporate responsibility—is currently under the focus of much public debate. In her profile, Dr. Li reflects on her own work and the future of environmental anthropology and provides some sound advice to students, including to "not shy away from controversial issues."

KEY TERMS:

- Environmental anthropology
- Nature
- Fortress conservation
- Protected areas
- Massai
- Disneyfication
- Land rights
- Environmental justice
- Anthropocene
- Climate change
- Climate ethnography
- Bicycling
- Sustainability
- Mineral extraction
- BP oil spill

8.1 Seeing Conservation Through a Global Lens

JIM IGOE

A common perspective on nature is that it is something void of human activity. Natural areas, national parks, and protected areas do not include humans, or so you may think. You may visit these places, but you should "take nothing and leave nothing but footprints." Doing so, the argument follows, is the best thing possible for both the natural world and its inhabitants. Igoe's discussion of "fortress conservation" in East Africa unravels this assumption, showing how Western fantasies about African wildlife have negatively transformed the landscape for the Maasai, destroying their traditional livelihood practices and connection to cattle and forcing them out of their homeland. Students will find multiple discussion points in this reading, including the effects of globalization and integration into the world economy on indigenous culture, the commodification of culture for tourists, to the relationship between origin myths and human-environment interactions.

Questions

1. Discuss the importance of cattle to the Maasai. What are the social and ecological functions of livestock exchange?
2. What has changed since the 1950s in terms of livestock holdings? How have these changes affected wealth and inequality?
3. What are the effects of Western fantasies of African wilderness on the Maasai and their ability to engage in traditional livelihoods? How have Western fantasies transformed the kind of work that Maasai do today?
4. What is "Disneyfication," and how does it play out in East Africa?
5. Compare the creation myth of the Maasai to that presented in Genesis. How do they produce distinct interactions with nature?

. . . This [piece] deals with a category of people who have resisted globalization: indigenous people. The most common definition of indigenous people is the original inhabitants of a particular place. However, this definition is being broadened to include those who have maintained their traditional ways of life in spite of the modernization and social change. . . .

Few people, if any, still live the idyllic indigenous lifestyle of the people in *The Gods Must Be Crazy*. The idea shown in the movie that people living in the Kalahari have never seen a bottle of Coca-Cola is simply preposterous. Coca-Cola is so widely available in Africa that it is easier to get than clean drinking water in many places. A more accurate portrayal of the Bushmen (or !Kung as they call themselves) can be seen in the anthropological documentary *N!ai: Portrait of a !Kung Woman* (the exclamation point stands for the clicking sound so common in the !Kung language). This film shows the making of *The Gods Must Be Crazy*,

Figure 8.1.1

Lobulu Sakita (center), one of my research assistants, is shown wearing his traditional ceremonial clothing. He is pictured with his wife, Flora, and his sister-in-law. . . . These clothes are worn for special occasions, or perhaps for tourists. Lobulu dressed in jeans and T-shirts most days. *Photo by Andrew Conroy.*

and the confusion of the !Kung actors about the ways in which the director wanted to portray their culture. Far from living an idyllic existence in the Kalahari, these actors have been forced to live on a reservation, where they rely on government handouts and tourist money, rather than on hunting antelope as portrayed in the movie. . . .

Introducing the Maasai

. . . Like other indigenous peoples, the Maasai are economically, culturally, and politically marginalized. Their traditional culture is distinct from the dominant cultures of Kenya and Tanzania, the two countries in which most Maasai live. Unlike most other Kenyans and Tanzanians, who speak English and/or Swahili, most Maasai speak their own language. . . .

The Maasai have also struggled to maintain their traditional herding economy, which revolves around the ability to keep large herds of cattle, sheep, and goats. . . . [I]t also requires a certain amount of mobility because the Maasai have traditionally moved their herds in search of pasture and water. This movement was informed by traditional environmental knowledge and seasonal cycles. . . .

. . . [T]he Maasai (at least the majority of them) no longer pursue their traditional herding economy. Increasingly they rely on subsistence farming, even though most of the areas in which they live are too arid to ensure a successful crop. Most Maasai can no longer be mobile because they have lost their traditional grazing lands to global processes. This change began with colonialism, when British settlers took over high-quality Maasai pasture for farms and cattle ranches. More recently the Maasai have lost land to African and foreign investors who have claimed large areas for bean farms, commercial hunting safaris, and wildlife viewing. These investors came into East Africa in recent years in response to policies designed to transform the economies of Kenya and Tanzania so that they could become more fully integrated into the world economy. The expectation, of course, was that Africans would also be transformed into wage-earning consumers instead of subsistence-oriented peasants. For the most part, however, this hasn't happened. The Maasai (in fact most rural Africans) have wound up left out of the process altogether. They have lost their land and their subsistence economy, but they haven't been able to benefit from the integration of their countries into the world economy.

Many of the elders I interviewed lamented that these processes were leading to the demise of their traditional values. In Maasai society, cattle are everything, in about the same way that money is everything in the United States. That is, although it may be a bit of an exaggeration to say that "it's everything," people certainly do spend a lot of time thinking about it and trying to accumulate it. The fact that Americans need to remind themselves that "money isn't everything" reflects the fact that they often behave as though it is. However, Americans don't have money in their creation myth: the Maasai creation myth holds that when God created the earth He gave cattle to the Maasai and proclaimed that they were the only people on earth with the right to own it. Throughout their history the Maasai have used this myth as a justification to raid neighboring ethnic groups and take away their cattle by force. If God proclaimed cattle to be the sole property of the Maasai, then other people must have obtained their cattle by less than honorable means. . . .

The central importance of livestock to the Maasai economy is reflected in its traditional (but diminishing) use as a medium of exchange in Maasai society. Gifts of livestock are presented to boys as they are initiated into warriorhood. Friendships, called stock associations by anthropologists, are cemented by periodic gifts of livestock. Wealthy men frequently lend animals to poorer men in an effort to build a loyal following of clients. Perhaps most important, livestock in Maasai society is used as a medium of marriage exchange. When a young man wishes to marry, he presents the parents of his potential bride with gifts of livestock. If the gift is acceptable, then he will periodically add new gifts of livestock to this original gift until the marriage is made official through a series of

rituals, also involving livestock exchange. Even once the marriage is complete the husband will continue to present his in-laws with livestock for the rest of their lives. These gifts . . . cement relationships between two social groups: the bride givers and the bride takers. If the marriage is dissolved then the livestock must be returned. As you can imagine, this creates huge pressures against divorce in Maasai society. . . .

The social exchange of livestock also serves ecological and group survival functions. One of the defining characteristics of Maasai country is its unpredictable weather patterns and periodic lack of rain. Rain may come for seven years to one area, and then not at all for another seven. . . . By giving and loaning livestock to friends and clients, Maasai herders effectively scatter their herds all over the place. When the area in which a herder lives is dry and several of his animals die, the area of his stock associates may receive abundant rains. Traditionally this means that this man's stock associates will present him with livestock, or if he is wealthy, his clients may return some of the animals he lent to them, allowing his herd to recover from the drought. . . .

Since the 1950s, however, the reputation of Simanjiro as a great place to keep livestock has declined immensely. Most of the pasture and water that were the foundation of Simanjiro's booming herding economy have been lost to other concerns. Because of the central importance of cattle to the Maasai of Simanjiro, the decline of this herding economy has had devastating effects on their culture. The ability to live the "pure pastoralist life style," which has been a central cultural value, is now enjoyed by only a handful of wealthy herders. As the herding economy declined, so did the number of livestock available for social exchange. Local people believe that social relationships within their society have suffered accordingly. Most important, for most Maasai, the tradition of wealthy herders sharing their animals with poorer ones has been steadily disappearing. The result has been increased wealth discrepancies within Maasai society as a few wealthy men, who are now able to hire laborers for cash, accumulate large numbers of animals, while many others decline into poverty. . . .

What About Conservation?

One of the central processes that have contributed to the displacement of Maasai herders in Simanjiro is conservation. Specifically, the creation of Tarangire

National Park has enclosed pasture and water resources essential to the herding economy, a process that has also contributed to ecological deterioration. Many of my informants described conservation as indistinguishable from any of the other global processes they confronted in their daily lives. Its bottom line was the alienation of traditional grazing lands for the benefit and enjoyment of other people, the majority of whom, from their perspective, were white and not even from Tanzania. As far as they were concerned, this was essentially unfair.

Of course this perspective is different from how most Americans imagine conservation. A student in my "Culture and the Environment" class once told me that for him the class had been as much about unlearning as it had been about learning. He had to unlearn things that he previously believed about conservation before he could begin to explore concepts addressed in the class. This process of unlearning is essential, because many people (myself included) hold preconceived ideas about conservation. Too often, these ideas are formed by popular notions that conceal the painful reality of how conservation affects indigenous communities around the world. . . .

Western Media Fantasies About Wildlife and the Maasai

Although you may not be able to find Tanzania quickly on a globe . . . you are probably familiar with conservation in Africa. Perhaps you have watched the Discovery Channel and [have seen] a pride of lions take down zebra on the Serengeti Plain. Or you may have seen video footage of the annual wildebeest migrations along the Great Rift Valley in Tanzania and Kenya. Tens of thousands of these animals plunge into flooded rivers, apparently oblivious to the racing current and the waiting crocodiles. Some drown and some are eaten, but most survive to complete the journey. Or possibly you are familiar with images of machine-gunned elephants, with gaping holes in their faces where poachers have crudely extracted their tusks. These images were indispensable to several highly successful fund-raising campaigns by American conservation organizations in the 1980s (cf. Bonner 1993). Through these popular media images, most Americans "know" that conservation in Africa is about animals. More specifically, it is about the preservation of endangered species, most notably rhino and elephants.

While I suspect that few Americans actually sit around and worry about African rhinos in their spare time, most associate Africa with wild animals.

Maasai are nearly as familiar to Westerners as the lions of the Serengeti. Whether you know it or not, you probably have an idea of what they look like. Maasai warriors, with their flowing red togas and spears in hand have become a quintessential symbol for vanishing Africa. They have appeared on the Discovery Channel, leaping into the air in exuberant dances and (in their calmer moments) leaning on their spears gazing out over a vast African landscape of waving savanna grasses. In the movie *Out of Africa* they appear racing across the arid savanna on a mysterious mission. A lighter movie, *The Air Up There,* presents an unlikely story of a college basketball coach who goes to Kenya to recruit a Maasai warrior for his school's team. The movie climaxes with a game between the "traditional" Maasai and some "nontraditional" urban Africans. (I won't spoil the ending by telling you who wins.) A recent commercial from Nissan features a group of Maasai warriors congratulating each other on the purchase of a brand new Altima. Standing in a row outside of their mud houses, they marvel at the latest in midsize family sedans while an elephant lazily wanders by in the distant background.

This bizarre scenario captures the essence of Western fantasies about Africa, which are frequently used to market something. Both African people and African wildlife are portrayed as exotic and inhabiting an unspoiled world that no longer exists in the West. Just as important, the two are portrayed as separate from one another. People exist in one realm, and animals in another. Viewers may see lions on the Discovery Channel, and viewers may see Maasai on the Discovery Channel. It is unlikely, however, that they will ever see lions and Maasai on the Discovery Channel at the same time. For most Westerners this seems like a "natural" arrangement: African wildlife exists in wilderness or nature, a place untouched by the ravaging effects of human activities. This imaginary vision is difficult to resolve with the reality of a traffic jam of zebra-striped safari vans converging on a rhino that happens to be wearing a collar that allows authorities to monitor his movements with a high-tech satellite tracking system. Nevertheless, it is an idea that many hold dear: national parks equal nature and nature does not include humans. If you are fortunate enough to

Figure 8.1.2

Elephants are an important national resource for Tanzania and other African countries, as tourists spend tens of millions of dollars every year to visit Africa and see these animals. Most Westerners are used to seeing elephants in this context—a group of elephants with no people in the frame (although if you think about it the photographer is a person and must have been pretty close by to get this picture). In reality there are human settlements within five miles of where this picture was taken. Elephants destroyed crops every year in the villages where I did my fieldwork, and local people regarded them as more of a nuisance than an asset. *Photo by Andrew Conroy.*

visit this nature, you should "take nothing but pictures and leave nothing but footprints." Westerners expect other cultures to conform to this imperative. . . .

These expectations raise important questions for the other half of the equation: the Maasai. If they don't live in nature along with wild animals, where exactly do they live? In one respect the answer to this question is a simple: somewhere else. If you examine Western stereotypes of the Maasai closely, however, this answer doesn't make much sense. . . . [T]he Maasai are commonly portrayed as living in a vast steppe, with nothing to see from horizon to horizon but tall savanna grasses. The reality of the situation is drastically different. A glimpse at a map of East Africa reveals that much of their rangeland has been encroached on by national parks and urban sprawl. Nairobi, a city of nearly 5 million people, sits squarely in the middle of traditional Maasai territory. I have seen Maasai herders grazing their livestock in the median of a major highway and by airport runways. In the rural areas, mechanized farms and commercial ranches have taken over much of the best grazing land outside of national parks. In short, the idea that the Maasai herd their cattle in wide-open spaces is largely inaccurate. . . .

Disneyfication and Ecocultural Tourism in East Africa

Obviously there are some serious discrepancies between Western media fantasies about wildlife and the Maasai and the "on-the-ground" realities of life in East Africa. . . . Is it possible for Western fantasies about people and the environment to be imposed on the "real world" and in effect become a reality? As bizarre as this proposition may initially appear, it is something with which Americans are intimately familiar, through institutions such as subdivisions, shopping malls, and especially theme parks.

Figure 8.1.3
This picture fulfills the Western fantasy about the Maasai homeland: wide open spaces with plenty of grass for grazing. In reality this space is shrinking. Rangelands are hemmed in by farms, parks, and urban sprawl. Elders I interviewed described moving their livestock hundreds of miles per year in the past. They now claim that they usually go no further than 10 or 15 miles afield, primarily because there is no place to go. *Photo by Andrew Conroy.*

So pervasive are the effects of theme parks on the ways that Westerners look at the world that some social scientists refer to the process by which artificial realities are constructed as "Disneyfication." . . . Disney World's African Safari Ride . . . simulates the African safari experience, to the extent of importing animals and people from Africa. Riders board a four-wheel drive vehicle that takes them through rutted dirt roads and swollen rivers before they finally encounter herds of animals listlessly grazing on an artificial savanna. An African man then runs up to the vehicle yelling, *"Bwana! Bwana!* The poachers are stealing the baby elephant!" The ride then becomes a high-speed chase, ending with the rescue of the baby elephant, which is a mechanical elephant's trunk sticking out of a wooden crate. The animals that the visitors encounter are not native; they were raised in captivity and descended from animals that were captured somewhere in Africa like the mechanical baby elephant who is "saved" from such a fate over and over again by the thousands of visitors who go on the ride every day.

In an article aptly entitled "The Maasai and the Lion King," anthropologist Edward Bruner (2001) describes how the types of fantasies produced by the "Disney dream machine" make their way back to Africa where they are repackaged and sold to Western tourists. Westerners usually go to East Africa on safari to see two things: animals and "traditional" Africans. To see animals they go to national parks. To see "traditional" Africans they don't even have to leave the comfort of their luxury hotels. Most resorts feature Maasai dancers at least a couple nights a week. What most tourists don't realize, however, is that many of these dancers are not actually Maasai. Tourists will pay to see "the Maasai." In a society with rampant unemployment, it only makes sense that young men should take advantage of this opportunity by dressing up like Maasai and learning "traditional" Maasai dances. More adventurous tourists might also visit "cultural villages," where they can see how the Maasai "really live" and pay to take some pictures for the folks back home. Unlike real Maasai villages, however, cultural villages lack cows, their manure, and the swarms of flies they inevitably attract.

Maasai "cultural villages" are exactly the type of controlled experience that Western tourists pay for when they purchase a luxury safari. Like the rides at Disney World, luxury safaris highlight the utopian and the romantic, presenting tourists with a world that is more like they imagined it would be. They are

Figure 8.1.4

This women's group has started their own cultural boma (homestead or village) in an effort to earn some income from Tanzania's tourist industry. This cultural boma lies on the road from Tarangire National Park to Serengeti National Park. *Photo by Andrew Conroy.*

met at the airport by an English-speaking guide in a safari suit who whisks them away to the Nairobi Hilton. They traverse the short distance from the van to the lobby with the assistance of porters dressed in brass-buttoned suits. The hotel shopping arcade offers everything from *The New York Times* to a pith helmet, without ever stepping outside. The same vehicle that brought them from the airport will transport them to a luxury lodge inside of one of Kenya's world-famous parks. From there they will be driven about, taking pictures of elephants, lions, and zebra. Then it's back to the Hilton, back to the airport, and back to the Western city from whence they came. With luck, the only Africans they will have encountered are servants and the "traditional" people who danced for their entertainment. Dangerous animals will have been viewed from the comfort and safety of their safari vehicle.

Also like the riders on Jungle Cruise and the African Safari Ride, these tourists will be spared the unpleasant realities of the real world that their "Disneyfied" experiences are modeled after. If they were only to step outside the Nairobi Hilton, less than a block away they would encounter 6-year-old boys sniffing glue on garbage heaps, shrouded lepers begging for money, and teenage girls forced into prostitution by poverty and despair. If they were only to stop outside the national parks that they came to visit, they would encounter whole communities of people who have been displaced and impoverished by those very parks. Because these people and their poverty are discreetly eliminated from the safari experience, very few tourists will make the connection between the luxury hotels, where they are spared from these unpleasant sights, and the vast wealth discrepancies that exist in countries like Tanzania and Kenya. . . .

Shedding My Fantasies About Africa, or Yet Another Ethnographer's Dramatic Entrance Tale

The depth of Western fantasies about traditional Africans and pristine wildernesses are reflected in my own experience of becoming an anthropologist. I will be the first to admit that I entered the field because it offered adventure. . . . One of the books [I read in "Introduction to Cultural Anthropology" in college] . . . was *The Forest People* by Colin Turnbull. His experiences among the Mbuti of Central Africa, living in a mud house and participating in the daily life of his host community, intrigued me. At the time, I was a dishwasher and selling plasma twice a week to make ends meet. Anthropological fieldwork appeared as an exciting alternative to my lifestyle of financial and intellectual impoverishment. I decided to become a cultural anthropologist. I never considered who would pay me to live among exotic people and write a book about it; I just decided it was the job for me.

As it turned out, I did get to live in a mud house. However, my experiences in the field were far more confusing and complex than those described by Turnbull. The Maasai warriors where I lived rode motorcycles, listened to reggae, and watched Jackie Chan movies on a portable video monitor. People were engaged in struggles with commercial farms and national parks that were encroaching on their land, and organizing their own NGOs. Through these NGOs, Maasai leaders were becoming active at the national and international levels. There was a great deal going on, not all of it was local, and none of it was easy to understand. . . . The reality of the situation was exceedingly different from my romantic expectations of fieldwork. . . . [M]y ideas of social change among the Maasai were naïve. I believed that I could find communities that were essentially unaffected by modernization. . . .

My views of African nature and wildlife were also essentially unexamined. I knew that my intended field communities were on the borders of a national park. This concerned me, because I imagined that a lion would probably eat me. Otherwise, I didn't give the matter much thought. I was there to study social and economic change among the Maasai. What could wildlife or national parks have to do with that? The animals were inside the park, where they belonged (except for the lions that might wander out and eat me). The people, and the processes of social change that I was interested in recording, were outside the park. This seemed reasonable to me. Of course, I now realize that it doesn't make sense. Even then I had begun to acknowledge that the whole arrangement seemed kind of funny. I suspected that at some point in time the Maasai must have lived in the area that was now the park. However, these niggling doubts were overridden by my uncritical assumption that parks were nature. I didn't consider conservation as part of the economic and social transformation that I wanted to study, until people in my study area complained so loudly and frequently about it that I couldn't ignore the issue any longer. . . .

Fortress Conservation . . .

. . . In East Africa (and many other parts of the world for that matter) national parks are a model of fortress conservation (Brockington 2002). This approach to conservation is based on the premise that the only way to save nature (and especially endangered species) is to forcefully exclude people from areas that are designated as wilderness. This perspective naturally assumes that this forceful exclusion is both desirable and possible. . . .

. . . The justification for this type of exclusion has changed over time. In the early 20th century, when English settlers first came to East Africa, it was enough to assert that Africans were too ignorant to appreciate the beauty of their natural surroundings (Neumann 1998). Because Africans did not appreciate the beauty of nature, they therefore had no right to be in nature. Nature was therefore set aside for the enjoyment of Europeans, who appreciated its aesthetic qualities and also enjoyed hunting the "big five" (elephant, rhino, buffalo, lion, leopard) without Africans cluttering up the landscape. Over the years, however, these racist ideas have become an unacceptable justification for excluding people from land in their own countries. These days the argument runs that parks must be protected inviolate in order to save rhinos and elephants from rampant poaching and, increasingly, to protect biodiversity.

Poaching in East Africa has become big business in the past 30 years. Rhino horn and ivory are particularly valuable commodities in the world market, and especially in East Asia. Ivory has traditionally been fashioned into jewelry and art objects. Rhino horn is highly sought after in China for its believed medicinal qualities. Essentially, it is the Chinese equivalent of Viagra. Because of the high value placed on these commodities, a single rhino horn or elephant tusk sells for tens of thousands of dollars on the black market. In countries where the minimum wage is around a dollar a day and most people can't find jobs, illegal poaching of elephants and rhinos is a tempting career option. A lucrative market also exists for bush meat, which is sold in African cities as a cheap alternative to domestic meats. In a region beset by civil wars (as in Somalia, Ethiopia, Sudan, Rwanda, and Burundi), it has also become increasingly easy for people to obtain state-of-the-art automatic weapons, which arrive in the form of Western military aid. Poachers using these weapons have become increasingly effective at wiping out entire herds of elephants, and of taking on park rangers, who sometimes are less well armed than [they are].

The increasing efficiency with which poachers can kill wildlife greatly exacerbated the fortress conservation mentality. The African Wildlife Foundation's (AWF),"Save the Elephant" campaign became one of the most successful direct-mail fundraisers in the history of American charities (Bonner 1993). Throughout the 1980s, Westerners were exposed to excruciating images of elephants and rhinos slaughtered by poachers and left to rot. . . . Rhinos in Tanzania's world-famous Ngorongoro Conservation Area were outfitted with radio collars and given around the-clock protection with funding from the Frankfurt Zoological Society. In theory, the special ranger unit created to protect the rhino knew where every animal was at any given moment. . . . In Zimbabwe, anti-poaching units were outfitted with airships, those big two-propellered helicopters made popular by movies such as *Apocalypse Now.* The war on poaching was beginning to look like a real war, and national parks were truly beginning to look like fortresses.

The social costs of these measures quickly became visible. Ranger units were rumored to have shoot-on-sight orders. Local people trapping meat to feed their families were frequently caught in the crossfire. As the Maasai of Simanjiro experienced, the growing presence of heavily armed, underpaid park rangers led to alarming levels of human rights abuses. . . .

It also appears that would-be poachers are beginning to target tourists as retribution for the stepped-up security around parks and other protected areas. During my time in the field, men with automatic weapons were attacking tourists inside Serengeti, as well as across the border in Kenya. Rumor had it that these men were poachers angered by the effects of fortress conservation on their livelihoods. Finally, fortress conservation has had the effect of alienating local people. Right before I left the field in 1997 an elephant was killed in Kenya's Tsavo National Park. The body was left to rot, but oddly the creature's tusks were left intact; also the animal had been killed with spears rather than with guns. This strange event led Western conservationists to speculate that Maasai warriors had killed the elephant as a way of protesting their exclusion from national parks. I was in a workshop when I heard of this tragic event. A representative of the AWF opined, "Well, we know which animals to show people when we want them to make donations, and they know which animals to kill when they want to make a point." Clearly, fortress conservation was not fostering the atmosphere of "good neighborliness" that Western conservationists envisioned for Tarangire and the Maasai of Simanjiro. . . .

Fortress conservation has fallen short of its objectives of protecting Tanzania's endangered species and their habitats. Some evidence suggests it might actually contribute to the decline of valuable endangered species. One particularly notorious example involves Ngorongoro Conservation game wardens and their head, Stephen Makacha. Makacha was implicated in the poaching of an Ngorongoro rhino named Amina, who was killed in August 1995. Even though game wardens had the technology to monitor the whereabouts of Ngorongoro rhinos at all times, a group of German tourists discovered Amina minus her life and her horn. During the period when Amina was shot, Makacha gave several wardens assignments outside of the Ngorongoro Crater and gave others three-day leaves of absence. . . .

This incident . . . is consistent with similar incidents that happen every day in countries like Tanzania . . . [and] reflects Tanzania's colonial history. . . . Suffice it to say here that the Tanzanian economy has been integrated into the world economy in such a way that it is difficult for Tanzanian elites to make money without resorting to illegal activities. During 1995 it also was reported in the Tanzanian press that an army colonel was cutting down trees in a forest reserve and transporting the timber with army trucks. Tanzanian officials, and indeed officials throughout the developing world, are notorious for taking bribes. This doesn't mean that they are all bad people. It means that there are few opportunities to make a living wage in Tanzania. Only a small group of wealthy Africans and foreign investors are actually in a position to profit from wildlife tourism, an activity that allows people to "consume" animals and scenery without actually consuming them. Parades of zebra-striped safari vans may be disruptive, but they don't contribute significantly to the demise of animal populations and habitats. Unfortunately, most people displaced by the park, along with those whose job it is to protect those animals, are in no position to profit from these kinds of "non-consumptive" activities. Still they have children to feed, and they are going to survive however they can. Unfortunately, this usually entails the illegal consumption of wildlife. For local people, who lack access to sophisticated weaponry, this consumption is usually minimal. For park rangers and game wardens, who are outfitted with AK-47s and M-16s, this consumption can be much more significant.

This phenomenon is difficult to document, since incidents like the poaching of Amina usually go unreported, and if reported almost always remain unprosecuted. . . . Obviously, protecting wildlife and biodiversity is especially difficult under such circumstances. While Western conservationists rarely address these adverse socioeconomic conditions, they are a driving force behind the massive techno-military buildup around African protected areas that have become the hallmark of fortress conservation.

The latest irony of fortress conservation is that Tanzania is now importing black rhinos from South Africa and Germany for reintroduction into protected areas. One such rhino reintroduction scheme is taking place within the Mkomazi Game Reserve. A self-styled conservationist named Tony Fitzjohn runs the rhino reintroduction scheme in Mkomazi. . . . Fitzjohn's presence in the game reserve has been continuously controversial. He lives in a modern house with a beautiful view and his own private airstrip and own private plane. He is not reintroducing the rhinos into the wild, but keeping them in a 15-square kilometer paddock enclosed by an electrical fence. The presence of such a fence raises questions about wildlife migration routes in Mkomazi (i.e., what happens when migrating wildlife run into the electric fence?). An American wildlife veterinarian working

in South Africa has also raised questions about the genetic viability of the rhino that are being flown into the Mkomazi Game Reserve by the South African Air Force (the rhino are descended from a small cohort of animals that were originally brought into South Africa from Tanzania). None of these problems has ever been adequately resolved. The controversy surrounding Fitzjohn's residency inside the game reserve, while all its former residents are now living in poverty somewhere else, also continues. . . .

The Problem of Wilderness and Eden

Obviously there is a fine line between conserving rhino in an electrified paddock inside a Tanzanian game reserve, and keeping them inside a zoo. If poverty in East Africa means that rhino can only be protected in small groups with radio collars or inside electric fences, can this activity really be called conservation? And if we do call this type of activity "conservation," what exactly is being conserved? Perhaps one day rhino reintroduction will lead to the recovery of East Africa's rhino population. Meanwhile, however, organizations like the Tony Fitzjohn/George Adamson Wildlife Survival Trust speak of "restoring a forgotten wilderness" (from the Trust's fund-raising literature). Since people have been living in and around Mkomazi for hundreds (and possibly thousands) of years, this statement prompts me to ask, "forgotten by whom?" Obviously Africans have known about this so-called wilderness for generations, and none of the people who have been evicted from Mkomazi have forgotten about it. This would seem to imply that African memories of Mkomazi are unimportant. It is Europeans who have forgotten about this wilderness, and it is Europeans who will restore it. . . .

Closely associated with this idea of a "forgotten wilderness" is the idea of a "vanishing Eden" (also from Tony Fitzjohn/George Adamson fund-raising literature). The idea of African national parks as Eden is a ubiquitous one, even among critics of national parks. . . . But the very idea of "Eden," and the idea that it should be preserved (even if this preservation somehow involves the participation of local people), prioritizes a Western way of looking at the world. . . .

This idea of Eden, of course, is derived from the creation account in Genesis, the first chapter of the Old Testament. Two aspects of the Genesis creation account are particularly relevant to this study: (1) the idea that human beings have some sort of special control over nature; and (2) the corollary idea that they are also separate from nature. In the six days in which God created this planet, Genesis reports that God produced sky, land, water, and all the plants and creatures that inhabit these domains. God then created Adam, to whom He gave a "dominion" over all those ecosystems and creatures. In short, God put Adam in charge of the Earth and told him that he could use all of the planet's natural resources in whatever way he saw fit, except of course the fruit from the "tree of knowledge." Genesis also reports Eve was tempted by a serpent (an early example of the anthropomorphizing of a nonhuman creature) to eat this very fruit. Eve in turn convinced Adam that he should try the fruit, and as a result God summarily evicted the pair of them from Eden. This account depicts a transformation from a state where human beings lived as one with nature (Eden) and coincidentally with God, to a state where human beings were cast out of nature (Eden) and forced to live as separate from it and, coincidentally,

God. This presents an ambivalent situation in which human beings are tainted and unworthy of being part of nature, while simultaneously being left in charge of nature and all of its plants and creatures.

This same ambivalence prevails in East African conservation projects, and in Western attitudes toward conservation generally. Westerners have already squandered their Eden. There are no wolves, bear, or elk left in Western Europe. Endless herds of bison no longer thunder over the prairies of North America. Westerners look to places like Africa to find the Eden that no longer exists in Europe and is quickly disappearing in most of North America. Americans who see the vast herds of wildebeest and zebra in Serengeti National Park frequently remark that they imagine this scene is similar to what the American prairies must have been like before the arrival of Europeans. But although the common sentiment is that Westerners have messed everything up, there is also a feeling that they are the only ones who possess the knowledge necessary to rescue the few remaining Edens in the world. . . .

References

The Air Up There. Directed by Paul M. Glaser. Hollywood Pictures Home Video, 1994.

Bonner, R. 1993. *At the Hand of Man: Peril and Hope for Africa's Wildlife.* New York: Alfred Knopf.

Brockington, D. 2001. *Fortress Conservation: The Preservation of the Mkomazi Game Reserve, Tanzania.* Oxford: James Currey.

Bruner, E. 2001. "The Maasai and the Lion King: Authenticity, Nationalism, and Globalization in African Tourism." *American Ethnologist* 28(4): 881–908.

The Gods Must Be Crazy. Directed by John Boshoff. 20th Century Fox, Sony Pictures Entertainmnet, 1984.

N!ai: Portrait of a !Kung Woman. Directed by John Marshall and Adrienne Miesmer. PBS, 1980.

Neumann, R. 1998. *Imposing Wilderness: Struggles over Livelihood and Nature Preservation in Africa.* Berkeley: University of California Press.

Out of Africa. Directed by Sydney Pollack. Universal Pictures, 1985.

Turnbull, Colin. *The Forest People.* Simon & Schuster, 1996.

8.2 Negotiating Land and Authority in Central Mozambique

MICHAEL MADISON WALKER

Anthropologists informed by political ecology, a theoretical approach that attends to the relationship between political and economic power and the environment, often frame their research around questions such as "Who has access and control over natural resources, and why? How do access and control vary by gender, class, race, or ethnicity? Who legitimates access, and how do people navigate their access and control in everyday practice? In the following case study, Walker asks these types of questions about land in post-colonial Mozambique. Comparing two individuals—one woman and one man—Walker illustrates how Mozambicans can make claims to land through multiple sources of authority; however, the navigational paths for making claims to land are gendered. Social relations play into property claims, and in a patriarchal culture women's land rights are tied into their male kin.

Questions

1. Which actors have the ability to allocate land and sanction its use in Mozambique?
2. How was land allocated before colonial rule? What role did kinship play in the distribution of land? What were the gendered effects of pre-colonial land allocation practices?
3. What is a machamba?
4. How did the conflict between Renamo and the Frelimo government affect settlement patterns and land use?
5. What does Walker mean by saying, "Mariana's land use rights are both secure and insecure"? How can land be both secure and insecure? What role does gender play in land security?
6. What is the difference between land access and property?

Concepts and definitions of property do not translate easily across cultures. In fact, property is better understood as a set of relationships as opposed to a specific thing, such as a parcel of land or a house. In other words, social relations underpin property rights, signifying who can claim a right to what, and under what conditions. When viewed through a cross-cultural perspective, property can entail a range of rights, duties, and obligations between individuals and groups over the control of specific things. Even in contexts where private property is the dominant form of property, an individual or corporation's property rights must be legitimated (i.e. by the market, the state,

etc.), implying a process of social and legal recognition. Put this way, property rights are claims that are recognized as legitimate by some form of authority whether it is a state, a court, a chief, a headman, or members of a specific community.

Access to material resources (land, water, forests, wildlife), needed to grow food or engage in subsistence activities, also legitimates certain forms of rule over people and the environment. In Mozambique, local struggles over land provide the basis for authority and recognition in the postcolonial nation-state where official state institutions overlap with kin-based leaders and culturally specific idioms and practices for establishing resource rights. In this reading I briefly discuss how women and men secure rights to land by navigating social relations, customary authority, local state institutions, and emerging informal markets in a community in central Mozambique. This case study demonstrates how the process of articulating claims to land also works to legitimate both customary and state authority over environmental resources in a postcolonial setting.

Mozambique's Overlapping Land Claims

Land provides the basis for rural livelihoods, identity, and belonging. Although Mozambique is not a land-scarce country, and in many districts the population density is low, there are communities where the history of colonial settlement, state intervention, armed conflict, and economic liberalization have created overlapping claims to land and installed multiple authorities who oversee land allocation and resolve land-related conflicts. All land is state property, and according to the land law, Mozambican citizens and foreign commercial entities can obtain state-recognized land use rights. But as this chapter demonstrates, the state is only one of several actors engaged in allocating land and sanctioning land use, thus linking land claims to implicit and overt recognition of authority.

Mozambique is predominantly a rural country with one of the lowest rates of urbanization in the world. It also has high rates of poverty. The United Nations 2014 Human Development Index, which measures socio-economic development, ranked Mozambique 178 out of 187, designating it as one of the poorest countries in the world, and despite its strong annual growth rates over the last decade, the national budget is heavily dependent on foreign aid. In Sussundenga (the site of this discussion) the town's residents are mostly subsistence farmers, cultivating maize, sorghum, cassava, groundnuts, and several varieties of beans on agricultural plots. These lands, along with the farmer's labor or hired labor, form the basis of rural livelihoods, enabling residents to grow food for home consumption and to sell in the local markets. Wealthier households combine off-farm income through wage earning opportunities with household food production, and some men engage in cash crop production, growing cotton, tobacco, paprika, or sunflowers through an out-grower scheme financed by an agricultural company or commercial farmer.

A small number of men fall into this latter category of commercial farmer, cultivating larger tracts of land and orienting most of their production for the market. Thus, everyone is dependent upon agriculture to some degree and use land for subsistence and material needs.

Prior to colonial rule in the Shona-speaking[1] areas of central Mozambique, customary authorities or chiefs governed land and people by allocating plots to the male household head who in turn gave portions of this land to his wife or wives to grow food for him and their children. Chiefs and their ancestral spirits were the rightful "owners" of the land, and by subjecting oneself to chiefly rule, a person gained land use rights. These rights could be transferred within and across generations through inheritance. In these patrilineal and patrilocal areas, household and community gender relations played a significant role in shaping land use rights at the household level where sons and brothers often inherited land, making women dependent on marriage or male relatives for access to land. Unmarried women cultivated their fathers' land until they married and moved into their husband's household. But with land plentiful, some women and men also obtained land use rights by negotiating with relatives, friends, and neighbors who were not using all of their land. When conflicts arose, chiefs and influential elders mediated land-related disputes.

From the 1960s to the mid-1970s, Portuguese settlers governed Sussundenga. The settlers expropriated land and labor from local residents, and with the support of the colonial state, established a European farming community. While Portuguese colonialism did not produce widespread land evictions (as was the case in other southern African colonial contexts), in Sussundenga, settlers became involved in land allocation and mediating land use, creating a new layer of authority over both land and local residents. In fact, some residents gained land use rights by working for individual Portuguese settlers in the area. For a small number of people, Portuguese colonial authority provided the basis for land use rights while others continued to rely on African customary authorities, such as chiefs, for land access and dispute resolution. But despite the effects colonial authority had on the area's land use rights, the European presence in Sussundenga was relatively short, as Mozambique would become an independent country in 1975.

Mozambique gained independence from Portugal after a long anti-colonial struggle, and the new socialist government instituted a vision of rural development that included redistributing former colonial landholdings to *camponêses* (peasant farmers) in the form of communal villages. The government's resettlement scheme, known as villagization, relocated many local families back to the lands from where the Portuguese settlers had displaced them a decade earlier. Households that received an agricultural and a residential plot now resided under the new government's authority, embodied by local party officials living in these newly constructed settlements. With residents now living in the confines of neighborhoods, the state could also deliver services, such as health clinics, schools, and potable water. But Mozambique's state-led development would soon be undermined by armed conflict. During the 1980s, Mozambique became embroiled in a protracted conflict between a resistance movement called by its Portuguese acronym Renamo, backed initially by Rhodesia and later apartheid South Africa, that attempted to destabilize the country governed by the ruling party Frelimo. The fighting caused widespread suffering and created a population of *deslocados* (displaced people) who fled their homes and communities because of the war. Many *deslocados* from other areas of the district resettled in and around the administrative center of Sussundenga where there was some semblance of security provided by Frelimo soldiers. The war caused a significant decrease in agricultural production, as people could no longer safely tend to their fields or abandoned them altogether. A peace accord ended the fighting in 1992, and the subsequent decade was marked by multi-party elections and capitalist-oriented growth. But while Mozambicans welcomed the end of armed conflict and the resulting political stability, many rural residents remained poor and did not see the benefits of the country's growing economy. Today, Mozambique's national development is often linked to questions of land use and access, raising the stakes for how land use rights are legitimated and by whom.

Mariana and Gendered Land Use Rights

Senhora Mariana[2] was born in the 1940s in Rotanda near the border with Southern Rhodesia (today Zimbabwe) at a time when Mozambique was under colonial rule. She married in the 1960s and moved with her husband to present-day Sussundenga, a small rural town in central Mozambique. In the 1960s Sussundenga was a Portuguese agricultural settlement where European settlers, with the support of the colonial state, expropriated land, conscripted male labor, and imposed new political authority in the countryside. Because Sussundenga was demarcated as a European settlement, Mariana and her family settled under the authority of a customary chief, *or mambo*, outside the nucleus of Portuguese farms. There Mariana, her husband, and young children cultivated maize, sorghum, and beans on a *machamba* (a small subsistence plot), relying on rainfall to irrigate their crops during the rainy season. When the rains stopped in late April, they cultivated a piece of land along a riverbank, using the river's water to irrigate a vegetable garden. Mariana's livelihood and land use practices were similar to her neighbors who lived in scattered settlements also under chiefly rule not far from the watchful eyes of the Portuguese settlers. Following independence, Mariana's husband received a new *machamba* located on land that formerly made up one of the Portuguese farms. Consequently, their family moved and established a new home inside of a villagization scheme under the authority of the postcolonial state. For several years, Mariana, her husband, and their children cultivated this land uninterrupted until her husband died during the armed conflict, leaving Mariana to raise their three children and make ends meet under precarious wartime conditions.

When I met Mariana in August 2006, she was still cultivating the land allocated to her husband by the state in the late 1970s. She was in her 60s and lived with one of her sons and his family. As Mariana and I sat on the edge of her *machamba* talking about her life history, I thought about the ways in which she and her husband had been able to make claims to land over the course of her life, and what type of authority had legitimated their rights to land, particularly as Mozambique transitioned from an extractive colonial economy, to state-led socialist development, to a free market economy shaped by international donors, banks, and commercial interests. In a setting where the majority of people depend on land and their own labor to sustain themselves, Mariana's story raises questions about how women and men gain the right to use land and who has the authority to sanction their land use rights.

Mariana's land use rights are both secure and insecure. On the one hand, Mariana and her son are long-standing residents, living under chiefly authority (since the 1960s) and the postcolonial state (beginning in the mid-1970s) and can articulate their claims to land within the community based on both of these authorities. This is important since Mozambique's growing market economy has created more opportunities for local elites to solidify their land claims by appealing to different forms of authority: state, customary, legal. Mariana and her son can also draw on multiple sources, including local culture and tradition and the state's authority to substantiate their claims. But on the other hand, Mariana's rights are enmeshed in the social and kin relations with her son who inherited his father's land after his wartime death. Because of the practice of patrilineal inheritance, Mariana's land use rights remain tied to her social relations with men, in this case her oldest son. These social and kin relations are legitimated by appeals to "customs" or "traditions" that place women's access to land under male authority. In the time that I knew Mariana and her family, I did not encounter evidence that her land use rights were threatened within the family; however, the fact that her access was contingent upon men may weaken her claims if her rights were ever contested within the household.

Joel and the Local State

Joel[3] spends most of his time cultivating a stream-bank garden off the beaten path. Although his primary house is located in one of Sussundenga's densely populated neighborhoods where he is the neighborhood secretary (a local functionary of the ruling party), he built a temporary structure near his garden at the boundaries of a state forest reserve. Like Mariana, Joel was born near the Mozambique-Zimbabwe border, but he moved to Sussundenga in 1972 when it was still under Portuguese rule. He obtained a job as a mechanic for one of the Portuguese settlers, and through this relationship, he gained access to the land where his garden is planted.

He is twice a widower and has six children: four sons and two daughters. His two oldest sons (ages 30 and 26) live in Zimbabwe where in the past they sent him money regularly to supplement his small pension and the money he makes from agriculture. But when I met him in 2006, he was no longer able to rely on his sons' remittances due to the economic hardships now facing Zimbabwe. Both of his daughters have married and moved out of his household, taking with them their labor and using it in their husbands' and

in-laws' respective fields. Joel works alongside his two teenage sons who balance their agricultural responsibilities with their schoolwork. During peak times in the agricultural cycle (plowing and harvesting) when the workload is the heaviest, Joel and his friend Pedro engage in a reciprocal labor exchange, helping each other plow and harvest their fields. While Joel was one of the most dedicated and knowledgeable farmers I met, he earned very little income through agriculture due to his lack of labor, capital, and low prices for agricultural commodities, but he was able to grow enough of the local staples to support himself and his two sons.

Joel is an *antigo combatante* (war veteran), and his service as a government soldier during the civil war took him to the provinces of Tete, Nampula, and Zambezia. When he returned to Sussundenga, he took up his current position as neighborhood secretary, as he demonstrated his loyalty to Frelimo during the war. It was upon his return to Sussundenga that he became, in his words, "serious about agriculture." Joel's land use rights are substantiated in two ways: the first is through the original allocation of land by a Portuguese settler, and the second is that he has been able to hold onto this land through his status as a war veteran and neighborhood secretary for the ruling party. His position as part of the local state and his social relations with individuals in its institutions legitimate his claims to this land. As a result, he cultivates a large and fertile riverine garden in an area where other residents are prohibited from clearing fields.

Property and Authority

The examples of Mariana and Joel highlight several broader patterns surrounding land, property, and authority in contemporary Mozambique. First, many Mozambicans use the state to legitimate their land use rights, but the state often takes the form of local level ruling party officials. While the land law is explicit in recognizing and protecting smallholder or peasant land use rights, it is the social relations with specific individuals within the local state that enable one's claims to stick. Second, in addition to the state, Mariana and others may also use customary authority in the form of chiefs or sub-chiefs to support their land claims. Chiefly authority varies in its prevalence and power, but in this part of central Mozambique, chiefs continue to play an active role in land allocation and legitimating land use rights. As new arrivals to Sussundenga in the 1960s, Mariana's husband originally received land use rights from a chief in exchange for pledging submission to chiefly authority. It was after independence that the state allocated her husband land within a new communal village. Many of the town's residents continue to rely on chiefly authority to substantiate their claims in cases of land conflict, giving chiefly authority a power and resilience within the postcolonial nation-state. After a long period of ostracism, the state officially recognized "traditional authorities" in 2000, enlisting them in local governance and expanding state authority into rural areas where state institutions were weak.

Because of Sussundenga's history of colonial settlement, postcolonial state re-settlement, and war-induced migration, depending on when and where a family or individual received land use rights, their claims may be legitimated by a different form of authority: a chief, a ruling party official, the district agricultural office, social relations with a relative or neighbor, or a combination of authorities. This, at times, leads to competing definitions of authority over land. In a pluralistic environment, the greater number and depth of ways one can appeal to authority—whether it's a chief, a claim of first settlement, pleas to culture and tradition, connections to ruling elites and local officials—the more likely one is able to substantiate and defend their land claims in cases of conflict. But, not everyone in the community is equally positioned to do so.

In Mariana's example, her ability to use and benefit from (i.e., access) the land she cultivates is embedded in social and kin relations while her son, as inheritor of his father's land, can articulate his land claims based on the authority of the postcolonial state. Therefore, Mariana lacks property rights in a sense that her claims may not be recognized if she and her son ever came into conflict with each other over their land. This reveals an important distinction between access and property; while access signifies the ability to benefit from land, property entails the power to control, make decisions, and exclude others from land. During the period of Mozambique's postwar economic growth, a small number of individuals have obtained land in Sussundenga through illegal buying and selling. While these cases are rare, there exists the potential for a new form of legitimation to emerge—the market—setting the conditions for some residents to profit from their control of land.

Conclusion

In many Western contexts we have the tendency to take property, and private property in particular, as self-evident. But when viewed through a cross-cultural perspective, property becomes a process, a set of social relations, a symbol, and an object that is made and re-made through social practice. Power relations are embedded in, and reproduced through, property rights, positioning some individuals and groups to benefit and profit through their control over resources. In central Mozambique women and men are enmeshed in overlapping and competing authorities sanctioning land use and access, and how local residents substantiate their land claims serves to legitimate particular forms of power and authority. As capitalist social relations shape more aspects of rural life in Mozambique, who can claim what will have important implications for poverty alleviation, the accumulation of wealth, and the perpetuation of various forms of inequality.

Notes

1. Shona is a Bantu language spoken in east and central Zimbabwe, and several dialects of Shona are spoken in central Mozambique. Chiteve and Chindau are the most common dialects spoken in Sussundenga.

2. Mariana is a pseudonym.
3. Joel is a pseudonym.

8.3 "If We Didn't Have Water": Black Women's Struggle for Urban Land Rights in Brazil

KEISHA-KHAN Y. PERRY

The environmental justice movement is concerned with addressing the linkages between racial discrimination, social justice, and access to environmental quality. Unlike the environmentalists that may come to mind for most readers, environmental justice activists are not concerned with conservation or the protection of biodiversity, but are focused on everyday living and the right to live, work, and play in a healthy community. The following selection not only provides a snapshot into environmental justice activism in Brazil, but it also explores a relatively underdeveloped topic of the connection between environmental justice and Afro-Brazilian religious traditions. In this reading, Perry draws on her ethnographic work in Gamboa de Baixo to show how religious traditions shape connections to the sea and rights to the land alongside it, and are thus intimately connected to their mobilization to defend their rights to coastal territory. Perry's work highlights the critical role of black women in neighborhood activism and the demand for material resources.

Questions

1. What does the sea represent in African religious traditions and environmental politics in Gamboa de Baixo?
2. What are terreiros? Why are they important for black women in Gamboa de Baixo?
3. What does it mean to say that "black matters are spatial matters"?
4. What does the author mean by saying that "black women's religious matters are political matters"? How does this connect to Dianne M. Stewart's notion of "the liberation motif"?
5. How is the environmental justice movement raced, classed, and gendered? Why are women of color at the forefront of the environmental justice movement?

Se não tiver água, se não tiver mata, se não tiver espaço de terra para a gente colocar o pé no chão, na terra, a gente não tem de onde tirar a nossa energia, a nossa força (If we didn't have water, if we didn't have the bush, if we didn't have land for us to put our feet on the ground, on the earth, we wouldn't have where to get our energy, our life force).

—MAKOTA VALDINA PINTO[1]

Keisha Perry-Khan. '"If We Didn't Have Water": Black Women's Struggle for Urban Land Rights in Brazil' 2009. *Environmental Justice* 2(1) Pp. 9–14. By permission of Mary Ann Liebert, Inc., Publishers.

n late December 2004, the tsunamis ravished South-east Asia and Africa, killing more than 140,000 people. In reading about the rescue and recovery efforts, I was struck by the statement of a Sri Lankan irrigation engineer that, "now people hate the sea, they hate it."[2] Although geographically distant, the devastation made me think differently about how Gulf Coast residents, many of whom have long since relocated from coastal cities such as New Orleans, might have viewed the ocean in the aftermath of Hurricane Katrina. Did they develop what Mike Davis calls an "ecology of fear" of living on the coast, or, similar to tsunami victims a few months prior, a hatred of the sea?[3]

These questions about the relationship to coastal landscapes provide a global framing for understanding the Brazilian fishing community and its female-led, grass roots movement against land expulsion that have been the focus of my anthropological work since 1999. Conducting research in Gamboa de Baixo, on the coast of the Bay of All Saints in the city-center of Salvador, Bahia, has challenged me to delve into the way I think about African descendants' simultaneous indictment and celebration of the sea that extends back to slavery. I am reminded of the testimony of abduction by an enslaved African woman, Mrs. Brooks, who recounted to missionaries in nineteenth-century Jamaica: "I was playing by the sea-coast, when a white man offered me sugar-plums, and told me to go with him. I went with him, first into a boat, and then to the ship. Everything seemed strange to me, and I asked him to let me go back, but he would not hear me; and when I went to look for the place where he found me, I could see nothing of land, and I began to cry. There I was for a long time, with a great many more of my own colour, till the ship came to Kingston."[4]

For black people in Brazil, the sea evokes similar memories of the journey and terror of the transatlantic slave trade but also represents a continuous geographic link to Africa that allows them to imagine a psychic return to "full freedom."[5] What drives the Gamboa de Baixo struggle for land rights during recent threats of mass eviction and forced displacement as a result of urban revitalization programs, or what neighborhood activists have termed a "wave of black clearance," is partly their love for and spiritual connection to the sea that is the backyard of their urban neighborhood. That collective memory of the blood in the waters between Africa and the Americas has not caused diaspora Africans to hate the sea inspires me whenever I think of the Bahian political context. In this article, I discuss the profound ways in which the sea in African religious traditions shapes everyday black culture and environmental politics in Gamboa de Baixo and in black neighborhoods throughout Salvador.

. . . Following in the diaspora feminist footsteps of [African]-American Brazilianist scholars such as historians Kim Butler and Rachel Harding, I highlight how black women in poor urban neighborhoods in Salvador carve out geographic, social, and political spaces for themselves while expanding notions of cultural belonging and citizenship rights at the levels of the city, the nation, and the diaspora.[6] It is significant that we see black women's central role in urban social movements as part of a larger diaspora pattern of black women's oppositional politics vested in property rights for both cultural and material gain.

Discussion

"If We Didn't Have Water . . . "

To begin to comprehend this inseparable connection between black women's religious culture and politics, the words of the late Brazilian literary scholar of Bahian culture, Jorge Amado, come to mind: "The ocean is large, the sea is a road without end, waters make up more than half the world, they are three-quarters of it, and all that belongs to Iemanjá." In the African diasporic religion of *candomblé*, practiced by the vast majority of Bahians, Iemanjá is the highly revered *orixá* (goddess) of the sea commonly known as the mother of the waters (*a mãe das águas*). Each year in Salvador, February 2 marks one of the most important days of celebration in *candomblé*, the Festa de Iemanjá, which takes place in the Rio Vermelho coastal neighborhood. With more resources today, particularly government sponsorship, the festival has been transformed from a community practice into a massive cultural project of local interest, as well as national and international tourism. However, the dominant ceremonial presence of black fishermen and *candomblé* religious leaders (most of whom are women) reminds us that, although Rio Vermelho is now a predominantly white, elite neighborhood, black fishing colonies have historically occupied the coastal lands of Salvador and have carried out these traditions since the slavery period. Gamboa de Baixo is now one of the few black urban fishing colonies that exist on the Bahian coast, and the

Iemanjá festival still occurs simultaneously within the neighborhood on a much smaller scale. Like in most fishing communities, local residents pay homage to the goddess of the sea for protecting the fishermen and fisherwomen while they work, and for supplying the sea with sufficient fish, an important natural resource that sustains the local economy and African-inspired culinary traditions. More important, Gamboa de Baixo residents express their gratitude to Iemanjá, who protects their children while they play on the neighborhood's beaches.

Approximately one week after the February 2 festivals, another Iemanjá festival is carried out in Gamboa de Baixo. Preta, a longtime activist and neighborhood association board member, organizes an offering of gifts to the *orixá* Iemanjá, a personalized celebration that has become a local custom. She receives relatives and friends from all over the city and state, as well as her *candomblé* family from Itaparica Island, located in the bay and visible from Gamboa de Baixo. The neighborhood association has been active in preparing Preta's offering each year, from raising funds to creating traditional gifts, many of which are biodegradable after much discussion within the organization about the harmful environmental effects of plastic presents such as dolls and perfumes. When I asked Preta why she joined the community struggle, she first explained that living in proximity to the resources of the city-center, such as schools and hospitals, was very important. Then she explained, chuckling, that few places in the city exist where she can have access to her own beach to carry out her yearly religious obligations to Iemanjá and celebrate with her neighbors. For this right to own and live on these coveted coastal lands, she will continue to fight. . . .

. . . [L]ocal activists assert that not only should the Iemanjá festivals in Gamboa de Baixo be understood within the context of African religious traditions and their reverence for the sea, but also as an aspect of black women's deliberate actions of staking claim to urban land on the Bahian coast. In *terreiros* (*candomblé* houses) throughout the city, not only have black women inherited African religious practices, but they have also inherited the rights to the land on which they practice these traditions. Historically, to speak of these *terreiros* has meant to speak of black women's land. Thus, black women have been uniquely positioned in these communities as having both collective memory and legal documentation of ancestral lands. This memory extends beyond the Bay of All Saints to the practice of women as landowners in Africa, where they served as the primary mediators of family relations within their communities, influencing the distribution of important resources such as land. Signifying more than just the physical space where families live, work, and forge political networks, urban land in contemporary Brazil represents the ability for black women to pass spiritual and material resources from one generation to the next. Land has become one of the greatest social and cultural assets for black people, and particularly for women, who are the most economically marginalized. In essence, the neighborhood fight for land rights has been able to integrate their political demands to legalize collective property rights with demands to preserve the material and the cultural resources the sea provides.

"If We Didn't Have Land . . ."

I am deliberate about not detailing *candomblé* practices nor its specific African-derived cosmologies and mythologies. Rather, the ethnographic examples of the Iemanjá festivals are intended to bring attention to the political formation of a black urban neighborhood located on the geographic and socioeconomic margins of a Brazilian city. . . . The case of Gamboa de Baixo supports my theoretical claim that African religious traditions are indissociable from black women's political actions in the local, national, and global black struggle for material resources such as land, employment, and education. . . . In other words, black women's religious matters are political matters, and black women's collective resistance against the violence of land evictions and displacement are deeply connected to what womanist theologian Dianne M. Stewart . . . terms "the liberation motif" of African-centered traditions in black diasporic communities.[7] This emphasis shows that black women in Brazil and throughout the black diaspora are cultural producers as well as political agents in their own right with their own African-inspired sensibilities of gendered racial liberation and social transformation in Brazilian cities. Spirituality, I reaffirm, must acquire a privileged space in the broader understanding of how black women have responded to the barbarous reality of class-based and gendered racism in Brazil and throughout the black diaspora.

. . . Kim Butler argues that adaptations of *candomblé* have been "rooted in the conscious choice of Afro-Brazilians to use African culture as a mode of support and survival in modern Brazilian society."[8]

The ethnographic focus on the political mobilization of black urban communities contextualizes black cultural practices within the ongoing processes of gendered racial and economic oppression that mark the black Brazilian experience. The black majority in Bahia and the predominance of African religious traditions does not obscure the lack of black women in positions of political and economic power, such as holding public office, executive positions in financial institutions, or even as store clerks in shopping malls. In many respects, the black population, particularly black women, carr[ies] the burden of centuries of enslavement and social marginalization. A legacy of the slave economy, 95 percent of domestic workers are black women who in their majority are underpaid and continue to live in poverty. Serving as spiritual spaces of racial and gender solidarity, the female-centered *terreiros* have been crucial to the maintenance of an African cultural identity and black community formation in the city of Salvador.

From this perspective, we cannot ignore that, historically, the main protagonists, such as Makota Valdina Pinto in Salvador, in antiracist environmental justice movements in Brazilian cities have been black women leaders (in their majority) of *candomblé* communities. Pinto, since her youth, has been a neighborhood activist and one of the city's most outspoken voices against environmental racism, linking the increased lack of public access to unpolluted lands and natural water sources to the widespread neglect of black urban communities. Pinto's actions echo Jomo Kenyatta and other diaspora scholar activists who argue that water and land are two of the greatest natural resources for black people socially, economically, and spiritually, and in Afro-Brazilian communities, gaining access to these resources or protecting them from privatization and destruction has been an ongoing focus of community-based activism. Black women environmentalists in Salvador have also focused heavily on the urgent need for environmental reform while also fighting for the eradication of the violent religious intolerance many Afro-Brazilian religious communities suffer. Violence against these communities has targeted the built environments of the *terreiros*, such as the defacement of the metal gates of the historic Casa Branca terreiro located in Ogunja and the encroachment on the lands of the Terreiro do Cobre in Federação. The state demolition of the Terreiro Oyá Onipó Neto (Imbuí) in March 2008 further illustrates the gendered implications of these violent attacks on black women's lands, and their organic leadership in combating such violence locally.

The leadership of black women in environmental justice movements should also be understood within the larger context of emerging neighborhood movements. Recently, I attended a housing rights forum during which Gamboa de Baixo activist and *candomblé* practitioner Ana Cristina boldly asked the audience, which included activists from other *bairros populares* and urban planning experts: "What kind of city do we live in that prepares architects and engineers to demolish homes and expel local populations in order to implement their urban development projects?" (Her public denouncement of destructive development policies would be later echoed in the cries of injustice in the aftermath of the demolition of the Terreiro Oyá Onipó Neto, which community activists fought to be rebuilt). She firmly asserted that "*a terra é do povo* [land belongs to the people]!" The affirmation of collective land ownership alludes to a serious question of why the *povo*, or the masses of blacks who occupy Salvador's poorest neighborhoods, have no legal right to own the land they have lived on and cultivated for generations. In the broadest sense, what does it mean for the likes of Ana Cristina—black women who occupy the racial, gender, and socio-spatial margins of the city—to make claims to it and work for its collective improvement? These questions force us to examine black women activists in Salvador, located at the center of political opposition to the racial social order, to include critiquing pedagogies and practices that integrate ideologies of exclusion into processes of urban planning and land distribution.

Within a city "structured in dominance," to borrow from Stuart Hall's formulation of the necessary relationship between racial domination and economic and political processes, black women carve out a geographic, social, and political space for themselves while expanding definitions of rights, citizenship, and national belonging.[9] Securing their citizenship rights to adequate water and sanitation also constitutes a necessary aspect of guaranteeing their permanence on the disputed coastal lands of the Bay of All Saints. In this sense, the political experiences of Gamboa de Baixo highlight the emergence of black women's militancy at the community level in struggles to improve the environmental and habitat conditions of Salvador's black neighborhoods. After the outbreak of cholera in Bahia in 1992, which caused several deaths in Gamboa de Baixo, the women organized themselves and founded the Associação Amigos de Gegê dos Moradores da Gamboa de Baixo [Association of Friends of Gegê Residents of Gamboa de Baixo]. They led Gamboa residents to radio stations to bring attention to the cholera outbreak and the contamination of their tap water. They demanded that the state test the natural water sources and the public water pipes in the neighborhood. Testing proved that the victims of cholera had died from contaminated water provided by the city and not from the neighborhood's natural water fountains. After these actions, the community received some social service interventions such as the construction of the *chafariz*, a central water fountain in the area. As founding leader of the neighborhood association, Boa Morte, recounted about this period:

> I was the first person to go to the radio stations. When I arrived home, EMBASA [the State water company] was already there investigating how to install the water fountain. What strengthened our movement more, was the death of Mr. Geraldo [known as Gêgê], the father of Lueci [ex-community leader]; in other words, I become mobilized at that time because families that I knew, mother and father, everybody young. . . . I was at home when I found out that he went to the hospital with symptoms of cholera and other residents had gone already. Another boy had died, so I thought that it was time for me to get moving. I called two other women, Tônia and Mel, and we went to the radio. Afterwards, other women began to arrive, Tinda, Solange, Hilda, and later Lueci. We took action and began to put water [in Gamboa]. It's from then on that the movement began to organize Gamboa, because before that, Gamboa was in a stand still, just being marginalized (my translation).[10]

Pioneer activist Dona Lenilda and Sr. Geraldo's widow also remembers that, "What led me to participate in the movement was that I wanted a better life for my family, for my children. We had just seen their father die, and other people, right? So, we wanted a more dignified life, with potable water, toilets so as not throw our feces just anywhere. That's why the disease [cholera] surfaced here, and that was what led me to the movement. If we are going to live in a place, we should treat it properly" (my translation).[11]

As Afro-Canadian geographer Katherine McKittrick frames it, "black matters are spatial matters."[12] In addition to making demands from the state for clean water and basic sanitation, local activists have found ways to treat their environment properly, to include scuba diving to remove garbage from the ocean and using biodegradable materials in *candomblé* ceremonies. Environmental reform and the building of sanitized spaces matter to poor people as much as it matters to the state to create sanitized, hygienic, modern cities, but black neighborhoods desire clean urban spaces that include them, rather than exclude them. Thus, environmental reform also should be viewed as intertwined with the struggle for the legalization of black urban lands, recognizing that property rights continue to be a crucial aspect of black claims to Brazilian citizenship. Furthermore, black women's political leadership in issues of land and sanitation in Salvador's *bairros populares* is an important field of understanding everyday grassroots actions of the black movement. . . .

Conclusions

"We Wouldn't Have Where to Get Our Energy . . . "

In my analysis of the political organization of Gamboa de Baixo around the urgent issue of rights to urban land, I have recognized that the sea, specifically its relationship to African cosmologies, yields an indispensable source of spiritual, material, and political nourishment in the lives of black women in Bahia. Many in the *candomblé* community have expressed their discontent with anthropological representations of African spirituality that fail to examine the role that antiblack racism and sexism play in the continuity of *candomblés* in Bahia and the institutionalization of black women's leadership in grassroots social movements. In this vein, I confront ethnographic paradigms that reduce black subjectivity in Bahia to a singular African religious essence. This approach to black Bahians' production of cultural knowledge is particularly salient when researching the lives of black women who are rarely considered cultural producers outside the realm of *candomblé*. Thus, my aim has been to theorize within the "liberation motif" of African diasporic religious traditions, which has given impetus to the political work of poor black women in Salvador's poorest neighborhoods. The women of the Gamboa de Baixo neighborhood association illustrate that black political movements imbricate the spiritual with the political.[13] In fact, I draw on the insights of the Iemanjá festivals as a way to examine how black women play vital roles in preserving African traditions while creating social networks and politicizing urban communities located on the Bahian coast. The nature of black women's agency in neighborhood-based social movements for land rights in Brazil is interconnected with black women's agency in Bahian *candomblé*. In Gamboa de Baixo, these cultural and political identities merge in the struggle over space, and in particular, the use and control of coastal lands and the sea.

It is not by accident that clean water continues to be a key political demand for neighborhood activists, and that black women lead this fight. As Makota Valdina Pinto suggests in the opening quote, land rights must be considered within the broader quest for water and an overall healthy, clean, urban environment. Politicizing the need for water has been integral to the Gamboa de Baixo's ongoing fight for urban land rights and neighborhood improvement amid state threats of land expulsion. Water, specifically the waters of the Bay of All Saints, has been a spiritual source of black women's political empowerment in Gamboa. Water has been at the center of Gamboa de Baixo's political organizing around issues of land and housing reform since its inception. Poor black women have been key to engendering and racializing political discussions around natural resources, and for broadening black collective claims to citizenship in dignified living conditions. As black feminist anthropologist Faye Harrison reminds us, "racism is an enduring social problem with serious implications for social and economic justice, political conflict, and struggles for *human dignity*" (my emphasis).[14] In Brazil and throughout the diaspora, black women's antiracism activism (as is also evident in post- Katrina New Orleans) is deeply rooted in the politics of the built environment, specifically how to use, protect, restore, and *own* spaces and places.

Notes

1. Makota Valdina Pinto is a black woman environmental rights activist and community and *candomblé* religious leader in Salvador, Bahia. This excerpt is from an interview conducted by Afro-Brazilian historian and director of the Palmares Foundation Ubiratan Castro in 1999, published in *Revista Palmares*, vol. 2 (Brasília: Fundação Palmares), 82.

2. Amy Waldman and David Rohde, "Fearing a Sea that Once Sustained, Then Killed," *New York Times*, January 5, 2005.

3. Mike Davis, *Ecology of Fear: Los Angeles and the Imagination of Disaster* (New York: Vintage, 1998).

4. Cited in Dianne M. Stewart, *Three Eyes for the Journey: African Dimensions of the Jamaican Religious Experience* (New York: Oxford University Press, 2005), 15.

5. Kim D. Butler, *Freedoms Given, Freedoms Won: Afro-Brazilians in Post-Abolition São Paulo and Salvador* (New Brunswick, NJ: Rutgers University Press, 1998).

6. Kim D. Butler, *Freedoms Given, Freedoms Won*; Rachel E. Harding, *A Refuge in Thunder: Candomblé and Alternative Spaces of Blackness* (Bloomington: Indiana University Press, 2003).

7. Dianne M. Stewart, *Three Eyes for the Journey*.

8. Kim D. Butler, *Freedoms Given, Freedoms Won*, 195.

9. Stuart Hall. "Race, Articulation, and Societies Structured in Dominance," in *Sociological Theories: Race and Colonialism* (Paris: UNESCO, 1980).

10. My translation of the original quote in Portuguese.

11. My translation from original in Portuguese.

12. Katherine McKittrick. *Demonic Grounds: Black Women and the Cartographies of Struggle*. (Minneapolis: University of Minnesota Press, 2006), xiv.

13. M. Jacqui Alexander, *Pedagogies of Crossing. Pedagogies of Crossing: Meditations on Feminism, Sexual Politics, Memory, and the Sacred*. (Durham: Duke University Press, 2005), 326

14. Faye Harrison, *Resisting Racism and Xenophobia: Global Perspectives on Race, Gender, and Human Rights* (Walnut Creek, CA: AltaMira Press, 2005), 9.

8.4 Gone the Bull of Winter? Contemplating Climate Change's Cultural Implications in Northeastern Siberia, Russia

SUSAN A. CRATE

In 2014, the Executive Board of the American Anthropological Association (AAA) received the final report from a 3-year task force focused on Global Climate Change. The AAA Statement on Humanity and Climate Change, which emerged out of this study, recognizes the global threat that climate change brings to all aspects of human life, including the spaces we call "home," our livelihoods, and cultures. Anthropologists are uniquely positioned to understand the impacts of climate change on human culture, and the ways in which local people make sense of their changing environment. The following selection discusses the significance of climate change for the Sakha horse and cattle breeders of northeastern Siberia. For the Sakha, winter is represented by a white bull, and the stories elders tell about the "Bull of Winter" explain temperature events. Crate wonders if these stories will soon become stories of the past, as she describes Sakha observations about the changing climate and its impacts on their culture. This "climate ethnography" is an example of advocacy or activist anthropology.

Questions

1. What does Crate mean when she says that hearing the story of Jyl Oghuhu was her "ethnographic moment"?
2. What are the cultural implications of climate change for the Sakha?
3. How is the Sakha's "sense of place" connected to their environment? How does climate change impact their sense of their homeland? How does climate change affect your sense of place?
4. What do the Sakha see as the causes for climate change?
5. How do global media shape Sakha elders' understanding of climate change? What role do the media play in your understanding of climate change?
6. What is an ethnoclimatologist?
7. What role can anthropologists play in addressing climate change?

The bull of winter is a legendary Sakha creature whose presence explains the turning from the frigid winter to the warming spring. The legend tells that the bull of winter, who keeps the cold in winter, loses his first horn at the end of January as the cold begins to let go to warmth, then his second horn melts off at the end of February and finally, by the end of March, he loses his head as spring is sure to have arrived. It seems that now with the warming, perhaps the bull of winter will no longer be. . . .

—MALE SAKHA ELDER, B. 1935

Sakha, Turkic-speaking native horse and cattle breeders of northeastern Siberia, Russia, personify winter in the form of the *Jyl Oghuha* (Bull of Winter), a white bull with blue spots, huge horns, and frosty breath. *Jyl Oghuha's* legacy explains the extreme 100°C annual temperature range of Sakha's sub-Arctic habitat. Accordingly, in early December the *Jyl Oghuha* arrives from the Arctic Ocean to hold temperatures at their coldest (−60° to −65°C; −76° to −85°F) for December and January. Although I had heard the story many times while working with Viliui Sakha[1] since 1991, in the summer of 2005 it had an unexpected ending. The realization that a cultural story, which for centuries had explained the annual temperature event of sub-Arctic winter, could perhaps become a story of how things *used to be,* alerted me to the cultural implications of global climate change. This elder's new way of recounting Sakha's age-old story of *Jyl Oghuha* was my "ethnographic moment" to enter the field of climate change research. In this chapter I explore Viliui Sakha observations of global climate change, bring to light the cultural implications of global climate change, and highlight anthropology's privileged approaches to understanding different ways of knowing to move anthropologists from impartial observers into the realm of action-oriented researchers.

Sakha's Turkic ancestors migrated from Central Asia to southern Siberia around 900, and then northward to their present homeland beginning in the 1200s. They inhabit a sub-Arctic region characterized by continuous permafrost with annual temperature fluctuations of 100° Celsius from −60°C (−76°F) in winter to +40°C (104°F) in summer. Viliui Sakha have adapted their southern agropastoralist subsistence to an extreme sub-Arctic environment and adapted to the throes of Russian colonization and Soviet and post-Soviet forces (Crate 2002, 2003a, 2006b). Today the majority of rural Viliui Sakha communities practice household-level food production via a system termed "cows and kin," focused on keeping cows and exchanging labor and products with kin (Crate 2003a, 2006b). They also rely heavily upon other subsistence production including gardens and greenhouses, forage (hunting, fishing, and gathering) and other domesticates including horses, pigs, and chickens. Theirs is a mixed cash economy, with most of their cash originating from state transfer payments in the form of state salaries, subsidies, and pensions.

Encountering Global Climate Change in Viliui Sakha Communities

In 2004,[2] 90 percent of the Viliui Sakha participants in my field research expressed their concerns about local climate change,[3] saying that they were seeing unprecedented change in their local areas and that they were concerned it threatened their subsistence (Crate 2006a).[4] In response to this result, in summer 2005 we worked with village youth, already engaged in our project's elder knowledge initiative (Crate 2006), to interview thirty-three elders about their local observations of climate change. We asked a simple set of questions about what elders observed, how their lives were affected, what the causes were, and what they thought the future would bring. The elders impressed upon us that they possess ecological knowledge about how the climate was and how it has changed. In lieu of availability of comprehensive local climatic data,[5] village elders' knowledge is vital. Most elders offered testimony similar to this:

> The climate is definitely different from before. When I was little, the winters were very cold, minus 50–60 degrees. When we spit, it froze before it hit the ground and flying birds sometimes would freeze and die. The summer was a wonderful hot temperature and the hay you just cut would dry very quickly. In the last few years the climate has changed. We have rain, rain, rain all the time and winter comes late and so does spring. For people who live with a short summer when there needs to be the right weather to accomplish all for the winter and there is cool rainy times so that the hay does not dry and has to sit and sit and the quality is bad because of that. It is the right time for haying but the conditions are all wrong. (male Sakha elder, b. 1938)

What are the changes people are observing? Sakha elders reported that they cannot read the weather anymore: "From long ago we could read the weather and know what weather would come according to our "Sier-Tuom" [Sakha sacred belief system]. But we can't do that anymore" (female Sakha elder, b. 1942). This is particularly urgent in the extreme environment of the Arctic where each day of summer is crucial to winter survival. Elders also commented that the timing of the seasons had changed, further jeopardizing winter survival. For the last decade, spring and fall have come several weeks late.

Elders also said that the climate had softened, referring again and again to *Jyl Oghuha:* "Winters have warmed and summers are not so warm. All is softer. The north is especially warming. It will be cold in winter and suddenly get warm in winter. It was never like this before. Strong cold held for months. We have the legend about the bull of winter losing its horns" (male Sakha elder, b. 1925). Additionally, two qualities of the climate, both critical to survival in the north, are reported to be different: a tendency toward long periods of calms and a relative lack of humidity. The summer heat is no longer dry, but laden with humidity that stifles in high temperatures: "Before it got very hot also, like it does now, but there was air—now it gets hot and you can't breathe [humidity]." Both the lack of calms and the humidity make the Viliui Sakha's environment that much more challenging to negotiate. Although these barriers are still surmountable, elders report that family members spend more time in the seasonal tasks, most notably haying and winter activities such as hunting and wood hauling, due to the increased challenge that these climate changes pose.

Several elders commented on the loss of familiar species and the arrival of new species from the south, including a variety of insects that prey on many of the garden and forage plants that Sakha depend on. They talked about other changes in their local environment, including increased rain during the haying season, too much winter snow, increased occurrences of thunder, and a change in the quality of sunlight. Many also correlated these changes with poorer health and more diseases among their people.

We next asked elders how climate change was affecting people s daily lives. First and foremost, they talked about the effects on harvesting forage for their animals:

It ruins the hay harvesting when it rains for two months solid. There is no winter forage for our cows and horses. Even if you plan to work every day at the hay, the weather keeps you from it. Every day it is raining. The land is going under water and the hay lands are smaller and smaller and if you keep a lot of animals, it is very hard. The hay itself has less nutrition and then when it is cut and lays and gets wet

and dries many times. It also loses its nutritious quality. (male Sakba elder, b. 1932)

They talked about the negative impact on their ability to raise enough food to see them through the long winter: "So much water is bad for the garden. Potatoes rot in the ground and there are many new insects. Gardens are very late. The water and cold mean we plant potatoes a month late and some not until July." (female Sakha elder, b. 1930)

Next elders talked about how difficult it has become for their horses which spend all winter outside and dig through the snow to find fodder. In the last decade elders have witnessed increasing amounts of snow due to warmer winter temperatures[6] and an impervious ice layer beneath the snow from a freeze/thaw that occurs commonly in the fall with warming and prevents the horses from reaching fodder. They also expressed concern about hunting, a supplemental source of food for many contemporary households especially in the post-Soviet context: "We hunters can't hunt. I go trapping in January when the snow is thinner. But as the snow is deeper I can't go and the deep snow is bad because dogs can't run and horses can't walk. In spring and fall hunters also can't hunt because there is so much mud and boggy land" (male Sakha elder, b. 1933). Not only are hay, hunting, and foraging areas diminished due to flooding, all land areas are threatened. In one of our four research villages, there is deep concern about how water is inundating the grazing and gardening areas in the village center, another source of sustenance in these communities: "All the water ruins the usable areas near our homes—it diminishes all our land—with all the water, no one has any land anymore."

Elders also mentioned that they noticed the land was sinking in places: "The flat fields are sinking in and we want to know why—perhaps the permafrost is melting?" The most graphic of these accounts of sinking land tell of how an island near the village of Kuukei is submerging: "We have an island on the lake but now it has fallen. I have been watching for the last ten years and I see this happening" (female Sakha elder, b. 1933). However important it is to understand whether the island is in fact sinking because of melting permafrost, and whether the melting is in fact due to climate change, when I heard these testimonies I was more concerned and curious about how the perception of the land actually sinking is affecting how Viliui Sakha orient themselves to their environment. Their sense of place and their understanding of "homeland" are both tied directly to an ecosystem dependent on water in its solid state. Although feeling "at home" in such icy confines is foreign to most of us, it is the familiar and the understood territory of comfort for northern inhabitants (Nuttall 1992). This was clear when we asked, "Isn't it good that it is not so cold in winter and not so hot in summer?" In response, elders unanimously argued to the opposite:[7]

> It is not bad to have warm winters, being an old person, it is great! But as Sakha people, we need strong cold here. It is how our lives are organized and how the nature works here. The big cold is good. The diseases are gone. When it is warm it snows too much and it is not warm or cold. The winter warmth affects people's blood pressure. And the heat in the summer is different, humid and very hard for people to go. It is bad for the way of life here and for survival. The nature, people, animals, and plants here are supposed to have very cold winters and very hot dry summers. That is the best for all life here. (female Sakha elder, b. 1929)

When we asked elders how they thought these changes would affect the future, all felt that conditions would progressively get worse: "As it gets warmer and warmer, the permafrost will melt and our land will be a permanent swamp and we won't be able to do anything—no pastures, no hay fields, just the high areas will remain. If it continues, then the permafrost areas will stop being frozen and it will all melt" (male Sakha elder, b. 1936). Many also made the connection between warming and its effects on health: "The worst part is that diseases will multiply in the future if it continues to get warmer and warmer. People's lives will get shorter with all the disease and no one will be able to keep animals here anymore" (female Sakha elder, b. 1944).

Some elders made a link between the local effects of global climate change and the breakdown of their contemporary social fabric: "People's attitudes will get worse and worse and things will go crazy. People's character and the way they relate has changed and I think it is because of the climate change. The way people are so violent these days I think is connected to the change in air and climate" (female Sakha elder, b. 1930). Making such connections is not unfounded. Similar cases of

contextualization, the ways in which people associate changes in the natural environment with changes in their social environment, can be found in different local settings in northern Russia (Karjalainen and Habeck 2004; Simpura and Eremitcheva 1997). There are also studies in the field of biometeorology that are making such correlations in other cultural contexts.

We also solicited elders' perceptions of the causes of global climate change. Many cited the presence of the reservoir of the Viliui hydroelectric station—constructed in the 1960s to supply electricity mostly for the then nascent diamond mining industry (Crate 2003b). However, studies have shown that the presence of the reservoir only results in a microclimatic change that would not include the extent of changes observed by the elders. Most elders agreed that the climate is changing due to a host of other reasons:

> They go into the cosmos too much and are mixing up the sky. When I was young they didn't go into the cosmos and we knew the weather. It rained when it was supposed to. Now it is all mixed up. Maybe from the mining activity and the electricity makers, the hydro stations, it all affects. They say the Sea [hydro station reservoir] affects us, but I don't agree. The natural climate is all mixed up. (male Sakha elder, b. 1933)

Elders commented that climate change is due to both natural and human induced causes. When they talk about the human causes, it is important to remember that in their lifetimes they have seen the introduction and the widespread use of technology. They were born and raised on remote homesteads without electricity and now live surrounded by most varieties of technology. It is an easy step to relate the changes in their physical environment with the entry and advancement of this technology. Explaining the changes as "caused by nature" also makes sense given that they live in a highly variable climate to begin with and also know there have been climatic changes in the past.

Natural causes elders talked about included changes from nature itself, the changing direction of the Earth and all planets, each with a magnetic pull that is affecting us, changing sky and clouds, and the melting of the ice on the Arctic Ocean, bringing lots of clouds and rain. Human-induced causes included the "breaking" of the atmosphere by rockets and bombs that go up into the sky, and by humans going into the cosmos too much and mixing up the sky; the changing of the atmosphere by something in the atmosphere that makes it all very warm, and by all the "technika" people are using that fouls the air; the holes in the ozone and the other wreckage done with all our technology; and too many atom bombs. Although at first consideration some of the contributing factors these elders mention seem irrelevant to Western scientific thought on the subject, their ideas are both relevant and culturally provocative: the former because many of their ideas are related to the anthropogenic drivers known to be partially causing global climate change, the latter because so much of their attention is focused on activities in the sky and outer space that have to do with Soviet technologies introduced in their lifetimes.

Some elders provided explanations that related to phenomena other than global climate change. One commented, "The elders said it was like this last century also and they say that every century the same conditions come around—one hundred years ago also the land was under water." Sakha also have a cultural understanding of there being dry and wet years:

> They said that we would be having dry years now, but it is the opposite. Very wet years have come, lots of rain. Not in the spring when we need it, but in the summer when it gets in the way. There are many times as much water as there should be in the wet years, and if it continues like this, we will all go under water. We had the wet years and so it should be dry by now. (male Sakha elder, b. 1932)

These are important historical events that need further investigation in order to tease out just how Sakha's ancestors adapted to and survived these cyclical changes prior to the Soviet period. Additionally, several elders explained that the waterlogged fields had more to do with Sakha's negligence to work the land as they did in centuries past: "Before—in the Soviet time and before that—since our ancestors first came to these parts, we would make the fields so they were free of water, but not now." However, understanding the inundation of fields by water in the context of other observed changes attributed to climate change refutes these explanations.

Many of the elders' testimonies reveal that they seek to understand local climate change not only based on their observations, but also by integrating knowledge

from other sources. One source was the ancient Sakha proverb "Tiiiekhtere ool uieghe, khachchagha Buus baiaghal irieghe," meaning, "They will survive until the day when the Arctic Ocean melts." Several elders recollected this proverb when they heard of the 2005 summer catastrophic flooding that occurred of the Yana River in the north of the Sakha Republic. Three villages were so heavily flooded that the residents had to permanently relocate. Reporting of this incident substantiated it not as an isolated phenomenon but directly related to the "fact" that the Arctic Ocean is no longer freezing up completely in the winters, resulting in increased water regimes for the entire republic.

In the summer of 2005, I identified only two media sources addressing global climate change that reached the villages. One was the British Broadcasting Company (BBC)'s airing of *The Day After Tomorrow*, the 2004 action/adventure, science fiction/fantasy thriller, on midday local television several times that summer. It is likely that many of the elders' comments about the global implications of local climate change were based on images and sound bites from this film.

The second media source was an article in the republic-wide *Komsomolskaia Pravda v Yakutii* by a Dr. Trofim Maksimov, a biologist and climate scientist in the capital city, Yakutsk (Ivanova 2005). His extensive research in the Sakha Republic shows that average temperatures have risen by 2–3.5°C in the last one hundred years and that average winter temperatures for the same time period are 10°C warmer. This correlates directly with the elders' observations. His findings also document the movement of floral species northward and more temperate species coming into the republic from the south. Again, elders have made similar observations. Despite Maksimov's outspokenness and comprehensive information, only a handful of Viliui inhabitants subscribe to this newspaper or have received either his message or other outside information about the extent and causes of global climate change.

The elders' testimonies reveal no debate about *whether* climate change is occurring. Like most indigenous cultures practicing subsistence, they are, by default, ethnoclimatologists. With a continuous stream of experiential data, they know things are changing. Working with these communities to facilitate adaptive responses to these physical changes is critical. Anthropologists have a unique role, as interpreters of culture, to understand and act in response to global climate change's cultural effects.

The Cultural Implications of Global Climate Change and Indigenous Peoples

Transformations of both symbolic cultures[8] and subsistence cultures such as the changes described here, reframe the implications of unprecedented global climate change. Global climate change, in causes, effects, and amelioration, is intimately and ultimately about culture: Global climate change is caused by the multiple drivers of our global consumer culture, transforms symbolic and subsistence cultures, and will only be forestalled via a cultural transformation from degenerative to regenerative consumer behavior. Accordingly, anthropologists are strategically well suited to interpret, facilitate, translate, communicate, advocate, and act both in the field and at home, taking action and responding to the causes of change and communities facing and adapting to change.[9] . . . [C]limate change is forcing not just community adaptation and resilience, but also relocation of human, animal, and plant populations. Lost with those relocations are the intimate human-environment relationships that not only ground and substantiate indigenous worldviews but also work to maintain and steward local landscapes. In some cases, moves also result in the loss of mythological symbols, meteorological orientation, and even the very totem and mainstay plants and animals that ground a culture.

We need not be over confident in our research partners' capacity to adapt. Although it seems completely plausible that highly adaptive cultures will find ways to feed themselves even if their main animals and plants cannot survive the projected climactic shifts, as anthropologists we need to grapple with the cultural implications of the loss of animals and plants that are central to daily subsistence practices, cycles of annual events, and sacred cosmologies (Crate 2008). The cultural implications could be analogous to the disorientation, alienation, and loss of meaning in life that happens when any people are removed from their environment of origin, like Native Americans moved onto reservations (Castile and Bee 1992; Prucha 1985; White 1983). The only difference is that while in some cases communities themselves will move, in other cases it is the environment that is moving.[10] As the earth literally changes beneath their feet, it is vital to understand the cognitive reverberations within and cultural implications for a people's sense of homeland and place.

If we agree, as Keith Basso convincingly argues, that human existence is irrevocably situated in time and space, that social life is everywhere accomplished through an exchange of symbolic forms, and that wisdom "sits in places" (1996, 53), then we need to grapple with the extent to which global climate change is and will increasingly transform these spaces, symbolic forms, and places. It follows that the result will be great loss of wisdom, of the physical make-ups of cosmologies and worldviews, and of the very human-environment interactions that are a culture's core (Netting 1968, 1993; Steward 1955).

Exploring Anthropological Research Approaches to Address Global Climate Change

Anthropologists can be most effective by using the tools of applied, advocacy-oriented, and public anthropology (Borofsky 2006; Chambers 1985; Gould and Kolb 1964; Kirsch 2002; Nagengast and Vélez-Ibáñez 2004; Rylko-Bauer et al. 2006). Advocacy is key not only in our collaborative relationship with communities but also in representing their best interests in policy and other advocacy contexts. In many parts of the world, indigenous peoples are actively advocating for themselves. However, there are places, such as northern Russia, where civil society and self-advocacy do not have the legacy that exists in Canada, Greenland, and Alaska, where indigenous groups are proactive on issues such as global climate change.[11] In such places anthropologists can work as communicators both to our indigenous research partners (what information they need about global climate change and in what proper form[s]) and by seeking out the local, regional, and national channels through which local voices can affect policy. Similarly, we can link our research partners with other communities who have gone through similar experiences (Cutter and Emrich 2006; Hoffman and Oliver-Smith 2002; Oliver-Smith 1996, 2005; Thomalla et al. 2006).

Research on climate change, the bulk of which to date is in the Arctic, does not address global climate change's cultural implications. Observations and perceptions of local effects of climate change, such as those of the Viliui Sakha presented here, reveal a need to develop research projects focusing on the cognitive/perceptual orientations of communities. Our research agendas must first investigate how our research partners perceive change (Crate 2008), and then use their understandings to encourage positive change. Now that many of our research partners are actively listening to their elders, the time is ripe for those elders' messages to inform the world and for anthropologists to take to heart and fully fathom the cultural implications and our innate responsibilities to act on all of our behalf. In the end we discover that each culture has its own *Jyl Oghuha* that is not only central to how that culture orients their daily/seasonal activities, worldview, and cultural identity, but is also part of the amalgamation of ethnodiversity that, like biodiversity, is intrinsic to the robust health and continued human, plant, and animal habitation of the planet.

Notes

1. Refers to Sakha inhabiting the Viliui River watershed of western Sakha Republic.

2. In context of my 2003–2006 NSF project entitled "Investigating the Economic and Sustainability, Gaining Knowledge," engaging local Viliui Sakha communities in defining sustainability and identifying barriers preventing them from realizing those definitions.

3. We administered surveys to a stratified sample of 30% (Elgeeii: $n = 63$, Kutana: $n = 24$) of all households surveyed by Crate in 1999–2000 (Elgeeii: $n = 210$, Kutana: $n = 79$). The survey instrument was developed based upon both the communities' definitions of sustainability generated during the first field season of the project and standardized questions used in the Survey of Living Conditions in the Artic project (http://www.articlivingconditions.org/).

4. This was a collaborative project involving myself, one research assistant from the United States, a research assistant in each of the four villages, and the direct involvement of the communities themselves. Hence, my use of the pronoun "we."

5. There are regional stations that provide data on a republic-wide level. However, these data are not translated into public information specific to the villages where these elders live.

6. Typically it snows in these areas from mid-September to mid-November and then again from mid-February to mid-March. In the deeper winter it is too cold to snow. In the last decade or so, as winter temperatures are milder, it tends to snow for longer periods in both the fall and spring and the cold period of no snow is increasingly briefer.

7. Granted, shorter winters may actually be beneficial for cattle and horse breeding. Horses and cattle will spend less time in the stables and barns (and more time on the pastures) if the annual average temperature increases. However, more precipitation (snow) and a higher frequency of freezing/thawing events will have an adverse effect.

8. In this article I use the term *culture* to refer to both the series of prescribed human activities and the prescribed symbols that give those activities significance; both the specific way a given people classify, codify, and communicate experience symbolically and the way that people live in accordance to beliefs, language, and history. Culture includes technology, art, science, and moral and ethical systems. All humans possess culture and the world is made up of a diversity of cultures. Accordingly, I use the term in both its singular and plural forms.

9. Although it is beyond the principle focus of this article to discuss the multiplicity of causes for and effects of the transformation of culture resulting from unprecedented global climate change, I do want to mention these larger implications as I see them. The causes and effects of global climate change are about people and power, ethics and morals, environmental costs and justice, and cultural and spiritual survival. Scholars are beginning to address the equity and just implications of climate change. See, for example, Thomas and Twyman (2005). On a temporal scale, the effects of global climate change are the indirect costs of imperialism and colonization—the "nonpoint" fallout for peoples who have been largely ignored. These are the same peoples whose territories that have long been dumping grounds for uranium, industrial societies' trash heaps, and transboundary pollutants. This is environmental colonialism at its fullest development—its ultimate scale—with far-reaching social and cultural implications. Global climate change is the result of global processes that were neither caused by, nor can they be mitigated by the majority of climate-sensitive world regions now experiencing the most unprecedented change. Thus indigenous peoples find themselves at the mercy of and adapting to changes far beyond their control.

10. I take poetic license here by saying that "the environment moves." It works well within the analogy. I fully acknowledge that the environment cannot move but that it changes.

11. I am not implying that it is necessary to install "civil society" in Viliui Sakha communities from scratch. I am emphasizing here that Inuit and other northern communities are far more successful when it comes to expressing their concerns and interests in the wider (global) public. Since the fall of the Soviet Union there has been a gradual increase in existing political institutions, NGOs, and researchers-cum-advocates in the Russian North. For example, in the case of the Eveny, local elites can articulate their concerns—at

least to some extent—via RAIPON (the Russian Association of Indigenous Peoples of the North). Vasilii Robbek and his team of researchers in Yakutsk have been trying to address several politically relevant issues in their research, and at least with some success (see http://www.sitc.ru/ync/narod1.htm). Places and spaces for self-determination in Sakha and the Russian North in general are very different from those in Alaskan or Canadian Northern communities. Local educational institutions, such as schools, libraries, houses of culture, etc., do play a significant role in ecological/environmental education and campaigning, and these institutions should be considered and included in the process of local "capacity building."

References

Basso, K. 1996. Wisdom sits in places: Notes on a western Apache landscape. In *Senses of place*, eds. K. Basso and S. Feld. Sante Fe, NM: School of American Research Press.

Borofsky, R. 2006. Conceptualizing public anthropology. http://www.publicanthropology.org/defining/defingingpa.htm (accessed May 30, 2007).

Castile, G. P., and R. L. Bee, eds. 1992. *State and reservation: New perspectives on federal Indian policy*. Tucson: University of Arizona Press.

Chambers, E. 1985. *Applied anthropology: A practical guide*. Englewood Cliffs, NJ: Prentice Hall.

Crate, S. 2002. Viliui Sakha oral history: The key to contemporary household survival. *Arctic Anthropology* 39(1): 134–54.

Crate, S. 2003a. Viliui Sakha post-Soviet adaptation: A sub-Arctic test of Netting's small-holder theory. *Human Ecology* 31(4): 499–528.

Crate, S. 2003b. Co-option in Siberia: The case of diamonds and the Vilyuy Sakha. *Polar Geography* 26(4) (2002): 289–307.

Crate, S. 2006a. Investigating local definitions of sustainability in the Arctic: Insights from post-Soviet Sakha villages. *Arctic* 59(3): 115-31.

Crate, S. 2006b. *Cows, kin and globalization: An ethnography of sustainability*. Walnut Creek, CA: AltaMira Press.

Crate, S. 2006. Elder knowledge and sustainable livelihoods in post-Soviet Russia: Finding dialogue across the generations. *Artic Anthropology* 43(1): 40–51.

Crate, S. 2008. Gone the bull of winter? Grappling with the cultural implications of and anthropology's role(s) in global climate change. *Current Anthropology* 49(4): 569–95.

Gould, J., and W. L. Kolb, eds. 1964. A dictionary of the social sciences. New York: The Free Press of Glencoe.

Hoffman, S. M., and A. Oliver-Smith, eds. 2002. *Catastrophe and culture: The anthropology of disaster*. Sante Fe, NM: School of American Research.

Ivanova, E. 2005. *Khvatit gasovat'* [Enough gassing]. *Komsolovkaia Pravda v. Yakutii*. 28 July–4 August: 1.

Karjaleinen, T. P. and J. O. Habeck. 2004. "When 'the environment' comes to visit: local environmental knowledge in the far north of Russia. *Environmental Values* 13)2): 167-86.

Kirsch, S. 2002. Anthropology and advocacy: A case study of the campaign against the Ok Tedi mine. *Critical Anthropology* 22: 175–200.

Nanengast, C. and C. G. Velez-Ibanez. 2004. *Human Rights: The scholar as activist*. Oklahoma City, OK: Society for Applied Anthropology.

Netting, R. M. 1968. *Hill farmers of Nigeria: Cultural ecology of the Kofyar of the Jos Plateau*. Seattle: University of Washington Press.

Netting, R. M. 1993. *Smallholders, householders: Farm families and the ecology of intensive, sustainable agriculture*. Stanford, CA: Stanford University Press.

Nuttall, M. 1992. *Arctic homeland: Kinship, community and development in Northwest Greenland*. Toronto: University of Toronto Press.

Oliver-Smith, A. 1996. Anthropological research on hazards and disasters. *Annual Review of Anthropology* 25: 303–28.

Oliver- Smith, A. 2005. Communities after catastrophe: Reconstructing the material, reconstituting the social. In *Community building in the 21st century*, ed. S. Hyland, 45–70. Santa Fe, NM: School of American Research Press.

Prucha, F. P. 1985. *The Indians in American society: From the Revolutionary War to the present*. Berkeley: University of California Press.

Rylko-Bauer, B., M. Singer, and J. van Willigen. 2006. Reclaiming applied anthropology: Its past, present, and future. *American Anthropologist* 108(1): 178–90.

Simpura, J. and G. Eremitcheva. 1997. Dirt: Symbolic and practical dimensions of social problems in St. Petersburg. *International Journal of Urban and Regional Research* 21 (3): 476–80.

Steward, J. H. 1955. *Theory of culture change*. Urbana: University of Illinois Press.

Thomalla, F., T. Downing, E. Spanger-Siegfried, G. Hand, and J. Rockstrom. 2006. Reducing hazard vulnerability: Towards a common approach between disaster risk reduction and climate adaptation. *Disasters* 30(1): 39–48.

Thomas, D., and C. Twyman. 2005. Equity and justice in climate change adaptation amongst natural-resource-dependent societies. *Global Environmental Change* 15: 115–24.

White, R. 1983. *The Roots of dependency: Subsistence, environment, and social change among the Choctaws, Pawnees, and Navajos*. Lincoln: University of Nebraska Press.

8.5 On the Mundane Significance of Bike Lanes . . . And the Pursuit of Anthropology in the Here and Now

LUIS A. VIVANCO

If there were more bike lanes, would more people ride bikes? Do bike lanes serve as symbols for sustainable cities? Bicycling advocates and transportation officials often argue, "If you build them, they will come," and see the bicycle not just as an alternative transportation medium but more generally as a symbol of sustainable living. Is this the case no matter where in the world one is? In what follows, Vivanco questions the popular notion that bicycling is unequivocally a decision to act "sustainably." Drawing on a study of urban bicycle culture and politics in Bogotá, Colombia, Vivanco illustrates the importance of cultural and structural dynamics that create connectivity and security for some bike riders and disconnection and insecurity for others, which inevitably impact both the ability and choice to use Bogota's cicloruta infrastructure. He uses this case study of a "mundane" practice like bicycling to demonstrate the value and relevance of anthropology today, calling for the pursuit of "an anthropology in the here and now."

Questions

1. What are examples of a "conducta vial" (i.e., culturally rooted "traffic behavior") in Bogotá? What about in your university's town? In your hometown?
2. What is "an anthropology in the here and now"? How does it contrast to an anthropology of the here and now?
3. What does the bicycle symbolize in Bogotá? What does the bicycle symbolize to you?
4. In Bogotá, bike lanes and other transportation infrastructure are not transparent or self-evident from the perspectives of their users. Do you think the same is true of streets, roads, and sidewalks in your town? How could you show that?
5. How is bicycling gendered, classed, and racialized/ethnicized in Bogotá? How does that compare to how bicycling is gendered, classed, and racialized/ethnicized in your home community?

A bike lane is not a bike lane is not a bike lane. I don't mean to suggest they don't exist, or that whatever you think about them is necessarily wrong. What I mean is that though they may have quite visible and definitely tangible presence, there is little that is self-evident, obvious, or necessarily predetermined about what lines marked on pavement, or special lanes protected by barriers, might mean to somebody riding a bicycle, much less how an individual on a bicycle might interact with them.

This point has become increasingly significant to me during ongoing ethnographic fieldwork on urban bicycle culture and politics in Bogotá, Colombia, which is one setting in a larger project I've been developing on the anthropology of bicycle mobility and its relationship with urban sustainability (Vivanco 2013a; 2013b).

A version of this essay was presented as the keynote address to the Northeastern Anthropological Association 2015 Annual Meeting at Franklin Pierce University. The research on which this essay is based was enabled by funding from the Fulbright Scholars Program and the University of Vermont. I am especially grateful to the Anthropology Department at the Universidad Nacional de Colombia, Bogotá Campus, for their generous collegiality and support for this research.

Bogotá is an Andean city of almost 9 million people, known as much for its chaotic streets and traffic jams as for its support to urban bicycle transportation to, at least partially, ease the pressures created by all those unruly and polluting automobiles and buses. Declared a "biking paradise" by the BBC (Wallace 2011), during the past fifteen years the city has implemented a number of progressive bicycle-related policies, among them expanding its weekly *ciclovía* in which 122 kilometers of its streets are closed to cars on Sundays and holidays, and holding an annual "car-free day" every February. It is especially known for its 376-kilometer *cicloruta* system—the largest network of protected bicycle lanes in the Americas—a city-wide network of lanes and paths for bicycle use based on a physical separation between bicycle users and motorized traffic. The system includes off-road paths that run parallel to main motorized traffic corridors, dedicated bike lanes that exist on sidewalks widened for the purpose, and bike lanes on streets that have bollards, planters, and other physical barriers or sometimes simply paint separating bicycles from motorized traffic. Thanks to these innovations and others, the city has received a lot of international media coverage and a steady flow of visits by people from all over the Americas and Europe—city officials, urban planners, journalists, and bicycle-renting tourists—who arrive seeking immersion in and grounded lessons from Bogotá's experience with the promotion of bike lanes and mass transportation by bicycle.

But on the countless occasions that I've ridden a bicycle around Bogotá—going to and from work or a meeting, running errands, heading some place for an organized group ride, or just out and about on city streets—I have been struck by the selective use, practical skepticism, and even avoidance tactics many bicycle users express about riding on the *ciclorutas*. Indeed, one of my first ethnographic introductions to the complex, even contradictory, set of attitudes emerged as I rode with two of the city's prominent young bicycle activists to a meet-up of other activists, on a ride that traversed some sixty city blocks north of the city center. For much of the trip, we rode with motorized vehicle traffic on a street parallel to one of the city's main *ciclorutas*, one of them explaining to me, "When you've mastered the road, the *cicloruta* shows itself to be what it is, slow and inconvenient. Too many people walking on it, and too many cross-streets." Not five minutes later, however, they made an instantaneous decision to

swerve onto the *cicloruta*. Riding at high speed on the narrow lane built on a sidewalk, we came upon a pair of pedestrians walking in the space of the *cicloruta*. One of the activists shouted over to me: "This is *our* space. They have their own space. If we don't protect it, we won't get it. They have to learn. We have to *teach* them to stay out of the way." She blew sharply into the whistle hanging on her helmet strap to get their attention, at which point they moved out of our way. We sped on, though we eventually moved back onto the street with motorized traffic.

This fleeting incident brought to my awareness an unfamiliar, even jarring, communication style (at least to me) in which the use of sharp whistles by cyclists is a common norm. More important, it pointed to certain subtleties—the ephemeral nature of tension between pedestrians and bicycle users, the creative and informal choreography of getting around the city by bicycle, the situational nature of involvement with *ciclorutas,* a context for political claims-making by cyclists, among others—all of which are embedded in what Argentine anthropologist Pablo Wright and his colleagues (2007) call a culture of "*conducta vial*," or culturally rooted "traffic behavior" guided by informal norms, codes, and practices well outside of formal law that are highly specific to countries, cities, and even neighborhoods. I would see a number of these subtleties bear out not just among other bicycle activists but also among the working class men who constitute the majority of Bogotá's daily riders, as well as growing numbers of middle- and upper-class individuals new to cycling who identify with the transnational hipster identity—"urban cyclist"—increasingly common to cities around the world.

So I've become an avid participant-observer of bike lanes, not just in Bogotá, but in other cities closer to home, and as a member of a bicycle advocacy group I'm pretty vocal in my own city about them and the possibility of building more. See, bike lanes are very much on the minds of people concerned with alleviating automobile traffic and promoting sustainability in U.S. cities, based on a "build-it-and-they-will-come" attitude that all the motivation people need to get on their bikes for everyday transportation is bike lanes. Beyond their potential for motivating and facilitating movement, one of the interesting things about bike lanes for me is that they also offer a lens into the dilemmas and opportunities of urban life in one of its most basic elements—an element that *all* people *everywhere* share—which is the need to get around in one's environment. Getting around in a crowded, chaotic, and car-choked city—a commonly familiar scenario given that more than half world's population are now urban dwellers—raises a number of big and important questions, about health, sustainability, quality of life, and so on.

But I have to admit that this interest in getting around cities by bicycles and bike lanes is pretty mundane stuff. Compared to what the Colombian anthropologists with whom I have worked do their own work on—cultures of violence, forced migration, racial discrimination, indigenous rights movements, human rights abuses, state terror and oppression, gender inequalities, and other themes of pressing human drama and danger—it might seem even frivolous. Though none of them have seen it that way. If anything, they have expressed to me on numerous occasions that they get it how complicated, significant—even frustrating and emotionally draining—are mundane matters of getting around a Third World megacity for its residents, and why the theme is ripe for anthropological attention.

Anthropology in the Here and Now

And yet it is important to remind ourselves that we live in a time in which the whole enterprise of anthropology, at least in North America, provokes a public response ranging from apathy to open dismissiveness. Indeed, certain prominent politicians and influential financial media outlets, among them the governor of Florida, *Forbes*, and *Kiplinger's Personal Finance*, have recently declared the study of anthropology as a whole to be frivolous and out of touch with the hard realities of the twenty-first century. These declarations emerge out of particular historically rooted concerns and contexts—of burgeoning student debt, changes in the entry-level job market, declining public investments in higher education as a result of neoliberal policies, among others. But the impression they give—of a discipline out of touch with the world in which it is practiced—is based on crude misunderstanding not just of the meaningful ways the study of anthropology enriches lives, but also what anthropologists actually do. Contrary to the image of a field beset by irrelevance and insensibility, most of us who practice it consider anthropology to be very much alive and vibrant, engaging in the worlds around us, producing

new species of knowledge, generating new theoretical discourses, and identifying new empirical interests and arguments (Lassiter 2005; Low and Merry 2010).

Especially important is to recognize that these activities are deeply embedded in, reflections of, and in dialogue with the "here and now," that is, of late-breaking, often newsworthy issues that erupt in our fluid and dynamic world and shape its everyday possibilities and contours. In spite of airy popular associations with the exotic and the socially marginal, cultural anthropology has, for quite a long time, occupied itself with the here and now. What are field notes but constructed fragments of a particular here and now? What are key historical paradigms of anthropology—salvage, applied, practicing anthropologies among them—but deliberate interventions in a here and now? What is ethnography but a flexible and adaptable set of methods that has been employed in literally every here and now imaginable? But today across the discipline there is a renewed creativity, sense of vigor, and opportunity to engage in the here and now through a merging with currents of public interest and concern. As Peggy Sanday (1998) suggests, this merging "is more than a focus for research; it is a paradigm for learning, teaching, research, action, and practice." From human rights to food justice, from biodiversity conservation to the trafficking of body parts and reconciliation in war-torn contexts, from problem solving to policy making, from the global to the local, the concerns shaping and informing these ongoing projects that merge anthropology with public currents are diverse and multifaceted.

The orientation that has taken shape here is not one whose sole normative goal is to produce accounts of a particular social group or ethnographic setting, or to simply comprehend, master, and control an existing body of knowledge from a perch of distanced and disengaged intellectualism—not to say that any of these things were ever simple. And they do and will continue to play a role in anthropology. Rather, it is an aspirational and problem-centered practice, an open-ended mode of questioning, philosophical inquiry, and apprehension of empirical worlds, all of which is directly immersed in the lived experiences and complex sociopolitical dilemmas of the communities with which we live and work. It is an anthropology *in* the here and now, not simply an anthropology *of* the here and now. It is an anthropology that realizes that the "here and now" is not a natural given, much less a particular geographic or temporal space, but constituted as much by the pressing and historically rooted issues confronting people as the social relationships we as anthropologists work hard to identify, create, and cultivate through our fieldwork practice. It is something more dynamic than any single label like applied, practicing, advocacy, activist, or public anthropology can lay exclusive claim to. Each of these terms carries particular connotations. Anthropology in the here and now crisscrosses these territories sometimes strategically, sometimes accidentally, but always with several characteristics that John Comaroff (2010) signaled as distinctive of what the anthropological perspective generates. These characteristics include a "critical estrangement" of the lived world, or the work of taking the familiar and taken-for-granted and making it seem strange, a deconstructing of its surfaces and a relativizing of its horizons; an appreciation of how the contradiction, the counterintuitive, the paradox can point us toward the situational and unstable character of subjective experience and social relations; and a focal interest in being-and-becoming, that is mapping the processes by which social realities are realized, materialities materialized, objects objectified with a reflexivity of how our own practices of knowledge production are implicated in those processes.

What motivates this anthropology in the here and now? Roy Rappaport (1994, 254) identified one of its key elements when he said, ". . . we cannot contribute to the formation of a pluralistic—and therefore more comprehensive or even holistic—public discourse by talking only to ourselves about issues that also matter to others." There is another, perhaps complementary way to frame the motive that we might want to also think about: that we cannot contribute to the formation of a pluralistic—and therefore more comprehensive or even holistic—*anthropological* discourse by talking to ourselves about issues that *don't matter* to others. And our contribution can start, I think, with a renewed attention to the mundane things that matter in people's lives, which brings me back to bike lanes.

The Mundane Significance of Bike Lanes

For me as an environmental anthropologist, one of the interesting things about the word "mundane" is that it has a double meaning that relates to both how we tend to use it—marking something as everyday

and quotidian—as well as one that derives from its Latin roots, *mundus*, "of or pertaining to the world or earth." As an everyday activity that imagines and constitutes particular worlds and earthly environments, riding a bicycle can be mundane in multiple and complex ways. For example, in his studies of metropolitan walking and pedestrianism, anthropologist Tim Ingold (2004, 333) drew attention to the idea that how we move about landscapes shapes our perception of them, and through walking landscapes are, he says "woven into life, and lives woven into the landscape, in a process that is continuous and never-ending." It is possible to say something similar about riding a bike, since cyclists develop very specific perceptions of urban space (Spinney 2007). The other key thing here about the word is that the conceptual world in which many urban cyclists live is one that makes explicit association between bicycle transportation and environmental virtue. In an era of public concern over global warming and peak oil, the bicycle has been reimagined as "vehicle for a small planet" and bicycle riding has come to represent a form of globally aware sustainable living and caring for the earth, an aspirational vehicle of ecological citizenship (Vivanco 2013b).

As much as something like connotations of "greenness" cycling carries exist in Bogotá, however, they do not provide a strong symbolic anchor for most riders. Bogotanos carry different meanings of using a bicycle for everyday transportation—especially for the poor majorities whose primary goal is inexpensive and flexible transportation—and as a result, the kinds of debates they have over the social and practical obstacles to it, as well as how to promote it, carry certain kinds of particularities.

In fact, if you ask them many Bogotanos resist the idea that they live in a "bike paradise," and find many reasons to mistrust the city's promotion of bicycles and its celebrated bike lanes. City bicycle counts seem to bear out that mistrust: of the 600,000 or so people who transport themselves daily by bicycle, less than 200,000 actually use the *ciclorutas* system. For me this point immediately raises a critical question: why, if they are available, would less than one-third of daily bicycle users actually use these facilities designed to aid their flow? The primary importance of this question is not so much that it reveals a gap between local practice and the image of success circulating internationally, but that it points us toward providing a deeper contextualization of how, why, and under what conditions individuals think about and engage with the infrastructure itself.

One element of the *cicloruta* story is, perhaps, that the "network" is not as extensive or consolidated as its potential users would expect or desire. It is certainly common among bicycle users and activists to hear that the system "is not big enough," and that riding on it can involve ducking, dodging, and weaving through pedestrians, stopping at intersections where priority often goes to cars, jumping steep curbs and ramps which requires strength and cultivated skill, and experiencing uncertainty where bike lanes end with no indication of where they pick up again. Nevertheless, one of the problems with purely quantitative indicators and factors like rider usage is their assumption that infrastructure is primarily a quantitative matter and that it is itself frozen and transparent. That is, that infrastructure is self-evident, manifest, and indisputable, and that if it is there, people use it in basically straightforward, rational, and unproblematic ways (Starr 1999; Larkin 2013).

As large scale infrastructure projects, roads and street projects tend to elicit these kinds of notions, which derives from their fetishistic qualities as symbols of emancipatory modernity. Paved streets and roads, bike lanes among them, typically carry dazzling possibilities for social change. They are viewed fundamentally as a social good and a manifestation of the modern promise of frictionless circulation, speed, connection, and flow; of political freedom and the aspiration for democratic process; of social equality and integration between social elites and the masses; and especially of economic prosperity with opportunities to increase trade and support the mobility of a labor force (Harvey and Knox 2012). All of these ideas, by the way, were put forward by the city leaders who pursued the creation of the *cicloruta* system.

In spite of the bicycle's relative potential for speed, however, among actual bicycle users, perceptions of risk, harm, and the threat of negative entanglements with others on the streets also play into their decisions to ride, route choice, and daily practice. Being on the streets in Bogotá has long been a marker not simply of social class (the poor walk, ride bikes, take public buses, or increasingly ride motorcycles, while the rich and upper middle classes use private automobiles), but also of differential levels of risk to physical attacks, muggings, and the like. Indeed, one of the principal narratives of life in Bogotá is that it is a chaotic and fearful city (Salcedo 1996), which is not simply a practical concern that shapes how individuals actually get around, but a kind of existential condition that one of my informants expressed to me as "a feeling I have when I leave apartment that something bad is likely to happen to me, even if it won't." For people on bicycle this narrative, along with its existential dimensions, has numerous manifestations. Fear of bicycle robbery and attacks runs especially high, and automobile-bicycle conflicts a somewhat distant second concern. It has not been uncommon for me in my fieldwork to encounter individuals, especially working class men, who traverse low income neighborhoods and have had their bicycles taken from them by armed individuals or been robbed at knifepoint, and in a few instances, had crashes with buses, trucks, or automobiles.

Given these possibilities, everyday bicycle users I interviewed expressed an acute sense of spatial awareness that quite literally focuses on the qualities of the infrastructure itself: how wide is that lane and how might it push them toward others; at what points might they be boxed in and unable to escape; where will they go when the lane ends suddenly; what especially dangerous neighborhood are they about to pass through; and so on. Women bicycle users often reported to me that these concerns loomed especially large in how they approached their daily practice. As expressed to me by a young woman who commutes ten miles to and from work every day: "As a woman I am always attentive to possibilities of getting attacked. Before whenever I'd see a bridge on a *cicloruta* I would get nervous. Not now. But still I get negative premonitions in certain places, like tunnels built into the *ciclorutas*, or in certain neighborhoods—as you know the dynamic can change very quickly from one street to another here in Bogotá. I will change my route dramatically to avoid problems."

So it is widely understood that *cicloruta* infrastructure can enable fluid movement and at the same time produce undesirable entanglements that cause slowdowns and personal insecurity, which bicycle riders experience as an embodied sense of fear, uncertainty, or as this woman expressed it, premonition. In practice, this recognition requires an ability to read the particularities of infrastructural conditions, flexibility in decision-making about one's route, and the making of micro-adjustments in speed or trajectory, all of which might barely rise to the surface of consciousness as decisions are made at speed.

Build It and They Will Come?

Back here in our own here and now, as I said, there is a lot of interest in pursuing the possibilities bike lanes can create for supporting greater levels of bicycle transportation, based in that old expression from the movie *Field of Dreams* (Robinson 1989) in which a somewhat crazed Iowa farmer tries to entice the ghosts of dead baseball heroes by building a baseball diamond on his land, explaining "If you build it, [they] will come." Indeed, when it comes to some transportation infrastructure, it is true, on some level, that if you build roads, at least automobiles will come. Have you noticed when a new road is built or expanded, it gets quickly filled with cars?

But when it comes to bikes . . . well, Bogotá's results are ambiguous, the judgment skeptical. Why? On one level the answer is complicated—as it always will be—by particularities of local history, legacies of urban planning, dynamics of social marginality embedded in each city. But on another, it is quite straightforward, at least from an anthropological point of view: "build it and they will come" implies a kind of technological determinism, an ability to make clear predictions through the instability and situational character of human action and belief. One of the central problems with this technological determinism is this: cycling in a city is sensitive to and shaped by a range of conditions, among them urban spatial form and the built environment to be sure, but also the political-economic and social hierarchies built into transportation systems, cultural perceptions and ideologies of urban space, and the embodied and performative demands, experiences, and informal codes involved in the movement itself (Vivanco 2013a).

The kind of culturally informed approach to bicycle advocacy I am developing in my own work is one that actively listens to people who use—and don't use— bicycles, to better understand their goals, practices, navigational challenges, ideas about urban space, symbolic understandings about infrastructure, and so on, instead of assuming that a bike lane designed and built by urban planners distant from everyday life is the best, or only, way to support an increase in bicycle transportation. People like to ride bikes (60% of Americans say they do, at least), but daily transportation needs and desires elicit a diversity of perspectives, concerns, and strategies—some of which may have little to do on the surface with transportation itself, but with peoples' aspirations, fears, social position, and other factors. Starting with a practical understanding of that diversity is a necessary place to build effective and inclusive public policy and infrastructure, as is a willingness to communicate these things to transportation planners, public officials, and other bicycle advocates. In the long term, it may mean we have to build different kinds of roads altogether, which is to say roads built with people and their needs—not automobiles—in mind. This will require a paradigm shift, but I'm convinced that to get there, anthropologists can play a key role in providing critical knowledge for developing a people-centered transportation system.

The issues I'm getting at here are not always easy to identify and can be difficult to raise; they are, after all, quite mundane. But if we remember that mundane refers as much to the everyday as it does to the earthly and world-making possibilities of everyday objects and technologies, these matters are really quite serious in terms of how we will experience and think about the worlds in which we lead our lives. And I think strengthened by a commitment to critical estrangement—that a bike lane is not simply a bike lane, it is a dream of flow and connection, but it can produce fear and insecurity—and an appreciation for the contradictory, and an interest in being and becoming, anthropology has a lot to contribute in the ongoing formation of a pluralistic, comprehensive, and holistic here and now.

References

Comaroff, John. 2010. "The End of Anthropology, Again: On the Future of an In/Discipline." *American Anthropologist* 112(4): 524–538.

Harvey, Penny, and Hannah Knox. 2012. "The Enchantments of Infrastructure." *Mobilities* 7(4): 521–536.

Ingold, Timothy. 2004. "Culture on the Ground: The World Perceived Through the Feet." *Journal of Material Culture* 9: 315–340.

Larkin, Brian. 2013. "The Politics and Poetics of Infrastructure." *Annual Reviews of Anthropology* 42:327–343.

Lassiter, Luke Eric. 2005. "Collaborative Ethnography and Public Anthropology." *Current Anthropology* 46(1): 83–106.

Low, Setha, and Sally Engle Merry. 2010. "Engaged Anthropology: Diversity and Dilemmas." *Current Anthropology* 51(S2): S203–S214.

Rappaport, Roy. 1994. "Disorders of Our Own: A Conclusion." In *Diagnosing America: Anthropology and Public Engagement*, edited by Shepard Forman, 235–285. Ann Arbor: University of Michigan Press.

Robinson, Phil Alden. 1989. *Field of Dreams*. Universal Pictures.

Salcedo, Andrés. 1996. "La Cultura del Miedo: La Violencia en la Ciudad." *Controversia*, No. 169. Centro de Investigación y Educación Popular.

Sanday, Peggy. 1998. "Opening Statement: Defining Public Interest Anthropology." Paper presented at the 97th annual meeting of the American Anthropological Association, Philadelphia, PA. Available at: http://www.sas.upenn.edu/~psanday/pia.99.html.

Spinney, Justin. 2007. "Cycling the City: Non-Place and the Sensory Construction of Meaning in Mobile Practice." In *Cycling and Society*, edited by Dave Horton, Peter Cox, and Paul Rosen, 25–45. Burlington, VT: Ashgate Publishers.

Starr, Susan Leigh. 1999. "The Ethnography of Infrastructure." *American Behavioral Scientist* 43(3): 377–391.

Vivanco, Luis. 2013a. *Reconsidering the Bicycle: An Anthropological Perspective on a New (Old) Thing*. New York: Routledge.

Vivanco, Luis. 2013b. "The Mundane Bicycle and the Environmental Virtues of Sustainable Urban Mobility." In *Environmental Anthropology: Future Directions*, edited by Helen Kopnina and Eleanor Ouimet, 25–45. New York: Routledge.

Wallace, Arturo. 2011. "Bogotá—Latin America's Biking Paradise." *BBC*. Accessed on July 2, 2012: http://www.bbc.co.uk/news/world-latin-america-14227373

Wright, Pablo, María Moreira, and Darío Soich. 2007. "Antropología vial: símbolos, metáforas y prácticas en el "juego de la calle" de conductores y peatones en Buenos Aires" ["Traffic anthropology: symbols, metaphors, and practices in the 'game of the streets' among drivers and pedestrians in Buenos Aires"]. Work prepared for el Seminario del Centro de Investigaciones Etnográficas, Universidad Nacional de San Martín del 23 abril, 2007. Available at: http://www.redseguridadvial.files.wordpress.com/2011/02/paper-vial-2.pdf.

IN THE NEWS BP Oil Disaster

On April 20, 2010, the BP-owned Deepwater Horizon oil rig exploded and sank in the Gulf of Mexico, resulting in an 87-day oil gusher flowing approximately 4.9 million barrels of oil into the waters (On Scene 2011). The BP oil spill is considered the largest accidental marine oil spill in history. It caused extensive and prolonged damage to marine and wildlife habitats, and to the local fishing and tourism industries. Numerous investigations found clear evidence that the spill was caused by negligence and cost-cutting decision at the expense of safety made by the oil industry. The sociocultural impacts of the spill in Louisiana and other nearby states are significant, deepening inequality within an already markedly economically disadvantaged region.

These short news articles from the *Houston Chronicle* and the *Times Picayune* discuss applied environmental anthropologist Dr. Diane Austin's testimony in the U.S. government's case against BP under the Clean Water Act. Dr. Austin was the second U.S. witness called in the case against BP. Like Adams' findings in post-Katrina New Orleans (Reading 9.3), Austin's research found that while there were efforts to aid people in the wake of the disaster, those who benefited the least were among the area's poorest families, businesses, and communities.

@ **Visit www.oup.com/us/brondo for weblinks.**

DR. SHIRLEY J. FISKE

Environmental Anthropologist, Former Research Program Manager for NOAA and U.S. Senate Legislative Advisor on Climate, Energy, Natural Resources

Figure 8.7.1

Shirley J. Fiske

How did you become interested in anthropology?

Never being comfortable with the "America-is-best" worldview that infused the United States in the post-World War II decades, I found a natural home in the field of anthropology—with its emphasis on understanding, if not reifying, the cultural logics and epistemologies of other worlds. Although there were no courses in high school, I was drawn to it in college where I graduated with a B.Á. in anthropology. My secondary concentration was in sciences—ecology, geology, botany and chemistry—training that provided a bridge to ecological anthropology and eventually environmental anthropology. When I graduated as a PhD from Stanford my areas were ecological anthropology and American Indians—specifically *urban* Indians—pan-tribal communities of Native American "relocatees" who were migrating in the '60s and '70s in increasing numbers to metropolitan centers. I launched my working career with the Los Angeles Indian Center, a community-based service organization in the skid-row area of Los Angeles where it became apparent that contemporary anthropology had to situate communities and people, and especially urban ones, in a nexus of power, political relationships, and public policy.

That is how I got into anthropology—the brief version, anyway. My next paid employment led me into academia as faculty in University of Southern California's (USC) School of Public Administration, and my experiences there were a major influence in turning to the practice of anthropology and to environmental and natural resource issues. In Public Administration, my colleagues routinely dealt with public policy and public affairs either as consultants or in community service, one colleague even running for political office. I was appointed by the Mayor to the Los Angeles County-City Native American Indian Commission, which was just being created, to enhance the political visibility of urban Indians.

I began to see the public sector not as a monolithic, intransigent bureaucracy, but as institutions that constantly change and evolve with issues and public pressure. I saw that anthropological approaches to both domestic and international issues were much needed across a number of sectors, from development assistance to managing natural resources, such as California's Coastal Zone. California had just passed its Coastal Zone law, which specified how far from the coast and what kinds of development would be permissible. This is how I gravitated to practice and to more environmental issues.

How did you end up at the National Oceanic and Atmospheric Administration (NOAA)?

The short answer is that I looked for and took an opportunity to work for a science agency in the executive branch of the federal government. I moved to Washington, DC, in the early 1980s while still teaching for USC in public administration. I received a fellowship that allowed me to interview with a variety of different federal agencies, and in the end I chose NOAA because of its scope, mission, and issue challenges. My background in sciences and ecology made it pretty easy for me to fit in with the NOAA crowd. NOAA runs civilian satellites, produces weather data and forecasts (National Weather Service) oceanographic services (such as nautical charts for ships), and has a number of world class laboratories for basic and applied research on atmospheric and oceanographic phenomena (like climate modeling). In natural resource management and in environmental issues, NOAA's mission included marine fisheries management, coastal zone management, and estuarine research reserve management (jointly with states).

What kinds of projects did you work on at NOAA?

When I started in the early '80s, I was based in the Policy and Planning Office, so I did analyses and evaluations on issues of concern to top management, such as user fees and peer review of science. I also occasionally advised issues such as whaling, which took me into the arena of "cultural takes" of bowhead whales by Inuit, a more traditionally anthropological realm. In a few short years I moved from policy and planning to the oceanographic and coastal research arm of NOAA with a position transfer to Sea Grant.

What Is Sea Grant?

The National Sea Grant College Program is a multidisciplinary, extramural research and extension program, focused on ocean and coastal science, development, and policy. The program is a matching funds program that works through state universities. I found fertile ground and receptive colleagues for the development of a social science program that funded

research and extension with fishing communities, among other priorities.

Each of us in the national office had a "portfolio" of issue areas and of universities—my portfolio quickly grew beyond social science; before I knew it I was also the Director of Marine Education, in which I guided and enabled a network of marine educators from across the nation, and a well-respected and popular fellowship program for graduate students in marine policy and sciences. The area of Marine Policy was added, which meant I was the go-to person for funding ocean and coastal policy studies; and ultimately I was asked to take on the directorship for Marine Extension, which locates agents and specialists in communities where fishing happens, like Brunswick, Georgia, or Galveston, TX, or downeast Maine, to work with them to bring the universities' research to bear on technical and policy issues for fishermen and coastal communities.

I have also learned that you worked as a senior legislative advisor in the U.S. Senate. Can you share more about that?

If there's one theme in my career, it's seeking bigger impact for anthropological input and insights through my work. After nearly 20 years in NOAA, I began to find the "coming and going" of administrations to be wearing, and I must say, particularly Republican administrations, because since the 1980s when President Reagan came into office, government in general and its growth have been labeled as the ultimate evil, and initiatives were undertaken to cut back on civil service, and cut back budgets. When President George W. Bush came into office twenty-one years later, I felt the onus of yet one more retrenchment, more sequestrations and more "contracting out" of government services. I pushed for a sabbatical to take a Brookings Fellowship to work on the Hill. I sensed that it might be possible to have a bigger bang for the buck working in the intestines of policy-making than working on the outside in the executive branch.

Was it a worthwhile experience? And did I make an impact? Absolutely—I worked on appropriations and I worked substantive issues, advising Senator Daniel K. Akaka (D-HI) on votes in the Senate and on issues from climate change to national parks; and from energy to fisheries. My experience in NOAA paved the way for a job offer from the office, leading to seven more years of legislative work. I learned the ropes and where the ropes were frayed; I learned how to make sausages.

On the impact side, I worked on the 2005 Energy Policy Act, the first bi-partisan omnibus energy bill in 20 years; I was able to expand and appropriate for national parks—cultural parks in particular; and I was one of the lead players and authors on a new law that protects paleontological resources on federal lands. Many staff never see a bill enacted into law, so I feel quite fortunate to have played such a strong part in a number of statutes, and I give lots of credit to the Fellows that I had working with me over the years.

What is the most meaningful initiative you've worked on over the course of your career? Why?

It's hard to choose just one project . . . but there are two that stand out.

The first is developing a sound base of marine fisheries and coastal anthropologists who focused their research on critically important social and policy issues facing marine fisheries and fishing communities. This was at a time when there was serious retrenchment in fisheries as the United States went from open access to limited access and a quota system for commercial fishing. Anthropologists were able to provide important information through the management process and through marine extension efforts to assist families and communities responding to the catch cut-backs and declines in their revenues. Ultimately this became the foundation for a much greater number of anthropologists being hired in the National Marine Fisheries Service and much greater attention paid to community impacts.

The second is helping develop the Human Dimensions program in the U.S. Global Change Research Program (USGCRP). I was appointed to represent the social sciences and insisted that the human dimensions program be more than "economic impacts" and include the broad spectrum of research that goes into understanding human drivers, or archaeological and paleontological past, human impacts writ larger than economics, and institutional decision-making and

feedback loops. NOAA has continued the human dimensions program to this day, although the focus has changed necessarily with new administrations, and my association with climate change continued from NOAA, to legislation on the Hill, and most recently as a co-PI on a climate change research project and Chair of the American Anthropological Association's task force on global climate change (http://www.aaanet .org/cmtes/commissions/CCTF/gcctf.cfm).

What does it mean to you to be an applied anthropologist, an environmental anthropologist, and a practitioner?

As a practitioner, it means I spent most of my career as an anthropologist employed outside of academia and anthropology but I stayed connected via the culture of my employer NOAA, since they supported academic research and scientific professional achievements. But when you call yourself a practicing anthropologist, or even an applied anthropologist, the terms refer to professional and disciplinary distinctions that the outside world—even related social sciences—often doesn't make. So I don't use these terms in normal conversation very often any more, unless one wants to de-rail a conversation about issues to explain the divisions within our discipline and in the United States.

What do you see as the most pressing issues for the future of environmental anthropology?

- Water governance in the face of a changing climate and neoliberal tendencies toward enclosure and privatization.
- Climate change, the Anthropocene and all its ramifications and drivers, as well as re-structuring the Kyoto Protocol.
- Identifying alternative models of economic growth that are sustainable and are not linked with income inequality and environmental in-justice.

ABOUT THE ANTHROPOLOGIST

Occupation: Research Professor, Department of Anthropology, University of Maryland
Education: PhD in Anthropology, Stanford University

Hobbies:

- Photography—Visual images are powerful tools for awareness, activism, and social change. I am on the constant lookout for ways to use photography for social and environmental change.
- Tree farming—I consider our fourth-generation family-owned sustainable timber tree farm in California to be a hobby because we love doing it but it is not a commercial success and in fact we have to pay out of pocket to keep it going.

CAREER ADVICE

Advice for students interested in environmental anthropology:

- Know a substantive field in addition to your primary focus. If environmental anthropology, get familiar with environmental law, policy, issues, and actors and players around the sector in which you will specialize—the agencies and state and local roles and advocacy groups and NGOs.

- Networking skills are important in locating and landing a job, and in doing your job well. Develop your networking skills and use them.
- It helps to stay involved and contribute to professional associations, whether local practitioner organizations (LPOs) or national organizations. They will learn from you; and you can get energized by comparing notes at annual meetings.
- Seek out and utilize fellowship and internship opportunities. Both times I have been fortunate enough to go that route, I have ended up being offered a job there.
- Be aware that most cultural anthropologists do not get jobs titled "anthropologist" right away. It takes time and sometimes patience to see where the opportunities for contributions exist in organizations.
- Know the communities involved. Recognize power.
- It helps to stay involved and contribute to professional associations, whether local practitioner organizations (LPOs) or national organizations. They will learn from you; and you can get energized by comparing notes at annual meetings.

DR. FABIANA LI

Environmental Anthropologist

Figure 8.8.1

Fabiana Li

What is your area of focus within anthropology?

I am a sociocultural anthropologist whose work focuses on conflicts over resource extraction, political ecology, the role of transnational corporations, and social movements in Latin America.

How did you become interested in anthropology?

As an undergraduate student, I envisioned working in international development or for an environmental organization. I was drawn to anthropology's cross-cultural perspective, and the way it brings together different dimensions of human life: social organization, ecology, belief systems, politics, economic structures, etc. After my first year of university, I took a year off to participate in a cultural exchange program to India with a non-profit organization called Canada World Youth. This opportunity opened my eyes to many things, including the experience of living with host families, being immersed in a different culture, and trying to understand worldviews and ways of doing things that were very different from what I was used to—a precursor to fieldwork, in a way. As I continued my university studies, I felt that anthropology— more than other disciplines— provided me with a critical perspective on issues related to global justice and inequality, and made me question my own assumptions about "development" and environmentalism. Anthropology didn't provide easy answers, but it inspired me to keep learning, exploring the world, and eventually embark on my own research as a graduate student.

What is the most meaningful project you've worked on over the course of your career? Why?

I have spent many years following the emergence of conflicts over mining activity in Peru, my country of birth. It was rewarding to rediscover the country my parents emigrated from when I was a child, and challenging to be both an insider (because of my familiarity with the country and language) and an outsider (because of my Chinese-Peruvian background, North American upbringing, and university education). During my fieldwork, I was also fortunate to meet many young activists, professionals, and community leaders who are working for social change and speaking out about the environmental problems generated by resource extraction projects.

Do you identify as an applied, engaged, or public anthropologist? What do these titles mean to you?

To me, these titles suggest a separation between these approaches and what some might see as a more theory-based form of anthropology. I do not think that "theoretical" and "applied" work should be placed on opposite ends of a spectrum—they should inform each other. Anthropology as a discipline has always concerned itself with issues that matter and that contribute to our understanding of the human condition. My own research on resource extraction deals with topics that are currently the focus of much public debate and popular interest. Our dependence on minerals and other resources implicates all of us, since we are linked to global commodity chains through our consumption habits, our economic policies, and our political actions.

What do you see as the future for environmental anthropology?

Climate change, deforestation, water scarcity, loss of biodiversity, urban pollution, resource conflicts—these are some of the most pressing issues we face. Environmental anthropology can help us understand how these problems are affecting people around the world and how social movements are working to counter environmental degradation.

Science and technology are at the heart of many environmental controversies (genetic engineering, renewable energy, etc.). Environmental anthropologists can shed light on the potential, limitations, and social dimensions of technology. Some anthropologists are also doing research into the culture of science, and can contribute to our understanding of environmental problems by showing that scientific research is not produced in a vacuum—it is influenced by the values, biases, and priorities that shape society at any given time.

ABOUT THE ANTHROPOLOGIST

Occupation: Associate Professor, University of Manitoba in Winnipeg, Canada
Education: PhD, Anthropology: University of California, Davis
Hobbies: In the summer, I enjoy gardening. The long, cold winters are a good time for reading, movies, art projects, and walks on the frozen river.

CAREER ADVICE

Advice for students interested in pursuing a career in environmental anthropology:

Don't shy away from controversial issues. At the same time, issues that don't receive a lot of media or academic attention can also make fascinating subjects of study. Seemingly uncontroversial topics are always more complex than they might appear at first, and a closer look can reveal the subtle workings of politics and power. Finally, dealing with environmental problems will require an interdisciplinary outlook and the ability to communicate across cultural, ideological, and disciplinary differences.

PART 9

Globalization, Development, and Culture

A defining characteristic of culture is that it is always changing. Cultures change due to the internal processes of invention and innovation, as well as through external forces such as when one culture comes into contact with another, through the diffusion of ideas, or by force associated with colonialism. The readings in this section explore culture change as shaped by colonialism, globalization, and development. Additionally, this section considers ways in which culture change via development efforts can be enhanced by attending to, and working within, culturally appropriate institutions.

Colonialism refers to the control of one country over another. Anthropology as a discipline took root in the colonial period of the late 1800s, and many early anthropologists were deeply engaged in research to either help colonial officials subordinate indigenous peoples or in studying the impacts of colonialism on colonial subjects. Expectations at the turn of the century were that indigenous populations would die off, and many anthropologists became involved in what is known as "salvage ethnography," or the study of indigenous ways of being to form a knowledge collection of disappearing ways of life. While indigenous peoples did not "die off," their total populations were indeed decimated and cultural institutions deeply affected. Globalization further exacerbated the negative effects of colonialism on indigenous peoples.

When anthropologists talk about globalization they are referring to the widening and deepening scale of cross-cultural interactions that have resulted from the increasing speed by which people, ideas, goods, money, and images move across national and international boundaries (Welsh and Vivanco 2014, 135). Closely connected to globalization is the idea of "development." Defining development is a tricky endeavor, with entire classes dedicated to unpacking its meaning and effects, but in general it refers to social, political, and economic actions made by institutions, states, international agencies, and businesses to modify the lives (economic, social, political, technical) of another place in the world. Development efforts typically focus on impoverished peoples and communities. There are two distinct traditions within anthropology that center on "development." Development anthropology is an applied tradition where anthropologists work to advance development programs in culturally appropriate ways. Anthropology of development is a critical approach that seeks to understand the impacts of development projects on local peoples.

The first two selections in this section explore the impacts of colonialism, development, and globalization on indigenous peoples. In the first selection (Reading 9.1), John H. Bodley shows that development, or "progress," comes at great costs to indigenous peoples. "The Price of Progress" argues that indigenous peoples are "victims of progress," with the "price" of the spread of industrialization and modernization projects being severe declines in quality of life, rising disease and malnutrition, land loss, and ecocide.

Bodley's article is followed by a piece from Cultural Survival, an organization formed to advocate for indigenous peoples throughout the world. In "Being Indigenous in the 21st Century" (Reading 9.2), Wilma Mankiller reflects on the diversity among, but also the connections between, indigenous peoples worldwide. Not only do indigenous peoples share similar values, including a close relationship to the natural world, but they also share strong resilience in the face of longstanding oppression. The individual and collective rights of indigenous peoples were recognized globally in 2007 under the United Nations Declaration on the Rights of indigenous peoples; Mankiller's speech (from which the selection is taken) was in commemoration of the first anniversary of the UN Declaration and the 60th anniversary of the Universal Declaration of Human Rights.

The remaining four pieces in this section look at the effects of "development" in different contexts. In "The Making of Disaster" (Reading 9.3), Vincanne Adams explores the aftermath of Hurricane Katrina, the Category 5 hurricane that devastated the City of New Orleans in 2005. In the selection, Adams explores the humanitarian crisis that ensued when the levees broke and flooded the city creating a "second-order disaster." Private industries ended up profiting from this human tragedy; meanwhile, poor racial minorities were unable to take advantage of recovery programs, causing social, economic, and health inequalities to deepen.

Natalie Bourdon's piece explores humanitarianism from another angle, one that may be very familiar to students. In "Whose Development? Service Learning Abroad and Discourses on 'Doing Good'" (Reading 9.4), Bourdon analyzes the rationale for service learning and volunteer programs where civic-minded university students go abroad to "give-back" through participation in development projects in impoverished communities. Drawing on her own experience as a faculty supervisor of one such program, Bourdon argues that while programs appear on the surface to be a win-win for all parties involved, they have the potential to extend neocolonial relationships between the north and south.

The final two selections are examples of applying anthropology in community development contexts. In "Housing Interests: Developing Community in a Globalizing City" (Reading 9.5), Jacqueline Copeland-Carson shares her work in housing development to design culturally appropriate mortgage tools for immigrant communities in Minnesota's Twin Cities. Similarly, Hsain Ilahiane applies his understanding of Islamic institutions in "Re-Working the Institution of *Waqf* (Islamic trust) for the Financial Sustainability of Information Technology Schemes in Morocco" (Reading 9.6) to propose a culturally appropriate manner in which to sustainably finance information technologies.

The section ends with the "Anthropology in Practice" portrait of action anthropologist Barbara Rose Johnston, a leading scholar on issues of environmental crisis and human rights abuses, especially as they arise within development contexts. In addition to the insights she shares in her interview, readers can learn more about her global public policy work on human rights abuses associated with nuclear weapons and reparation for dam-affected communities on www.oup.com/us/brondo.

 Visit www.oup.com/us/brondo for weblinks.

KEY TERMS:

- Globalization
- Development
- Development anthropology
- Anthropology of development
- Colonialism
- Neocolonialism
- Indigenous rights
- Cultural survival

- Hurricane Katrina
- Humanitarianism
- Disaster capitalism
- Service learning
- Community development
- Housing
- Transnational migration
- Action anthropology

9.1 The Price of Progress

JOHN H. BODLEY

"Development" is often associated with the word "progress," and most commonly is taken to mean economic growth and modernization. Some anthropologists work to advance development agendas (known as "development anthropologists"), while others take a critical view, analyzing the effects of "development" on local cultures (and fall in the "anthropology of development" camp). This selection falls within the latter, as Bodley points toward the many impacts of modernization and development projects on indigenous peoples. The "price" indigenous and tribal peoples pay range from declining quality of life, to disease and malnutrition, to land loss and ecocide.

Questions

1. What is progress? How do you define it? How is it defined in terms of "development"?
2. Discuss the range of ways indigenous peoples have been impacted by development.
3. What role could applied, engaged, and public anthropologists play vis-à-vis development?

Until recently, government planners have always considered economic development and material progress beneficial goals that all societies should want to strive toward. The social advantages of progress—as defined in terms of increased incomes, higher standards of living, greater security, and better health—are thought to be positive, universal goods to be obtained at any price. Although one might argue that indigenous peoples should not be forced to sacrifice their own cultures and autonomy to obtain these benefits, government planners historically felt that the loss of cultural autonomy would be a small price to pay for such obvious advantages.

. . . [A]utonomous indigenous peoples have not chosen progress to enjoy its advantages and . . . the real reason governments have pushed progress upon them was to obtain resources, not primarily to share the benefits of progress with indigenous peoples. . . . [T]he price of forcing progress on unwilling recipients included the deaths of millions of indigenous people, as well as their loss of land, political sovereignty, and the right to follow their own lifestyle. . . .

Progress and Quality of Life

. . . It is widely recognized that standard of living, which is the most frequently used measure of progress, is an intrinsically ethnocentric concept that relies heavily upon indicators that lack universal cultural relevance. As a less ethnocentric alternative, the Happy Planet Index, which uses self-reported life satisfaction levels, life expectancy, and ecological footprint to rank nations, shows that some of the smallest, least developed nations rank as the happiest.[1] Vanuatu, the "happiest" country in the world, had just over two hundred thousand people in 2007, and a per capita GDP of under three thousand dollars. More than half (65 percent) of the population derived its living from the subsistence sector.[2] A top ranking on Happy Planet Index requires

John H. Bodley. 2008. *Victims of Progress.* AltaMira Press, Lanham, 167–184.

high satisfaction, good life expectancy, and a very small ecological footprint. Such factors as GDP and per capita income may be especially irrelevant measures of actual quality of life for autonomous indigenous peoples. . . .

A more useful measure of the benefits of progress might be based on a formula for evaluating cultures devised by Walter R. Goldschmidt.[3] According to these less ethnocentric criteria, the important question to ask is: *Does progress or economic development increase or decrease a given society's stability or its ability to satisfy the physical and psychological needs of its population?* This question is a far more direct measure of quality of life than are the standard economic correlates of development, and it is universally relevant. Specific indication of this standard of living could be found for any society in the nutritional status and general physical and mental health of its population, incidence of crime and delinquency, demographic structure, family stability, and the society's relationship to its natural resource base. We might describe a society that has high rates of malnutrition and crime and one that degrades its natural environment to the extent of threatening its continued existence as having a lower standard of living than another society in which these problems do not exist.

Careful examination of the data, which compare on these specific points the former condition of self-sufficient indigenous peoples with their condition following their incorporation into the world-market economy, leads to the conclusion that their standard of living is often lowered, not raised, by economic progress—and often to a dramatic degree. This is perhaps the most outstanding and inescapable fact to emerge from the years of research anthropologists have devoted to the study of culture change and modernization. Despite the best intentions of those who have promoted change and improvement, all too often the results have been poverty, longer working hours, much greater physical exertion, poor health, social disorder, discontent, discrimination, overpopulation, and environmental deterioration—combined with the destruction of the small-scale culture.

Diseases of Development

Perhaps it would be useful for public health specialists to start talking about a new category of diseases. . . . Such diseases could be called the "diseases of development" and would

consist of those pathological conditions which are based on the usually unanticipated consequences of the implementation of developmental schemes."[4]

Economic development increases the disease rate of affected peoples in at least three ways. First, to the extent that development is successful, developed populations suddenly become vulnerable to all of the chronic "lifestyle" diseases suffered almost exclusively by "advanced" peoples,[5] including diabetes, obesity, hypertension, and a variety of circulatory problems. Second, development disturbs existing environmental balances and may dramatically increase some bacterial and parasite diseases. Finally, when development goals prove unattainable, an assortment of poverty diseases may appear in association with the crowded conditions of urban slums and the general breakdown in small-scale socioeconomic systems.

Outstanding examples of the first situation can be seen in the Pacific, where some of the most successfully transformed small-scale societies are found. In Micronesia, where development has progressed more rapidly than perhaps anywhere else, the population doubled between 1958 and 1972. However, the number of patients treated for heart disease in the local hospitals nearly tripled, the incidence of mental disorders increased eightfold, and by 1972 hypertension and nutritional deficiencies began to make significant appearances for the first time.[6]

Although some critics argue that the Micronesian figures simply represent better health monitoring due to economic progress, rigorously controlled data from Polynesia show a similar trend. The progressive acquisition of modern degenerative diseases was documented by an eight-member team of New Zealand medical specialists, anthropologists, and nutritionists, whose research was funded by the Medical Research Council of New Zealand and the World Health Organization. These researchers investigated the health status of a genetically related population at various points along a continuum of increasing cash income, modernizing diet, and urbanization. The extremes on this acculturation continuum were represented by the relatively traditional Pukapukans of the Cook Islands and the essentially Europeanized New Zealand Maori; the busily developing Rarotongans, also of the Cook Islands, occupied the intermediate position. In 1971, after eight years of work, the team's preliminary findings were summarized by Dr. Ian Prior, cardiologist and leader of the research team, as follows: "We are beginning to observe that the more an islander takes on the ways of the West, the more prone he is to succumb to our degenerative diseases. In fact, it does not seem too much to say our evidence now shows that the farther the Pacific natives move from the quiet, carefree life of their ancestors, the closer they come to gout, diabetes, atherosclerosis, obesity, and hypertension."[7]. . .

Government development policies designed to bring about changes in local hydrology, vegetation, and settlement patterns and to increase population mobility, and even programs aimed at reducing some diseases, have frequently led to dramatic increases in disease rates because of the unforeseen effects of disturbing the preexisting order. . . .

Self-sufficient populations in general have presumably learned to live with the endemic pathogens of their environments, and in some cases they have evolved genetic adaptations to specific diseases, such as the sickle-cell trait, which provided immunity to malaria. Unfortunately, however, outside intervention has entirely changed this picture. In the late 1960s, the rate of incidence of sleeping sickness suddenly increased in many areas of Africa and even spread to areas where the disease had not formerly occurred, due to the building of new roads and migratory labor, both of which caused increased population movement. Forest-dwelling peoples such as the Aka in central Africa explicitly attribute new diseases such as AIDS and Ebola to the materialism associated with roads and new settlements.[8]

Large-scale relocation schemes, such as the Zande Scheme, had disastrous results when natives were moved from their traditional disease-free refuges into infected areas. Dams and irrigation developments inadvertently created ideal conditions for the rapid proliferation of snails carrying schistosomiasis (a liver fluke disease), and major epidemics suddenly occurred in areas where this disease had never before been a problem. DDT-spraying programs have been temporarily successful in controlling malaria, but there is often a rebound effect that increases the problem when spraying is discontinued, and resistant strains of the malarial mosquitoes are continually evolving.

Urbanization is one of the prime measures of development, but it is a mixed blessing for most small-scale cultures. Urban health standards are abysmally poor and generally worse than in rural areas for the former villagers who have crowded into the towns and cities throughout Africa, Asia, and Latin America seeking wage employment out of new economic necessity. Infectious diseases related to crowding and poor sanitation are rampant in urban centers, and greatly increased stress and poor nutrition aggravate a variety of other health problems. . . .

The Hazards of Dietary Change

The diets of indigenous peoples are admirably adapted to their nutritional needs and available food resources. Even though these diets may seem bizarre, absurd, and unpalatable to outsiders, they are unlikely to be improved by drastic modifications. Given the delicate balances and complexities involved in any subsistence system, change always involves risks, but for indigenous people the effects of dietary change have been catastrophic. The benefits of traditional subsistence-based diets are dramatically demonstrated by the negative health effects explicitly connected with the "Nutrition Transition," the shift to diets based on highly processed commercial foods.[9] . . .

Under normal conditions, food habits are remarkably resistant to change, and indeed people are unlikely to abandon their traditional diets voluntarily in favor of dependence on difficult-to-obtain exotic imports. In some cases it is true that imported foods may be identified with powerful outsiders and are therefore sought as symbols of greater prestige. This may lead to such absurdities as Amazonian Indians choosing to consume imported canned tuna fish when abundant high-quality fish is available in their own rivers. Another example of this situation occurs in tribes where mothers prefer to feed their infants expensive and nutritionally inadequate canned milk from unsanitary, but high-status, baby bottles. The high status of these items is often promoted by traders and clever advertising campaigns.

Aside from these apparently voluntary changes, it appears that more often dietary changes are forced upon unwilling indigenous peoples by circumstances beyond their control. In some areas, new food crops have been introduced by government decree or as a consequence of forced relocation or other government policies designed to end hunting, pastoralism, or shifting cultivation. Food habits have also been modified by massive disruption of the natural environment by outsiders—as when sheepherders transformed the Australian Aborigines' foraging territory or when European invaders destroyed the bison herds that were the primary element in the Plains Indians' subsistence patterns. Perhaps the most frequent cause of diet change occurs when formerly self-sufficient peoples find that wage labor, cash cropping, and other economic development activities that feed resources into the world-market economy must inevitably divert time and energy away from the production of subsistence foods. Many indigenous peoples in transforming cultures suddenly discover that, like it or not, they are unable to secure traditional foods and must spend their newly acquired cash on costly and often nutritionally inferior manufactured foods.

Overall, the available data seem to indicate that the dietary changes that are linked to involvement in the world-market economy have tended to reduce rather than raise the nutritional levels of the affected peoples. Specifically, the vitamin, mineral, and protein components of their diets are often drastically reduced and replaced by enormous increases in starch and carbohydrates, often in the form of white flour and refined sugar.

Any deterioration in the quality of a given population's diet is almost certain to be reflected in an increase in deficiency diseases and a general decline in health status. Indeed, as indigenous peoples have shifted to a diet based on imported manufactured or processed foods, there has been a dramatic rise in malnutrition, a massive increase in dental problems, and a variety of other nutrition-related disorders. Nutritional physiology is so complex that even well-meaning dietary changes have had tragic consequences. In many areas of Southeast Asia, government-sponsored protein supplementation programs, which supplied milk to protein-deficient populations, caused unexpected health problems and increased mortality. Officials failed to anticipate that in cultures where adults do not normally drink milk, they no longer produce the enzymes needed to digest it, resulting in milk intolerance.[10] In Brazil, a similar milk distribution program caused an epidemic of permanent blindness by aggravating a preexisting vitamin A deficiency.[11]

Teeth and Progress

There is nothing new in the observation that savages, or peoples living under primitive conditions, have, in general, excellent teeth. . . .

Nor is it news that most civilized populations possess wretched teeth which begin to decay almost before they have erupted completely, and that dental caries is likely to be accompanied by periodontal disease with further reaching complications.[12]

Anthropologists have long recognized that undisturbed indigenous peoples are often in excellent physical condition. And it has often been noted specifically that dental caries and the other dental abnormalities that plague globalscale societies are absent or rare among indigenous peoples who have retained their diets. The fact that indigenous food habits may contribute to the development of sound teeth, whereas modernized diets may do just the opposite, was illustrated as long ago as 1894 in an article in the *Journal of the Royal Anthropological Institute* that described the results of a comparison between the teeth of ten Sioux Indians and a comparable group of Londoners.[13] The Indians, who were examined when they came to London as members of "Buffalo Bill's Wild West Show," were found to be completely free of caries and in possession of all their teeth, even though half of the group was over thirty-nine years of age. The Londoners' teeth were conspicuous for both their caries and their steady reduction in number with advancing age. The difference was attributed primarily to the wear and polishing caused by the Indian diet of coarse food and the fact that they chewed their food longer, encouraged by the absence of tableware.

One of the most remarkable studies of the dental conditions of indigenous peoples and the impact of dietary change was conducted in the 1930s by Weston Price,[14] an American dentist who was interested in determining what contributed to normal, healthy teeth. Between 1931 and 1936, Price systematically explored indigenous areas throughout the world to locate and examine the most isolated peoples who were still living relatively self-sufficiently. . . . The study demonstrated both the superior quality of aboriginal dentition and the devastation that occurs as modern diets are adopted. In nearly every area where traditional foods were still being eaten, Price found perfect teeth with normal dental arches and virtually no decay, whereas caries and abnormalities increased steadily as new diets were adopted. In many cases the change was sudden and striking. Among Inuit (Eskimo) groups subsisting entirely on traditional food he found caries totally absent, whereas in groups eating a considerable quantity of store-bought food, approximately 20 percent of their teeth were decayed. This figure rose to more than 30 percent with Inuit groups subsisting almost exclusively on purchased or government-supplied food and reached an incredible 48 percent among the native peoples of Vancouver Island. Unfortunately for many of these people, modern dental treatment did not accompany the new food, and their suffering was appalling. The loss of teeth was, of course, bad enough in itself, and it certainly undermined the population's resistance to many new diseases, including tuberculosis. But new foods were also accompanied by crowded, misplaced teeth, gum diseases, distortion of the face, and pinching of the nasal cavity. Abnormalities in the dental arch appeared in the new generation following the change in diet, while caries appeared almost immediately even in adults .. . .

In New Zealand, the Maori, who in their aboriginal state are often considered to have been among the healthiest, most perfectly developed of peoples, were found to have "advanced" the furthest. According to Price: "Their modernization was demonstrated not only by the high incidence of dental caries but also by the fact that 90 percent of the adults and 100 percent of the children had abnormalities of the dental arches."[15]

Malnutrition

Malnutrition, particularly in the form of protein deficiency, has become a critical problem for indigenous peoples who must adopt new economic patterns. Population pressures, cash cropping, and government programs have all tended to encourage the replacement of previous crops and other food sources that were rich in protein with substitutes high in calories but low in protein. In Africa, for example, protein-rich staples such as millet and sorghum are being systematically replaced by high-yielding manioc and plantains, which have insignificant amounts of protein. The problem is increased for cash croppers and wage laborers whose earnings are too low and unpredictable to allow purchase of adequate amounts of protein. In some rural areas, agricultural laborers have been forced systematically to deprive nonproductive members (principally children) of their households of minimal nutritional requirements to satisfy the need of the productive members of the household. . . .

One of the most tragic, and largely overlooked, aspects of chronic malnutrition is that it can lead to abnormal brain development and apparently irreversible brain damage; chronic malnutrition has been associated with various forms of mental impairment or retardation. Malnutrition has been linked clinically with mental retardation in both Africa and Latin America,[16] and this appears to be a worldwide phenomenon with serious implications.[17]

Optimistic supporters of progress will surely say that all of these new health problems are being overstressed and that the introduction of hospitals, clinics, and other modern health institutions will overcome or at least compensate for all of these difficulties. However, it appears that uncontrolled population growth and economic impoverishment will likely keep most of these benefits out of reach for many indigenous peoples, and the intervention of modern medicine has at least partly contributed to the problem in the first place. . . .

Ecocide

"How is it," asked a herdsman, . . . "how is it that these hills can no longer give pasture to my cattle? In my father's day they were green and cattle thrived there; today there is no grass and my cattle starve." As one looked one saw that what had once been a green hill had become a raw red rock.[18]

. . . The introduction of new technology, increased consumption, reduced mortality rates, and the eradication of all previous controls have combined to replace what for many indigenous peoples was a relatively stable balance between population and natural resources with a new system that is unbalanced. Economic development is forcing ecocide on peoples who were once careful stewards of their resources. There is already a trend toward widespread environmental deterioration in indigenous areas, involving resource depletion, erosion, plant and animal extinction, and a disturbing series of other previously unforeseen changes. . . .

Swidden systems and pastoralism, both highly successful economic systems under former conditions, have proven particularly vulnerable to increased population pressures and outside efforts to raise productivity beyond its natural limits. Research in Amazonia demonstrates that population pressures and related resource depletion can be created indirectly by official policies that restrict swidden people to smaller territories. Resource depletion itself can then become a powerful means of forcing indigenous people into participating in the world-market economy—thus leading to further resource depletion. For example, Foley C. Benson and I[19] showed how the Shipibo Indians in Peru were forced to further deplete their forest resources by cash cropping in the forest area to replace the resources that had been destroyed earlier by the intensive cash cropping necessitated by the narrow confines of their reserve. In this case, some species of palm trees that had provided critical housing materials were destroyed by forest clearing and had to be replaced by costly purchased materials. . . .

The settling of nomadic herders and the removal of prior controls on herd size have often led to serious overgrazing and erosion problems where these had not previously occurred. There are indications that the desertification problem in the Sahel region of Africa was aggravated by programs designed to settle nomads. . . .

The environmental hazards of economic development and rapid population growth have become generally recognized only since worldwide concerns over environmental issues began in the early 1970s. Unfortunately, there is as yet little indication that the leaders of nations in transformation are sufficiently concerned with environmental limitations. On the contrary, governments are forcing indigenous peoples into a self-reinforcing spiral of population growth and intensified resource exploitation, which may be stopped only by environmental disaster or the total impoverishment of the indigenous peoples.

The reality of ecocide certainly focuses attention on the fundamental contrasts between small- and global-scale systems in their use of natural resources. In many respects the entire "victims of progress" issue hinges on natural resources, who controls them, and how they are managed. Indigenous peoples are victimized because they control resources that outsiders demand. The resources exist because indigenous people managed them conservatively. . . .

The ecocide issue is perhaps most dramatically illustrated by two sets of satellite photos taken over Brazilian rainforests of Rondônia.[20] Photos taken in 1973, when Rondônia was still a tribal domain, show virtually unbroken rainforest. The 1987 satellite photos, taken after just fifteen years of highway construction and "development" by outsiders, show more than 20 percent of the forest destroyed. The surviving Indians were being concentrated by FUNAI into what would soon become mere islands of forest in a ravaged landscape. . . . [T]he fact is that for the past two hundred years rapid environmental deterioration on an unprecedented global scale has followed the wresting of control of vast areas of the world from indigenous peoples by resource-hungry commercial societies. The reality is that nearly 80 percent of the world's primary forest (tropical, temperate, and boreal) is gone.[21] It is also no accident that the areas with the richest and/or best preserved ecosystems in the world are occupied by indigenous peoples.

Deprivation and Discrimination

Contact with European culture has given them a knowledge of great wealth, opportunity and privilege, but only very limited avenues by which to acquire these things.[22]

Unwittingly, indigenous peoples have had the burden of perpetual relative deprivation thrust upon them by acceptance—either by themselves or by the governments administering them—of the standards of socioeconomic progress set for them by the commercial world. By comparison with the material wealth of commercial societies, small-scale societies become, by definition, impoverished. They are then forced to transform their cultures and work to achieve what many economists now acknowledge to be unattainable goals. Even when the modest GDP goals set by economic planners for the impoverished nations during the "development decades" that began in the 1960 were met, the results were hardly noticeable for most of the indigenous people involved. Population growth, environmental limitations, inequitable distribution of wealth, and the continued rapid growth of national societies have all meant that both the absolute and the relative gap between the rich and poor in the world is steadily widening. In 2000 the top 10 percent of the world's households held 71 percent of household net worth in purchasing power parity dollars, measured in standard commercial values.[23] Viewed from the bottom up, the four hundred wealthiest Americans held more personal wealth than 2.5 billion people in the poorest eighty-one countries in the world.[24] . . .

It is of course quite incorrect to consider indigenous people "impoverished" when they enjoy cultural autonomy with full ownership over their territories. . . .

Indigenous peoples may feel deprivation not only when the economic goals they have been encouraged to seek fail to materialize, but also when they discover that they are powerless second-class citizens who are discriminated against and exploited by the dominant society. At the same time, they are denied the satisfaction of cultural autonomy when it has been lost in the process of globalization. . . .

Notes

[1.] Nie Marks, Saamah Abdallah, Andrew Simms, and Sam Thompson, 2006, *The Unhappy Planet Index: An Index of Human Well-Being and Environmental Impact*, London: New Economics Foundation.

[2.] CIA, World Factbook, https://www.cia.gov/library/publications/the-world-fact-book/index.html (accessed July 11, 2007).

[3.] Walter R. Goldschmidt, 1952, "The interrelations between cultural factors and the acquisition of new technical skills," in *The Progress of Underdeveloped Areas*, ed. Bert F. Hoselitz, Chicago: University of Chicago Press, 135.

[4.] Charles C. Hughes and John M. Hunter, 1972, "The role of technological development in promoting disease in Africa," in *The Careless Technology: Ecology and International Development*, ed. M. T. Farvar and John P. Milton, Garden City, NY: Natural History Press, 93.

[5.] World Health Organization, 2003, *Diet, Nutrition and the Prevention of Chronic Diseases*, Report of a Joint WHO/FAO Expert Consultation, WHO Technical Report Series 916, Geneva: WHO.

[6.] U.S. Department of State, 1959, *Eleventh Annual Report to the United Nations on the Administration of the Trust Territory of the Pacific Islands (July 1, 1957, to June 30, 1958)*; U.S. Department of State, 1973, *Twenty-Fifth Annual Report to the United Nations on the Administration of the Trust Territory of the Pacific Islands (July 1, 1971, to June 30, 1972)*, statistical tables.

[7.] Ian A. M. Prior, 1971, "The price of civilization," *Nutrition Today* 6(4): 2.

[8.] Hughes and Hunter, "The role of technological development in promoting disease in Africa.".

[9.] Barry S. Hewlett and Bonnie L. Hewlett, 2007, *Ebola, Culture and Politics: The Anthropology of an Emerging Disease*. Belmont, CA: Wadsworth/Thompson.

[10.] A. E. Davis and T. D. Bolin, 1972, "Lactose intolerance in Southeast Asia," in *The Careless Technology: Ecology and International Development*, ed. M. T. Farvar and John P. Milton, 61–68. Garden city, NY: Natural History Press.

[11.] George E. Brunce, 1972, "Aggravation of vitamin A deficiency following distribution of non-fortified skim milk: An example of nutrient interaction," In *The Careless Technology: Ecology and International Development*, ed. M. T. Farvar and John P. Milton, 53–60. Garden City, NY: Natural History Press.

[12.] Earnest A. Hooton, 1945, "Introduction," in *Nutrition and Physical Degeneration: A Comparison of Primitive and Modern Diets and Their Effects*, by West A. Price, Redlands, CA: Author, xviii.

[13.] Wilberforce Smith, 1894, "The teeth of ten Sioux Indians," *Journal of the Royal Anthropological Institute* 24: 109–16.

[14.] West Andrew Price, 1945, *Nutrition and Physical Degeneration: A Comparison of Primitive and Modern Diets and Their Effects*, Redlands, CA: Author.

[15.] Ibid., 206.

[16.] F. Monckeberg, 1968, "Mental retardation from malnutrition," *Journal of the American Medical Association* 206: 30–31.

[17.] Ashley Montagu, 1972, "Sociogenic brain damage," *American Anthropologist* 74(5): 1045–61.

[18.] J. D. Rheinallt Jones, 1934, "Economic condition of the urban native," In *Western Civilization and the Natives of South Africa*, ed. I. Schapera, 159–92. London: George Routledge and Sons.

[19.] John H. Bodley and Foley C. Benson, 1979, *Cultural Ecology of Amazonian Palms*, Reports of Investigations, no. 56, Pullman: Laboratory of Anthropology, Washington State University.

[20.] William Albert Allard and Loren McIntyre, 1988, "Rondonia's settlers invade Brazil's imperiled rain forest," *National Geographic* 174(6): 772–99, 780–81.

[21.] United Nations Food and Agriculture Organization, 2006, *Global Forest Resources Assessment 2005: Progress towards Sustainable Forest Management*, PAO Forestry Paper 147, www.fao.org/forestry/site/32039/en (accessed December 11, 2007).

[22.] Ron Crocombe, 1968, "Bougainville! Copper, C. R. A. and secessionism," *New Guinea* 3(3): 39-49.

[23.] James B. Davies, Susanna Sandstrom, Anthony Shorrocks, and Edward N. Wolff, 2006, *The World Distribution of Household Wealth*, Helsinki, Finland: World Institute for Development Economics Research.

[24.] John H. Bodley, 2008, *Anthropology and Contemporary Human Problems*, Lanham, MD: Altamira Press, chap. 7.

9.2 Being Indigenous in the 21st Century

WILMA MANKILLER

Indigenous, tribal, native, or first peoples make up approximately 5 percent of the world's popula-
tion. While there is debate over a universal definition for the word "indigenous," most agree that
Indigenous Peoples worldwide share certain characteristics. The individual and collective rights of
Indigenous Peoples are protected under the 2007 United Nations Declaration on the Rights of Indig-
enous Peoples, which emphasizes their rights to maintain and strengthen their own cultural institu-
tions and traditions, affirms their right to self-determination, and recognizes the close relationship
between the continuation of cultural traditions and control over traditional land and territory. The
following selection, by Wilma Mankiller, the first female principal chief of the Cherokee Nation, is
excerpted from a speech she gave one year after the Declaration on the Rights of Indigenous Peoples
and on the 60th anniversary of the Universal Declaration of Human Rights. She highlights how
Indigenous Peoples everywhere are connected by their values, by a shared experience of oppression,
and by their resilience. This piece comes from Cultural Survival, an organization formed to advocate
for Indigenous Peoples throughout the world.

Questions

1. According to this piece, what is an indigenous relationship to the natural world?
2. What misconceptions exist about Indigenous Peoples?
3. What challenges lie ahead for Indigenous Peoples?

 Additional resources may be found at www.oup.com/us/brondo.

There are more than 300 million indigenous people, in virtually every region of the world, including the Sámi peoples of Scandinavia, the Maya of Guatemala, numerous tribal groups in the Amazonian rainforest, the Dalits in the mountains of Southern India, the San and Kwei of Southern Africa, Aboriginal people in Australia, and, of course, the hundreds of Indigenous Peoples in Mexico, Central and South America, as well as here in what is now known as North America.

There is enormous diversity among communities of Indigenous Peoples, each of which has its own distinct culture, language, history, and unique way of life.

Despite these differences, Indigenous Peoples across the globe share some common values derived in part from an understanding that their lives are part of and inseparable from the natural world.

Onondaga Faith Keeper Oren Lyons once said, "Our knowledge is profound and comes from living in one place for untold generations. It comes from watching the sun rise in the east and set in the west from the same place over great sections of time. We are as familiar with the lands, rivers, and great seas that surround us as we are with the faces of our mothers. Indeed, we call the earth Etenoha, our mother from whence all life springs."

Wilma Mankiller. "Being Indigenous in the 21st Century." 2009. *Cultural Survival Quarterly* 33 (1). Online.

Indigenous people are not the only people who understand the interconnectedness of all living things. There are many thousands of people from different ethnic groups who care deeply about the environment and fight every day to protect the earth. The difference is that indigenous people have the benefit of being regularly reminded of their responsibilities to the land by stories and ceremonies. They remain close to the land, not only in the way they live, but in their hearts and in the way they view the world. Protecting the environment is not an intellectual exercise; it is a sacred duty. When women like Pauline Whitesinger, an elder at Big Mountain, and Carrie Dann, a Western Shoshone land rights activist, speak of preserving the land for future generations, they are not just talking about future generations of humans. They are talking about future generations of plants, animals, water, and all living things. Pauline and Carrie understand the relative insignificance of human beings in the totality of the planet.

Aside from a different view of their relationship to the natural world, many of the world's Indigenous Peoples also share a fragmented but still-present sense of responsibility for one another. Cooperation always has been necessary for the survival of tribal people, and even today cooperation takes precedence over competition in more traditional communities. It is really quite miraculous that a sense of sharing and reciprocity continues into the 21st century given the staggering amount of adversity Indigenous Peoples have faced. In many communities, the most respected people are not those who have amassed great material wealth or achieved great personal success. The greatest respect is reserved for those who help other people, those who understand that their lives play themselves out within a set of reciprocal relationships.

There is evidence of this sense of reciprocity in Cherokee communities. My husband, Charlie Soap, leads a widespread self-help movement among the Cherokee in which low-income volunteers work together to build walking trails, community centers, sports complexes, water lines, and houses. The self-help movement taps into the traditional Cherokee value of cooperation for the sake of the common good. The projects also build a sense of self-efficacy among the people.

Besides values, the world's Indigenous Peoples are also bound by the common experience of being "discovered" and subjected to colonial expansion into their territories that has led to the loss of an incalculable number of lives and millions and millions of acres of land and resources. The most basic rights of Indigenous Peoples were disregarded, and they were subjected to a series of policies that were designed to dispossess them of their land and resources and assimilate them into colonial society and culture. Too often the policies resulted in poverty, high infant mortality, rampant unemployment, and substance abuse, with all its attendant problems.

The stories are shockingly similar all over the world. When I read Chinua Achebe's *Things Fall Apart*, which chronicled the systematic destruction of an African tribe's social, cultural, and economic structure, it sounded all too familiar: take the land, discredit the leaders, ridicule the traditional healers, and send the children off to distant boarding schools.

And I was sickened by the Stolen Generation report about Aboriginal children in Australia who were forcibly removed from their families and placed in boarding schools far away from their families and communities. My own father and my Aunt Sally were taken from my grandfather by the U.S. government and placed in a government boarding school when they were very young. There is a connection between us. Indigenous Peoples everywhere are connected both by our values and by our oppression.

When contemplating the contemporary challenges and problems faced by Indigenous Peoples worldwide, it is important to remember that the roots of many social, economic, and political problems can be found in colonial policies. And these policies continue today across the globe.

Several years ago Charlie and I visited an indigenous community along the Rio Negro in the Brazilian rainforest. Some of the leaders expressed concern that some environmentalists, who should be natural allies, focus almost exclusively on the land and appear not to see or hear the people at all. One leader pointed out that a few years ago it was popular for famous musicians to wear T-shirts emblazoned with the slogan "Save the Rainforests," but no one ever wore a T-shirt with the slogan "Save the People of the Rainforest," though the people of the forest possess the best knowledge about how to live with and sustain the forests.

With so little accurate information about Indigenous Peoples available in educational institutions, in literature, films, or popular culture, it is not surprising that many people are not even conscious of Indigenous Peoples.

The battle to protect the human and land rights of Indigenous Peoples is made immeasurably more difficult by the fact that so few people know much about either the history or contemporary lives of our people. And without any kind of history or cultural context, it is almost impossible for outsiders to understand the issues and challenges faced by Indigenous Peoples.

This lack of accurate information leaves a void that is often filled with nonsensical stereotypes, which either vilify Indigenous Peoples as troubled descendants of savage peoples, or romanticize them as innocent children of nature, spiritual but incapable of higher thought.

Public perceptions will change in the future as indigenous leaders more fully understand that there is a direct link between public perception and public policies. Indigenous Peoples must frame their own issues, because if they don't frame the issues for themselves, their opponents most certainly will. In the future, as more indigenous people become filmmakers, writers, historians, museum curators, and journalists, they will be able to use a dazzling array of technological tools to tell their own stories, in their own voice, in their own way.

Once, a journalist asked me whether people in the United States had trouble accepting the government of the Cherokee Nation during my tenure as principal chief. I was a little surprised by the question. The government of the Cherokee Nation predated the government of the United States and had treaties with other countries before it executed a treaty with one of the first U.S. colonies.

Cherokee and other tribal leaders sent delegations to meet with the English, Spanish, and French in an effort to protect their lands and people. Traveling to foreign lands with a trusted interpreter, tribal ambassadors took maps that had been painstakingly drawn by hand to show their lands to heads of other governments. They also took along gifts, letters, and proclamations. Though tribal leaders thought they were being dealt with as heads of state and as equals, historical records indicate they were often objects of curiosity, and that there was a great deal of disdain and ridicule of these earnest delegates.

Tribal governments in the United States today exercise a range of sovereign rights. Many tribal governments have their own judicial systems, operate their own police force, run their own schools, administer their own clinics and hospitals, and operate a wide range of business enterprises. There are now more than two dozen tribally controlled community colleges. All these advancements benefit everyone in the community, not just tribal people. The history, contemporary lives, and future of tribal governments [are] intertwined with that of their neighbors.

One of the most common misperceptions about Indigenous Peoples is that they are all the same. There is not only great diversity among Indigenous Peoples, there is great diversity within each tribal community, just as there is in the larger society. Members of the Cherokee Nation are socially, economically, and culturally stratified. Several thousand Cherokee continue to speak the Cherokee language and live in Cherokee communities in rural northeastern Oklahoma. At the other end of the spectrum, there are enrolled tribal members who have never been to even visit the Cherokee Nation. Intermarriage has created an enrolled Cherokee membership that includes people with Hispanic, Asian, Caucasian, and African American heritage.

So what does the future hold for Indigenous Peoples across the globe? What challenges will they face moving further into the 21st century?

To see the future, one needs only to look at the past. If, as peoples, we have been able to survive a staggering loss of land, of rights, of resources, of lives, and we are still standing in the early 21st century, how can I not be optimistic that we will survive whatever challenges lie ahead, that 100 or 500 years from now we will still have viable indigenous communities? Without question, the combined efforts of government and various religious groups to eradicate traditional knowledge systems has had a profoundly negative impact on the culture as well as the social and economic systems of Indigenous Peoples. But if we have been able to hold onto our sense of community, our languages, culture, and ceremonies, despite everything, how can I not be optimistic about the future?

And though some of our original languages, medicines, and ceremonies have been irretrievably lost, the ceremonial fires of many Indigenous Peoples across the globe have survived all the upheaval. Sometimes indigenous communities have almost had to reinvent themselves as a people but they have never given up their sense of responsibility to one another and to the land. It is this sense of interdependence that has sustained tribal people thus far and I believe it will help sustain them well into the future.

Indigenous Peoples know about change and have proven time and time again they can adapt to change. No matter where they go in the world, they hold onto a strong sense of tribal identity while fully interacting with and participating in the larger society around them. In my state of Oklahoma alone, we have produced an indigenous astronaut, two United States congressmen, a Pulitzer Prize-winning novelist, and countless others who have made great contributions to their people, the state, and the world.

One of the great challenges for Indigenous Peoples in the 21st century will be to develop practical models to capture, maintain, and pass on traditional knowledge systems and values to future generations. Nothing can replace the sense of continuity that a genuine understanding of traditional tribal knowledge brings. Many communities are working on discrete aspects of culture, such as language or medicine, but it is the entire system of knowledge that needs to be maintained, not just for Indigenous Peoples but for the world at large.

Regrettably, in the future the battle for human and land rights will continue. But the future does look somewhat better for tribal people. Last year, after 30 years of advocacy by Indigenous Peoples, the United Nations finally passed a declaration supporting their distinct human rights. The challenge will be to make sure the provisions of the declaration are honored and that the rights of Indigenous Peoples all over the world are protected.

Indigenous Peoples simply do better when they have control of their own lives. In the case of my own people, after we were forcibly removed by the United States military from the southeastern part of the United States to Indian Territory, now Oklahoma, we picked ourselves up and rebuilt our nation, despite the fact that approximately 4,000 Cherokee lives were lost during the forced removal. We started some of the first schools west of the Mississippi, Indian or non-Indian, and built schools for the higher education of women. We printed our own newspapers in Cherokee and English and were more literate than our neighbors in adjoining states. Then, in the early 20th century, the federal government almost abolished the Cherokee Nation, and within two decades, our educational attainment levels dropped dramatically and many of our people were living without the most basic amenities. But our people never gave up the dream of rebuilding the Cherokee Nation. In my grandfather's time, Cherokee men rode horses from house to house to collect dimes in a mason jar so they could send representatives to Washington to remind the government to honor its treaties with the Cherokee people.

Over the past 35 years, we have revitalized the Cherokee Nation and once again run our own school, and we have an extensive array of successful education programs. The youth at our Sequoyah High School recently won the state trigonometry contest, and several are Gates Millennium Scholars. We simply do better when we have control over our own destiny.

9.3 The Making of Disaster

VINCANNE ADAMS

In 2005, Category 5 Hurricane Katrina, one of the deadliest in U.S. history, devastated New Orleans, and the humanitarian crisis that ensued when the levees broke and flooded the city created a "second-order disaster." In this selection, taken from her book Markets of Sorrow, Labors of Faith: New Orleans in the Wake of Katrina, Vincanne Adams adopts Naomi Klein's notion of "disaster capitalism" to show how private industries took advantage of this major disaster, profiting from human tragedy. This case study reveals the negative effects of privatizing what once were government-controlled social services—private subcontractors are driven first and foremost by making money for their shareholders rather than being motivated by a human-rights agenda to provide humanitarian aid to those most in need. Those hurt the most in the recovery process were poor racial minorities, as they were not "market-visible," and therefore not positioned to take advantage of recovery programs. Thus, inequalities were deepened through this "second-order disaster," and continue to be felt by the New Orleanians.

Questions

1. What was the structure of recovery assistance in post-Katrina New Orleans? What kinds of companies were subcontracted to provide relief efforts? What worked about it? What didn't?
2. What are the drawbacks of private-sector companies subcontracting with the government?
3. What is disaster capitalism? Where have you seen other examples of disaster capitalism?
4. Discuss the racialization of recovery and prioritizing of those who were already market visible.

It is now well established that the impact of the storm when it hit New Orleans and the subsequent flooding were both man-made catastrophes. The elaborate system of channels, canals, and levees that wound through Greater New Orleans . . . was originally designed to augment what William Freudenburg and colleagues call the growth machine of the region, or the low of river-sea traffic and maritime commerce. By 2005 many of the waterways were no longer used and had created problems from the start. The U.S. Army Corps of Engineers was responsible for building and maintaining the levees in New Orleans, but locals had been increasingly worried for years that signs of deterioration in the levee walls were being ignored. Local newspapers and engineers had previously warned about the potential damage that a hurricane like Katrina could cause.

When Katrina hit, the problem was twofold: first, the Mississippi River Gulf Outlet . . . , a 1.8-mile-wide channel created by the U.S. Army Corps of Engineers to expedite shipping, had destroyed Greater New Orleans's natural land barrier, and it created a funnel that would direct storm surges right into the city. The canals had become a known menace to the fragile wetlands stretching over the 8,176-square-mile coastal area that had served as a natural protective buffer zone for the Crescent City. Because the canals prevented the inflow of fresh water to feed the foliage and replenish sediment, the wetlands had been losing approximately thirteen square miles per year, or about one football field of marshland every hour. By 2005, New Orleans had little protection against major storms. Previous Gulf storms of Katrina's magnitude would have landed much farther from the city and were subsequently reduced in size before hitting Greater New Orleans itself. With the wetlands gone, storms moved directly inward from the Gulf and made landfall closer in. Moreover, the storm surge traveled with much greater intensity through a man-made channel system, directing the worst effects of the hurricane into the city itself.

Second, most locals knew that even though the Army Corps of Engineers had known about the problem for decades, just as it knew that the levees would not hold up against anything over a Category 2 storm, it did not repair them. In fact, as early as 1998, engineers and local environmentalists warned that levee walls were not sufficiently rigid, strong, or stable enough to withstand predicted storms. Despite political debate among city, regional, and state officials and the media about the severity of the situation and the possibility that the levees could be compromised by a large storm, no repairs or strengthening projects were done before it was too late.

One reason for the deferred maintenance of the levees was that the Army Corps of Engineers had been undergoing internal changes for at least two decades prior to Hurricane Katrina. Private-sector companies, including the Shaw Group, Bechtel, Halliburton, HNTB, Titan, Blackwater, and KBR Associates, had developed relationships as legacy contractors with the federal government. The wall between the subcontractors and the federal Corps had become more like a revolving door between public and private sectors,

with former Corps engineers working in key executive positions at these companies. Few saw or raised concerns over the conflict of interest in this situation; those who did were often fired. As a result, throughout the 1990s, the Corps became increasingly invested in helping subcontractors undertake waterway projects that had less to do with protecting the public (by repairing levees) and more to do with augmenting the oil industries in the Gulf region. By 2003, the war in Iraq paid subcontractors much more than they could earn in New Orleans, and most Corps work in the area dried up. The levees still went unrepaired.

Without the protection from the wetlands that once stretched from city to ocean, the Greater New Orleans area was impacted harder than expected by the hurricane on August 29, 2005. In fact, the storm passed mostly to the south of the city, causing minor water damage in the city itself, but within the next twenty-four hours the levees failed and the real damage took place. . . . Eighty percent of the Greater New Orleans area was flooded, with whole neighborhoods submerged under more than ten feet of water, and some neighborhoods were nearly entirely washed away.

With more than 350,000 people affected, the federal government declared a state of emergency. Because the Federal Emergency Management Authority (FEMA) had merged with the Office of Homeland Security only two years before, many of the same firms that subcontracted to the Army Corps of Engineers (such as Blackwater and the Shaw Group) were called upon to provide disaster relief through noncompetitive contracts, despite the fact that they had no experience or training in humanitarian assistance operations.

Rescue and Relief

The debacle of the lack of immediate relief after this catastrophe is by now a very familiar story. More than 455,000 people were evacuated, and for those unable to evacuate before the flood—upward of 50,000 people, with roughly 25,000 at the Superdome alone—survival was difficult. Rescue operations were late, disorganized, and misguided. Floodwaters remained in the city for up to three weeks. Within a month, Hurricane Rita followed, reflooding the already inundated Lower Ninth Ward and other low-lying areas, tearing off roofs, and felling trees onto houses and cars in the few neighborhoods that were not previously flooded. This forced thousands of people into secondary evacuations to locations even farther away from their homes.

No one escaped the storm's impact. All told, more than a million people in the region were displaced; up to 600,000 people were still displaced a month afterward. Hurricane evacuee shelters housed 273,000 people, and FEMA eventually housed 114,000 households in their now-infamous trailers. At the five-year mark after Hurricanes Katrina and Rita, more than 100,000 fewer people lived in the Greater New Orleans area. . . . The highest estimates of death from these 2005 events exceed the official numbers offered by the government. Hurricane and levee failures most likely were the cause of the officially documented deaths of at least 1,464 Louisiana residents, with major causes including drowning (40 percent), injury and trauma (25 percent), and heart failure (11 percent). Nearly half of all victims were over the age of seventy-four. Most of these deaths occurred in homes, in attics, and from rooftops where people were stranded or swept away. Most of those who stayed behind did so because they could not evacuate, did not have transportation, or, despite their efforts to leave, had to return to the city with family members who were too sick or infirm to survive the long waits in traffic jams and the distances they had to travel to find hotels or shelters with vacancies. Some people didn't know they were supposed to evacuate because they did not have televisions, radios, or enough contact with neighbors. A few refused to leave because they felt safer "weathering" the storm in their homes than leaving them. . . . Some stayed behind because they didn't want to abandon their pets.

No matter the reasons they stayed, the poor, the elderly, and the infirm were among the first to die. Many children died, too, some from the tragedy of slipping from their parents' arms into the raging water. Some people perished while waiting for rescue in the city's Superdome and at the convention center. With 50,000 people in these places, the disaster was worsened by the fact that there was not enough food, water, or medical assistance for evacuees. The majority of these people, though certainly not all, were African American and poor. Those who did not make it to the Superdome or the convention center were stranded in their homes or on freeway overpasses, bridges, and the tops of high-rises. Hundreds awaited rescue on dry stretches of freeway for days. People from one such freeway location, informally known as "Causeway Camp," described harrowing conditions filled with thousands who were forced to stand for hours or to sit in mud and trash under the watch of National Guard guns, reminiscent of African American relocation camps that were set up during the 1927 Mississippi River Flood. Although under guard by military and aid personnel, people in Causeway Camp reported poor organization and a total lack of communication. When buses came sporadically, people were herded on with no knowledge of destinations, and in many cases they were separated from both friends and nuclear family members. Sally, a fifty-six-year-old Caucasian woman from St. Bernard Parish, was still living in a FEMA trailer fifty miles from her original home when she told her story two and a half years after the storm.

Prior to Katrina I worked as a housekeeper in [a] nursing home down at St. Bernard, Louisiana, and . . . we got all our people out of there Friday, but the staff stayed like me. . . . [After the storm began, we] heard a big boom, and we said, "What was that?" And we looked to the right. I don't know if you have ever seen that movie The *Poseidon Adventure,* but there was this wall of water coming at us . . . the wall of water was maybe, I'd say, two city blocks away, but of course you could see it because it was so large. Well, we didn't know it at the time, but the levee had just broke, so we had just two minutes to run up maybe. I would say two minutes because by the time we got to the second flight, the water was right here on us. . . . We stayed like eight hours [like that], and we realized we didn't have any TV; everything was out then, you know. So, we didn't actually know that the levee had broken in three places. We knew it broke here, you know, we saw everything floating and everything, so it was pretty bad. Our cars floated off, got washed out.

Finally we saw flat boats . . . coming around. We didn't see any police. . . . We didn't see any of that, but finally . . . the little boys in the neighborhood, they came around. They had stolen the flat boats and all, and they came around and started rescuing people. . . . So when they did rescue us (I use the term loosely), they took us to St. Bernard High School. OK? Well, we stayed there three days and three nights, and we had like a pack of crackers one day, like this, and a bottle of water that had to last you all day 'til the next day. And, the next day, if they found something, then you got another pack of crackers. The third day we had to share a bottle of water with three people like that. No sewage, no water, no toilet, no nothing. OK. Well, by the third day the world finally caught on that there is something going on down here, so then they sent in the National Guard, whoever they sent in. So, that was after three days and three nights.

. . . It was like something you read about, you know . . . it was real, real bad; I am going to tell you, real, real bad. So, when the National Guard came in on the third day, they decided they was going to take us out of St. Bernard High School, which is right over there to the left, and they were going to ship us somewhere.

[Outside] it was flooded, everything, dead bodies tied to trees, you couldn't see the tops of the houses, I mean, it was something like out of a war movie, but nobody my age saw it before, and it was real bad, I am telling you, when I say real bad, real bad. . . . [A]t that time everybody's nerves were gone; they were more stressed out than you because they lost their homes, and they are trying to help you too, and they are worried about their own people. There were a lot of people dying and everything; they never found out what happened to them, or anything. So, they didn't want to hear, you know, that you couldn't do what you had to do at the time.

So, then we hear bang, bang, bang. I said, "Oh, Jesus." There was a sniper. He was shooting over us. So, everybody as much as they could, they hit the deck. . . . The National Guard made you get down on the ground. I went back to the same position. I was trying to tell them, "I cannot bend. I use a cane." I said, "I can't lay down." So he puts an M-16 to my head. I said, "Let me explain something to you." I mean, he couldn't have been more than twenty years old. You know they called them in, and I said I hurt my leg. What I did, I just lay down as well as I could, and then they . . . they threw a tarp over all my group that was there. And then we had to get on the trucks. . . . We drove all the way out from [St. Bernard] to the interstate with M-16s in our heads, and all the guys looking out for snipers and all. So, finally we get to

[the docks]; it's 99 degrees and I am going to starve. I knew I was going to die right there in the truck.

And so we get to Metairie [a suburb that was less damaged]. OK, praise the Lord, we get to Red Cross; get all the buses lined up. Well, thank God; I don't know if it was Red Cross, or Salvation Army, but as soon as you got off the truck everybody got a bottle of cold water. And, let me tell you, that tastes like champagne after three days. So, everybody got a bottle of that because it was cold, you know. So, now, what did I see? I thought I'd lose my mind in Metairie. They had the mammas, the daddies, the children, OK, in, like, four buses at a time. What I didn't understand, and to this day nobody will make me understand, is this: the mammas went on this bus, the daddies went on this bus, and the children went on this bus [i.e., they were put on separate buses]. I mean, these kids are screaming and howling. . . . And I thought I'd lose my mind right there. They actually pulled, pulled the children out of . . . I mean, I can't understand that, and nobody is going to explain that to me. After I saw it on TV they said some of them children have never been reunited. That's horrible, and seeing the dead bodies, and the dead animals, d I am sorry, but it was . . . disrespect for the dead, you know. So, we get on the bus. Nobody knows where they are going. You are just shuttled like cattle, you know. They just wanted to get us out for some reason. You couldn't ask questions; they tell you to shut up. So, I said, OK. I am going to sit down, I am going to the Third World, you know. But, I said, OK. And now, in the midst of all of this you don't know if any of your family is living or dead, or whatever, you know. . . . We go to Houston, and that's a long ride. No food, no water, not while you're on this bus, anything, except the bottle of water they gave you.

After days of waiting in an abandoned evacuated city, the first official help to arrive on the ground in some parts of the Greater New Orleans area were the Canadian Mounties, who got to Chalmette and St. Bernard Parish first.[1] When the U.S. National Guard finally arrived some three to five days after the hurricane left, they found desperate people who were suffering from dehydration and starvation. They were disoriented and scared. The situation brought out the best in some people. Victims tried to help each other, wading through water and using any sort of boat to get supplies of food and water from stores or homes and bring it back to where people waited. Locals with boats helped transport people from rooftops to freeways and city exits. Informal neighborhood groups like the "Soul Patrol," a crew of working-class African American men from the Seventh Ward, spent days patrolling their neighborhood by boat. They rescued residents and provided aid to neighbors.

However, the situation also brought out the worst in some people. Elderly survivors talked about having their clothes, and even their shoes, stolen from them while they slept at the Superdome. A middle-aged white woman told us that her sister was raped while stranded under the freeway at the edge of the floodwaters. Another asserted that she had been sexually assaulted by a local sheriff who had patrolled the shelter she was staying in. Whites were told they were refused on buses filled with black evacuees, and black residents were told that they would not be allowed on white buses. . . . Stranded survivors recall being more harassed than helped by law enforcement for their refusal to leave any of their neighbors behind before they themselves could be evacuated. Rescue crews hired by military and security companies began to see themselves as gunmen on the attack against an enemy force, although it was not always clear who the enemy really was.

Disaster Capitalism

Media coverage began to show the magnitude of the evacuation failure early on. Delays in responsiveness were blamed on the federal government and the Louisiana governor's office, but less well documented were delays caused by the companies who were subcontracted by the government to help with rescue and relief. Buses and ships from surrounding areas, from local school bus drivers to cruise lines and even USS carriers had arrived on their own to help transport the stranded out of the city. But they were turned away by government authorities because private companies had already been contracted by FEMA/Homeland Security to rescue people, even though these subcontractors had

not yet arrived. Halliburton, for example, with its long history of subcontracting with the military in overseas operations, had been hired to provide buses, and this deterred the arrival of other volunteer bus services that were ready to help. The people of New Orleans became double victims, first of the hurricane, and then of crime that ensued as military and private business operations turned a bad situation into a worse one by treating innocent victims as if they were a potential enemy.

Many of the troops identified as National Guard by locals were in fact hired security personnel working for the private-sector subcontractors. Blackwater Security, or what is now called Xe Services, was one such company. Despite the fact that this private-sector military company founded by Erik Prince and Al Clark had already been made infamous by its killing of innocent civilians while on duty in Fallujah, Iraq, it was hired, along with fifty other private security groups, including an Israeli company called Instinctive Shooting International (ISI), to help with rescue and relief.

According to some sources, Blackwater was paid $250,000 a day to help with the recovery in New Orleans. . . . Armed men had hit the streets of New Orleans in armored cars, patrolling with machine guns and no official explanation as to who they were and why they were there. Innocent people wandering the streets and trying to find food, transport, or medical assistance were met with harassment, terror, and, in some cases, incarceration instead of help.

Testimony from those who remained in the city suggests that humanitarian relief was actually slowed, if not undermined, by the government's subcontracting, which gave for-profit companies the responsibility for carrying out FEMA's tasks. While people were stranded on rooftops waiting for help, military and "rescue" personnel were building makeshift prisons in empty parking lots in order to incarcerate suspected "terrorists," a story captured vividly by Dave Eggers in *Zeitoun,* his biographical account of the New Orleans resident Abdulrahman Zeitoun's arrest in the days following the hurricane. Even after the floodwaters receded, Blackwater continued to work under a federal contract through the Department of Homeland Security to provide armed guards to FEMA reconstruction projects in ways that resembled more of a military tactical operation in a war zone than a civilian recovery process in a beloved American city. The racial contours of this criminalization of stranded victims only augmented the degree to which rescue operations were transformed into a new sort of disaster discrimination. . . .

. . . The existing infrastructure of subcontractors, and particularly the close relationships between the Army Corps of Engineers and groups like Halliburton, Blackwater, and the Shaw Group, enabled companies to secure large contracts and funds up front, with virtually no check on their past performance history in the delivery of humanitarian relief . . .

Bechtel and Halliburton won lucrative contracts not just in the immediate aftermath but also in the years of recovery following Hurricane Katrina. In fact, some estimates say that Halliburton earned far more than the reported $124.9 million in assorted contracts with the Department of Defense, FEMA, the U.S. Navy, and the Army Corps of Engineers.[2] Despite criticism over its handling of contracts in Iraq for poor performance, and its pending twenty investigations for wrongdoing, law violations, bribery, bid rigging, and overcharging, this company was given multiple Katrina contracts even after its initial fiasco of rescue. . . .

Racialization of Recovery and the Profile of Dispossession

Displacement affected New Orleanians of all social classes and all racial groups, but the degree to which both the hurricane and floods led to dispossession and impoverishment in the years afterward was racially uneven and exacerbated by the way that recovery was organized; specifically, the poor were disproportionately hurt more than those with financial resources. . . . Market-oriented strategies for recovery that sought to use fiscal resources where they were most likely to bring profits, rather than using them where the need was greatest, fueled a situation in which African Americans would be offered less than others. Existing inequalities in socioeconomic starting points helped fuel a racialization of recovery that meant African American communities would be the least likely to return and the last to recover. . . .

For instance, federally funded resources that were made available to help residents in New Orleans put African Americans at a disadvantage because they often had fewer financial resources or fiscal visibility to begin with. African Americans were less likely to have money in saving and were more likely not to have insurance. They constituted the largest group of renters. They were least likely to have, or to know how to access, assistance from federal or state agencies and the most likely to be turned away from these resources when they did apply for help. Even among homeowners, fewer African Americans than other groups had the paperwork evidence they needed to obtain Road Home funding, and this was because they often were excluded from traditional sources of funding for home mortgages on the basis of their race.

African American families, for instance, were the most likely not to be in possession of title documents that federal relief services required. Even when they had them, homeowners found that such documents often had not been changed from deceased family members' names from whom they had inherited their property. . . .

Worse still, even when Road Home provided rebuilding funds to African Americans, these recipients were more likely than others to have their homes undervalued in the assessment process. Using assumptions that African American neighborhoods had property values that were uniformly lower than white neighborhoods, insurance companies and recovery assistance programs like Road Home offered financial support that was far below what homeowners should have received. Reports that the Road Home Program unfairly discriminated against African American homeowners were verified by the courts in 2010 which reported that prejudice occurred specifically with the calculations of lower pre-storm home values in neighborhoods that were predominantly African American than in neighborhoods that were predominantly white. The ways in which the market has always worked unequally for different racial groups was only made worse in a recovery that relied on strategies for rebuilding that favored fiscal measures of worthiness above other measures, such as humanitarian or human rights–based assumptions about need. Thus many people who were qualified for assistance were denied adequate funding because of race-based assumptions about their fiscal worthiness. Recovery processes in New Orleans revealed in this sense the ways in which basic citizenship rights were filtered through a grid of market concerns and, as a result, based on race, rights were denied to some more than others.

One of the main routes to dispossession among African Americans in the recovery period was that of the organization of recovery in ways that prioritized those who were already market visible—that is, people who already had a foot in the game by owning a home that had a paper trail within the banking system. For people who could not show the specific paperwork of a title used within the mortgage industry (even if they could show that they had paid taxes on their property), there was little help. The African-American community was more reliant on the informal economy to begin with, whether in the ways they bought homes (without bank mortgages), the ways they held titles to homes, or in the ways they made a living. These informal strategies for homeownership and income generation (whether in skilled construction or other part-time labor) go a long way to explaining the degree to which a market-driven recovery would exclude African Americans.

More significantly, the large population of New Orleans renters (roughly 54 percent, with some 22 percent of whom were low income and living in publicly subsidized housing) were not offered Road Home funds or much other support that would help them return. Middle and low-income renters and people who lived in federally subsidized housing were the most impacted by dislocation. Renters were given FEMA trailers only if they had access to private property upon which to put the trailers, or if they had access to the few public spaces that were converted to trailer parks in the city and a means of justifying their return to the city by volunteering as a first responder or as a person whose rental home was being rebuilt or was inhabitable.

Many renters who did not own property were initially housed in large trailer lots several hours outside the city. . . . Some of these FEMA trailer parks were the modern equivalent of relocation camps, with chain-link fences and National Guardsmen posted at their entrances. Some were in locations where there were no public transportation services, schools, or jobs. Left to sort out how to make a living, many were forced to give up even the seasonal or itinerant labor they were able to do in New Orleans and simply lived off of federal welfare. When the last of these parks closed down in 2009, few of the people who had been living there were able to return to New Orleans, where rental prices had in most cases doubled from their pre-storm rates.

In fact, the storm and floods were used by local New Orleans government officials as an excuse to eliminate a large percentage of its working-class and welfare-class poor, many of whom were African American,

and to welcome the arrival of less well-paid immigrant laborers (largely Hispanic) to take their place. The fact that rental homes themselves were difficult to impossible to find after Hurricane Katrina could also be traced to the market-driven recovery plan. Public housing units that were not even flooded were closed down by the city and boarded up with steel plates within weeks of the storm, and inhabitants were never allowed to return to them (not even to retrieve belongings).

All but one of the nine public housing units were torn down by the Housing Authority of New Orleans by the third year after Katrina. . . . The majority of units in these projects were to become privately owned condominiums, severely limiting the city's supply of rental housing.

. . . Despite public protests and calls for more rental housing . . . and despite the fact that the one remaining unit, Iberville, had been functioning successfully and had been murder-free during its last year due to effective resident-organized crime protection, the city went ahead with redevelopment.

The hurricane and floods, in essence, set in motion an eviction of the poor through the machinery of disaster capitalism. . . .

Wayne Bodrian's story is typical. He was forty when Katrina hit. When we spoke in late 2008, he talked about the city's growing homeless population that was one of the most visible consequences of the displacement of working-class African-American renters like him. When we first met Wayne in early 2007, he had been living in a FEMA trailer in an open lot on the University of New Orleans campus. Before the storm, he had a job working at the convention center. After the storm, he got a trailer because he was considered a "first responder," and he helped to clean up the same convention center that had housed stranded residents. Wayne knew it would be only a matter of time before FEMA would ask for the trailer back. Even though Wayne held two jobs, he still did not earn enough to afford the rising cost of rental housing. He feared that he would end up among the city's growing ranks of those homeless since Katrina, camped out under the freeway overpass near Claiborne Street.

I'm working, so I'm gonna try my best to do what I gotta do, but some people can't work. You know what I'm saying? They got children. They got women, children, pregnant women under the Claiborne Bridge, sleeping in a tent. And some of them been there two years. And they're just starting to help them people. I'm talking about children! I'm talking about three years old, four years old! The mayor, he say he wanna help, but he . . . I don't know what to say about it. Also, the people that's still out of town, that's trying to get back home. . . . They tore the projects down. The people at home now, some of 'em that came home, they be in front of City Hall, picketing, talking about where they gonna live at? That's what the big fight was about. They had a big fight in front of City Hall two weeks ago. There are people still had furniture in their homes. They still had their family pictures and memories, and they tore it down [the public housing units]. They just tore it down. They didn't let them go back in. I mean, like, I know one thing: by them putting the rent that skyhigh, black folk can't handle it. Not Uptown. I'm gonna say middle I can't think of what I want to say the less income people, they know we can't handle that. So, I guess, where this gonna leave us at? Under the overpass in a tent.

Wayne's complaint that there was an open expression of relief on the part of government officials over the fact that large numbers of poor African Americans had been essentially "evicted" from the city by the hurricane, and the fact that some saw this as "a blessing," was borne out by the statements heard in the first year following the storm. The notion that God had done what city administrators couldn't do on their own to eradicate poverty was uttered by officials in New Orleans and by wealthy citizens alike[3], leading some to believe that the levees were deliberately "blown" to hit African American communities the hardest. . . .

As he predicted, in March 2009, Wayne received a notice from FEMA that he would have to vacate soon. FEMA was working with city officials to clear out all of the trailers. When we asked Wayne where he would go once he left his trailer, he explained that he didn't know. Rents had nearly doubled. . . . The unresolved problem for him was where the rent money would come from once the assistance stopped, now that rents had doubled but jobs still paid around minimum wage. Wayne interpreted the creeping housing crisis in terms of the racial consequences he envisioned it producing: "they want a white city.". . .

Wayne's perceptions of the racial inequalities of dispossession in the years after Hurricane Katrina were validated in actual demographic patterns (which show declines in African American residents) and increased rates of violence in the urban African American communities of New Orleans. Adding insult to injury, the recovery period was also marked by augmented white racism toward African Americans. In the immediate aftermath of the floods, white families often expressed hostility toward African Americans regarding the inordinate amount of attention paid to the black racial profile of the disaster, noting that whole neighborhoods of white families had also been displaced. Not seeing their own relative advantages in the recovery process, white residents often talked about the benefits of Katrina in terms of this racial "cleansing," a language that former residents in the Lower Ninth Ward said contributed to a form of "genocide."

It is important to remember that people of all race and class groups were affected by the hurricane and floods. At the same time, the arrangements of recovery, like the arrangements of inequality before the disaster, were such that they made these inequalities worse. . . .

Notes

[1.] See Cardé, *American Betrayed*. DVD. New York: First Run Features, 2008.

[2.] Halliburton Watch, http://halliburonwatch.org.

[3.] See Lipsitz, "Learning from New Orleans," which offers this quote from the Republican congressman Richard Baker from Baton Rouge: "We finally cleaned up public housing in New Orleans. We couldn't do it but God did" (453).

References

Lipsitz, George. "Learning from New Orleans: The Social Warrant of Hostile Privatism and Competitive Consumer Citizenship." *Cultural Anthropology* 21(3) (2006): 451-468.

9.4 Whose Development? Service-Learning Abroad and Discourses on "Doing Good"

NATALIE J. BOURDON

Service-learning and volunteerism opportunities both home and abroad have become a major part of the college experience for U.S. students. Many programs are designed in ways that enable civic-minded students to "give back" through the delivery of social or medical services, technical assistance, or construction projects in impoverished communities. While such programs seem on the surface to be a win-win for all parties involved, Bourdon points out that these programs have the potential to extend neocolonial relationships between the North and South. Bourdon describes her involvement in, and interviews about, Mercer University's "Mercer on Mission" programs, raising questions about the rationale behind "doing good" in foreign places. To what extent do students driven by compassion understand the linkages between their own ability to "help" and the sociopolitical and economic circumstances that created the need they travel to address?

Questions

1. What are the goals of service-learning?
2. Why do students at Mercer engage in service-learning?
3. Who benefits from "Mercer on Mission" and how?
4. What does it mean to say that Mercer on Mission programs are depoliticized?
5. Have you ever participated in a service-learning class at home or abroad? How was the experience linked to course content?

Service-Learning and Poverty

For the past two decades, colleges and universities across the United States have been developing programs and classes that integrate experiential and service learning as components of their educational initiatives. In some cases, these programs have come to serve as cornerstones that reflect the institution's commitment to developing informed, innovative, and civic-minded students while at the same time aiming to "give back" to a particular community. The concept of service-learning in higher education has roots in the beginning of the twentieth century where a model of education combined with service provided "real world" opportunities to college students that would prepare them for employment after graduation. The Cooperative Education Movement, founded at the University of Cincinnati in 1903, was one such early initiative with a structured method of combining classroom-based education with practical work experience. "Folk schools" in Appalachia and the Northeast that sought to combine work, service, and learning took up this model. Since the Great Depression, different U.S. administrations have promoted national-level initiatives as ways for young people to use their education in service to the nation or to be rewarded with education for their service.

Historically, service-based educational models lacked a clear connection between what was being taught in the classroom and what was being pursued outside of it. Today, short-term overseas service-learning initiatives also oftentimes fall short of preparing students by clearly linking in- and out-of-classroom learning. The reciprocity of service learning—hands-on skills and civic insight for students, and something of objective value for the community—is the hallmark of service learning at Mercer University, a liberal arts college in middle Georgia. One of Mercer's emerging service-learning opportunities involves students studying on campus for two weeks before carrying out a three-week service-learning project in a developing country. Service learning for Mercer students is in part defined as "another way of learning course content—not from a textbook or a lab but through community-based projects or research" and as ". . . a chance to exercise the knowledge you are gaining in the classroom, to test theory against practice, to accomplish goals that are meaningful to the community, and to develop as much personally as intellectually (Mercer University 2015).

There are strong affinities between service learning, development work, and humanitarian initiatives. Bornstein and Redfield (2011, 4) note that "Alongside development and human rights, the humanitarian impulse to alleviate suffering constitutes a central element in international moral discourse. . . ." Academic institutions attempt to address the "humanitarian impulse" through service learning. Like humanitarian work, international service-learning initiatives must carefully measure the benefits and complications that might result in such short-term, drop-in engagements. How faculty and students understand the multifaceted and contextualized nature of poverty and how they envision suffering and "doing good" will influence how we envision-with-others sustainable solutions to some of those problems. As an anthropologist who has worked in the areas of human rights and development, I am keenly aware of the possibilities for short-term service-learning projects to advance neo-colonial relationships and reify students' assumptions about the Global South. As an educator and social justice advocate, I am at the same time interested in the possibilities that lie within the realm of informed engagement.

This case study engages with my own experiences in designing and carrying out two service-learning programs in Tanzania and Ghana and research with other faculty who have led "Mercer on Mission" (MoM) programs. The following snapshots from this research are intended to provoke reflection and discussion for students and faculty engaged in similar service-learning initiatives.

MoM Background—"Crossing Cultures, Changing Lives"

Mercer University describes itself as an institution that is "committed to an educational environment that embraces intellectual and religious freedom while affirming values that arise from a Judeo-Christian understanding of the world." Mercer's website describes its service orientation, in part, as follows:

> Service to humankind is *ingrained* in Mercer culture. It is found in academic units to signature programs like Mercer on Mission that deploy students and faculty across the world to alleviate human suffering. It is found in programs like Mercer Service Scholars, which engages diverse undergraduate students in substantive service to local and international communities. . . . It is found in more than 200,000 hours of volunteer service that students . . . contribute to their communities each year.

The Mercer on Mission program was launched in 2007 and was the result of conversations between the University President and the Director of Religious Life Studies, who subsequently became the Director of the Mercer on Mission program. Despite the program's name and the fact that many programs have partnered with faith-based organizations, Mercer on Mission programs are open to all disciplines and have no requirement to include a faith-based component. In the words of the director, it is a program where "everyone can participate," including people from all disciplines and faith perspectives. As of 2012, 56 service-learning abroad courses had been undertaken, with the majority of programs ($n = 23$) in Africa.

Development, Service-Learning, and Moral Rhetorics of Caring for Strangers

The lines between humanitarianism and development are becoming increasingly blurred as each field has practitioners as diverse as trained economists, medical professionals, faith-based volunteers, celebrities, philanthropists, and non-expert altruists who want to "do good." While Bornstein and Redfield propose that development, human rights, and humanitarianism all have an "impulse to alleviate suffering," Calhoun distinguishes development from humanitarianism as having an agenda for improving the human condition, clarifying that it is not simply a human response to immediate suffering but that there is a larger and longer term goal to improve people's lives (2008, 90). Development, as Bornstein and Redfield (2011, 6) note, "seeks to confront poverty, which is usually defined through material lack, while humanitarianism emphasizes the physical and increasingly psychological condition of suffering people above all else." The authors argue that there is a sensibility that perceives suffering as a preventable tragedy and that humanitarianism includes a structure of feeling, a cluster of moral principles . . . and a call for action" (Bornstein and Redfield 2011, 17). There is no objective definition of suffering, making it difficult for practical actors to agree on courses of actions and schemes of evaluation (Calhoun 2008, 72). This matters because the way we "see" and understand suffering will lead us to envision markedly different solutions to, and our own role in, alleviating or perpetuating suffering and injustice. Faculty leaders on service-learning programs strongly influence or frame how students see suffering, in part through pre-departure coursework. Hypothetically, while students may go on a trip to build a water well in a rural Indian village, they might learn about the lack of water in a village and the consequent health problems that result from a lack of clean drinking water. However, they are not necessarily taught about how Coca Cola has drained and contaminated the water table, or about the gendered and class struggles over access to natural resources that well-building may either alleviate or exacerbate.

The following is an example of what I hope serves as a more contextually aware service-learning course I developed with a colleague in the school of music titled "Tanzania, HIV/AIDS, and Music for Social Change." For the program, we developed a number of learning goals for the two pre-departure courses we taught. We wanted students to become knowledgeable about the layered causes and effects of the spread of HIV in East Africa and how culture, economics, gender relations, and policy all contribute to and work to prevent the spread of HIV/AIDS. We also chose texts to study how musical performance and artistic creation function in the East African context and studied how East African musical and artistic performance initiatives have been used to promote greater health and to combat HIV/AIDS. Being familiar with Tanzanians' subjective narratives on HIV/AIDS, our students were able to be conversant in the lives of Tanzanians and worked with Tanzanian youth to develop plays and musical performances that were then performed at an annual health fair. Our hope is that this type of engagement keeps Tanzanian experiences as/at the center of our service-learning initiatives.

When Mercer on Mission faculty members discuss the goals of the program, they do not speak in terms of reducing suffering but most often foreground the benefits that our students will derive from their participation. When talking about the program's goals, one professor remarked, ". . . the first goal really selfishly is for the benefit of our students . . . but then you know the ethical component is that I don't want to use other people just for the benefit of our students, so my hope is that there is some benefit. . . to the population where we actually go." Another remarked, "The program is set to give students an experience to develop some of their skills and knowledge in a way that utilizes how they've developed in their undergraduate experience and to serve other people." While most faculty members recognize that students are being developed in more ways than the people we serve, a majority also emphasized the aim or hope that we are doing significant development work.

While MoM faculty largely recognize that students are being developed more than our beneficiaries, faculty leaders often challenge the neat separation between development and humanitarianism. For example, in the Mozambique program that worked with artisanal gold miners to reduce their exposure to mercury poisoning, faculty leaders recognized that the long-standing physical suffering involved in exposure to mercury was being compounded by a developmental problem resulting from the trans-border migration of newly impoverished Zimbabweans in search of employment.

Visions of poverty and development are often accompanied by a moral rhetoric to alleviate the suffering of even distant strangers. Lacqueur (2009, 32) notes, "We are . . . more likely today to have sympathy for and even to do something to alleviate the suffering of people . . . distant from ourselves—geographically [and] culturally . . . than were men and women three centuries ago." A strange moral geography arises when students are able to care for strangers far and away while being perfectly capable of ignoring or being ignorant of political injustices like racism and classism that are tied to poverty in their own backyards. Worried, based on my own experiences with students, that poverty is seen as inscribed on the bodies of black- and brown-skinned people in developing countries in a way that is divorced from the global political structures that lead to such deepening inequalities, I asked faculty about why we conduct service projects abroad rather than down the street, in a city that made the national news in 2009 when Forbes named it the seventh poorest city in the United States, and where nearly 30 percent of the adult population is illiterate. In response, nearly all faculty spoke in terms of the "special space," "vantage point," or "liminality" that being in a "totally different context" provides students while at the same time tying these liminal spaces to our students' abilities to see our "common humanity."

These concerns are not lost on other faculty who run programs. The director of Mercer on Mission explained the promise and problems of this liminal space in the following terms:

> Sometimes it takes seeing [poverty] in a foreign context to be able to come back home and see that the same thing is happening here. The levels of impoverishment and injustice are more prominently observable in other contexts. Here's what I mean. In Cambodia, [where Mercer operates a medical clinic] one of the values of this program is that you see advanced pathologies that would never have gotten that far in the U.S. . . . There may be some truth across the program in that the pathologies that we see in other countries are more advanced than perhaps we see them in the U.S., which I hope would sound a warning to our students . . . because this is how bad it can get. I would say that I know that we've failed in our MoM program for the student who comes back and says, "Boy, we've sure got it good here. I'm sure glad I'm home." I know it didn't work for that student.

The causes of poverty discussed by faculty members predominantly echo developmental discourses on "lacks," or what Ferguson describes as depoliticized manifestations of development problems (Ferguson 1999). For example, saying that Cambodians "lack" access to good medical care naturalizes and normalizes this problem without coming to understand the social, political, and economic reasons why this is so.

One professor responded that the causes of poverty in the African country he has brought students to can be explained in terms of "geography, disease, and lack of health care and clean water," while a psychologist's remarks included "the whole issue of women, uneducated women, the fact that when you have impoverished families the kids need to work and can't get educated, sometimes it's resources, like lack of irrigation."

While localizing problems may aid us to focus on envisioning solutions to the particularities of local issues, it also holds the danger of obscuring questions about uneven development, overconsumption by the Global North, and the historical and contemporary geopolitics that contribute to the production of poverty. It can also lead service learners to think along the same lines of one faculty member, who told me, "the thing they need most is our money." Only one faculty member discussed that this depoliticization was a problem, explaining that the Mercer prosthetics program in Vietnam doesn't do enough to explore why we are there in the first place. He remarked, "There's no connection between our engagement in Vietnam and the current market opportunities for U.S. companies or why people there don't have limbs." Envisioning poverty and suffering mainly in terms of developmental lacks can give service-learning students the impression that they have fixed a problem, that the well or house they built has been "finalized" and along the way, students' sense of moral engagement and "doing good" has been satisfied.

Sympathizing and Caring for Strangers as "Doing Good"

I have observed that a visual and aesthetic engagement in caring for strangers through service learning may lead particular programs to gain more traction with donors and for students and faculty alike to feel as though they have "done good." As Kleinman, Das, and Lock note (1997), efforts to reduce suffering have habitually focused on control and repair of individual bodies. Indeed, the program most often mentioned in any university-wide or public event has been the Vietnam program, where medical and engineering students and faculty have designed low-cost prosthetics for Vietnamese amputees. Other popular programs include medical services or housing that result in a visual display of the "good" that has been done. If, as

Rieff (2002) argues, our approach to suffering requires a more personal response grounded in human sympathy, this research suggests that we must be careful to discern how images and vision draw out our sympathies and are tied closely to how we envision caring for strangers and doing good.

Faculty felt it was somehow easier for students to sympathize with people in poverty abroad rather than at home, remarking both on the temporal nature of sympathy involved in a three-week program and because students perceive those in developing countries as the "worthy poor." As a geographer who works in international development stated,

> I think most of our students have a Protestant
> inclination to reach out and help people. It's
> quite different when you see a kid standing in
> dusty Malawi, begging for water. I mean, the
> extremity of that. And to think that you had
> some positive influence to help that one image,
> that one kid, has more power in making you
> feel good about yourself than helping the black
> family down the street who can't pay the water
> bill because they can't do it for themselves.
> That's one reason the international has more
> attraction.

This comment largely resonated with students' narratives about their engagement with international poverty in relation to the program they participated in.[1] Students' responses can be organized into three categories. The majority spoke in terms of students themselves as primary beneficiaries of the program, while the fewest spoke in terms of working with community members. Some of the more common language used in their descriptions are in brackets: The *students as primary beneficiaries* of the program [made me feel gratitude . . . it was eye opening . . . it was challenging . . . it gave me hope . . . it gave me a well-rounded education . . . the kids in Greece taught me . . . It taught me: to love others . . . to give back . . . to cooperate . . . to help people . . . to learn about others. It taught me selflessness. It has warmed my heart. It has helped me grow as an individual]; the *students as givers/educators* [we taught gold miners . . . we "taught about" . . . we fit amputees . . . we gave out medicine . . . we gave food]; and students who spoke in *relational terms/working with host people and communities* [I established friendships and bonds . . . I worked with local doctors].

The language of compassion and the need to care for strangers was structured by faculty leaders of Mercer on Mission programs in terms of developmental progress, a Christian imperative to help the less fortunate, because the stranger acts as a reminder that ours is not the only way, and because strangers are a "blank slate," making it harder for us to bring our assumptions about them to the table. The idea being expressed here was that it might be easier to find compassion for a person whose circumstances you know *less* about, because not knowing will prevent you from bringing your prejudices to bear on "why" they are poor. The stranger, in the words of one faculty, helps us to be more honest. Only one faculty member spoke of caring for strangers as a pathway to link up to issues of social justice. She stated, "If caring for a stranger enables you to see others equally deserving of care and concern *and* your political activism, to recognize structural and racial inequality, yeah, then it's a great gateway." Students, on the other hand, most often spoke in terms of developmental utilitarianism, bettering people's lives, or filling a need that moves people from point A to point B. Faculty and students in the United States engaged with service learning would do well to think along the lines of the director of the MoM program, who responded to the value of caring for strangers in this way:

> I benefit from helping the stranger. Because
> I'm able to assert and confirm my own capacity
> to be of value to another person. There's an
> additional value of the decentering that happens
> when you help someone else. When you
> use the word "sympathize." If you are really
> *cum pathos*, if you are feeling with them, then
> there's a sense in which your world has expanded.
> You've taken into your own soul, mind,
> whatever, the experiences of another. I go back
> to our conversation about Margaret Mead's first
> sign of civilization, the healed femur. There is
> something that enlarges my world when there's
> more than just me. And being able to put the
> interests, the well-being, of another person in
> conversation with my own self-interest, keeps
> me away from the terminal egotism that makes
> my life very small when it's only me, and I'm
> consumed by self-interest. I'm trying to grow
> into the awareness that there is no stranger.
> Stranger is a concoction of the darker side of
> my fears and ignorance that allows me to see

someone else as other, when I'm not sure that's a distinction that I can live with. I want to be increasingly aware of the us-ness of all of humanity. So stranger is having less and less currency with me. . . . I think it was Maya Angelou who said, "I am a human, and nothing human can be alien to me."

This type of caring is a starting point, a cultivated disposition, that must be complemented by rigorous study, the willingness to listen, and the humility to recognize that our hosts are often doing it better than we can. In my interviews with students, a majority did not comment on their course preparation for their service projects and when prompted to, nearly 50 percent said that they did not find it very useful. There were however, a specific few programs that were lauded by students for their in-class preparation beforehand. Faculty leaders have a great responsibility to carefully link coursework with service activities and in requiring and encouraging students toward substantial background reading

before departure. It is a lot to ask for a two-week pre-departure course, but ethical engagement demands at least this much from us.

Conclusion

At its best, service-learning abroad encourages students to undertake the type of active, slow, engaging seeing that Lacqueur claims is central to the creation of sentiment, in keeping someone else within ethical range (2009, 40). Anthropologists and other scholars of humanitarianism and development are poised to contribute to such programs in our ability to at once link the local, subjective experiences with poverty to the broader global forces that help shape and produce those lives. At the same time that our students learn about our "common humanity" they can be encouraged to think hard about the social, political, and economic injustices that have led some to be able to more fully express their humanity than others.

Notes

[1.] This data is based on surveys with students and MoM student videos, many of which you can find on YouTube. The survey question

evaluated here was: "Do you think the [country] program was a success? If so, in what ways? If not, why?"

References

Bornstein, Erica, and Peter Redfield. 2011. *Forces of Compassion: Humanitarianism Between Ethics and Politics*. Santa Fe: SAR Press.

Calhoun, Craig. 2008. "The Imperative to Reduce Suffering: Charity, Progress, and Emergencies in the Field of Humanitarian Action." In *Humanitarianism in Question: Politics, Power,Ethics*, edited by Michael Barnett and Thomas G. Weiss, 73–97. Ithaca, NY: Cornell University Press.

Ferguson, James. 1999. *The Anti-Politics Machine: Development, Depoliticization and Bureaucratic Power in Lesotho*. Minneapolis: University of Minnesota Press.

Kleinman, Arthur, Veena Das, and Margaret Lock (eds.). 1997. *Social Suffering*. Berkeley: University of California Press.

Lacqueur, Thomas W. 2009. "Mourning, Pity, and the Work of Narrative." In *Humanitarianism and Suffering: The Mobilization of Empathy*, edited by Richard Wilson and Richard Brown, 31–57. Cambridge: Cambridge University Press.

Mercer University. 2015. "A Student Guide to Service-Learning." Retrieved from https://community.mercer.edu/mu-community/service/upload/Student-Guide-to-Service-Learning.pdf.

Rieff, David. 2002. *A Bed for the Night: Humanitarianism in Crisis*. New York: Simon and Schuster.

9.5 Housing Interests: Developing Community in a Globalizing City

JACQUELINE COPELAND-CARSON

Globalization, or the widening, deepening, and quickening movement of people, ideas, images, money, and goods across and within national borders, has accelerated cross-cultural interaction. The social, political, and economic fabric of U.S. cities is being reshaped due to rising numbers of immigrants, refugees, and transnational migrants, who bring with them their own cultural behaviors, norms, and beliefs. Minneapolis-St. Paul (the Twin Cities area), in Minnesota, which is featured in this section, has undergone terrific transformations with respect to the rising number of African immigrant communities. Practicing anthropologist Jacqueline Copeland-Carson details how, as part of her work with the U. S. Department of Housing and Urban Development (HUD), she sought to design culturally appropriate mortgage tools for immigrant communities, addressing their cultural prohibition against paying or receiving interest. Her account shows the immense value and practical impact anthropologists can have in the public and private sectors to advance social justice goals in access to housing and other basic needs.

Questions

1. How did Copeland-Carson employ her skills as an anthropologist during her work as a community development fellow with HUD?
2. What is riba-free financing, and why is it important culturally?
3. How is globalization affecting the nature of cities?

. . . Global flows of people, technology, ideas, and capital have fundamentally changed local communities, and the U.S. is no exception. Immigrants and refugees, especially from countries in Africa, Asia, and Latin America, are reshaping the face of U.S. communities. Newcomers, like generations of U.S. immigrants before them, bring new energy and resources to communities, revitalizing declining urban neighborhoods and increasing tax revenues. At the same time, their language and cultural diversity can present new challenges for public and private institutions attempting to provide basic housing and other services. Migration has long been a key force in globalization. However, reactions to the increasing immigration of racial and religious minorities such as Muslims in the late twentieth century have created especially visceral tensions. Today U.S. community development anthropologists work to help cities adapt to this new diversity, including expanding housing and economic opportunity to immigrants. . . .

An Anthropological Perspective on U.S. Community Development

Community development is a multifaceted field with varied definitions. Essentially, it is the planned, systematic effort to improve a place or people's quality of life, power, or economic opportunity. Although in the U.S. the field has roots in the early twentieth-century settlement house movement, community development became a movement in the post–Civil Rights era as the country attempted to address Jim Crow's legacies of concentrated ghettos and rural poverty.

Today, like its international development counterpart, it has become a full-fledged industry with many disciplines and subfields. Some community development anthropologists focus on housing, economics, environment, social services, or some combination of issues. Cutting across these subfields is the array of public and private institutions that implement such activities, including multilateral bodies, government agencies, for-profit or nonprofit corporations, grassroots voluntary organizations, religious groups, and others. . . .

Regardless of the particular type of community development that anthropologists engage with, there are common ties that bind us. Community development anthropologists specialize in the social and cultural dynamics of housing and economic development and change—what is often called "the human factor." As is the case with applied anthropologists working in many fields, we recognize that cultural values, power, and social structures all influence community prospects. Thus, instead of just developing urban policy, buildings, or finance, we consider how different institutions and social groups have diverse agendas, needs, or interests that need to be considered. . . .

The impact of sociocultural issues is becoming more recognized in community development as globalization and migration intensify. Immigrants and refugees not only bring new languages, foods, and ethnicities. They also bring new community development practices. For example, although this is obvious to the handful of scholars who study these issues and residents who practice them, immigrants, refugees, and people of color give money and time—called "philanthropy" and "volunteerism"—for collective goals and projects just as the majority community does. Often these are ancient practices adapted to contemporary needs. For example, rotating savings clubs are a major immigrant and refugee resource for community development off the radar screen of many professionals in the field. Immigrants and refugees send remittances not only to assist extended family members, but also to build schools and clinics and provide other services in the world's poorest regions. . . . Globalizing cultural influences do not stop at community development finance. For example, foundations and other public funders are very interested in knowing whether the nonprofit agencies they fund are representative of their communities. Their leaders, however, are not necessarily knowledgeable about clan or ethnic dynamics that might influence nonprofit governance and representation, and foundations are not typically diverse enough to have experts from these communities on their staffs or boards, which deprives them of an important source of cultural knowledge and competence.

Community development anthropologists can help cities resolve globalization's challenges in many ways, including identifying new needs; uncovering social innovations from many cultures to address them; creating policies, programs, and procedures for the times; and designing, managing, or evaluating such programs. The case presented here examines how I convened Muslim and Christian religious leaders, activists, nongovernmental organizations (NGOs), foundations, bankers, the Minneapolis Federal Reserve, and the U.S. Department of Housing and Urban Development (HUD) to understand and accept non-interest-based finance, a longstanding, ancient practice in Islamic countries, to promote homeownership and business opportunities for its growing Somali immigrant community as well as others who had cultural prohibitions against paying or receiving interest.

Case Example: Profile of a Globalizing City (ca. 2000)

In the 1990s, the Twin Cities of Minnesota, the largely liberal land of Vice President Hubert Humphrey and Governor Jesse Ventura as well as Senators Paul Wellstone and Al Franken, lovingly gibed in the stories of Garrison Keillor, underwent a dramatic demographic shift that is still reshaping its civic discourse and culture.

During the 1990s, Minnesota's unemployment rate was about 2 percent—the lowest in the country. There was a labor shortage even for the most entry-level positions, with companies providing signing bonuses to attract bank tellers and meat packers. These booming economic conditions, including one of the highest concentrations of Fortune 500 companies (Target, Land O' Lakes, General Mills, and Medtronic are all headquartered there), relatively low crime levels, strong public infrastructure, an active religious community, and a longstanding Scandinavian-based ethic of "Minnesota Nice" emphasizing civic engagement, social responsibility, philanthropy, and mutual support, attracted millions of people from throughout the U.S. and the world. Notwithstanding the fact that in July 2011, Minnesota had to shut down many basic government services due to budget shortfalls, from the 1970s through 1990s it had a well-deserved national reputation as what a 1973 cover story from *Time* magazine titled "Minnesota: A State that Works" (American Scene 1973).

Starting in the 1990s, the region experienced a dramatic growth in its African refugee and immigrant population, including mostly Somalis but also significant numbers of Ethiopians, Sudanese, Nigerians, Kenyans, Sierra Leoneans, Ghanaian, and others. By the 2000 U.S. Census, the Twin Cities had the nation's most diverse black population based on ethnicity and country of origin, including one of the highest concentrations of college-educated blacks as well as the country's largest Somali, Hmong, Tibetan refugee, and urban Native American communities. Not all newcomers were immigrants or refugees from other countries. Overall, during a two-decade period, Minnesota had one of the country's highest levels of in-migration. Included were professionals from all over the country, as well as low-income people from declining industrial areas in midwestern cities such as Gary, Indiana, and Chicago, diversifying the region politically, culturally, and ethnically and drawing it more tightly to the global economy.

Although the newcomers were seeking the good life in Minnesota, long-time Minnesotans were not always so sure how much they wanted to share it. It is easier to be liberal and accepting in a community where, as a *Wall Street Journal* reporter writing about the state's unprecedented demographic changes in a 1999 article noted, "a mixed marriage once meant the marriage of a Norwegian and a Swede" (Johnson 1997). This globalizing urban area began experiencing new pressures that were even more challenging, given its different racial makeup, than the Great Migration of mostly Europeans to the area in the early twentieth century. Employers had to determine how to allow

Muslim employees to pray during the work day, as required by Islam, while respecting the rights of non-Muslim workers too; YMCAs had to decide whether to let Muslim girls swim in their scarves and full body coverings, as required by Islam's modesty principles; high schools had to resolve sometimes violent tensions between African-American and African immigrant students, while school districts had to educate students representing almost 80 different languages. Lawyers had to determine how to advocate for Hmong women escaping arranged or polygamous marriages. Bankers had to figure out if and how to open checking accounts for undocumented Latino business owners. City health officials had to determine whether African hair-braiding shops should be subject to cosmetology laws that did not take such practices into account. And social service officials had to respond to a growing and alarming Native American teen suicide rate as young people felt caught between the worlds of the hardcore inner city and the reservation.

This period of accelerated social change was fraught with challenges but also new possibilities. The fabric of Minnesota's good life was seriously tested as its communities responded to the new diversity as the 1990s and 2000s unfolded. A racially charged mayoral race unseated the two-term African-American female mayor of Minneapolis. So-called "white flight" from urban public schools grew as neighborhoods and student bodies became more diverse and, coincidentally, public education funding declined, eroding the state's once touted educational system. There were growing and alarming disparities between minority and white Minnesotans along almost every social indicator.

Social Innovation in the Twin Cities

Despite these pressures . . . enterprising newcomers, along with their more established Twin Cities partners, created new ways to build communities. During this period, a number of high-profile initiatives emerged as leaders attempted to shape these new public issues. These efforts attempted to build bridges between newcomer and established communities, incorporate immigrants and refugees, and address the growing concentrations of poverty, especially in communities of color. Immigrants and refugees opened small businesses along declining inner city commercial corridors, slowly reviving them and their surrounding neighborhoods. Service providers, with the help of public and private funders, convened to address unmet immigrant/refugee service needs. Corporate leaders recognized that newcomer communities were also new markets that they could tap. . . .

Supported by a booming economy and expanded philanthropic funding, Hmong, African, and Latino newcomers also created nonprofits to address their community needs and tap the new markets they brought for social innovation donations. . . . The combined entrepreneurial and social sector activity in this then-thriving economy, along with gains in education, eventually catapulted many new immigrants/refugees into the middle class at the same time the concentration of poverty in the region's U.S.- and foreign-born communities of color continued. . . .

Unlearning Mortgage "Sins"

Since my anthropology and urban planning graduate school days in the early 1980s, I had studied and practiced community development with a focus on housing, first in Nigeria, West Africa, and later throughout the U.S. I was particularly interested in culturally appropriate housing development as well as diversity, community formation, and social networks in cities throughout the world. . . . I had worked for many years as a foundation executive who designed, managed, and funded initiatives to address social issues, such as reducing poverty and promoting homeownership, jobs, and other wealthbuilding strategies. But despite all my exposure to cross-cultural community development issues, I was not quite prepared for what I encountered when I started working with HUD's Twin Cities office.

In the late 1990s, the Clinton/Gore administration, recognizing that the new pressures of globalization and demographic and other socioeconomic change in U.S. cities might have outpaced federal agencies' capacity to keep pace, created the Community Builders Fellowship Program. This was part of the administration's effort to reform and improve federal services. . . . Fellows were selected from a national applicant pool of interdisciplinary development professionals to be full-time two-year internal consultants who would create new initiatives that integrated and updated HUD's programs.

I was selected to be one of these Community Builders Fellows. Given my interest and experience in housing development, I decided to support FHA's Faith-based Homeownership Initiative, created by the administration to do outreach about FHA mortgages and other tools to expand homeownership in low-income communities.

Thinking like a typical anthropologist, I interpreted "faith" in broad terms to mean the various religious traditions represented in a community. I developed a list of diverse religious leaders, including Christian ministers, Muslim imams, rabbis, and others, to whom I should speak to let them know how FHA-backed mortgages could help low-income congregants become successful homeowners. I also wanted to learn more about their communities' housing issues and get advice on how FHA could better publicize and explain its programs.

I was initially shocked and confused when a prominent Somali Imam whom I interviewed early on told me, "Well, it's great that the government has all these ways to help struggling people buy homes. But in my community, all these mortgages and interest will just send people to hell. Getting a mortgage is a sin" (Somali imam explaining the community's reluctance to take on mortgages, personal communication, 1999).

Others explained that there was great ethical conflict and debate among Minnesota Muslims about how to resolve the conundrum of a growing need and market demand for homeownership and the lack of culturally appropriate mortgage products. Some segments of the community took a "when in Rome do as the Romans do" approach, sometimes receiving special dispensation from their imams to take on the sin of a mortgage because no other finance options were available in the U.S. Others would pool resources with extended family members and attempt to pay cash for a home. I even met a devout Muslim and successful architect, earning well into six figures, who was still a renter because he had been saving money for almost 15 years so he could pay cash to buy a house in Minnesota's thriving and increasingly expensive market.

As I continued my conversations with many imams and activists in the state's diverse Muslim community, I discovered that for many the Koran prohibited both the payment and receipt of interest. In fact, a rabbi also told me of a small Orthodox Jewish community in a Minneapolis suburb with a similar interpretation of the Talmud. He explained that "strictly speaking, Judaism renders all interest as inherently usurious because it . . . just involves a privileged class taking advantage of a poor class. It creates permanent debtors and creditors and is not good for society" (Twin Cities rabbi explaining Judaism's perspective on usury, personal communication, October 1, 1999).

Through outreach to ministers active in the housing justice movement, I also learned that this same strict interpretation of the Bible was a driving force in the original formation of Habitat for Humanity, the Christian-based housing NGO made famous by Jimmy Carter that uses sweat equity, donations, and grants to build houses for low-income families throughout the world and provides interest-free mortgages. So a social equity philosophy, rooted in faith, was the basis of many Minnesota Muslims', Orthodox Jews', and some Christian groups' aversion to either paying or receiving interest.

. . . As I continued my exploration, I decided to talk with an African-American imam who also happened to be the director of a nonprofit housing development agency. . . . He explained, "You see, for many Muslims the Koran teaches that this time value of money thing is just a way that rich people made up to rip off poor people. Money is just a piece of paper. It has no tangible value on its own, unlike this chair or this table that has a real value" (African-American Imam and director of a nonprofit housing development agency, personal communication, 1998).

The look of consternation on my face must have been clear, because he went on to give me an example that helped me to finally grasp the issue.

> Maybe this will help you understand. You are a *homeowner,* right? But think about it, do you really *own* that house? Every month you pay the bank more than the house is worth for the right to live there. And you'll probably end up paying for the next 30 years. So, you don't really own anything right now. The bank really owns your house. This is the fundamental problem many Muslims have with paying interest period—for a house, a car, a business. They know they don't necessarily own anything; they just own debt (African-American Imam and director of a nonprofit housing development agency, personal communication, 1999).

Although certainly an overstatement for educational effect, with hindsight, the irony and wisdom of this imam's core cautions about the potential dangers of interest-bearing mortgages seemed prophetic of the 2007–2010 U.S. foreclosure and predatory lending crises. This moment of epiphany helped me to understand how something as seemingly fundamental as paying interest—an article of faith for most Americans and certainly anyone in the community development field—was a real religious and cultural taboo for many Minnesota Muslims and others. The Minnesota housing industry, and indeed, most of the country, was proceeding as if interest-based mortgages were the universal means of purchasing a home, although clearly they were not.

From Epiphany to Systems Change

However, making the case to HUD officials—let alone banking and philanthropic leaders—would require more than my sharing the stories of Minnesota religious minorities who felt the system did not provide the tools necessary for them to become homeowners. . . . Despite some staff members' initial reservations, fortunately, the HUD office's senior leadership was committed to ensuring that it was serving the entire public, as were other public officials who eventually became partners.

Essentially, I mixed anthropological methods such as ethnographic interviewing, participant observation, and cross-cultural comparisons with the compilation of demographic and market data to prove my case and build alliances. The first step was to further my knowledge of cross-cultural finance, particularly in Muslim countries and communities throughout the world, as interest-free loans were not yet a common option in the United States. . . .

Without getting deeply into all the technical details of interest-free or, in Arabic, riba-free financing, there is an ancient tradition of equitybased financing in all the world's major religions. Essentially, riba-free principles prohibit not only the payment of interest but all potentially exploitative financial practices, such as derivatives and predatory lending. A financier would buy a house, business, or other capital asset at what might be best understood as a wholesale price, adding a markup that would include fees for concrete administrative services and a profit.

The financier would sell the house to a buyer, who is considered a coinvestor; the buyer then pays back the loan and fees in agreed-upon installments. Because these various fees are for real assets—that is, not for what would be considered an artificial commodity like interest, the time value of money—they are considered an equity investment, which is allowed in Islam, producing an ethical and legitimate profit. It is broadly similar to a lease-purchase agreement in U.S. terms. . . .

Riba-free Islamic finance has been growing worldwide, fueled both by the growth of Islam as well as concerns about escalating national and personal debt, as Western-based finance systems penetrate the world's markets. . . .

After providing myself a basic education in riba-free financing, the second step was to assemble the demographic data to describe the United States' and Minnesota's potential riba-free mortgage market. I convened an advisory body of Muslim clerics, activists, nonprofit leaders, and realtors as well as non-Muslim foundation officials, bankers, and federal agency representatives, most notably the Minneapolis Federal Reserve Bank and Fannie Mae, establishing a "Cross-Cultural Mortgage Finance Working Group."

Although recruiting Muslim clerics and activists was not difficult, as they were delighted that someone was taking up their cause, attracting bankers was another matter altogether. Let's just say that even the term "non-interest-based mortgage" was an oxymoron to many in the initiative's formative stages. Eventually, however, I was able to sustain the working group, which met for a year under HUD auspices to learn about the cultural barriers to homeownership for religious minorities and the various types of alternative finance strategies. This involved my acting as a sort of research center, compiling and translating cross-cultural finance information and data about Minnesota's growing Muslim market.

I did not, of course, use the terms "anthropological" or "ethnographic" in any of this work. Instead, various euphemisms such as "culturally appropriate financing," "cultural markets," or "cultural communities" were sufficient to convince public officials and bankers that the need for riba-free mortgages was real for this "market" even though this was only a semantic issue for non-Muslims. Basically, I facilitated what anthropologists would call an "emic" perspective on mortgage finance.

Part of our strategy was to build a public profile for our work to legitimize religious minorities' homeownership needs as a tool of inclusion and not special interests. The initiative was designed to organize a series of high-profile public meetings about the community's homeownership needs, put in terms of both new market opportunities as well as the need to expand economic opportunity for low-income minorities. Meeting agendas typically involved participants sharing stories of "culture clashes," as devout Muslims of various backgrounds attempted to finance their mortgages in a system that did not provide a sufficient array of options. One participant, a Muslim Nigerian realtor, shared the stories of clients who were perpetual renters because of these barriers. Another, a Somali single mother with a household that included six children and two elders, and whose husband had died in her home country's long civil war, told of the inherent challenges of finding suitable rentals that would accept large families. . . .

Over time, these stories—auto-ethnographic vignettes, really—combined with my research briefs documenting similar issues in other cities to create a kind of culturally immersive experience for public officials and funders. It had the practical effect, as well, of extending and diversifying all participants' social networks, providing more direct access to the community's leadership for the grassroots participants, and more connections to a new constituency's leadership for the public officials. . . .

During the course of our year-long cross-sector education and industry awareness process, the Hennepin County Government, also a working group member, created a non-interest-based financing tool for its tax-forfeited sale program (homes essentially repossessed by the government for long-term failure to pay property taxes). This was probably the first such program by a branch of Minnesota government and by a member of our working group. Our collaborative study and outreach led to our holding a technical conference co-hosted by the Federal Reserve in 2000. Much of my conference design work involved selecting presenters who could credibly present a range of new non-interest-based mortgage models that were emerging in various parts of the United States. Several of the expert presenters were U.S.-born Muslim converts, including African Americans and white Americans who were experts in culturally appropriate financing vehicles. Other conference design challenges were providing for Muslim prayer and dietary restrictions while being sensitive to the needs of nonMuslim participants, all in a conference and catering center located at the Minneapolis Federal Reserve building. In addition, advised by the Muslim participants, I was careful not to choose a date that conflicted with religious observances, especially Ramadan, a period requiring fasting during the day for Muslims. Prayer needs were accommodated using a technique I had witnessed in religiously diverse regions of Nigeria. I set aside gender-specific contemplation rooms that anyone could use for activities that required some level of privacy, including nursing, meditation, or prayer.

Thus, even the meeting design required cultural sensitivity, listening to both the needs and ideas of diverse working group participants. . . .

Soon after the conference, my HUD fellowship expired. However, an expanded working group continued to meet, sponsored by the Federal Reserve's community relations department, ultimately culminating in a non-interest-based mortgage pilot developed by the Fannie Mae Foundation, a key working group partner. And, as noted by Wafiq Fannoun, one of our working group members and a Muslim community development specialist interviewed for this case study, "Today there are many riba-free tools for Muslims. But that wasn't true in these early days. The HUD working group brought the issue to the attention of the broader community, making it possible to do something about it" (Mutombu 2005). Later in the 2000s, an enterprising Somali banker, Hussein Samatar, who had been an officer with a major bank in the region, created the African Development Corporation (www.adc.org), a nonprofit development corporation specializing in these riba-free financing instruments. This organization has become a major force in promoting homeownership and small business development in the region's African immigrant community. Also, a long-time community development advocate, Mike Temali, director of the Neighborhood Development Center (www.ndc.org), created one of the country's first domestic riba-free business finance loan programs, although Saudi-backed banks in the United Kingdom had been providing such loans in the U.S. since the 1990s. A booming economy no doubt made it easier for both nonprofit and corporate financiers to create such products. Despite 9/11, growing prejudice against even law-abiding Muslims, and the economic decline, interest-free finance programs became an established alternative to conventional financing by the end of the first decade of the new millennium, albeit still used by a minority of Minnesotans and other Americans.

Islamic finance, because it did not charge interest, escaped some of the pitfalls of the conventional, interest-based finance systems that almost brought down the world's economy. By 2010, there were $500 billion in riba-free loan assets in the United States, and the market was booming.

However, it is not without controversy. There are those who argue that the fees and markups charged by these loans are merely interest in other cultural clothing. Furthermore, some claim that fees charged to U.S.-based riba-free purchasers is either just as expensive or, in some cases, more expensive than their conventional finance counterparts. Thus, Islamic or other alternative finance may, in some cases, be as exploitative as the supposedly usurious loans they are supposed to counterbalance. Moreover, it is not clear if such riba-free financed loans in the United States have lower foreclosure rates than interest-based ones. Nonetheless, at least in Minnesota, religious minorities and others with interest-free requirements have an expanded set of choices, all monitored by federal agencies and fair-lending activists, to finance businesses and homes.

Lessons Learned for Applied Global Anthropology and Beyond

Searching for Inclusion

Even though anthropology does not always practice it well, the field is strongly shaped by a social justice philosophy. Anthropology students are taught that diversity is a cultural resource. Sometimes in a particular power system or historical moment, cultural difference can become a barrier to social justice or even basic survival. Our basic orientation as anthropologists, however, is to promote inclusion, pushing the public—as presented through policies, institutions, and officials—to encompass all social groups. One never knows when what was once seen as a "fringe" or marginal cultural practice, such as the growing worldwide use of interest-free loans or microfinance during credit-restricted times, might help a broader constituency. Just as biologists promote biodiversity as a natural resource, anthropologists promote diverse cultural practices as a way to help people survive and adapt to changing times. We not only celebrate and promote cultural variation, but we also, as the cliché goes, promote "unity in diversity"—the notion that people from different backgrounds can define common goals and interests. Working together, they can learn from each other, breaking down barriers of race, class, religion, and ethnicity to build mutual networks of support and community. Certainly, these basic anthropological principles of diversity and inclusion drove my initial interest in ensuring that the needs of religious minorities were included in homeownership financing policies and products. In the community development and philanthropy field, this cross-cultural bridge-building is often called either "community convening" or "cross-sector convening." Using the terms familiar to the nonprofit, philanthropic, and corporate stakeholders involved in the project was critical to its success, even though the anthropological side of my brain certainly conceptualized it as a means to increase cross-cultural understanding while expanding economic opportunity.

The Power of a Cross-Cultural Lens

. . . The basic culture concept in anthropology—that social groups have differing worldviews that are true for them even if they contradict the researcher's own experience—is fundamental to understanding and addressing the cultural barriers that can arise as cities become more diverse and global. This principle enabled me to eventually understand that riba-free mortgages were a legitimate need in the Somali market. The approach also helped me to present interestbased mortgages not only as an economic tool, but as a "culturally specific way of financing the purchase of capital assets," as I often explained it to bankers. Furthermore, it enabled me to translate these needs into the cultures and languages of the government, foundations, and banking to craft a legitimate social justice and business argument for interest-free housing. A cross-cultural lens also allowed me to patiently listen to the perspective of some development industry peers that it was a temporary community need that would pass with assimilation. Applying the culture concept as a framework to understand and build common ground across these conflicting interests and perceptions was essential to the initiative's success. . . .

Conclusions: Toward a Translocal Community Development Praxis

In the past 30 years, U.S. community development has become an industry with a wide range of conventional

wisdom and core practices that are often taken for granted. But cultural change has accelerated for everyone in the globalizing city. Just as anthropologists can no longer take for granted that the majority represents a community's needs and norms, community development specialists cannot presume that their conventional tools will work in diverse cultural populations. . . . Community development practitioners, whatever their training and background, need to become more cross-culturally competent to be effective in globalizing contexts, even in such seemingly "culture-proof" arenas as housing finance and economic development. . . .

The Twin Cities have become what anthropologist Arjun Appadurai describes as "translocalities," world cities at the nexus of global flows of people, ideas, and resources (Appadurai 1996; Copeland-Carson 2004). . . . Today, more than ever before, social life in U.S. neighborhoods is at once local and global. Basic community development notions, such as "community" as geographically defined, or interest-based finance, are not givens. People are remixing their concepts of identity, community, and development itself as the global and local meet in America's cities. . . .

A "translocal" perspective, sensitive to cultural and other innovations emerging in globalized cities and how they can be used as tools of resistance and social transformation, can expand opportunities, not only for immigrants but for all residents. To work effectively in globalizing contexts, we must practice a kind of translocal anthropology: sensitive to the intersections, intercultural collisions, and new energy created when the local and global meet. . . . With such a lens, we can help policy makers and even grassroots leaders see and resolve emerging community challenges that may be hidden in plain view. . . .

References

American Scene. 1973. Minnesota: A State that Works. Time Magazine, August 13. Available at: http://www.time.com/time/magazine/article/0,9171,907665,00.html (accessed July 7, 2011).

Appadurai, Arjun. 1996. Modernity at Large: Cultural Dimensions of Globalization. Minneapolis: University of Minnesota Press.

Copeland-Carson, Jacqueline. 2004. Creating Africa in America: Translocal Identity in an Emerging World City. Philadelphia: University of Pennsylvania Press.

Johnson, Dirk. 1997. Ethnic Change Tests Mettle of Minneapolis Liberalism. *Wall Street Journal*, October 18, pp. A1 , A8.

Mutombu, Chingwell. 2005. Notes from Case Study Interview with Wafiq Fannoun, Former Cross-Cultural Mortgage Finance Working Group Member, U.S. Department of Housing and Urban Development, 2000.

9.6 Re-Working the Institution of *Waqf* (Islamic Trust) for the Financial Sustainability of Information Technology Schemes in Morocco

HSAIN ILAHIANE

Assuming technology may be a facilitator of community development, how do anthropologists help address deficiencies in technology adoption in places without sufficient economic resources and infrastructure support? The following case study provides a concrete example of applied anthropology, allowing students to track a project from its conception (research goal) to an anthropologist's chosen methods for data collection, to the study's findings and practical outcomes. In this selection, Hsain Ilahiane reports on a project he conducted in Morocco while serving as a visiting researcher for the People and Practices Research Lab of Intel Corporation. He considers how the Muslim institution of waqf, or the endowment of personal property for the benefit of some good cause, may serve as a mechanism to provide sustainable exposure and adoption of these new technologies. This piece pairs well with Copeland-Carson's consideration of culturally appropriate financing in the Twin Cities.

Questions

1. Define the religious institutions *zakat* and *waqf*. What are their roles in social service provisions?
2. Discuss the role of ICT in community development.
3. What are the purposes of *madrasas*? Why are they being reformed in Morocco?
4. How did Ilahiane "put anthropology to use" in addressing his research problem?

Research Problem

This case study explores the potentially productive relationship between Islamic charitable institutions and information technology to grow and to support self-sustaining community development throughout the Muslim world. There are more than 1.5 billion Muslims worldwide. To non-Muslims, Islam may appear just like any of the other world religions. It is mostly understood as consisting of going to services on one day, practicing daily religious rituals, and perhaps reading a holy book through the week for the most pious. However, in Muslim countries, Islam informs and structures the daily socio-cultural, economic and political lives of Muslims,

from food habits and dress code to dating and marriage practices, to worship guidelines and finance arrangements, to politics, friends and family ethos. Islam is not *just a religion; it is a way of life*. In fact, Islam strives to direct the lives of individuals, as well as societies, to the worship of the One God (called Allah in Arabic) and to leave no domain, in the unfolding human activities, exempt from the authority of the divine law embodied in the *Qur'an* (Muslim holy book) and *Sunnah* (deeds and sayings of the Prophet Mohamed). Ideally, this means that no community or society can possibly have any institutions other than religious ones (Rahman 2002).

Two of these religious institutions are *zakat* and *waqf*. *Zakat* (alms-giving) is an obligatory charity and a vital element of community building and strengthening. As the only "tax" demanded of Muslims by Quranic law, its amount is fixed, according to the nature of goods, at 2.5% of one's yearly gains among Sunni Muslims. *Zakat* is also one of the five basic tenets of Islam and it is handed over to the public agency of Islamic endowments and affairs (Mannan 1986). Connected to the practice of *zakat* is the institution of *waqf* or mortmain endowments. *Waqf* is an endowment of personal property which is dedicated in perpetuity for the benefit of some good cause and represents an elaborate pattern of institutional religious foundations also called Islamic Trust or pious foundations. The institution of *waqf* is one of the most typical institutions of Muslim society. A waqf asset cannot be sold or bought and its benefits are used for specific purposes, which are charitable in nature. Revenue yield is essential to the institution of *waqf*. Ever since the advent of Islam, *zakat* and *waqf* have served as major providers of social services and economic assets in a decentralized approach to Muslim society. While obligatory and voluntary charity deals with economic inequalities by adopting a redistributive framework, *waqf* can be used to enhance the capabilities of the poor by providing them access to education, health, and other resources and skills for sustainable livelihood systems (Çizakça 2000). *Zakat* and *waqf* assets are estimated to total between $250 billion and $1 trillion annually (USAID 2005, 1).

Separately and much more recently, an increasing number of researchers and practitioners have identified information and communications technologies (ICT) as a key tool for community-based economic development (Heeks 2008 and 2002; ITU 2006; Siochrú and Girard 2005; UNDP 2001). Digital technologies (e.g., Internet, CD-ROMs, personal digital assistants, interactive television and voice response systems, telecenters and information kiosks, wireless computing, mobile phones, and community radios) have been shown to improve services and create added-value applications that in turn foster local development. Digital platforms offer the potential for enhanced reach to underserved and poor populations, at relatively low cost, offering scalability, time efficiency, and ability to customize. Improvements in livelihoods at the household and community levels not only benefit from improved access to communication and information but may also contribute to the social and economic sustainability of digital initiatives.

Unfortunately, most of the existing models provided by international donor agencies for community-based

ICT have not been sufficient to foster widespread adoption and tend to produce a very low ratio of benefits to costs in the context of the poor. It has also been recognized that donors investing in the developing world tend to favor large-scale, capital- and foreign exchange–intensive projects (Best and Kumar 2008; Hudson 2006; James 2006 Sen 1985). Equally important is the role played by donors' oversight of existing institutions and unawareness of the potential value of these institutions to sustainable business models of technology diffusion and adoption. The fundamental problem is that while some aspects of this technology transfer can be useful, others simply tend to be irrelevant to the technology needs of the poor and their socio-economic and cultural system. Limited availability of capital and lack of appreciation of culturally embedded institutions prevent widespread technology investment. Beyond capital there are other barriers as well. These include limitations of access based on gender, age or simply location; irregular electricity supply; lack of connectivity; lack of requisite forms of literacy; or simply lack of familiarity with technology. As a result, many community technology initiatives (e.g., telecenters or village kiosks), while promising, have failed to reach self-sustainability or generate momentum to scale beyond initial implementations.

My goal was to address a significant current deficiency in technology delivery systems and platforms in rural and urban applications by examining the linkages between digital interventions and sustainable financial models. Specifically, I identified a viable and predictable business model for engaging self-sustaining community development appropriate to the realities of Muslim societies. My objective, which was the next step toward attainment of my long-term goal, was to assess the social and economic consequences of *waqf* principles on the financial sustainability and replicability of technology delivery interventions. My rationale was that its successful completion will allow for the development of a new business model appropriate for technology diffusion and adoption as well as provide donor-funded initiatives a new approach to account for existing organizations and resources, resulting in productive and self-sustaining communities. To accomplish the overall objective of this proposed work I pursued the following specific objectives:

1. To understand and identify best practices of *waqf* and *zakat* funded institutions.

2. To discover new opportunities and approaches to engage these time-honored institutions for technology adoption.

3. To generate a new business model for sustainable ICT projects in resource-poor areas of the Muslim world and beyond.

In sum, *waqf* presents an opportunity to change this situation. By leveraging both large financial assets and culturally embedded institutions, *waqf* might enable much wider technology adoption and diffusion throughout the Muslim world. As a facilitator of community development, technology could come to be seen as a legitimate destination for charitable donations. Technology implementations associated with charitable organizations and institutions in the community might better overcome the cultural and educational obstacles to the adoption of computing. In addition, proper placement of technologies in established institutions might overcome a lack of infrastructure, and ensure exposure and sustainability.

Why Morocco?

Morocco is located on the northwest coast of Africa, with a population of 31 million, in a geographic climate that ranges from the southern Saharan deserts, through the mountain highlands, to the arable northern coastal plains and plateaus (similar to California geography and climate). Morocco's population has become increasingly concentrated in urban areas, primarily in centers of industrial activities, crafts production, mining, agriculture and fisheries, and tourism development.

Morocco is a Muslim-majority country and has a rich *waqf* heritage (Ministère des Habous et des Affaires Islamiques 2007). Property gifted to *waqf* is of many types, movable and immovable. According to Luccioni (1956), the list of *waqf* assets is composed of about 40,000 objects, these include houses, shops, baths, mills, bakeries, agricultural land, gardens, olive groves, single books or entire libraries, salt pits, and sections of water and underground irrigation canal systems. The administration of *waqf* has, down the centuries, provided the working capital and the construction costs of mosques, universities, sanctuaries, religious lodges, hospitals, asylums, and cemeteries. Today, *waqf* assets consist of about 84,840 hectares of agricultural land, 195,850 farming parcels, and 49,547 urban properties. There are

all together about 10,000 beneficiaries, and *waqf* total assets are estimated to be around 100 billion dirhams (US$1 equals 9.96 Moroccan dirhams) (TelQuel 2007; La Vie Economique 2005).

Equally important is that Morocco has witnessed an astonishing explosion in the deployment of mobile technologies in the last several years. Information technology services and goods make the current period appear very different from previous decades. While half of Morocco's population is still rural and a majority of its villages and towns have yet to get electricity, fixed phone lines, paved roads or running water, the country has one of the highest rates of ICT usage in Africa and the Middle East, 13 Millions mobile phone users and 316 thousand Internet users (ITU 2006).

Research Methods and Design

To achieve my research objectives, I used a wide range of data based on archival, ethnographic, and survey methods. This united application of methods consisted of academic and popular literature review, consultations and interviews with decision-makers, religious scholars, university researchers, and civil society activists. In phase one of this research, I conducted structured and semi-structured consultations with policy makers at the Ministry of Awqaf and Islamic Affairs, Secrétariat d'Etat à la Poste et aux Technologies de l'Information, Agence Nationale de Réglementation des Télécommunications, non-government organizations, and the research community. Consultations and interviews with these actors provided: perceptions of *waqf* and its feasible use in promoting technology adoption, legal and political opportunities and constraints on the implementation of an ICT pilot project, a narrative of the information and communications policy context in Morocco, and sectorial profiles of users and rates of usage.

In phase two, I targeted a nationally known Quranic school, Sidi Zouine *madrasa*, relevant to the stated research objectives. There, I conducted intensive field observation with the director of the *madrasa* to document *waqf* properties and technology-based activities and users' understanding of mobile technology devices, assess students' technological base, and map out the *madrasa's* financial flows and activities. In phase three, I analyzed my field data and developed a *waqf*-based business model for the potential financial sustainability of technology projects in Morocco and beyond.

Findings

Description of the Quranic *Madrasa* of Zawiya Sidi Zouine

What is a *zawiya*? This Arabic term refers to the corner or angle of a building. In North Africa, the term is used interchangeably with *ribat*, for "the abode," meaning a religious lodge or order. It is usually associated with a saintly man (or woman in rare cases), or *murabit* or *marabout*. It provides a space for the practice of localized forms of Islam, which are dominated by the mechanical repetition of certain invocatory words and phrases as well as Quranic texts (*dhikr*), liturgical chanting, passages of mystical writings and poetry, music, and rhythmical movements or dancing, all producing a state of common trance (*al-hal*). There are also a few *zawiyas* known for religious study that struggled to combine mystical learning methods and scholastic thought and established some of the finest theology schools or *madrasas* as in the case of Sidi Zouine *madrasa*. Usually a *zawiya* stands for a place where a saint is buried, and its simple architecture consists of a whitewashed shrine with a cupola (*qubbah*). Its location constitutes an inviolable space open to those seeking refuge from enemies or the public authorities (Ilahiane 2004).

The Sidi Zouine *madrasa* is located near Marrakech where, in 2007, 397 male students aged 13 to 55 years were in attendance. The *madrasa* was founded by Sidi Zouine (1796–1894 CE) in 1830 CE. He was a holy man whose real name was Mohammad Ben Mohammad Ben Ali Ben Qanan Al-Zarari Al-Fahli Al-'Umari, with a genealogical link to one of the founding fathers of the Islamic state and a close companion of the Prophet Mohammad, the second and rightly-guided Caliph, 'Umar (634–644 CE). The nickname Sidi Zouine was given to him by his *sheikh* Al-Tuhami al-Awbari of the al-Sharradiya religious lodge, where he learned the science of *qiraat al-Qur'an* or traditions of Quranic memorization and recitations. While religious learning is universally accepted and the participation of girls is not excluded from the preschool settings of the *kuttab/msid*, *madrasa* training has been for the most part limited to boys. The argument is that such training for girls was of little economic utility since women were also barred from such male-dominated and defined Islamic occupations as the posts of imam (prayer leader in a mosque) and notary. However, historical exceptions to this belief were actually made. Topics of study include reading, writing, memorization and recitation, and rituals associated with the basic pillars and understanding of the Islamic faith.

Tradition and Modernity in the *Madrasa*

Sidi Zouine specializes in the memorization of the Quran, *al-qiraat* or the different traditions of recitation and their rules (of which there are fourteen although they mostly teach from seven to ten *qiraat*), *riwaya* or the science of correct Quranic pronunciation, and the standard books in hadith, such as the *Sahihs* of Bukhari and Muslim; in law and legal thought (*fiqh*, *furu'*, and *usul*), in Quran exegesis, such as Zamakhshari's *al-Kashshaf*; in the Prophet's biography (*sirah al-nabawiyah*), and in Arabic language and grammar, such as the *Ajarumiyah*, the *Tuhfat*, and the *Alfiyya*. As for Qur'an recitation, its presence in the curriculum is pervasive, being a daily requirement of the students. In 2006, the *madrasa* added new subjects to its curriculum such as French, mathematics and introduction to basic computing skills.

Ever since the tragic events of September 11, 2001, in the United States, *madrasas* have received increasing scrutiny and criticisms by Muslim and non-Muslim policy makers and the media, often characterizing them as breeding grounds for terrorists and as being associated with the promotion of violence and the spread of radical and extremist views of Islam. Based on ethnographic data, I suggest that the educational mission of the Sidi Zouine Quranic *madrasa*, with Quranic memorization at the heart of its curriculum, is to provide a sound and traditional Islamic alternative to public education, when the quality and availability of public schooling is limited or beyond the financial capacities of the poor. In light of these negative critiques leveled against traditional Quranic education as well as the Casablanca terrorist suicide bombings of May 16, 2003, the Moroccan policy makers have embarked on *al-islah* or reform drive of Quranic schools. The reform policies of the religious field seek to modernize the school's curriculum and to bring them to par with secular public education in terms of structure and organization.

In Sidi Zouine this has meant, at least for now, the teaching of French and mathematics. Basic computing lessons, although not part of the curriculum at this point in time, are given on a voluntary basis by the teacher of French and mathematics who uses his own laptop computer. Because the school has no computers, both the director and the new subjects' teacher expressed the felt need to integrate computers into the school. They thought that computers would aid students in Quranic memorization, provide a window on global society, and equip them with practical and entrepreneurial skills that they can mobilize upon leaving the school. I was also told that other initiatives are on their way to the *madrasa*, especially building new classrooms with desks, a multi-media room, and books for the library. These changes are part of the growing transformation of the Quranic school system in Morocco.

A remarkable aspect of the teaching of these new subjects is their new pedagogical technique. They have ushered in a slight, but transformative, shift in the instruction from the *luha* writing slate to the individual student to the collective whiteboard in the mosque, even though students still sit on the floor mats and the activity is referred to as a lesson circle or *halaqa*. The *luha* is not just a highly personalized and intimate device—each of the slates being different in size—it also clearly indicates that students work at diverse paces and levels, with varying capacities applied to different sections of text. By contrast, the whiteboard, now standard equipment in the mosque, in its distance from the student and in its control by the standing *sheikh*, illustrates a remote and recalls a standardized approach of instruction. A *sheikh*-to-circle relationship mediated by the whiteboard co-exists with the rich and complex *sheikh*-to-*taleb* relationships mediated by *luhas*. This slight culture change goes to the heart of the traditional model of knowledge transmission, which is sustained by a one-to-one mode of delivery, on a *taleb* being formed 'in the hands' of the *sheikh*.

How does *Waqf* Fund the School Today?

Historically, the endowments of the *madrasas* have varied considerably in size and educational scope, depending on the wealth and goals of the endower (Ministère des Habous et des Affaires Islamiques 2007). But, since most *madrasas* were founded by influential people and holy men and women, most *madrasas* could depend on substantial revenues from marked endowments that would keep them functioning for a long time. Endowments might consist of daily food donations, shops, mills, houses, baths, land, or all of these. In addition to other donations, the proceeds of working or renting these places were used to cover all expenses of the *madrasa*, from the employees' wages to the cost of replacing the *madrasa's* furniture and repairing its buildings. What makes the *madrasa* unique is its identity as an educational

institution. In this it is, unlike the mosque in its primary conception, organized, formal, and, above all, residential. As such, the *madrasa* has an administrative structure, a defined body of residents, and a distinct curriculum (see Afsaruddin 2005; Eickelman 1978; Houtsonen 1994; Metcalf 1978; Tawil 2006; Wagner and Lotfi 1980).

Architecturally, the school consists of six buildings. These buildings are the shrine of the Sidi Zouine where the founder of the school and some of his offspring are buried; a remodeled and spacious mosque with a minaret overshadowing the shrine; and the administration building housing the office of the director, a small library, and two *sheikh* rooms used for the memorization of the Quran and correction of wooden slates used by students. The remaining three are residential buildings; these are the Haj Brahim complex built by a *muhsin* (good doer) of the same name in the early 1980s, with 113 rooms . . . at the center of which there is a squared structure in which a sanctified well is carved out for ritually washing wooden slates; the Hassanian complex built in the name of the late king of Morocco in 1991 which has 100 rooms; and the *Shuyukh* or teachers quarters built by a Saudi Arabian *muhsin*, with 23 rooms.

Additionally, students benefit from daily donations of bread and milk. A *muhsin* from the Souss region supplies a loaf of bread to every student in the morning; the offspring of the holy shrine also donate another loaf of bread every afternoon; and the milk cooperative of Marrakesh gifts 100 liters of milk a day to the school. Students also receive more than a free education; they also are given stipends by the Ministry of *Awqaf* and Islamic Affairs, 300 dirhams per trimester per student (US\$1 = 9.30 Moroccan dirhams). The faculty is salaried, with their monthly income supplied by the Ministry of *Awqaf* and Islamic Affairs. The same ministry also covers repairs, potable water, sewage, phone, and electricity expenses of the *madrasa*.

In sum, the funding of the Sidi Zouine *madrasa* is supported by the endowments of the religious lodge or *zawiya*, the Ministry of *Awqaf* and Islamic Affairs, royal gifts, private donations, zakat, and sporadic parental financial support (see Figure 9.6.1).

Outcomes

I am proposing the use of cash *waqf* for the promotion of sustainable ICT development (see Figure 9.6.2). This method is as follows. The relevant stakeholders will

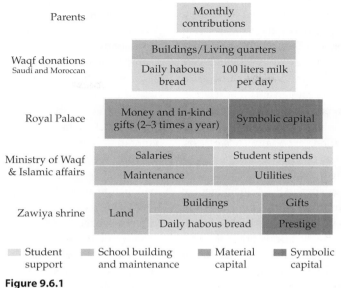

Figure 9.6.1

Funding model of a Quranic *madrasa*.

design ICT projects for socio-economic development. These projects will be proposed to the Waqf Authority (WA) of the country concerned. The WA will then prepare project profiles and invite voluntary cash *waqf* to finance ICT projects (see also Sadeq 2002). The cash *waqf* may be raised by producing *waqf* certificates of different denominations against the planned projects, so that a large number of individuals and institutions may buy them and thus join together to finance the planned schemes. Separate cash *waqf* may be raised for each individual *waqf* activity (facility, computers, various components and so on). This will have a resource-pooling effect to implement a *waqf*-based ICT project, which would otherwise be unattainable by a single attempt. For example, a Knowledge and Business Center may be established by raising cash *waqf*.

One might also note that in some cases, the founding of the primary project will not be adequate, but rather it will need continuous flows of cash to cover operational costs and expenses. Its financing will need secondary projects or working assets in the form of commercial real estate to generate a regular flow of revenue. For instance, a Knowledge and Business Center is a primary project. In order to finance the operations of the center, secondary working assets as in rental properties may be established by cash *waqf* funds. The revenue or rents

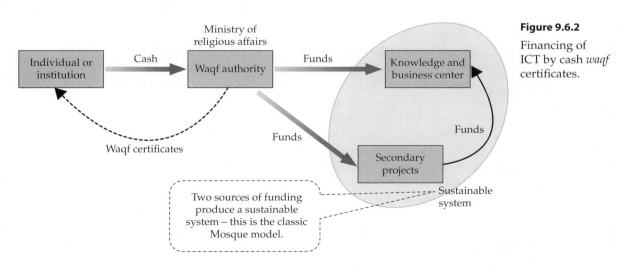

Figure 9.6.2

Financing of ICT by cash *waqf* certificates.

generated from these properties may then be used to finance the operations and activities and the salaries of the staff of the primary project. Thus, in this approach, the institution of *waqf* provides *sustainable* revenue streams for the planned projects, rather than depending on unpredictable flows of foreign aid.

Within the *madrasa* context, I encountered a complex and strategic research problem in Quranic schooling in Morocco. Quranic education, especially in *madrasas*, has become the focal point of policy makers. *Madrasas* and their reform bring together a set of key issues facing the Islamic world: Islam and the management of its image internally and externally, education and radicalism, and ICT and their benefits to social and economic development. Although, at this point in time, I am indecisive about the feasibility and potential of Islamic telecenters in dealing with such a constellation of issues, the Sidi Zouine *madrasa* provides a concrete start from which to explore barriers and stimulants to technological change in a Muslim space. Sidi Zouine *madrasa* presents an opportunity to leverage both financial and charitable assets and culturally embedded institutions, which might enable much wider technology adoption and diffusion throughout the wider Muslim world. As a facilitator of community development, technology could come to be seen as a legitimate destination for charitable donations. Technology implementations associated with charitable organizations and institutions in the *madrasa* might better overcome the cultural and educational obstacles to the adoption of computing. In addition, proper placement of technologies in established institutions might overcome a lack of infrastructure, and ensure exposure and sustainability.

The Anthropological Significance and Difference

Applied anthropology is simply defined as the use of anthropological theory, methods, comparative perspectives, and data to identify, evaluate, and solve social, economic, political, and environmental problems facing people (van Willigen 2002; Ervin 2005). In this project, firstly, I supplemented the existing historical and ethnographic accounts of Islamic education with data collected from my own ethnographic observations of the Sidi Zouine Quranic School activities and open-ended interviews with a diverse set of consultants and stakeholders. One of the most valuable tools of doing applied anthropology is being able to take part in the

events and activities we study in order to understand how people reconcile what they say with what they do.

Secondly, having grown up in a Muslim culture, being aware of the role of charitable Islamic institutions in Muslim societies, and being multilingual allowed me to obtain reliable and clean data to build a charity or *waqf*-based business model for the potential of financial sustainability of technology projects for community development.

Thirdly, equally significant is the focus of applied anthropology on home-grown institutions that outsiders or national development planners tend to ignore because they think these institutions are either ahistorical or it is just a matter of time before they disappear. Through ethnographic fieldwork and appreciation of the potentiality and relevance of local institutions to development, this case study will hopefully breathe new life into time-honored and culturally appropriate institutions, will minimize dependency and reliance on outsiders for assistance, and will provide new ways of rethinking sustainable development—a development that is economically viable, socially just, and institutionally sound.

Finally, applied anthropology provides a holistic approach to the study of information technology in the development arena because it helps development practitioners and organizations to not only appreciate context-specific and culturally appropriate forms of services delivery but to also understand the importance of local institutions for the financial sustainability of introduced new technologies. Repurposing community-based development models, such as *waqf* and its *madrasa* system model, that can provide stimulants to the use of mobile technology is a critical component of the anthropological difference.

Questions for Further Thought

1. Why do you think local institutions such as *waqf* are overlooked in development thinking and planning?
2. Should development planners take into account local institutions when designing development interventions in the developing world?
3. Should governments and international donors (like USAID) encourage the use of religious institutions to promote social and economic development?
4. Could you think of similar institutions in your community that could be repurposed for community development?

Acknowledgments

This research was carried out during my tenure as a visiting senior researcher at People and Practices Research Lab of Intel Corporation in 2006–2007. I would like to express my gratitude to Intel Corporation for funding this research project, and to my colleagues at Secretariat d'Etat auprès du Premier Ministère Chargé de la Poste et des Technologies des Télécommunications et de l' Information, and the Ministère des Habous et des Affaires Islamiques. Special thanks go to the staff and students of the Quranic *madrasa* of Zawiya Sidi Zouine for their time and willingness to share their knowledge of Islamic educational and charitable institutions with me.

References

Afsaruddin, A. 2005. "Muslim Views on Education: Parameters, Purview, and Possibilities." *Journal of Catholic Legal Studies* 44: 143–78.

Best, M., and Kumar, R. 2008. "Sustainability Failures of Rural Telecenters: Challenges from the Sustainable Access in Rural India (SARI) Project." *Information Technologies and International Development*, 4(4): 31–45.

Çizakça, M. 2000. *A History of Philanthropic Foundations: The Islamic World from the Seventh Century to the Present*. Istanbul: Bogazici University Press.

Eickelman, D. 1978. "The Art of Memory: Islamic Education and Its Social Reproduction." *Comparative Studies in Society and History* 20 (4): 485–516.

Ervin, A. 2005. *Applied Anthropology: Tools and Perspectives for Contemporary Practice*. Second Edition. Boston: Pearson Education, Inc.

Heeks, R. 2002. "Information Systems and Developing Countries: Failure, Success, and Local Improvisations." *The Information Society* 18: 101–112.

Heeks, R. 2008. "ICT4D 2.0: The Next Phase of Applying ICT for International Development." *IEEE Computer Society* (June): 26–33.

Houtsonen, J. 1994. "Traditional Quranic Education in a Southern Moroccan Village." *International Journal of Middle East Studies* 26 (3): 489–500.

Hudson, H. 2006. *From Rural Village to Global Village: Telecommunications for Development in the Information Age*. Mahwah, NJ: Lawrence Erlbaum Associates.

Ilahiane, H. 2004. *Ethnicities, Community Making, and Agrarian Change: The Political Ecology of a Moroccan Oasis*. Lanham, MD: University Press of America.

International Telecommunication Union (ITU). 2006. "World Information Society Report." http://www.itu.int/osg/spu/publications/world informationsociety/2006/report.html

James, J. 2006. *Information Technology and Development: A New Paradigm for Delivering the Internet to Rural Areas in Developing Countries*. New York: Routledge.

La Vie Economique. 2005. *La fortune des Habous (The Habous (Islamic endowments) Fortune)*. November 5.

Luccioni, J. 1956. *Les Fondations Pieuses, Habous, au Maroc (The Pious Foundations, Islamic Endowments, in Morocco)*. Rabat: Imprimerie royale.

Mannan, A. M. 1986. *Islamic Economics: Theory and Practice*. Boulder, CO: Westview.

Metcalf, B. 1978. "The Madrasa at Deoband: A Model for Religious Education in Modern India." *Modern Asian Studies* 12 (1): 111–134.

Ministère des Habous et des Affaires Islamiques. 2007. L'enseignement traditionnel au Maroc.

(Medersas) (Traditional Education in Morocco (Madrasas). http://habous.gov.ma/fr/derniere-actualite/56-Les-Ecoles-Traditionnelles/213-les-ecoles-traditionnelles-apercu-general.html

Rahman, F. 2002. *Islam*. Chicago, IL: University of Chicago Press.

Sadeq, A. 2002. "Waqf, Perpetual Charity, and Poverty Alleviation." *International Journal of Social Economics* 29(1/2): 135–151.

Sen, A. 1985. *Commodities and Capabilities*. Amsterdam: North-Holland.

Siochrú, S., and B. Girard. 2005. "Community-Based Networks and Innovative Technologies: New Models to Serve and Empower the Poor." New York: United Nations Development Programme" http://p-ced.com/reference/community-based_nets.pdf.

Tawil, S. 2006. "Quranic Education and Social Change in Northern Morocco: Perspectives from Chefchaouen." *Comparative Education Review* 50 (3): 496–517.

TelQuel. 2007. "Patrimoine des Habous. Un trésor, un gâchis (Heritage of Islamic Endowments. A Treasure, a Waste), No. 266." March 24–30. http://ykzxlck.telquel-online.com/archives/266/economie1_266.shtml.

United Nations Development Program (UNDP). 2001. "Human Development Report. Making New Technologies Work for Human Development." http://hdr.undp.org/reports/global/2001/en/

United States Agency for International Development (USAID). 2005. "The Idea and Practice of Philanthropy in the Muslim World. PPC Issue Paper No. 5." http://www.csis.org/media/csis/pubs/the_idea_of_philanthropy_in_the_muslim_world.pdf

van Willigen, J. 2002. *Applied Anthropology: An Introduction*. Second Edition. Westport, CT: Bergin and Garvey.

Wagner, D., and Lotfi, A. 1980. "Traditional Islamic Education in Morocco: Socio-Historical and Psychological Perspectives." *Comparative Education Review* 24 (2): 238–51.

DR. BARBARA ROSE JOHNSTON

Environmental Anthropologist; Senior Research Fellow and Director of the Center for Political Ecology, an independent education and action-research institute

Figure 9.7.1

Barbara Rose Johnston. (2015; photo used with author's permission)

What kind of work do you do, and how do you put anthropology to use in your work?

I use anthropology's holistic approach, participatory and collaborative methodologies, and critical environmental social justice frameworks to conduct action-research. I study ulcerating crises, part of a broader transdisciplinary effort to engage and ideally transform human environmental crises. It is termed by some as political ecology, though I generally think of it as simply environmental quality/social justice. In short, I examine the conditions that generate environment health inequities and, conversely, the conditions that allow the enjoyment of the right to a healthy environment. This means (1) exploring the historical conditions, societal relationships, and driving forces that give rise to ulcerating events or situations;

(2) documenting the anatomy and dynamic meanings in experiencing human environmental crisis; and (3) articulating and advocating for meaningful remedy—including acknowledgement, apologies, transformative public policy, and other concrete remedial actions that strive towards "never again."

How did your career evolve over time?

This has not been an easy path. My interdisciplinary training and scholar/advocate approach did not fit the position announcements in my early post-doc years. Encouraged to reapply once I had more publications, my interest in the problem-solving realm led me to write for applied and interdisciplinary audiences, publications that prompted the advice from colleagues in hiring departments that, should I get an interview,

I should avoid using terms like "human rights" or "applied anthropology." My inability to secure a tenured position and the demands of a growing family made job decisions complicated. For me, family comes first, thus when positions were offered that would require splitting the family and commuting between homes, it was no-brainer. My passionate commitment to a socially responsible anthropology led me to shape and to encourage a community-based action-research oriented "backyard anthropology." It is my firm belief that anthropologists can and should work in their own back yard; not simply because it is a place we know so well, but also because the relative lack of distance between the issues and problems that structure work and the ramifications resulting from our engagement encourages a sense of social responsibility.

Thus, I have come to realize and celebrate the immense richness of my artisanal life. I am someone who is happiest when busily engaged in doing multiple things at once, a product I suspect of coming from a very large family. In addition to my applied professional appointments, at various points in my life I have worked as a cook, cannery worker, receptionist, bookkeeper, archaeologist, boat crew, naturalist, dance teacher, gymnastics coach, writer, editor, environmental planner, and more. I spent a decade living in the Caribbean, and have traveled and worked in Europe, Southeast Asia, North and Central America, and Oceania. I do what I can to support and sustain my larger commitment to lead a socially responsible life. While I have spent an immense amount of time delving into and documenting horrific human tragedies and the related consequences of a world seemingly driven by plunder, I remain an optimist. It has been my experience to see and appreciate the fact that individuals can and do make a difference in this world.

What is the most meaningful project you've worked on over the course of your career? Why?

This is a hard question to answer, as every project I have gotten myself involved in has taken on deep meaning for one reason or another and each initiative seems to fold into (and be further informed by) the next. Just when I think closure has been achieved, new developments draw me back into an action-researcher role.

My work documenting the consequential damage of nuclear testing and related human subject experimentation in the Marshall Islands is a case in point. Focused work on this history and its consequences began in 1990, when I helped organize an effort to develop social science contributions to a United Nations Human Rights Special Rapporteur human rights and environment investigation. Our human rights and environment committee compiled case studies and produced a series of reports summarizing some of the many injuries suffered by indigenous peoples and ethnic minorities whose place-based ways of life made them extraordinarily vulnerable when displaced from traditional homelands, collective community, and critical resources. One of the more egregious examples of relationship between environmental degradation and human rights abuse was the case of nuclear testing, fallout, and the consequences for the environment, health, and traditional ways of life in the Marshall Islands, especially injuries suffered by the people of Rongelap Atoll whose heavy radiation exposures and related health problems were the subject of four decades of classified study by U.S. Atomic Energy Commission scientists.

I published a summation of the Rongelap case in the mid-90s, and this led to an invitation in 1999 from Public Advocate Bill Graham to advise the Marshall Islands Nuclear Claims Tribunal on culturally appropriate and legally defensible ways to define and value the damages associated with nuclear weapons testing and related fallout. In essence, I was asked to consider the meaning and value of life, the means by which life is damaged or destroyed, to envision what meaningful remedy might possibly be and how might it be achieved. And, I was fortunate enough to take on these questions at a time where new tools allowed previously unimaginable access to information: computers, web-based word-searchable declassified archives, the ability to easily communicate with an international array of scientific peers and cultural experts, including (most importantly) experts in the Marshallese community. I developed a consequential damages research methodology to help organize and contextualize the evidentiary record through archival and participatory fieldwork, organized a research team and began work with a Marshallese advisory committee.

Our resulting study, "The Rongelap Property Damage Claims Study: Efforts to Seek Redress for Nuclear

Contamination and Loss of a Way of Life," prompted a request by the NCT Public Advocate to take a more exhaustive look at the human radiation experiment history and its consequences, resulting in an expert witness report and October 2001 testimony to the Nuclear Claims Tribunal on "Hardships Endured by the People of Rongelap as a Result of the U.S. Nuclear Weapons Testing Program and Related Biomedical Research." Subsequent research into the human radiation experimentation history prompted briefing memos to the Tribunal in 2004-05 and again to help implement award decisions announced in 2007. The history, continuing suffering, and resonance of the case with larger world events (the Fukushima nuclear disaster, resurgent nuclear militarism) continues to prompt my periodic involvement as a researcher, writer, and advocate working with civil society, governments, and in varied public arenas in support of efforts to secure meaningful remedies.

I met you in the early 2000s on one of your visits to Michigan State University, where you serve as an adjunct professor in anthropology. In addition to research presentations and collaborations with faculty, you would also participate in methods class discussions about "unspoken fieldwork dilemmas." Can you share one or two pieces of advice with readers here?

The ability to see the world through other eyes is perhaps the biggest outcome of anthropological fieldwork; the dilemma is how one gets there. Some of those dilemmas include how one goes about fashioning a professional persona whilst juggling the realities of personal and social life. Anthropologists are typically trained as individuals through an intensive process that prioritizes and rewards the unique contributions of an anthropological voice; an ego-centric, self-centered training that makes many folks ill-prepared to handle the realities of field work—be it in communal settings or team-work with interdisciplinary partners.

While we are trained to think and articulate, we do so within a hierarchical system that rarely values the ability to listen, carefully, with respect; to engage in response to the needs of others, rather than needs of our funded endeavor. This training can leave you ill-prepared for the dynamic realities of being an outsider in the homes and the lives of the studied or host community. Friendships help bridge sociocultural differences; they can also generate complex personal, social, and political dramas with

potentially messy, painful outcomes. Point being, take care in your approach and manner. The obligations that arise as a result of your engagement may be life-changing, for you and others. You may find yourself privy to all sorts of information about all sorts of goings on, legal and otherwise. . . . Eyes wide-open is a useful policy, and ethical codes (disciplinary, international human rights law, etc.) are important sources for guidance.

CAREER ADVICE

Advice for students interested in pursuing action-oriented anthropology:

- Action-oriented research is work done in the public interest, often conducted by interdisciplinary or transdisciplinary teams in partnership with affected or host communities engaged in citizen science, as a means to secure an independent analysis that helps clarify issues and identify meaningful remedy.
- The role of the anthropologist in this partnership is multifaceted; overarching goals include to educate, facilitate, and empower a rights-protective research and advocacy process.
- Collaborative and participatory approaches to the problem, definition of goals, assignment of duties, analysis and dissemination of research outcomes, and other facets of decision-making, communication, and work are key.
- Scope of work agreements (formal and informal) help to insure transparency and accountability; the ability for all parties to revisit and revise terms by common agreement as conditions and understandings change is essential.
- Success is relative: The process of doing action-oriented research generates complex changes that may be the most important outcome of the initiative, more important than the idealized project goal. Relationships, sociopolitical performance, and capacity building are all examples of sustaining outcomes and are important indicators of project success.

For more information on the Marshall Islands Nuclear Claims Tribunal research, see Barbara Rose Johnston and Holly Barker, 2000, "Nuclear Compensation in the Marshall Islands," *Cultural Survival Quarterly,* 24(1): 48–50.

PART 10

Violence, Conflict, and Mobility in the 21st Century

Violence is an assertion of power; it is the use of force to harm some-one or something. When anthropologists study violence, they approach it not as a natural expression of humanity, but as a learned social behavior. Thus, anthropologists consider the particular historic and social circumstances that produce violent acts or actions. In recent years, news outlets have reported major increases in violence, conflict, and acts of terror across the globe. While mainstream media pundits often refer to these acts as "mindless" or chaotic, anthropologists counter that such acts are never "meaningless" but rather full of meaning, both to victims and perpetrators. For the latter, they are political strate-gies intended to lead to specific, culturally significant outcomes (Welsh and Vivanco 2014, 254–256).

The "War on Terror" in the early 2000s was justified on the basis of a belief that different cultural values generate geopolitical conflict (Welsh and Vivanco 2014, 149). Thus, those in support of this perspective believed that ideological divisions necessitated military actions in order to bring democracy from the enlightened West to the Middle East, which was dominated by what was perceived to be a closed and oppressive culture, arising from Islamic faith. In the first piece in this section, Lila Abu-Lughod takes on the ethnocentric notion of Western freedom, asking, "Do Muslim Women Really Need Saving? Anthropological Reflections on Cultural Relativism and Its Others"

(Reading 10.1). Drawing on her knowledge of the *burqa*, Abu-Lughod challenges the Western idea that veiling is a symbol of female subordination, showing instead that for most Muslim women it is a public symbol of piety and the separation of women's and men's spheres, and sometimes also a sign of sophistication and modernity.

Closely connected to war, conflict, and violence is the mobility of people. Readings 10.2 and 10.3 explore mobility resulting from experiences of violence in one's home country. In "Dispelling the Myths: Unaccompanied, Undocumented Minors in U.S. Immigration Custody" (Reading 10.2), Susan Terrio addresses child migration, revealing the harsh realities that children face in their home communities, leading them to cross the border in the first place, and then the poor conditions they face once detained in the United States. In "The Non-National in Jordan: Statelessness as Structural Violence Among Gaza Refugees in Jordan" (Reading 10.3), Michael Perez explores the lives of Gaza refugees in Jordan. Refugees are migrants who are forced to move due to political oppression or war; they often have legal permission to stay in their new location. However, Gaza refugees are *stateless* refugees; they lack citizenship and as a result suffer from structural violence and oppression, creating difficulties in obtaining employment, housing, and healthcare services. Perez raises a key point about the fundamental problem of living in a world in which the gateway to securing rights is through citizenship, rather than the ability of all humans everywhere to be afforded the same rights, regardless of where they live.

The section then turns to a collection of articles, profiles, and news pieces that interrogate the role of anthropologists within conflict zones. While anthropologists have a long history of involvement with government agendas, from colonialism to development projects to military operations, the role of anthropology in these contexts made headlines in the late 2000s when the U.S. Department of Defense established the Human Terrain System (HTS). HTS embedded applied social scientists with U.S. troops in war contexts; anthropologists were hired as part of these teams to help troops understand the local cultural and linguistic context. The program has been surrounded by controversy, and the reasons for alarm are detailed across several pieces at the close of this section. One central concern among critics is that working for the military makes it impossible for anthropologists to uphold their primary commitment to be trustworthy and open with their informants. Trust-building in war contexts is the focus of Patricia Omidian's piece, "Living and Working in a War Zone: An Applied Anthropologist in Afghanistan" (Reading 10.4).

This section's "In the News" feature explores the controversy over the HTS and links to both an interview with Roberto González, a leading critic of HTS, and the homepage of the Network of Concerned Anthropologists (NCA), an independent network of anthropologists that formed in response to the "war on terror" in order to promote ethical anthropology in the face of what appeared to be significant efforts to militarize the discipline of anthropology.

Finally, the section's "Anthropology in Practice" piece features Dr. Laura McNamara, an organizational anthropologist employed in the Department of Energy's Sandia National Laboratories. In her interview, McNamara reflects on her experiences working within this nuclear weapons engineering laboratory, and the challenges of working at the intersection of science and foreign policy. McNamara has written extensively on working in national security environments, and spent years serving on the AAA's Commission for the Engagement of the U.S. Security and intelligence Community (CEAUSSIC), examining the ethical risks and issues related to anthropologists in the security sphere. She is also a signer of the Network of Concerned Anthropologists Statement to Congress opposing the Human Terrain System.

The section closes with an additional "In the News" piece that explores another form of mobility and violence: the trade in human organs. Nancy Scheper-Hughes spent over a decade investigating the illegal organ trade, uncovering extensive corruption surrounding international kidney trafficking.

 Visit www.oup.com/us/brondo for weblinks.

KEY TERMS:

- Violence
- War on Terror
- Cultural relativism
- Colonial feminism
- Mobility
- Child migration
- Immigration policy
- Refugees

- Conflict
- Humanitarian aid
- Human Terrain System
- Network of Concerned Anthropologists
- National security
- Organ trade
- Ethics

10.1 Do Muslim Women Really Need Saving? Anthropological Reflections on Cultural Relativism and Its Others

LILA ABU-LUGHOD

Is "liberating" Muslim women a valid justification for going to war? What did First Lady Laura Bush mean in her 2002 speech arguing that the War on Terrorism is a fight for the dignity of women? Do Muslim women need to be saved from their own culture? Abu-Lughod takes on the ethnocentric notion of Western freedom through the exploration of the differential meanings associated with the burqa and the way in which veiling was invoked in the justification to go to war in Afghanistan. For many Westerners, the burqa is understood as a symbol of female subordination. But to most Muslim women it is a public symbol of piety and the separation of women's and men's spheres, enabling women to move freely in public space where strangers mix. Moreover, certain styles of veiling are understood as signs of sophistication and modernity. This piece points toward the role anthropology can play in encouraging an appreciation for cultural difference among global women and in valuing that difference is produced by unique historical circumstances and social desires.

Questions

1. Discuss the different symbolic meanings attached to veiling. What do distinct practices reveal about social status, professional occupation, religious beliefs, and so on?
2. What does the burqa represent in the "War on Terrorism"?
3. What is "colonial feminism," and how did Laura Bush's speech about the War of Terrorism emancipating women reflect colonial feminism?
4. What does this discussion about the burqa reveal about cultural understandings of freedom, choice, and human rights?

What are the ethics of the current "War on Terrorism," a war that justifies itself by purporting to liberate, or save, Afghan women? Does anthropology have anything to offer in our search for a viable position to take regarding this rationale for war? . . . Like many colleagues whose work has focused on women and gender in the Middle East, I was deluged with invitations to speak—not just on news programs but also to various departments at colleges and universities, especially women's studies programs. Why did this not please me, a scholar who has devoted more than 20 years of her life to this subject and who has some complicated personal connection to this identity? Here was an opportunity to spread the word, disseminate my knowledge, and correct misunderstandings. . . .

I want to point out the minefields—a metaphor that is sadly too apt for a country like Afghanistan, with the world's highest number of mines per capita—of this obsession with the plight of Muslim women. I hope to show some way through them using insights from anthropology, the discipline

Lila Abu-Lughod. "Do Muslim Women Really Need Saving? Anthropological Reflections on Cultural Relativism and Its Others." 2002. *American Anthropologist* 104 (3), 783–790. Reproduced by permission of the American Anthropological Association. Not for sale or further reproduction.

whose charge has been to understand and manage cultural difference. . . .

It is easier to see why one should be skeptical about the focus on the "Muslim woman" if one begins with the U.S. public response. I will analyze two manifestations of this response: some conversations I had with a reporter from the PBS *NewsHour with Jim Lehrer* and First Lady Laura Bush's radio address to the nation on November 17, 2001. The presenter from the *NewsHour* show first contacted me in October to see if I was willing to give some background for a segment on Women and Islam. . . . The questions were hopelessly general. Do Muslim women believe "x"? Are Muslim women "y"? Does Islam allow "z" for women? I asked her: If you were to substitute Christian or Jewish wherever you have Muslim, would these questions make sense? . . . [The] question is why knowing about the "culture" of the region, and particularly its religious beliefs and treatment of women, was more urgent than exploring the history of the development of repressive regimes in the region and the U.S. role in this history. Such cultural framing, it seemed to me, prevented the serious exploration of the roots and nature of human suffering in this part of the world. Instead of political and historical explanations, experts were being asked to give religio-cultural ones. Instead of questions that might lead to the exploration of global interconnections, we were offered ones that worked to artificially divide the world into separate spheres—recreating an imaginative geography of West versus East, us versus Muslims, cultures in which First Ladies give speeches versus others where women shuffle around silently in burqas.

Most pressing for me was why the Muslim woman in general, and the Afghan woman in particular, were so crucial to this cultural mode of explanation, which ignored the complex entanglements in which we are all implicated, in sometimes surprising alignments. Why were these female symbols being mobilized in this "War against Terrorism" in a way they were not in other conflicts? Laura Bush's radio address on November 17 reveals the political work such mobilization accomplishes. On the one hand, her address collapsed important distinctions that should have been maintained. There was a constant slippage between the Taliban and the terrorists, so that they became almost one word—a kind of hyphenated monster identity: the Taliban-and-the-terrorists. Then there was the blurring of the very separate causes in Afghanistan

of women's continuing malnutrition, poverty, and ill health, and their more recent exclusion under the Taliban from employment, schooling, and the joys of wearing nail polish. On the other hand, her speech reinforced chasmic divides, primarily between the "civilized people throughout the world" whose hearts break for the women and children of Afghanistan and the Taliban-and-the-terrorists, the cultural monsters who want to, as she put it, "impose their world on the rest of us."

Most revealingly, the speech enlisted women to justify American bombing and intervention in Afghanistan and to make a case for the "War on Terrorism" of which it was allegedly a part. As Laura Bush said, "Because of our recent military gains in much of Afghanistan, women are no longer imprisoned in their homes. They can listen to music and teach their daughters without fear of punishment. . . . The fight against terrorism is also a fight for the rights and dignity of women" (U.S. Government 2002). These words have haunting resonances for anyone who has studied colonial history. Many who have worked on British colonialism in South Asia have noted the use of the woman question in colonial policies where intervention into sati (the practice of widows immolating themselves on their husbands' funeral pyres), child marriage, and other practices was used to justify rule. As Gayatri Chakravorty Spivak (1988) has cynically put it: white men saving brown women from brown men. The historical record is full of similar cases, including in the Middle East. In Turn of the Century Egypt, what Leila Ahmed (1992) has called "colonial feminism" was hard at work. This was a selective concern about the plight of Egyptian women that focused on the veil as a sign of oppression but gave no support to women's education and was professed loudly by the same Englishman, Lord Cromer, who opposed women's suffrage back home.

Sociologist Marnia Lazreg (1994) has offered some vivid examples of how French colonialism enlisted women to its cause in Algeria. . . . She describes skits at awards ceremonies at the Muslim Girls' School in Algiers in 1851 and 1852. In the first skit, written by "a French lady from Algiers," two Algerian Arab girls reminisced about their trip to France with words including the following:

Oh! Protective France: Oh! Hospitable France! . . .
Noble land, where I felt free
Under Christian skies to pray to our God . . .

God bless you for the happiness you bring us!
  And you, adoptive mother, who taught us
  That we have a share of this world,
  We will cherish you forever! [Lazreg 1994, 135]

These girls are made to invoke the gift of a share of this world, a world where freedom reigns under Christian skies. This is not the world the Taliban-and-the-terrorists would "like to impose on the rest of us."

Just as I argued earlier that we need to be suspicious when neat cultural icons are plastered over messier historical and political narratives, so we need to be wary when Lord Cromer in British-ruled Egypt, French ladies in Algeria, and Laura Bush, all with military troops behind them, claim to be saving or liberating Muslim women.

Politics of the Veil

I want now to look more closely at those Afghan women Laura Bush claimed were "rejoicing" at their liberation by the Americans. This necessitates a discussion of the veil, or the burqa, because it is so central to contemporary concerns about Muslim women. This will set the stage for a discussion of how anthropologists, feminist anthropologists in particular, contend with the problem of difference in a global world. . . .

It is common popular knowledge that the ultimate sign of the oppression of Afghan women under the Taliban-and-the-terrorists is that they were forced to wear the burqa. Liberals sometimes confess their surprise that even though Afghanistan has been liberated from the Taliban, women do not seem to be throwing off their burqas. Someone who has worked in Muslim regions must ask why this is so surprising. Did we expect that once "free" from the Taliban they would go "back" to belly shirts and blue jeans, or dust off their Chanel suits? We need to be more sensible about the clothing of "women of cover," and so there is perhaps a need to make some basic points about veiling.

First, it should be recalled that the Taliban did not invent the burqa. It was the local form of covering that Pashtun women in one region wore when they went out. The Pashtun are one of several ethnic groups in Afghanistan and the burqa was one of many forms of covering in the subcontinent and Southwest Asia that has developed as a convention for symbolizing women's modesty or respectability. The burqa, like some other forms of "cover" has, in many settings, marked the symbolic separation of men's and women's spheres, as part of the general association of women with family and home, not with public space where strangers mingled.

Twenty years ago the anthropologist Hanna Papanek (1982), who worked in Pakistan, described the burqa as "portable seclusion." She noted that many saw it as a liberating invention because it enabled women to move out of segregated living spaces while still observing the basic moral requirements of separating and protecting women from unrelated men. Ever since I came across her phrase "portable seclusion," I have thought of these enveloping robes as "mobile homes." Everywhere, such veiling signifies belonging to a particular community and participating in a moral way of life in which families are paramount in the organization of communities and the home is associated with the sanctity of women.

The obvious question that follows is this: If this were the case, why would women suddenly become immodest? Why would they suddenly throw off the markers of their respectability, markers, whether burqas or other forms of cover, which were supposed to assure their protection in the public sphere from the harassment of strange men by symbolically signaling to all that they were still in the inviolable space of their homes, even though moving in the public realm? Especially when these are forms of dress that had become so conventional that most women gave little thought to their meaning.

To draw some analogies, none of them perfect, why are we surprised that Afghan women do not throw off their burqas when we know perfectly well that it would not be appropriate to wear shorts to the opera? At the time these discussions of Afghan women's burqas were raging, a friend of mine was chided by her husband for suggesting she wanted to wear a pantsuit to a fancy wedding: "You know you don't wear pants to a WASP wedding," he reminded her. New Yorkers know that the beautifully coiffed Hasidic women . . . are wearing wigs. This is because religious belief and community standards of propriety require the covering of the hair. They also alter boutique fashions to include high necks and long sleeves. As anthropologists know perfectly well, people wear the appropriate form of dress for their social communities and are guided by socially shared standards, religious beliefs, and moral ideals, unless they deliberately transgress to make a point or are unable to afford proper cover. . . . What had happened in Afghanistan under the Taliban is that one regional style of covering or veiling, associated with a certain respectable but not elite class, was imposed on everyone as "religiously" appropriate, even though previously there had been many different styles, popular or traditional with different groups and classes—different ways to mark women's propriety, or, in more recent times, religious piety. Although I am not an expert on Afghanistan, I imagine that the majority of women left in Afghanistan by the time the Taliban took control were the rural or less educated, from nonelite families, since they were the only ones who could not emigrate to escape the hardship and violence that has marked Afghanistan's recent history. If liberated from the enforced wearing of burqas, most of these women would choose some other form of modest headcovering, like all those living nearby who were not under the Taliban—their rural Hindu counterparts in the North of India (who cover their heads and veil their faces from affines) or their Muslim sisters in Pakistan.

Even the *New York Times* carried an article about Afghan women refugees in Pakistan that attempted to educate readers about this local variety. The article describes and pictures everything from the now-iconic burqa with the embroidered eyeholes, which a Pashtun woman explains is the proper dress for her community, to large scarves they call chadors, to the new Islamic modest dress that wearers refer to as *hijab.* Those in the new Islamic dress are characteristically students heading for professional careers, especially in medicine, just like their counterparts from Egypt to Malaysia. One wearing the large scarf was a school principal; the other was a poor street vendor. The telling quote from the young street vendor is, "If I did [wear the burqa] the refugees would tease me because the burqa is for 'good women' who stay inside the home" (Fremson 2001, 14). Here you can see the local status associated with the burqa—it is for good respectable women from strong families who are not forced to make a living selling on the street.

The British newspaper *The Guardian* published an interview in January 2002 with Dr. Suheila Siddiqi, a respected surgeon in Afghanistan who holds the rank of lieutenant general in the Afghan medical corps (Goldenberg 2002). A woman in her sixties, she comes from an elite family and, like her sisters, was educated. Unlike most women of her class, she chose not to go

into exile. She is presented in the article as "the woman who stood up to the Taliban" because she refused to wear the burqa. She had made it a condition of returning to her post as head of a major hospital when the Taliban came begging in 1996, just eight months after firing her along with other women. Siddiqi is described as thin, glamorous, and confident. But further into the article it is noted that her graying bouffant hair is covered in a gauzy veil. This is a reminder that though she refused the burqa, she had no question about wearing the chador or scarf.

Finally, I need to make a crucial point about veiling. Not only are there many forms of covering, which themselves have different meanings in the communities in which they are used, but also veiling itself must not be confused with, or made to stand for, lack of agency. As I have argued in my ethnography of a Bedouin community in Egypt in the late 1970s and 1980s, pulling the black head cloth over the face in front of older respected men is considered a voluntary act by women who are deeply committed to being moral and have a sense of honor tied to family. One of the ways they show their standing is by covering their faces in certain contexts. They decide for whom they feel it is appropriate to veil.

To take a very different case, the modern Islamic modest dress that many educated women across the Muslim world have taken on since the mid-1970s now both publicly marks piety and can be read as a sign of educated urban sophistication, a sort of modernity (e.g., Abu-Lughod 1995, 1998; Brenner 1996; El Guindi 1999; MacLeod 1991; Ong 1990). . . .

Two points emerge from this fairly basic discussion of the meanings of veiling in the contemporary Muslim world. First, we need to work against the reductive interpretation of veiling as the quintessential sign of women's unfreedom, even if we object to state imposition of this form, as in Iran or with the Taliban. (It must be recalled that the modernizing states of Turkey and Iran had earlier in the century banned veiling and required men, except religious clerics, to adopt Western dress.) What does freedom mean if we accept the fundamental premise that humans are social beings, always raised in certain social and historical contexts and belonging to particular communities that shape their desires and understandings of the world? Is it not a gross violation of women's own understandings of what they are doing to simply denounce the burqa as a medieval imposition? Second, we must take care not to reduce the diverse situations and attitudes of millions of Muslim women to a single item of clothing. Perhaps it is time to give up the Western obsession with the veil and focus on some serious issues with which feminists and others should indeed be concerned.

Ultimately, the significant political-ethical problem the burqa raises is how to deal with cultural "others." How are we to deal with difference without accepting the passivity implied by the cultural relativism for which anthropologists are justly famous—a relativism that says it's their culture and it's not my business to judge or interfere, only to try to understand. Cultural relativism is certainly an improvement on ethnocentrism and the racism, cultural imperialism, and imperiousness that underlie it; the problem is that it is too late not to interfere. The forms of lives we find around the world are already products of long histories of interactions.

We need to look closely at what we are supporting (and what we are not) and to think carefully about why. . . . I do not know how many feminists who felt good about saving Afghan women from the Taliban are also asking for a global redistribution of wealth or contemplating sacrificing their own consumption radically so that African or Afghan women could have some chance of having what I do believe should be a universal human right—the right to freedom from the structural violence of global inequality and from the ravages of war, the everyday rights of having enough to eat, having homes for their families in which to live and thrive, having ways to make decent livings so their children can grow, and having the strength and security to work out, within their communities and with whatever alliances they want, how to live a good life, which might very well include changing the ways those communities are organized.

. . . For that, we need to confront two more big issues. First is the acceptance of the possibility of difference. Can we only free Afghan women to be like us or might we have to recognize that even after "liberation" from the Taliban, they might want different things than we would want for them? What do we do about that? Second, we need to be vigilant about the rhetoric of saving people because of what it implies about our attitudes.

Again, when I talk about accepting difference, I am not implying that we should resign ourselves to being

cultural relativists who respect whatever goes on elsewhere as "just their culture." I have already discussed the dangers of "cultural" explanations; "their" cultures are just as much part of history and an interconnected world as ours are. What I am advocating is the hard work involved in recognizing and respecting differences—precisely as products of different histories, as expressions of different circumstances, and as manifestations of differently structured desires. We may want justice for women, but can we accept that there might be different ideas about justice and that different women might want, or choose, different futures from what we envision as best? We must consider that they might be called to personhood, so to speak, in a different language.

Reports from the Bonn peace conference held in late November to discuss the rebuilding of Afghanistan revealed significant differences among the few Afghan women feminists and activists present. RAWA's [Revolutionary Association of the Women of Afghanistan] position was to reject any conciliatory approach to Islamic governance. According to one report I read, most women activists, especially those based in Afghanistan who are aware of the realities on the ground, agreed that Islam had to be the starting point for reform. Fatima Gailani, a U.S.-based advisor to one of the delegations, is quoted as saying, "If I go to Afghanistan today and ask women for votes on the promise to bring them secularism, they are going to tell me to go to hell." . . .

One of the things we have to be most careful about in thinking about Third World feminisms, and feminism in different parts of the Muslim world, is how not to fall into polarizations that place feminism on the side of the West. I have written about the dilemmas faced by Arab feminists when Western feminists initiate campaigns that make them vulnerable to local denunciations by conservatives of various sorts, whether Islamist or nationalist, of being traitors (Abu-Lughod 2001). As some like Afsaneh Najmabadi are now arguing, not only is it wrong to see history simplistically in terms of a putative opposition between Islam and the West (as is happening in the United States now and has happened in parallel in the Muslim world), but it is also strategically dangerous to accept this cultural opposition between Islam and the West, between fundamentalism and feminism, because those many people within Muslim countries who are trying to find alternatives to present injustices, those who might want to refuse the divide and take from different histories and cultures, who do not accept that being feminist means being Western, will be under pressure to choose, just as we are: Are you with us or against us?

My point is to remind us to be aware of differences, respectful of other paths toward social change that might give women better lives. Can there be a liberation that is Islamic? And, beyond this, is liberation even a goal for which all women or people strive? Are emancipation, equality, and rights part of a universal language we must use? . . . [M]ight other desires be more meaningful for different groups of people? Living in close families? Living in a godly way? Living without war? I have done fieldwork in Egypt over more than 20 years and I cannot think of a single woman I know, from the poorest rural to the most educated cosmopolitan, who has ever expressed envy of U.S. women, women they tend to perceive as bereft of community, vulnerable to sexual violence and social anomie, driven by individual success rather than morality; or strangely disrespectful of God. . . .

Let us return, finally, to my title, "Do Muslim Women Really Need Saving?" The discussion of culture, veiling, and how one can navigate the shoals of cultural difference should put Laura Bush's self-congratulation about the rejoicing of Afghan women liberated by American troops in a different light. It is deeply problematic to construct the Afghan woman as someone in need of saving, When you save someone, you imply that you are saving her from something, You are also saving her *to* something, What violences are entailed in this transformation, and what presumptions are being made about the superiority of that to which you are saving her? Projects of saving other women depend on and enforce a sense of superiority by Westerners, a form of arrogance that deserves to be challenged. All one needs to do to appreciate the patronizing quality of the rhetoric of saving women is to imagine using it today in the United States about disadvantaged groups such as African American women or working-class women. We now understand them as suffering from structural violence. We have become politicized about race and class, but not culture. . . .

A first step in hearing their wider message is to break with the language of alien cultures, whether to understand or eliminate them. Missionary work and colonial feminism belong in the past. Our task is to critically explore what we might do to help create a world in which those poor Afghan women, for whom "the hearts of those in the civilized world break," can have safety and decent lives.

References

Abu-Lughod, Lila. 1995. Movie Stars and Islamic Moralism in Egypt. Social Text 42:53–67.

Abu-Lughod, Lila. 1998. Remaking Women: Feminism and Modernity in the Middle East. Princeton: Princeton University Press.

Abu-Lughod, Lila. 2001. Orientalism and Middle East Feminist Studies. Feminist Studies 27(1):101–113.

Ahmed, Leila. 1992. Women and Gender in Islam. New Haven, CT: Yale University Press.

Brenner, Suzanne. 1996. Reconstructing Self and Society: Javanese Muslim Women and "the Veil." American Ethnologist 23(4):673–697.

El Guindi, Fadwa. 1999. Veil; Modesty, Privacy and Resistance. Oxford: Berg.

Fremson, Ruth. 2001. Allure Must Be Covered. Individuality Peeks Through. New York Times, November 4: 14.

Goldenberg, Suzanne. 2002. The Woman Who Stood Up to the Taliban. The Guardian, January 24, Electronic document, https://www.theguardian.com/world/2002/jan/24/gender.uk1.

MacLeod, Arlene.1991. Accommodating Protest. New York: Columbia University Press.

Lazreg, Marnia. 1994. Accommodating Protest. New York: Columbia University Press.

Ong, Aihwa. 1990. State Versus Islam: Malay Families, Women's Bodies, and the Body Politic in Malaysia. American Ethnologist 17(2):258–276. Papanek: Hanna.

Papanek, Hanna. 1982. Purdah in Pakistan: Seclusion and Modern Occupations for Women. In Separate Worlds. Hanna Papanek and Gial Minault, eds. Pp. 190-216. Columbus, MO: South Asia Books.

Spivak, Gayatri Chakravorty. 1988. Can the Subaltem Speak? *In* Marxism and the Interpretation of Culture, Cary Nelson and Lawrence Grossberg, eds. Pp. 271–313. Urbana: University of Illinois Press.

U.S. Government. 2002. Electronic document, http://www.whitehouse.gov/news/.

10.2 Dispelling the Myths: Unaccompanied, Undocumented Minors in U.S. Immigration Custody

SUSAN TERRIO

While migration to the United States by unaccompanied migrants is not a new phenomenon, the stories of youth arriving alone captured the public's attention in 2014 through major stories in the mainstream media. Susan Terrio confronts four myths that were perpetuated in the media about unaccompanied and undocumented minors entering the United States. Contrary to popular belief, most youth are not arriving in the United States in search of legal status, nor are they better off being returned to the homes they came from or held in detention centers "for their own protection." Drawing on ethnographic interviewing with dozens of youth migrants, Terrio reveals the harsh realities these children face, in their home communities, en route to cross the border, and once detained in the United States.

Questions

1. What are the structural causes of youth migration?
2. What dangers do child migrants face en route? How are migrant experiences gendered?
3. What attachments do child migrants have in their home communities? What is life like back in their home communities?
4. Compare and contrast life in the home communities of youth migrants to that in the Office of Refugee Resettlement. Which is preferable and why?
5. What is "family reunification," and what have been the critiques of it from advocates?
6. How can immigration policies be reformed in a way that is culturally sensitive and advances the rights of global children?

 Visit www.oup.com/us/brondo for press on youth crossing the U.S.-Mexico border alone.

I met Mirabel in 2011, four years after she had left her home in San Pedro Sula, Honduras, a city reputed to be the murder capital of the world. She, her sisters and mother had been terrorized by an alcoholic father who abused them and stole the earnings from her mother's struggling grocery store to spend on liquor and women. The tipping point came when Mirabel, then 16, confronted her father after a drunken rampage, and he nearly killed her with a machete. When an uncle offered to pay for a smuggler to take Mirabel to the United States, her mother begged her not to go. "We all know the stories of girls who get raped or die in the desert," Mirabel told me. "But I couldn't stay. I had no life there." She told her mother she loved her, boarded a bus with her teenage cousin and headed north, hoping for a better life in "*El Norte.*"

Mirabel made it to the United States just 15 days later. But this outcome was unusual and could have

Susan Terrio. "Dispelling the Myths: Unaccompanied, Undocumented Minors in US Immigration Custody." 2015. *Anthropology Today* 31 (1), 15–18. By permission of John Wily & Sons, Inc.

ended differently. Mirabel made this hazardous journey in 2007, at a time when underage migrants from Mexico and Central America were largely hidden from public scrutiny and absent from immigration debates. The huge numbers of child migrants crossing the U.S. border suddenly became breaking news in the spring and summer of 2014. During the first 10 months of the fiscal year 2014 (1 October 2013–31 July 2014), the Border Patrol took into custody an unprecedented 62,998 unaccompanied children. Although current apprehensions have sharply declined, in July 2014 nearly 500 children were crossing the border every day, some with parents or relatives and many who travelled on their own.[1]

Shocking pictures of kids in detention centres began circulating in the media in 2014. Over the summer, news reports galvanized public attention, creating both sympathy and alarm. On the one hand, the public has heard stories of Central American migrants as young as four or five packed into overcrowded holding cells, and has read reports of children arriving alone and running toward—not away from—immigration authorities in the hope of rescue. On the other hand, the public has witnessed anti-immigrant protesters banning these children from entering their communities, blocking buses, or even passing resolutions to keep out unwanted aliens. Facing what the President called an "urgent humanitarian crisis," the Obama administration scrambled to set up additional shelters for unaccompanied minors and for undocumented parents with young children. The President promised to "stem the tide" of further migration, by warning Central Americans to stop sending their children north because they would be sent back.

Figure 10.2.1

Unaccompanied child in care of the U.S. Customs and Border Protection agency at the South Texas border into the United States. *Photo: Eddie Perez/US Government.*

The frenzied coverage of the young migrants in the mainstream media, the blogosphere, rallies, community centres, and coffee shops, has created a number of powerful myths about who these children are, why they are coming to the U.S., and what happens to them after they are apprehended by immigration authorities and placed in one of the 114 government facilities for children under 18 years old who are without a parent or guardian in the country able and willing to provide care for them.

In this article I confront and dispel these myths based on the research I have conducted on the U.S. custodial system between 2009 and the present. The Office of Refugee Resettlement (ORR)—the Department of Health and Human Services agency that operates the custodial system—granted me rare access to 20 federal facilities and six foster care facilities between 2009 and 2012. . . .

Myth #1: Young Mexican and Central American Migrants Are Coming to the U.S. to Get Legal Status

None of the young people I interviewed or met in government custody said that they left home because they expected to win protective status. In fact, most of them knew nothing about U.S. immigration law and were unaware that they could petition for asylum or apply for a visa designed to protect those who had been the victims of trafficking, crime, or abuse, abandonment, or neglect by parents in the home country.

My research indicates that child migrants leave their countries because they feel that they have no choice. They do this knowing that the journey north is perilous and that they could die en route. An analysis last year by the human rights group the Washington Office on Latin America found that there were at least 463 migrant deaths at the U.S. border in the fiscal year 2012. The massive build-up of border security in terms of personnel, technology, and new fencing—what migration analysts call the "formidable machinery" of immigration enforcement—has forced immigrants to cross in increasingly dangerous sectors, and many die crossing the Rio Grande or from exposure and dehydration in the desert.[2] And that's only counting those who make it that far.

These migrants travel alone or in groups, hire smugglers or venture into uncharted areas without help, often carrying only a change of clothes, a phone number in the U.S. scribbled on a scrap of paper, and cash hidden in the soles of shoes or sewn inside the linings of their clothes. They witness or survive robberies, fall victim to brutal attacks or sexual assaults, outrun or hide from federal police and border patrol agents but also fall prey to criminal gangs and drug cartels whose specialty is kidnapping and extortion. NGOs (non-governmental organizations) in the United States, Central America and Mexico have reported that cartels kidnap young migrants in order to extort money from their families or traffic them for sex and labour. Of the 40 young people I interviewed, nine—seven boys and two girls—told me they were captured by the Zetas cartel in Mexico on their way to the United States. Rape is so common that many migrant girls get birth control injections[3] before they leave home.

A United Nations High Commissioner for Refugees (UNHCR) study, based on 404 interviews with migrants aged 12–17 who entered the United States in the autumn of 2011 or later, concluded that 58 percent of them had been forcibly displaced by threats in their home countries.

Consider the case of Ernesto. He told me he fled horrific abuse in Honduras and migrated with two friends, hitching rides and travelling by foot through Guatemala and Mexico. They avoided Mexican freight trains because people can fall off them and die. "I mean, you just don't care about the odds or you wouldn't do it," Ernesto says of his journey. "How did I decide? It was the American Dream." Ernesto worked his way north until he was seized by members of the Zetas cartel outside a Mexican border town. He was starved and beaten, while the Zetas extorted $4,000 from his family back home in Honduras. He escaped, but three of his companions were killed when they balked at the cartel's demands.

Carlita, a 13-year-old Salvadoran girl, fled gang violence. She told me she was also kidnapped by the Zetas in Mexico, used for sex and forced to transport drugs for them, before escaping and ultimately making it to the border.

Myth #2: "They Need to Go Back to Their Families Where they Belong!"

The child migrants arriving in large numbers are viewed with ambivalence—in contrast to their American-raised counterparts, the "Dreamers"—and they tend to be categorized in one of two ways. First, they are, as anti-immigrant activists in Arizona put it, "illegal aliens." When informed in mid-July 2014 that the government intended to transfer 40–60 unaccompanied minors to Oracle, Arizona, the local sheriff, Paul Babeu, told CNN: "These children should be returned to their home country where they belong." Second, they are seen as a vulnerable population who, despite their "illegal status," need protection and assistance. One Oracle resident, Frank Pierson, worried that the town would be seen as anti-children: "We think the angels of our better nature need to be reflected through efforts like this one."[4]

These contradictory perspectives ignore some basic facts. In my visits to these detention facilities and in interviews with former detainees, I heard many stories like that of Maribel. Many children and youths lack families who are able to provide adequate care and support. Many have been severely abused and neglected or abandoned. Others seek refuge and new attachments after violence back home tore their families apart, leaving them without parents or siblings and forcing them to face the terrors of life on the street. Others live with a caretaker like a grandparent after their parents are forced to migrate to the U.S. in order to provide for them. When these arrangements break down, many young people set out alone, some with or without the help of guides or smugglers.

Unaccompanied child migrants are younger than ever before, with 24 percent under the age of 14 in 2013, up from 17 percent in 2012. In 2014 the average age for youth migrants from Honduras and El Salvador was 14, and for those from Guatemala [it] was 15. A government official reported seeing children as young as four years old coming into the country alone or with a sibling or cousin who was slightly older.[5] There has also been an upswing in the number of girls undertaking this arduous journey, with girls comprising 27 percent of the youth entering ORR custody in 2013, compared to 23 percent in 2012. Most notably, the number of unaccompanied girls under the age of 14 and making the journey alone has increased, and this accelerated rate is expected to continue.[6]

Child and adolescent migrants come from countries where social inequality is high, living wages are scarce, and violence is a scourge in the home and the community.[7] The vast majority in U.S. federal custody (88 percent) come from Central America—Guatemala, El Salvador, and Honduras in search of family, work, education, or refuge from domestic abuse, political violence, criminal gangs, or drug cartels. Mexican children and youth are underrepresented in immigration custody (only 3 percent in 2013) because most are returned within 72 hours. Travelling through Mexico, many Central American migrants face an intensely violent economic enterprise that generates enormous profits from kidnapping, human smuggling, drug trafficking, extortion, and killings.[8] The spread of criminal gangs and the grab for drug trafficking profits have spawned new cartels, creating murderous competition over smuggling routes and distribution networks. Young people in Central America and Mexico experience firsthand the intensification of lawlessness, the political corruption, and the gang violence that infect all spheres of social life.[9] Migration is a calculated wager as a hedge against domestic abuse, predatory police, forced gang conscription, drug traffickers and the certainty of a social or physical death if they remain at home.

Insisting that child migrants return to their families ignores the fact that the families of many of these young people are, in fact, already in the United States. Structural violence and poverty at home have forced their parents to migrate to the U.S. in order to provide their children with food and clothing. Huge investments in border enforcement along the U.S.-Mexico border have not kept migrants out but sealed them in, separating them from their families on the other side. The vast majority of children and youth who are designated as unaccompanied, and have been detained and released, will either live without legal status, leave, or be removed from the U.S., even though it is estimated that nearly 40 percent could be eligible for legal relief.

Myth #3: The 2014 Crisis Is Not New

This crisis involving child migrants didn't need to happen, and in fact detention and deportation weren't always the norm. In 1984, during the Salvadoran civil war, there was another large-scale migration of children to the United States as thousands of youth fled violence at home and headed north. Until that time, U.S. immigration authorities had routinely released detained children to parents or family already living in the United States, pending immigration court hearings.

But, citing the need to protect vulnerable children caught up in a humanitarian emergency, and using their broad powers to detain non-citizens, in 1984, authorities in the western division of the Immigration and Naturalization Service—the precursor to the ICE (Immigration and Customs Enforcement), CBP (Customs and Border Protection) and other agencies within the Department of Homeland Security—made automatic detention the new norm and release became the exception. These authorities continued to defend detention, even when legal aid organizations in southern California sued them in 1985 for confining children under the punitive conditions usually reserved for violent offenders. Children as young as 14 who posed no security threat or flight risk were incarcerated with adult criminals and adjudicated youths, subjected to shackling and strip searches and deprived of legal, educational, and social services.

After years of litigation, the Supreme Court in 1993 affirmed the government's right to detain undocumented children in secure facilities for unspecified and sometimes prolonged periods of time, pending release to approved sponsors and an appearance in immigration court. Faced with continuing legal challenges, the federal government agreed in 1997 to establish minimum standards for their humane treatment, to hold them in the least restrictive setting and to ensure their prompt release. In 2008, passage of the Trafficking Victims Protection and Reauthorization bill added protections for unaccompanied children seeking asylum or juvenile visas and required ICE agents to notify ORR officials after the apprehension of a young migrant and to transfer custody of that child to the ORR within 72 hours.[10]

Myth #4: Unaccompanied Children Apprehended Alone Need Detention for Their Own Protection

Despite the jarring images of young children in overcrowded holding cells, little is known about what happens to children after they are apprehended by the U.S. Border Patrol. Twenty-four of the youth I interviewed, including Ernesto and Carlita, spoke at length about their experiences in CBP custody. They were grateful for the life-saving interventions of the Border Patrol but described being subjected to coercive arrests, physical discomfort such as frigid temperatures and inadequate food, and both verbal and physical abuse.

Their stories round out civil and human rights groups' 2012 and 2014 allegations that the CBP systematically abused unaccompanied children. The CBP insists that "mistreatment or misconduct is not tolerated" and that it "strives to protect unaccompanied children with special procedures and safeguards."

Child migrants are allowed to remain in CBP custody for only 72 hours. Those from Mexico are deported quickly unless they express a fear of persecution or trafficking, but migrants from Central America or other countries who are designated as unaccompanied minors are transferred to special facilities for underaged children and youth operated by the ORR. First, officials from the enforcement branches of the Department of Homeland Security, CBP, and ICE make the critical determination of whether each child is 18 and without family in the United States to care for him or her. ICE officials gather data on each child's family background, identify potential security risks such as a criminal background or gang affiliation, and make a preliminary recommendation for placement in the ORR-operated facilities. The profile that emerges is frequently based on incomplete, misleading, or incorrect information that obscures the existence of family relationships and mischaracterizes the child's personal history.[11]

Government facilities are privately run and contracted by the ORR and are classified by three security levels—low, medium, and high. These facilities typically house large numbers of children (200) and are located in remote border areas in order to reduce costs and to facilitate the children's eventual removal. Government regulations call for children to be held "in a non-institutional home-like atmosphere of care." But I saw firsthand that custody is not anything like home. Although the ORR has introduced more alternatives to institutionalized settings such as group homes, independent living, and foster care, it also has greatly expanded contracts with large-scale detention facilities that require controlled entry, exit, and movement, 24-hour camera surveillance, and continuous supervision. In such facilities, children attend school inside the shelter, play sports within fenced areas, and only leave the facilities under "escort" for court appearances, special medical or psychiatric treatment, and occasional community outings. Until recently they were subjected to rigid behavioural management programmes that were both punitive and infantilizing. Those misbehaving could be moved to more restrictive facilities and held for longer periods and/or diagnosed with psychological disorders and managed with psychotropic medicine.[12]

For many of these children, the strict regulations within the facilities were a shock. Fernanda, a 22-year-old from Guatemala, recounted to me the litany of rules enforced in the minimum-security Texas facility where she stayed for six months:

> We had to keep an arm's length from another person and to maintain this distance without touching. We couldn't play rough, talk loud, run around, touch the windows or send messages to other kids. We had about 15 minutes to pee and brush our teeth in the morning, and the same time to take a bath at night. There were always two workers in each house. They were watching us all the time. Lights went out at 9.30 pm. If you sleep a certain way at night and then turn over, they write it down. If you wake up in the middle of the night, they write it down.

Carlos, a young Salvadoran who crossed the Rio Grande to enter the United States, was initially placed in a low-security shelter in Washington State, given a legal screening and deemed to be eligible for legal relief. He liked the shelter but described that, after getting into a fight, he was transferred to a more secure facility that resembled a prison:

> When they told me the rules, I thought, "This is not a jail!" They gave me clothes, took me on trips, and we took turns cleaning the bathrooms and the kitchen. They explained the point levels. There was level 1, 2 and 3. You start at one level, and if you behave OK, you stay there. But if you say bad words, if you don't go to your room when they tell you, if you touch a friend anywhere, they lower your level and they can kick you out. I got sent to a different place. I was locked up all the time. They had levels too. The best level had TV, CD and radio, but the level I started on had nothing—no movies on Friday nights, no radio. The rooms for my level were the oldest and the dirtiest. It was bad, and I was there for four months. I couldn't qualify for a foster care family because I got stepped up [to a more restricted level]. Then I turned 18, and they sent me to the adult detention centre. I really suffered there.

Being locked up with no set endpoint creates feelings of helplessness among children who are already suffering from trauma. Maribel captured this sense of desperation when she described being detained for six months in a federal facility in Los Fresnos, Texas: "It was clean and had a nice enough living room, but I realized that I couldn't leave. There was no life—life ended there. The shelter was near the main road and I could see cars going by, and I wanted to be in that car." Ernesto also remembered his feelings of disorientation: "You don't know what's going to happen. I asked, 'Why do they send me here?' We were so afraid. Were they going to take us somewhere and kill us?"

In 2012, the length of stay in ORR facilities for unaccompanied children averaged 60 to 75 days. And the longer the children stay, the more anxious they tend to feel and the more likely they are to misbehave. Some who qualified for protective status instead choose to self-deport in order to escape prolonged confinement. In a 2009 report, the Women's Refugee Commission estimated that half of those in detention are medicated for mood disorders, depression, or post-traumatic stress disorder.[13] The government does not systematically track what happens to children once they are released to families in the United States or returned to the home country.

The process of release from custody is termed family reunification, even if the child is not approved to join family members in the United States or had not previously lived with the sponsor. Family reunification—defined broadly as joining or rejoining blood relations or surrogate family—was, and remains, the ostensible goal of the federal custody and the primary means by which undocumented children are permitted to stay in the United States. Federal staff members have portrayed family reunification as modelled on national child welfare standards that prioritize identifying risk factors that threaten a safe release, such as domestic violence, substance abuse, or financial insecurity. Academics and advocates have contested this assertion arguing that the process of reunification has functioned as a system of control closely tied to immigration enforcement. Decisions about suitable sponsors have been determined as much by security considerations—criminal history and legal status—and financial solvency as by emotional bonds and family connections. Being undocumented, poor, and having a criminal record could trump even the closest blood relationship. The intrusive government scrutiny of prospective sponsors before release—including parents and close relatives—expresses strong anxieties about national culture, race, and ethnicity in the nation of the future.

The ORR's decision about whether to release children to families or sponsors in the United States is entirely separate from the decision, by an immigration judge, about whether to grant them protective status. The children are required to be placed in removal proceedings after their apprehension, but they are not entitled to government-funded attorneys or child advocates. In detention, they struggle to find volunteer or pro bono attorneys; only 28 percent of children in detention manage to do so, according to a report by the Vera Institute of Justice. Nearly 90 percent of children in detention are released to sponsors within the United States, but the ORR does not track the outcome of their cases in immigration court, meaning that while these children find a place outside detention to stay temporarily, their long-term status in the United States is uncertain.

Carlos' attorney, for instance, worked with the local ICE office to get him released, and helped him apply for a Special Immigrant Juvenile visa based on the severe abuse he endured at home. He is now a legal permanent resident living and working in Washington State. But Ernesto, the young man from Honduras who had been seized by the Zetas en route to the United States, faced more complications. He was sent to a minimum-security shelter in Texas and hoped that it would offer refuge from the horrors of his journey. Instead, it was the beginning of a painful ordeal where he was sexually abused by a shelter worker who was sentenced on state charges of child abuse to a seven-year prison term. Ernesto spent 14 months in two different federal facilities before being granted a U visa (non-immigrant status) and released to a foster family in Virginia.[14] His green card (permanent residence card) petition is still pending.

Today, the federal custodial system built up to house these migrants is an expanding leviathan that costs taxpayers hundreds of millions of dollars each year and affects thousands of families. For many years the number of children apprehended, designated as unaccompanied, and detained annually in the U.S. was 6,000–8,000. From 2009 to 2013, that number tripled. The custodial system administered by the ORR was designed for approximately 8,000 children per year, so the dramatic increase in new arrivals in 2014 (57,496) has placed considerable strain on facilities and personnel.

Before 2014, critics of the federal custodial system complained about long periods of detention—especially for children with special physical, psychological, and behavioural problems; the overuse of secure facilities; a shortage of specialized therapeutic facilities; and the long-standing trend of locating facilities in remote border regions to reduce costs or to keep children in close proximity to the border and ready for deportation if ordered.[15] I found that immigration custody continues to be plagued by systemic problems. It takes an ad hoc approach that undermines consistency and fairness, lacks coordination in data collection, restricts information flows, enhances redundancy, and concentrates power in the hands of senior government administrators whose decisions are difficult to review or appeal. Complaints about the abuse of children by facility staff have continued. Government officials have been slow to report abuse and have repeatedly failed to hold abusers accountable.[16] More troubling is the lack of independent oversight to track the government's compliance with its own detention standards—those who oversee operations are supervisors working for the ORR.

. . . Prior to 2014, the length of immigration custody averaged 60 days but in a chaotic response to the increased arrivals, average stays have been reduced to less than 30 days for children without family in the United States and to approximately 10 days for those with parents living in the country. During the summer of 2014, the government even removed the requirement that sponsors be fingerprinted as part of the background check. There have been cases of children falling into the hands of smugglers or traffickers and situations of exploitation—the very harm that the system was instituted to prevent.

In the wake of failed attempts to implement comprehensive immigration reform and a continued focus on enforcement, it is instructive to hear from young people who were detained, released from custody, awarded legal status and are building lives in the U.S. I asked Mirabel what she would say to people who want all undocumented immigrants to go home. She replied:

> I understand the American point of view that it is unfair for immigrants to come here and to take advantage. They don't think immigrants have the right to get benefits when they weren't raised here and didn't paid taxes [*sic*]. But I would tell them that I came here to change

my crazy life and to provide for my children. I wanted to come to a place with laws. People don't understand what we suffer to get here. I had to leave my country, my father and my mother because she couldn't help herself. But I can and I am strong.

She had this advice for young people like herself:

> Don't be too scared to change. You may cry and want to go back to your country but stay, be independent, and work hard. You have opportunities here. Don't throw them away. Don't live like you are back in your home country. Your children will be born here and they will make their life here. I can see my whole life in my past and in my present and I am accomplishing my dream.

On 15 June 2012, late in the presidential campaign and under pressure from Latino groups, Obama issued an executive order that offered a temporary reprieve from deportation and short-term work authorization for young immigrants who were brought to the U.S. as children, were enrolled in school, and had no criminal record. On 19 November 2014, Obama once again used his executive authority to announce a new deferred action programme, this time for the undocumented parents of U.S. citizens and Legal Permanent Residents who will get temporary relief from deportation and work authorization.[17] However, the White House insisted that the administration's "aggressive and coordinated Federal response" to the 2014 influx of unaccompanied children to the U.S.-Mexico border would focus on "heightened deterrence, enhanced enforcement, stronger foreign cooperation and greater capacity to secure our borders." The new order directed immigration courts to prioritize the removal cases of recent border crossers, a direct reference to unaccompanied children and single mothers with young children.[18]

While the government works to address the challenges at the U.S. border, the country should also ask itself if it makes sense to continue to prosecute and detain large numbers of unaccompanied minors in order to ensure their safety. This policy puts the U.S. at odds with international norms in Europe and with domestic practice. After all, who benefits if the country spends millions of dollars to inform children of their rights, improve their health, and teach them English only to put them in removal proceedings and cut them loose after their release? Why build insurmountable hurdles to legal status and deny them the opportunity for legal work? Why shouldn't the U.S. protect young people who escape violence and who work hard to realize the tantalizing promise of the American Dream?

Notes

1. The Customs and Border Protection (CBP) agency reports that in the first two months of the fiscal year 2015, the apprehensions of unaccompanied children at the southwest border had dropped by 40 percent compared to the same time period in 2014.

2. Meissner, D. et al. 2013. 2013. *Immigration enforcement in the United States: The rise of a formidable machinery.* Washington, DC: Migration Policy Institute

3. United States Conference of Catholic Bishops (USCCB) 2014. Mission to Central America: The flight of unaccompanied children to the United States. Report of the Committee on Migration of the USCCB, Washington, DC.

4. "Growing protests over where to shelter immigrant children hits Arizona." http:// www.cnn .com/2014/07/15/us/arizona-immigrant-children/.

5. Statements by government officials at the meeting of the Interagency Working Group on Unaccompanied Minors, 22 May 2014.

6. Roundtable on Detention and Removal, Institute for the Study of International Migration, Georgetown University, 7 October 2014.

7. Ward, P. 2004. From the marginality of the 1960s to the 'new poverty' of today. *Latin American Research Review* 39(1): 183–187.

8. Vogt, W. 2013. Crossing Mexico: Structural violence and the commodification of undocumented Central American migrants. *American Ethnologist* 40(4): 764–80.

9. Adams, T.M. 2012. Chronic violence and its reproduction: Perverse trends in social relations, citizenship and democracy in Latin America. Latin American Program. Woodrow Wilson International Center for Scholars.

10. Terrio, S.J. 2015. *Whose child am I? Unaccompanied, undocumented children in U.S. immigration custody.* Berkeley, CA: University of California Press.

11. Terrio 2015.

12. Terrio 2015; see also Heidbrink, L. 2014. *Migrant youth, transnational families, and the state: Care and contested interests.* Philadelphia, PA: University of Pennsylvania Press.; Women's Refugee Commission 2009. Halfway home: Unaccompanied children in immigration custody. http://womensrefugee commission.org / resources/document/196-halfway-home-unaccompanied-children-in-immigration-custody Zatz, M.S. & N. Rodriguez 2015. *Dreams and nightmares: Immigration policy, youth and families.* Berkley, CA: University of California Press

13. Women's Refugee Commission 2009.

14. To be eligible for a U visa, the undocumented applicant must provide certification from federal, state, or local authorities that he or she has been the victim of a crime and is likely to assist law enforcement in the investigation and prosecution of the crime. http://www. uscis.gov/sites/default/ files/files /pressrelease/U- visaFS2_05Sept07.pdf.

15. Young, W. & M. McKenna 2010. The measure of a society: The treatment of unaccompanied refugee and immigrant children in the United States. *Harvard Civil Rights–Civil Liberties Law Review* 45: 252..

16. See note 12.

17. This executive order expanded the 2012 Deferred Action for Childhood Arrivals (DACA) benefit of temporary relief from deportation to those who came to the U.S. before 1 January 2010, regardless of how old they are at the time of application..

18. Zatz & Rodriguez 2015.

10.3 **The Non-National in Jordan: Statelessness as Structural Violence Among Gaza Refugees in Jordan**

MICHAEL VICENTE PEREZ

Refugees are people who have migrated because of war or political oppression. While refugees typically have legal permission to live in another country, that does not mean they hold the same rights as the citizens of the nation-state to which they have migrated. This point becomes quite clear through the following case study of Gaza refugees in Jordan. In this selection, Michael Perez argues that statelessness is a form of violence that denies certain Palestinians of their basic human rights. Violence, here, is used not to describe physical oppression, but rather to describe the structural oppression that Gazans suffer as a result of lacking citizenship. This selection points to the fundamental problem of living in a world in which the gateway to securing rights is through citizenship, rather than the ability of all humans everywhere to be afforded the same rights, regardless of where they live.

Questions

1. What does the concept of social suffering emphasize?
2. How does the fact that Gaza refugees are excluded from Jordanian citizenship impact their lives? How does statelessness expose the limits of human rights? Provide specific examples from the reading.
3. To what degree are humanitarian aid regimes helpful in the lives of Palestinian refugees? Where do they fall short?

Abu Asad lives in one of the older sections of Amman. His home sits on a narrow alleyway off a staircase leading up from the City Center to Jabal Amman. Our encounter was pure luck. I didn't know Abu Asad from my previous fieldwork in Jordan. Our meeting was a chance encounter determined by a combination of anthropological curiosity and Arab hospitality. Climbing the steps that hot summer day, I was drawn to the conspicuous presence of two Palestinian flags and the word "Gaza" spray-painted on the wall leading to his home. This was an unusual bit of street art. In Amman, it's uncommon to see Palestinian flags outside of the tourist shops in the downtown. For historical and political reasons, the Jordanian government is mostly intolerant of Palestinian displays of nationalism. Thus finding explicit displays of Palestinian

national symbols is generally a difficult task. Yet on this obscure street in Old Amman, two Palestinian flags defied the norms of Palestinian invisibility. And this caught my attention.

After photographing the flags, I was ready to continue my trek up to Rainbow Street on the top of the hill. At the steps, however, I saw an older man making his way up the stairs with a cane. The man smiled as I offered customary salutations. His demeanor was gentle yet confident. From the look on his face, he seemed as interested in our presence as we were in the Palestinian art down the street. Following a scripted exchange about our backgrounds, he asked me about the purpose of my visit to his neighborhood. I blamed the Palestinian flags for our pause. With a hint of excitement, the old man told me we were looking down his street and invited me to join him at his house at the end of the alley. I enthusiastically accepted.

Along the short walk to his house, Abu Asad offered a brief account of his home and neighborhood. The house, he explained, was built in the early 1900s during the end of Ottoman rule. As he continued his narrative, my mind drifted elsewhere. I couldn't help but draw connections between the conditions of his neighborhood and the conditions of Jordan's refugee camps. The similarities were striking. The decrepit homes, the sewage-soaked streets, and the concrete aesthetic all reminded me of Palestinian camps I'd visited years ago. When I arrived at his home, the situation was no different. It was a ramshackle house with a series of makeshift arrangements: curtains functioned as walls, barrels of water served for bathing, and cinder blocks upheld furniture. The bare concrete floors were unevenly paved and pools of water formed throughout the living room. Like the Palestinian camps, their poverty was conspicuous and anything but accidental.

Abu Asad and his family are ex–Gaza refugees. Like thousands of Palestinians, they fled the Gaza Strip during the 1967 Arab-Israeli war. Many of these Palestinians were doubly displaced: forced from their homes in Palestine in 1948 to Gaza, the new war compelled them to join a second wave of displacement to Jordan. Since their arrival in Jordan, they have lived the status of stateless refugees unable to enjoy the rights of Jordanian citizens. This particular status has placed the Gaza refugees in conditions of vulnerability that exposes them to particular forms of discrimination and thus social suffering. The concept of social suffering points to the nexus between human suffering and political, economic, and institutional power (Kleinman, Das, and Lock 1997). It emphasizes the non-accidental nature of pain, poverty, ill health, and even death. Moreover, the lived condition of statelessness Gazans have experienced for over 40 years underscores their status as victims of structural violence. As stateless refugees, Gazans suffer from an oppressive social structure that results in the systematic reduction of their rights and human potential. The violence against Gazans, in other words, is built into the social structure that excludes them as refugees—the structure that makes their statelessness a lived experience. As such, it is an indirect form of violence that is both the product of human agency and avoidable (Galtung 1969). Gazans don't have to suffer this way.

In this chapter, I argue that the situation of Gaza refugees demonstrates how statelessness is a particular form of violence maintained through the legal boundaries between citizens and non-citizens. Using the concept of structural violence (Farmer 2003), I situate the Gazans' experience within a larger historical and institutional context that has systematically deprived certain Palestinians of their basic human rights. These exclusions constitute a form of violence rooted in a social order whose effects include the social and economic impoverishment an entire class of people as *stateless refugees*. Their statelessness, in other words, is not the reason for their suffering. The condition of being stateless alone is insufficient for the kinds of suffering Gazans experience in Jordan. The human rights framework suggests that refugees and stateless peoples *should* enjoy the protection of their rights regardless of their non-citizenship status. Thus it is not that being stateless limits one's human rights; rather, it is the specific systems of exclusion enforced by states that render statelessness a condition of rightlessness. In other words, it is the social structure that turns the experience of statelessness into a condition of rightlessness that makes the Gazans and other stateless people suffer.

In this sense, this chapter not only shows the contradiction between Jordanian domestic law and international human rights but also reveals the larger problem inherent within a world where human rights are dependent on, and thus limited by, sovereign states. Living in what Agamben described as the state of exception (Agamben 2000), in which refugees are expelled from the order of the nation-state and thus subject to exceptional rules, we can see that statelessness exposes the limits of human rights. It tells us that the predicament of those whom Hannah Arendt called the rightless is not that they don't have rights but that, as stateless people, no state exists to protect them. Expelled, as it were, from nowhere, they belong to no one. It is this tension between the idea of transcendental rights and the order primacy of the nation-state that led Arendt to conclude that statelessness was tantamount to rightlessness. As she observed:

> [It] is not that they are deprived of life, liberty, and the pursuit of happiness, or of equality before the law and freedom of opinion— problems that were designed to solve problems *within* given communities—but that they no

longer belong to any community whatsoever. Their plight is not that they are not equal before the law, but that no law exists for them; not that they are oppressed but that nobody wants even to oppress them. (Arendt 2000, 26)

Palestinian Refugees as "Historically Given"

Writing about the context of Haiti, Paul Farmer suggested that understanding violence as a structural phenomenon required attention to history. According to him, suffering is "structured" by historically given and often economically driven processes and forces that conspire—whether routine, ritual or, as is more commonly the case, the hard surfaces of life—to constrain agency (Farmer 2003 40). In the Gazans' case, history is critical. Their status as refugees is the "historically given" effect of the Israeli national project in Palestine. Indeed, the very existence of *Palestinian* refugees is the direct outcome of Israeli settler colonialism in the Middle East. Thus any effort to approach the particular situation of Gazans in Jordan must begin with the larger context of Israel's creation and Palestine's destruction.

From the establishment of the state of Israel in 1948 to the contemporary occupation and colonization of the West Bank (Piterberg 2013, 18), Palestinians' encounter with Zionism has been shaped by violent processes of Jewish territorial expansion and Palestinian territorial loss. The dynamics of this settler colonial project culminated in the 1948 Palestine war and creation of the state of Israel on approximately 70 percent of former Palestinian territory. During this war, over 700,000 Palestinians were ethnically cleansed (Pappe 2006) from their homes and denied the ability to return. Compelled by conditions of war and, in some cases, deliberate expulsion by Zionist forces, Palestinian displacement reflected the logic and effort to create an exclusively Jewish state emptied of its original inhabitants. As Morris noted:

> [The] refugee problem was caused by attacks by Jewish forces on Arab villages and towns and by the inhabitants' fear of such attacks, compounded by expulsions, atrocities, and rumors of atrocities—and by the crucial Israeli Cabinet decision in June 1948 to bar a refugee return. (Morris 2007, 38)

The 1948 refugees fled to areas in what remained of Palestine and to surrounding countries including Lebanon, Syria, and Jordan. For these Palestinians, displacement was intimately tied to the ongoing project of Zionist colonization. Thus after the 1948 war and, particularly, [during] the period of 1965–1969, the Israel Land Administration authorized the demolition of hundreds of former Palestinian villages in an effort to "clear the land" of its Palestinian past (Shai 2006, 87) and preclude Palestinian return.

The situation of Gaza refugees in Jordan must therefore begin with its connection to the process of Zionist settler colonization. Displaced from Palestine in 1948 to Gaza and again in 1967 to Jordan, their particular situation is the outcome of Zionist settler colonialism, two Arab-Israeli wars, Israeli territorial expansion, and Israel's refusal to acknowledge Palestinian refugees' right to return. More specifically, their existence as *stateless* refugees is rooted in the absence of a sovereign Palestinian state. Without a state of Palestine, in other words, Palestinians remain subject to external regimes of power that structure their lives according to the exceptional condition of having no state of their own. Understanding the circumstances of Gazans in Jordan thus requires attention to the larger historical processes that not only made Palestinians *refugees* but also the ongoing restrictions on the creation of a Palestinian state.

Statelessness as Rightlessness: The Structural Violence of Exclusion

The structural limits imposed upon Gazans result from two particular refusals: the refusal to extend Jordanian citizenship and the refusal to recognize Gazans' human rights as stateless refugees. Like most states in the world, the Jordanian government grounds its exclusionary policies in the idea that state sovereignty entails the right to decide who can become a citizen and under what conditions. Thus from the government's perspective, whether Gazans can or should be offered Jordanian citizenship is at the discretion of the state; Gazans have no right to citizenship. The historical context of this decision extends back to the Arab-Israeli War of 1967. Palestinians fleeing to Jordan generally fell into two categories: those displaced from the West to East Bank of Jordan (internally displaced refugees) and refugees displaced from Gaza. For the first group, their displacement had no effect on their national status; they were already Jordanian citizens. For refugees fleeing Gaza, however, crossing the Jordanian border had very different results. Because the Gaza Strip was under Egyptian administration before the war, the Jordanian government treated the refugees as Egyptian subjects and thus unassimilable. The terms of this policy suggested that Gazans had no right to Jordanian citizenship and they were therefore categorized as legal foreign residents. The decision not only excluded Gazans from the benefits of Jordanian nationality but also perpetuated their status as stateless refugees.[1] Ineligible for citizenship, the Jordanian government offered the Gazans one-year temporary passports. More recently, Jordan has extended the duration of these passports to three years.

Since their arrival in Jordan over 40 years ago, Gazans have thus lived the dual status of foreign residents and stateless refugees. Circumscribed by these two statuses, Gazans have encountered a variety of barriers that complicate their ability to experience the rights enjoyed by other Palestinians who have Jordanian citizenship. This is not to say that other Palestinian refugees have it easy. Indeed, like the Gazans, many Palestinians still live within refugee camps administered by the United Nations Relief and Works Agency (UNRWA). For these refugees, life entails various challenges that are directly linked to their status as refugees living within camps. In terms of income, housing, education, health, and general living conditions, for example, significant disparities exist between the experience of Palestinian camp refugees and non-camp Palestinian refugees (Tiltnes and Zhang, 2013). In the Gazans' case, however, matters are much worse. Their status as stateless foreign residents *and* camp refugees results in particular hardships that distinguish them from other refugees. Indeed, virtually every aspect of socio-economic life for Gazans is plagued by discriminations that set them apart from the majority of Palestinians in the Kingdom. Thus Gazans are not only poorer than other refugees but are also more than three times as likely to be amongst the very poorest and most destitute living on less than $1.25 USD a day (Tiltnes and Zhang 2013, 8). Gazans are also most likely to live in the worst conditions of all Palestinians. A 2007 European Union survey of living conditions in the Gaza camp, for example, found that approximately 60 percent of Palestinians dwellings were "structurally unsafe." According to a 2011 report on the living conditions in Palestinian camps, issues of overcrowding were highest in the Gaza camp. Defined as "three or more persons sharing one room," about 24 percent of Gaza camp homes have been identified as overcrowded. The same report found that the Gaza camp suffered from major sewage problems linked to the absence of an underground sewage network. These findings were reconfirmed in 2013 when a similar report found that:

> Grey water generated in the households sometimes contaminated with leaks of sewage from old cesspools, runs along open collection ditches all around the camp. . . . Children play in streets with ditches and close to the pools, which results in an inflated incidence of (blood) diarrhea and hepatitis. A dilapidated and undersized water supply network exacerbates the situation as the water may be of poor quality, and the scarcity of water impedes hygienic behavior. (Tiltnes and Zhang 2013, 63)

In the following section, I will take the accounts of several Gazans I met in Jordan during my fieldwork in 2006–2007 and again in 2015 to show how some of the limitations outlined previously translate into particular forms of suffering. This is not to say that all Gazans confront the same hardships or experience them the same way. It is, however, an attempt to elucidate how structural limitations produce specific effects on people's lives that, when taken together, demonstrate conditions of shared suffering and oppression.

My first encounter with the predicament of Gazan refugees occurred during my fieldwork in Amman in 2006–2007. I was in the Wihdat camp conducting interviews with Palestinians about their experience as refugees in Jordan and ideas about the Palestinian homeland. Our escort, Im Ayman, was a local Palestinian from Wihdat. With extensive contacts in the camp, she introduced me to numerous Palestinian families willing to share their stories with a foreign researcher. After several visits in the camp, Im Ayman brought us to a small dwelling with a large steel door. Upon entering the home, we were struck by the austere conditions. Two foam mattresses functioned as a couch in the only shared space of the house. The owner of the home, a woman who appeared to be in her sixties, graciously seated us while she prepared a meal on a small stovetop directly connected to the gas canister that fueled it. Sitting next to us were her two sons, one of which she described as "miskeen," which meant he suffered from mental illness and was unable to work. Her husband died years ago.

During our discussion, I learned that the woman, whom I will call Im Shadi, was a Gaza refugee. Since their arrival in Jordan, Im Shadi and her family have received special services under the Social Safety Net Program. Designed by UNRWA to address the needs of families identified as the "abject poor," the program provides quarterly assistance in the form of food commodities and cash subsidies. Although the program supports any refugees living below a specific poverty metric, various reports on the socio-economic conditions of refugees in Jordan suggest that Gazans constitute a significant number of the program's recipients. In a 2009 assessment on the Gaza camp, for example, approximately 513 families qualified for assistance linked to their status as "special hardship cases." In this sense, the conditions of Im Shadi's home and her life more generally, which she vividly described as "hard," "a struggle," and "without dignity," can be seen as structurally given. That is, the difficulties of Im Shadi's life and her need of assistance were the structural outcome of her position as a non-citizen Gaza refugee.

Im Shadi wasn't the only Gazan I met during my fieldwork. The more time I spent in Amman's refugee camps, the more I learned about the specific experiences of Gaza's refugees. While conducting interviews in the Hitteen camp, for example, I met another Gazan family. Like Im Shadi, they too lacked Jordanian citizenship and thus struggled to satisfy their basic needs. Because of their statelessness, I was told, life was much more difficult. Their educational options were limited, their healthcare was largely dependent on the basic services provided by UNRWA, and employment was hard to come by. Their poverty, in other words, resulted in a set of limits that precluded access to critical resources in Jordan. Post-secondary education, for example, was impossible for the family in Hitteen. According to them, there aren't enough scholarships available for Gazans—about 26 out of 300 government scholarships are reserved for Gazan students each year. The limited number of scholarships is supposed to reflect their comparatively smaller population. This, however, ignores that fact that Gazans like this family are the poorest of all Palestinian refugees in Jordan. Thus the combination of limited scholarships, high university costs, and Gazans' low income means that

post-secondary education is simply too costly an ambition. The family I spoke with in Hitteen thus saw the labor market as the only option for their children after graduation. Yet, for this family, even work options were limited. As foreign residents, they could not expect to find most work available to Jordanian citizens. Rather, they had to compete for jobs available to other foreign workers. This presents a structurally limited range of opportunities for advancement since foreign laborers often work for lower wages than Jordanians and fill temporary labor positions.

Abu Marwan was one of several Gazan refugees I met in the Gaza camp. Located in the northern city of Jarash, the camp houses approximately 25,000 refugees displaced from Gaza in 1967. Introduced by a mutual friend who was also a Gaza refugee, Abu Marwan offered one of the most vivid accounts of social suffering I'd heard. During our discussion, he described a series of limits, vulnerabilities, and injuries that were inseparable from his status as a stateless refugee. One of the challenges he described concerned employment. Labor laws in Jordan require that employers purchase a permit from the Ministry of Labor for any foreign employees. Because Gazans are legally categorized as foreign residents, hiring them also requires permit. According to Abu Marwan, this means that Gazans are structurally disadvantaged in several ways. First, Gazans have to compete within a limited job market primarily reserved for foreign laborers. This, Abu Marwan suggested, was a significant problem since the influx of Egyptian labor has limited the jobs available to Gazans. Second, if an employer does hire a Gazan, they may deduct the cost of the permit from his wages. Finally, some Gazans may choose to avoid the permits altogether and work illegally. While working illegally may get around the problem of securing a permit, it nonetheless opens them to other disadvantages including lower wages inconsistent pay, poor job security, and the legal consequences of violating the law. The cumulative effect of these challenges was such that, for Gazans, earning an income was plagued by precarious possibilities—possibilities rooted in their structural position as stateless refugees.

In addition to employment, one of the key issues Abu Marwan highlighted concerned the problem of healthcare. In Jordan, only Gazan children under six years of age are entitled to the Civil Insurance Program (CIP), which covers healthcare costs for government employees, the disabled, and the poor. Unable to work in the government or register their poverty as Jordanian citizens, Gazans are ineligible for CIP coverage and must therefore purchase medical insurance from the private sector or seek treatment at government hospitals. In both cases, however, Gazans are structurally disadvantaged: the wide-scale poverty among Gazans means that most medical options are simply unaffordable. This reality was forcefully conveyed by Abu Marwan during our interview. For him, the inability to afford medical treatment for his son had tragic results.

> My eldest son was diagnosed with cancer (pause); he died in 2006. Because I didn't have a national number,[2] no one helped me. I went to the Royal Palace for help. I went to the Ministry of Health. I asked for help from the United Arab Emirates. I even sent a letter to [Yasser] Arafat to help me! The UNRWA health services didn't cover my son's treatment. After a year, I relied on God. Finally, Princess Basma offered me Royal Insurance . . . after my son died. There are many stories like this. The people of [Gaza] camp, we die and then the insurance follows us to the cemetery.

Despite the government's willingness to pay for 60 percent of the costs, Abu Marwan said the remaining costs were still too expensive. Thus like other Gazans unable to afford the high costs of serious medical treatments, he was forced to watch his son slowly die from the painful effects of cancer.

The brief accounts offered [herein] are not unique. Many of the Gazans I met highlighted the connection between their experiences of poverty and their status as stateless Gazans. Poverty, however, was never simply an economic category. Rather, it was a lived experience of suffering that resulted from a disadvantaged position in a system where citizenship is paramount. As many Gazans insisted, the absence of a national number precluded their access to critical resources in society that were available to other Jordanians. Specifically, their non-citizen status rendered them vulnerable to particular forms of suffering that were manifest in their inadequate living conditions, limited educational opportunities, poor health care options, and restricted chances of earning a living in a marginal and uncertain economy.

My return to Jordan in 2015 allowed me to meet more Gazan refugees. Almost ten years after my original fieldwork, these encounters were an important opportunity to see how, if at all, things had changed for the stateless. From the Gazans I met, it seemed that the hardships of the past persisted into the present. Abu Jihad, for example, was a Gaza refugee living on the outskirts of Amman. He and I met at the Wihdat camp in Amman during the month of Ramadan. Every year he travels to Wihdat to sell clothing to Palestinians in the camp. This was part of a larger economic migration he performs throughout the year to earn a living. With few economic opportunities, he explained, he loads his truck with cheap clothing every morning at sunrise and moves throughout the country to poor areas to sell his goods. Poor himself, it is amongst the poor that he earns his income. This daily economic ritual, he suggested, was the result of a failed dream: he spent years trying to leave Jordan in order to acquire citizenship in a foreign country. As a stateless refugee, his vision of a dignified life entailed the search for citizenship. Constrained by a life of statelessness, he understood that rights were inseparable from nationality. He therefore pursued several opportunities to become a citizen in whatever country . . . might accept him. His efforts, however, did not succeed: today he remains a stateless Gazan struggling to carve out a decent life on the margins of a social order that deprives him of equal recognition and participation.

As previously mentioned, I met Abu Asad during the summer of 2015. It was a serendipitous encounter but one that resulted in a warm friendship. After our first visit to his home, he and his family invited us to join them for lunch later in the week. Our return was affectionately received and hours of conversation gave me deeper insight into the problems Abu Asad's family face as Gazans. Neither he nor his family has Jordanian citizenship. They thus lack a national number and, like the Gazans discussed earlier, live as foreign residents. Abu Asad's parents were originally from Haifa. Like other Palestinians, they were forced from their lands in 1948 to Gaza where they became refugees for the first time. Displaced again in 1967, they came to Jordan.

Today, their lives reflected many of the same issues I witnessed among other Gazans during my previous fieldwork. Their living conditions, for example, resembled the situation of many Gazans in Palestinian camps: inadequate building structures, makeshift furniture, and poor insulation. Educational and work opportunities were clearly constrained by a poverty that was inseparable from the limits they shared with other stateless Gazans. For example, I learned that Mahdi, one of Abu Asad's sons, didn't pursue higher education. Given their poverty, this was no surprise. Mahdi was thus on the labor market struggling to find fulltime work. At the time, he told us his employer didn't have enough work to offer him consistent hours. He therefore spent countless hours throughout the week waiting for labor's call. Abu Asad's wife, Im Asad, also complained about the high costs of hospital visits and treatment for non-citizens like herself. Their limited income meant that healthcare was a burdensome cost, one that left me wondering about Abu Asad. He is a cripple. One of his legs was injured and he thus carries an old stick that functions as a cane. Knowing the circumstances of Gazans, I speculated about his condition. Did his leg betray the effects of statelessness on his health? Did his crippled body reflect the crippled system that forces Gazans into conditions of care that are inadequate for the bodies of Gaza's displaced? Were he and his family living in what Joao Biehl described as a zone of abandonment, where people are caught between encompassment and abandonment, memory and non-memory, life and death (Biehl 2005, 4)?

The Rights of the Rightless

The situation of Gaza refugees in Jordan is the product of historical and contemporary problems specific to the plight of Palestinian refugees. Their general statelessness is the result of Israeli settler colonialism and the international community's indifference to the Palestinian struggle. For over 100 years, Zionist colonization in Palestine has diminished territorial, economic, and political possibilities for Palestinian statehood and, in the refugees' case, for return. Thus Palestinians throughout the world today remain subject to humanitarian aid regimes like UNRWA and/or the policies of states in which they live. In the case of Jordan, these policies have had mixed results. On the one hand, the Jordanian government has extended citizenship to all 1948 Palestinian refugees living within its contemporary borders. This is a unique privilege among Palestinian refugees given that, in Syria, Lebanon, or Egypt, Palestinians remain stateless. On the other hand, the exclusion of Gaza refugees from Jordanian citizenship has resulted in various hardships that constitute particular forms of social inequalities and suffering that

violate a variety of basic human rights. Of all the problems Gazans face, poverty, in particular, has been the greatest issue. Poverty, in this case, however, is not as the result of a general condition of a limited economy in an equitable playing field. It is, rather, the structural outcome of a deliberate policy of exclusion that positions Gazans unequally in social order where citizenship is tantamount to rights.

Writing about the connection between poverty and human rights, Kathleen Ho suggests that "poverty consists of a systematic or structural denial of basic freedoms resulting in agency constrained to the extent that individuals are unable or lack the 'capability' to meet their basic needs (Ho 2007, 9)." Poverty, in this sense, not only limits individuals' ability to pursue certain opportunities accessible to others but also creates particular vulnerabilities that they disproportionately face. Structurally produced, this kind of poverty thus constitutes a basic violation of human rights. It is the de facto negation of human rights since "those living in poverty, on balance, have less access to the kind of economic resources that are necessary for adequate healthcare, education and welfare services, which may in turn effect the degree to which they [can] enjoy their civil and political rights" (Ho 2007, 9). In the Gazans' case, poverty is anything but an historical accident. Produced by their systematic exclusion from the rights enjoyed by citizens, their poverty is the structural outcome of a policy that leads to suffering by exception. It is not, in other words, that Jordan seeks to oppress Gazans by direct forms of violence. Rather, it is by exclusion that they suffer. As stateless refugees, they exist in a liminal status wherein rights are deprived by omission, not denial.

While the Gazans suffer from the specificities of their status as Palestinian refugees, they are also not unique. Indeed, their general problem reflects the larger tension between the efforts to secure *human* rights in a world where citizenship provides the fundamental gateway to rights. According to international human rights principles, all humans have rights. It is by virtue of their being human, not citizens, that they are entitled to rights. Refugees are no exception to this idea. Within the international human rights system, specific rules exist to protect the rights of refugees wherever they might be. Thus the Convention Relating to the Status of Refugees, the 1954 Convention Relating to the Status of Stateless Persons, and the 1967 Protocol Relating to the Status of Refugees all provide a framework for addressing the needs and rights of displaced peoples regardless of their citizenship status. In this respect, the Jordanian government, like many states, is violating the rights of refugees on two fronts. First, by denying Gazans citizenship, it is simultaneously denying them access to the key mechanism by which rights are fully realized in Jordan. In effect, it is placing the sovereignty of the state above the rights of humans. This has created the situation Gazans currently face: the maintenance of Gazans' statelessness results in a particular liability and suffering that underscores their status as non-citizens. Second, by ignoring the rights enshrined in the principles, declarations, and covenants created to protect the rights of refugees, it is reinforcing the link between citizenship and human rights. The Jordanian government's treatment of the Gazans, in other words, contributes to a structural limit on human rights imposed by the priority of states and citizens over human rights. More specifically, it is undermining the possibility of a world in which rights, not citizenship, are the shared privilege of humanity.

Notes

1. Under Egyptian rule, Gazans were never extended citizenship.

2. In Jordan, only citizens have a national number (raqam wattani).

References

Agamben, Giorgio. 2000. *Means Without Ends: Notes on Politics*. Minneapolis: University of Minnesota Press.

Arendt, Hannah. 2000. "The Perplexities of the Rights of Man." In *The Portable Hannah Arendt*, edited by Peter Baehr, 31–45 New York: Penguin Books.

Biehl, Joao. 2005. *Vita: Life in a Zone of Social Abandonment*. Berkeley: University of California Press.

Farmer, Paul. 2003. *Pathologies of Power: Health, Human Rights, and the New War on the Poor*. Berkeley: University of California Press.

Galtung, Johan. 1969. "Violence, Peace, and Peace Research." *Journal of Peace Research*. 6(3): 167–191.

Ho, Kathleen. 2007. "Structural Violence as a Human Rights Violation." *Essex Human Rights Review* 4(2):1–17.

Kleinman, Arthur, Veena Das, and Margaret M. Lock, eds.1997. "Introduction." In *Social Suffering*, ix–xxvii. Berkeley: University of California Press.

Morris, Benny. 2007. "Revisiting the Palestinian Exodus of 1948." In *The War of Palestine: Rewriting the History of 1948*, edited by Eugene L. Rogan and Avi Shlaim, 37–59. Cambridge: Cambridge University Press.

Pappe, Ilan. 2006. *The Ethnic Cleansing of Palestine*. Oxford: Oneworld Press.

Piterberg, Gabriel. 2013. "The Zionist Colonization of Palestine in the Context of Comparative Settler Colonialism." In *Palestine and the Palestinians in the 21st Century*, edited by Rochelle Davis and Mimi Kirk, 15–34. Bloomington: Indiana University Press.

Shai, Aron. 2006. "The Fate of Abandoned Arab Villages in Israel, 1965–1969." *History and Memory* 18(2): 86–106.

Tiltnes, Åge A., and Huafeng Zhang. 2013. *Progress, Challenges, Diversity: Insights into the Socio-Economic Conditions of Palestinian Refugees in Jordan*. Fafo Report 2013:42. Oslo: Fafo Research Foundation.

10.4 Living and Working in a War Zone: An Applied Anthropologist in Afghanistan

PATRICIA A. OMIDIAN

In 2007, the U.S. Department of Defense established the Human Terrain System (HTS), teams of applied social scientists who accompanied U.S. troops into war contexts. Anthropologists were hired as part of these teams to help troops understand the local cultural and linguistic context. The program has been surrounded by controversy, and the American Anthropological Association (AAA) Executive Board found that the HTS comes into direct conflict with the AAA Code of Ethics. One central concern among critics is that working for the military makes it impossible for anthropologists to uphold their primary commitment to be trustworthy and open with their informants. The following selection offers a window into trust-building in war contexts. Patricia Omidian, an anthropologist living and working in Afghanistan before and after the 2001 destruction of twin towers, argues that anthropologists must remain separate from armed actors in order to maintain their ethical standards for research and safety.

Questions

1. Why did Omidian never carry a weapon or hire armed security?
2. Why is it not a good idea to use military to provide humanitarian aid? What are the impacts on anthropologists and NGO workers?
3. Discuss the concept of "do-no-harm" within anthropology. Provide examples of how Omidian worked to "do-no-harm."
4. Omidian offers several reasons for why she finds the notion of militarized anthropology to be inappropriate. What are they?
5. What is Omidian's stance on HTS? Do you agree or disagree?
6. How is this selection an example of action anthropology?

. . .

This [chapter] is a discussion of action anthropology as it has unfolded for me in a region of the world that went from obscurity to the center of the world's attention in 2001 when the [twin towers of the] World Trade Center were destroyed in the United States. . . .

Action anthropology, as delineated by [Sol] Tax, was an important contribution to the development of anthropology as a discipline. He advocated an approach that combined theory with practice—that one's work should be practical as it advances theory and that it helps solve local problems (Hill 2000). Public anthropology holds a similar perspective of doing anthropology for the public good, and not just for the sake of an academic career (Purcell 2000). These approaches highlight the need for applied anthropologists to work collaboratively with local populations to help them solve problems they identify as important.

Omidian, Patricia. "Living and Working in a War Zone: An Applied Anthropologist in Afghanistan." 2009. *Practicing Anthropology* 31 (2), 4–11.

. . .

Applied anthropologists struggle to stay safe, build culturally appropriate programs and to speak for those who are without power or resources. The anthropologist, like the development or emergency aid worker, and unlike the soldier or other military personnel, must depend on the largess and the protection of the local community. Militarized anthropology subverts our work and puts us on an ethical slippery slope. It also increases the danger to us as the local people with whom we work find it difficult to distinguish between combatants and non-combatants, the soldiers and the civilian aid workers. It jeopardizes personal safety and development work, while increasing the likelihood of future violence.

Without Guns: Living and Working in a War-Zone (2001–2006)

. . . Working in Afghanistan under the Taliban had many challenges though safety was not one of them. For the most part, it did not feel like war because people seemed too frightened or disheartened to fight.

In 2001, I was working for an Afghan NGO that had development projects inside Afghanistan but was based in Peshawar [Pakistan] when the World Trade Center [was] blown up on September 11. Within days I was evacuated and sent back to the US to wait. I was in touch with my colleagues in Peshawar as they waited for the US to begin bombing. At that time most Afghans wanted the US and coalition forces to come to Afghanistan and force the Taliban out of their country.

By Christmas, I had returned to Peshawar and flew almost immediately to Kabul to join my colleagues there. I lived between Kabul and Peshawar for the next four months, until I moved out of Pakistan and based myself in Kabul in March, 2002. . . .

That first winter in Kabul was unforgettable as a time of great excitement, hope. and the sharing of bittersweet memories. I shared my colleagues' pain and joy of returning to Kabul after their years of exile: joy at returning and the pain of seeing the nearly complete destruction of most of city. There were miles of bombed out buildings with whole neighborhoods destroyed. One of my colleagues cried as he pointed at a ruined three-story structure:

There! See what is left of my high school. When I was a student it was known as the best school in the whole city. Now there is no glass left in the windows and children can fall through the holes in the walls of the third floor.

. . .The city of Kabul still had a ghostly feeling about it that first winter. There were few cars and almost no electricity. Yet, it was no longer the silent city it had been under the oppressive Taliban.

The painful memories were contrasted with the sheer energy and excitement of post-Taliban life. For example, as we traveled to a Kabul market for curtain fabric for our office we were met by many women covered head to foot in the blue *chadari* (burqa) that became the center of world attention under the Taliban. As I walked through the narrow alleyways of the fabric market, women would come to me, pull the cloth of the *chadari* back over their heads so that I could see their wonderfully smiling faces. Everyone shook my hand and asked me to come home with them for tea. This was a middle class area and the mood of the place was celebratory. Taliban had just left Kabul and President Karzai arrived in their place. Hope was high and everyone was ready for change. . . .

In December, 2001 women, Afghan and foreign, traveled throughout the city without a headscarf, but by the spring of 2002 it was clear that Kabul had become a very conservative and nervous city. By the summer even the most determined women in my office asked me to wear a headscarf when I was in public. Women's head covering became a topic of conversation at many expatriate gatherings. As the war increased in the south between the Americans and opposition groups, there were enough anti-government actions in Kabul to keep people from relaxing. A bomb that exploded in a nearby market injured one of our office guards. Yet, we all felt like we were contributing to a process that was important, the rebuilding of a nation.

The biggest problem faced by the residents of Kabul was where to house all the returning Afghans. . . . Kabul was destroyed, with many areas flattened by the internecine conflict that followed the departure of the Russians in 1989 and the collapse of the Najib government in 1992. The houses that remained were old, drafty and incredibly expensive—at over US$10,000 a month in an exclusive area of Kabul called Wazir Akbar Khan, where INGOs traditionally had their offices. I lived in the NGO office where I worked; my bed was a cotton mat that would be stored during the day and brought out at night and placed by my desk. Middle class people struggled for places to live but returnees and the poor had no options. Housing was scarce; winter bitterly cold, summers hot and dusty.

Before my Afghan "family" could return to their home in Kabul they had to move the family that was there out and repair the place. This took most of spring. I continued to live in my office until summer when they arrived from Peshawar—the whole family, parents and six children. I felt like I had a home again. Their home was near the airport in an apartment complex that survived the war. We lived another two years together before I moved into my own apartment. Adjustment was hard for all of us in the early days. The children struggled with a school system that was barely functioning, overcrowded and corrupt. Electricity in Kabul came regularly from March to July and then would fade to a 2–4 hour period every third day in winter. Heating was a problem in winter and I think I never warmed up between November and March. I wore several layers of clothing and a winter coat indoors, adding gloves and boots when I went outside. Stories of people freezing were constant reminders of how difficult life was for the poor who lived without proper housing. Security problems, curfews and robberies also impacted everyone's lives.

During this period I conducted a large survey for the UN and the CDC (Omidian 2002). In this survey I was mandated to do a qualitative study of maternal mortality in five districts where verbal autopsies were carried out by the quantitative team (cf. Bartlett et al., 2005). . . . I did this survey as a project within the Afghan NGO where I was employed. With the help of the staff, we hired four surveyors, two sister/brother teams (Fatima and Nasir Khan, Rana and Kabir[1]). Fatima and Rana had survey experience. Nasir Khan and Kabir were to act as escorts for their sisters and to conduct surveys with the men in the villages we would visit. . . . Because the areas we would be visiting were remote, we had to get the information in one visit. . . .

. . . As members of the NGO world we would be traveling without guards or weapons; our protection depended on local knowledge and sometimes luck.

For four weeks the five of us traveled to remote areas of Afghanistan by car with a driver from the NGO, seeing some places that are no longer accessible because of the escalation of the war. Our first trip was to a remote area of Badakhshan in the north.

The area was breathtaking and gave one the impression of being on the roof of the world. It was August, yet each morning there was ice on the stream near where we stayed. We had so much fun that we believed the whole survey would be as easy. We were told there were security problems but we did not feel it. Our only problem was finding enough food to eat in the local village.

Our next stop was in the eastern province of Laghman, close to Pakistan. In the evening of our first night there, as we settled into a routine, the men went out to get water for cooking and washing. Fatima, Rana and I were sitting talking when we heard shouts and fighting beyond the wall of the compound where we stayed. I could not understand the dialect but it was clearly trouble. Fatima was close to panic as she listened to the voices. The noise increased then stopped. So did our hearts. Within minutes the men of our group returned, but things had clearly gone from bad to worse. Nasir Khan had been stabbed. Fortunately, he blocked the knife with his arm or it would have been a stomach wound. He and the others had inadvertently stumbled across a robbery in progress—by men dressed as police. The driver and Kabir rushed Nasir Khan to the local hospital where his wound was bandaged. Because of the tribal issues in this war torn area, and because we were strangers, we did not want to take the chance of further violence, but we had to wait until morning before we could travel. After a sleepless night, we left for Kabul as soon as we heard the morning *azaan* (call to prayer). I cancelled the survey for this province. Nasir Khan healed quickly and was ready to travel again after a short rest.

The third province on our program was Kandahar, where we were to travel to Maiwand district with a UN staff person, a Japanese woman, to conduct more surveys. UN logistics for Kandahar chose the villages for us to visit. Maiwand was dangerous even in 2002 and my NGO did not want us there, but we were assured that the US forces were in control. The first village we entered turned out to be about five kilometers from an Al Qaida training camp. Most of the village was empty, as families had relocated to other areas to avoid the fighting. Women who remained in the village took Fatima and Rana to a nearby hill and pointed out a place where a nomad camp had been bombed by US fighter jets killing most of the men, women and children in camp. We could not verify the story but it sent chills through all of us in spite of the lovely fall weather. We conducted the interviews and mapping exercises and left for the long drive back to Kandahar.

The next day we visited another village, not far from a dried riverbed and across from vineyards that had died because of the very severe drought. Upon arrival we started to interview a group of women in a home when Nasir Khan called us out of the house and told us to quickly get into the cars. We had to leave immediately. Once in the cars and on our way, he angrily told us that UN logistics had selected a village that was pro-Taliban and pro–Al Qaida. He overheard some of the village talking about kidnapping the UN woman who was traveling with us. Being Japanese, she looked like a Hazara woman, an ethnic group despised by the Taliban.

Our third day was no better for surveying. We were again told the village to visit and headed off on the long bumpy drive over dirt roads and riverbeds. When we arrived the place was deserted. The night before US troops had come to the village and arrested every male over 15, leaving only one old man and the pre-adolescent boys to guard all the women and children. The women wanted to talk to us so we conducted our interviews with them but left as soon as we could. There was the possibility of angry people attacking us out of frustration. This was truly an active war zone and we were intruders. I was feeling that each day's trip in this area was getting us into more dangerous predicaments. . . .

Security conditions in the south were already deteriorating by the fall of 2002, and by 2005 only those traveling in armed caravans felt safe. In 2008, those would be targeted as well. Each year Afghanistan moved toward more chaos, with fewer areas where roads were safe. I returned again to Laghman in 2003 to complete a different survey, yet; shortly after my visit the office where I stayed was bombed. By 2004, Laghman was far too dangerous and many NGO offices in that province were forced to close. Nationally, security continued to deteriorate, so that by 2006 Ghazni, a short drive from Kabul, proved too dangerous for AFSC staff to visit. In 2008, no road out of Kabul was safe. War and chaos had engulfed most of rural Afghanistan.

As areas became more dangerous for the delivery of reconstruction and humanitarian aid because of the war, the US government and NATO increased their use of Provincial Reconstruction Teams (PRT), military groups that tried to engage in reconstruction activities, including the building of schools, clinics or water systems. Most NGOs (both local and international) worked hard to distance themselves from military actors, including the PRTs. It was standard procedure for NGOs to have signs on their offices and cars prohibiting weapons. There was an active campaign by the NGO community to try to discourage NATO from expanding the system, but it failed. It was important to signal a clear separation between military work (and even USAID) and civilian/non-governmental work. Although the idea of using the military to provide aid sounds like a good idea, it is removing the symbolic boundary that aid workers (and anthropologists) need to stay safe and which allows us to be seen by local communities as neutral. That boundary no longer exists in Afghanistan. The military bid for Afghan "hearts and minds" means that there is no longer a distinction between armed and non-armed actors. Afghanistan has since become one of the most dangerous countries for aid workers.

In 2004 I became the country representative for the American Friends Service Committee (AFSC) in Afghanistan, a position I held until leaving the country in 2007. . . .

Shortly after starting work with AFSC, I moved into my own flat in an area of the city where no other expats (international workers) lived. My language ability and understanding of the culture, thanks to the seven years with my Afghan family, allowed me to pass as an Afghan who had returned from the West. This was important, not to confuse locals, but to allow me the security of anonymity in a city that was always insecure. Those who knew me, including all my neighbors in my apartment block, knew I was not Afghan. This period had its dangers and the international community was constantly bombarded with warnings or threats. My neighbors protected me numerous times by telling people who searched for "foreigners" that none lived in our area. I was again dependent on the local community for my safety.

As head of the AFSC office in Afghanistan, we followed the same rules as most aid agencies and did not allow guns on the premises. This occasionally led to problems. For example, once a consultant from the US, funded by US State Department, wanted to visit our office. I was looking forward to seeing her but the regulations for her safety as a US contractor demanded that she be in sight of her armed guards when traveling anywhere outside of her office compound. . . . Unfortunately we were at an impasse. No guns or soldiers were allowed in our compound and she was not allowed to enter if her guards did not come with her. We held the meeting elsewhere.

In another incident, thieves climbed the wall and entered our office compound in the night. Our unarmed guards were alerted and because of the noise they made, the robbers climbed back over the wall without taking anything. No one was hurt on this occasion. Our guards then asked if we would supply them with or allow them to carry weapons. As a Quaker organization, the answer was no. But we also breathed a sigh of relief that our guards were not armed when we later learned the robbers were part of the local police. They thought our compound was empty after dark and had planned to make a few dollars quickly. Had our guards been armed someone might have been shot or killed, which would have left our agency in trouble with the local government for wounding or killing police. Our office rule was that if armed thieves came into the compound to rob the place, our guards (local men with large families to support who make a low but steady wage) should not resist. We would joke and say that if armed robbers enter the compound, the only thing the guards would do is offer them tea, something Afghans do for any guest.

In the three years as the country representative for AFSC (2004–2007), I was able to travel throughout Afghanistan, conducting surveys on health, education and mental health. But the greatest joy was in working in remote provinces, trying to promote education and some form of change as identified by local communities. This work was not without struggle. Yet, had we been armed, the trust we developed with local communities would have been impossible. Most of these areas are governed by warlords with militias or traditional tribal leaders who have an armed following. Many NGOs in Afghanistan had stickers on their cars showing that there were no weapons in the vehicle. It was, and is, important to distance oneself and one's agency from armed actors in any conflict zone. A few NGO workers with guns would not alter the situation in a positive way.

In the summer of 2006, I realized that I was burning out from the stress of security issues. . . . I could no longer judge safety for myself or my office colleagues and friends who were willing to put their lives on the line for me. There were several incidents where my local friends hid me, such as when Kabul erupted in violent riots that targeted INGOs. My staying could add to their risk. It was time to leave. . . .

Afghanistan 2007–2008

Something about Afghanistan and the resiliency of the Afghan people makes for an unbreakable cord, pulling me back again and again. The countryside is devastated by the joint terrors of war and drought. . . . Afghanistan sits at the crossroads of trade and threat; currently India and Pakistan fight their battles there and Iran uses it to overstretch the US military by supporting the enemies of their enemy. The situation has become steadily worse, yet, I find I return to visit friends and former colleagues, trying to come in time to share in the Muslim holidays or Persian New Year.

The economy of Afghanistan also suffers from war, and is based on drug trafficking in opium and heroin. Corruption finds itself all the way to the highest levels of the government. . . . [T]he country has almost no accountability or rule of law and remains in the control of warlords. There is an absence of justice or safety. In September, 2008, I spent five days in Kabul and stayed with three families whom I have known for many years, and talked to a number of others. At that time security was uppermost on their minds. Each family had a family member (uncle, cousin or son) or knew someone who had been kidnapped for ransom. Some were released, others killed. . . . These cases tended to be men in their later years who had wealth or attracted attention because of political status. One family was asked to pay three million US dollars, another US$40,000. In a country where the average salary is less than $50 a month, these kidnappings demonstrate a new kind of economic activity.

Even more frightening for families of the middle class were the kidnapping and murder of young men between the ages of 15 and 30. The boy or man would be taken while on his way to school, work or shopping for the family. Most were killed with the excuse that they said or did something against another ethnic or political group. These killings occurred frequently enough that all families felt at risk. When one man (a distant relative of a family I stayed with) was kidnapped, his kidnappers told the story that he was arguing with someone and made a rude remark about Ahmad Shah Masoud—a war hero from the north. He was killed and his family did not find out the truth until well after his body was buried. When the family went to the police to file a report, they were told that their son was one of 171 missing youth in that area of Kabul city.

These cases were the most worrisome because there was a feeling in Kabul that ethnic divisions motivated many of the issues around security. Many felt that ethnicity was being used to divide various groups in Afghanistan and that the divisions were being supported by popular media and US/Karzai policy. . . .

Afghans, generally, were tired of the war and have been for decades, but there was a major shift in 2006 toward American policy in Afghanistan. Before this, people would complain but would add that the US needed to stay because the Karzai government would not be able to cope with all the problems. In 2008, they told me that the US was making the same mistakes that the Russians made years before. As I talked to people I found no distinction being made between ISAF forces, NATO and the US military. All were seen as making things worse not better, though people were afraid that if any of these groups pulled out of Afghanistan the results would be catastrophic. They expressed anger at the way the US continually failed to respect Afghan culture. The killing of civilians was unforgivable and played into the hands of anti-government groups (AOG). . . .

. . . Many people told me horror stories of the Kandahar/Kabul road, now too dangerous for anyone but the poorest of people to travel. There were frequent roadblocks and Taliban checkpoints (sometimes Taliban dressed as police) where everyone was checked. They looked for signs that the person worked for the government or an NGO. One method was to take the numbers from the person's cell phone to find where he worked. When they found numbers of foreigners on the phone the owner of the phone could be beaten or killed. Also, members of certain ethnic groups were at risk, including Hazaras and Panjshiris (those from the area where Ahmad Shah Masoud lives). . . .

I found the country growing steadily tenser as armed actors operate from every sector. The anti-government groups are fully armed, as are the warlords, drug lords and mafia groups. The government has its army and police, and has been arming local militias to help combat anti-government groups. Guns are seen by locals as having become part of the aid sector as well, with more PRTs building schools or hospitals. Into this mix of military and para-military units, weaponry, factions and violence, anthropologists (and other social scientist) have stepped in to add to the confusion. Confusing non-military activities with military actors is a dangerous slippery slope, one that anthropologists must avoid.

Militarized Anthropologists

The US government has introduced a system called The Human Terrain System (HTS), in which social scientists, including anthropologists, work for them in Afghanistan and Iraq. The goal is to help the military understand local communities and to reduce the number of deaths. . . . Trust is hard to establish but critical to any field endeavor. As an applied anthropologist I work for the people I "study" not for those who pay my way. To do otherwise hurts more than me, it also damages the profession and the anthropological position to "do no harm." Peacock et al. note:

> Anthropologists' engagements with military and intelligence agencies have the potential to damage relationships of trust with the people studied as well as the reputation of the discipline. (2007, 17)

Because our work is grounded in participant observation and a dependence on those we study for our survival, I find the whole notion of a militarized anthropology to be inappropriate for many reasons. Leaving aside the whole question of the reputation of anthropology as a discipline, the first point one must consider is "who is being studied and what is the purpose of the study." Interwoven in this is the whole issue of trust.

In Afghanistan, goals and beneficiaries were always clearly stated at the onset of any project. When doing the study for the UN in 2002, as described [previously], I and my team were paid through the UN on a CDC-initiated study of maternal mortality (Bartlett et al. 2005) with myself and my team doing the qualitative portion that looked at knowledge, attitudes and practices (KAP) (Omidian 2002). In Kandahar we found one unexpected cause of maternal mortality that was not liked by the agency funding the study. It was that US military action was a leading contributor to the death of women of childbearing age in the areas we visited. I was asked by my contact person in the UN in Kabul to remove this information from my final report, as it would upset the US donor. I refused. Consequently my study was not circulated with the quantitative study, though European and Canadian colleagues working in the area of maternal health were given the document. They were asked not to share it with Americans. As an anthropologist I felt an obligation to be honest regarding my data and to report my findings. It was not for me to censor my work for fear of insulting the donor;

rather, it was important to give voice to those whom I had met and interviewed.

The purpose of the study was to understand maternal and infant deaths in rural and urban populations of four areas of the country. The information was to be used to develop culturally appropriate and critically needed health care that would target the populations being served. As with most research, other information comes that is not expected and may even be unwelcome. What we do with that data is important. The reason for this study was to understand how Afghan women and their families tried to prevent deaths from occurring and how they dealt with it when it did. To know that military action was negatively impacting their chances of survival was important. As the anthropologist it was my task to help give them a voice so they can be heard. The Afghan agency with whom I worked needed to know, also, that I (an American) could be trusted to write that information into my report. In the end it was about trust and intellectual honesty. Had I been working for the US military, I would not have been able to maintain either.

The second point in this debate relates to power configurations. How does the militarized anthropologist deal with the imbalance of power? When I enter a village, it is by local transport, whatever that might be, possibly by foot, donkey, horseback, jeep, car or van. But I come with a group of Afghan aid workers by invitation of the local community or by a representative. I am not naïve and I know that there is a clear imbalance of power in any relationship I establish but those lines of power actually work both ways. The local community may or may not protect me while I can leave when I want. The community can also ask me to leave, refuse to speak to me or invite me to stay a while. Based on what is happening around me, I can usually respond appropriately.

The HTS of the military works by different rules. . . .

If our task is to understand the day-today lives of people and we are to "do no harm," how does a militarized anthropology fit our definition of anthropology? To enter a community as a member of the military, a person with power and the weight of the US army behind her/him brings about a level of power that the local person cannot act against since any reaction can get them arrested or killed. The imbalance is so great that it is easy to overlook.

. . .

Conclusion

As we work, we have to remember that our work can be used against the people we study. . . . We have to do the best we can to protect those whom we study, with whom we share lives and to whom we owe our profession. Militarized anthropology is about a gross imbalance of power, as well as the subversion of a discipline that has an ethical challenge to do no harm as we work among those who may lack power in the global setting. The American Anthropological Association clarified its stance on this (though they did not go as far as I would have liked):

> Our framework for evaluating the ethics of anthropologists' engagement with US intelligence and defense communities is grounded in four basic principles: to do no harm; to provide disclosure of one's work and role / not to deceive; to uphold the primary responsibility to those involved in one's research; and to maintain transparency, making research accessible to others to enhance the quality and potential effects of it as critique. (Peacock et al. 2007, 14)

Any work an anthropologist does can be used against the community studied by those in power. Though we cannot control how our data are used once published, we can control how we maintain loyalty to the populations who share their lives with us. In this [chapter] I have tried to give concrete examples of action anthropological techniques and applications in an active conflict zone.

Applied anthropology is aptly suited to help address peace-building processes, program design, implementation and assessment. As anthropologists we can offer a nation coming out of war insights into ways international programs can be locally adapted. Participant observation affords us the opportunity to understand people in the way that other aid workers cannot match. The anthropologist tries to understand things from the local point of view and this is our biggest contribution. I cannot list all the times I had to let someone know that the word for a person from Afghanistan is Afghan and the money is Afghani. And that Afghans do not necessarily dislike their daughters but if you ask them in Iranian Farsi how many children they have, in Dari the same words ask how many sons. Sometimes the information is as simple as how rude it is to slam a door. But it all comes together to allow for program development that meets culturally specific criteria.

. . .

In the declared "war against terror" many ethical standards (including human rights and freedom from torture) have been set aside. Militarized anthropology is just one more in the long list. This is a slippery slope that reminds me that the damage may not show right away. Yet, I have no doubt it will come back to haunt us. I was speaking at a seminar in Karachi in December 2008 when I was asked to explain why anthropologists helped the British subjugate the Indian sub-continent and then worked against the Muslims. This man was referring to the way social anthropology was introduced and used in the first half of the twentieth century, but his question was fair. Just as those who were perceived to support colonialism in British India, the militarized anthropologists will be seen to act on behalf of the army they serve and not for the good of the local community they study.

Note

1. Not their real names.

References

Bartlett, Linda A., Shairose Mawji, Sara Whitehead, Chadd Crouse, Suraya Dalil, Denisa Ionete, Peter Salama. 2005. Where giving birth is a forecast of death: maternal mortality in four districts of Afghanistan, 1999–2002. The Lancet 365 (9462):864–870.

Omidian, Patricia A. 2002. Qualitative Maternal Mortality Study in Four Areas of Afghanistan. Kabul: CDCs and UNICEF Health Sector.

Peacock, James (Chair), Robert Albro, Carolyn Fluehr-Lobban, Kerry Fosher, Laura McNamara, Monica Heller, George Marcus, David Price, and Alan Goodman (ex officio). 2007. "AAA Commission on the Engagement of Anthropology with the US Security and Intelligence Communities." Final Report.

IN THE NEWS Human Terrain

This "In the News" feature continues the conversation from Reading 10.4, Patricia Omidian's reflections on living and working in a war zone. In "Army Enlists Anthropology in War Zones," *New York Times* writer David Rhodes explores the controversy over the U.S. Department of Defense's Human Terrain System (HTS), the teams of applied social scientists who accompanied U.S. troops into war contexts. Rhodes tracks the work of one anthropologist embedded within a counterinsurgency operation in a Taliban stronghold in eastern Afghanistan in 2007, illustrating both potential positive outcomes of having an anthropological perspective within military forces as well as the strong critique from the anthropology community.

After reviewing the article, students can read an interview with Roberto González, Professor of Anthropology at San Jose State University, and founding member of the Network of Concerned Anthropologists (NCA). The NCA is an independent network of anthropologists that formed in response to the "war on terror" in order to promote ethical anthropology in the face of what appeared to be significant efforts to militarize the discipline of anthropology. Dr. González has written extensively on the use of social science in the military including the book *American Counterinsurgency: Human Science and the Human Terrain* (Prickly Paradigm Press, 2009). In the interview, González discusses the history of the Human Terrain System (HTS) and its ethical and political problems it creates.

@ **Visit www.oup.com/us/brondo for links to the news article and interview. Other resources available online include the official website of the Network of Concerned Anthropologists and for the documentary film about the HTS, "Human Terrain: War Becomes Academic."**

DR. LAURA MCNAMARA

Organizational Anthropologist

Figure 10.6.1

Laura McNamara. (Photo: Laura A. McNamara/Paul Johnson)

Where do you work, and what do you do?

I've spent the past 18 years in the Department of Energy's national laboratory system as an anthropologist with an organizational and policy bent. I started at the labs in 1997, as a graduate student at Los Alamos National Laboratory, where I wrote my dissertation about nuclear weapons design and engineering at the end of the Cold War. I also spent a couple of years as a staff member in the statistical sciences group before accepting a position at Sandia National Laboratories in 2003. For the past 12 years or so, I've been a research staff member at Sandia.

Most of my work deals in some respect with design and evaluation of human-information interaction systems across a wide range of domains. I'm very interested in how we evaluate the correctness of computational modeling and simulation systems and how people make decisions using those tools. These days, when people ask what I do, I explain that I'm a mixed-methods researcher with expertise in software design and evaluation, visual cognition and human-information interaction.

Sandia's history is as a nuclear weapons engineering laboratory. It seems like a challenging fit for a cultural anthropologist.

Well, the national laboratories are multi-program facilities, very interdisciplinary, with research in areas from energy to intelligence data analysis to remote sensing to nuclear weapons—which makes them a very rich place to work. I actually never intended to stay at the national laboratories for a career. Los Alamos was "just" a field site. However, while doing my dissertation fieldwork, I fell in love with the inter-disciplinary research environment at Los Alamos. I had minimal formal training in physics or engineer-ing, so my doctoral fieldwork was a vertical learning curve—every field observation or interview that I did required me to go find an article or a book that would provide me domain context so I could put what I was learning into better context. However, my interlocutors were extremely supportive and helped me find the resources I needed—that is, if they didn't actually sit down and tutor me themselves. Also, I was a foreign service major at Georgetown University, and as an undergraduate I was always fascinated by the intersection of science and foreign policy. The combination of a challenging research environment and the mission space became pretty irresistible for me, and I stayed.

Are there other anthropologists in the Department of Energy?

Yes. There are a handful of archaeologists at most of the DOE sites, and I've met a few other cultural anthropologists, but we're definitely a minority. However, the national laboratories have a long history of hiring people in human factors, industrial engineering, and psychology; there are also political scientists and economists, so social scientists aren't entirely absent from the workforce. But it can be rather intimidating to integrate oneself as a qualitative researcher into a math-heavy engineering environment. Fortunately, when I was transitioning from being a graduate student to a professional researcher, I had a wonderful ethnographic mentor and role model, Dr. Mary Meyer. She was the first anthropologist hired at Los Alamos and she was a researcher in the Statistical Sciences group. She did lot of really groundbreaking methodological work on human judgment in probabilistic risk assessment. Dr. Meyer helped me understand what ethnographic practice could bring to a physics and engineering environment; for example, helping scientific software teams prioritize workflow requirements to ensure that a mathematical model or a physics simulation would be genuinely useful to domain experts.

How does anthropological practice in an engineering laboratory differ from, say, doing anthropology in an academic environment?

Well, I've never been in an academic environment, so I'm not entirely sure what it's like these days. I was never really interested in going into academic research. I always wanted to work in interdisciplinary teams and on problems that had real-world implications, so this isn't an accident. I think the biggest difference is what I alluded to previously: the national laboratories are very interdisciplinary and I'm always working outside my intellectual comfort zone. This isn't just because I'm an anthropologist in an engineering laboratory—everyone I know at Sandia agrees that our work always requires one to think outside one's training. Our research and development projects are always team-based and your colleagues bring an impressive array of skills to the table, from

software engineering to materials science. Sometimes I work with other social scientists, but regardless I'm constantly reading outside my discipline. I like figuring out how to be an effective partner in knowledge domains that I might not otherwise encounter. And inevitably I end up with interests and skills I never realized I'd find interesting, or want to acquire.

Can you give an example?

A couple of years ago, I began working with the Synthetic Aperture Radar (SAR) programs at Sandia. I knew absolutely nothing about SAR systems, but some of the researchers in the group were seeking feedback on options for presenting SAR data in different types of imagery. I gave the team some basic advice on how to engage the user community in an evaluation exercise; for example, making sure that the new image was presented in the same way they'd use it in their existing workflow, to promote informed comparisons and judgments. Long story short, I ended up running the study with a couple of my colleagues and I've continued working with the SAR imagery analysis teams ever since. I've learned a lot about remote sensing and electronic image formation, but I've also had to teach myself a lot about human visual perception and cognition. These days, our group is doing a lot of gaze research using eye tracking systems, so I'm learning a lot out eye tracking from my psychologist colleagues. In return, they've come to appreciate that ethnographic observation is really useful in experimental work—ethnographic team observation ensures that future experimental designs address the salient features of the relevant work environment. Working on an interdisciplinary visual cognition team is not what I expected to do in my forties, but it's great fun.

Anthropologists tend to hesitate about working in national security environments. That's an intersection you've been working for a long time. Care to comment on those debates?

In the wake of the 9/11 attacks and the subsequent wars in Afghanistan and Iraq, a lot of anthropologists rightly questioned the ethical implications of engaging in national security careers. I was on the AAA's Commission for the Engagement of the US Security and Intelligence Community (CEAUSSIC), which spent several years examining the ethical risks and issues related to anthropologists in the security sphere. It's easy to forget that the "national security" realm isn't a monolithic institution. Instead, national security describes a conglomeration of epistemic communities, many of which aren't involved in the "sharp end of the spear" activities so concerning to anthropologists. I think we did a good job balancing the fact of public sector employment in the national security realm, vis-à-vis the ethical requirements of anthropological practice. I would like to see more anthropologists go into public sector careers, period—I find that anthropologists bring a set of critical thinking and communication skills that can really benefit these organizations.

What advice do you have for a young anthropologist seeking a practice-oriented career?

Besides developing a relationship with a skilled and generous mentor, I think the most important thing any researcher can do is develop some methodological chops. You'll need a problem-solving toolkit that makes you an effective contributor in interdisciplinary research projects. Internships and research assistantships can be a wonderful way to get skills outside your traditional training, even if they're not anthropology per se. Also, take extra classes if you can find the time. I took several semesters of statistics in grad school. Some anthropologists eschew quantitative methods, but I find that my very basic skills in descriptive and inferential statistics are among the most useful skills I've got, if only for deciphering research literature. Human factors and decision science researchers have developed some very useful frameworks that can provide some structure to anthropological fieldwork in organizations. Researchers have developed many wonderful toolkits that we can all use—go find them, read about them, integrate with your ethnographic practice, and document what you've learned so others can learn, too. It's what makes work joyful.

ABOUT THE ANTHROPOLOGIST

Occupation: Principal Member of Technical Staff, Sandia National Laboratories, Albuquerque, New Mexico
Education: BS in Foreign Service, Georgetown University; MA and PhD in Ethnology and Cultural Anthropology, University of New Mexico
Hobbies: Dogs, llamas, scuba diving, birdwatching, hiking, travel, and running . . . slowly.

CAREER ADVICE

Advice for students seeking practicing careers:

- Find a skilled and generous mentor.
- Build your problem-solving toolkit.
- Develop competency in quantitative methods; take statistics.
- Pursue internships and research assistantships

PART 11

Visual and Media Anthropology

Visual anthropologists study and produce visual culture, asking questions about how visual images and objects reflect and shape the world in which we live. Visual representations of culture come in many forms, including, for example, film, photography, museum exhibits, dance, cave paintings, tattoos, and graffiti. Media anthropologists, on the other hand, study mass media. Readers likely have heard of the scholarly discipline known as "media studies"; what makes media anthropologists different from media studies scholars is their ethnographic approach to the study of media, especially in their application of participant observation.

One theme that cuts across all of the following selections is the emphasis on our changing social landscape in the digital age. While most students reading this book will likely have grown up in a world where screens dominate all aspects of our lives, from work to entertainment, and thus know no other way of being, the widespread adoption of technology and its impact on culture is only recently being studied and theorized by anthropologists. The authors in this section collectively ask questions such as: How will the fact that people spend approximately half (or more) of their waking hours engaging with screens change humanity? How does participation in a virtual world shape actual world behavior? To what degree does "reality television" reflect "real" cultural patterns? How does reality TV impact or change culture? What do social media posts say about culture? And, what does participation in virtual activism through social media outlets like Twitter or Facebook say about social activism on the ground?

In "Everyday Second Life" (Reading 11.1) Tom Boellstorff presents his ethnographic fieldwork in the computer program Second Life. Boellstorff favors a position that Internet worlds are indeed profoundly human worlds. Unlike some scholars of virtual technology who worry that we are entering into an uneasy terrain of the "posthuman," with technology allowing us to overcome the human form, Boellstorff demonstrates that virtual worlds like Second Life impact actual life, reworking what it means to be human in the actual world.

If virtual worlds like Second Life shape actual life, what about participation in social media? In "#Ferguson: Digital Protest, Hashtag Ethnography, and the Racial Politics of Social Media in the United States" (Reading 11.2), Yarimar Bonilla and Jonathan Rosa consider the use of social media platforms as a field site for engaging in social activism. Focusing on the "hashtag activism" that emerged through #Ferguson in response to police brutality and the misrepresentation of racialized bodies in the mainstream media after the fatal police shooting of Michael Brown in Ferguson, Missouri, the authors consider what participation in social media platforms says about those who post, contrasting participation in Twitter to posting in Facebook. Further, they explore the degree to which "hashtag activism" reflects "actual" social activism.

The question of the degree to which media reflect or shape "actual" life continues through "Policing Childhood Through The Learning Channel's *Toddlers and Tiaras*" (Reading 11.3), with Andrea Freidus's analysis of the relationship between "reality television" and mothering practices. Analyzing Internet dialogue surrounding The Learning Channels' *Toddlers and Tiaras*, a reality television program about child beauty pageants, Freidus shows how both mothering and childhood are policed, but policed along classed and racialized lines. She argues that reality shows like *Toddlers and Tiaras* and its spinoff *Here Comes Honey Boo Boo*, make the actions and behaviors of working class people public for scrutiny, surveillance, and discipline by those of higher social and economic classes.

Reading 11.4, "Bootlegged: Unauthorized Circulation and the Dilemmas of Collaboration in the Digital Age," moves our focus from mass media television production to ethnographic film-making and its effects, which can be unanticipated. While ethnographic film-making has long been part of our discipline, we have entered new terrain in the digital age. Digital media have both increased opportunities to collaborate with others on the direction of a film—including with those representing the culture under study—as well as increased opportunities for the widespread circulation of the films once they are produced. But what happens when a film gets circulated beyond the anthropologist's original intent, or when third parties begin to profit from a film but the film's subjects or producers do not? Noelle Stout tackles these and other key ethical questions by reflecting on her production of *Luchando*, a film she produced in collaboration with Cuban sex workers that ended up circulated beyond her intention.

This section's "In the News" piece features another form of visual anthropology: native rock art. In an article linked to this feature entitled "No, It's Not 'Cool' to Deface Native Rock Art," Chip Colwell-Chanthaphonh speaks out against recent spikes in the defacement of native art, a felony offense. Native rock art provides us with clues into the history of first peoples, documenting their experiences and beliefs. They also serve as monuments for contemporary Native Americans to revere their ancestors. This "In the News" feature also links to publically available interviews of and news articles by Dr. Colwell-Chanthaphonh, a public archaeologist who specializes in Native American culture and history.

Part 11 ends with two "Anthropology in Practice" snapshots of academically based researchers who each work in collaborative visual ethnography. Dr. Neera Singh, an Assistant Professor in the Department of Geography and Planning at the University of Toronto, shares her work with participatory video ethnography on people's relationship to nature in Odisha, India. Dr. Karen Nakumura reflects on her career as a visual anthropologist doing work on issues around disability and sexuality in contemporary Japan.

Additional Resource: The website companion includes links to the Virtual Casebook Project at New York University. Developed by Barbara Abrash and Faye Ginsburg, this project explores areas of cultural activism in which tactical media play a key role. The first casebook focuses on 9/11 and After; subsequent casebooks will focus on HIV/AIDS activism and human rights.

 Visit www.oup.com/us/brondo for more information.

KEY TERMS:

- Visual anthropology
- Media anthropology
- Digital age
- Virtual worlds
- Social media
- Reality television
- Electronic panoptican

- Virtual activism
- Hashtag ethnography
- Ethnographic film-making
- Participatory video
- Public archaeology
- Native rock art

11.1 Everyday Second Life

TOM BOELLSTORFF

It is likely that a large percentage of students in your class spend major chunks of their days online, in virtual worlds. Maybe you, the reader, are one those of people. Anthropologists and other scholars wonder, how will such regular engagement with technology change humanity? In the following selection of his book Coming of Age in Second Life: An Anthropologist Explores the Virtually Human, *Tom Boellstorff draws on two years of ethnographic fieldwork in Second Life, a computer program that connects people over the Internet in what Boellstorff argues to be a profoundly human world. While some scholars of virtual technology worry that we are entering into an uneasy terrain of the "posthuman," with technology allowing us to overcome the human form, Boellstorff offers the opposite analysis, showing how worlds like Second Life are reworking what it means to be human in the actual world.*

Questions

1. What is a "virtual world"?
2. When and how do real and virtual worlds blend together in Second Life? Provide specific examples from the readings.
3. What negative assumptions did Boellstorff encounter about virtual worlds? What other critiques can you think of?
4. Are you a "resident" in any virtual worlds? How does your world online shape your actual life?

Everyday Second Life

A man spends his days as a tiny chipmunk, elf, or voluptuous woman. Another lives as a child, and two other persons agree to be his virtual parents. Two "real"-life sisters living hundreds of miles apart meet every day to play games together or shop for new shoes for their avatars. The person making the shoes has quit his "real"-life job because he is making over five thousand U.S. dollars a month from the sale of virtual clothing. A group of Christians pray together at a church; nearby another group of persons engages in a virtual orgy, complete with ejaculating genitalia. Not far away a newsstand provides copies of a virtual newspaper with ten reporters on staff; it includes advertisements

for a "real"-world car company, a virtual university offering classes, a fishing tournament, and a spaceflight museum with replicas of rockets and satellites.

This list of occurrences does not begin to scratch the surface of the myriad ways those who spent time in Second Life interacted with each other and the virtual world. During the time of my fieldwork, the level of "real"-world news coverage of Second Life increased dramatically, often focusing on aspects of the virtual world seen as sensational (for instance, that over US$1,000,000 of economic activity was occurring daily, or that a "real"world musician was performing in-world). But events seen as exceptional are of limited value; they take place in the context of broader norms that at first glance may seem uninteresting, but are the true key to understanding culture. For this reason it will prove helpful to introduce Second Life not by means of some infamous incident, but through a portrait of what an uneventful afternoon might have looked like during the time of my fieldwork. I do not intend this portrait to be representative of everyone's experience, just one example of what life in Second Life could be like during my fieldwork. Readers with experience in virtual worlds may find the description obvious, but I would ask such readers to consider what kinds of cultural assumptions are encapsulated within these apparently banal details of everyday Second Life.

Imagine yourself suddenly teleported into Second Life, alone in your home. You already have a Second Life account and thus an "avatar," which we will call Sammy Jones. On a computer—at home, at an office, or on your laptop at a café—you start the Second Life program just as you would an email program, word processor, or web browser. After logging on with your avatar name and password, you see your avatar, who never needs to eat or sleep, standing in your home (Figure 11.1.1). You built this house out of "primitives" (or "prims"), as objects in Second Life are known. You did so after practicing with Second Life's building tools in an area known as a "sandbox," where you can build for free but everything you build is deleted after a few hours. The piece of land upon which your house sits is 1,024 square virtual meters in size; you paid a virtual real estate agent about thirty dollars for it, conducting the transaction in linden dollars or "lindens." For the right to own land you paid Linden Lab, the company that owns Second Life, $9.95 a month for a "premium account" and an additional $5 a month for the ability

to own up to 1,024 square meters of land; this is known as a "land use fee" or "tier fee."

Using your mouse and keyboard you walk around your house, adorned with furniture, paintings, and rugs. You purchased some of these furnishings from stores in Second Life; others you made yourself. Deciding you are tired of the white rug in your living room, you open your "inventory," which appears on your screen as a "window" filled with folders containing items within them. . . . You drag an icon named "green rug" from your inventory window and, as if by magic, it materializes in your living room. You then right-click on the white rug: a "pie menu" appears with commands arranged in a circle. You choose "take" and the white rug disappears from your home; at the same time an icon named "white rug" appears in your inventory.

Now you walk out your front door and, pressing the "F" key on your keyboard, you begin to fly. Gaining altitude and speed, you see a landscape of green hills receding into the distance; as you move forward, buildings, trees, and other objects appear before you (Figure 11.1.2). Persons in Second Life typically say objects are "rezzing" into existence, a verb that dates back to *Tron* (Steven Lisberger, Disney, 1982), one of the first movies to use computer-generated graphics and to represent a virtual world. The reason it takes a few seconds for objects to "rez" is that the Second Life program on your computer is a "thin client" providing only the basic interface (Kushner 2004, 53): almost all of the data about the objects making up Second Life is transmitted to your computer over the Internet. In a sense, of course, the objects and the data about them are the same thing. Almost all of these objects are, like your

Figure 11.1.1

Standing at home (image by author).

Figure 11.1.2

Flying across the landscape (image by author).

house, not created by Linden Lab: Second Life is based upon the idea of user-created content (Ondrejka 2004). Linden Lab maintains the basic platform for Second Life: a landscape with land, water, trees, and sky; a set of building tools; and a means to control, modify, and communicate between avatars. Nearly everything else is the result of persons or groups of people spending millions of hours every month in acts of creation. Much of this creation is for personal or informal use, but since people in Second Life can earn "real" money in the virtual world and retain intellectual property rights over anything they create, individual entrepreneurs and even corporations create objects for sale.

Continuing to fly away from your home you see three people—more precisely, three avatars—rezzing into view. You knew they would be here because you pressed "control-M" to open a window with your "world map" and noticed three green dots on the square of land your avatar was about to enter (Figure 11.1.3). This square of land, 264 meters on a side, is known as a "sim" (short for "simulator"). Four sims are typically stored on one actualworld computer server; as your avatar enters a sim your computer receives information about the sim via the Internet. These servers retain all of the information about the sim's landscape as well as created objects or buildings, so that the virtual world persists when individuals turn their computers off.

The three avatars you now approach are being controlled by people who, like you, are currently logged onto Second Life: they could be next door to your physical location, a hundred miles away, or on another continent; there could even be two people controlling a single avatar together as they sit in front of a shared computer. During the time of my fieldwork it was only possible to speak audibly using third-party software, and this was rarely used. However, once you are within thirty virtual meters of these three avatars they will be able to "hear" what you "say": if you type something into your chat window, the text you type will appear on their computer screens when you press the "return" key. By clicking on an avatar with your mouse you can obtain a "profile" which tells you something about the person—a short paragraph they have written about themselves, a list of their favorite places in Second Life, the groups to which they belong. All of this information refers to a "screen name"; rarely do you discover someone's "real" name. As you look through your computer screen at the back of your avatar's head and these other avatars, the persons controlling them are looking at you through their own computer screens and can click on your profile.

"How are you doing?" you type to these three persons. "Good," replies one of them, named Judy Fireside. "We are just thinking about going to the Cool Club for their 80s Dance Club Hour." You continue

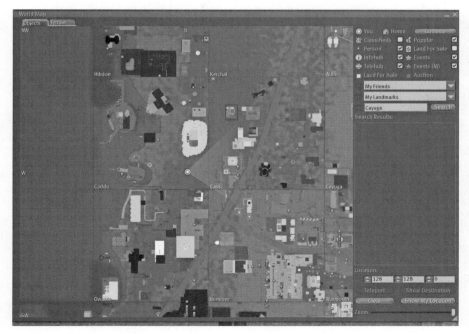

Figure 11.1.3

Looking at the world map, local area (image by author).

talking for a few minutes before deciding that you want to say something specifically to Judy Fireside, so you click on her avatar and choose "send IM" from the pie menu that appears. This opens up a window that allows you to type an "instant message" or "IM" solely to Judy. For several minutes you carry on two conversations at once—you are part of a group of four people chatting with each other, and also one of two people carrying on an instant-message conversation, perhaps commenting on what one of the other two people is saying. It is like being able to talk and whisper at the same time. You realize you want to stay in touch with Judy Fireside, so you right-click on her once again and choose "add friend" from the pie menu. This causes a message to appear on Judy's computer screen saying "Sammy Jones is offering friendship." She chooses "yes." Judy will no longer be an anonymous green dot on the world map or the "mini-map" that can be used to show your local area; you will be able to find her location and receive notification whenever she logs on or off.

Now you decide you want to go shopping for a shirt for your avatar. You say goodbye to Judy and the other two people to whom you were speaking. Opening the world map once again, you see the sim where your avatar is located and a couple others nearby. You zoom out on the map until you see Second Life in its entirety: over two thousand sims (at this point) laid out into a series of continents floating on a blue sea, known as the "mainland," and thousands of additional sims separate from the continents, known as "islands" (Figure 11.1.4). Over ten thousand green dots cover the mainland and islands, each representing the location of a person currently logged on to Second Life. Some dots are isolated; perhaps someone is building a house, strolling through a mall, or just sitting in a forest. You see pairs of dots: two friends catching up with each other, perhaps, or a couple having sex, or a real estate agent showing a plot of land to someone. You also see clusters of as many as seventy dots: perhaps a popular dance club, a casino, even a philosophy discussion.

Where was that favorite shirt store again? You type "control-F" on your computer and a window called "Find" appears on your screen, with tabs for locating people, places, and events. Selecting the "Places" tab you type "shirt": several hundred stores selling shirts appear in the window and you recognize one as the store you had in mind. You hit the button marked "teleport" on the Find window and after a few seconds of blackness you are half a continent away with a store rezzing around you. On the wall are squares with images of shirts and prices for each: 70 lindens, 150 lindens, 95 lindens. You see a shirt you like and right-click on the square with its image, choosing

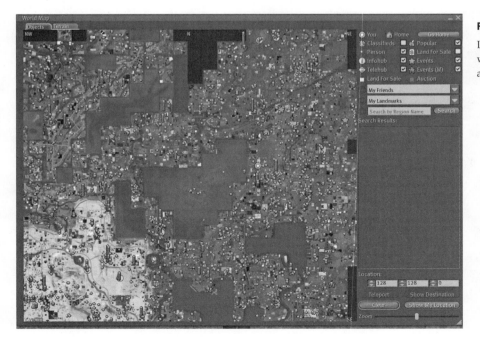

Figure 11.1.4

Looking at the world map, wider view (image by author).

"buy" from the pie menu that appears. Seventy lindens (about twenty-five cents during the period of my fieldwork) is deducted from your Second Life account, and the shirt is moved into your inventory. You open your inventory window, find the shirt, and choose the command "wear"; after a few seconds your avatar is wearing the new shirt. Then you notice that a store next to this one, designed to look like a medieval castle, is selling "textures," which can be added to the surface of prims. You have been meaning to add a deck to your house and as you stroll through this second store one of its owners, his avatar sitting on a stone staircase, asks, "can I help you?" You say that you are looking for a plank texture and the owner shows you a set of wood textures on sale for 300 lindens. They look great, so you purchase the textures like you purchased your shirt a few minutes ago.

The new textures safely in your inventory, you teleport home, walk outside your house, and choose the "create" command. A box appears in front of you on the ground. You choose "edit" and turn the box into a square ten meters wide, long, and tall—normally the maximum allowable size for a single prim—then flatten it to half a meter thick. The number of prims you have to work with depends on the size of your land: you have about 450 prims available on your plot, with only 300 currently used, so there is no harm in adding a bit more to your deck. You move the square flat prim just created up against the back of your house, and then create two more prims in the shape of poles to hold up the deck. In this virtual world a deck would stay up without poles, but like most people you create structures that accord visually with the laws of physics, more or less. Now you open your inventory and select one of the recently purchased wooden plank textures, dragging it onto your newly created deck and poles.

You are moving your deck a bit to the right so that it lines up with your home's back door when the instant message window pops up on your screen. It is Judy Fireside, asking "whatcha doing?" You tell Judy to come see the new deck and she teleports over with a friend, George Walker. Before long you are all deep in conversation and George is telling you and Judy about how his "real" mother has been ill lately. "But enough about that," George says, "a friend of mine is having a wedding. I just im-ed her and she said that you and Judy can come!" You and Judy both say you would be happy to attend.

Looking in your inventory you find a tuxedo you bought a couple of months ago, but have not had an opportunity to wear. You put it on your avatar as Judy and George find formal clothing for their own avatars. Judy chooses a gorgeous red and black gown, made from "flexible prims" that give the appearance of silk flowing in the Second Life breeze: it was made by a well-known designer who earns over three thousand U.S. dollars a month from her creations. Once everyone is ready, the three of you teleport to a steepled church on a virtual mountainside. Pools with fountains and schools of fish bracket the church's front door; inside there are garlands of flowers on the pews and soft piano music in the air. There are already twenty people inside the church, sitting on pews, with a best man, maid of honor, and officiant at the altar. You, Judy, and George take seats on a pew and send instant messages to each other so as not to disturb the solemnity of the occasion: "I've never been to this church before—it's stunning!" After a few minutes, the bride and groom prepare to walk down the aisle. They have been lovers for over a year in Second Life but have never met in the "real" world. In fact, they have not shared any information about their real-world lives—the bride might be a man, the groom a woman, either might already be married in the "real" world—but you feel genuinely happy as they exchange vows. Finally each types "I do" to the other. On your screen you see the officiant say "the bride and groom may now kiss" and each opens their inventory window to click on an icon for what is known as an "animation" a program that causes avatars to move. The avatars embrace as the audience in the pews types "yay!" "congratulations!" "I'm so happy for you!"

After the ceremony there is a party in a large club next door to the church. You click on a ball hanging from the ceiling of the club and it animates your avatar so that you dance together with the other guests, all the while chatting about the ceremony and congratulating the bride and groom. After a few songs, you glance up at the top of your computer screen and realize that you have been online for two hours; your "real" body is hungry and it is time to eat dinner. So you take your leave of the bride and groom, tell Judy and George that you will see them again soon, and quit the Second Life program as you would quit any program on your computer. Second Life disappears from your computer screen, but as you go to your kitchen to chop

vegetables, you think about all those people still dancing away in a club with a bride and groom, watching a
virtual sun set over a virtual sea.

. . .

This composite vignette . . . describes a mere frac-
tion of the thousands of ways people spent time in
Second Life during the period of my fieldwork. Some
were loners; others were members of groups with hundreds of members. Some had intense emotional and
sexual relationships; others came to Second Life to sail
a boat across a virtual lake, dance at a club, or play a
board game, without intimacy beyond the casual
acquaintance. Virtual worlds provide the opportunity for many forms of social interaction, and this can
include anthropological research. Just as I can attend
a wedding or build a house in Second Life, so I can
interview those in Second Life about their experiences
and also engage in "participant observation," following people around in their daily lives as a member of
the community. . . .

Terms of Discussion

. . . [V]irtual worlds are places of human culture realized
by computer programs through the Internet. Another
good definition for "virtual world" is "any computer-
generated physical space . . . that can be experienced
by many people at once" (Castronova 2005, 22).
My definition and Castronova's both presume three
fundamental elements to be present in all virtual
worlds: they are (1) places, (2) inhabited by persons,
and (3) enabled by online technologies.

[The] pivotal terms for my analysis are "virtual"
and "actual." In colloquial contemporary English, a
prominent meaning of "virtual" is "almost," as when
someone says "she's virtually my sister" to refer to
a close friend (Lévy 2001, 56). The Oxford English
Dictionary phrases this meaning of "virtual" as referencing something "that is so in essence or effect,
although not formally or actually. Virtuality can
thus be understood in terms of potentiality (Massumi
2002, 30); it can be said to exist whenever there is a perceived gap between experience and "the actual." This
is now the most important meaning of "virtual" with
regard to virtual worlds; "virtual" connotes approaching the actual *without arriving there.* This gap between
virtual and actual is critical: were it to be filled in, there
would be no virtual worlds, and in a sense no actual
world either. This is ultimately a reconfiguration of

the binarism between nature and culture, and its
boundary-marker is the distinction between "online"
and "offline."

. . . It is incorrect to associate virtual with culture
and actual with nature. Humans make culture in virtual and actual contexts; since humans are part of nature,
and the virtual is a product of human intentionality, the virtual is as "natural" as anything humans do
in the actual world. . . .

During my fieldwork, those in Second Life often
referred to "real life," "first life," "the physical world,"
or "the real world." Such terms are imprecise ant-
onyms for "virtual world" because they imply that
technology makes life less real: . . . a phrase like "in real
life" often "demarcates 'those experiences that occur
offline'" (Markham 1998, 115). In other words, "real"
often acts simply as a synonym for "offline," and does
not imply a privileged ontological status: "online
worlds are [not] spaces in which we simply work out
offline issues and once sorted, happily leave. . . . What
happens in virtual worlds often is just as real, just as
meaningful, to participants" (Taylor 2006, 19). Virtual worlds increasingly have "real" ramifications—a
business, an educational course, an online partner becoming a "real" spouse. As one person in Second Life
put it, "our virtual relationships are just as real as our rl
[real life] ones." Such ramifications take advantage of
the gap between virtual and actual. They do not blur
or close that gap, for their existence depends upon the
gap itself.

In short, "the virtual is opposed not to the real but
to the actual. . . . I do not oppose "virtual" and "real";
I refer to places of human culture not realized by computer programs through the Internet as parts of the
"actual world." "Actual" is also imperfect, but I find
it the best provisional term and additionally one used
fairly often by those in Second Life.

. . . Debates as to whether or not Second Life
was a game were common and sometimes heated
during my fieldwork. One Second Life resident offered this analysis: "Stadiums and Casinos. Venues
for games? Yes. Games? No. Canvas and paint?
Artistic medium? Yes. Game? No. A neighborhood
bar? Social scene? Yes. Game? No . . . Don't confuse the container with the contents. SL is no more
a game than a box of crayons." As this resident
noted, virtual worlds are not in and of themselves
games, and assuming that theories about games and
play are necessary foundations to understanding

virtual worlds leads to serious misinterpretations. This includes a conflation of online sociality with entertainment, obviating the consequential forms of intimacy, community, and political economy in virtual worlds. Scholars have long noted how a virtual world "is not goal-oriented; it has no beginning or end, no 'score' and no notion of 'winning' or 'success.' . . . [Such a world] isn't really a game at all" (Curtis 1992, 122). As a result, "virtual worlds are not games. Even the ones written to *be* games aren't games. People can play games *in* them, sure, and they can be set up to that end, but this merely makes them venues. . . ."

. . . There is no way to claim virtual worlds are games without trapping oneself in a definition of "game" so vague as to include most of our actual lives. For some, spending time in virtual worlds like Second Life means spending less time gaming. On those occasions during my fieldwork when persons termed Second Life a game, what they really meant was that it was a place of play, reflecting the centrality of creativity to understandings of the virtual world. For these reasons I will refer to someone logged into Second Life as a "resident" (a term used within Second Life) rather than "user," "player," or "gamer."

. . . Without wishing to engage in hyperbole, we may be on the verge of another massive transformation linked to technology, the creation of societies on the Internet: "for the first time, humanity has not one but many worlds in which to live" (Castronova 2005, 70). This could involve new forms of culture and selfhood, ones shaped in unpredictable ways by actual-world sociality: . . . I am not interested in questions like "is humanity going virtual" or "will we all live our lives online?"; such phrasing invites hype and casts the debate in polarizing terms. At issue is the simple fact that not so long ago, the percentage of human social life spent in virtual worlds was zero, that percentage is increasing, and social inquiry must follow this movement online. Drawing upon the work of a range of scholars of technology and society, I will develop a theory of this virtual world-view as *techne,* and of the person who engages in techne not just as *homo faber* ("man the maker") or *homo ludens* ("man the player"), but above all as *homo cyber.* The human online, the virtual human. In using the term "techne," I will draw upon a philosophical distinction between knowledge (episteme) and technology or art (techne), examining how virtual

selfhood is becoming predicated on the idea that people can craft their lifeworlds through intentional creativity.

During the writing of this [piece], I returned to Indonesia to study HIV/AIDS prevention, research that was intentionally distinct from my work in Second Life. Yet I continued to think about Second Life while doing this research; many sentences in this book, including this one, were written on a laptop in the city of Makassar on the island of Sulawesi. I found that maintaining a program of research in an actual-world context while conducting virtual anthropology was helpful in indicating what aspects of cultures in virtual worlds are truly unprecedented, and which are not. Through my ethnography of Second Life I work to pinpoint what is distinctive about virtual worlds. . . .

When presenting my research to audiences with limited experience in virtual worlds, I have found two negative assumptions to be particularly common. The first is that virtual worlds are hopelessly contaminated by capitalism. Such a response is often triggered by the reality that many virtual worlds are owned by for-profit companies, and also by the fact that some allow residents to earn actual-world money. . . . Questions of labor, consumption, and class are important in any discussion of virtual worlds. However, allowing such questions to consolidate a negative impression overestimates their influence and elides the degree to which such questions are no less important with regard to actual-world cultures. Indonesia, for instance, is highly capitalist, but no one has ever told me to stop studying it for that reason.

A second common negative interpretation I have encountered from those with limited experience in virtual worlds is that they are just a form of escapism from the actual world: . . . Such naïve realists "see computer systems as alien intruders on the terrain of unmediated experience. . . . Reality, they assert, is the physical world we perceive with our bodily senses [and] . . . the computer is . . . a subordinate device that can distract us from the primary world" (Heim 1998, 37).

. . . It is true that some persons spend time in virtual worlds to be something different: women becoming men or men becoming women, adults becoming children, disabled persons walking, humans becoming animals, and so on. However, many who participate in virtual worlds do not seek to escape from their actual lives. Such negative views of virtual worlds fail to consider forms of escapism in the actual world, from rituals to amusement parks to daydreaming: the degree to which an activity is "escapist" is independent of whether it is virtual or actual. . . .

The Posthuman and the Human

On January 16, 2006, I—more precisely, my Second Life avatar, Tom Bukowski—was sitting at home, enjoying the view across the water channel that lies below the steep slope on which I built my house, when Dara, a recent acquaintance, stopped by to say hello. I invited her to have a seat on my front porch and we started talking (chatting via text, of course). Soon Dara said, "by the way, I read your profile and I think what you're doing is really interesting. I like intellectual activities too, not just shopping all day long." I responded by telling her about some discussion groups:

> ME: There is the Thinkers group, and also my group Digital Cultures—join those groups.
>
> DARA : From what I saw in your group meeting, I found it very interesting
>
> ME: Oh, you're already a member of Digital Cultures
>
> DARA: You already made me a member, don't you remember?
>
> DARA: Or are there a few other people running your av [avatar] too
>
> ME: Yes, I made you a member of Digital Cultures, I just forgot lol [laugh out loud]
>
> ME: It's just me lol, me forgetting things
>
> DARA: Good, hate to get to know one and a new attitude appears

This innocuous exchange reveals a social error—I had forgotten that Dara had attended a meeting of Digital Cultures, a discussion group in Second Life that I moderated during my fieldwork, and that I already had made her a member of the group. Learning from moments of failure has a long history in anthropology. Yet there is something distinct to this innocuous exchange: confronted with my lapse in memory, one possible conclusion Dara draws is that I have not been

forgetful at all. Instead, different actual-world people might be inhabiting the avatar Tom Bukowski at different times, so that what is at issue is a disjuncture between avatar and actualworld person. Dara knows that the avatar Tom Bukowski is always being controlled by a computer in some actual-world location, and that someone other than Tom Boellstorff might be sitting in front of that computer. Dara indicates that she has experienced such a situation before; she "hates to get to know" someone and then a "new attitude appears" because the person controlling a particular avatar has changed.

Throughout this book I investigate changing notions of personhood linked to the emergence of virtual worlds, with a particular interest in debates over the "posthuman." This term usually refers to ways in which "technology can enable us to overcome the limits of human form" (Nayar 2004, 71; see also ibid., 11; Foster 2005,:xi) . My discomfort with the notion of the posthuman is partially a disciplinary effect: anthropology defines its object of study as *anthropos,* the human (Rabinow 2003). It might be possible to define "posthuman" in such a way as to make it theoretically productive, but in my view the term is misleading. . . . The notion of the posthuman conflates the human with the subject of liberal humanism, and thus with disciplinary debates in the humanities. It is an overly narrow and ethnocentric definition that effaces the variability of human lifeways.

While some see virtual worlds as marking the emergence of the posthuman, through terms like *homo cyber* I argue that the forms of selfhood and sociality characterizing virtual worlds are profoundly human. But while the emergence of virtual worlds "does not necessarily mean the end of the human . . . we need to see the human as re-configured and organized differently" (Nayar 2004, 21). This is one meaning of the phrase "virtually human"—in virtual worlds, we are not quite human. The relationship between the virtual and the human is not a "post" relationship where one term displaces another; it is a relationship of coconstitution. Far from it being the case that virtual worlds herald the emergence of the posthuman, . . . I argue that *it is in being virtual that we are human.* Virtual worlds reconfigure selfhood and sociality, but this is only possible because they rework the virtuality that characterizes human being in the actual world.

References

Castronova, Edward. 2005. *Synthetic Worlds: The Business and Culture of Online Games.* Chicago: University of Chicago Press.

Curtis, Pavel. 1992. [1997 reprint]. "Mudding: Social Phenomena in Text-Based Virtual Realities." In *Culture of the Internet,* ed. Sara Kiesler, 121–42. Mahwah, NJ: Lawrence Erlbaum Associates.

Foster, Thomas. 2005. *The Souls of Cyberfolk: Posthumanism as Vernacular Theory.* Minneapolis: University of Minnesota Press.

Heim, Michael. 1998. *Virtual Realism.* Oxford: Oxford University Press.

Kushner, David. 2004, "My Avatar, My Self." *Technology Review* 107,3 (April): 50-55.

Lévy, Pierre. 2001. *Cyberculture.* Minneapolis: University of Minnesota Press.

Markham, Annette N. 1998. *Life Online: Researching Real Experience in Virtual Space.* Walnut Creek, CA: Altamira Press.

Massumi, Brian. 2002. *Parables for the Virtual: Movement, Affect, Sensation.* Durham, NC: Duke University Press.

Nayar, Pramod K. 2004. *Virtual Worlds: Culture and Politics in the Age of Cybertechnology.* New Delhi: Sage Publications.

Ondrejka (Linden), Cory R. 2004a. "Escaping the Gilded Cage: User Created Content and Building the Metaverse." Available at: http://papers.ssrn.com/sol3/papers.cfm?abstract=555661 (accessed December 1, 2004).

Rabinow, Paul. 2003. *Anthropos Today: Reflections on Modern Equipment.* Princeton: Princeton University Press.

Taylor, T. L. 2006a. *Play Between Worlds: Exploring Online Game Culture.* Cambridge, MA: MIT Press.

11.2 #Ferguson: Digital Protest, Hashtag Ethnography, and the Racial Politics of Social Media in the United States

YARIMAR BONILLA AND JONATHAN ROSA

Visual media both reflects and shapes how people understand the world in which they live. Today, much of the world has access to several forms of visual media, and the numbers of cell phone users— even in the poorest and most marginalized communities—continue to grow rapidly. The role of cell phone technology and social media outlets, in culture change and cultural expression, is ripe for anthropological analysis. But, can a hashtag itself serve as an anthropological field site? Here Yarimar Bonilla and Jonathan Rosa consider the use of social media platforms as a field site for engaging in social activism. They focus on the "hashtag activism" that emerged through #Ferguson in response to police brutality and the misrepresentation of racialized bodies in the mainstream media in the wake of protests after the fatal police shooting of Michael Brown in Ferguson, Missouri, in 2014.

Questions

1. Is Twitter a non-place or a virtual world or something else? Explain.
2. Do social media distort or reflect reality? Explain.
3. Can a hashtag serve as an anthropological field site? Why or why not?
4. Compare and contrast participating in #Ferguson with posting about Ferguson on Facebook. What does each say about social activism?
5. Analyze the images that were circulated in the wake of #Ferguson. How were black bodies represented, and what did participation in specific postings reveal about those who posted?
6. Does "all that is tweeted melt into the air"?

On Saturday, August 9, 2014, at 12:03 p.m., an unarmed black teenager named Michael Brown was fatally shot by a police officer in Ferguson, Missouri, a small town on the outskirts of St. Louis. Within the hour, a post appeared on the Twitter social media platform stating, "I just saw someone die," followed by a photograph taken from behind the beams of a small wooden balcony overlooking Canfield Drive, where Michael Brown's lifeless body lay uncovered, hands alongside his head, face down on the asphalt.

Immediately following the incident, community members assembled to demand an explanation for why this unarmed 18-year-old had been seemingly executed while reportedly holding his hands up in a gesture of surrender, pleading "don't shoot." The impromptu gathering soon turned into a sustained protest marked by daily demonstrations and violent confrontations with highly armed local police—all of which were documented in detail across social media platforms like Twitter, Instagram, YouTube, and Vine.

Occurring on the heels of other highly publicized killings of unarmed black men—such as Eric Garner (who died as a result of an illegal chokehold by New York City police just weeks before the events in Ferguson), Oscar Grant (whose death was emotionally portrayed in the award-winning film *Fruitvale Station* (Ryan Coogler, The Weinstein Company, 2013) released just one year prior), and 17-year-old Trayvon Martin (whose 2012 killing sparked national outcry and spurred numerous forms of activism)—the death of Michael Brown quickly captured the imagination of thousands across and beyond the United States. Protestors from around the nation flocked to Ferguson to participate in demonstrations calling for the arrest of the officer responsible for the fatal shooting. Television viewers tuned in across the country to watch live news coverage of the violent confrontations between the protestors and the highly armed local police. Images of these confrontations circulated widely in national and international news coverage, and news of these events quickly went "viral" across social media. During the initial week of protests, over 3.6 million posts appeared on Twitter documenting and reflecting on the emerging details surrounding Michael Brown's death; by the end of the month, "#Ferguson" had appeared more than eight million times on the Twitter platform.

These statements are simple facts, but the meaning and consequences of these facts will be occupying social analysts for years to come. Much will be written about Michael Brown: about his portrayal in the media, his treatment by the police, and both the circumstances and consequences of his death. Much will also be written about the protestors who immediately gathered at the site of his killing and about those who remained, under intense police harassment, long after the media spotlight faded.[1] But what are we to make of the eight million tweets? What do they tell us about this event, its place in the social imagination, and about social media itself as a site of both political activism and social analysis?

In 1991, a homemade VHS tape of Los Angeles resident Rodney King being brutally beaten by four police officers sparked outrage across the country and galvanized thousands in what is widely recognized as one of the most influential examples of citizen journalism in the United States (Allan and Thorsen 2009).[2] Today, 56 percent of the U.S. population carries video-enabled smartphones, and the use of mobile technology is particularly high among African Americans.[3]

The increased use and availability of these technologies has provided marginalized and racialized populations with new tools for documenting incidents of state-sanctioned violence and contesting media representations of racialized bodies and marginalized communities. In many cases—such as police officers' use of a chokehold in the murder of Eric Garner—the use of mobile technology to record and circulate footage of events has played a key role in prompting public outcry.[4] In the case of Ferguson, video footage of the fatal shooting of Michael Brown has yet to surface, but informal journalism was used to document the scene in the direct aftermath of his murder, to publicize the protests that ensued, and to bring attention to the militarized police confrontations that followed. Through social media, users were able to disseminate these accounts to a broad audience and to forge new mediatized publics that demand anthropological attention. In this [chapter], we explore how and why platforms like Twitter have become important sites for activism around issues of racial inequality, state violence, and media representations. . . .

Can a Hashtag Become a Field Site?

. . . Is Twitter the ultimate "non-place" (Augé 2009) of super modernity, a transient site of fleeting engagement, or is it an instance of a "virtual world" (Boellstorff 2008), with its own set of socialities and forms of engagement? And is the study of an event through social media a return to a previous era of "armchair anthropology"? Or is hashtag ethnography the next logical step in an anthropology of the 21st century . . . ? To answer these questions, it is necessary to begin by distinguishing the town of Ferguson, Missouri, from "hashtag Ferguson" and to recognize how each of these contributed to the formation of the larger "event" of Ferguson. As those familiar with Twitter know, the hashtag symbol (#) is often used as a way of marking a conversation within this platform. The hashtag serves as an indexing system in both the clerical sense and the semiotic sense. In the clerical sense, it allows the ordering and quick retrieval of information about a specific topic. . . . Similar to the coding systems employed by anthropologists, hashtags allow users to not simply "file" their comments but to performatively frame what these comments are "really about," thereby enabling users to indicate a meaning that might not be otherwise apparent. Hence, someone could write, "Decades of racial tension and increasing suburban poverty boiled to the surface last night" followed by the text "#Ferguson," as a way of creating a particular interpretive frame. Hashtags thus operate in ways similar to library call numbers: They locate texts within a specific conversation, allowing for their quick retrieval, while also marking texts as being "about" a specific topic.

In addition, hashtags have the intertextual potential to link a broad range of tweets on a given topic or disparate topics as part of an intertextual chain, regardless of whether, from a given perspective, these tweets have anything to do with one another. Thus, a tweet in support of Ferguson protestors and a tweet in support of Officer Darren Wilson could both be coded and filed under #Ferguson. Moreover, a tweet about racial disparity in Missouri, such as "racism lives here," and one about a night out on the town in St. Louis could both be marked #STL.

This insight requires anthropologists to carefully consider the variety of uses in play for any given hashtag as well as the stances and perspectives associated with any given use. In the case of #Ferguson, patterns emerged in which Twitter became a platform for providing emergent information about the killing of Michael Brown and for commenting on the treatment of the officer who shot him. For example, one user posted, "Prosecutors get real friendly when they have to adjudicate one of their own. But they'll move heaven and earth hunting POC down. #Ferguson."[5] In contrast, other tweets recontextualized the situation in Ferguson as part of global affairs (e.g., "#Egypt #Palestine #Ferguson #Turkey, U.S. made tear gas, sold on the almighty free market represses democracy"), while others critiqued the appropriation of this event (e.g., "seriously though, @FCKH8 never posted ANYTHING on their Facebook page in support of #Ferguson until it was time to sell some t-shirts"[6]). . . .

In addition . . . hashtags also have the interdiscursive capacity to lasso accompanying texts and their indexical meanings as part of a frame. Linkages across hashtags and their accompanying texts—which comprise both other hashtags (e.g., #Ferguson, #MichaelBrown, #HandsUp, etc.) and additional commentary—frame #Ferguson as a kind of mediatized place.[7] It is in this sense that much like one could go to the library, stand in front of a call number, and find texts on a particular subject, one could go onto Twitter, type #Ferguson, and find a large number of posts on the subject at hand. But what is the relationship between this mediatized place—as it is experienced from outside the boundaries of the geographical context with which it is associated—and everyday life in what might be understood as Ferguson proper? How does the mediatization of Ferguson, Missouri, through #Ferguson lead to the formation of new "ad hoc publics" (Bruns and Burgess 2011)?

The types of publics created by Twitter emerge from the hashtag's capacity to serve not just as an indexing system but also as a filter that allows social media users to reduce the noise of Twitter by cutting into one small slice. However, this filtering process also has a distorting effect. Social media create a distorted view of events, such that we only get the perspective of the people who are already in our social network (Garret and Resnick 2011; Pariser 2012; Sunstein 2009). This effect should signal one of the first cautions for anthropologists interested in social media: We must avoid the common slippage made by journalists and others who tend to represent Twitter as an unproblematized "public sphere" without taking into account the complexity of who is on Twitter, as well as how people are on Twitter in different ways (e.g., some are constant users, others tweet infrequently, some do so from their phone, some from their office, etc.).

Part of the problem of engaging in hashtag ethnography, then, is that it is difficult to assess the context of social media utterances. Moreover, a simple statement of fact—for example, that there were eight million Ferguson tweets—tells us very little. How many were critical of the police? How many were critical of the protestors? How many were posted by journalists (both professional and amateur)? Beyond knowing that people tweeted, we know little about what those tweets meant to their authors and their imagined publics. We do not know, for example, how many of the eight million tweets were aimed at a national audience (and thus appropriately hashtagged for quick retrieval and retweet) versus how many were aimed at a smaller group of followers with the contextual information necessary to assess both the explicit and implicit uses of hashtags and other references.

In thinking about the hashtag as a field site, these questions and the competing perspectives they highlight demonstrate the importance of reorienting social media ethnography from an emphasis on "network and community" toward a focus on individual experiences, practices, and socialities (Postill and Pink 2012, 124). . . .

In the case of Ferguson, it is worth noting that, at least initially, the most common use of the #Ferguson hashtag was to convey information about the unfolding events. Before the mainstream media had caught up to what was happening, the mass of hashtagged tweets was a way of calling attention to an underreported incident of police brutality. . . .

. . . [R]ecognizing that hashtags can only ever offer a limited, partial, and filtered view of a social world does not require abandoning them as sites of analysis. Rather, we must approach them as what they are: entry points into larger and more complex worlds. Hashtags offer a window to peep through, but it is only by stepping through that window and "following" (in both Twitter and non-Twitter terms) individual users that we can begin to place tweets within a broader context. This kind of analysis requires us to stay with those who tweet and follow them after hashtags have fallen out of "trend." . . .

The Whole World Is Tweeting

Social movements have long used media and technology to disseminate, escalate, and enlarge the scope of their struggles: Transistor radios allowed Cuban guerrilla fighters to transmit from the Sierra Maestra; television coverage transformed the riots in Selma, Alabama, into a national event; and e-mail accounts allowed Zapatistas in Chiapas to launch global communiqués. #Ferguson did what many of these other tools did: It allowed a message to get out, called global attention to a small corner of the world, and attempted to bring visibility and accountability to repressive forces.

One of the differences between Twitter and these earlier forms of technology, however, is its multivocality and dialogicality (Bakhtin 1981). Twitter does not just allow you to peer through a window; it allows you to look through manifold windows at once. On #Ferguson, you could watch six simultaneous live streams. You could read what protestors were tweeting, what journalists were reporting, what the police was announcing, and how observers and analysts interpreted the unfolding events. You could also learn how thousands of users were reacting to the numerous posts. In the era of transistor radios and television sets, one did

not necessarily know what listeners or viewers yelled back at their machines, but on Twitter one can get a sense of individual responses to mediatized events.

E-mail, television, radio, and print have long managed to open up windows into the experience of social movements, but the dialogicality and temporality of Twitter create a unique feeling of direct participation. Twitter allows users who are territorially displaced to feel like they are united across both space and time. . . .

#Ferguson and its attendant live streams created a . . . feeling of shared temporality—particularly during the protests and confrontations with police. As opposed to someone who might *post about* Ferguson on Facebook, users on Twitter felt like they were *participating in* #Ferguson, as they tweeted in real time about the unfolding events, rallied supporters to join various hashtag campaigns [(discussed later in this chapter)], and monitored live streams where they could bear witness to the tear gassing and arrests of journalists and protestors. Engaging in these activities is akin to participating in a protest in the sense that it offers an experience of "real time" engagement, community, and even collective effervescence. Through this form of participation, users can experience the heightened temporality that characterizes all social movements: the way days marked by protest become "eventful," distinguishing them from quotidian life. . . .

Hashtag Activism Versus "Real" Activism?

. . . [I]t is important to examine how and why digital activism has become salient to particular populations. It is surely not coincidental that the groups most likely to experience police brutality, to have their protests disparaged as acts of "rioting" or "looting," and to be misrepresented in the media are precisely those turning to digital activism at the highest rates. Indeed, some of the most important hashtag campaigns emerging out of #Ferguson were targeted at calling attention to both police practices and media representations, suggesting that social media can serve as an important tool for challenging these various forms of racial profiling.

The first of these campaigns was inspired by eyewitness reports that Michael Brown had his hands up in the air as a sign of surrender and had uttered the words *don't shoot* just before he was shot and killed by Officer Darren Wilson. Initial activism around Michael Brown thus revolved around the hashtag

#HandsUpDontShoot, often accompanied by photos of individuals or groups of people with their hands up. One of the most widely circulated images from this meme was that of Howard University students with their hands up (see Figure 11.2.1).

Through this campaign, users sought to call attention to the arbitrary nature of racialized policing, the vulnerability of black bodies, and the problematic ways in which blackness is perceived as a constant threat. Because Michael Brown was allegedly shot while holding his hands up, #HandsUpDontShoot also became a tool for contesting victim-blaming or respectability narratives rooted in the belief that one can control the perception of one's body and the violence inflicted on it. These efforts echoed a previous "meme" that emerged in response to the killing of another unarmed African American teenager, Trayvon Martin, two years earlier.[8] Shortly following Martin's killing, a recording of the 911 call made by George Zimmerman, the killer, describing Martin as someone "suspicious" wearing a "dark hoodie," circulated widely in the press. Fox News commentator Geraldo Rivera suggested that the hoodie was "as much responsible for Trayvon Martin's death as George Zimmerman" (Rivera 2012). Rivera argued that hoodies had become emblematic of criminal behavior, given their ubiquitous presence in crime-suspect drawings and surveillance footage of petty theft. This argument elides the role that race plays in structuring the hoodie's alternate status as an innocuous piece of clothing versus a sign of criminality or deviance. That is, hoodies

are only signs of criminal behavior when they are contextualized in relation to particular racialized bodies.[9] Many commentators sought to draw attention to this point. In the wake of Trayvon Martin's death, the hoodie became a powerful symbol, with events like the "Million Hoodie March" drawing hundreds of supporters. Online activism at the time included the circulation of images of users wearing hoodies, marked with the hashtags #HoodiesUp and #WeAreTrayvonMartin in a sign of solidarity.

Immediately following Trayvon Martin's killing, many social media users changed their profile pictures to images of themselves wearing hooded sweatshirts with the hoods up. Similarly, in the wake of Michael Brown's death, many posted profile pictures of themselves with their hands up. These instances show how the seemingly vacuous practice of taking "selfies" (i.e., photos of oneself) can become politically meaningful in the context of racialized bodies. These images represent acts of solidarity that seek to humanize the victims of police brutality by suggesting that a similar fate could befall other similarly construed bodies.[10]

Two of the other popular memes that emerged in the wake of #Ferguson also focused on representations of black bodies and, specifically, on media portrayals of Michael Brown. The first of these emerged as a response to the photograph that mainstream media initially circulated in the wake of his death. The image sparked controversy because it showed Michael Brown making a hand gesture that, for some, represented a peace sign and, for others, a gang sign. Like Trayvon Martin's hoodie, the very same hand gesture could be alternately interpreted as a sign of peace or criminality depending on the racialized body with which it is associated. In response, Twitter users began using the hashtag #IfTheyGunnedMeDown to post contrasting pictures of themselves along with various versions of the question "which picture would they use?" For example, 18-year-old Houston native Tyler Atkins (featured in a *New York Times* article about the meme) posted a picture of himself after a jazz concert in his high school, wearing a black tuxedo with his saxophone suspended from a neck strap. This was juxtaposed with a photo taken while filming a rap video with a friend, in which he is wearing a black T-shirt and a blue bandanna tied around his head and his finger is pointed at the camera (see Figure 11.2.2).

Figure 11.2.1

Image of students at Howard University with their hands up. Posted to Twitter on November 16, 2014, by David Flores with the text "#100DaysOfInjustice #Ferguson #HandsUpDontShoot." (Image courtesy of David Flores.)

#IfTheyGunnedMeDown which picture would they use.

RETWEETS 92   FAVORITES 134

6:11 PM - 10 Aug 2014

Figure 11.2.2

Image tweeted on August 10, 2014, by Tyler Atkins with the post "#IfTheyGunnedMeDown which picture would they use." (Photo courtesy of Tyler Atkins)

Once again, these images represent an act of solidarity. They suggest that anyone could be represented as either respectable and innocent or violent and criminal—depending on the staging of the photograph. This campaign speaks to larger concerns over privacy in an era when private photos and surveillance footage are routinely leaked, hacked, and repurposed to nefarious ends. More importantly, it also speaks to an acute awareness among young African Americans of how black bodies are particularly vulnerable to misrepresentation by mainstream media (Vega 2014).

The final hashtag campaign we mention here speaks directly to this issue. It emerged in response to a *New York Times* profile of Michael Brown released on the day of his funeral, which described the 18-year-old as "no angel" (Elignon 2014). The piece suggested that Brown "dabbled in drugs and alcohol" and had been involved in "at least one scuffle with a neighbor." Many saw this as a tasteless, unfair portrayal and an extension of the attempted smear campaign carried out by the local police, who had released what they themselves admitted was "unrelated" surveillance video of a purported act of shoplifting at a convenience store. In response, Twitter users began using the hashtag #NoAngel to highlight the mainstream media's inability to acknowledge the possibility of black victimhood or innocence. For example, one person tweeted, "I am #NoAngel, so

I guess I deserve to be murdered too. Yep, perfectly acceptable to gun down a person if they aren't a Saint."

The use of hashtags such as #HandsUpDontShoot, #IfTheyGunnedMeDown, and #NoAngel speak to the long history of inaccurate and unfair portrayal of African Americans within mainstream media and to the systematic profiling and victim blaming suffered by racializied bodies. Their use suggests that while social media might seem like a space of disembodied engagement, for many, social media can become an important site in which to foreground the particular ways in which racialized bodies are systematically stereotyped, stigmatized, surveilled, and positioned as targets of state-sanctioned violence. These hashtag campaigns, which seek to identify the insidious nature of contemporary racism, can thus be understood as a powerful response to the "racial paranoia" (Jackson 2008) associated with African Americans' ongoing experiences of abject inequality in an age of alleged colorblindness.

The effort to bring attention to this inequality is powerfully captured by the hashtag #BlackLivesMatter, which emerged in July 2013, after George Zimmerman was acquitted of Trayvon Martin's murder. Many Twitter users also drew on this hashtag in response to the killing of Michael Brown. It is important to understand #BlackLivesMatter not simply as a general statement about the inherent value of black life in the face of state-sanctioned racial violence but also as a reflection of the ways that social media can become a site for the revaluation of black materiality. As illustrated in the memes described above, participants often used photos of themselves to contest the racialized devaluation of their persons. Whereas, in face-to-face interactions, racialized young people like the ones described [earlier] might not be able to contest the meanings ascribed to their bodies (or impede the deadly violence exerted on them by the police), through their creative reinterpretations on social media, they are able to rematerialize their bodies in alternative ways. With these creative acts, they seek to document, contest, and ultimately transform their quotidian experiences by simultaneously asserting the fundamental value and the particularity of their embodiment both on- and off-line.

All That Is Tweeted Melts into Air?

It is clear that platforms like Twitter have become essential to contemporary social actors, but the long-lasting effects of digital modes of activism remain hotly debated. For some, these acts represent fleeting moments of awareness, quickly replaced by the customary innocuousness of social media pleasantries. For others, however, participation in forms of digital activism prove transformative in unpredictable ways. . . .

As Johnetta Elzie, a 25-year-old protestor profiled in the magazine *The Nation*, explained, "We saw it with Trayvon Martin. We saw it with Jordan Davis—but I always felt away from everything. Then I saw Brown's body laying out there, and I said, 'Damn, they did it again!' But now that it happened in my home, I'm not just going to tweet about it from the comfort of my bed. So I went down there" (Hsieh and Rakia 2014). Elzie's words hint at how face-to-face and digital forms of activism work in interrelated and aggregative ways. Although she draws a distinction between tweeting from the comfort of her home and physical presence at an event, her narrative shows how these contexts are interrelated and build on each other—even beyond the confines of one particular historical event or hashtag campaign.

The article goes on to describe how Elzie encountered other activists involved in the protests through their shared use of social media, stating, "They quickly developed a tight-knit community, sustained by their addiction to social media. Together, they live-tweeted, Vined and Instagrammed every protest, through the sweltering days and tumultuous nights, as well as the direct actions taking place elsewhere in the St. Louis area." The group eventually took on the name Millennial Activists United and shifted their role from "documenting" their actions to "generating" new forms of social community, for instance, through the use of #FergusonFriday to create a space for reflection on the movement, the creation of a daily newsletter *This Is The Movement* to spread news and reflection pieces about unfolding events, and the organization of national "fireside" conference calls during which activists based in Ferguson could speak directly with those following the events from afar.[11] The ways these activists shift seamlessly across spaces and modes of engagement underscore the slippery boundary between analog and digital forms of activism. Indeed, it is unclear if #HandsUpDontShoot and #JusticeForMichaelBrown represent the use of political slogans as hashtags or if they represent the use of hashtags as slogans. . . .

Postscript

On November 24, 2014, after a grand jury released its decision not to indict Darren Wilson, Ferguson went viral once again, with over 3.5 million tweets appearing in a matter of hours under the hashtag #FergusonDecision. That evening, and in the days that followed, protestors took to the streets across the nation and beyond to decry the decision, the overall handling of Michael Brown's case by the justice system, and racialized police brutality more broadly. Demonstrators staged "death-ins" at city intersections and shopping malls, they lined suburban sidewalks face down in memory of Michael Brown's lifeless body, and they brought traffic in several cities across the United States to a halt, shutting down multilane highways, bridges, tunnels, and modes of public transportation. Many wore T-shirts proclaiming "I am Mike Brown" and held signs calling for the need to "Indict America." These demonstrations led social media users to claim that "#Ferguson is everywhere," emphasizing the connection between online and offline forms of protest.

The release of the grand jury hearing transcripts also offered a new view of the events as narrated by Darren Wilson, who had until that moment remained silent. His testimony—particularly his description of Michael Brown as "a demon," as a larger-than-life figure, and his use of the pronoun *it* to refer to the 18-year-old—offered further insight into the distorted lens through which black bodies are read by representatives of the state. Michael Brown and Darren Wilson were both 6'4" tall and weighed 290 pounds and 210 pounds, respectively, yet, in his testimony and in television interviews, Wilson said he felt like "a 5-year-old holding on to Hulk Hogan." Wilson's characterization of himself as a child and of Brown as a superhuman monster became part of an exculpatory narrative in which the unarmed teenager was framed as the true threat, not the police officer who shot and killed him. In his testimony, Darren Wilson affirmed that he had done nothing wrong and expressed no remorse for his actions. Describing the moment of Michael Brown's death, he stated that, as the bullets entered the young man's body, "the demeanor on his face went blank, the aggression was gone, it was gone, . . . the threat was stopped." Wilson's reverse logic, sanctioned by the state, presents a narrative in which an unarmed teenager is a terrifying aggressor and an armed police officer is an innocent victim. This inversion underscores the significance of affirming that #BlackLivesMatter in a context where they are disproportionately viewed as threats by state forces and mainstream institutions.

The same week of the Ferguson grand jury decision, news broke of the fatal shooting of 12-year-old Tamir Rice by Cleveland police after a 911 caller reported a "guy" with a gun. The gun was probably fake, the caller had said, and "it" (referring to Rice) was "probably a juvenile," but, still, the mere sight of the boy with a toy gun "is scaring the shit out of me," the caller insisted. Police were dispatched, and they shot the boy dead within two seconds of encountering him. This event made clear once again state agents' distorted views of black Americans, especially teenagers—how their very bodies are perceived as looming, larger-than-life threats and how any objects in their possession (e.g., candies, sodas, toys, articles of clothing) are read as weapons.

Once again, the media focused not on state action but on the worthiness of black bodies. Local news immediately ran profiles of Rice's parents, noting that they both had "violent pasts" (his father had been charged with domestic violence and his mother with drug possession). This history, reporters argued, could help explain why Tamir Rice would be inclined to play with a toy gun in a public place. Under fire for its coverage, the Northeast Ohio Media Group claimed, "One way to stop police from killing any more 12-year-olds might be to understand the forces that lead children to undertake behavior that could put them in the sights of police guns." There was no discussion of a national "gun culture," as there often is in incidents involving youth and guns (though, in this case, the "gun" was a toy), nor was there any discussion of the structural violence that Rice and his family engaged with on a daily basis or of the distorted ways young black bodies are viewed when they end up "in the sights" of police guns.

Within this context, social media participation becomes a key site from which to contest mainstream media silences and the long history of state-sanctioned violence against racialized populations. Upon announcing the Ferguson grand jury decision, St. Louis prosecutor Robert McCulloch claimed that media coverage, and particularly social media, had posed "the most significant challenge" to his investigation. Social media cast a spotlight on this small Missouri township, but more importantly, by propelling Ferguson into a broader, mediatized, virtual space, social media users were able to show that "#Ferguson is everywhere"—not only in the sense of a broad public sphere but also in the sense of the underlying social and political relationships that haunt the nation as a whole. . . .

Notes

1. The protests in Ferguson did not quickly fade. Indeed, as this article was being drafted, a new hashtag, #FergusonOctober, began trending as people from across and beyond the United States gathered in Ferguson from October 10 to October 13, 2014, "to build momentum for a nationwide movement against police violence." See Ferguson October 2014.

2. One could go even further back historically and examine how the image of Emmett Till, released by his mother for publication in *Jet* magazine, served as an important catalyst for the Civil Rights movement. . . .

3. A recent study by the Pew Research Center (Smith 2013) indicates that 53 percent of white Americans, 64 percent of African Americans, and 60 percent of U.S. Latinos/as own smartphones.

4. While some audiences have interpreted increased mediatization of such events as a sign of increased rates of police brutality, many others have pointed out that police brutality has always been rampant in communities of color, particularly African American and Latina/o communities. . . .

5. POC is an acronym for people of color.

6. "@FCKH8" is the Twitter handle of a company that sells T-shirts with activist themes. The author of this tweet is accusing the company of using the events in Ferguson as an opportunity to generate profit.

7. John Postill (2014) has noted the ways that the use of multiple, novel hashtags reflects savvy social media users' understanding that Twitter rewards novelty over raw numbers in its trending algorithms. . . .

8. Memes might be best understood as mediatized tropes. That is, memes are citational representations that circulate in forms such as hashtags, photos, and videos. In some cases, such representations are explicitly recognized as memes. See Know Your Meme 2007–14.

9. Like Trayvon Martin's hoodie, whose sign value was construed in relation to race, the meaningfulness of the bag of candy and can of iced tea he was carrying

with him at the time of his death were also racially construed and, in fact, rematerialized altogether as weapons and drug paraphernalia. George Zimmerman, Trayvon Martin's killer, allegedly thought that the candy and can of iced tea were potentially guns or other weapons; other commentators speculated that Martin was using these items to make recreational drugs. Here, ideas about race transform not just a sign's value (e.g., as a relatively unremarkable piece of clothing or a sartorial practice associated with criminality, as in the case of the hoodie) but the fundamental ontology of a given sign (e.g., as a bag of candy or a gun, a can of iced tea or drug paraphernalia), thus reflecting the semiotic power of race and racialization (Rosa 2010).

10. Perhaps the most recognizable of these images was a photo of the Miami Heat basketball team wearing hooded sweatshirts with the hoods up that famed NBA player Lebron James posted to Twitter with the hashtag #WeAreTrayvonMartin. See ESPN.com 2012.

11. The phrase #Ferguson has been used not only on social media but also on other canvases such as posters and T-shirts. During October 2014, #Ferguson morphed into #FergusonOctober as a temporal rallying cry for demonstrations against police violence held in Ferguson throughout the month in preparation for the announcement of whether Officer Darren Wilson would be prosecuted for the killing of Michael Brown. In addition to this adaptation of #Ferguson, #HandsUpDontShoot has been invoked on posters and other organizing materials urging interested parties to text "HANDSUP" to a particular number for updates on what is going on in Ferguson and in the broader effort to eradicate police violence. Thus, there are powerful coordinating relationships between digital and offline contexts such as #Ferguson and Ferguson proper as well as relationships between digital modalities such as the circulation of information via Twitter and cellular text messages.

References

Allan, Stuart, and Einar Thorsen, eds. 2009. Citizen Journalism: Global Perspectives. New York: Peter Lang.

Augé, Marc. 1995. Non-Places: Introduction to an Anthropology of Supermodernity. John Howe, trans. New York: Verso Books.

Bakhtin, Mikhail. 1981. The Dialogic Imagination: Four Essays. Caryl Emerson and Michael Holquist, trans. Austin: University of Texas Press.

Boellstorff, Tom. 2008. Coming of Age in Second Life: An Anthropologist Explores the Virtually Human. Princeton: Princeton University Press.

Bruns, Axel, and Jean Burgess. 2011. The Use of Twitter Hashtags in the Formation of Ad Hoc Publics. Paper presented at the European Consortium for Political Research conference, Reykjavik, August 25–27.

Elignon, John. 2014. Michael Brown Spent Last Weeks Grappling with Problems and Promise. New York Times, August 24, 2014.

ESPN.com. 2012. Heat Don Hoodies after Teen's Death. ESPN.com, March 24. http://espn.go.com/nba/truehoop/miamiheat/story/_/id/7728618/miami-heat-don-hoodies-response-death-teen-trayvon-martin (accessed October 15, 2014).

Ferguson October 2014. About. http://fergusonoctober.com/about/ (accessed October 15, 2014).

Garret, Kelly R., and Paul Resnick. 2011. Resisting Political Fragmentation on the Internet. Daedalus 140(4):108–120.

Hsieh, Steven, and Raven Rakia. 2014. After #Ferguson. Nation. October 27, 2014.

Jackson, John L. 2008. Racial Paranoia: The Unintended Consequences of Political Correctness: The New Reality of Race in America. New York: Basic Civitas.

Know Your Meme. 2007–14. Know Your Meme Home. http://knowyourmeme.com (accessed October 15, 2014).

Pariser, Eli. 2012. The Filter Bubble: How the New Personalized Web Is Changing What We Read and How We Think. New York: Penguin Press.

Postill, John. 2014. Democracy in an Age of Viral Reality: A Media Epidemiography of Spain's Indignados Movement. Ethnography 15(1):51–69.

Postill, John, and Sarah Pink. 2012. Social Media Ethnography: The Digital Researcher in a Messy Web. Media International Australia 145:123–134.

Rivera, Geraldo. 2012. "Leave The Hoodie At Home" YouTube video, 3:02, from Fox New Broadcast on March 23. Posted by tpmtv. https://www.youtube.com/watch?v=2Yyqkcc-a8U (accessed October 15, 2014).

Rosa, Jonathan. 2010. Looking Like a Language, Sounding Like a Race: Making Latina/o Panethnicity and Managing American Anxieties. Ph.D. dissertation, Department of Anthropology, University of Chicago.

Smith, Aaron. 2013. Smartphone Ownership 2013. Pew Research Center, June 5. http://www.pewinternet.org/2013/06/05/smartphone-ownership-2013/ accessed October 15, 2014.

Sunstein, Cass. 2009. Republic.com 2.0. Princeton: Princeton University Press.

Vega, Tanzina. 2014. Shooting Spurs Hashtag Effort on Stereotypes. New York Times, August 12.

11.3 Policing Childhood Through The Learning Channel's *Toddlers and Tiaras*

ANDREA FREIDUS

To what degree does television—and "reality television" in particular—reflect, influence, or "discipline" and control the lives of others? In the following piece, Andrea Freidus analyzes Internet dialogue surrounding The Learning Channel's Toddlers and Tiaras, a reality television program about child beauty pageants. Freidus argues that the television show operates as an "electronic panopticon," whereby the actions and behaviors of working-class people are made public for security, surveillance, and discipline by those of higher social and economic classes. The panopticon refers to Jeremy Bentham's nineteenth-century prison design that created the "perfect prison" whereby cells would be open to a central panoptic (pan = all and optic = seeing) tower where guards could see out (if they are in the tower) but prisoners could not see in, thus resulting in a feeling of being under constant surveillance since the prisoners would never know when someone was looking. In this selection, Freidus shows how both mothering and childhood are policed, but policed along class and racialized lines. In addition to considering the piece as an example of media ethnography, this chapter works well in conversation with Part 4 on family and kinship (especially Scheper-Hughes' discussion of mothering in Brazilian shantytowns, Reading 4.2) and with Part 5 on race, ethnicity, and class (and particularly with Low's and Jackson's discussion of whiteness and class privilege, Readings 5.2 and 5.4).

Questions

1. How is childhood idealized in Western cultures?
2. Why are women to "blame" for the "exploitative enterprise" of child pageantry?
3. What does Freidus mean by saying that the bloggers participate in "policing of proper whiteness"?
4. In what ways do reality shows (and their associated blogs) in general function as an "electronic panopticon"?

Introduction

Beauty Pageants have long been examined as sites of cultural production, contestation, and commodification (King-O'Rain 2008). Similarly, child beauty pageants, originating in the 1960s, are considered sites of cultural production. A growing industry, child pageants boast an annual estimated participation rate of nearly 3 million children, primarily girls, from toddlers and babies to adolescents. Blitz Pageants that allow contestants the use of make-up, flippers (dentures), false eyelashes, colored contacts, ornate costumes, and fake tans have grown to become a 5 billion dollar industry. The number of child beauty pageants worldwide has reached close to 3,000. While the child pageant industry is burgeoning, so, too, are the critiques. The 1996 murder of JonBenét Ramsey is credited with bringing the world of child beauty pageants to the national consciousness, and the light shone on these beauty princesses, and their mothers, has not been flattering (Heltsley and Calhoun 2003).

Toddlers and Tiaras is a reality television program on The Learning Channel (TLC) that explores child pageants. While popular in viewership, it has generated a firestorm of Internet and media discourses about the industry and child participants with the majority of online discussions targeting mothers of child contestants. The tone and content have been almost exclusively negative. This chapter explores the ways in which *Toddlers and Tiaras* functions as a cultural script illuminating issues of class, gender, race, geography and parent-child relations.

I draw on data collected from watching episodes of *Toddlers and Tiaras* as well as following a variety of blogs, Internet forums, and news stories dedicated to the show. There are drawbacks concerning this type of data collection including issues of sampling, anonymity, and Internet user bias. While a systematic sampling is difficult with such a vast database, this should not preclude using Internet forums, blogs, and interactive news venues. Points of saturation can be met, and triangulation with other sources makes the Internet a more reliable tool for ethnographic work. These circulating discourses are relevant because of their reiteration and because they reveal something about on-line users' cultural, social and moral meaning-making.

This is not meant to be a definitive study of systematized and quantified narratives, but rather a snapshot of dominant themes needing further investigation. It is a study of reality television that provides a site for exploring how the normalization of gender roles, childhood, and class get articulated, critiqued and reproduced via the juxtaposition of that deemed proper, good, and productive against that which is considered deficient, inappropriate and criminal (Sears and Godderis 2011; Skeggs 2005, 2009). Television and the Internet combine in this work as an "electronic panopticon," as coined by Lyon, whereby the lives, behaviors, and choices of "ordinary" working class people are made public and open to surveillance, scrutiny, and discipline (Lyon 1993; Sears and Godderis 2011).

Mothering

Embedded within the narratives surrounding *Toddlers and Tiaras* is a focus on mothers and their role in (im)proper parenting. Evident throughout is a naturalization and normalization of a particular type of "modern" childhood that is threatened by pageantry. Discourses construct children as innocent, asexual, pure, passive beings in need of protection and nurture from parents. The overwhelming number of reactions to child pageantry articulates a moral opprobrium focused on the perceived loss or threat of loss of childhood. Responses demonstrate that sexualization in particular disrupts the naturalized notions of childhood innocence.

Mothers, not children, involved in these activities are perceived of as deviant. In particular, white, lower or working class women are publically critiqued as pathological and dysfunctional examples that challenge proper motherhood. There are repeated rhetorical references to "white trash" or "trailer trash" which codes participants as being from rural, poor, predominantly Caucasian communities with the associated stereotypes including being dirty, criminal, amoral, sexually promiscuous and/or perverse (Newitz and Wray 1997; Wray 2006). They become moral subjects circumscribed for surveillance and policing critiqued in an effort to defend and define normative notions of middle and upper class motherhood and "modern" childhood.

Making Modern Childhoods

The industrial revolution is a watershed moment that engendered the shift to a sacred childhood space in large part constituted by the codification of a gendered division of labor pivoting around the construction of the ideal modern family (Foucault 1980). A "modern" childhood assumes a nuclear family, provides a protected space of nurture for future economic production, and emphasizes the psychological worth of the child (Stephens 1995). Women were expected to "keep the home" and reproduce the industrial labor force, which revolved around childcare (McDowell 1999).

McDowell (1999) notes that during this time the home was imbued with spirituality and women were constructed as "angels" meant to nurture, protect, and ensure purity—both moral and physical. It was sacrilegious to denigrate the scared space of the home, and it was the responsibility of women to protect the sacred. These conventional gender roles and the perceived polarization of men's and women's working lives went largely unchallenged until the feminist movements of the 1970s (Connell 2005).

This period of childhood became a time of seclusion as parents protected and prepared children for their futures. Only upper-class members of society were able to actualize the ideal modern form of childhood because they had the financial freedom to invest heavily in the development of their children (Aries 1962). It has been well documented that the children of lower and working class backgrounds worked to support themselves and their families.

Within this Western paradigm, children are developing subjects needing strict surveillance, often by mothers, and discipline in order to ensure an economically productive and morally responsible future (Christensen and Prout 2005). Children are conceptualized as passive recipients with no agency in these modern constructions (Egan and Hawkes 2008; Giroux 1998). These are the roots of contemporary idealized modern childhoods that are evident in circulating meta-narratives examined in this chapter. While this was an archetype for modern childhood it remains elusive to many in the United States. Cook (2009, 8) posits "that a sequestered childhood of innocence is something of a privilege, a bourgeois privilege" yet it still remains the aspiration of most people who desire to be "good" Americans. Inherent within these hegemonic constructions is a privileging of whiteness as social domination.

"Whiteness" as a category is not homogenous, but socially stratified and hierarchical. There are boundaries within whiteness that create social marginalization for some whites. In what follows we see the heterogeneity of whiteness and the antagonism that exists between marked groups within this racial construction. In this chapter, the "other" whiteness being critiqued is referred to as "white trash" and is characterized along geo-economic lines, or a rural-urban divide (Hartigan 1997, 2003).

The geopolitical spacing of white trash as predominantly characteristic of southern states is tied to the period of Reconstruction when white northern travelers visited the defeated postbellum South (Winders 2003). Theses voyeurs reported extensively on rural southern poverty in travelogues, magazines, and journals describing scenes of degeneration, crudeness, lechery, filth, perversion, and vulgarity (Winders 2003). It is within this context that northern observers were attempting to make sense of class in the newly ordered racial South where poor blacks occupied the marginalized position (Winders 2003).

These constructions continued to be pervasive during the 1880–1920s eugenics movements when poor, rural whites were seen as "genetically defective" (Newitz and Wray 1997; Wray 2006). "As Nicole Hahn Rafter puts it, the central image these studies created was 'the degenerate hillbilly family, dwelling in filthy shacks and spawning endless generations of paupers, criminals, and imbeciles" (Rafter 1988 in Newitz and Wray 1997, 2). Fear of contamination and the degeneration of the gene pool by poor, rural, predominantly southern whites described as "exhibiting higher levels of criminality, feeblemindedness, sexual promiscuity, and alcoholism" led to the *Buck v. Bell* Supreme Court decision in 1926 to allow forced sterilization of "unfit" people without their consent (Wray 2006, 19).

While the eugenics movement was discredited following World War II, the white trash stereotype and social category persists. Scholars of whiteness attempting to unpack the traditionally assumed monolithic approach to whiteness have identified white trash as one social category that serves as an intra-racial form of Othering used to express social contempt (Hartigan 1997, 317). These distinctions have consequences. Newitz, in her analysis of white trash in popular films, argues that these characterizations serve several purposes that reify class distinctions and justify inequality. Poor whites, according to Newitiz (1997, 136), are perceived as "trash" and therefore "don't deserve the benefits of social welfare, sympathy, or national power." The poor can be blamed for their poverty along with a variety of social ills. She also argues that there is a deliberate "othering" happening; "Civilized" whites can measure and define themselves against degenerate, white trash. "White trash, by occupying the position of 'bad' Other, offer a perspective from which 'good' whites can see themselves as a racial and classed group" (Newitiz: 1997, 136). In the following section I illuminate this process of "othering" and how these historically rooted notions of childhood, gender roles, and class antagonisms get played out in the contemporary discourses specific to *Toddlers and Tiaras*.

Threatened Childhood

Shows such as *Toddler and Tiaras*, broadcast to millions, disrupt our constructed notions of childhood and serve as an obvious form of surveillance and discipline as blogs incessantly focus on the moral degradation of TLC participants. Any version of childhood that appears to pervert the normalized notion of an innocent childhood creates a moral panic. Today, this modern construction of childhood has become so pervasive it is perceived of as a biologized and naturalized state. Turning to *Toddlers and Tiaras*, this is especially evident in blogs berating child pageants that specifically argue a "natural" childhood is being degraded or that modern childhood is under threat. One blogger wrote:

> Why do we even have "pageants" for children? This is ridiculous! No child needs to be paraded around like a piece of meat. Little girls wearing make-up, fake teeth, hair extensions, etc. are being exploited by their mothers trying to live their own lives through their daughters. Disgusting! Let kids be kids—they already grow up way to fast! TLC = Trashy Living Channel.

This blogger is upset because the perceived natural state of childhood is under threat as child contestants are dressing and behaving in ways that the blogger imagines to be adult-specific. The assumption is that these children are interpreting their pageant activities as an attempt to be "adult-like," which is not necessarily how children experience pageants. Another theme in this blog that is repeated on nearly all Internet sites focused on *Toddlers and Tiaras* is that mothers are at fault for contaminating the natural, innocent period of childhood. The threat of a loss of childhood is evident when "Caroline" wrote:

> Kudos to all parents who let their children BE children and appreciate them in their natural, cute and innocent state.

Threats to childhood are evident when children are seen as crossing into adult worlds. One *Toddlers and Tiaras* participant sparked controversy when her dress and behavior were considered appropriate only for adults. Destiny, a 4-year-old girl, appeared on stage in a child pageant mimicking Olivia Newton-John's character "Sandy" from *Grease*. She wore a leather jacket, teased her hair, and puffed on a prop cigarette. Bloggers who commented on the numerous news stories that reported on the controversy called for Destiny's mother to be jailed or for child protective services to intervene. The bulk of outrage was against what is perceived as the exploitation of children by mothers for celebrity status. Central to this panic is the threat

of lost childhoods and the long-term negative consequences for children and by extension society. As one blogger stated in response to this controversy,

> This is Absolutely unbelieveable. What's next? A martini? Why can't these parents let their kids, just be kids? Or was this beauty pageant for kids just a failure of these mothers' dreams? A failure. And now these kids will be so screwed up, with phony cigarettes, they will be like their mom. A failure.

Another blogger wrote, "And people are wondering why there are so many problems in society?" Bloggers regularly comment on the future of these children, with the most common reference being that of a deviant female sexuality culminating in a career as a prostitute or stripper. In reference to Destiny, one blogger stated, "I'd bet there's a pole in that girl's future."

The apparent sexualization of girls, not boys, and associated loss of innocence litters Internet forums. While emerging in the historical context, the notion of innocence is deeply ingrained in our contemporary construction of ideal childhoods. It is not that these children look like adults; it is that they are sexualized (Egan and Hawkes 2008). That which threatens such innocence is "abhorred" as blogger Ingrid states:

> Innocence and childhood is a very brief time in a girl's life. It can be stolen so easily and so quickly. Our cultural Sodom in America takes this innocence ever earlier. As the mother of daughters, it enrages and terrifies me when I see the monstrous assault on all that is precious and good in girlhood. *Toddlers and Tiaras* is the crystallization of all that is wrong morally in our culture. As a mother, my job is to love and protect my daughter by giving her what is good and wholesome and raising her to resist and abhor what is wrong and twisted. I am supposed to keep her away from filthy people who would use her for their own foul entertainment and pleasure. Mothers who participate in the pimping out of their daughters for fame and fortune are child abusers, simply put.

Drawing on outrage over the perceived sexualization of girls serves two purposes. First, it stresses the natural state of innocence of children, which includes their lack of agency. Second, it reifies the role of the parent as protector, which further embeds and polarizes the world into the adult-child binary. In these constructions the notion that women are responsible, almost solely, for childcare and child development is evident.

When men do appear in the blogosphere they are either critiqued negatively as being dominated by women or are criminalized as pedophiles. In one blog exchange on CNN, a debate about the degradation of TLC and parenting ensued. Some critics did blame TLC, but most shifted the blame for this "exploitative enterprise" on the mothers. Some responses mentioned "parents," which led to the following post:

> Please stop using "parents." Women—this is all on you. No man does this to his daughter, and if a man is watching it—it is either b/c his woman is forcing him to or he's a pedophile.

So the man is not "man" enough to tell his wife he disapproves, or he is a perverse criminal. On that same blog, another wrote:

> All you have to do is watch 1 minute of this show and you'll see two things: most dads are not there and the mom's [*sic*] are all fat cows living vicariously through their 4 year olds. Grow up, you uneducated skanks!

There is a lot at stake in these assertions as evidenced by the case of Madisyn Verst. She was 5 years old when she appeared on *Toddlers and Tiaras*. She received attention when she was featured on the cover of *People* magazine with an associated exposé-type article that was the result of her dressing in a Dolly Parton outfit that included a padded bra in an episode. ABC news reported that Maddy's father, Bill Verst, had taken his ex-wife, Lindsay Jackson, to court seeking sole custody on charges that Lindsay was sexually exploiting their daughter. One blogger responded to this, stating:

> Why is this kind of thing even allowed? What kind of women will these young girls become? Teaching them about make-up and how to make your body sexy seems to me that is inviting trouble now and in their teen yrs. Don't teens today have enough problems without Mothers forcing them to act like little grown ups? I hear everyday about pedophiles

searching out young ladies. Isn't this an invitation? I side with the Father on this one. It is just plain sick in my opinion. A little girl should be allowed to be a child.

This blogger's reaction is rooted in a clear dichotomy that distinguishes adult from child with associated notions of how childhood is defined and characterized in relation to adults. Her reaction is not surprising given the way in which children in the West are constructed as innocent, passive, and developing subjects with limited agency in need of the guidance and protection of adults, especially mothers (Foucault 1980; Zelizer 1985). Also evident in many of these tirades is the notion that children, when asked to walk, wave, smile, or turn in a certain way or are dressed in certain types of clothing, are assumed to be internalizing an adult-centric notion of sexuality. It is unclear if children perceive their behavior as encouraging sexual attention, suggesting actual sexual behavior, or signaling sexual attraction in an adult-sense. We don't know if they understand these behaviors in adult terms (Egan and Hawke 2008).

A consistent theme on the blogs is that these mothers need to be punished in a punitive way. One blogger associated this infiltration of children into adult worlds with child neglect, stating:

> Let Maddy have her childhood. Making her be a miniature adult is child abuse.

It is common to find reactions that call for child protective services to become involved. One ABC news article reader commented on the story, "'Toddlers and Tiaras' Controversy: Mom Defends Feeding Daughter "Pageant Crack', "This is absolutely disgusting! Where is child services? Why do these people have children?"

A twitter feed dedicated to the spinoff show "Here Comes Honey Boo Boo" jokingly reads:

> "Here Comes Honey Boo Boo" is good, but the spinoff "Here Comes Social Services" is gonna be better. #HoneyBooBoo

Policing White Trash

The Western ideal of childhood has been constructed by and for upper- and upper-middle-class families. This constructed ideal of childhood was not the reality for the majority of the population in the U.S. or Europe in the eighteenth and nineteenth centuries, and continues to be an ideal achieved only by those in positions of power with access to resources (Lareau 2003). This sets the stage for class conflict. As Hymowitz argues, "the disquiet over sexualization is, in part, catalyzed by the fear of class contamination. The discourse on sexualization paints a picture of overly sexual displays of "low culture" rupturing the innocence of middle- and upper-class girls and transforming them into "Britney [Spears] wannabes" (Hymowitz 2002 referenced in Egan and Hawkes 2008, 306).

TLC's *Toddlers and Tiaras* participants are targets of a fairly sweeping moral outrage that tracks along class and geographic lines. These distinctions allow viewers to "other" those involved in pageants and subsequently blame them for a host of societal ills. Or, as Newitz and Wray (1997, 1) suggest, "the white trash stereotype serves as a useful way of blaming the poor for being poor. The term white trash helps solidify for the middle and upper classes a sense of cultural and intellectual superiority." The blogs revealed that TLC participants are homogenized as all belonging to the lower class despite the fact that many TLC participants may actually come from the middle class. In a blog entitled, "In defense of Honey Boo Boo," Gautreau challenges the class distinctions and associated moral outrage:

> A fair amount of criticism of the show comments on the idea that "those people" are somehow horrible or that the show is similar to watching a trainwreck. This criticism is more revealing about popular attitudes than it is about the show itself. . . . There is certainly an element of classism in these remarks, as much commentary centers on how the family chooses to spend their money and their appearance, and tends to revolve around the idea that such people do not "deserve" a television show. Who, then, does deserve a show? Attractive, white, middle-class families who refrain from potty humor and show off their wealth with material goods?

TLC uses a deliberate mapping of their subjects or a "moral subject semiotics" that leads the audience to "read" participants in a specific way (Skeggs 2009). *Toddlers and Tiaras* participants are primarily coded in ways that reference white, working-class culture much like the examples of reality TV that Skeggs (2009) analyzes. In both cases, participants are read "euphemistically, as slob, scrounger, slacker, or locating them in a context of chaos, dirt, and disorder" (2009, 630). In the case of TLC, some participants are quite literally located in dirt. The family of Lynsie from Clarksburg, West Virginia was featured "mud blogging" (driving a four wheel jeep through mud pits) exclaiming their identity as "rednecks." Lynsie's mother said, "You don't have to be missing your teeth to be a redneck. It is a state of mind."

Aside from structural indicators, the families themselves engage in behaviors that signal a particular class status. Alana, also known as Honey Boo Boo, epitomizes "redneck" positionality. Internet commentators note that her mother has children by three different men. Her father, also known as Sugar Bear, is overweight, inarticulate, and chews tobacco. Her mother, June, is obese, slovenly dressed, and has bad teeth. Their speech is considered indecipherable so TLC uses subtitles. Expletives are a common part of their speech, and Alana regularly makes scatological references. In many ways they embrace this identity calling themselves "white trash." Alana is known for popularizing the phrase, "You better redneckognize." In one episode the police inform the family that there is road kill knowing that they will happily retrieve the carcass (in this case it is a deer), clean it, and consume it. Alana's sister gave birth to a child with an extra thumb, which led many bloggers to reference inbreeding and incest, a characterization found in the lexicon of white trash.

Many of the episodes of *Toddlers and Tiaras* that I viewed would be described as being situated in working class communities. Despite the participation by middle class families, the observations made by bloggers either explicitly referenced "white trash" or made reference to codes associated with white poor or working class participants. One blogger stated,

> Kiddie pageants, secret go go juice, hoarders, couponers, white trash, and a pregnant teen. They hit the TLC motherload.

The moral subject semiotics that defines white trash and distinguishes it with disdain from proper forms of whiteness is evident in the characteristics depicted by this blogger that strings together and relates child pageantry, "go-go juice," hoarding, and teenage pregnancy. Another stated,

> Oh my, what can you say about such a massive train wreck of white trash, redneck, morbidly obese cast members? TLC scraping the bottom of the barrel? Yes indeedy! And you can bet I'll watch at least one or two episodes of this freakshow for the same reasons you crane your neck to see an accident scene!

These assertions signal that bloggers attempt to define and describe participants along racial and geo-economic lines despite the presence of participants that did not fit the white trash stereotypes. One blogger on the justmommies.com web forum explained how situating child participants, their families, and the pageant industry in the South was a gross misrepresentation of child pageantry,

> As a girl who grew up in the pageant circuit, let me say that this show is a horrible example of child pageantry. This show focuses more on competitions in the south such as the Southern Majestic Glitz Girls. Texas, Alabama, Tennessee, and South Carolina are a joke in the pageant community. I won over 80 crowns as a child and never had to wear a flipper or a spray on tan once. That show is nothing but a bunch of hillbillies using their welfare checks to pay for stuff they don't need. And yes, I feel like I have the right to say so because I'm considered a hillbilly by most having grown up in southern Missouri.

TLC's use of a moral subject semiotics that this blogger alludes to encourages class-based antagonism for mass consumption. Through these blogs we are privy to the policing of proper whiteness and the reification of distinct class boundaries meant to prevent contamination. Everything from body weight, family structure, how and what to spend money on, what to wear, how to speak, and how to comport oneself falls under the gaze of the electronic panopticon and the naturalized innocent modern child is attempted to be rescued. As one blogger stated,

> TLC should be ashamed for exploiting an innocent child who comes from an obviously poor family who doesn't have a clue about manners or etiquette. It is quite obvious the child doesn't have the typical "pageant" look and she will be ostracized by others.

Here we see the blogger attempt to protect the child drawing on her innocence while also signaling that the child's class positionality will lead to her being ostracized because she does not fit what is considered to be a proper child pageant contestant, or even a proper child, for that matter.

Conclusion

Despite the overwhelming disapproval registered in online forums, both *Toddlers and Tiaras* and *Here Comes Honey Boo Boo* elicit a high viewership. A testament to *Honey Boo Boo*'s popularity is that a reported 2.9 million viewers tuned in on Wednesday, August 29, 2012, outranking the Republican National Convention by 1.7 million viewers.

Viewers enjoy both programs for a host of undisclosed reasons—reasons not necessarily addressed in weblogs, chat forums, or news stories. . . . those who defend the show or admit, doggedly, that they are behind the scenes fans draw on a few reasons for their dedication including; watching it to gawk because it is a "train wreck"; watching for mindless entertainment; supporting participants who resist the hegemony of upper and middle class ideals evident in their counter-hegemonic display of ways of being; or, are past pageant participants who watch in remembrance of the benefits they gleaned from participation.

Most common is the notion of watching "train-wrecks." Viewers say they watch these shows in a way that purposefully reifies distinctions between what is proper, and what is grotesque. One blogger stated,

> I'm shocked, abhorred [sic] and disgusted, yet drawn in like a 5 car pile up on the opposite side of I-95 during rush hour to these types of shows.

Another blogger on the same forum mentioned watching it with her children, stating,

> This is totally my guilty pleasure! My daughters and I sit and watch this, pointing and staring like we're at the zoo or something.

This mother is using the program to teach her children what is appropriate and what is worth ostracizing or alienating. Evident across blogs is a sense of moral superiority. In these types of discourses people tune in to feel better about their proper whiteness. Regardless of how viewers discussed their support of these shows—whether being regaled as a counter-hegemonic display meant to challenge dominant notions of gender, childhood, or class distinctions or if it is used to teach about improper ways of being—there is a recognition of class warfare.

The moral backlash against mothers who support and encourage their children to participate in these pageants is situated within broader discourses of power predicated on idealized notions that reflect upper- and middle-class constructions of family. In the process of these circulating critiques women are actually forcing (other) women and their daughters into certain roles of inequality (as men are perceived as innocent bystanders). Moreover, female sexuality continues to be reflected as subversive and in need of strict surveillance and control (Egan and Hawkes 2008). It is something to be feared.

The construction of white trash and the associated stereotypes that are consumed via shows such as *Toddlers and Tiaras* have real social, cultural, economic, and political implications. As Kipnis and Reeder (1997, 114) argue,

> Bodies that defy social norms and properties of size, smell, dress, manners, or gender conventions; or lack the proper decorum about matters of sex and elimination; or defy bourgeois sensibilities by being too uncontained and indecorous—these bodies seem to pose multiple threats to social and psychic order.

Viewers watch the grotesque unfold and blame women for the sexualization and commodification of their children instead of questioning the more insidious structural factors that shape inequitable gender relations and unequal childhoods. Discourses are targeting a certain "class" of women for their deviance and immorality instead of actually challenging the dominant gender paradigm that works to sexualize and objectify women systemically. This process leads to the reification of certain power relations that afford no agency to children, limit women's agency more broadly, and sublimate female sexuality.

References

Ariès, Philippe. 1962. *Centuries of Childhood: A Social History of Family Life*. London: Jonathan Cape.

Christensen, Pia, and Alan Prout. 2005. "Anthropological and Sociological Perspectives on the Study of Children." In *Researching Children's Experience: Approaches and Methods*, edited by Sheila Greene and Diane Hogan, 42–60. London: Sage.

Connell, Raewyn. W. 2005. *Masculinities*, 2nd ed. Berkeley: University of California Press.

Cook, Thomas. 2009. "Editorial: When a Child Is Not a Child, and Other Conceptual Hazards of Childhood Studies." *Childhood* 16(1):5–10.

Egan, R. Danielle, and Gail L. Hawkes. 2008. "Endangered Girls and Incendiary Objects: Unpacking the Discourse on Sexualization." *Sexuality and Culture* 12:291–311.

Foucault, Michel. 1980. "The Politics of Health in the Eighteenth Century." In *Power/Knowledge: Selected Interviews and Other Writings, 1972–1977*, 166–182. New York: Pantheon.

Giroux, Henry A. 1998. "Nymphet Fantasies: Child Beauty Pageants and the Politics of Innocence." *Social Text* 57:31–53.

Hartigan, John. 2003. "Who Are These White People? 'Rednecks,' 'Hillbillies,' and 'White Trash' as Marked Racial Subjects." In *White Out: The Continuing Significance of Racism*, edited by A. W. Doane and E. Bonilla-Silva, 95–112. New York: Routledge.

Hartigan, John1997. "Unpopular Culture: The Case of 'White Trash.'" *Cultural Studies* 11(2):316–343.

Heltsley, Martha, and Thomas Calhoun. 2003. "The Good Mother: Neutralization Techniques Used by Pageant Mothers." *Deviant Behavior* 24(2):81–100.

Hymowitz, K. 2002. "Thank Barbie for Britney: She's Not That Innocent." *National Review Online*.

King-O'Rain, Rebecca Chiyoko. 2008. "Making the Perfect Queen: The Cultural Production of Identities in Beauty Pageants." *Sociology Compass* 2(1):74–83.

Kipnis, Laura, and Jennifer Reeder. 1997. "White Trash Girl: The Interview." In *White Trash: Race and Class in America*, edited by M. Wray and A. Newitz, 113–130. New York: Routledge.

Lareau, Annette. 2003. *Unequal Childhoods: Class, Race, and Family Life*. Berkeley: University of California Press.

Lyon, David. 1993. "An Electronic Panopticon? A Sociological Critique of Surveillance Theory." *The Sociological Review* 41(4):653–678.

McDowell, Linda. 1999. *Gender, Identity, and Place.* Minneapolis: University of Minnesota Press.

Newitz, Annalee. 1997. "White Savagery and Humiliation, or a New Racial Consciousness in the Media." In *White Trash: Race and Class in America,* edited by M. Wray and A. Newitz, 131–154. New York: Routledge.

Newtiz, Annalee, and Matt Wray. 1997. "Introduction." In *White Trash: Race and Class in America,* edited by M. Wray and A. Newitz, 1–12. New York: Routledge.

Rafter, Nicole H. 1988. *White Trash: The Eugenic Family Studies 1877–1919.* Boston, MA: Northeastern University Press.

Sears, Camilla A., and Rebecca Godderis. 2011. "Roar Like a Tiger on TV? Constructions of Women and Childbirth in Reality TV." *Feminist Media Studies* 11(2):181–195.

Skeggs, Beverley. 2005. "The Making of Class and Gender through Visualizing Moral Subject Formation." *Sociology* 39(5): 965–982.

Skeggs, Beverley. 2009. "The Moral Economy of Person Production: The Class Relations of Self-Performance on 'Reality' Television." *The Sociological Review* 57(4):626–644.

Stephens, Sharon. 1995. "Introduction: Children and the Politics of Culture in Late Capitalism." In *Children and the Politics of Culture* edited by Sharon Stephens, 1–48. Princeton, NJ: Princeton University Press.

Winders, Jaime. 2003. "White in All the Wrong Places: White Rural Poverty in the Postbellum US South." *Cultural Geographies* 10:45–63.

Wray, Matt. 2006. *Not Quite White: White Trash and the Boundaries of Whiteness.* Durham, NC: Duke University Press.

Zelizer, Viviana A. 1985. *Pricing the Priceless Child: The Changing Social Value of Children.* Princeton, NJ: Princeton University Press.

11.4 Bootlegged: Unauthorized Circulation and the Dilemmas of Collaboration in the Digital Age

NOELLE STOUT

The digital age has produced unprecedented opportunities for the production and widespread circulation of ethnographic images and films. What happens when images get circulated beyond the anthropologist's original intent? What about if some parties begin to—or appear to—be making money off the images the anthropologists filmed? Noelle Stout reflects on these and other key ethical questions surrounding ethnographic filmmaking in the digital era by reflecting on her production of Luchando, *a film she produced in collaboration with Cuban sex workers that ended up being circulated beyond her intention.*

Questions

1. How has the landscape changed for anthropologists making ethnographic films?
2. Why does Stout feel that traditional informed consent agreements no longer apply in the digital age? What new forms should replace them?
3. What role did geopolitics play in the circulation of Luchando? Why was there an "appetite" for images of Cuba?
4. What is "disidentification," and how does it figure into what Stout was trying to do with the film Luchando?

Introduction

"I want gays around the world to see my life, to see how we live in Cuba, but I don't want to show up on CNN," Diosa said. "I have a *travesti* friend who ended up on CNN saying things about the Cuban government. No, no, no, that would be suicide."[1]

"Of course not," I assured her. "I would never sell this footage to news outlets or use it in a politicized way." We were sitting in Diosa's cramped, scorching living room during an August heat wave in Havana. I had spent the day filming scenes that Diosa, a 22-year-old *travesti*, had devised—a typical Saturday of her cooking, cleaning, and walking to the market.[2] She had proudly paraded me around the neighborhood to show her friends the making of "her documentary." Now she was donning her tight jeans and off-the-shoulder top for work in the sex trade and this process inspired a conversation about whether or not I should film her as she spent the evening flagging clients. She was concerned about how my presence might affect business and I was worried about how the Cuban police could use these images against her in a context in which prostitution and filmmaking without state permission were both criminalized.

A year later, I completed the resulting documentary *Luchando* (Noelle Stout, Film Study Center at Harvard, 2007), which chronicles the lives of Diosa and three other sex workers in Havana's queer *ambiente* [subculture]. The film made its way around the

Noelle Stout. "Bootlegged: Unauthorized Circulation and the Dilemmas of Collaboration in the Digital Age." 2014. *Visual Anthropology Review* 30 (2), 177–187. By permission of John Wiley & Sons, Inc. Notes have been renumbered.

Figure 11.4.1

Still from *Luchando*. Diosa faces hecklers on the street.

film festival circuit[3] and I fought to keep my promise to control the use of the footage. I traveled with the film to discuss the importance of collaboration in its production, detailing the conflicts and confluences of perspective with my interlocutors. To my producer's disappointment, I passed on two distribution offers because I wanted to confine the audiences to those vetted by my collaborators who participated in the film—academic and film festival viewers. Given my goal of keeping the footage from becoming part of a decades-old propaganda battle between the United States and Cuba, the Miami festival screenings were especially challenging. I turned down appearances on television talk shows and radio programs hosted by conservative Cuban American journalists who were eager to politicize the existence of prostitution in Cuba. On their programs, they often implied that Fidel Castro had starved the island to the point that men were forced to have sex with other men to earn the money to survive. After brief conversations with their production staff, it quickly became clear that they wanted to use my film to support these implicitly homophobic and reductive narratives of Cuban erotic economies.

Given the care I took with the film's distribution, I was shocked when three years later I received an e-mail from a Miami lawyer requesting payment on Diosa's behalf for proceeds from the sale of the documentary. In keeping with our original agreement, I had never sold the film and there were no profits to distribute. A frantic phone call to the attorney revealed that since the film's release, Diosa had moved to Miami. She had walked into a bodega and seen pirated versions of *Luchando* for rent on the dusty shelves next to bootleg copies of Cuban soap operas. My producer and I began calling every bodega in Miami, asking if they had a copy of *Luchando* we could rent or buy. "We have four copies," a teenage boy said on the phone, speaking Spanish with a thick Cuban accent, "but they're all rented. Try back in a few days."

I had taken every precaution possible to protect the festival copies, but DVDs were somehow available for purchase from an online distributor who sold Cuban films otherwise unavailable outside of the island. A quick search online revealed that a bootleg version of *Luchando* was featured on his Web site for $19.95; a still taken from the film's Web site was used as the cover of the DVD. A heated argument with the unauthorized distributor ensued, in which he tried to convince me that I was a Cuban filmmaker (I am not) and that because of the embargo restrictions on commerce between the two countries, copyright laws did not apply to work that I had created. After I threatened a lawsuit, he agreed to remove the film from his Web site. Along with our attorney, my American producer and I sent a flurry of cease-and-desist letters to the bodegas carrying the film. The project had never made any profits, but I told Diosa's lawyer that I was happy to give her money out of pocket. He explained that this offer would "cut him out of the deal" and refused to give me her contact information. Then, months after I had managed to halt the unauthorized distribution of the film in Miami, a student of mine discovered it on YouTube with two pages of viewers' comments. My attorney contacted the man who had posted it, but my attempts to police *Luchando*'s circulation began to feel futile.

Figure 11.4.2

Still from *Luchando* used as the bootleg DVD cover.

I start with this story of my failed efforts to control *Luchando*'s distribution to illustrate how ethnographic video circulation is increasingly rapid and promiscuous. This intractability in a moment when the reproduction and circulation of ethnographic media are faster and easier than ever before presents a fundamental, yet relatively underexplored emergent component of contemporary ethnographic filmic collaboration. In this article, I trace the cultural biography of *Luchando*, focusing on the politics surrounding the circulation of anthropological representations of Cuban sex workers outside of Cuba to elucidate how the changing landscape of anthropological digital media distribution demands new collaborative strategies. I maintain that long-standing discussions of how best to cooperate with our interlocutors—particularly those whose marginal status makes them especially vulnerable—are given new life in an age when the unauthorized reproduction and circulation of stills and clips are escalating at a dizzying speed. . . . I argue that the traditional agreements of informed consent that have governed the production of ethnographic film fail to address these emergent dynamics of circulation.[4] . . .

. . . The case of *Luchando* illuminates how the democratization of media circulation, such as personal computer DVD burning, YouTube streaming, and inexpensive online distribution, presents new capacities for ethnographic collaboration while also creating obstacles to guaranteeing the protection of our interlocutors.[5] . . .

Extrapolating the lessons learned from collaborations between anthropologists and their indigenous interlocutors, I turn to the piracy of *Luchando* to provide a concrete example in which the unauthorized distribution of ethnographic media can endanger the fragile bonds of cooperation and trust between anthropologists and subjects, while also depriving politically marginalized and economically disadvantaged communities of royalties. The unruly circulation of *Luchando* shows how the reach of distribution continues to intensify with significant implications for anthropological collaboration and practice.[6] In mapping the multiple and unintended life trajectories of *Luchando*, I show how advances in digital technology have expanded the possible meanings and potential of ethnographic film by making it more affordable and accessible but also by increasing the stakes and responsibilities that anthropologists hold in this changing milieu.

The *Mise-en-Scène* of Production

Given the anonymous nature of online social worlds, it is difficult, if not impossible, to discern the specific identities and practices of those who pirated *Luchando*. Pirates most likely obtained the film from unscrupulous festival staff or videotaped it during a festival screening. Nevertheless, it is possible to analyze how their actions reflect broader structural factors and cultural assumptions that inform the circulation of media, which is not an ephemeral flow of self-propelled, "free" information, but is shaped by sociopolitical dynamics. Not everyone lives in the same "digital age," and it is important to contextualize the dissemination of ethnographic media within these uneven sociopolitical realities (Ginsburg 2008). Attention to the slippery nature of circulation necessitates consideration of geopolitics, which fueled appetites for images of Cuba, including *Luchando*, among the Cuban diaspora and non-Cubans alike.

The digital divide between Cuba and the United States was acute at the time of my research in Havana between 2001 and 2007. With few exceptions the Cuban government did not allow Internet access, and citizens needed special state permits to acquire Internet access in their homes. There was a significant black market in e-mail correspondence in which one person with access to e-mail would charge people to send and receive messages on their behalf. Similarly, cell phone use was prohibitively expensive, with a 10-minute phone call costing a week's worth of salary in a state job. Cubans were also required to have foreigners cosign to acquire cell phone contracts. Video equipment such as cameras, DVD players, and laptop computers could not be brought into the country. Television programming and cinemas were heavily censored and monitored by government agencies. A handful of Cubans smuggled in cable antennas and accessed outside cable networks, but it was considered extremely risky and the government often cracked down on homes with hidden antennas. Despite these restrictions, a significant Cuban blogosphere emerged beginning in 2007, as Cuban bloggers used surreptitious means to publish their work and quickly rose to international prominence.[7] While few Cubans on the island could access these blogs, their existence attests to the ability of digital information to circulate despite government sanctions. . . .

These battles over access to information and technology were part of the post–Cold War transformation of Cuban society, which opened the island to capitalist foreigners, incited massive waves of Cuban migration, and fostered a global market for Cuban cultural commodities and images. After the loss of Soviet subsidies in the 1990s, Cuba entered into an unprecedented economic crisis and the Cuban government turned to international tourism as a development strategy to salvage the economy. As the island opened to capitalist foreigners for the first time since the 1959 revolution, journalists, photographers, and scholars descended on Havana and incited an "image boom" of documentaries and photographic volumes, first from Europe—primarily France, Italy, and Spain—and later from the United States (Dopico 2002, 464). A representational regime began to coalesce in the 1990s that framed Cuba's reentry into the global capitalist markets through tropes of dystopic decay, couching it as a country "frozen in time," and through the overtly sexualized images of black Cuban women's bodies, which served as "proof" that Cuba had slipped into its prerevolutionary state as the "brothel of the Caribbean."

Beginning in the 1990s, major U.S. news networks including ABC, CNN, and NBC likewise focused on the rise of Cuban sex tourism as an emblem of late-socialist demise. The fact that sex work, rather than other emergent tourist-Cuban relationships, formed the central imagery of these accounts was significant because it overlaid gendered and raced assumptions about power onto stories of Cuba's post-Soviet transition. The *mulata* sex worker and white male sex tourist offered a familiar shorthand for political economic narratives that presented Cuba as vulnerable, destitute, and exotic and Western capitalist nations as powerful, affluent, and white. More than symbolically suspect, these reports were often deceptive. Cuban women hailing taxis, sitting in city parks, or dancing at nightclubs were presented as sex workers summoning clients without any evidence that the women were in fact linked to erotic economies. Moreover, the presence of homoerotic relations that might complicate the perspectives of dominant heteronormative and racialized narratives was duly erased. These American representations of Cuban erotic labor fingered the communist government for the rise of sex tourism rather than the evacuation of state services as Cuba adjusted

to a global capitalist economy at a moment in which the U.S. government claimed victory in the Cold War.

As U.S. media outlets focused on the rise of the sex trade as a way to attack the policies of Cuban government officials, tourist erotic economies became controversial in Cuba. Cuban socialist programs had largely eradicated the sex industry in Cuba by the early 1960s, so its return in the 1990s was especially fraught. While journalists and government leaders in the United States, including President George W. Bush, blamed Fidel Castro and his government for the rise of the sex trade and promised to end prostitution by bringing democracy to Cuba, Cuban officials and pundits blamed Cuban women for the rampant nature of sex tourism. The prevalent trope of the white tourist and *mulata* sex worker became a symbol for the weakness of Cubans to maintain their loyalty to socialist principles in the face of hardship. In the Cuban press, academic accounts, and society at large, many Cubans described sex workers as antisocial, materialistic, and delinquent.[8]

Contesting from Within: Making *Luchando*

My own presence in Havana was part of this post-communist moment in which the island opened to capitalist foreigners and their cameras. Likewise, my attraction to the stories of sex workers in Havana's queer nightlife was, in part, motivated by a desire to disrupt dominant narratives of Cuban prostitution that were becoming omnipresent—from special reports airing on major news networks to photographs in artistic volumes and galleries. Shooting from 2003 to 2004 and again during 2007, I used a process that Jose Muñoz (1999) describes as "disidentification": I set out to resignify popular gendered, sexed, and raced representations of the Cuban sex trade not by abandoning them but, as Stuart Hall (1997, 274) describes, by "contesting them from within"—by taking dominant images as a principal site for creative intervention. Constant negotiation over the direction of *Luchando* was therefore a cornerstone of production because it enabled sex workers to speak back to these mainstream representations in ways that I could not have scripted when I began filming. The four protagonists used the filmmaking experience to highlight different aspects of their lives that challenged prominent misconceptions about sex workers. Collectively, my protagonists counteracted these accusations through their

Figure 11.4.3

Discussing the direction of a scene while shooting Diosa.

interviews and through particular scenes that they suggested shooting. In their scenes, they emphasized the difficulty of finding well-paying employment, their hard work ethic, and the responsibilities of family and children that they shouldered.

Given the conditions of extreme poverty that plagued my interlocutors, finding a fair system of payment seemed critical. The Harvard Film Study Center had provided a modest amount of funding to cover equipment and costs and I chose not to pay participants directly for their participation, a system in which they might "earn" a fixed amount for each day of shooting. Per diem payments often leave subjects feeling as though they are "acting" for the camera and tend to place the filmmaker in a position to direct them (Taylor and Barbash 1997). Instead, I developed ongoing systems of reciprocity more typical of relationships and friendships between foreigners and Cubans in which I would pay for food, drinks, and taxis; give money and gifts when requested; and then provide a substantial sum of cash before I left the island. . . . While never made explicit during shooting, I assumed that should any money be made from the film, unlikely in the case of restricted distribution, all royalties would be divided among the protagonists.

. . . I immersed viewers in the daily lives of the protagonists, introducing their families, lovers, and mundane routines, to show their humanity and counteract sensationalist representations in popular media that reduced sex workers to their experience in the sex trade. The film showed how *luchando*, or struggling, encompassed erotic labor, but that these men, women,

and *travestis* also participated in a range of economic activities through which they could make ends meet. In editing their stories, I also aimed to reflect the participants' intentions rather than sanitize their stories to make the characters more sympathetic to an international audience. If a participant wanted to portray himself as a womanizer, for instance, I respected his performance for the camera and allowed that to guide the story rather than present the protagonists as victims or one-dimensional heroes. Questions of sexual identity and desire were likewise left open in their complexity, rather than explained for audiences.

The dissemination of *Luchando* in festivals and academic contexts garnered widespread attention and more incisively counteracted dominant American representations of Cuban sex work than textual accounts, which would have reached a smaller audience, could have. The difficulty of filming in Cuba and the scarcity of Cuban-produced media available internationally fueled interest among Cubans living abroad and non-Cuban audiences. Through international screenings, my ethnographic research on Cuba and the lives of the film's protagonists traveled in ways otherwise unimaginable. A feature story about the film that suggested the complexities of Cuban sexual labor, for example, became the most read story of the day in April 2009 on the *Nuevo Herald*'s Web site, a widely circulated news outlet that had previously politicized Cuban prostitution, even doctoring images to suggest that the Cuban government was "pimping" women to foreign tourists.

While digital storytelling allowed Cuban sex workers to speak back to prominent representations in

Figure 11.4.4

Still from *Luchando*. Masciel braids a French tourist's hair for one dollar.

Figure 11.4.5

Setting up for a festival screening in Miami.

popular culture, these technologies also enabled the unauthorized distribution of the film as illegal DVDs on Web streaming sites, in the aforementioned bootleg video rentals throughout Miami bodegas, and on YouTube. Because of the U.S. embargo against Cuba, Cuban films were not subject to copyright laws in the United States and vice versa. The online distribution company that pirated *Luchando*, Kimbara Cine Cubano Inc., had been deploying these immunities to distribute Cuban films and television shows that were not available for sale. In ways that I never imagined, the illicit distribution of *Luchando* revealed that digital technologies enable anthropologists to reach wider audiences, increasing the impact of our work—but not always in a manner that we intend. This sea change in turn raises key questions about informed consent and how ethnographer and subject, author and collaborator imagine the afterlives of ethnographic media.

Consenting to the Unimaginable

. . . Through a robust state-subsidized arts program, Cubans have been widely exposed to documentaries, both on television and in Havana's frequent film festivals. While my collaborators signed standard consent forms that allowed me to use their images in any way I saw fit in perpetuity, these contracts were a vehicle through which I initiated more detailed conversations about what was safe to show on camera and whom they imagined as their ideal audience. Through these ongoing discussions and by viewing the daily footage

together, I felt that the resulting documentary reflected our mutual and overlapping narrative agendas. Yet we did not predict how the film would slip beyond my control in an age of inexpensive and easy reproduction and distribution through social networks and Web [media] such as YouTube.

Given the growing sophistication of pirating technologies for digital forms, agreements to limited forms of circulation are quickly becoming anachronistic. Anthropologists can use safeguards such as protected DVDs and anticopying software, but more useful are frank discussions about the potential obsolescence of these precautions. When stylistically possible, producers can include these dialogues with interlocutors about the risks and benefits of visibility within the work itself. When a producer includes reflexive moments in an ethnographic film or digital storytelling project, audiences will gain a better sense of how visibility was negotiated with the participants, thereby suggesting the stakes and local contexts within which the media was produced. . . .

If the possibilities of exposure in a media landscape that cannot be contained are too great, ethnographers can explore alternative forms of representation, which may provide some sense of either anonymity or control. For example, if revealing a person's identity creates a problem, ethnographers can work with audio material to create podcasts or use voiceover narration over images or stills that evoke the story. Media producers can take advantage of interlocutors' involvement with new media forms to curate their self-generated work.

Figure 11.4.6

The line stretching around the cineplex as spectators waited to see *Luchando* in Miami (photo by Sandra Dong).

Piggy-backing on contemporary forms of self-publicity, anthropologists can reframe and contextualize this material in innovative ways.

Traditional anthropological notions of informed consent must expand to include unanticipated technological futures. . . . [A] growing number of anthropologists are deploying photographic images and video production in their research and circulating these objects in professional presentations, through social media, in film festivals, and on the Web sites of anthropological journals. Hence, rethinking the guidelines for circulating ethnographic media is all the more pressing given the increasing popularity of media making and anthropologists' continued focus on marginal and vulnerable communities who are most often the subjects, rather than the chroniclers, of their own stories.[9] Yet, at the same time, an ethics of visual and sensory research must remain informal and ad hoc, responding to the unique situations in which anthropologists find themselves, rather than relying on institutional boards and oversight committees. Institutional measures can lead to unproductive restrictions on anthropological inquiries and, perhaps more dangerously, to a false sense of security that can allow scholars to "avoid the more painful moral and political questions" inspired by our work (Fassin 2006, 524).

Embracing Creativity and Crisis

For anthropologists working with communities that are criminalized and ostracized, questions of how to protect our collaborators from further stigma and legal prosecution have always loomed large. Today, it is all the more important to consider the consequences of these images going viral, as media finds its way through online social networks that can be used to implicate or exonerate. . . .

. . . [It] is important to attend to how people understand and imagine the possibilities of circulation. How people imagine their "right" to bootleg, consume, or purchase these images likewise reveals useful insights about cultural imaginaries framing digital technology and information. Even the language our collaborators use to describe the dissemination of work—flow versus distribution or sharing versus selling—can help anthropologists to understand the shifting interpretations of media landscapes as they have become ingrained in everyday life.

The advantages of including audiovisual or sensory, in addition to textual, media in the production of anthropological knowledge are numerous, including reaching wider audiences, fostering new cultural epistemologies, and providing innovative forms of collaboration. . . .

Given the power of these digital platforms to foster new modes of thinking, create accessible archives, and reach wider audiences, rather than being dissuaded from producing ethnographic media because of the unruliness of digital reproduction and circulation, I advocate reevaluating the promises anthropologists can make to interlocutors. In the case of *Luchando*, the illicit copying and dissemination of the film fractured my ties with Diosa, a key collaborator. Once in the United States, Diosa only reached out to me through her lawyer and to date my attempts to locate her through mutual friends and Internet searches have proved futile. It is easy to imagine her feelings of betrayal lingered even with the knowledge that *Luchando* had been distributed without my consent and that I have not profited from the film's distribution. In thinking about the responsibilities that come with the possibilities of circulation, anthropologists collaborating to produce media can initiate honest discussions with their interlocutors that can, in many circumstances, become part of the story itself.

Notes

1. *Travesti* identity for Diosa, like her peers, meant that she had been born a gay man and had begun living as a woman. I refrain from translating this term as "transgender" because in the United States, transgender often implies being born into the incorrect gender identity. At the time of my research, *travestis* did not seek sex-reassignment surgery.
2. During production, my methods of collaboration were inspired by Jean Rouch's notions of *anthropologie partagée* (shared anthropology), a process in which ethnographer and participants jointly create and critique visual representations of their lives. While the logistics of production prevented collaboration during editing, I sought to maintain my participants' intentions in the stories I constructed.
3. A literal translation of "*luchando*" is "fighting." Traditionally, the term has been used by the Cuban government to mean the fight for the Cuban revolution, but sex workers have appropriated the word to describe the struggle of sex work to survive.

4. In this article, I draw on my experiences filmmaking in Cuba between 2001 and 2007 and festival and academic distribution between 2007 and 2009. My perspective is also informed by teaching a yearlong video production course for doctoral candidates in anthropology over the last six years through the Graduate Certificate Program in Culture and Media at New York University.

5. My analysis has likewise been inspired by recent scholarship suggesting that Web 2.0 technologies such as Wikis, blogs, and embedded videos form a new online landscape that, while providing user-generated content and connectivity, deserves greater critical attention (Coleman 2010; Shirky 2008; Weinberger 2007).

6. While issues of bootlegging predated these developments, with large markets of bootleg VHS tapes, for instance, their scope and speed have greatly intensified.

7. The most famous among the blogs is "Generation Y," penned by Yoani Sánchez (http://generacionyen. wordpress.com/).

8. For an important discussion of ethics in anthropological studies of urban gay life, see Hersker and Leap (1996).

9. Research projects have life histories and the current institutional structure for human subjects protocols focuses on informed consent, which is only one moment of interaction with a respondent (Brenneis 2006, 539). While more nuanced than this bureaucratic model, anthropological guidelines for ethnographic film have likewise focused on moments of contact and collaboration with our subjects during production, but the afterlives of these images as they circulate and transcend and escape our control may prove to be just as central.

The following are other new ethnographic films that use digital technologies. These were referenced within Noelle Stout's full-length article (p. 184):

Kim Fortun's "Asthma Files" (http://theasthmafiles .wikispaces.com/. Subject: Ashma
Christine Walley's "The Exit Zero Project" (http://www.exitzeroproject.org/). Subject: deindustrialization in Southeast Chicago.

Philippe Bourgois and Jeff Schonberg's *Righteous Dopefiend*. (https://slought.org/resources/ righteous_dopefiend). Subject: Homeless drug users in San Francisco.
Lucien Taylor's *Sweetgrass* (2009). codirected with Ilisa Barbash. Subject: modern-day cowboys
Leviathan. (2012). codirected with Verena Paravel. Subject: North American fishing industry.

References

Banks, Marcus. 2001. Visual Methods in Social Research. London: Sage.

Banks, Marcus. 2007. Using Visual Data in Qualitative Research. London: Sage.

Brenneis, Don. 2006. Partial Measures. American Ethnologist 33(4):538–540.

Coleman, Gabriella. 2010. Ethnographic Approaches to Digital Media. Annual Review of Anthropology 39:487–505.

Dopico, Ana Maria. 2002. Picturing Havana: History, Vision, and the Scramble for Cuba, in *Nepantla: Views from the South* 3.3.

Fassin, Didier. 2006. The End of Ethnography as Collateral Damage of Ethical Regulation? American Ethnologist 33(4):522–524.

Ginsburg, Faye. 2008. Rethinking the Digital Age. *In* The Media and Social Theory. David Hesmondhalgh and Jason Toynbee, eds. Pp. 127–144. New York: Routledge.

Hall, Stuart. 1997. The Spectacle of the Other. *In* Representation: Cultural Representations and Signifying Practices. Stuart Hall, ed. Pp. 223–290. London: Sage.

Hersker, Alan L., and William Leap. 1996. Representation, Subjectivity and Ethics in Urban Gay Ethnography. City and Society 8(1):142–147.

Muñoz, Jose. 1999. Disidentifications: Queers of Color and Performance Politics. Minneapolis: University of Minnesota Press.

Shirky, Clay. 2008. Here Comes Everybody: The Power of Organizing without Organizations. New York: Penguin.

Taylor, Lucien. 1996. Iconophobia: How Anthropology Lost It at the Movies. Transition 69:64–88.

Taylor, Lucien, and Ilisa Barbash. 1997. Cross-Cultural Filmmaking: A Handbook for Making Documentary and Ethnographic Films and Videos. Berkeley: University of California Press.

Weinberger, David. 2007. Everything Is Miscellaneous: The Power of the New Digital Disorder. New York: Henry Holt.

IN THE NEWS Defacing Native Rock Art: Not "Cool"

For tens of thousands of years, humans have engaged in art production. Some of the earliest expressions of art are found on cave walls in the form of what archaeologists call "rock art" (i.e., engravings and paintings on natural stone. Native rock art provides us with clues into the history of first peoples, and the meanings and symbolism attached to rock art images are an important area of scholarly research. Rock art sites found on public lands and Indian lands are protected under the Archaeological Resources Protection Act of 1979, and defacing them is a felony. Unfortunately, there are enough people out there who do not recognize and appreciate the sacred, and in 2011 there was a huge spike in reports of damages to Native art, despoiled by graffiti, gang tags, and bullet holes.

In a guest commentary for the *Denver Post* entitled "No, It's Not "Cool" to Deface Native Rock Art," Chip Colwell-Chanthaphonh explains the significance of ancient rock art. Rock art represents the cultural archive of first peoples, documenting their experiences and beliefs, and serve as monuments for contemporary Native Americans to honor their ancestors. Readers may also be interested in hearing more about the work of Dr. Colwell, the Curator of Anthropology, at the Denver Museum and Nature and Science. He has a long-standing career in public archaeology, focusing on Native American culture and history. The museum website links to several interviews with Dr. Colwell as well as several of his articles for the popular press.

 **Visit www.oup.com/us/brondo for links.**

DR. NEERA SINGH

Human Geographer focusing on human-nonhuman relations

Figure 11.6.1
Neera Singh.

How would you describe the nature of the work that you do?

Wary of disciplinary labels, I think of myself as an academic-activist, most interested in understanding what happens in the hyphen that bridges nature and culture. I came to academia after a long career as an NGO practitioner and activist in India. My work as an activist guides my current work as an academic. The core question that animates my work is: How can we (humans) come to care for "nature"? For me this question—of how can we care for our environment—is connected to the question—or the challenge—of how can we transform our modes of being human and of relating to nature and to each other? In view of the deep ecological crisis that we face, our only hope lies in being able to change our modes of being human and become more attentive to processes of "co-becoming" and flourishing with others.

Tell us a bit about your work in India as a practitioner.

In 1990, after a Masters' degree in Forestry Management, I went to Odisha to work with a consulting firm managing a Social Forestry Project. I found that, unnoticed by this Project, rural communities were protecting state-owned natural forests (which the Project was trying to protect from these local people). I became very interested in supporting these community-based forest conservation initiatives and founded a non-profit organization, *Vasundhara* (which means Mother Earth in Oriya), to advocate for community rights over forests. For almost a decade, I worked with Vasundhara on community forestry and sustainable livelihood issues.

The lessons that I have learned (and continue to learn) from rural communities in Odisha are helping me appreciate the importance of nurturing "affective ecologies"—which to me means deep appreciation of our dependence on other beings and an expanded sense of the "self."

What is the most meaningful project you've worked on over the course of your career? Why?

I see most of my professional life, as continuation of engagement with the phenomena of community-based forest conservation efforts in Odisha. Trying to understand local people's motivations to invest their labour and love to conserve forests in the absence of formal rights or financial incentives. Some of this work, indirectly, led to the enactment of India's Forest Rights Act, which provides for individual and collective rights over forests. It is now estimated that almost half of India's forests can potentially come under community control due to this law. That is deeply satisfying. I am now working on a book based on this work—which I am quite excited about.

You are a geographer, but one who I know has had significant training in anthropology, and someone who regularly publishes in and participates in anthropology circles. What is it about anthropology that speaks to the work that you do?

I am drawn to anthropology as it helps ask these fundamental questions about the nature of humans. What kinds of beings are we? What possibilities for alternate ways of being—and becoming—are open to us? Ethnography helps us learn from other cultures (and our own) and helps us explore the full range of possibilities available to us. I am convinced that the current socio-ecological crisis arises due to our enacting the story of humans as rational economic actors maximizing "self" interest. While we do so, we never question the stable self that comes from the Western perspective about the subject that underpins this "self-interest" maximization story. To me, learning from other cultures and practices about other ways is critical. This is where anthropology is helpful. It helps us understand other ways of being, while at the same time urging us to focus on the dynamic processes of becoming.

I draw heavily from anthropological theory and methods in my work to understand how different societies value things (and processes) differently and how different ways of valuing lead to different ways of organizing social and economic relations. For me this understanding is fundamental to envisioning alternatives to the current neoliberal economic order—and to radical revisioning of human–nature relations.

I use qualitative research, using anthropological sensibilities of "participant observation" in my work. Of late, I have been using participatory videos or visual ethnography in Odisha.

How are you using video ethnography?

I've used participatory videos to explore affective dimensions of people's relation to nature. I worked with a local media team in Odisha, who trained women and men in three villages to use video cameras. The villagers then filmed their daily lives over several months focusing on researching and documenting their village's history and forest conservation efforts. Our goal was to do the entire editing at the village level and do detailed documentation of the editing decisions that villagers make—what to show and what not to show to an external audience. However, we were only able to do some editing at the village level—as "fatigue" with the process set in and villagers were happy to hand over control to external technology-savvy people for editing. In one village, in addition to the videos, the villagers also wrote up the village history and poems about the village and they plan to publish this as a book to share with other communities, and to have has a record for the future generations.

What drew you to participatory video ethnography? Are there any challenges to the approach?

I decided to use participatory videos to get past the limitations of "talk and text" methods, which I find to be inadequate in getting to people's feelings and emotions. Even though I got interesting insights into the affective terrain of local lives, I found that the villagers saw their everyday life and practices as mundane and not worthy of representation. It was difficult to get past this problem. They tended not to focus on their everyday life and affective dimensions of it. I also felt "uncomfortable" watching their footage as it seemed intrusive—to get into the everyday lives of people uninvited (through the cameras).

I am still in the process of working through these dilemmas and fine-tuning the use of this method. The idea was to destabilize an external gaze and give authorship over representation of their lives to local people. One film that is almost finalized seems to have achieved this "insider" focus and is telling the village's story at their own terms. But a lot of work needs to be done to upscale this work into a cross-learning and advocacy tool. It requires an extensive network of local volunteers to work with villagers and use this as a story-telling tool that sheds light on the stories of oppression, resistance, re-imagination and everyday living—and helps these stories travel and create empathy.

In what ways would you say your work is applied, engaged, activist, or public?

I strive to do work that is all of the above—applied, activist, engaged, and public—but I don't think I have achieved that yet in my work (or maybe my standards are too high!). I think my work is deeply theoretical and applied at the same time. It is applied in the sense that it seeks answers to questions that are of practical relevance. It is also activist in the sense that it seeks to destabilize hegemonic ways of thinking.

For me, "acting" and "thinking" are intertwined. For me, thinking takes place or should take place, in (and through) our daily actions of trying to make the world a better place and reflect on what gets in the way of doing so.

ABOUT THE ANTHROPOLOGIST

Occupation: Assistant Professor, Department of Geography and Planning, University of Toronto.
Education: Ph.D., Michigan State University
Hobbies: Read, write, travel

DR. KAREN NAKAMURA

Cultural and Visual Anthropologist

Figure 11.7.1

Karen Nakamura. (photo by Hisako Matsuo)

Who are you?

I'm a cultural and visual anthropologist who does work on issues around disability and sexuality in contemporary Japan.

Where did you grow up?

I was born in Jogjakarta, Indonesia. Both of my parents are anthropologists and I was their "field baby." They took me around the world as a child, so I grew up in Indonesia, Australia, the United States, and Japan. As a result of moving around so much, I quickly learned to be a chameleon to fit in anywhere, but conversely no place really feels like home. This is maybe why I study identity as my central research question.

What is it about identity that puzzles you?

I don't feel any strong allegiance to any particular identity. So I have to try to understand why people have identities. Why do they hold so strongly onto feelings of gender, sexuality, nation, religion, disability-status, and so forth? How did they come to have these identities, and how has that affected their lives both socially and politically?

How did you become interested in the discipline of anthropology?

To tell the truth, I rejected it for the longest time. In college, I refused to take anthropology courses because that was what my parents did. Instead, I took social psychology and sociolinguistic classes. In my senior year, my advisor in social psychology told me to my horror that if I was interested in graduate school that my interest in identity politics and social movements would find a better home in cultural anthropology. It took me a while to realize that maybe my parents weren't so nuts after all and anthropology really was a good discipline to both ask the types of questions I wanted to ask, as well as a way to provide cross-cultural answers that would go outside of the implicit ethnocentrism of psychology and sociology.

What are your profession, current place of employment, and job title?

I am a sociocultural and visual anthropologist at the University of California Berkeley. My formal title is Professor of Anthropology and the Robert and Colleen

Haas Distinguished Chair in Disability Studies. I just took up this position after spending the past decade at Yale University.

How did you become a visual anthropologist?

I didn't receive any formal training in visual anthropology in graduate school. Because my first research project was about the deaf community in Japan and my informants used sign language, I had to videotape all of my interviews. When I switched to my second project on psychiatric disabilities, I was convinced that I wanted to make ethnographic films along with a written ethnography. Most people don't know what someone who has schizophrenia looks like or talks like—or what it might look like for them to live in the community. We only have very inaccurate stereotypes from the media. I wanted to make an ethnographic film that would show the reality of how they lived. At the same time, I knew that a short film couldn't reveal many of the complexities of their life and their past experiences, so I paired the film with the text in my book to balance the two forms.

What is the most meaningful project you've worked on over the course of your career? Why?

I put a great deal of myself into that second book about psychiatric disabilities in Japan, titled: *A Disability of the Soul* (University of Cornell Press, 2013). This is not only because I've struggled with my own mental health, but also because I've seen so many promising students have their college plans derailed by symptoms of depression, bipolar disorder, and schizophrenia. In Japan, we recognize these mental illnesses as psychiatric disabilities and there are some protections around them. In the United States, we've been very slow to extend protection to mental illness as a disability, especially at colleges and universities. We will go to great extent to make a dorm room accessible to a student who is blind or who is using a wheelchair, but not only will we not help a student with psychiatric disabilities, we often force them to drop out of school by taking a medical leave. Can you imagine the uproar if we asked a deaf student to do the same?

I wrote that book because I had heard about a community in Japan where people with psychiatric disabilities were able to live full and fulfilling lives and I wanted to explore as an anthropologist what they needed to do to have a functional community. I wrote the book in jargon-free language and produced the films so that they could be read broadly by people other than academics and anthropologists. I want there to be a conversation about how we can improve the situation for people with psychiatric disabilities in the USA.

Please tell us a little about your forthcoming work on transsexuality. What does that have to do with disability?

In the United States, we're used to thinking of trans as part of the broader LGBT movement. I became interested in the question of transsexuality-as-disability when I noticed trans activists in Japan in the late 1990s rejecting affiliation with sexuality and instead identifying as part of the disability movement. They embraced the psychiatric diagnostic category of "Gender Identity Disability" (GID) as a cover for transsexuality and started mobilizing as people with disabilities. This enabled them to achieve a great deal of political and social change in the last two decades. The book I'm currently writing is about what happens when the T breaks off of the LGBT movement and joins the disability movement.

Do you identify as an applied, engaged, or public anthropologist? What do these titles mean to you?

I identify as a public anthropologist. I believe that anthropologists (and academics in general) have a responsibility to educate the public. We are given tenure so that we can ask troubling questions about how society and its institutions exist or should exist. Because many anthropologists exist in two cultures (their home ones and the communities they study), they have responsibilities to both.

Which is your home community?

My primary audience is people in the United States. I write the books that I do because I want people to think about the various identity categories that I've looked at (deafness, mental illness, transsexuality) in new ways. I've also worked hard to make my books accessible to the general public. I want them to see other worlds, gain new perspectives, and ask different sets of question. That's how I hope my work can drive positive social change.

Is public anthropology supported in academia?

It varies greatly. At the small liberal arts college where I taught at the very start of my career, there was a strong emphasis in service learning. There, I felt that public anthropology was supported in the classroom. The private university where I spent the last decade was not as supportive of public and applied anthropology, and that was one of the attractions of moving to a public university.

What advice do you have for students who wish to pursue a career in visual anthropology?

We are at a strange time for visual anthropology. Because of the ubiquity of digital cameras, it's easier than any other time in history to shoot a lot of footage if you want to make an ethnographic film. But it's still just as difficult to edit it into a coherent narrative— and even more so, perhaps, given that people are no longer receiving training in traditional filmmaking and editing skills. Non-filmmakers don't realize how much work goes into editing a film and most people utterly underestimate the work needed to distribute one as well. While there are more venues to publish

ethnographic films, there's much more material out there and the noise-to-signal ratio is perhaps higher than ever. I've always paired my visual work with textual narrative as I think it's very difficult to be a visual anthropologist who only makes films.

What do you see as the future for anthropology and disability studies?

There are still too few disabled anthropologists and academics—especially those who are doing their fieldwork outside of the United States. The American Anthropological Association is beginning to realize that it needs to do more for scholars with disabilities—especially graduate students—and beginning conversations on how we can make the discipline as a whole more accessible. There's still so much about disability—and all of the intersectional identities that it bisects—that we don't know. I'd like to encourage students with disabilities to think of careers as anthropologists, and especially as applied anthropologists.

ABOUT THE ANTHROPOLOGIST

Occupation: Cultural and Visual Anthropologist
Education: Cornell BA 1993. Yale PhD 2001.
Books: Deaf in Japan (Cornell University Press, 2006); *Disability of the Soul* (University of Cornell Press, 2014)
Hobbies: Making weird and wonderful gadgets in my home laboratory.
Favorite Food: Undecided. I haven't eaten them all.

PART 12
Careers in Engaged and Applied Anthropology

The introduction to this book oriented your reading by providing an overview of the ways in which anthropologists have defined and framed their work as "engaged," "applied," and "public" in contrast to traditional ethnography. Doing so may have helped to situate the individual chapters within specific traditions. At times, the authors were very intentional about identifying their work within a particular approach; others may not have made their approach explicit, but the reader might have imposed on them a particular slant given what they have come to think about as "applied," for instance, as compared to "critically engaged."

Regardless of how one identifies, what we all must confront at some point is finding the right language to communicate the value of our discipline and the work that we do to the broader public, whether it is to effect policy change or to find a job post-graduation. The first piece in this section takes up these practical points. In "So, You Want to Be an Anthropologist" (Reading 12.1), Carol Ellick and Joe Watkins provide advice to students transitioning from college life to professional careers, including helping to frame the skills that anthropologists possess for potential employers. This reading also includes a selection of career stories, including the authors' own, to illustrate the diversity in career options for professional anthropologists.

The remaining pieces bring us back to consider the various forms of anthropological practice—engaged, public, applied, activist, collaborative, and so forth. In "Moving Past Public Anthropology and Doing Collaborative Research" (Reading 12.2), Luke Lassiter calls upon us to stop worrying about what label we fall under and instead focus on what is important to all anthropologists: addressing and ameliorating social problems. From here, he advocates for the adoption of a collaborative approach, with students and scholars working alongside of community members on issues of shared concern. Such an approach, for Lassiter and others, is bound to make a positive difference for the world.

For others, our role as "witness"—or engaged observers—is paramount to authorizing and legitimizing the painful realities of marginalized communities. And so, the process of documentation is a worthy endeavor, and perhaps being an "engaged observer" is just as effective as co-producing research outcomes with community members under a collaborative approach. While powerful and well-intentioned, in "Expert Witness: Notes Toward Revisiting the Politics of Listening" (Reading 12.3), Asale Angel-Ajani asks us to confront the fact that sometimes the ways in which anthropologists are called to act as a witness are not always noble. Drawing on her own research documenting the experiences of incarcerated African immigrant women in Italy, Angel-Ajani reveals that it is not just the public that may question the authority of anthropological work. Anthropologists also police one another's work, and their own preconceived notions may lead them to question the truth statements of others.

The final reading, "The Future of Practice: Anthropology and the Grand Challenge" (Reading 12.4) by Riall Nolan, calls upon anthropologists to work to address the world's "grand challenges," the major global problems we face such as health inequalities, energy shortages, climate change, and poverty. Nolan sees the future of our discipline to be one where the "ivory tower" is left behind and more and more students of anthropology will be working as practitioners to bring sociocultural data and cultural perspectives to bear on addressing global challenges.

This section's "In the News" story features the growing job market in business and design anthropology. More and more companies are beginning to recognize the value anthropologists bring in shedding light on what people really want (not just what they say they want) and how people go about using products in their daily lives. Employment within this subfield has come under critique by some anthropologists who question if working to advance a company's profit is consistent with our discipline's ethical code. Links to these debates are provided in the website companion.

The final "Anthropology in Practice" feature in this collection of readings highlights design anthropologist Melissa Cefkin. Her story is a perfect end to this book as it reflects the nonlinear paths that anthropologists take in developing their careers. From a passion for folk dancing and the Middle East to working on the design of future driverless automobiles for Nissan, our paths seem like a series of non-sequiturs. But as Dr. Cefkin and others throughout this text have shown, the underlying current of most anthropologists is a commitment to social justice and cultural understanding. Dr. Cefkin, like many contemporary anthropologists, refuses to be placed in a box; she is not applied nor public, and has never liked these terms, but as she astutely points out, she does "not know a single anthropologist who is not 'engaged.'"

KEY TERMS:

- Careers
- Practicing anthropology
- Collaborative anthropology
- Engaged anthropology
- Public anthropology
- Business anthropology
- Design anthropology

12.1 So, You Want to Be an Anthropologist . . .

CAROL ELLICK AND JOE WATKINS

The following excerpts are taken from a career book oriented toward students who are transition-ing from their university lives to professional careers. In this short selection, the authors provide students with a general sense of the kinds of skills that an anthropology degree provides and how to translate those skills to potential employers. Additionally, the excerpt includes career stories from working anthropologists which capture the wide range of professions in which anthropology is practiced.

Questions

1. What skills do anthropologists have that make them attractive to future employers?
2. How might you go about expanding you skillset during your time in college?
3. Based on what you read, what level of degree do you need to achieve your current career goals?

What skills has your background in anthropology given you? Citing a paper by the American Anthropological Association (http://www.aaanet.org/profdev/careers/Careers.cfm), Kedia (2008, 23) notes that anthropologists are "careful observers of humans and their behavior" and that anthropology students are exposed to a "range of social, behavioral, biological and other scientific research methods [that supplement] statistical findings with descriptive data gathered through participant observation, interviewing, and ethnographic study." These skills, in conjunction with "careful record-keeping, attention to details, analytical reading . . . social ease in strange situations, [and] critical thinking" are marketable skills that many employers need.

Jana Fortier, Ph.D., Department of Anthropology, University of California, San Diego, responded to our request for helpful advice for students entering the field of anthropology with a wonderfully written, detailed list of anthropological skills. She presented it as a "gift" toward the book project. And it is an incredible gift to share with you.

Dr. Fortier's Statement on Developing Skills

Students of anthropology invariably take classes concerning research methods, but once you leave academia, it is time to look for work in the marketplace. If you do a search in a jobs database, such as monster.com, you might type in the key phrase "cultural anthropologist," yet only a handful of job offerings will pop up onto your computer screen. Analogous to disciplines such as mathematics, philosophy, and history, it is more the skills you have acquired rather than the degree title that are needed by potential employers. So for those of us who love to work using our skills as applied cultural anthropologists, it is important to develop skills that are recognizable and sought after by employers.

In my case, it turned out that the employers mostly have been government agencies who need someone to write reports or other documents after having done ethnographic research. Some of these agencies have been the City of San Diego, the California Transportation Department (Caltrans), the local Marine Corps Air Station, the local Naval Facilities; and some private groups, including museums, CRMs (cultural resource management firms), and some non-profits. What these employers have in common is that they seek someone who can do cultural and historical research, conduct valid interviews and surveys, write excellent reports, and do it all with common sense, enthusiasm, and professionalism.

Each ethnographer develops a distinct method, based on his or her past experience and interests. In *my* case, these are some of the "skills" that I have in my kit (and ones you could type into "monster.com" and find jobs). They are not all necessary for any one contract, but I have used these in many cases.

Records searching—The government agencies with whom I have worked require research into certain databases. These have included Sacred Lands file searches, California Historic Resources Information System research, searching records in the San Diego Historical Society, artifact searches in the local anthropology museum, review of information in the National Register of Historic Places, review of laws involving CRM such as NAGPRA. One skill you will learn is to transform your library database search skills as a student into one of competence using other professional databases.

Videography and photography—I used to say that I specialize in taking pictures of people working. Studs Terkel would have been proud of me. Ethnographers need to take well-composed pictures and videotaped interviews, but we especially need to be able to stuff as much cultural information into our images as possible. Practice taking pictures of "congealed knowledge" more than of peoples' faces. In my work, I have images of people cutting usable plants, transforming them into rope, shoes, and other cultural artifacts; of people doing pottery, ironsmithing, pipe making, growing grains, threshing, teaching children, building irrigation ditches, and recreating ancient Andean terraces. When it comes time to write reports, a handful of well-composed photos illustrating your main points will bring high quality and authenticity to your work.

Design structured interviews—This is when research design classes come in handy, but also you may want to keep a research design folder of articles and some books on hand for reference. You can effectively translate your studies of various types of research into a carefully structured research proposal for a client. I've had to use such methods as daisy-chain interviews, sampling to ensure equal numbers of diverse social classes, sets of key issues to be discussed, and key vocabulary such as native plant names. Other methods such as time allocation studies are useful, but the time frame for contract work may not allow for these more time-consuming methods. Your interviews are precious moments. Let your interviewee talk as much as they want. Don't rush and say, "I have to go at 5 pm." Respect the lovely sliver of memories that you are collecting. Remember how important it is to prepare; think about how to conduct your interviews, and leave yourself enough time to carry out as many interviews as possible. My usual regret is that I only got x number of interviews or that I interrupted someone while they were speaking. In applied work, we often have less time and yet the reports need to be of high quality.

Transcription and data analysis—This is the place for ethnographers to slow down, spend more time reviewing the material. Transcribe all the important conversations; look for key ideas, phrases, and bits that will have the most impact in a report. Think about the goals of the report and the contracting agency.

Report writing—Don't be afraid to write that "lame first draft." Just start writing! Then polish, polish some more, and review it for sentence flow and simplicity. When busy people read your report, the paragraphs have to have "hooks" and "anchors" and other edges for your reader to remember. Use memorable quotes from interviews; devise beautiful word-images; use alliteration and other rhetorical devices from your favorite non-fiction writers.

It's never too late to stretch yourself and learn more skills. For example, I found that recording cultural geographic information using a GPS handheld device has proved useful. I have recorded information about plant gathering sites, sites of stories and myths, sites with natural resources such as vernal pools, and toponymic sites with significant cultural information about these special places. The GIS map specialists with whom I've worked have enjoyed putting together maps of these places, and they bring an additional dimension to agency reports.

There are jobs out there for those of us who choose to study cultural anthropology. But we do not always have to call ourselves "anthropologists." We can use our anthropology skills in such work as program coordinator, program manager, clinical research specialist, cultural research specialist, records analyst, grants specialist, science writer, etc.

The trick, as many practicing anthropologists will tell you, is to help convince the prospective employer that your anthropology skills will help you do the job better than a non-anthropologist would. Your degree and knowledge are composites of the classes you took, the internships you held, and the background you acquired. . . .

To the Nth Degree

A question that hangs over most students' heads (and that we often get asked) is "What degree do I need to get a job?" If you haven't asked yourself that question, you might. If your aspiration is to develop an archaeologically based seasonal round that would move you from summer projects in the Pacific Northwest to winter field projects in the Arizona sun, or if you want to do short-term ethnographic research for marketing companies so that you can stay on ski patrol at Snow Basin in the winter, then you may not need more than a bachelor's degree. If you want to direct these projects, then you will probably need at least a master's degree. If you want to become the next Jane Goodall or Dian Fossey and study nonhuman primates in the hopes of throwing additional light on human behavior, then you should count on completing a doctorate.

The preceding examples are *generalizations*. There are people who have made successful careers moving from technician to supervisor to director who have a bachelor's degree coupled with years of experience. But in today's culture, that is the exception rather than the rule. Even in a government setting, you can only climb so high on the General Schedule (GS) pay scale before you have to either move on to a new region and a new job or add a degree. It takes *both* education and experience to build a successful career. Look at the jobs that actually interest you before deciding that you want to take your education to its ultimate completion by getting a Ph.D. Make sure that by getting a Ph.D. you will not walk into the job market overqualified for the positions that interest you.

What You Can Do with a Bachelor's Degree

What you do with a B.A. or B.S. degree depends on your area of interest, but no matter what field you've entered, be prepared to be hired in an entry-level position. The actual work you do will depend on the employer and the project. If, for example, you plan to become an archaeologist, a bachelor's degree would qualify you to work as a laboratory technician or a field technician. Those entering cultural anthropology might find a position as a poll taker, market researcher, or assistant caseworker. Going into biological anthropology? You might look for positions in public health, at museums, zoos, or agencies conducting forensic studies. Entry-level jobs for linguistic anthropologists can be found primarily in the social services and governmental research programs.

What You Can Do with a Master's Degree

At most academic institutions, an M.A. or M.S. can be earned in as little as two years. Some master's programs require a minimum number of classes before the student must pass a set of comprehensive exams aimed at demonstrating knowledge. Other programs require internships and a research paper or thesis for graduation, in addition to the classes.

A master's degree will get you a middle-management type of job. This may not sound very appealing when phrased this way, but in practical terms it means that you would have the qualifications to work at the project management level, do your own research, or coordinate programs. This said, we would not recommend walking out of a college or university and into a management position without first gaining some field experience in that area. Field experience gives you practical knowledge that you simply cannot gain any other way. . . . Believe us when we say that skipping the field experience prior to becoming a crew chief or project manager will not only be frustrating to you, it will create frustration and animosity among the crew. Those entering master's-level positions will need not only technical knowledge of a specific topic, but also the ability to analyze and synthesize information for site or project reports. Some community colleges or schools that focus on undergraduate degrees will hire professionals with a master's degree, but competition at that level is getting more intense, and more and more professors at the community college level have a Ph.D. Basically, if being a professor is your goal, then you will need a Ph.D.

What You Can Do with a Doctorate of Philosophy

A Ph.D. is the highest degree awarded by departments of anthropology. According to the ideal timeline, a Ph.D. can be completed in as few as two years following the master's. In reality, very few individuals complete their coursework and dissertation within this time frame. When planning your path, think realistically. Will you be devoting all of your time to getting a degree? If not, it might take you five to seven years to accomplish the coursework, the research, and the writing required to produce a dissertation.

The successful completion of a doctorate indicates the ability to conduct independent research, to analyze, synthesize, and evaluate information, and to write and defend a dissertation. A doctorate will get you a management-level job and put you at the top of the employment food chain. With a Ph.D., you have the credentials to be considered for a tenure-track position at the university level. Outside of the university context, you could be a research director or principal investigator and manager of your own consulting firm.

Mixing and Matching

Before we venture into the discussion on applied versus academic careers, we'd like to mention the benefits of mixing and matching interests, programs, and degrees. [Earlier], we talked about the old-fashioned four-field approach that still exists in many anthropology departments. We touched on the interdisciplinary major, but we would like to reinforce the idea that getting a double major, or a second concentration, or even degrees in related disciplines gives you more options. The strongest careers we've seen are from people who brought two distinct professions together: an R.N. and a cultural anthropology M.A.; M.D. and biological anthropology Ph.D.; anthropology B.A. and education M.A.; anthropology B.A. and Native American Studies M.A. All of these individuals created their own unique careers based on their unique qualifications.

That said, you need not go so far as obtaining a second degree. If you have a talent or specialized

training, think how it can fit together with your formal education to make you stand out in the eyes of potential employers. . . .

Career Stories

There are more career options in applied anthropology than you can imagine. Perhaps the easiest way to highlight the diversity is to describe our own career paths and present you with some career stories of others who have pursued an applied path. . . .

Joe Watkins, Ph.D. Director, Native American Studies, University of Oklahoma

My first job out of college within the field of anthropology was as an archaeologist for a federal agency. I was able to take advantage of my field experience and my education to influence the practice of archaeology in the southeastern United States. The area where I worked had three large reservoir projects going: the Tennessee-Tombigbee Waterway, the Richard B. Russell Reservoir, and the Tellico Dam projects. While I wasn't doing field work, I was able to get into the field to review the work that other archaeologists were doing. I also learned a great deal about federal contracting and the types of archaeological research that could be done with federal assistance.

After leaving the federal agency, I started my own archaeological consulting firm in Oklahoma. I was able to get some small contracts primarily in the southern and central Great Plains, but also in other parts of the United States. I was responsible for obtaining the contract, doing the fieldwork, analyzing any artifacts found during the fieldwork, and writing up the final report, all while working on the finances. I also worked as a crew member and crew chief for other contracting firms when I didn't have my own contracts.

For a time I was out of archaeology, working for a nonprofit legal services organization and a museum, but I eventually went back to doing what I enjoyed the most. I worked for large and small private consulting firms, as an archaeologist for the University of Oklahoma doing cultural resources inventories for the Oklahoma Department of Transportation, and then as an agency archaeologist in the Southern Plains Region of the Bureau of Indian Affairs. In all those jobs, I was responsible for writing large and small reports to agencies, to supervisors, or to interested groups, as well as writing clear, concise letters outlining what I had done or was proposing to do.

After I completed my Ph.D. in 1994, I felt the need to "give back" to the discipline. I wrote about my experiences as a Native American archaeologist; I revised my dissertation and got it published; I got involved in national anthropological organizations and local tribal ones; I "gave back" with a vengeance! Ultimately, as a result of all these activities, I landed a job at the University of New Mexico and now at the University of Oklahoma. I love the students and the teaching (but could do without the administrative aspects of it). I now struggle to find time to write and to conduct research, but I still find archaeology to be as rewarding as it was more than 40 years ago when I started.

Carol J. Ellick, M.A. Archaeology and Cultural Education Consultants

I was lucky. My first paid position in anthropology was the summer prior to the completion of my B.A. I spent that summer and part of the fall working as a laboratory technician and as an assistant pedologist (soil scientist) on a large contract archaeology project. It was my first taste of fieldwork, and perhaps not my best, but overall it was exactly what I'd hoped for— outside, in the sun, using my mind, and getting paid for it. This job was my first in cultural resource management (CRM), the area in which I would end up spending the majority of my time for the first 30 years of my career. It sounds simple, but it hasn't been. Working as a field technician or crew chief took applying to every possible agency and organization that may have won contracts during the previous season.

During my career as a field archaeologist, I worked for CRM programs in anthropology departments and for private companies. If a field project was only a few weeks long, I could find myself working for two, three, and possibly four employers in one year. Some years, I worked in three different states! The only part that wasn't fun was sending letters of application and filling out federal and state forms during tax season. And, when I use the term "field archaeologist," I don't just mean digging holes in the dirt. I spent my summers on crews walking survey, excavating, drawing stratigraphy, gridding sites, and doing cartography. I stamped bags in the lab, processed artifacts, and prepared samples for analysis. I worked as a field and lab technician,

crew chief, lab manager, and project supervisor. During the off-season, I used my artistic talents and illustrated artifacts and finalized maps for publication. I worked for the Forest Service, Bureau of Land Management, three major universities in Washington State, an uncountable number of archaeological consulting firms, and a school district. The way I figured it, my mark of success was staying out of the unemployment lines.

The longer I worked, the more specific my area of interest became, until I ultimately settled into archaeological education and public outreach. While working in this field, I worked for for-profit and not-for-profit companies and organizations. I also held workshops, lectured at universities, and taught university classes. Over time, this all added up to a career.

Robynne Locke ICF International

About halfway through my M.A. in cultural anthropology at the University of Denver, I began to be concerned about what I was going to do after graduation. I wasn't sure if continuing on to a Ph.D. program was something I was ready for, but I had a hard time imagining an alternative. Who would pay me to do what I am passionate about?

When it came to finding my dream job, I had several counts against me. First, I owed a significant amount in school loans that I would have to start repaying after graduation. Second, the country was deep in the midst of a recession, and every day I heard more and more news on the growing unemployment rates of young professionals. Third, I wanted to return to Vermont to be closer to friends and family, but the small rural state has few opportunities for someone pursuing a career in international research. If I wanted a career in anthropology, I knew I would need to plan ahead.

My first decision was to delay my fieldwork until the fall (by taking independent research and study credits) and to use the summer to get an internship in a place I might want to work after graduation. I started by doing a Web search of areas of interest to me, but all I could find were a handful of small nonprofits who were either not hiring, would not pay enough for me to pay back my loans, or would not allow me to use the skills I learned in graduate school. Then, finally, I came across a company called ICF International, a research and consulting firm with an office in Burlington, Vermont. As a "do-gooder," I never considered working in the private sector, as I had the perception that doing so would somehow conflict with my overall goal of helping others. But after looking closely into the company, I found that they worked in the areas that I care passionately about: health, education, development, energy, and social justice. Although the company had no formal internship program or temporary positions available, I sent in my résumé and requested an interview. The company decided to give me a chance, and I found the opportunity I was looking for. At the end of the summer, they encouraged me to apply for a full-time position after graduation, and I did just that. I am now a Research Assistant/ Analyst with ICF Macro International, and looking forward to building my career with the company.

There are several benefits to working for a large company in the private sector. I earn enough to slowly pay back my school loans, I know there is opportunity to move up in my career, and I am gaining the hands-on business and management experience that was previously lacking in my mostly academic résumé. Most importantly, the wide scope of ICF's work allows me to participate in a variety of interesting projects. I was even recently approached with the opportunity to assist with research on human trafficking, which was the topic of my M.A. thesis.

There are also some drawbacks to this work. It is not the career I originally imagined for myself. In my current position, "the field" is in my office, not in some remote village; data collection consists of hundreds of thousands of surveys completed by mail or by phone, not through years of establishing a relationship with a community; and analysis is completed by a team of statisticians, and not the intimate experience I had with my own M.A. thesis. But as the office anthropologist, I have found my supervisors to be incredibly supportive, encouraging me to bring my unique interests and skills to the company, and I know that eventually I will make my own way.

I would encourage anyone graduating with a B.A., M.A., or Ph.D. in anthropology to consider a career in the private sector. Companies like ICF are doing important work in areas of critical interest to anthropologists, and I believe the opportunity to work together in these areas is a mutually beneficial one.

Jennifer Cardew Kersey Intrepid Consultants in Seattle, WA

Not too long ago, someone referred to me as a "practicing anthropologist," and I realized . . . I'm not a student anymore, I'm really an anthropologist! It sounds silly, but the question of "When am I an anthropologist versus a student of anthropology?" is one that is asked in departments across the country. My journey has been stressful at times, but it's been fun. And doing great research that benefits consumers makes it all worthwhile.

My graduate courses at the University of North Texas (UNT) really prepared me to use anthropology outside of academia by providing hands-on experience in the courses and in my practicum. I undertook my practicum with a small market research boutique, Intrepid Consultants in Seattle, Washington, and I've worked there for two years now. I started conducting interviews after just a few months on the job, and I now lead multidisciplinary teams researching everything from physicians' perspectives on health and wellness, to what "local" means to children, to Web developers' habit and practices. A lot of my fieldwork consists of in-depth telephone interviews and focus groups in facilities and in homes. I have ventured into the world of virtual ethnography and social media monitoring in order to contextualize offline research and provide a more holistic view to our client.

The path I took to get to where I am now was untraditional at the time. I completed my degree in the UNT online Master's in Anthropology Program. I can honestly say that I got a great education and successfully entered into the anthropology community of praxis (CoP) by attending the Society for Applied Anthropology (SfAA) and American Anthropological Association (AAA) annual meetings, reaching out to others, and connecting with people online.

I actually found my practicum internship through a post on Twitter in 2006. It was an offer from an anthropologist working at Intrepid who had been following my Twitter feed. In the age of social networking, connecting with anthropologists is easier than ever. Being an anthropologist is wonderful because it means you're a part of a community, and it's a community that will support you throughout your career by giving you feedback or answers when you need them, connecting you with jobs, and giving you a sound body of theory to apply in your research.

The important thing to remember is to go into something you enjoy, with people you enjoy working with. If you don't, you'll only find frustration.

12.2 Moving Past Public Anthropology and Doing Collaborative Research

LUKE ERIC LASSITER

The introductory chapter of this book reviewed current movements toward "engaged," "applied," and "public" anthropology. Proponents of the various approaches sometimes argue over the meaning of each of the labels. In this piece, Lassiter advocates that we move beyond those debates by recognizing that what cuts across all of them is collaboration. Collaborative research offers an opportunity for students and scholars to work closely with local communities on an issue of shared concern. The piece closes with sound advice for students wishing to pursue collaborative work.

Questions

1. What does the label "public anthropology" represent, and why has it emerged in recent years?
2. Is there a meaningful distinction between public anthropology, applied anthropology, and collaborative research? Discuss your position.
3. What are benefits of doing collaborative anthropological research? What are the risks associated with the approach?
4. Do you see yourself doing collaborative research in your career? Why or why not?

. . . In recent years, "public anthropology" has become one of the many labels used to describe a growing and ever-more ubiquitous concern with anthropological relevance, public engagement, and action. . . . In another but closely related sense, public anthropology may also imply an amplification of action or activist anthropology, a "public interest anthropology" that challenges the theory/practice divide; reconfigures an anthropological praxis established on equity and social justice; and augments moral, ethical, and political action, which, again, may or may not be meant to influence public policy (see, e.g., Sanday 1976, 1998; cf. Basch et al. 1999; Hill and Baba 1999). In this same vein, this practice may employ a kind of participatory action research that plants roots in locality, and assembles cooperative cocitizenships and coactivisms built on the counderstandings emergent in the collaborative research partnerships between and among anthropologists and local publics (see, e.g., Lassiter 2001a, 2003, 2005b; cf. Checker and Fishman 2004).

Obviously, the issues revolving around public anthropology—whether called "public interest anthropology," "public archaeology," "public ethnography," or just "engaged anthropology"—are very closely aligned with applied and practicing anthropology (see Lamphere 2004). After all, they all draw from the same sources of inspiration: Franz Boas, Ruth Benedict, and Margaret Mead are a few oft-cited examples. Given this, though, many applied and practicing anthropologists argue that many of those who espouse a public anthropology are ignoring and usurping the important role that applied anthropology has long played in our field (see, e.g., Singer 2000). . . .

Barbara Rylko-Bauer and colleagues (2006) echo this sentiment, noting that while "recent movements toward a more public anthropology have done a useful service for the general discipline" (186), "critiques grounded in labeling and othering or those based on dismissal of large portions of anthropologically informed work and erasure of disciplinary history are counterproductive, because they overlook significant areas of creative accomplishment" (187). . . .

Les Field and Richard Fox argue in *Anthropology Put to Work* (2007) that such divisions and the recent calls for a public anthropology are out of touch with contemporary practice. Field and Fox point out that the disintegration of such divisions—such as that between "pure" and "applied" research—has already happened, mainly because the contemporary work conditions of anthropology require an ever-expanding range of conceptual and practical expertise. . . . Students today, then, must be prepared to be expert theoretical, applied, public, and practicing anthropologists all at the same time, no matter where their career trajectories take them, in or out of academia.

Simply put, rather than worrying about on which side of the argument you fall, or more precisely, rigidly demarcating what you do as applied, public, practicing, or academic anthropology, students should be charting, as *anthropologists*, how best to connect with the central questions and problems of a larger anthropological project (Lamphere 2004, 432)—questions such as, to borrow from Rylko-Bauer and colleagues (2006, 186) again, "How do we operationalize the goals of addressing and ameliorating social problems? How do we translate knowledge successfully into pragmatic action? Which strategies work?"

One of the ways we can engage such questions is through collaborative research, to which I now turn.

Collaborative Research

. . . Collaborative research can have a variety of names, including "community-based research," "action research," "participatory action research," or "participatory community research" (Wali 2006, 6). Although the various labels for collaborative research may denote a wide and diverse range of applications, and implement collaboration to varying degrees, the "underlying spirit is that of working, learning, and

moving toward positive social change together" (Wali 2006, 6).

My own interests along these lines have focused on doing and writing *collaborative ethnography*—a very specific kind of ethnography that builds on the cooperative relationships already present in the ethnographic research process (i.e., between ethnographers and informants/consultants) and endeavors to engender texts that are more readable, relevant, and applicable to local communities of ethnographic collaborators (i.e., local publics). . . . I define collaborative ethnography as

> an approach to ethnography that *deliberately* and *explicitly* emphasizes collaboration at every point in the ethnographic process, without veiling it—from project conceptualization, to fieldwork, and, especially, through the writing process. Collaborative ethnography invites commentary from our consultants and seeks to make that commentary overtly part of the ethnographic text as it develops. In turn, this negotiation is reintegrated back into the fieldwork process itself. Importantly, the process yields texts that are co-conceived or cowritten with local communities of collaborators and consider multiple audiences outside the confines of academic discourse, including local constituencies. (Lassiter 2005a, 16)

Collaborative ethnography implies more than what this brief definition might at first glance suggest. . . . [C]ollaborative ethnography . . . is founded on four main commitments:

1. Ethical and moral responsibility to ethnographic consultants—whereby moral and ethical commitments between researcher(s) and research participant(s) frame the contours of many ethnographic projects;
2. Honesty about the fieldwork process—whereby the ethnographic fieldwork experience (including that of both the ethnographer[s] and interlocutor[s]) is honestly discussed, explored, and evaluated within the context of collaborative research partnerships;
3. Accessible and dialogic writing—whereby the ethnographic account not only represents diverse

experiences and voices, but is clearly written, free from the highly specialized discourse of the academy, so that ethnographic consultants can actually read, engage, and respond to ethnographic texts; and subsequently,

4. Collaborative reading, writing, and co-interpretation of ethnographic texts with consultants—whereby ethnographer(s) and research participant(s) work together (via, for example, focus groups, community forums, editorial boards, ethnographer/consultant research and writing teams) to co-interpret ethnographic representations as they develop and evolve. (see Lassiter 2005a, 77–154)

Such collaboratively based commitments are not the final step in practicing collaborative research and practice, however. These cocommitments have the potential to establish a foundation for community-based collaborative action as well, where ethnographers and consultants choose to work together to make a difference in their local communities via the coproduction of ethnography. . . .

. . . In the *Other Side of Middletown* project (see Lassiter et al. 2004), to offer a more recent example from my own research experience, faculty, students, and community members worked to coproduce a text that addressed a community-based concern, in this case, about the exclusion of black experience from both classic and ongoing studies of Middletown (which had largely ignored the contributions of African Americans to the city of Muncie, Indiana). We were charged, as a group, to write a text to rectify this problem. And as its completion was so important to many in the community—in fact, some had already begun the work years before we started—its very collaborative inscription was a powerful way to engage in collaborative action from the very beginning (see Miles 2004). This initial collaborative process yielded still other collaborative actions, though, as members of the community guided faculty and students into the realm of larger community-centered issues, concerns, and activisms. Several of the students, for example, became closely involved in community debates, forums, and protests that surrounded a contentious community conflict to rename a local city street to Martin Luther King, Jr., Boulevard (see Williams 2003). . . .

Doing Collaborative Research: Some Advice

. . . *Familiarize yourself with the history and broad range of collaborative and community-based research.* Many will be happy to know that practitioners across several disciplines, not just in anthropology, are doing collaborative research. . . .Be especially aware, however, that different disciplines and their various scholar-activists have a diversity of visions for what this collaborative research practice should look like. These different visions, of course, are often based in the history and traditions of any given discipline. In anthropology, for example, calls for a more collaborative ethnography materialized, as is well-known, in the vibrant discussions of ethnographic authority emanating from critical theory, feminist, and postmodern anthropology in the 1960s, '70s, and '80s; but the roots of collaborative research go much deeper than this (see Lassiter 2005a, 25–47). . . . In the end, though, we cannot presume to know everything about every historical moment or every collaborative research model. But we can push ourselves to appreciate—and this is the point—that doing collaborative research is part of a much larger project in the social sciences, past and present. And that when we choose to do this kind of research, we are, first, not alone in our efforts, and second, in the company of many fellow travelers who have much to offer each other in our common efforts to realize a more equitable social science. If you can, get to know these "fellow travelers" and their collaborative researches. There is much for all of us to learn.

Choose your methods with care. Being familiar with the history and broad range of collaborative research, of course, provides the foundation for choosing collaborative research methods that best suit the goals of you and your collaborators in any given project or partnership. For me, collaborative ethnography has often worked extremely well for apprehending the common goals that emerge in collaborative inquiry: whether researching drug addiction and recovery, Kiowa song, or black Muncie, collaborative ethnography seemed the best approach for articulating multicultural understanding and, my collaborators and I have hoped, social change. In other cases, however, my consultants and I have sought out other methods and procedures that were best suited to the context of the collaborative partnership in which we worked. I have mentioned this elsewhere—for example, doing more traditional ethnographic surveys for Muncie's African American community in the wake of *The Other Side of Middletown* collaboration (see Lassiter 2004a, 8–9). Most recently, in my job as the director of a program closely associated with a school of education, I am now working to varying degrees with a diversity of local teachers and administrators, school districts, service agencies, state officials, higher education faculty, and students in the context of a wide range of collaborative research projects meant to improve teacher training and student learning (see Lassiter 2007). In these partnerships, we have pulled together several different research approaches, from quantitative and qualitative methods to collaborative ethnography and action research. While these combined research approaches deploy collaboration in very different ways, they share a commitment to community-based collaborations that are responsive to the needs and goals of the parties involved. What this requires, of course, is openness to and the careful selection and utilization of multiple approaches that allow for diverse collaborative research partnerships and projects.

Acknowledge that collaborative research is challenging and that it requires time. Of all the research approaches available to anthropologists and other social scientists, collaborative research is perhaps the most time-consuming. Collaboration rests, first and foremost, on trust, and building trust does not happen overnight; it grows—often, over the course of years—as any given project or partnership develops and evolves. For example, in a recent publication of the Field Museum's Center for Cultural Understanding and Change, *Collaborative Research* (Wali 2006), the authors line out for both scholars and community-based organizations seven steps for doing participatory action research: finding a partner, forming a research question, planning, conducting research, analyzing the data, sharing the findings, and taking action. As each of these steps is built on cooperation and mutual respect for varying viewpoints, each of these steps accordingly requires time and the ongoing nurturing of relationships: "Planning meetings, hosting social events in each other's neighborhood and homes," the authors point out, "and openness to constructive criticism all help to create bonds during the research process" (Wali 2006, 33). Such commitments to collaboration, of course, require that we learn to work effectively with many different people, to listen, and to take others seriously. I have already mentioned . . . that the negotiation

of diverse visions, agendas, and expectations can be challenging intellectually. But collaborative research can also be challenging on a personal level. It often requires us to surrender authority and control, shifting the role of the researcher(s) from one of "expert" to one of "facilitator." This can be hard for some, especially as collaborative research may necessitate that we put aside our own egos in order to bring about more multidimensional, dialogic understandings.

Look for and take opportunities to collaborate. While not all research will fit well within the contours of collaborative research, plenty does. And once you start looking for opportunities to collaborate, the opportunities tend to only multiply—in my experience, at least, collaborative research projects seem to beget more collaborative research projects. . . . A collaborative museum exhibit on African American pioneers originated the partnership that would eventually establish the *Other Side of Middletown* project (see Lassiter et al. 2004, 4–5), which, in turn, produced—in addition to the already mentioned collaborative actions—collaboratively based undergraduate and graduate theses, a video documentary, a photo exhibit, a library digitization project, public school programs, a range of community events, and another state museum exhibit (see, e.g., Indiana State Museum 2007). The possibilities for collaboration can thus be endless. Indeed, one could spend a lifetime doing collaborative research: if we are open to the collaborative process, then we need only look for and take opportunities when they arise.

But when to get started? This raises another set of issues, and summons some advice that may be unpleasant to bear in mind; but important nonetheless for any student considering collaborative research now or in the future.

Start early, but proceed cautiously. Doing collaborative research is not just for the seasoned practitioner. In my mind, students who are interested in doing collaborative research should start as early as possible. It may not always be feasible, though: academic environments, especially, are not at all times as open as we think they might (or should) be. I now realize that I was extremely fortunate to "come of age" as both an undergraduate and graduate student in departments of anthropology that supported and encouraged collaborative research practice (see Lassiter 2004a, 5–8). When I wrote my dissertation on Kiowa song, for example, my Kiowa consultants—particularly Billy Evans Horse, tribal chairman and key consultant—insisted that Kiowas be able to read the dissertation and comment on its evolution. My dissertation committee was open to this idea and allowed the student training inherent to the dissertation process to unfold accordingly as we negotiated a middle ground. But after leaving graduate school and working in other academic environments, I discovered that this kind of openness to student collaborative research—and for that matter, open-ended cooperation with one's professors—does not always proceed this smoothly (see, e.g., Lassiter 2005b, 102). Many academics, including anthropologists, still seem suspicious of collaborative research approaches: while it can be theoretically appealing to many, in practice collaborative research still seems to pose, for some, a threat to academic privilege, authority, and control. Given this, though, the validity and value of collaborative research seems to be growing, and I suspect that students will have less trouble doing collaborative research earlier in their career as our field, as many predict, steadily turns once again toward more public and applied emphases. In the interim, students should be especially cognizant that while many academic environments support and nurture collaborative research, others may not, and in fact, may actively discourage it.

Be aware of the larger risks. A closely related issue is how collaborative research situates your overall work as an anthropologist. Put another way, the work you do as a student, especially as a graduate student, will define your career trajectory (at least in its earliest stages). On the one hand, doing collaborative research as a student may enhance your future job prospects if you envision doing applied anthropology outside academia. On the other hand, doing collaborative research as a student *may* pose a risk to future job prospects (and future job security) if you envision yourself doing this kind of applied anthropology within the context

of academia. Right now, and perhaps for some time to come, multisited, theoretically couched, and academically situated research is king in anthropology. As anthropologist and educator Douglas Foley writes about critical ethnography, for example, "the technical, theory-driven academic ethnography remains the standard through which young scholars must aspire. The senior scholars who control the machinery of academic production and promotion maintain a tight grip on the conventions of social scientific writing. This surely will be the last bastion to fall, if it ever does. In the meantime, the social sciences remain a rather elitist, 'high culture' form of social commentary" (Foley and Valenzuela 2005, 224). . . .

Conclusion

The discussions about public anthropology will no doubt continue for some time, especially as many anthropologists maintain—in some cases, convincingly—that "public anthropology is not just old wine in new bottles" (McGranahan 2006, 256). These dialogues will no doubt, too, continue providing "a useful service for the general discipline" (Rylko-Bauer et al. 2006, 86). But if we are to get beyond public anthropology (particularly those arguments and debates that separate out this anthropology from that anthropology), and chart the central questions and problems of the larger anthropological project, then we—students included—must resist the temptation of academic solipsism and together build more deliberate opportunities for public engagement. A powerful way in which we can do so is through collaborative research. Such research—and the partnerships on which it is based—can press theory and practice into service in ways more direct and immediate in our common search to make a difference in our world, however small or large.

References

Basch, Linda G., Lucie Wood Saunders, Jagna Wojcicka Sharff, and James Peacock, eds. 1999. Transforming Academia: Challenges and Opportunities for an Engaged Anthropology. Washington, DC: American Anthropological Association.

Checker, Melissa, and Maggie Fishman, eds. 2004. Local Actions: Cultural Activism, Power, and Public Life in America. New York: Columbia University Press.

Field, Les, and Richard G. Fox, eds. 2007. Anthropology Put to Work. Oxford: Berg.

Foley, Douglas, and Angela Valenzuela. 2005. Critical Ethnography: The Politics of Collaboration. In The Sage Handbook of Qualitative Research, 3rd ed. Norman K. Denzin and Yvonna S. Lincoln, eds. Pp. 217–234. London: Sage.

Hill, Carole E., and Marietta L. Baba, eds. 1999. The Unity of Theory and Practice in Anthropology: Rebuilding a Fractured Synthesis. Washington, DC: American Anthropological Association.

Lamphere, Louise. 2004. The Convergence of Applied, Practicing, and Public Anthropology in the 21st Century. Human Organization 63(4):431–443.

Lassiter, Luke Eric. 2001a. Engaging a Localized Public Anthropology. Anthropology News 42(2):7–8.

Lassiter, Luke Eric. 2003. Theorizing the Local. Anthropology News 44(5):13.

Lassiter, Luke Eric. 2004a. Collaborative Ethnography. AnthroNotes 25(1):1–9.

Lassiter, Luke Eric. 2005a. The Chicago Guide to Collaborative Ethnography. Chicago: University of Chicago Press.

Lassiter, Luke Eric. 2005b. Collaborative Ethnography and Public Anthropology. Current Anthropology 46(1):83–106.

Lassiter, Luke Eric. 2007 On the Job: Applied Anthropology in a Graduate Humanities Program. Society for Applied Anthropology Newsletter 18(3):8–10.

Lassiter, Luke Eric, Hurley Goodall, Elizabeth Campbell, and Michelle Natasya Johnson. 2004. The Other Side of Middletown: Exploring Muncie's African American Community. Walnut Creek, CA: AltaMira Press.

McGranahan, Carole. 2006. Introduction: Public Anthropology. India Review 5(3–4):255–267.

Miles, James, dir. 2004. Middletown Redux. DVD documentary. Walnut Creek, CA: AltaMira Press.

Rylko-Bauer, Barbara, Merrill Singer, and John van Willigen. 2006. Reclaiming Applied Anthropology: Its Past, Present, and Future. American Anthropologist 108(1):178–190.

Sanday, Peggy Reeves. 1976. Anthropology and the Public Interest. New York: Academic Press.

Sanday, Peggy Reeves. 1998. Opening Statement: Defining Public Interest Anthropology. Paper presented at the 97th annual meeting of the American Anthropological Association, Philadelphia, December 2–6.

Singer, Merrill. 2000. Why I Am Not a Public Anthropologist. Anthropology News 41(6):6–7.

Wali, Alaka, ed. 2006. Collaborative Research: A Practical Introduction to Participatory Action Research (PAR) for Communities and Scholars. Chicago: Field Museum.

Williams, Marco, dir. 2003. MLK Boulevard: The Concrete Dream. New York: Discovery-Times Channel.

12.3 Expert Witness: Notes Toward Revisiting the Politics of Listening

ASALE ANGEL-AJANI

One often hears anthropological work described as a form of "witnessing," although the meaning attached to the act of witnessing and the method of communicating what one had witnessed is differentially understood. In this selection, Angel-Ajani not only reflects on the role of anthropologist as "witness," but she also raises thought-provoking questions about the role of anthropologist as "police" of one another's witnessing. Here the use of "witness" and "police" bear special importance as her research focus was to explore the experiences of African immigrant women incarcerated in Italy. Angel-Ajani explores how her work was questioned and critiqued by colleagues for its truth statements, and unpacks the role that a researcher's positionality, meaning of "field experience," and preconceived ideas about a subject population play in the presentation of "truth."

Questions

1. What makes research "valid" in the eyes of other anthropologists? What about in the eyes of the public? Are these the same thing?
2. What is the role of critical reflection in sharing ethnographic research?
3. How might your positionality impact the work that you do?

One confesses—or is forced to confess.

—MICHEL FOUCAULT, HISTORY OF SEXUALITY

A Confession

I am haunted by voices. There is one voice in particular that calls to me day in and day out, and unlike the loud rambling voices of the others that I hear, her voice is a distinct whisper that licks at my ears. I try to ignore the voices, but hers sits before me like a starving child. Her bloated stomach repels me. She cries to me at all hours. I hate to be alone with her, but she sits on my brain, pounding on my skull for attention. She keeps me up at night, and during the day her whispers make my skin crawl. I cannot be alone with her, and yet I dare not stray too far away.

Her voice demands to know if I can remember what it was like. She questions my memory's ability to return to that horrible place that is the prison. Can I, she wonders, walk back into my mind's eye and conjure up the images of the dark cold corners, the smells of cat shit, and the noise of heavy metal doors clanging shut? Can I return to the shouts of the angry guards or the embattled women? Can I remember the faces that held my deepest respect and affection, can I return to the women as they once were? Mostly, she wants to know if I will be able to live with myself for walking away from them.

She is teaching me that, maybe, for most people who work with "real flesh and blood," who negotiate the horrors that envelop people, maybe there is no salvation. It is one thing to do research safely from the archives and it is quite another to make a living off of the everyday suffering of women.

Two or three things I know for sure: I cannot live with the fact that I peddle the flesh of women's stories for academic consumption, making them pretty, because the reality of their lives is too difficult to bear. I know that through incorporation of "theory" I have learned to water down difficult emotional moments so as not to appear too sentimental. Another thing that I know is that working with African women detained in one of Italy's largest female prisons, Rebibbia Femminile, numbed many of my emotional sensibilities. I am not certain that, despite my commitment (and my privilege) to struggle with these women for recognition and dignity, I have the strength to walk back into that space where the horrors of unspeakable trauma, institutional and societal violence, and individual suffering live. However, even though every moment was shaped by the institution and even small acts of resistance were bundled in reprisals, there were happy times, even feelings of utter joy. On very special days, many women were motivated by the promise of prospects for the future, for friendships and lives lived beyond the walls of Rebibbia. And on those days, I (and I am sure all of us) silently hoped that the world could be a different place for Black women who, forced by social conditions and their social positions, lived just beyond the confines of the fluctuating and unequal rules of dominant society.

I quickly learned that in spite of the lack of knowledge about how carceral systems actually operate, society imagines and even pleasurably envisions powerfully vivid images of crime, criminals, and prison life. These images are, of course, fed to people by academics and the media and because of this, stories of inmates, women inmates in particular, seem already familiar. "Incarcerated women" is the story that has already been told; they are old news. Both public and academic discourse about female criminals represents them as poor women of color, single mothers, and addicted to drugs. More sophisticated accounts identify imprisoned women often as survivors of physical violence and sexual abuse, who are less often detained for violent offenses than men. In spite of whatever truth these theories and ideas might hold, as imprisoned women, activists, and a few scholars have long argued, the lives of imprisoned women are much more complex than these mere "facts."

When I began my research in 1996, I had, as a daughter of parents who had been incarcerated, long understood the quiet respect of not asking people who had been or were in prison why they were there. So, while I was in Rebibbia I did not ask. Because of this, I was shocked by some of the women's willing admission of what brought them to Rebibbia. I realized that because the prison officials introduced me as a researcher there seemed to be little question of why I was there and what information I was deemed as "needing to know." Many of the women had become very familiar with the rules and routine of being an interview subject. This unsettled me. Even though I knew that I was, by the nature of my position in the university, part of the machine that produced the often negative representations of prisoners to the world "outside," I hoped that I was more than just a narrator of other Black women's lives. I hoped I was more than just a mere anthropologist. I believed that I belonged to a group of activist scholars who, through writing, research, and organizing are working toward the abolition of prisons as we know them and, through this process, exposing the broader racist, sexist, and classist social structures that criminalize and demonize poor Whites and people of color.

Firm in my commitment not to participate in furthering the criminalization of African women, whenever I shared my research I did not mention why women that I worked with in Rebibbia were imprisoned. Needless to say, this frustrated several audiences. I had failed the first duty as an anthropologist and as an academic. I learned that as an anthropologist, I had a *particular* professional duty to translate my observations about the lives of women who are forced to live in cages. But by discussing the toll that imprisonment, violence, and forced prostitution (among many other traumas) had on the lives of women—without ever having mentioned their crimes, or worse, by not confirming the veracity of some women's seemingly "outlandish" stories—I had not met the demands and expectations of my audience. As much as representation and the practice of fieldwork have been debated, the anthropologist has not entirely rid herself of the role of "recovering the truth," the role of being the one who assembles evidence, and then testifies in a (court) room of her "peers."

Ethnographic Authority (again)

. . . In this chapter I think through the promise and the limitations of engaged observation, especially the form of anthropological engagement some have called "witnessing." . . . I believe that especially for ethnographers who work with and write about survivors of many forms of violence, the figure of the witness becomes a powerful space in which to authorize and legitimate the painful and often devastating histories that we anthropologists are allowed to listen to and sometimes see with our own eyes. Nevertheless, despite good intentions, we do not recognize both the responsibility of the witness and the many ways in which being called to act as a witness are not always noble. With the full-hearted embrace of the notion of the anthropologist as witness, we fail to fully question the conditions that make our work possible as well as critically assess the consequences of our ethnographic production.

I want to contemplate how we who are critical of the more traditional forms of social science data gathering and reporting often turn to courtroom metaphors, or worse. The metaphors that I will be discussing sit between the anthropologist as witness and the anthropologist as police. . . .

Between the Witness and the Police

The notion of the anthropologist as witness is widely used and often referenced, but not always under the sign of engaged observation. For some, the anthropologist as witness is what all anthropologists do. For others, the discipline of anthropology itself is a mode of witnessing. As Ruth Behar writes: "Anthropology . . . is the most fascinating, bizarre, disturbing, and necessary form of witnessing left to us at the end of the twentieth century" (1996, 5). Clearly Behar's sentiments about anthropology as a form of witnessing do not expressly speak about forms of engagement with the people who are subjected to the eye of the witness/anthropologist. But she elevates the status of witnessing not only as necessary but also as seemingly one of the few viable options "left to us." Nancy ScheperHughes goes even further by positioning the witness as a noble actor. In the introduction to *Death Without Weeping*, she argues that "the act of witnessing is what lends our work its moral (and at times its almost theological) character"

(1992, xii). Scheper-Hughes's account of witnessing underscores a form of anthropological engagement that she implies is active and committed.

In similar fashion, the mission statement for the series on Public Anthropology published by University of California Press and edited by Robert Borofsky claims that "the series seeks to affirm ethnography as an important public witness of today's world." According to the statement, the goal of this series, titled "Public Anthropology," is to bring ethnographic analysis to the fore of "the world's public discussions" and to "position ethnography as a central way of knowing in public intellectual life." At the heart of ethnographic witnessing, then, at least for Borofsky, is the desire to heighten anthropology's status in the domain of public affairs and to return anthropology (as an expert witness of culture) to its former valorized place on the world scene.

Though very different, the articulations by Borofsky, Behar, and ScheperHughes of the witness firmly establish the centrality of the anthropologist by suggesting that as a witness she not only bears witness (was there) but has testimony to give. Although this is certainly provocative, it leads to at least two questions: what and for whom does this form of observation advocate, and who benefits from this mode of engagement?. . .

. . . Liisa Malkki (1997) explored alternative ways of positioning anthropologists in relation to the field and the written production of fieldwork. . . . Through her work with Hutu refugees from Burundi living in Tanzania, she challenges more typical ethnographic norms that anthropologists are supposed to adhere to. . . . For Malkki, being a witness implies a greater sense of responsibility, presumably to the subjects of the ethnography. She writes, "being a witness implies both a specific positioning and a responsibility of testimony, 'a caring form of vigilance'" (94). Malkki goes on to argue that being a witness and giving testimony would be a "workable strategy" against producing the more typical ethnographic accounts of "cultures, peoples, communities and ways of life" (95). . . .

. . . With few exceptions, most anthropologists are third-party chroniclers of events who have not experienced (from beginning to end) what they write about.[1] As third-party chroniclers, the act of witnessing that anthropologists engage in is ultimately juridical in nature. Like material witnesses, anthropologists provide information about a "case," culture, or community that significantly affects the understanding (negatively and positively) of that community.

If the possibility of "anthropological witnessing" or the anthropologist as witness exists, then the question of responsibility and ethnographic authority must be grappled with. . . .

I believe that Malkki's call for anthropologists to consider the connections between police work and fieldwork signals the need to think more critically about the choices one makes as an anthropologist. What are the differences between the anthropologist as investigator/inquisitor/police and the anthropologist as witness? Are there differences? [Are] our will to knowledge and our methodologies (interviews, observations, and the archive, among others) so fatally flawed . . . that we cannot help but be police? Of course, because I do critical work on the criminal justice system, terms such as "police" and "witness" are not lighthearted words. It goes without saying that the police and witnesses can produce evidence that can both condemn and exonerate. But when one works in a prison and listens to and observes the sharp contrast between those who confine and those who are confined, the line between the witness and the police is not philosophical. Being in and of the world, as anthropologists are, should only heighten our awareness that while police work involves police informants (who may act as witnesses), and evidence, clues, and privileged information, police also employ suspicion, fed by the larger discourse of criminalization, labeling, or racial profiling, and ideologies of racism, sexism, homophobia, and classism. Indeed, as reports from global human rights organizations such as Human Rights Watch and Amnesty International, as well as local human rights groups and social justice activists from all over the world have evidenced, much of police work relies on coercive measures that can be deadly, especially to the mentally ill, women, people of color, poor people, and immigrants.

Not All Fields Are Created Equal; Neither Are Anthropologists

The moment I crossed the threshold between the "free world" and the world of confinement, I assumed that I was the one who chose between being an anthropologist who witnesses and one who polices. I did not know that the institution and its agents would quickly make that choice for me. Prior to my arrival at Rebibbia, I was a female researcher from a prestigious university in the United States. Over the phone, a friendly administrator from the prison director's office scheduled a morning meeting between us. After the meeting with the warden, I was to be introduced to the core staff (including social workers, health professionals, and senior prison guards), followed by a formal tour of the facility, where I could meet women and make arrangements to interview them according to their work schedules.

On a hot August morning in 1996, armed with a permission letter from Italy's minister of justice and a rather official-looking letter from my university, I announced myself to the guard manning the reception desk. I knew that he had seen me approach and I could tell that he was eyeing me with curiosity. As I slid my documents to him through the thick glass partition, I watched as he grew confused then suspicious. He eyed my passport and picked up the phone. I could not hear what he was saying, but I remember hoping that he would hurry up because I did not want to be late for my appointment. He was gesturing rapidly with my passport in his hands. He hung up the phone and turned back to the window. He called to another guard who I had not seen earlier. The two of them stood at the window reviewing my documents. I looked past them to the clock. "So you are an American?" the first guard asked. I dragged my eyes from the clock to him and back to the clock, trying to be obvious. "Yes." He leaned forward and I looked him in the eye. "Well, you don't speak [Italian] with an American accent." He pushed a button to his right and the large blue doors that separated the prison from the outside slowly opened up. "No," he said without missing a beat, "you have an Arabic accent." Knowing full well what his comment meant, I thanked him by saying that I agreed that American accents were awful in any language, including English. I walked through the prison doors and was greeted by the second guard, who informed me that I was allowed to bring in only a pen and paper. As I went through the metal detector the second guard called after me, "You are here to speak to the Nigerian girls?" "Yes," I replied. "Well tell your compatriots that they should stop bringing drugs into Italy." He added, "Maybe they will listen to you." By the time the guard and I arrived at the main office, my entire morning schedule had been revised. I no longer had a meeting with the warden, my staff introductions were going to be limited to a social worker and a guard who would be present at every interview and whose main duty would be to "escort" me everywhere-from the office where I did my interviews to the bathroom door. As I prepared to leave the prison that afternoon, I was told that I had to get official verification from the American embassy stating that I was truly a U.S. citizen.

It was clear from the start that as an "other" American who had an "other" name, I was seen as being on the side of the inmates. As a Black woman, I apparently had nothing in common with those who ran the facility. Not that I minded, and nor was I shocked, at how easily my race and apparent difference put me squarely in the corner of the detained African women in the eyes of the administration. Although I had convinced myself that any good anthropologist would be wary of approaching her work with bias (in graduate school I had been trained to stay away from the stuff—of bias) but I knew long before entering the facility, long before touching down in Italy, that my affinities were and would be with the inmates. My bias was built on the knowledge that my status as an "other" American (who did not appear to be authentically from the United States) would greatly affect my experience. . . .

Anthropologists are, of course, very big on experience. Whether we are writing about the experiences facing the communities with which we work or are evaluating our own experiences, it is clear that "experience," particularly that which is gained in the field, is what makes one an anthropologist. As Gupta and Ferguson note, "we would suggest that the single most significant factor determining whether a piece of research will be accepted as . . . 'anthropological' is the extent to which it depends on experience in the field" (1997, 1). Though they are mostly concerned with the strictures and practices of fieldwork and its valorized place within the discipline of anthropology in their essay, Gupta and Ferguson are referring to the widely known (yet unwritten) criterion that one must spend a significant amount of time in the field (a year or more). Wrapped innocently in their language is the profound question of who determines what is anthropological experience. Beyond the question of length of time spent in the field and where in fact that field is, the issue of experience, it seems, is uncontroversial here.

The question is, why? Why is it that despite the numerous critical anthologies and self-reflective essays, we still reify "Experience" as if it is something that can be duplicated and universally understood? Is one really a good anthropologist because one has spent years in the field, speaks the language fluently, and crafts beautifully written ethnographies? Perhaps these are the trappings of a good anthropologist, but I reckon that if all of these traits were bundled in an ethnography that was counterintuitive to what the audience thinks they know (regardless of whether they have any "experience" in the area) the anthropologist in question may be deemed "unanthropological." Is there an assumption in anthropology that the amorphous space known as the field is necessarily level? Here I am encouraged to reflect upon the experience of France Winddance Twine, who sought guidance in how to address the murky waters of what her brown body signified for both Blacks and Whites in Brazil. . . . As she puts it: "After decades of self-reflexivity among ethnographers analyzing the practice of writing and conducting field research, the lack of sustained attention to racialized dilemmas is particularly note worthy, considering the degree to which other axes of power have been theorized" (Twine 2000, 5). For as long as there has been anthropology, the race, gender, age, and social position of the anthropologist has affected the ways in which they are received in the field and in the discipline, among their peers. What has long been clear but seldom discussed is that where one works and how one looks when conducting that work factors in significantly. It is an old story that one's race, gender, sexuality, and social position can (and do) determine what kind of information one might receive, and influence the kind of knowledge produced. At the risk of stating the obvious, and as Donna Haraway (1991) reminded us, knowledge, like experience, is situated.

Politics of Listening

The she that opens up this essay, the one who taught me about the politics of ethnographic production and challenged my easy ability to name myself and my work "activist" was an inmate at Rebibbia. Her name, which is not her name, was given to her by the anthropologist/author who hopes to protect her identity and her dignity. She, "Esther," is no longer imprisoned but it does not change the fact that she will always be considered a condemned woman, an exconvict. When telling her story through the transcription of events that combines her memory, my remembering of our meetings, and an untrustworthy pen and note pad, I am often pushed by anthropologists (and other academics) to reveal more and more about her life. Her story, particularly the story of her arrest is, yes, a potholed windy road on a foggy night. Hers is like the story of Eros and Psyche, of love under the cover of darkness, thrilling, naive, and full of burning questions. The contours of her life are an enigma, but the minutiae are as big as everyday. The combination of elusiveness and vivid description feeds the pungent imagination of the listener.

The potholes in Esther's story, the seemingly inconceivableness of her experiences, created dilemmas for academics, scholars of all varieties, who have listened to my rendition of her life as an African woman imprisoned in Italy. Before she was incarcerated she had been a member of an elite family, most of whom were killed in a massacre; she had been a refugee, a sex worker, and an unwitting drug courier. Once, after I shared these details of Esther's story with a group of academics, one woman asked me how I evaluated the veracity of it—after all, the anthropologist added, "she is in prison."

Now I am not so naive that I thought that Esther's story would provoke collective soul-searching in the body politic. I was hoping, I admit, that this woman, a fairly progressive individual by any standards, would be moved to disbelief because Esther had suffered more trauma than it would seem that anyone should endure. I was hoping that she would be enraged at a world that could accommodate this magnitude of human suffering. But no—for this woman and several other anthropologists, Esther and all of the women that I worked with were casualties of the contingencies of life. Furthermore, they were suspected of not telling the truth, simply because they had been confirmed by the state as criminals, regardless of the circumstance that brought them to prison. I am reminded here of a similar discussion by Luana Ross, who works with incarcerated Native American women in Montana. She writes: "Because I was interested in how racism and sexism function inside prison and affected imprisoned women, I concentrated on the women's subjective experiences of

prison. Some critics of my work and of other qualitative research argue that prisoners do not tell 'the truth'" (Ross 1998, 5). Indeed, academics tend to be an arrogant lot, and we believe that the world is an open book that must be analyzed and judged by the elite cadre known as "us."

I often wondered how people would respond to my research if I did not work in prisons but, say, in a refugee camp or a shelter. Would there be the same concerns about truth telling? Would it be easier to accept the violence and the pain that mark many of the women's lives if they had been in a shelter and not in a prison? I am struck by the ways that "crime" still defines the criminal, to crudely paraphrase Foucault. When I choose not to write about a woman's particular crime, or if I flatly state that it is not my goal to confirm the veracity of a woman's "testimony," which would require me to go through their court papers, initial police reports, and lawyers' notes, I am often met with sideways glances and questions about my methodology. . . .

To be sure, Esther's "story" is not a story but a testimony, and my story of her testimony is and was in some ways a small act of witnessing. But I wonder why my anthropology audience couldn't see that the listener enters into the contract of testimony (Laub 1992). . . . If we think we know it all before a word is uttered, then what does that say about our ability to receive the details of another person's experience or testimony? What does this say about the possibilities for ethical engagement (Chun 1999)? Can we be engaged scholars or activist intellectuals if we do not know how to listen or if we seek or even demand knowledge that confirms what we already think we know?

To be the receiver of testimony, as some anthropologists are, is to be, in part, a witness, but it is also to assist in that witnessing process. . . . When I think through the practice of ethnography, I see that we have concerned ourselves with the authoritative act of what it means to witness. That authoritative act is the act of speaking, giving voice, reclaiming and reconstructing an event. Ironically, however, an anthropologist's job is supposedly based on the act of listening. Listening does not imply that the listener is an expert or an authority. I believe that there are valuable lessons to be learned if we open our ears to experiences that might not fit what we think we know. Critical reception might just lead to ethical engagement.

Note

1. Of course there are notable exceptions, but this charge applies to most North American anthropologists who write about violence in Africa, Latin America, Asia, Eastern Europe, and urban centers in the United States. Part of the reality that we need to face as academics, in the United States, Europe, and Australia, including the Ph.D.-holding elites from the global south living and working in the United States or Europe, is that we are not only a privileged class but that often, in part because of funding constraints (few foundations are willing to support research that places individuals in dangerous locations), we are part of the collective of people who "witness" the aftermath of violence. There is promise in this, one that has the potential to recognize the tremendous responsibility we have.

References

Behar, Ruth. 1996. *The Vulnerable Observer: Anthropology That Breaks Your Heart.* Boston: Beacon.

Borofsky, Robert. n.d. http://www.publicanthropology.org/.

Chun, Wendy Hui Kyong. 1999. "Unbearable Witness: Toward a Politics of Listening." *Differences: A Journal of Feminist Cultural Studies* 11.1: 112–149.

Gupta, Akhil, and James Ferguson. 1997. "Discipline and Practice: 'The Field' as Site. Method, and Location in Anthropology." In *Anthropological Locations: Boundaries and Grounds of a Field Science.* Berkeley: University of California Press.

Haraway, Donna. 1991. "Situated Knowledges: The Science Question in Feminism and the Privilege of the Partial Perspective." In Hanaway, *Simians, Cyborgs, and Women.* New York: Routledge.

Laub, Dori. 1992. "An Event without a Witness: Truth, Testimony and Survival." In *Testimony: Crises of Witnessing in Literature, Psychoanalysis, and History,* edited by Shoshana Felman and Dori Laub. New York: Routledge.

Malkki, Liisa. 1997. "News and Culture: Transitory Phenomena and the Fieldwork Tradition." In *Anthropological Locations,* edited by Akhil Gupta and James Ferguson. Berkeley: University of California Press.

Ross, Luana. 1998. *Inventing the Savage: The Social Construction of Native American Criminality.* Austin: University of Texas Press.

Scheper-Hughes, Nancy. 1992. *Death without Weeping: The Violence of Everyday Life in Brazil.* Berkeley: University of California Press.

Twine, France Winndance. 2000. "Racial Ideologies and Racial Methodologies." In *Racing Research, Researching Race: Methodological Dilemmas in Critical Race Studies,* edited by France Winndance Twine and Jonathan Warren. New York: New York University Press.

12.4 The Future of Practice: Anthropology and the Grand Challenge

RIALL NOLAN

As this book's introduction and Lassiter's chapter illustrated, there exists an ongoing tension surrounding the role that anthropology should play vis-à-vis the public, where anthropologists should find employment, and how anthropological knowledge should be put to use. In this selection, Riall Nolan makes the case that the future of anthropology is a "future of practice." He calls upon us to put the theory–praxis divide behind us; doing so will help solve the "grand challenges" affecting humankind and facilitate better training for our students, who are more than likely going to work as practitioners and not within the "ivory tower."

Questions

1. What is the difference between a profession and a discipline?
2. Should anthropology be an applied science?
3. Where do you see yourself working as an anthropologist?

. . . I want to look briefly at several linked issues: what we as a society need to pay attention to these days, what anthropology has done to help us with this, and how anthropology might become more useful to us in the future.

Today's World

Our world, it hardly need be said, is becoming more diverse and complex with every passing day. Communication and transport have moved difference in next door to each of us, both literally and metaphorically. We value this diversity; we celebrate and extol it. And yet, to a large extent, we remain profoundly ignorant of the cultural worlds of others, even as we try to connect with them. Pico Iyer cautioned us:

> Insofar as we try to love our neighbors as ourselves, we have to admit that our neighbors are people with whom we share no common language, or past, or value. (1994, 13)

What we *do* share, however, are predicaments, the ones we've come to call "grand challenges." These include such problems as climate change, sustainable energy, global health, and poverty. These problems are not merely "grand," they are wicked. "Wicked" problems share a number of characteristics: they are hard to formulate and resolve; every solution brings consequences of its own; stakeholders disagree about almost every aspect of the problem, from its shape to its solution; and wicked problems are intertwined and connected in dynamic ways. Perhaps the worst—and most important—characteristic of wicked problems is that we can't afford not to address them.

Our current attempts to deal with these wicked problems are spearheaded by disciplines such as science, engineering, and agriculture, which in turn are

Riall Nolan. "The Future of Practice: Anthropology and the Grand Challenge." 2013. In *A Handbook of Practicing Anthropology*, Riall Nolan, ed., 391–396. Wiley Books. By permission of John Wiley and Sons, Inc.

driven by a mindset that is highly empirical, focused on efficiency, profit, and speed, in which cultural factors, if they appear at all, tend to be considered as obstacles.[1]

We've seen this mindset at work, for example, with two of our biggest problems—war and poverty—issues which in many parts of the world are linked, in both straightforward and highly complex ways. Our attempts to confront these problems have tended, on the whole, to be highly technical in nature, and, for the most part, these approaches have failed. Ambrose Bierce once remarked that war was the way God taught Americans about geography. I believe that war and poverty are also teaching us, in rather painful ways at times, about culture.

Human culture—its nature and its consequences—are a huge missing piece our attempts to create better and more sustainable futures for ourselves and others. Whatever their accomplishments thus far, science and technology alone are unlikely to be sufficient for resolving the problems and challenges which now confront us.

This presents clear and enormous opportunities for anthropology, which works to situate objects, events, and ideas within a broader context. . . .

Anthropology's Response So Far

Many universities—and some entire disciplines—now speak of repositioning themselves to confront these "grand challenges" in a strategic manner, developing programs and curricula, and organizing the work of faculty differently. Anthropology would seem to have much to contribute here, but in many institutions so far seems muted. Although anthropology takes as its brief all human issue, the people actually writing about these issues—and whose books reach the public—are rarely anthropologists. We have no disciplinary project, so to speak, for addressing any of our global problems in coherent, coordinated, intentional ways. Our discipline does not talk collectively about "grand challenges" or "wicked problems." Indeed, with respect to war and poverty in particular, the discipline has sometimes seemed intent on marginalizing the anthropologists actually working in those areas, thus ensuring that anthropology's contribution to—and learning from—these difficult problems will remain minimal.

. . . It's not that we haven't been involved in global issues (see Checker 2009, for example). It's just that we haven't been very effective in that arena. We need to actively figure out how to bring anthropology into the global conversation. Instead, we've chosen to focus on other things. Controversy continues among academics concerning the proper role of practice, and the appropriate status to be accorded practitioners. In the conference halls there is still intense debate over how far anthropology should go in pursuit of public goals, what means and methods should be used, and what roles anthropologists should adopt. But there's very little in the way of a coherent plan. . . .

Today, more graduates are choosing practice, rather than being pushed into it. In the fields in which they work, they are increasingly skilled and influential. These practitioners, for the most part, have made their peace with issues of engagement. Practitioners now look outside the academy for inspiration, validation, and professional satisfaction. Practitioners are slowly transforming the public face of anthropology into something that looks much more like a profession. To do this, however, they will need to connect more effectively with each other, by creating communities of practice. And this they are beginning to do.

The disconnect between the academy and the world of practice is neither as dire nor as pronounced as many might think, but it is still significant, and particular so when we consider the present stagnation in academic employment and the fact that most of our graduate students are still being prepared for academic careers. There is an obvious synergy here between the strengths of practitioners and the strengths of the core discipline, but this synergy is not, for the most part, being captured.

Where We Go from Here

The main task in the future for anthropology, it seems to me, is to succeed in bringing sociocultural data and perspectives into our efforts to address global problems. To do this, anthropology needs to be much more involved with public life. Erve Chambers reminded us years ago that anthropology is more than a science: "it must also be a form of participation in human affairs" (1985, 189). If we want to be more influential in the wider society, we will need to enter into that society more fully. We will be listened to because of our skill and experience, not as anthropologists per se, but as problem-solvers. Action does not challenge anthropology's traditional role—it extends it.

We will also need to repair the split we have created between academia and practice. We're not the only discipline which needs to do this, of course. Ernest Boyer (1997), who wrote extensively on the role and mission of the university in today's society, believed in what he called the "scholarship of application." He felt strongly that it should have equal place in the academy beside research.

But sadly, many of us continue to feel that practice is what anthropologists do if they're not good enough to be academics. And many of us also feel that it is unethical to work for change, at whatever level. We seem preoccupied with disciplinary purity, focused on controversies which seem irrelevant to many, and increasingly isolated in significant ways from what's actually going on out on the street, so to speak.

As long as we continue to believe these things, anthropology will have little or no effective voice in world affairs. As Pat Fleuret, a development practitioner, said years ago:

> The notion of a value-free, non-directed applied science that is uninterested in achievement is absurd. Most anthropologists . . . are cripples as applied scientists because they are unwilling—or simply unable to accept service in the search of improvement as a measure of professional performance. (1987, 271)

More recently, Kamari Clarke framed the issue this way:

> Such compartmentalization [between theory and praxis] is false and has no place in the context of an unfurling new world order in whose presence anthropology has: far from public face and risks becoming divided between those in "ivory towers" and those who are exiled from academia because of the work they do. (2010, 5311)

Whereas a discipline generates knowledge, a profession puts it to use, within specific domains, for clients (Greenwood 1957). Bringing the academy and the world of practice together will involve conscious recognition of the professional, as opposed to purely disciplinary, face of anthropology.

The longer we delay advancing the profession of anthropology, the higher the risks to the discipline. As the recognition of the need for social knowledge grows, so do the opportunities for anthropologists. But if we don't promote our discipline professionally, then others will eventually own what we do, and how we do it. And at that point, there will be no further need, so to speak, for our services. Choosing to remain on the sidelines will all but ensure that others will seize these opportunities, imposing their preferred solutions. "The dogs bark;" as they say, "but the caravan moves *on*."

Becoming more involved with public life will also have the effect of allowing us to develop a true theory of practice—a set of propositions and principles for bringing anthropology to bear on real life situations, which is intellectually sound, practically relevant, and effective. Essential to the development of theory is of course a supporting literature of practice—"thick description" accounts of how practitioners actually work. Practice is an unfolding field test of anthropological method and theory, and understanding how practitioners do what they do will greatly enrich our discipline.

Thanks to practitioners, anthropology is today increasingly present and influential in our public life. Practitioners are involved at every level with the issues of our time. As a result, our students now have more options available to them regarding what to do with what they have learned. Years ago, Laura Nader (1972) exhorted us to "study up," and it's still good advice. But for many practitioners, it's now also a case of "studying in"—of looking at these organizations from the inside out. And while I'd freely admit that not everyone has to "go inside," I'd also maintain that without that authentically insider's viewpoint, we're missing much of the picture. So—to be direct about it—not all of us have to work for the World Bank, or for the military, or for a corporation. But we need to listen to our colleagues who do, learn from them, and put that knowledge to good use.

> We have no other way, ultimately, to effect change on a global scale than through our institutions. They are human creations, built by us, products of our minds. As we created them, so can we reshape them. (Nolan 2002, 281)

Anthropology today is very different from anthropology of 20 or 30 years ago. We now have a majority of practitioners, and they work at every conceivable job. It's time we made use of their collective skill and experience to find more effective ways to speak truth to power. Because if we don't take up this challenge, we're going to get what we've gotten so far—institutions that find it very difficult to think across cultural boundaries.

No one would call that a desirable state of affairs. The ability to work productively and sustainably with culture and cultural difference is very clearly central to America's story in the twenty-first century—to our democracy, to our values, and to our continued economic prosperity. It is also central to our attempts to join with others across the globe to address our common problems. Helping our institutions transform themselves into global learning organizations will not be done easily or quickly, but it can be done if we—academics and practitioners alike—work together, and with others, carefully and confidently.

It has always seemed to me that anthropology unites two very basic human impulses: a curiosity about the people living over the next hill, and a desire to make a lasting contribution. Anthropological practice is in many ways a fulfillment of these impulses, and I believe that it has a very bright future.

Note

[1] I've characterized this mindset as "technicist thinking," and have elsewhere explored its manifestations and implications in development work (Nolan 2002: 45–50, 233–234).

References

Boyer, Ernest. 1997. *Scholarship Reconsidered: Priorities of the Professoriate.* San Francisco: Jossey-Bass.

Chambers, Erve. 1985. *Applied Anthropology: A Practical Guide.* Prospect Heights, IL: Waveland Press.

Checker, Melissa. 2009. "Anthropology in the Public Sphere, 2008: Emerging Trends and Significant Impacts." *American Anthropologist* 11: 162–169.

Clarke, Kamari M. 2010. "Toward a Critically Engaged Ethnographic Practice." *Current Anthropology* 5l (S2): S301–S312.

Fleuret, Patrick. 1987. "Comment on Natural Resource Anthropology." *Human Organization* 46: 271–272.

Greenwood, Ernest. 1957. "Attributes of a Profession." *Social Work* 2: 44–55.

Iyer, Pico. (1994) "Strangers in a Small World." *Harper's Magazine* (Sept.), 13–16.

Nader, Laura. 1972. "Up the Anthropologist—Perspectives Gained from Studying. In Dell H. Hymes (ed.), *Reinventing Anthropology.* New York: Pantheon Books, 284–311.

Nolan, Riall. 2002. *Development Anthropology.* Boulder, CO: Westview Press.

IN THE NEWS Corporate Anthropology

In March 2013 and then again in March 2014, anthropologists' social media networks blew up with the news that *The Atlantic and The Business Insider* published articles describing the value of anthropological insights to corporations. Family members, worried that their young relatives were pursuing a degree that would relegate them to minimum wage employment for the rest of their lives, were suddenly relieved. Or at least some were. The articles "Anthropology Inc." by Graeme Wood and "Here's Why Companies Are Desperate to Hire Anthropologists" by Drake Baer focus on the role of applied anthropological methods in uncovering the role products play in people's lives, pointing out how companies like Google, Intel, and Microsoft have cued into the fact that what people say they want or do is not always what they actually want or do. Each highlights ReD Associates, an ethnographic consulting firm, as an example of one of many such firms popping up to serve the needs of the business community.

Some anthropologists are highly critical of corporate ethnography, finding private-sector ethnography to be compromised and unethical because its ultimate goal is to advance a profit for company stakeholders, which may mean "duping" people into consumerism and even potentially causing harm to humans and community well-being. For a blog discussing and contesting these perspectives see "Ethnography Matters" on the website companion.

The website companion also includes links to the Career Center website of the American Anthropological Association where a PowerPoint is available for those interested in anthropology for businesses as well as the blog "Anthropologizing" where Amy Santee (M.A. in Anthropology) regularly posts essays and interviews with anthropologists working in design ethnography and user experience.

 Visit www.oup.com/us/brondo for more information.

DR. MELISSA CEFKIN

Design Anthropologist; Principal Scientist at Nissan Research Center, Silicon Valley

Figure 12.6.1

Melissa Cefkin (photo by Mazya Lotfalian)

Where do you work, and what do you do?

I currently work in the belly of the beast, Silicon Valley, conducting research related to autonomous vehicle development. I am a social and interpretive scientist operating in a world most profoundly shaped by the goals and approaches of artificial intelligence, engineering, and computational solutions. This makes for some exciting if at times unsettling work!

By autonomous vehicles, you mean cars that can drive themselves? What is the role of anthropology in this work?

Yes, vehicles that can operate on their own. (Though just how "on their own" is yet to be determined and concerns technical, regulatory, insurance, and social considerations.)

In terms of putting anthropology to work, the most tangible thing to point to is that I perform ethnographically informed studies focused on the social and cultural lives of products, consumption, processes of production, and the people and social forms that give rise to and emerge from these practices. I then translate these understandings into implications for action, working hand in hand with designers, engineers, system developers, program designers, strategists, and others.

That is the most visible way I apply my anthropological training. However, I view my primary agenda and key role somewhat more broadly. And that is, to decenter often taken for granted ideas about the relationships between people and technology, some of which, I believe, do not serve society as well as they should. The model that posits people as the "other" to technology, as "users" of products and services, is an example of the mindset I hope to disrupt. I see my role (as do many of my peers in this line of work) as putting consideration of people's lived experience and broader social forms at the center.

The everyday work that I do may not look that distinct from that of my corporate colleagues—I attend the same meetings, play many of the same managerial roles. My contributions as an anthropologist are as much about the questions I pose and how I frame considerations of business and the workplace. "You see things differently" is what I've often heard from my colleagues, though it sometimes takes some time working together before they come to appreciate what that can offer.

How did you get into this line of work? It is my understanding that you began your career as an anthropologist with an interest in performance and the Middle East? Perhaps you can begin by sharing how you became interested in the discipline of anthropology.

I suspect that anyone who has found their way into anthropology by way of their own experiences of marginality always find this a loaded question.

In my case it relates to having grown up in Colorado as the youngest of four children to parents who transplanted from New York for professional reasons. We were one of just a small handful of Jewish families in Fort Collins where my father was a professor of Political Science at Colorado State University.

My family was very oriented toward concerns of social justice and international awareness. My father's area of specialty was international relations and especially Africa and the Middle East, and when I was three years old we moved to Rhodesia (Zimbabwe) for my father's sabbatical. My family's roots and my father's profession meant there was a steady stream of visitors from around the world through our home. I remain humbled and inspired by my siblings who pursued careers in teaching, nursing, counseling, the Foreign Service, the Peace Corps, and international relief. Not only were these familial influences especially strong, but after following my sister to an evening of recreational folk dancing one summer as a young teenager, I became an avid folk dancer, infusing me not only with the sounds and movements of song and dance from around the world but introducing me further to people of many backgrounds.

The fact that I went from a BA to a PhD in Anthropology had everything to do with having read Marcus and Cushman's "Ethnographies as Text" as an undergrad at UC Santa Cruz. The reflective questioning of the epistemological basis of knowledge—not just our knowledge, but any knowledge claims —was heady and profound. Since I intended to focus on topics related to Islam and the Middle East, the fact that Michael Fischer was also at Rice University with George Marcus made it an obvious choice for my PhD.

This was an extraordinary time (late 1980s, early 1990s) in anthropology with the rethinking of the ethnographic endeavor, the attention to performativity, and the intermingling of perspectives from other fields from philosophy to feminist studies to architecture to biology. This was also the period in which Science and Technology Studies was gaining ground. As a period aiming to grapple with the contemporary in all its forms and catalyzed by a spirit of experimentalism, it is perhaps no surprise, looking back, that I found my way into business, design, and technology. My route there came by way of a chance to work with the not-for-profit, the Institute for Research on Learning on an ethnographic study of back-office corporate practices through a rubric of social learning. The rest, as they say, is history.

What is the most meaningful project you've worked on over the course of your career? Why?

Let me name two. The first concerns changing forms of work driven through digitally enabled work marketplaces. The space of "open and crowd work platforms" (as I've dubbed it) includes a spectrum from large-scale, grand challenges (e.g., the X-Prize) to micro-task crowdsourcing (e.g., Mechanical Turk) and the freelancer and project-based app-driven work exchanges found in between (think Uber for work). What is notable about these mechanisms is how they create fissures in traditional terms of employment, in the model of "rented" labor and the (regulated) right to assign tasks to that labor. These marketplaces shift labor further from an "owning" to "accessing" model, and disrupt the authority of assignment. They also disrupt the security of identity, wages, and benefits of full-time job assignment.

Beyond that I have to point to what I'm doing now. The potential of a future with autonomous vehicles is evocative, powerful, and troubling. I'm optimistic, but questions abound. For instance, do we get to a future of fully autonomous vehicles broadly accessible to all, or just some subset of that? How will the rewards accrue, and what happens to the economic shifts in terms of job displacements, etc.? Street life and road use has been profoundly shaped by automobility; what does the future hold? As we examine vehicles as social objects that occupy, move through, and are fellow travelers in our social spaces, I am close enough to have the potential to effect aspects of what happens.

Do you identify as an applied, engaged, or public anthropologist? What do these titles mean to you?

Though I've engaged in organizational roles defined by anthropology in the service of making change, I've never particularly identified as an "applied anthropologist." In general I am not very attracted to these terms. While in any given moment the subject position one occupies can be vital to her ability to perform, I'm not sure how much it helps to view these as fixed subject positions. I do not know a single anthropologist who is not "engaged."

I applaud those who make explicit efforts to extend their reach and exhort others to do the same. I welcome the move for more anthropologists to speak in a voice that is widely accessible. And yes, I can get as annoyed as anyone at the insularity of much anthropological talk, at talk that speaks as if changing the world but is spoken to nobody but ourselves. But who am I to say that doesn't count? I don't know, and don't think we can fully know, what voices make their way into action. Every voice is a voice in conversation with some more than others, which is heard by some and not others. There is no one "public." It takes all kinds.

CAREER ADVICE

Advice for students interested in organizational or design anthropology:

- Learn about organizations. Understand different functions.
- Get your head around the fact that producing interesting findings, building new understandings, is rarely enough. These are worlds of action. The question is, what should happen (be built, implemented, designed, replaced) based on that understanding?

Glossary

action anthropology: An approach in which the research is intended to lead to social change.

AIDS: Acquired immune deficiency syndrome.

anthropocene: The period in which human activities have profoundly altered geological conditions and processes, serving as the primary driver of global ecological change.

anthropology of development: A critical approach that seeks to understand the impacts of development projects on local peoples.

assisted reproductive technology (ART): Technology that is used to achieve pregnancy, including artificial insemination, fertility medications, in vitro fertilization, and surrogacy.

biocitizenship: Citizenship based in the age of biomedicine and biotechnology.

biomedicine: Medicine based on principles of Western natural sciences.

BP oil spill: The largest accidental marine oil spill in history, occurring in 2010; also known as the Deepwater Horizon oil spill.

business anthropology: Applying anthropological theories and methods to the needs of private sector organizations.

child migrant: A child who leaves his or her home to travel to work or live in another region or country without adult accompaniment.

class: The ranking of social groups based on attributes of achieved status, such as wealth, occupation, or social standing.

climate change: A long-term change in the state of global or regional climate, largely attributed to increased levels of carbon dioxide and other greenhouse gases in the atmosphere that have largely resulted from rises in burning fossil fuels to produce energy.

climate ethnography: Ethnographic study of a community's observations and understanding of the changing climate and its impact on their culture.

community development: Process of improving community well-being through action.

community-supported agriculture (CSA): An alternative, locally based model of agriculture where a network of individuals pledge support to one or more local farms and share in the risks and benefits of food production.

collaborative anthropology: An approach that builds on cooperative relationships between anthropologists and research informants and emphasizes collaboration throughout the ethnographic process.

colonial feminism: Term coined by Leila Khaled to describe the appropriation of women's rights and selective expression of concern for women's well-being in order to advance colonial interests.

colonialism: The practice of one country exercising control or governing influence over another, less powerful country and its people.

colorblindness: Also known as "racial blindness"; used by proponents to describe ignoring racial characteristics in making decisions about a person's participation or selection for an activity or service. This approach has been heavily criticized as being racist and grounded in white privilege, and ignoring the structural causes of racial inequality.

conflict: A struggle or serious disagreement.

critical medical anthropology: An approach that highlights the linkages between social, political, and economic processes to human health and illness.

cross-cultural communication: The study of how people from different cultural backgrounds communicate.

cultural capital: Forms of knowledge acquired by individuals through their social and economic class.

cultural relativism: Understanding another culture in its own terms, according to its worldview, ethics, and values.

cultural survival: An advocacy organization formed to defend the human rights and cultural heritage of Indigenous Peoples throughout the world.

design anthropology: Field of study that merges design and anthropology to create new products and services.

development: The process of change or act of improving or advancing something.

development anthropology: An applied tradition where anthropologists work to advance development programs in culturally appropriate ways.

dialect: Regional or class variation of a language.

digital age: The information age or computer age; new media age.

disaster capitalism: The practice of taking advantage of a major disaster to adopt neoliberal economic policies that the population may not have accepted under normal circumstances.

discourse: Verbal and spoken communication.

disease: Forms of biological impairment explained by biomedicine.

Disneyfication: The construction of artificial realities to appeal to Western desires and fantasies.

Ebola: An infectious and often fatal disease spread through infected body fluids that leads to severe internal bleeding.

electronic panopticon: Where the behaviors and actions of working-class people are made public for surveillance and discipline by higher socioeconomic classes.

emic perspective: An insider's perspective; using the concepts and categories of the culture under study to describe cultural phenomena.

engaged anthropology: An approach that emphasizes collaboration and support, public education, social critique, advocacy, and activism.

environmental anthropology: The study of the relationship between culture and the natural world.

environmental justice: A movement concerned with addressing the linkages between racial discrimination, social justice, and access to environmental quality.

etic perspective: An outsider's perspective; using the concepts and categories of the researcher's culture to describe another culture.

ethics: Ideas about what is morally right and wrong and standards and codes of conduct for appropriate behavior.

ethnicity: Belonging to a social group that shares a distinctive history and customs.

ethnographic film: A non-fiction film resulting from anthropological fieldwork, usually organized in the form of a lineal narrative.

ethnographic method: Long-term and intensive participant observation in the life of a community or culture.

ethnography: The anthropological description of a culture through fieldwork.

female genital mutilation: Female circumcision; the removal of all or part of the clitoris and/or labia.

Ferguson: A city in the greater metropolitan area of St. Louis, Missouri, where Michael Brown, an unarmed black teenager, was shot and killed in August 2014 by a white police officer, prompting protests and raising the debate about brutality and extrajudicial killings of black people by police forces.

fetish: Worship for an inanimate object.

fieldwork: Immersion in the daily life of a culture for the purpose of collecting data about that culture.

foodways: The cultural practices and traditions surrounding food production and consumption.

fortress conservation: An approach to conservation based on the assumption that the best and only way to preserve nature is to forcefully exclude people from designated wilderness areas.

gender: Social and cultural expectations about how men and women should behave, and how they are perceived and evaluated.

genderlect: Linguistic differences by gender.

genotype: The genetic makeup of an organism.

globalization: The deepening and widening scale of interaction and integration of people, ideas, exchanges, and other components of culture across and within national borders.

habitus: Personal dispositions, both conscious and unconscious.

hashtag ethnography: ethnographic study of the social media platform Twitter which employs the hashtag symbol (#) to mark and share a conversation.

Human Terrain System: A program of the U.S. Department of Defense where teams of applied social scientists were embedded with U.S. troops in war contexts.

humanitarian aid: Assistance designed to save lives and alleviate human suffering after human-made crises or natural disasters.

humanitarianism: Promoting human welfare; a moral imperative to care for human beings and to alleviate suffering.

Hurricane Katrina: The 2005 hurricane that devastated the Gulf coast from central Florida to Texas, with levee failure and storm surge; the costliest and one of the five deadliest hurricanes in the history of the United States.

illness: The social and psychological experience a patient has of a disease.

Indigenous: Original or native to a particular region or area.

indigeneity: The quality of being indigenous.

indigenous rights: Rights and protections afforded to indigenous inhabitants of a region whose cultures and ways of life are threatened by forces of development.

intersex: Individuals who exhibit sex organs between male and female, and often of both.

language: Communication system consisting of words, sounds, or signs used to express and communicate meaning.

language ideology: Widespread assumptions about the degree to which some languages or dialects are superior or more sophisticated than others.

language revitalization: Efforts to preserve or revive languages that are on the verge of extinction.

LGBTQ: Lesbian, gay, bisexual, transgender, and queer or questioning.

lifeboat ethics: Garrett Hardin's model for resource distribution that describes a lifeboat with limited space and compares the lifeboat to rich nations and swimmers to poor nations.

magic: A set of beliefs and practices designed to control the world; manipulation of supernatural forces for the purpose of intervening in human activity or natural events.

marriage: A socially approved institution that formalizes relationships—economic, political, and sexual—between adult partners within a family.

marriage equality: Equal acceptance of same-sex and heterosexual marriages.

Maasai: An ethnic group of semi-nomadic people inhabiting northern Tanzania and southern Kenya.

meatpacking: The industry that slaughters, processes, and distributes livestock such as cattle, pigs, and other animals for consumption.

media anthropology: The study of mass media.

midwifery: The health profession that deals with pregnancy, childbirth, and postpartum care.

national security: The concept that a government should protect its citizens against crises that would impact the nation-state; extension of the use of political, economic, and military power for the protection of a singular country.

native ethnography: Ethnographic work where there is a close cultural and linguistic familiarity between the anthropologist and the community they are studying.

native rock art: Engravings and paintings on natural stone by native peoples.

neocolonialism: The dominance of strong nations over weaker nations through cultural imperialism and economic influence.

neoliberalism: A set of political and economic policies and programs that presume human well-being can be best enhanced through encouraging efficient economic markets, free trade, and strong property rights, while also limiting the role of the state by privatizing public services and engaging in massive governmental deregulation.

Network of Concerned Anthropologists (NCA): An independent network of anthropologists that formed in response to the "war on terror" in order to promote ethical anthropology in the face of what appeared to be efforts to militarize the discipline of anthropology.

organ trade: Trade of human organs for use in transplant surgery.

participant observation: A research method in which anthropologists live with the people under study and observe and participate in their everyday activities.

participatory video: A form of participatory media in which a community collaborates with the researcher on the making of the film.

passive infanticide: Indirect act of causing death to an infant, usually through inadequate nutrition or neglect of a sick baby.

phenotype: The physical characteristics of an individual, resulting from the interaction of the genotype and environment.

political ecology: Theory that focuses on the linkages between political and economic power, social inequality, and environmental issues.

polyandry: A form of plural marriage where a woman marries two or more brothers at one time.

polygamy: Plural marriage.

positionality: The conditions of a given social situation, and the ways in which gender, race, class, sexuality, and other aspects of identity are markers of relational positions rather than essential qualities.

practicing anthropology: The professional practice of anthropology.

protected area: A geographical area that is designated for protection due to its natural, ecological, and/or cultural assets and managed to achieve long-term conservation.

public anthropology: An approach that promotes bringing anthropological knowledge to a primarily non-academic public; focused on expanding anthropology's public image.

public archaeology: Sharing information discovered through archaeological methods with people outside of the profession; communicating archaeological and heritage issues to the wider public.

race: A social and cultural construct that reflects categorizations of people into groups based on specific physical traits.

racialized geography: Neighborhood-wide patterns of segregation by race.

racism: The systematic oppression through unequal and repressive practices and beliefs of one or more socially defined race by another race.

reality television: A genre of television in which people are continuously filmed in unscripted ways, and then the footage is edited to provide entertainment to viewers.

refugees: Migrants who are forced to move due to political oppression or war, and who often have legal permission to stay in their new location.

religion: A system of ideas and practices surrounding the belief in supernatural forces that provides meaning and purpose, and explanation for unexplainable phenomena.

reproductive health: A state of physical, mental, and social well-being in all aspects related to the reproductive system.

reproductive justice: An approach that emphasizes reproductive health alongside social, economic, and political equality and power enabling individuals to make healthy decisions about their own bodies, sexuality, and reproductive health.

ritual: Repetitive social practices of a sequence of symbolic activities that are closely tied to culturally significant ideas, to gain an understanding of a culture's worldview.

service learning: A teaching approach that integrates community service with learning; designed to teach civic responsibility and enrich the learning experience while strengthening communities.

sex: Used to describe sex organs and reproductive functions of the body.

sexuality: Sexual preferences and practices.

sociolinguistics: A branch of anthropological linguistics that studies the relationship between language and culture, with attention to how language use differs by social context.

stratified reproduction: An insight from critical medical anthropology referring to how higher social strata are supported in their efforts to reproduce while those in marginalized social strata are actively discouraged from reproduction.

structural violence: The systematic ways in which the political and economic organization of our social world harms or disadvantages certain individuals or populations.

subjectivity: The way in which a person experiences things in his or her own mind; based on personal feelings, beliefs, and opinions.

sustainability: Ability to maintain an activity forever; sustainable practices can meet the needs of people in the present without jeopardizing the potential to meet the needs of future generations.

taboo: A rule or custom that prohibits or restricts a behavior or action.

transnational migrants: People who migrate from one nation-state to another but continue to participate in the social relations of their place of origin, living social lives across the borders of more than one nation-state.

universal human rights: The rights to which one is entitled by virtue of being human.

urban agriculture: Cultivating, processing, and distributing vegetables, herbs, and fruits in cities; can also involve raising animals, fish, and beekeeping.

urban foraging: Reclaiming "wasted" food through scavenging of dumpsters and waste containers.

violence: Intentional use of physical force to harm someone or something.

virginity testing: The practice of determining whether or not a girl or woman is still a virgin by inspecting the hymen; based on the assumption that the hymen can only be torn through sexual intercourse.

virtual activism: Internet activism through digital campaigning, online organizing, and advocacy.